VIRGINIA LAW BOOKS

Conway Robinson (1805-1884)

VIRGINIA LAW BOOKS

ESSAYS AND BIBLIOGRAPHIES

Edited by

W. Hamilton Bryson

American Philosophical Society
Philadelphia ❖ Independence Square
2000

Memoirs
of the
American Philosophical Society
Held at Philadelphia
For Promoting Useful Knowledge

Volume 239

ISBN:0-87169-239-2
US ISSN: 0065-9738

Virginia law books: essays and bibliographies / edited by W. Hamilton Bryson.
p. cm. -- (Memoirs of the American Philosophical Society ; v. 239)
Includes bibliographical references and index.
ISBN 0-87169-239-2 (cloth)
I. Law--Virginia--Bibliography. 2. Legal literature--Publishing--Virginia--History. I. Bryson, William Hamilton, 1941-
II. Series.

KFV2401 .V567 2000
016.349755--dc21 00-060582

TABLE OF CONTENTS

PREFACE

THERE HAS BEEN much constructive collaboration among the various contributors to this volume and with our professional colleagues. All of us would like to acknowledge the patient advice and the generous sharing of knowledge and professional expertise by the following scholars in the field of Virginia bibliography: Frances Pollard and Janet Schwarz of the Virginia Historical Society; Margaret Cook of the College of William and Mary; Sarah Huggins of the Library of Virginia; Steven D. Hinckley, Lucinda Harrison-Cox, Allen R. Moye, formerly of the University of Richmond School of Law; John Jacob of Washington and Lee University School of Law; Donna K. Bausch of the Norfolk Law Library; Susan Trask and Susan Welch of the William and Mary Law School; Joyce Manna Janto, Sally H. Wambold, John R. Barden, and Robert R. Weertman of the University of Richmond School of Law; and James S. Presgraves of Wytheville. The title pages used as illustrations have been reproduced here with the kind permissions of the Alderman Library of the University of Virginia, the Virginia Historical Society, the Library of Virginia, and the Leyburn Library of Washington and Lee University. The portrait of Conway Robinson by Thomas Sully has been reproduced as the frontispiece with the kind permission of the Virginia Historical Society.

INTRODUCTION

THE MAKING OF THIS COLLECTION was inspired by two phenomena. The first was the publication in 1990 of Erwin Surrency's book, *A History of American Law Publishing*. This book was enthusiastically received as the first comprehensive book on law publishing in America. I join in the praise of Professor Surrency, and I have valued his friendship for many years. However, his book is the beginning, not the end, of the study of the subject; it is the pathbreaker and the guide to further research. This collection of essays and bibliographies attempts to provide another piece of the larger picture. Whereas Professor Surrency's book is broad, this one is deep, so far as our limited resources of time and energy have permitted. We have benefitted greatly from Professor Surrency's work, and we have attempted to add the details as to the Commonwealth of Virginia.

Very little Virginia legal bibliography has preceded this book. Therefore, these essays and lists are, more or less, the beginning, and they are designed as beacons to point the way to further research in this fascinating field. This book might well have been called a trial bibliography had that title not been preempted.

The importance of legal bibliography is that it makes available easy access to the foundation stones and the building blocks of legal scholarship. The understanding of law, as much as any intellectual endeavor, depends upon the ideas and experiences of the past. This is equally true for judges, legislators, lawyers, and law teachers. The entire legal profession is dependent upon its books, for the law is an intellectual and a bookish profession. The future of serious legal scholarship must depend on its memory, and it is better to trust to the written rather than the oral memory.

Legal bibliography can be seen as a part of legal history. For that matter, all law can be seen as a part of legal history because the line between current law and legal history is an elusive one. Perhaps legal history is antiquated rules that once were but are no longer in force. But the antiquated rules must be remembered for two reasons. First, they influenced the formation of the current rules of law; they are the background of the current law. Second, the old rules of law were superseded or rejected for some good reason. If these developments are forgotten, we may unwittingly repeat mistakes. Change is not necessarily good, and much folly is sold to the gullible and ignorant as "reform."

The second motivation behind this book is an appalling practice among librarians that is referred to euphemistically as weeding. Weeding is the removing of books from library collections and discarding them. When a librarian to whom the care and custody of a book has been entrusted decides that it is more efficient to throw a book away rather than to preserve it for some future reader, that book, that receptacle of thought and human experience, is unceremoniously deaccessioned and murdered. Why? Perhaps it is because a new book needs the shelf space and the board of trustees will not build an extension onto the library building; because the librarian believes that the book has been superseded; because the temporary custodian of the book thinks that no one has used the book recently and no one is likely to use it during his or her tenure as librarian; or because the book expresses ideas that are presently unorthodox and politically incorrect. Libraries full of old books are the repositories of wisdom and of folly, and it is not always clear which is which. Therefore, we must preserve them all so that future generations can come to their own conclusions.

The relationship of the newly invented electronic storage of the written word and the old established method of recordation in book form, now referred to by the sociologists as print culture, is presently being evolved by the time-honored method of trial and error. The electronic technicians are predicting a book-free world where all knowledge will be preserved only in some electronic form. These people, however, are inexperienced in the work of in-depth research, and they do not understand the limitations of electronic storage and retrieval, nor the utility of the book in its codex form.

This is not to denigrate the usefulness of the electronic storage of information. Electronic data banks have some advantages over books. Furthermore, electronic typesetting has recently revolutionized book production in the same degree of magnitude as did the invention of moveable type in the fifteenth century.

However, the point being belabored here is that books and electronic data banks both have their legitimate places in the service of scholarship. Both have their relative advantages. And both must be used, and thus books must be kept, preserved, and made available.

It is hoped that this book will demonstrate the continuing value of Virginia law books and convince librarians to retain the works discussed and listed herein. If this purpose fails, then we hope that bibliophiles and other collectors will pick up those that may have been discarded and preserve them for posterity.

In 1863, West Virginia was made into a new and separate state, and thus, after that date, it made good sense to make combined legal indexes, digests, and encyclopedias for both Virginia and West Virginia because the common and statute law of Virginia before 1863 is the common law of West Virginia. (West Virginia Code § 2-1-1.) It was also economically wise because the bar of West Virginia was too small to support the publication of many law books without a broader market for them. And thus many of the law books in this bibliography reflect these intellectual and financial economies.

However, at the present, this combination has outlived its usefulness. Today the laws of Virginia and West Virginia are no longer uniquely similar. This is especially true in the area of civil procedure, because the West Virginia state courts use a slightly modified version of the *Federal Rules of Civil Procedure*. In the last 130 years, a large independent body of case and statutory law has grown up, which is not very relevant or useful to the legal practitioners of the other state. Today, it is very annoying and frustrating to have this combined treatment of the separate laws of Virginia and West Virginia. The future of successful law publishing is the separation and specialization of law books by individual jurisdiction.

Constitutions and constitutional conventions are not included in this book because they have been treated in Earl G. Swem, "A Bibliography of the Conventions and Constitutions of Virginia," *Bulletin of the Virginia State Library*, vol. 3, no. 4, pp. 359-441 (Oct. 1910). Note also A. E. Dick Howard's *Commentaries on the Constitution of Virginia* (1974), which gives the historical background of the present Constitution of Virginia, and Professor Howard's article " 'For the Common Benefit': Constitutional History in Virginia as a Casebook for the Modern Constitution-Maker," *Virginia Law Review*, vol. 54, pp. 816-902 (1968), which discusses the Virginia constitutions of 1776, 1830, and 1851. Furthermore, the creation of a constitution is a political phenomenon even though the result is the establishment of the fundamental law.

Treatises, monographs, continuing legal education materials, and such like publications that appeared after 1950 have not been included here because the large quantity of these books requires a separate volume to list them all. This bibliography will have to await another day for compilation and separate publication.

TABLE OF ABBREVIATIONS

DAB — *Dictionary of American Biography* (1928-1958). 22 vols.

Hening's Statutes — W. W. Hening, *Statutes at Large . . . of Virginia* (1820-1823, rept. 1969), 13 vols.

Legal Education in Va. — W. H. Bryson, *Legal Education in Virginia 1779-1979: A Biographical Approach* (1982).

Q.L.J. — *Quarterly Law Journal* (1856-1859). 4 vols.

Q. L. Rev. — *Quarterly Law Review* (1860-1861). 2 vols.

Tyler's Qtly. — *Tyler's Quarterly Historical and Genealogical Magazine* (1920-1952), 33 vols.

Va. L. J. — *Virginia Law Journal* (1877-1893). 17 vols.

Va. L. Reg. — *Virginia Law Register* (1895-1928). 34 vols.

Va. L. Rev. — *Virginia Law Review* (1913 to present).

Va. Law Reporters — W. H. Bryson, *The Virginia Law Reporters Before 1880* (1977).

Va. Mag. Hist. Biog. — *Virginia Magazine of History and Biography* (1893 to present).

Va. State Bar Ass'n Repts. — *Report of the Virginia State Bar Association* (1888-1975). 85 vols.

Wm. & Mary Qtly. — *William and Mary Quarterly* (1892 to present).

LIST OF CONTRIBUTORS

REBECCA G. BATES
Attorney at Law, Shelbyville, Kentucky

ELLEN FIRSCHING BROWN
Senior Counsel, Dominion Resources Services, Inc., Richmond, Virginia

W. HAMILTON BRYSON
Professor of Law, University of Richmond

ANNE P. CATALINE
Associate Member, Flin Austin, Marlton, New Jersey

COURTNEY A. CHRISTENSEN
Attorney at Law, Charlotte, North Carolina

A. GRAY COLLINS, III
Attorney at Law, Richmond, Virginia

FRANCIS N. CRENSHAW
Counsel, Crenshaw, Ware and Martin, P.L.C., Norfolk, Virginia

JAMES S. HELLER
Director of the Law Library and Professor of Law, College of William and Mary

JOHN B. JENKINS, JR.
Former Partner, Jenkins and Jenkins, Norfolk, Virginia

JAMES N. JORGENSEN
Associate Member, Bode, Call and Stroupe, L.L.P., Raleigh, North Carolina

MICHAEL L. LOY
Member, Virginia State Bar

KENNETH D. MCARTHUR, JR.
Director, Durrette, Irvin and Bradshaw, P.L.C., Richmond, Virginia

KENT C. OLSON
Assistant Law Librarian and Lecturer in Legal Research, University of Virginia

DAVID W. PARRISH, JR.
Retired President, The Michie Company, Charlottesville, Virginia

BRANDON D. QUARLES
Director of the Law Library and Assistant Professor of Law, Baylor University

E. LEE SHEPARD
Assistant Director for Manuscripts and Archives, Virginia Historical Society

ROBERT F. STROHM
Associate Director for Administration, Virginia Historical Society

MARSHA TRIMBLE
Curator of Special Collections, Law Library, University of Virginia

GAIL WARREN
State Law Librarian, Commonwealth of Virginia

SARAH K. WIANT
Director of the Law Library and Professor of Law, Washington and Lee University

STATE CODES

Kent C. Olson

I. *Introduction*

IN 1992 the Michie Company released *Virginia Law on Disc*, a CD-ROM product containing the entire text of the Code of Virginia, in addition to court rules and appellate judicial decisions. This and online databases have revolutionized access to Virginia law, but they have not supplanted the published versions of Virginia statutes. They are simply the latest of many innovations in the development of Virginia codes, a story that began in 1612.

Virginia lawyers and legal researchers are usually quite familiar with the *Code of Virginia 1950*, the set of black volumes that has been the source for Virginia statutes for fifty years. For many research needs, the current code is the only statutory source necessary. There are times, however, when it is expedient to consult other resources for historical research, to trace the development of laws now in force, or to determine the laws in effect when potential legal rights or liabilities were created. This chapter is focused on the 1950 Code and its predecessors, the sources with which to begin most historical research.

Since 1619, legislative power in Virginia has resided in the General Assembly, which makes enactments or statements of law. These enactments are then published in various forms. They are collected and published at the end of each session in the form called session laws. They are also arranged by subject matter and published as codes of law. Codes can be official enactments of the legislature or collections of statutes published by a private person. It is better to cite to an official code or an official publication of session laws than to an unofficial code, however easy of use the latter may be.

The term "code" is applied to documents of varying scope. There can be a codification of the law of or statutes on a specific branch of the law, such as the Uniform Commercial Code, the Probate Code, or the criminal code. Secondly, there can be a codification of all of the statutes in force, such as the Code of Virginia.[1] Finally, there can be a codification of an entire system of law, such as the codes of continental Europe and most of Latin America.[2]

---

[1] Another example is the Code of Justinian (A.D. 534).

[2] The most famous examples are the French *Code Napoleon* (1804-1810) and the German *Burgerlischesgesetzbuch* (1900).

II. *Acts of Assembly*

In addition to the codes, it is often necessary to consult the session laws, known as the *Acts of Assembly*. This series contains all the laws enacted by the General Assembly, arranged chronologically. A volume is published at the end of each session of the legislature.[3] Manuscript session laws exist from the seventeenth century, but the first printed Acts of Assembly were advertised by William Parks in 1730 and the oldest surviving volume dates from 1732. Laws from the early sessions occupied only a few dozen pages; in recent years there have been over 2,000 pages each year.[4]

The Acts of Assembly is the source to use in order to find the text of a particular act or to analyze the activities of a single session of the legislature. Its text is often the only way to determine exactly when a specific change was made in a statute. Using older volumes can be quite frustrating, for it is rarely clear just what change has been made in an amendment. The new act may simply refer to an earlier session law, and a careful comparison of the two provisions is necessary to find changes. This problem was partially alleviated in 1950 when the Acts of Assembly began to use *italics* to show new or changed language. Since 1970 the volumes have also shown the language being deleted from a provision, so that the ~~old~~ and *new* language can be compared and the change determined easily.

The first index to an annual volume appeared in 1770, printed by William Rind. This innovation lasted only until 1772, and the annual index did not become a regular feature until 1788. In addition to the annual indexes, there are several covering longer periods. The first of these, *Index to Enrolled Bills of the General Assembly of Virginia, 1776 to 1910*, by John W. Williams (1911), indicates the year in which to find legislation, but for some reason its references are to the original bound parchment sheets rather than to the printed session law volumes. The researcher then needs to check the index in the annual volume for the appropriate page number. This index has two parts; the first, covering 1776 to 1862, was first published separately in 1908, and the second covers 1863 to 1910. The next volume, *Index of Acts of the General Assembly of the Commonwealth of Virginia 1912-1959* (1959), was compiled by Alice Clark Pierce, Deputy Clerk of the House of Delegates, who according to the preface "displayed an unusual aptitude as an indexer." One welcome indication of this aptitude is that this

[3] Va. Code Ann. § 30-34.5.

[4] The Virginia *Acts of Assembly* and legislative journals are listed in W. H. Bryson, *Bibliography of Virginia Legal History Before 1900*, pp. 221–237 (2d ed. 1997).

volume, unlike the 1776-1910 index, does cite to the chapter and page of the published Acts of Assembly. Later cumulative indexes have covered 1960 to 1965 and subsequent five-year periods through 1986 to 1990.

III. *The Development of Code Publication*

Because the Acts of Assembly contain only newly enacted laws, they do not provide a cohesive or systematic view all of the statute law in force at any given time. For this purpose, one must turn to the Code of 1950 or one of its predecessors.

As one goes backward into Virginia history, generally the codes get more rudimentary and less accessible. The features taken for granted in modern codes tend to disappear. The familiar subject arrangement of statutes has been used only since 1819; earlier collections arranged laws in force chronologically by date of enactment. Several major features which make the codes useful in research developed gradually over the years. A code must be revised or updated frequently or it will quickly become obsolete. Because case law is frequently so important in interpreting statutes, references to cases, or annotations, provide essential information complementing the statutory text. To facilitate historical research, a code must also provide references to the sources from which each section derives. Finally, a code must have a thorough and detailed subject index to be of much value at all. This section explores the development of each of these features in Virginia codes.

A. *Revision and Updating*

There are two types of collections of laws published: revisions and compilations. The preface to the Code of 1919 explains this distinction:

> The statutes of this State of a general nature have been revised and codified but three times since the year 1819. These codifications consist of the Codes of 1849, 1887, and the present Code. There have been other publications called Codes, to wit: the Codes of 1860, 1873 and 1904, and two supplements of the last mentioned, but these publications were not codifications. They were mere compilations of statutes by private persons, and while declared by statutes to be *prima facie* evidence of the statutes embraced therein, they were only *prima facie* evidence, and if they varied from the original statutes, the latter always prevailed. Not so of the Codes. In each instance the Code is enacted as a new law

> embracing all statutes of a general nature, civil and criminal, and all such statutes as are not embraced in the Code or kept in force by some provision thereof are repealed. The present volume was enacted by the legislature as a single act of assembly, and, except as therein provided, contains all statutes of a general nature, civil and criminal, in force in this Commonwealth on January 9, 1918. All others of that class are repealed. The statutes contained in this Code are original statutes, not copies.

For centuries, Virginia struggled every generation or so to organize its laws into a revision. The problems of the committee working on the revision of 1706 were typical: "The assignment was taking longer than had been anticipated. The members of the committee found that the job required `great care diligence & study, sedate quiet thought & the most intense application of minds not disturbed with business of another nature'."[5] Finally with the current Code of 1950 the legislature stopped worrying about revising the entire code and began revising its individual titles. Under this method parts of the code are periodically modernized in a more manageable fashion, and the 1950 code remains reasonably current.

Another problem over the centuries has been the quick obsolescence of the codes. The General Assembly never stops enacting laws once a code is published. To find the current law, one would often have to use both the code and several volumes of later session laws. Many attorneys would note new laws and amendments in the margins and endpapers of their copies of the codes. Within a few years the need for a new code would be painfully obvious.

This situation improved only in this century, when regular supplementation of the codes finally began. John Garland Pollard, editor of the 1904 code, began issuing biennial supplements, and this tradition was picked up by the Michie Company once it published its first code in 1924. A committee studying a new code format in the 1940s recommended pocket part supplementation, a format being used by the *United States Code Annotated* and codes in several states. Pocket parts to the *Code of Virginia 1950* were first issued biennially after each regular session.

When the General Assembly began meeting every year in 1970, the frequency of the pocket parts was increased to match. They are now published each June, to be in place when the new laws take effect on

[5] H. F. Rankin, *Virginia Laws: Codification and Printing*, I-30 (1957, published on microfiche in 1989) (quoting *Executive Journals of the Council of Colonial Virginia*, vol. 2, p. 87 (1927)).

July first. As individual pocket parts became unwieldy, they are superseded by replacement volumes.

The Roman jurists illustrated the doctrine of corporate continuity though the individual membership changed with the story of the ship of Theseus, which was preserved in a museum in Athens. As the individual planks rotted, they were replaced with new ones, and the new ones thus became part of the old ship. Eventually, all of the original parts were replaced, and yet the historic old ship continued in existence.[6] So it is also with the Virginia Code of 1950. Eventually, all of the sections will be amended or replaced. However, because the Code of 1950 is continually being kept up to date in a serviceable way by means of pocket parts and replacement volumes, this Code of Virginia can continue in existence indefinitely.

B. Annotations

The terms of a statute rarely stand alone. They must be read as interpreted by the courts. Yet for years the codes contained no mention of decisions affecting the statutes. It was left to attorneys to mark up their own copies of the code. As a book notice at the end of the nineteenth century remarked, "It is the rule rather than the exception, that the lawyer has annotated his Code quite thoroughly."[7]

Brief citations to cases were introduced in the Code of 1849, but these were limited to marginal notes indicating simply the name of the reporter, volume, and page. By 1887, little had changed. Most case citations still appeared in the margins, although a few chapters had footnotes indicating the names of the cases and one-line descriptions of the holdings. The revisors explained: "It was much desired that the references to adjudged cases should be by their titles in full, but it was found that references in that form would greatly increase the size of the volume, and therefore they were not thus made, except in a few instances."[8]

The need for information on case law was met by the digest, a publication that summarized the statutes by subject and provided extensive footnotes describing relevant cases. This approach was used by Joseph Tate in 1823 and by James Matthews in 1856. By the time

[6] *Digest*, 5.1.76; A. Watson, *Law Making in the Later Roman Republic*, pp. 189-190 (1974); Sir Matthew Hale in *The History of the Common Law*, p. 40 (C. M. Gray, ed., 1971), makes the same analogy in reference to Jason's ship, *Argo*.

[7] *Va. L. Reg.*, vol. 1, p. 939 (1896).

[8] Va. Code of 1887, "Preface," p. v.

of Matthews's final edition in 1890, he had abandoned his subject arrangement and was printing the code sections in numerical order accompanied by judicial references. The distinction between code and digest was blurring.

In 1895, Abram C. Eby published a work entitled *Citations to the Code of Virginia*. His volume did not reprint or summarize the statutes themselves; instead section by section it described cases decided under each section of the code. He listed cases chronologically, but sought to avoid merely cumulative listings of cases, "as the value of a work of this kind will depend upon its concise statement of an authoritative decision on each point which has been questioned."

By the end of the nineteenth century, more than half of the states had published annotated codes, combining the text of the statutes with case summaries. Virginia's first annotated code was published in 1904 by John Garland Pollard. George Bryan enthused about the benefit Pollard provided to the attorney: "We have now, for the first time, an *Annotated Code*. Where, in the others, there have been a few blind citations of cases construing the several sections, we now have not only the names of the cases, but a summary of their rulings."[9] Pollard's work established a standard for all subsequent editions of the Virginia code.

C. Parallel References

Often a researcher needs to study the development of a law over a period of years or centuries, either to determine what happened to a section of an outdated code or to trace the predecessors of a current code section. In the early years of Virginia law, it was necessary to find the appropriate provisions in each code by browsing or by using subject indexes. In modern times tables and cross-references have greatly simplified this work.

Nowadays researching back into time is usually a straightforward process, although it frequently requires handling several large code volumes. If there is a law in the current code, its origin is indicated in parentheses at the end of the statutory language. Sections enacted or amended since the most recent revision of a title are cited to the Acts of Assembly. Sections carried over from the earlier title are cited to the previous section number, and sections predating the Code of 1950 are cited either to the 1919 code or to subsequent session laws and the Michie Code of 1942.

To continue back further requires access to the Code of 1919 or to

[9] *Va. L. Reg.*, vol. 10, p. 757 (1904).

one of the Michie codes published between 1924 and 1942. The 1919 section numbers cite to their predecessors in the Code of 1887. This code in turn provides references to the Code of 1849, which leads to the Revised Code of 1819 and to Hening's *Statutes at Large*. Finally, the Revised Code of 1819 contains a wealth of references to earlier codifications dating back to the seventeenth century.

Research tracing the history of early statutes requires more patience, for older codes were not very precise about designating the sources of their contents. As Hening noted in 1810: "Unfortunately, in the various revisals which we have had of our laws, but two (the edition of *Pleasants & Pace*, in 1803, and of *Pleasants*, in 1807) have any references to the laws from which they were originally taken."[10]

Working forward in time, trying to learn the fate of a code provision found in an older reference, has become a simple task in this century. The "Tables" volume of the Code of 1950 lists each section of the 1919 code, indicating its location or disposition in the current code. Similar tables, showing the disposition of sections in the 1887 code, are found in the Code of 1919 and in each of the Michie codes.

D. *Indexing*

Ever since the Purvis collection in the 1680s included an "alphabetical table" of its contents, it has been clear that a useful index is a key element in access to the statutes. As T. Munford Boyd wrote,

> The practical utility of any law book, and particularly a compilation of statutes, depends in no small degree upon the completeness of its index. The difference between a law book with a good index and one lacking this advantage is literally equivalent to the proverbial difference between order and chaos.[11]

While a few early collections were published without indexes, most code editors have understood this need and have advertised the clarity and improved nature of their indexes. Early compilations with indexes proudly noted the fact on their title pages. The preface in the Code of 1803 states:

> All the gentlemen of the law, with one voice, complained of the imperfections of the former index. A new one has been entirely

[10] Hening's Statutes, vol. 2, p. v.

[11] Book Review, *Va. L. Rev.*, vol. 15, pp. 521-522 (1929).

The Revised Code

OF THE

LAWS OF VIRGINIA:

BEING

A COLLECTION OF ALL SUCH ACTS

OF THE

GENERAL ASSEMBLY,

OF A PUBLIC AND PERMANENT NATURE, AS ARE NOW IN FORCE;

WITH A GENERAL INDEX.

TO WHICH ARE PREFIXED,

THE CONSTITUTION OF THE UNITED STATES;
THE DECLARATION OF RIGHTS;
AND
THE CONSTITUTION OF VIRGINIA.

Published pursuant to an act of the General Assembly, entitled "An act providing for the re-publication of the Laws of this Commonwealth," passed March 12, 1819.

VOLUME I.

RICHMOND:
PRINTED BY THOMAS RITCHIE,
PRINTER TO THE COMMONWEALTH.

1819.

> wrote over again, and at a very considerable expense, for the present edition. In the former, there were, under the letter A, only *twenty-six* different heads. In this edition, there are *forty-nine*.

By modern standards, these early indexes were rudimentary affairs. Under each heading, references were simply listed in the order in which they appeared in the volume making it necessary at times to scan through several columns for relevant material. A book notice in 1856 complained: "There is now no legal work more needed in Virginia than a complete and perfect index to the statutes of the State. The man who will accomplish it, will deserve and will receive the profound gratitude of the profession."[12]

Yet the problem endured for almost forty more years. A review of the 1887 code notes:

> The index seems to be full and accurate enough, but only actual use can sufficiently test that. We regret exceedingly, however, that it was not differently arranged. It would be difficult to overestimate its increased usefulness if the entries had been made in alphabetical order under the titles, after the manner of the admirable index to Barton's Chancery Practice. As it is we experience a painful sense of discouragement upon turning, say to the title "Clerks of Courts," and finding six and a half columns of index to toil through.[13]

Another reviewer commented,

> Since the publication of the Code of 1887 there has been a very general regret on the part of the profession in the State, and all those who have to consult that work, that the learned revisors did not see fit, or were unable for want of the necessary time, to prepare a fuller and more comprehensive index thereto . . . . Since the one affixed to Code of 1849, we have not enjoyed the advantages of a proper index to our Codes, nor was that one all that could be desired.[14]

This writer was reviewing a vastly improved index prepared by Overton Howard of the Virginia bar, *Howard's Index to the Code of Virginia of 1887* (1895). Howard's preface explained that his work was

---

[12] *Q.L.J.*, vol. 1, pp. 189-190 (1856).

[13] Editorial, *Va. L. J.*, vol. 12, pp. 294-295 (1888).

[14] *Va. L. Reg.*, vol. 1, p. 939 (1896).

similar to indexes in Minor's *Institutes* or Barton's works.

> If, for example, you wish to find the law, that payment of the tax is required before probate of a will you will look for *Wills —probate—tax prerequisite*. You find wills in its alphabetical place, skipping over all intervening references under *wills*, you find in its alphabetical place, *probate*; and skipping over all intervening letters under *probate*, you find *tax* in its alphabetical place, where you find what you want.

Howard's enthusiasm about his index only became excessive when he recommended that students read it in its entirety as a way of reviewing the Code.

Howard's index was 203 pages; the index to Pollard's annotated code in 1904 covered 356 pages. It too was hailed by a reviewer:

> Last, and to many minds the most important feature of all, is the Index. We really have now an index which indicates—a scientific system of inclusion and exclusion, prepared by the expert in that line of the West Publishing Company, by means of which we can find every phase of each subject indexed under at least one head, if not under two or more.[15]

Similar claims of scientific precision were made when the preface of Michie's *Virginia Code of 1936* introduced a new index:

> It is with pardonable pride that reference is here made to the Index to this compilation. Many months have been spent to the end that the Bench and Bar of this State may have in this Code an index that will compare favorably with that in the Code of any other State. Rigid tests to which the present index has been subjected indicate that it is thorough and accurate.

By 1950, the index had grown to over 1,400 pages, supplemented with an ever larger pocket part. In 1963 it was split into three volumes with over 2,800 pages, and in 1975 Michie began publishing new index volumes each year. In 1994 the publisher again introduced a newly revised index, this time reset in smaller type and occupying only two volumes.

Despite steady indexing improvements, researchers have continued to have problems finding statutes. Well aware of widespread frustration with statutory indexes, Michie provides postcards in the back of each volume, on which users can complain or recommend

---

[15] G. Bryan, Book Review, *Va. L. Reg.*, vol. 10, p. 757 (1904).

improvements. It also maintains toll-free telephone and fax numbers for index assistance. F. D. G. Ribble's comments of seventy years ago, however, remain true today: "The indexes of codes are often among the most troublesome of the devices which aid or confound the lawyer, as few indexes seem thoroughly logical except to their makers."[16]

IV. *Conclusion*

The following annotated list of major Virginia statutory publications includes both official revisions and private compilations. It is divided into three parts: first codes and then other collections, abridgments, and digests, the latter being private publications designed to help researchers make sense of the forest of statutes. The final part gives the reports of revisors of codes.

In addition to the general works listed here, there have been hundreds of publications of Virginia statutes on specialized subjects. These began as early as 1808, with Thomas Nicolson's publication of *The Militia Laws of This Commonwealth, and of the United States.* These specialized works have been published both by state agencies in the areas of their specialty and by private publishers. Some have been published on a regular basis, such as the State Corporation Commission's collections of banking and corporation laws. Others, such as *Laws of Virginia Relating to the Insane, Epileptic, Feeble-Minded and Inebriate* (Legislative Reference Bureau, 1920), appeared only once. The Michie Company, publisher of general Virginia codes since 1924, has printed collections in over fifty subject areas, usually under the auspices of state agencies. These range in length from the seven-page *Agricultural Lime Law* (Virginia Department of Agriculture and Commerce/Michie, 1974) to the three-volume *Police, Crimes and Offenses and Motor Vehicle Laws of Virginia* (Department of State Police/Michie, 1988). Most of Michie's collections simply reprint statutes from the official code, usually without annotations, but some include other material such as the State Corporation Commission's Rules of Practice and Procedure, forms, and indexes. This class of statutory publication has not been included in the following bibliography.

[16] Book Review, *Va. L. Rev.*, vol. 11, p. 500 (1925).

BIBLIOGRAPHY

I. *Codes*

Code of 1612

For the Colony in Virginea Britannia. Lawes Divine, Morall and Martiall, &c. London: Walter Burre, 1612; ed. by Peter Force in *Tracts and Other Papers*, Washington, D.C.: W. Q. Force, 1844, vol. 3, no. 2; New York: P. Smith, 1947; Gloucester, Mass.: Peter Smith, 1963; ed. by David H. Flaherty, Charlottesville: University Press of Va., 1969; facsimile ed. Amsterdam: Theatrum Orbis Terrarum, and New York: Da Capo Press, 1972.

> This was the first legal code for English-speaking America, but an anomaly in Virginia law. It provided a severe code of conduct for the struggling colony, with the death penalty imposed for offenses ranging from bearing false witness to stealing crops. These rules were put into force when Sir Thomas Gates arrived as Acting Governor in 1610, and the following year they were enlarged to include martial laws by Sir Thomas Dale. In 1612 the collected laws were published in London with a foreword by William Strachey (c. 1572-1621), who had been secretary of the colony. Their application ended in 1619 when the new Assembly began making laws. David H. Flaherty's introduction to the 1969 reprint edition provides a thorough discussion of this code.

Code of 1632

> By 1632, the body of enacted laws had already grown confusing. The Assembly organized the first official revision of the laws, in order to provide "a clearer explanation of some of them, as likewise some additions and alterations." Hening's Statutes, vol. 1, p. 179. This revision is printed in Hening's Statutes, vol. 1, pp. 179-202. Note that this is a true code in that it repealed all previous statutes so that it remained the only statute law in force.

Code of 1643

> Ten years after the codification of 1632 it was necessary once again to reduce the laws "into a more exact method and order." Hening's Statutes, vol. 1, pp. 239-240. Again, the General Assembly repealed all previous statutes so that all of

the statute law would be contained in this single compilation. This revision is printed in Hening's Statutes, vol. 1, pp. 238-282.

Code of 1652

During the Commonwealth of Oliver Cromwell there were two further revisions. The first, in 1652, was unknown to Hening, but is printed in Warren M. Billings, ed., "Some Acts Not in Hening's *Statutes*: The Acts of Assembly, April 1652, November 1652, and July 1653," *Va. Mag. Hist. Biog.*, vol. 83, pp. 27-72 (1975).

Code of 1657

The second revision of the code during the Interregnum, in 1657, is printed in Hening's Statutes, vol. 1, pp. 429-495.

Code of 1662

The Lawes of Virginia Now in Force. Collected Out of the Assembly Records, and Digested into One Volume. London: E. Cotes for A. Seile, 1662.

The 1662 revision was made necessary by the Restoration of Charles II in 1660. It was clear that the acts and ordinances of the Interregnum in England were void in that they never received the Royal Assent, but the legality of the acts of the General Assembly was unclear because they had been approved the Governor of Virginia although he had not been appointed by the king. To clarify the situation, a new code was prepared under the supervision of Francis Moryson, deputy governor, and Henry Randolph, clerk of the General Assembly. The revision was enacted in March 1662 and sent to London for printing. It is more widely accessible as reprinted in Hening's Statutes, vol. 2, pp. 41-148. This code is substantially larger than any that had gone before.

Code of 1684

A Complete Collection of All the Laws of Virginia Now in Force. Carefully Copied from the Assembly Records. To Which is Annexed an Alphabetical Table. London: T.J. for J.P., [1684].

A private compilation was published without date but dedicated to Lord Howard, governor from 1684 to 1687. The work is attributed to John Purvis, commander of the ship *The Duke of York*. The book appeared shortly after William Nuthead had been prevented from printing Acts of Assembly without authorization and further printing was banned from Virginia. In April 1684 Purvis was reprimanded for producing a work that was "found to be very false and imperfect" and for printing without license, and Lord Howard (despite the dedication) ordered that the publication be suppressed and inadmissible in any county court. *Journals of the House of Burgesses 1659/1660-1693*, pp. 201, 203 (1914). The collection was also severely criticized by Hening for its omitted acts, missing sentences, and innumerable typographical errors. Hening's Statutes, vol. 1, p. v. Nonetheless it provided access to the laws, included a brief index, and remained in use in the colony until 1733. A 1699 act appointing a revision committee recognized that "the whole body of the laws . . . do lie in great disorder and confusion by reason that many of them are repealed, others obsolete and out of use some expired and many made in the infancy of this country inconsistent and hardly intelligible." Hening's Statutes, vol. 3, p. 181. The Assembly finally passed a revision in 1706, but two of the most important statutes were vetoed by the governor, and another failed when the House of Burgesses and the Council could not agree on its provisions. As a result, the Assembly refused to print the laws and for a hundred years this revision existed in manuscript only. It is printed in Hening's Statutes, vol. 3, pp. 229-481.

Code of 1727

Acts of Assembly, Passed in the Colony of Virginia, from 1662, to 1715. London: John Baskett, 1727.

This compilation, known as Baskett's Edition, was first published in 1727 with "Volume I" on the title page, and then reprinted the following year without the added "to 1715" and with no volume designation. It is an obscure work, apparently unknown to Jefferson and Hening and not mentioned in the codes of 1819 or 1849. Not limited to acts in force, it also included numerous repealed and obsolete provisions. The entire volume was already twelve years out of date when printed. It has no subject index.

Code of 1733

A Collection of All the Acts of Assembly, Now in Force, in the

Colony of Virginia. Williamsburg: William Parks, 1733; rept. Baltimore: Gateway Pr., Inc., 1976.

This book was the first domestic publication of Virginia law and one of the first books published in the colony. The compilation was edited by George Webb, who three years later would produce the first Virginia law text, *The Office and Authority of a Justice of the Peace* (1736). It was printed by William Parks, who as Maryland's public printer had published *A Compleat Collection of the Laws of Maryland* in 1727. In Williamsburg in 1730 he established Virginia's first press since William Nuthead was enjoined from printing in 1683. Parks published the first printed Acts of Assembly, and was named public printer in 1732. According to its title page, this collection was published pursuant to an order of the General Assembly and was "examined with the records, by a committee appointed for that purpose." It was, however, a private venture as indicated by its list of over 200 subscribers. It is considered one of the finest examples of colonial printing as well as the "first adequate compilation of the laws of colonial Virginia." H. F. Rankin, *Virginia Laws: Codification and Printing,* II-12. It was reprinted in 1976 by the Bicentennial Committee of the Virginia State Bar.

Code of 1752

The Acts of Assembly, Now in Force, in the Colony of Virginia. Williamsburg: William Hunter, 1752.

This was the second revision of the laws to be published as a printed code. A joint committee of the Council and the House of Burgesses was appointed in 1745, and George Webb, editor of the 1733 compilation, was named clerk of the committee. The committee issued its report in 1748 and the revision was passed that year. The laws appear in Hening's Statutes, vol. 5, pp. 408-558, and were published in 1752 by William Hunter, who had been journeyman printer under William Parks and purchased Parks's press from his estate. The laws had already been printed when it was learned that the king had repealed ten of the sixty-seven acts by royal proclamation, so this important fact was noted in an appendix. The repeal forced the publication, in 1752 or 1753, of a fifty-eight page supplement of older laws which would otherwise have been superseded by the new acts.

Code of 1769

Acts of Assembly, Now in Force, in the Colony of Virginia. Williamsburg: W. Rind, A. Purdie, & J. Dixon, 1769.

> This final collection of statutes before the revolution was published by order of the General Assembly but did not revise the laws in force. It updated the 1752 compilation but did not differ much from its predecessor in content or style.

A Collection of All Such Public Acts of the General Assembly, and Ordinances of the Conventions of Virginia, Passed Since the Year 1768, As Are Now in Force. Richmond: Thomas Nicolson and William Prentis, 1785; rept. Wilmington, Del.: Michael Glazier, Inc., 1982.

> Commonly known as the "Chancellors' Revisal," this publication was a stopgap effort to provide access to statutes of the new commonwealth. Compiled by Edmund Pendleton, George Wythe, and John Blair, the judges of the High Court of Chancery, it merely updated the 1769 compilation and needed to be used in conjunction with that work. The Chancellors' Revisal is a disappointing work because much more was attempted in the early years of independence. In 1777 Pendleton, Wythe, and Thomas Jefferson began work on a comprehensive revision of the law. Jefferson in particular sought to create a new, republican code of laws, with radical changes in the law of descent and religious freedom. The revisors submitted their report in June 1779, but their work was not adopted by the General Assembly. Instead selected acts were singled out and enacted over the course of the next several years. The revision as a whole was considered at the October 1785 session, but only about a third of the bills were passed. A few more were enacted at the October 1786 session, but the entire revision was never adopted. The proposed revision was published in *Report of the Committee of Revisors Appointed by the General Assembly of Virginia* (1784). Julian P. Boyd's "Editorial Note" in *The Papers of Thomas Jefferson,* vol. 2, p. 305 (1950), provides an extensive overview of these developments.

Code of 1792

A Collection of All Such Acts of the General Assembly of Virginia, of a Public and Permanent Nature, As Are Now in Force. Richmond: Augustine Davis, 1794.

Following the failure of the Jefferson revision, it took several committees to secure finally a comprehensive revision of Virginia acts. Committees of revisors were appointed in 1787 and 1789, but they only completed preliminary work in the revision process. Finally a committee appointed in October 1790 completed the task, and a revision was adopted in 1792. Unlike Jefferson's proposed revision, this work merely collected the existing laws rather than attempting to change them. The volume published in 1794 was a chronological collection of acts, but it includes the 1792 revision at pages 61-305. Charles T. Cullen, "Completing the Revisal of the Laws in Post-Revolutionary Virginia," *Va. Mag. Hist. Biog.*, vol. 82, pp. 84-99 (1974), discusses this revision process.

A Collection of All Such Acts of the General Assembly of Virginia, of a Public and Permanent Nature, As Are Now in Force. Richmond: Samuel Pleasants, Jun. and Henry Pace, 1803; 2d ed. Richmond: Samuel Pleasants, 1814.

This compilation updating the 1794 collection was published pursuant to an 1802 Act of Assembly. Shepherd's *Statutes*, vol. 2, p. 386. The compilers noted in the preface: "It would be the summit of frivolity to expatiate upon the importance of a work like this; because it is plain, that every family in the Commonwealth should, if possible, possess a copy of it." It was, nonetheless, little different from its predecessor. It did include six acts predating the 1792 code but omitted from that publication, which were "selected, and inserted by the special advice and desire of Governor Monroe." It was republished in 1814 with additional notes and an expanded index.

A Collection of All Such Acts of the General Assembly of Virginia, of a Public and Permanent Nature As Have Passed Since the Session of 1801. Richmond: Samuel Pleasants, Junior, 1808.

This book updated the 1803 collection and included fifty-seven more acts passed since 1785 but omitted in the 1794 and 1803 collections.

Supplement Containing the Acts of the General Assembly of Virginia, of a Public and Permanent Nature As Have Passed Since the Session of Assembly [in 1807]. Richmond: Samuel Pleasants, 1812.

Code of 1819

The Revised Code of the Laws of Virginia. Richmond: Thomas Ritchie, 1819, 2 vols.

> The first effort in Virginia to classify the statute law by subject matter, this code was prepared by Benjamin Watkins Leigh (1781-1849), with the assistance of William Waller Hening (1767-1828) and William Munford (1775-1825). Leigh had been a member of the House of Delegates in 1811-13, and from 1829 to 1841 would be the reporter of the Court of Appeals. Leigh was charged by the General Assembly to "prescribe the order, in which the several laws shall be published in the code, carefully classing them according to their subject matter, without reference to the time of their passage." Act of March 12, 1819, ch. 35, 1819 Va. Acts, pp. 50, 63. Although at least eight other state codes were already arranged by subject, Leigh understood that Virginia's conservative bar might object to the new subject arrangement, and he wrote: "This novel order of publication rendered it impossible to designate the year of the Commonwealth, at the top of the page, as in all the other publications of our laws since the revolution. Loath to deviate from the custom of dating all public acts from the epoch of our independence, (a custom grateful to public feeling, and, in my opinion, of real utility,) I have placed the year, of the foundation of the republic, as well as the year of our Lord, in the side margin." Preface, p. iii. The code was adopted by the General Assembly in 1819, and all existing acts of a general nature not included in the code were at the same time repealed as of January 1, 1820. It was published in two volumes and contained 262 chapters arranged in twenty-three subject titles. For each section the code indicated the original act or acts from which it was compiled, and it provided references at the beginning of most chapters to former general laws relating to the same subjects. An appendix includes a three-page account of earlier publications of Virginia law. A century later, Earl G. Swem noted in "A Bibliography of Virginia, Part II," *Bull. Va. St. Lib.*, vol. 10, pp. 1, 169 (1917): "The code of 1819 is as valuable to historical students as Hening's statutes. The footnotes are numerous and elaborate. On the subjects of many chapters the notes give an historical survey from 1619. There is a complete index of nearly 200 pages."

Supplement to the Revised Code of the Laws of Virginia. Richmond: Samuel Shepherd & Co., 1833.

This volume contained acts passed since 1819 and the new Constitution resulting from the convention of 1829-30. It too arranged the laws by subject, but it did not attempt to incorporate the new acts into the code's numbering system. Instead it simply assigned them new chapter numbers from 1 to 401.

Code of 1849

The Code of Virginia. Richmond: William L. Ritchie, 1849.

Perhaps the most thorough revision of Virginia law to be enacted into law, the Code of 1849 was principally the work of John M. Patton and Conway Robinson. Patton (1797-1858) had served in the U.S. House of Representatives (1831-1838) and on the Virginia Council of State (1938-1841). Robinson (1805-1884) was a respected legal scholar, author of the three-volume *Practice in the Courts of Law and Equity* (1832-1839), and official reporter of Court of Appeals from 1842 to 1844. In 1836 he married the daughter of Benjamin Watkins Leigh, editor of the 1819 code. Whereas Leigh simply combined multiple acts into single statutes, the General Assembly asked Patton and Robinson to "suggest such contradictions, omissions or imperfections, as they may perceive in the statutes" and to execute the revision "in such a manner as in their opinion will render the said general statutes most concise, plain and intelligible." Act of Feb. 20, 1846, ch. 33, 1845-46 Va. Acts, pp. 26, 26-27. Their five reports presented to the General Assembly between 1847 and 1849 summarize the difficulties they encountered in trying to make sense of the statutes. Some arcane distinctions elude them; in a section dealing with lumber inspections, they shrug their shoulders and note, "What is the difference between `white oak staves' and `rough white oak staves,' we do not know. In the existing law, the dimensions of both are the same, and yet they are carefully repeated as to both." *Report of the Revisors of the Code of Virginia*, vol. 2, p. 480 (1848). By 1849, however, they were proceeding much more confidently. In their fourth report, they note, "A marked difference will be perceived on comparing this and the last report with the two which preceded it. The subjects on which we have latterly acted, having come a good deal before us in professional life, we have had less reluctance to propose changes in the laws respecting them than in relation to others with which we were less familiar; and even in respect to these, the stage of the work at which we acted on them, has probably led us to go farther than we might have done if they had been taken up in the first or second report." *Report of the Revisors*, vol. 4, p. iv (1849). They even begin acknowledging differences of opinion, as in this footnote to a section on an attorney's liability to his client: "One of us thinks this section may be omitted as of no value." *Id.* at p. 826. For the first two years Patton and Robinson focused their attention on the state's civil laws, as a revision of the criminal laws had been in progress for over a decade. Chapman Johnson began work on this revision in 1836. When his health failed, Robert G. Scott took over and issued a *Revision and Digest of the Criminal Code of Virginia* in 1846. The following year the criminal laws were turned over to Patton and Robinson for incorporation in the code; after substantial revision, they were covered in their final report in July 1849. Ever mindful of the cumbersome and prolix two-volume 1819 code, Patton and Robinson were pleased that their code could be published in a single volume of under one thousand pages. They wrote in 1848: "To attain this result is a work of great labour; a hundred fold greater than would be required to have a Code of three or four volumes. But such a result we regard as so desirable that we shall not relax our endeavours to accomplish it." *Report of the Revisors*, vol. 2, p. v (1848). After numerous, mostly minor amendments by the General Assembly's Joint Committee of Revision, the code was passed in 1849 and entered into force on July 1, 1850. It was generally accepted as a modernization of Virginia statutory law, but some felt it had gone too far. An article published in 1857 commented: "The Code of Virginia, of 1849, contains much that is new to the jurisprudence and legislation of the Commonwealth; and unfortunately, its faults are about of equal magnitude with its novelty. Its framers seem to have labored under a delusion as to the nature of their duties. Too many of its provisions seem to have been enacted merely under the influence of a restless desire for change. . . ." "Imprisonment for Debt," *Q.L.J.*, vol. 2, pp. 209, 214 (1857). The code consists of 216 chapters in fifty-six titles, with sections in each chapter individually numbered. Marginal notes indicate the source for each section, providing references to the Acts of Assembly, the Revised Code of 1819, and Hening's *Statutes at Large*. For some sections, terse case citations are also provided in the margins. The code provides a variety of historical information, including a lengthy preface summarizing the history of Virginia codifications and footnotes tracing the development of major institutions and legal doctrines back to the seventeenth century. The code of 1849 remained in force for almost forty years.

The Code of Virginia. Second Edition, Including Legislation to the

Year 1860. Richmond: Ritchie, Dunnavant & Co., 1860; rept. Westport, Conn.: Negro Universities Press, 1970.

The Code of 1849 was updated in 1860 by George W. Munford, Secretary of the Commonwealth. This edition included the new Constitution of 1851. This book was not an official revision of the statutes, but it was authorized by the General Assembly by 1859-60 Va. Acts, ch. 85, p. 191; and 1861 Va. Acts, ch. 32, p. 56.

Third Edition of the Code of Virginia: Including Legislation to January 1, 1874. Richmond: James E. Goode, 1873.

The Code of 1849 was updated again by George W. Munford in 1873. Note 1872-73 Va. Acts, ch. 228, p. 205. It included the new Constitution of 1870. In these compilations new acts were assigned section numbers and inserted where Munford thought most reasonable, but these assignments were not official and neither edition was adopted as a revision. Meanwhile the code swelled in size from 898 pages to 1,022 pages to 1873s unwieldy 1,546 pages. A critic of the third edition wrote that "Repetitions, often once, sometimes twice, not never thrice, of the same matter in the same words, increases the bulk of the volume, till we are made to *feel* that `a great book is a great evil.' While, on the other hand, some enactments and other matter which should be contained therein are omitted totally." William Green, "Editions of the Code," *Va. L. J.*, vol. 3, pp. 709, 712-713 (1879).

Code of 1887

The Code of Virginia. Richmond: James E. Goode, 1887.

This revision of the laws was prepared by Judge E. C. Burks, Judge Waller R. Staples, and Major John W. Riely. They were asked to correct contradictions, omissions, and imperfections in the statutes "without producing a radical change in the present system." Act of March 18, 1884, ch. 523, 1883-84 Va. Acts, pp. 702-703. This time the revisors issued no printed reports, but simply submitted their proposed code in manuscript to the General Assembly in 1887. The code was passed by both houses without amendment, received the governor's approval, and went into effect May 1, 1888. It is cited as the Code of 1887. The new code's major innovation was in numbering the 4,205 sections of the code in one consecutive sequence. This followed the system used in the

Revised Statutes of the United States in 1873 and was specified in the 1884 act authorizing the revision. It was a relatively minor change, but one that simplified citation to Virginia statutes.

General Laws of Virginia. 1887-'94. Ed. Jno. Garland Pollard. Richmond: J. L. Hill, [1894].

In 1894 a young Richmond attorney named John Garland Pollard published *Amendments to the Code of Virginia, 1887,* printed on slips of paper intended to be pasted over the sections affected, as well as a volume of new acts, *General Laws of Virginia 1887-'94.*

Supplement to the Code of Virginia. Ed. Jno. Garland Pollard. Richmond: J. L. Hill, 1898.

Pollard improved on his method by publishing a *Supplement to the Code of Virginia,* which printed amended sections, assigned new laws appropriate locations in the code, and noted citations of cases and *Virginia Law Register* articles. His approach of printing only affected sections was innovative enough that the preface explains it in italics: "*The book omits entirely all sections of the Code that have neither been changed by the legislature nor considered by the Supreme Court of Appeals.*" Pollard (1871-1937) was well on his way to being one of the most important figures in Virginia code publication, although this work would eventually be overshadowed by his career in politics and government.

An Annotated Pocket Code of Virginia. By Sam N. Hurst. Pulaski City, Va.: Hurst & Co., 1898; 2d ed., 1905; 3d ed., 1913; 4th ed., 1920; 5th ed., 1928.

In 1898 the General Assembly gave Sam Hurst authority "to publish on his own account and at his own cost and expense a pocket codification . . . provided, that the size of said Code shall not be larger than seven inches long by five inches wide, and the type used shall not be larger than minion." Act of Feb. 2, 1898, ch. 196, 1897-98 Va. Acts, p. 218. The resulting 498-page volume was limited to those parts of the code that Hurst felt an attorney would need in everyday practice. It also provided brief citations of cases and an index to the entire code. Hurst's pocket code was updated several times, in a 1905 second edition, a 1913 third edition, and a 1920 fourth edition, growing larger each time. The fifth and final edition in 1928, now titled *A Pocket Code and Form Book for Virginia Attorneys*, no longer had annotations but had swelled to an unwieldy 1,442 pages and included 320 pages of model forms.

Supplement to the Code of Virginia. Ed. by Jno. Garland Pollard. Richmond: Everett Waddey Co., 1899.

Code of Virginia as Amended to Adjournment of General Assembly, 1904 . . . Annotated. Ed. by Jno. Garland Pollard. St. Paul, Minn.: West Publishing Co., 1904, 2 vols.

In 1904 John Garland Pollard provided his greatest contribution to the field of code publication, a two-volume annotated edition of Virginia statutes. His code was basically a second edition of the 1887 code, published under legislative authority. Act of Dec. 18, 1903, ch. 471, 1902-3-4 Va. Acts, p. 733. It was, however, the first ever to include extensive descriptive annotations after each section. Cases from Virginia and federal courts were summarized, and references were also provided to major Virginia legal periodicals and treatises. The annotations for some sections were quite extensive; § 3455, explaining when appeals were prohibited, was followed by twelve pages of case notes. The profession received the annotated code enthusiastically. George Bryan wrote: "It is far and away the best Code the state has ever had." Book Review, *Va. L. Reg.*, vol. 10, p. 757 (1904). In a "History of Virginia Codification" the following year, William E. Ross called the work "the most ambitious of the kind ever undertaken in Virginia upon individual effort. The value of an *Annotated Code* has for the first time been demonstrated to the Virginia lawyer, and having once seen the practical advantage of such a work, it is not probable that the profession will ever be content with anything but an *Annotated Code*." *Va. L. Reg.*, vol. 11, pp. 79, 98-99 (1905). The 1904 code was West Publishing Company's only foray into Virginia statutory publication. Bryan's review praised West's participation, noting its contribution to the typographical appearance and the indexing, but for some reason it was a one-time shot. From the start, West had no part in the code's supplements, which were printed locally by Richmond's Everett Waddey Company.

Pollard's Code Biennial: Containing All Statutes of a General and Permanent Nature Passed by the General Assembly of Virginia at its Session of 1906: Also Annotations to the Code of Virginia 1904 and the Constitution and Tax Bill. Ed. by Jno. Garland Pollard. Richmond: W.

E. Ross, 1906.

> Pollard's first update came in 1906 with *Pollard's Code Biennial*, which provided acts from the new legislative session.

Garnett, Christopher B[rowne], and Robert N. Pollard. *The Business Man's Code of Virginia Laws*. Pulaski, Va.: B. D. Smith & Bros., 1907.

> This is an abridged edition of the code. It contained "such statutes as every business man needs and should have access to; and excluding the statutes relating to crimes, governmental functions, matters of jurisprudence, and other matters not relating to business," and included forms and annotations. The publishers noted that these statutes were "not liable to change for some years to come," but promised to supply any amendments in a convenient form. True to their word, they issued a pamphlet supplement in 1910.

Pollard's Code Biennial 1908. Richmond: Everett Waddey Co., 1908.

Pollard's Supplement to the Code of Virginia. Richmond: Everett Waddey Co., 1910.

> This cumulated the new acts through the 1910 session of the legislature and is designated on the spine as code volume 3. This same pattern was followed with biennials in 1912 and 1914, and another cumulative supplement (volume 4) in 1916.

Pollard's Code Biennial 1912. Richmond: Everett Waddey Co., 1912.

Pollard's Code Biennial 1914. Ed. by Louis C. Phillips. Richmond: Everett Waddey Co., 1914.

> When Pollard became Attorney General of Virginia in 1913, he turned his publications over to Louis C. Phillips, a member of the bar of James City County. G. Stanley Clarke of the Richmond bar assisted Phillips in this work.

Bumgarner, S[imeon] C[olumbus] *Bumgarner's Pocket Code of Virginia for Magistrates*. Harrisburg, Pa.: United Evangelical Church, 1914.

> This volume was even smaller than Hurst's work, but it included forms, a guide to notaries, and "a list of reliable attorneys in every town" in Virginia.

Pollard's Supplement to the Code of Virginia. Ed. by Louis C. Phillips. Richmond: Everett Waddey Co., 1916.

Pollard's Code Biennial 1918. Ed. by Robert N. Pollard. Richmond: Everett Waddey Co., 1918.

Code of 1919

Code of Virginia. Richmond: Davis Bottom, Superintendent of Public Printing. Unannotated ed., 1918; annotated ed., 1919, 2 vols.

> Despite Pollard's continuing efforts to keep Virginia statutory law accessible, the old Code of 1887 creaked under the weight of added legislation and extensive changes required by a new 1902 constitution. Under an act of March 14, 1914, the governor appointed a revision committee: Samuel A. Anderson, Martin P. Burks, and Francis B. Hutton. Their proposed code passed with few amendments and was approved by governor in March 1918. It would have taken effect on January 1, 1919, but the General Assembly delayed its effective date until January 13, 1920. It is, nonetheless, known as the Code of 1919. The new code consisted of sixty-three titles, with 6,571 consecutively numbered sections. It was published in both an unwieldy one-volume unannotated edition and a two-volume annotated version. In both versions, parenthetical references after each section provide its source in the 1887 Code or in later session laws, and a Table of Sections shows disposition of Code 1887 sections. The 1919 code's annotations in the code were taken with permission from Pollard's earlier works. The new § 6337, dealing with prohibited appeals, now had fifteen pages of annotations, but these simply reprinted Pollard's notes followed by summaries of new cases.

Pollard's Code Biennial 1920. Ed. by Morton L. Wallerstein. Richmond: Everett Waddey Co., 1920.

Pollard's Supplement to the Code of Virginia, 1922: Containing All Statutes of a General and Permanent Nature Passed by the General Assembly at the Sessions of 1918, 1919, 1920 and 1922, Also Annotations to the Code of Virginia, 1919. Ed. by Jno. Garland Pollard. Richmond: Everett Waddey Co., 1922.

> Pollard continued to publish his biennials in 1918 and 1920.

His *Pollard's Supplement to the Code of Virginia 1922*, purporting to be volume 3 of the annotated code, was a confusing volume in which acts not directly amending code provisions were printed in chronological order. This unfortunate approach was one Pollard himself had abandoned back in 1898. The bar would not have to wait long for a more convenient method.

General Laws of the Commonwealth of Virginia, As in Force July 1, 1923. Ed. by C. H. Morrissett. Charlottesville: Surber-Arundale Co., 1923.

Within a very few years the 1919 code was already badly out of date, and Pollard's 1922 supplement did little to ease the confusion. In 1923 Carlisle Havelock Morrissett (1892-1976), who had worked on the annotations for the 1919 code and was director of the State Legislative Reference Bureau, adopted a more effective approach by reissuing the entire code and assigning section numbers to new statutes. The new Workmen's Compensation Act, for example, was squeezed in and assigned the section numbers 1887-1 to 1887-79. As Morrissett noted in his preface, "This is an age of statutes. In Virginia, as elsewhere, the codification of the law continues apace. . . . The increased and increasing volume of legislation, much of it on vital subjects, requires a more frequent publication of the statutes than formerly sufficed." Although Morrissett recognized the need for more frequent publication, he issued just one edition of his work. His volume was greeted as a timely and useful collection of statutes, but its annotations were criticized as inadequate since they only covered the five years since the completion of the Code of 1919. Richard R. Florance, Jr., Book Review, *Va. L. Rev.*, vol. 10, pp. 413-414 (1924). The reader would still have to refer to the 1919 edition to find older cases, and the new volume in effect did little to simplify the work of statutory research.

The Code of Virginia as Amended to Adjournment of General Assembly 1924. Charlottesville: The Michie Co., 1924.

In 1924 the Michie Company issued its first edition of what would popularly become known as the "Michie Code." The company, which was formed in 1897 when it took over publication of *American and English Corporation Cases* and *American and English Railroad Cases*, had begun publishing Virginia law in 1900 with *Virginia Reports Annotated*, a recompilation of Virginia cases from 1730 to 1880. Like Morrissett's *General Laws*, this publication continued the section numbering of the 1919 code; unlike Morrissett, Michie provided extensive, newly revised annotations. The large black volume was a success, and Michie Codes became the standard sources of Virginia law until the 1950 revision. The 1924 edition was prepared under the supervision of Thomas Johnson Michie, one of the founders of the firm and editor of its early works. The 1924 code was supplemented in 1926 and 1928.

Pollard's Code Biennial 1924. Ed. by Jno. Garland Pollard. Richmond: Everett Waddey Co., 1924.

Pollard's Code Biennial 1926. Ed. by Jno. Garland Pollard. Richmond: Everett Waddey Co., 1926.

1926 Supplement to the Virginia Code of 1924. Charlottesville: The Michie Co., 1926.

1928 Supplement to the Virginia Code of 1924. Charlottesville: The Michie Co., 1928.

The Code of Virginia As Amended to Adjournment of General Assembly 1930. Charlottesville: The Michie Co., 1930.

This new edition of the Code was compiled and annotated in 1930 by the editorial staff of The Michie Company under the supervision of A. Hewson Michie. This in turn was supplemented twice before *The Virginia Code of 1936*, edited by A. Hewson Michie and Charles W. Sublett.

1932 Supplement to the Virginia Code of 1930. Charlottesville: The Michie Co., 1932.

1934 Supplement to the Virginia Code of 1930. Charlottesville: The Michie Co., 1934.

The Virginia Code of 1936. Charlottesville: The Michie Co., 1936.

1938 Supplement to the Virginia Code of 1936. Charlottesville: The Michie Co., 1938.

Special 1939 Supplement to the Virginia Code of 1936. Charlottesville: The Michie Co., 1939.

1940 Cumulative Supplement to the Virginia Code of 1936. Charlottesville: The Michie Co., 1940.

The Virginia Code of 1942. Charlottesville: The Michie Co., 1942.

> This edition was edited by A. Hewson Michie, Charles W. Sublett, and Beirne Stedman.

1944 Supplement to the Virginia Code of 1942. Charlottesville: The Michie Co., 1944.

1945 Supplement to the Virginia Code of 1942. Charlottesville: The Michie Co., 1945.

1946 Cumulative Supplement to the Virginia Code of 1942. Charlottesville: The Michie Co., 1946.

1948 Cumulative Supplement to the Virginia Code of 1942. Charlottesville: The Michie Co., 1948.

Code of 1950

Reorganization Provisions of the Code of Virginia. Richmond: Div. of Purchase and Printing, 1948.

Code of Virginia 1950. Charlottesville: The Michie Co., 1949, 10 vols. As of 1995: 24 vols. (1986-1994).

> By the 1940s the old classification system was beginning to show signs of strain; a law dealing with industrial loan associations, for examples, was assigned §§ 4168(11½)a to 4168(11½)e. Meanwhile the single-volume code had grown to over three thousand pages. In 1944 the General Assembly began investigating the creation of a revised code with a new numbering system and "a method whereby changes in the statute law may be incorporated into the official Code or statutes so as to keep such official Code or statutes complete and current at all times." House Joint Resolution No. 28, 1944 Va. Acts, p. 809. By this date over two-thirds of the states had multivolume annotated codes regularly supplemented with pocket parts. A committee looked at the other states' codifications, sent a questionnaire to bench and bar, and returned a recommendation for a multivolume code (it estimated that four would be the proper number of volumes), decimal numbering to indicate titles and sections, and

provision for pocket part supplementation. *Recodification of the Code of Virginia: Report of the Virginia Advisory Legislative Council*, 1946 House Doc. No. 19. A Commission on Code Recodification was created in 1946, and it submitted its report in December 1947. The code was passed in 1948 and became effective on February 1, 1950. The new code contained 65 titles, arranged alphabetically except for "General provisions" in Title 1. Following each section were references to its source in the Code of 1919 or in subsequent session laws and the 1942 Michie Code. The code was extensively annotated by the Michie Company, by now well familiar with Virginia statutes, under the direction of George P. Smith, Jr. In 1948, the recodification commission has been renamed the Virginia Code Commission and made a permanent body responsible for publishing and maintaining the Code. The 1950 Code had not rewritten the laws or made substantive changes. In 1952, Title 38, "Insurance," was completely repealed and replaced by a new Title 38.1. The following year, the Code Commission recommended that the General Assembly continue to revise the law on a title-by-title basis rather than contemplate a wholesale revision of the Code, noting that this was the method followed by Congress in revising the *United States Code*.[17] The General Assembly in turn gave the Code Commission the responsibility for drafting recodification bills.[18] To date over forty titles have been repealed and replaced by successor titles, and eight of these have been replaced a second time. One title, covering "Justices of the Peace," has been repealed, and new titles have been added to cover the "Commercial Code," "Persons with Disabilities," and "Youth and Family Services." Each volume of the code was updated with a pocket part, at first biennially and then annually once the General Assembly began meeting every year in 1970. As the pocket parts have grown cumbersome, volumes have been recompiled or replaced. The first replacement volume was published in 1953 to incorporate the revised "Insurance" title. Since then over a hundred new volumes have been issued, and every one of the original ten volumes has been split into two or more parts. The set now contains twenty-four volumes, none published before 1986.

II. *Other Collections, Abridgments, and Digests*

An Abridgement of the Laws in Force and Use in Her Majesty's

[17] *Revision of the Code of Virginia*, Report of the Virginia Code Commission, 1953 House Doc. No. 29.

[18] Act of April 8, 1954, 1954 Va. Acts, ch. 706, p. 934; Va. Code Ann. § 9-77.11.

Plantations; Virginia, Jamaica, Barbadoes, Maryland, New-England, New-York, Carolina, &c. Digested under Proper Heads in the Method of Mr. Wingate, and Mr. Washington's Abridgements. London: John Nicholson, R. Parker & R. Smith, and Benj. Tooke, 1704.

In the 1690s abridgments of Virginia law were prepared by William Fitzhugh and Philip Ludwell, but neither was published at the time. Fitzhugh's was sent to London in 1694, but is known only from his letters attempting to secure publication. "Letters of William Fitzhugh," *Va. Mag. Hist. Biog.*, vol. 4, pp. 176, 180-181 (1896), pp. 310-311, 415-416 (1897), vol. 5, pp. 297-302 (1898). Ludwell's *An Alphabeticall Abridgment of the Laws of Virginia,* also prepared in 1694, existed only in manuscript until it was published over two hundred years later. It summarized the laws in force under forty-nine subject headings, and included helpful aids such as a table of acts "repealed, expired, or disused," and lists of regnal years, governors, and assemblies. "An Abridgment of the Laws of Virginia," *Va. Mag. Hist. Biog.*, vol. 9, pp. 273-288, 369-384 (1902), vol. 10, pp. 49-64, 145-160 (1902), pp. 241-254 (1903); reprinted in pamphlet form by the Virginia Historical Society (1903). The first published abridgment of Virginia law appears in this large work covering several colonies, published for "Gentlemen trading to, or concern'd in Her Majesty's Plantations, having frequent Occasion to consult the various Laws of each Place." Preface. The volume was published in 1704 but only covered Virginia law up to 1682. It was little used in Virginia, and passed unmentioned by contemporaries and Hening. Its subject arrangement of the early statutes may nonetheless be of some use in researching seventeenth-century law.

An Abridgement of the Publick Laws of Virginia, in Force and Use, June 10, 1720. London: F. Fayram & J. Clarke, and T. Bickerton, 1722; 2d ed. London: F. Fayram & J. Clarke, and T. Saunders, 1728.

This abridgment is usually ascribed to Robert Beverley, author of *History and Present State of Virginia* (1705), member of the committee revising the laws in 1705, and county court magistrate. The dedicatory preface explains that the abridgment was prepared for private use but is being printed in response to the people's desires to obtain the printing of their laws. It is arranged chronologically, with a short subject index. A "second edition" was published in 1728, with no change except a new title page.

Mercer, John. *An Exact Abridgment of All the Public Acts of Assembly, of Virginia, in Force and Use.* Williamsburg: William Parks, 1737; 2d ed. Glasgow: John Bryce and David Paterson, 1759.

Mercer, John. *A Continuation of the Abridgment of All the Public Acts of Assembly of Virginia.* Williamsburg: William Parks, 1739.

> The first abridgment to be printed in Virginia was prepared by John Mercer (1704-1768), a prominent lawyer in Stafford County. His work was modeled after Edmund Wingate's 1655 abridgment of English statutes and has been called "the most complete and most correct attempt ever privately made to abridge in convenient form all the titles of Virginia law necessary to the layman and the lawyer." William H. Martin, "Some Virginia Law Books in a Virginia Law Office," *Va. L. Reg.* n.s., vol. 12, pp. 279, 284 (1926). Mercer's abridgment was advertised to potential subscribers in the weekly newspaper that William Parks began publishing in 1736. That fall it was noted that Mercer would be adding laws from the latest Assembly session, "and only desires the Subscribers, if they think fit, to make up their Subscription Half a Pistole." *Virginia Gazette*, Sept. 17, 1736, p. 4. A few months later, it was announced that he would also be adding "A Collection of Forms and Precedents, of all Sorts, peculiarly adopted to the Laws and Customs of this Colony; and very necessary for all Magistrates, and other Officers: Which will make it the most useful Book, of its Kind, that ever was published in this Part of the World." *Virginia Gazette*, Feb. 18, 1736/37, p. 4. Two years later Mercer published a brief continuation to his abridgment, and in 1759 a second edition was published in Glasgow by John Bryce and David Paterson. This edition includes a 60-page index and useful features such as lists of Virginia counties and towns, showing the years they were created by the Assembly, and a table of legislative sessions indicating regnal years, governors, and speakers of the Assembly.

Akten Welche in der General Assembly der Republik Virginien Passirt Warden Sind. G. F. Goetz, comp. Philadelphia: C. Cist, 1795.

> This is a German translation of ten acts dating from 1792 to 1794. It has a certificate by Charles Hay and H. Broke, the clerks of the two houses of the General Assembly.

Abridgment of the Public Permanent Laws of Virginia. Richmond: Augustine Davis, 1796.

Akten,

welche

in der General-Assembly

der

Republik Virginien

paßirt worden sind.

Aus dem Englischen übersetzt
durch
Gustav Friedrich Goetz.

Philadelphia:
Gedruckt bey Carl Cist, No. 104, in der Zweyten-straße,
nah bey der Rehs-straße, 1795.

Based on the plan of John Mercer, this abridgment was designed as a substitute for the 1794 revised code. It is sometimes known as "Randolph's abridgment," but it was unsigned and the authorship is uncertain. In "History of Virginia Codification," *Va. L. Reg.*, vol. 11, pp. 79, 91 (1905), William E. Ross attributes it to Edmund Randolph, who had recently resigned under fire as Secretary of State, but biographical sources on Randolph make no mention of the abridgment. In "Some Virginia Law Books in a Virginia Law Office," *Va. L. Reg.* n.s., vol. 12, pp. 385, 400 (1926), William H. Martin says it was probably the work of the reporter Peyton Randolph, Edmund's son, but according to Randolph's biographer he would have been fifteen years old at the time. John J. Reardon, *Edmund Randolph: A Biography*, p. 40, n. 48 (1974).

Hening, William Waller. *The Statutes at Large; Being a Collection of All the Laws of Virginia from the First Session of the Legislature, in the Year 1619.* 13 vols. 1st ed., Richmond: Pleasants, 1809, 1810, 1812, 1814 (vols. 1-4); 2d ed., New York: Bartow, 1823 (vols. 1-2), Philadelphia: Desilver, 1823 (vol. 3), Richmond: Franklin, 1820 (vol. 4); 1st ed., Richmond: Franklin, 1819 (vols. 5-6), 1820 (vol. 7), Richmond: Cochran, 1821 (vols. 8-9), 1822 (vol. 10), 1823 (vols. 11-12), Philadelphia: Desilver, 1823 (vol. 13); rept. Charlottesville: Univ. Press of Va., 1969, 13 vols.; vol. 1 was reprinted: John D. Cushing, ed., Wilmington, Del.: Michael Glazier, Inc., 1978, as *Colony Laws of Virginia 1619-1660* (2 vols.).

Hening's *Statutes at Large* remains the essential source for early Virginia legislation. John Stewart Bryan, "Report of the Committee on Library and Legal Literature," *Va. State Bar Ass'n Repts.*, vol. 11, pp. 58, 62 (1899), hailed it as "[b]y far the most important Virginia law [book] published in this century." Covering all session laws Hening could find from 1619 to 1792, it preserved a vast collection of laws that had been available previously only in manuscript and that would undoubtedly have been lost to later historians. Hening (1767-1838), author of *New Virginia Justice* (a handbook of procedure for magistrates, first published in 1795), and reporter with William Munford of four volumes of Virginia Supreme Court of Appeals reports (1808-1811), was a neighbor of Thomas Jefferson and had access to his collection of rare, often deteriorating manuscripts. In addition to the statutes, several volumes include other historical documents such as charters, proclamations, and state papers. Each volume is separately indexed. Hening intended to publish a general index to the whole set, but none was ever completed. He wrote in the preface to the final volume that the index "would certainly have been made" had not the legislature limited the number of volumes in the set and specified that Hening include acts through the end of 1792. These constraints forced him to omit the general index, "which the editor was sincerely desirous to introduce." Hening's Statutes, vol. 13, p. iii. Although he complained publicly, perhaps Hening privately was relieved to abandon this ambitious goal. No one since has completed a general index to the complete set. It is partially indexed in Joseph J. Casey, *Personal Names in Hening's Statutes at Large of Virginia, and Shepherd's Continuation* (1896), an index to names, but not to subjects, which was prepared for genealogists over seventy years later. Note also E. G. Swem, *Virginia Historical Index* (1934-1936), in two volumes, which partially analyzes Hening's great work.

Winfree, Waverly K[eith]. *The Laws of Virginia, Being a Supplement to Hening's Statutes at Large.* Richmond: Virginia State Library, 1971.

Acts dating from 1701 to 1749 that were omitted from Hening's Statutes have since been found and published in this book. Some had been forwarded to England for approval and no full text survived in this country. These were printed from copies in the British Public Record Office. There is an editorial note by Randolph W. Church. Earlier laws have been published periodically as they come to light, most frequently in the *Virginia Magazine of History and Biography*.

Shepherd, Samuel. *The Statutes at Large of Virginia, from October Session 1792, to December Session 1806, Inclusive.* Richmond: Samuel Shepherd, 1835-1836, 3 vols.; rept. New York: AMS Press, 1970, 3 vols.

Hening's set was updated to 1806 by Samuel Shepherd in a three-volume set. Again, each volume is separately indexed. It is also partially indexed in Casey's *Personal Names in Hening's Statutes at Large of Virginia, and Shepherd's Continuation* (1896).

Tate, Joseph. *A Digest of the Laws of Virginia.* Richmond: Shepherd & Pollard, 1823; 2d ed. Richmond: Smith & Palmer, 1841.

With the publication of the 1819 code, in which statutes were arranged by subject rather than chronologically, there was a less pressing need for a separate subject abridgment. The laws were voluminous and duplicative, however, so there was a market for Tate's 385-page work simplifying and paraphrasing the statutes. More significantly, Tate also provided footnotes summarizing cases applying the statutes, a feature altogether lacking in codes of the day. A second edition was published in 1841 by Smith & Palmer of Richmond.

Matthews, James M[uscoe]. *Digest of the Laws of Virginia, of a Civil Nature.* Richmond: J. W. Randolph, 1856, 1857, 2 vols.

This was reviewed in *Q.L.J.*, vol. 1, pp. 75, 189-190 (1856).

Matthews, James M[uscoe]. *Digest of the Laws of Virginia, of a Criminal Nature.* Richmond: West & Johnston, 1861; 2d ed., Richmond: J. W. Randolph & English, 1871; supp., Richmond: J. W. Randolph & English, 1878; 3d ed., Richmond: J. W. Randolph & English, 1890.

The final comprehensive digest of Virginia statutory law. The civil volumes summarized the statutes under 104 alphabetical headings and provided extensive footnote discussions of cases. The criminal volume provided similar treatment of criminal laws under 24 headings. Only the criminal digest was republished after the first edition. It next appeared in an 1871 second edition, which was reprinted seven years later with appendices containing the new criminal procedure law passed in 1878 and annotations of recent cases. A third and final edition in 1890 simply presented the code sections in numerical order with judicial references, making the digest in effect an annotated edition of the code.

III. *Reports of Revisors*

Report of the Committee of Revisors Appointed by the General Assembly of Virginia in MDCCLXXVI. Richmond: Dixon & Holt, 1784.

Johnson, Chapman, and Robert G[ourmain] Scott. *Revision and Digest of the Criminal Code of Virginia.* Richmond: Shepherd & Colin, 1846.

Patton, John M[ercer], and Conway Robinson. *Report of the Revisors of the Civil Code of Virginia.* Richmond: Samuel Shepherd, 1846-1849.

This report was issued in five parts. The last two parts were printed by W. F. Ritchie. A volume of *Selection from the*

Reports of the Revisors was printed by J. W. Randolph in 1856.

Report of the Commission to Revise the Code of Virginia. Richmond: Davis Bottom, 1917.

Cohoon, Willis E., et al. *Report of the Commission on Code Recodification and Proposed Code of Virginia.* Charlottesville: The Michie Co., 1947, 2 vols.

> This was prepared under the authority of 1946 Va. Acts, ch. 400, p. 940, and submitted in 1948. Since the adoption of the Code of 1950, the Virginia Code Commission has issued numerous reports on the revision of individual titles. These are published by the General Assembly as House Documents.

MUNICIPAL AND COUNTY CODES

Sarah K. Wiant

THE COMMONWEALTH OF VIRGINIA is, and has since 1634 been, subdivided into counties.[1] In addition to the counties, there are various types of municipal corporations in Virginia: towns, cities, and service districts.[2] The first municipal corporations in Virginia were James City, the City of Williamsburg, and the Borough of Norfolk.

The local government divisions included in this bibliography fall within three broad categories, those of counties, cities, and towns. Cities and towns comprise the two types of municipal corporations found within Virginia and are differentiated from one another by their populations. The Virginia Constitution stipulates that a municipality with one thousand to five thousand inhabitants is a town, while a city is a municipality with more than five thousand inhabitants.[3] In addition, a city with five thousand to ten thousand inhabitants is considered a city of the second class, while cities of more than ten thousand inhabitants are cities of the first class. A town, upon reaching a population of five thousand inhabitants, may choose to retain its current status, and as a result, a municipality's status is not always indicative of its size.

Incorporated towns exist within counties. However, cities are completely independent of county government, as was the tradition in England. Virginia is, in fact, the only state in the Union in which cities are independent of counties. Cities of the first class have courts for themselves, while cities of the second class may elect to have their own courts, or they may choose to be included in the county court system.

Municipalities act as agents of the state and are organized and governed as provided by general state law or by charter. Most municipalities are governed by their charters. Municipal charters are granted by the General Assembly; they delegate state authority to the

[1] See generally, A. O. Porter, *County Government in Virginia: A Legislative History, 1607-1904* (1947); *Michie's Jurisprudence*, vol. 5A, "Counties."

[2] See generally C. W. Bain, *"A Body Incorporate" The Evolution of City-County Separation in Virginia* (1967); A. E. D. Howard, *Commentaries on the Constitution of Virginia*, "Local Government," vol. 2, pp. 781-876 (1974); P. M. McSweeney, "Local Government Law in Virginia, 1870-1970," *U. Rich. L. Rev.*, vol. 4, pp. 174-222 (1970); *Michie's Jurisprudence*, vol. 13B, "Municipal Corporations."

[3] Va. Const., Art. VII, § 1 (1971).

municipalities and, like general laws, may be amended or repealed by the General Assembly without the consent of the city or town.[4]

The charters are the constitutions of the municipal corporations. Cities and incorporated towns can and do enact ordinances and bylaws that govern themselves and their inhabitants, and these are often published in printed compilations.[5] Moreover, many individual parts of city codes and county and municipal ordinances that regulate specific activities, such as building codes, are published separately for the convenience of those involved in the trades and activities that are being regulated. Because of the ephemeral nature of these publications, this bibliography cannot pretend to be complete.[6]

BIBLIOGRAPHY

Abingdon

Bye-Laws of the Town of Abingdon: Together With the Acts of the Legislature of Virginia, Relating to the Said Town. Abingdon: Statesman Office, 1837. 38 p.

The Charter and the Code of Ordinances of the Town of Abingdon, Virginia, 1950 and an Appendix Containing Rules of Order. Code of Ordinances Enacted as a Whole, May 31, 1950; Effective Date of Code of Ordinances, July 15, 1950. Charlottesville: Michie City Pub., 1950. vi, 233 p.

Albemarle County

The Code of the County of Albemarle, Virginia: the General Ordinances of the County. Charlottesville: Michie City Pub., 1967.

Alexandria

The Laws of the Corporation of the Town of Alexandria: to Which are Prefixed, the Acts of the Legislature of Virginia, and the Acts of Congress, Respecting the Said Town. Alexandria: Samuel Snowden, 1811. 213, [5], 222-294, [5] p.

---

[4] These charters and the amendments thereto are published in the *Acts of Assembly*. In addition, many of them have been printed separately by the municipalities themselves.

[5] In addition to this bibliography, see also L. F. Chanin, P. J. Gregory, and S. K. Wiant, *Legal Research in the District of Columbia, Maryland, and Virginia*, pp. 3-57, 3-155 to 3-157 (1995).

[6] These publications have not been systematically collected and preserved in any library or location.

Charter of the Town of Alexandria, With the Revised Code of Laws of the Corporation of Said Town. Alexandria: Rounsavell and Pittman, 1821. 14, 119, [1] p.

Laws of the Corporation of Alexandria, Passed Since the Revision on the Twentieth of January, Eighteen Hundred and Twenty-One. Alexandria: S. Snowden and W. F. Thornton, 1825. 95 p.

The Laws of the Corporation of the Town of Alexandria, D.C. Revised and Published, by Authority of the Common Council of Alexandria. Alexandria: Alexandria Gazette Office, 1844. 124 p.

The Charter and Laws, of the City of Alexandria, Va., and an Historical Sketch of Its Government. Published by the City Council. Alexandria: Gazette Book and Job Off., 1874. 163 p.

The Code of the City of Alexandria, Virginia, 1953. The Charter and the General Ordinances of the City, Enacted as a Whole, June 23, 1953, Effective August 1, 1953. Charlottesville: Michie City Pub., 1953.

The Code of the City of Alexandria, Virginia, 1963. The Charter and the General Ordinances of the City. Charlottesville: Michie City Pub., 1963.

The Ordinance to Amend Section 7-8 of Chapter 7 of the Code of the City of Alexandria, Virginia, 1963. Alexandria: n.p., 1963. 69 p.

Building Code of the City of Alexandria, Virginia, Enacted by Ordinance No. 1169. Charlottesville: Michie City Pub., 1964.

Zoning Use Digest: a Condensation of Use and Zoning Requirements Contained in Chapter 42 of the 1963 Edition of the Code. Alexandria: Dept. of City Planning and Urban Renewal, 1967.

Ordinances of the City of Alexandria, 1976. Alexandria: n.p., 1976.

Zoning Code, City of Alexandria; Section 42, 1963 City Code With Revisions Through April 1980. Alexandria: n.p., 1980.

The Code of the City of Alexandria, Virginia: the Charter and the General Ordinances. Washington, D.C.: PRM Law Pub., 1981.

Amherst County

Code of the County of Amherst, Virginia: General Ordinances of the County. N.p., 1987.

Arlington County

Plumbing Code. Adopted May 14, 1935. Arlington: Arlington Press, 1935. 58 p.

Plumbing Code. Adopted May 14, 1935. Arlington: Arlington Press, 1936. 53 p.

Gas Code. Adopted April 29, 1944; Amended June 7, 1947. Arlington: n.p., 1947. 46 p.

Ordinances, September 1, 1948, Arlington County. N.p., [1948]. x, 118 (i.e. 119) p.

Arlington County Code: as Recodified on January 28, 1978, With Amendments, to be Known as 1978 Arlington County Code, as Amended. Arlington: County Clerk's Office, 1978.

[Ordinances] Adopted by the Arlington County Board. Arlington: n.p., 1980.

Zoning Ordinance: As Contained in the Appendix of the Arlington County Code. Arlington: n.p., 1982.

The Code of the County of Arlington County, Virginia. Tallahassee, Fla.: Municipal Code Corp., 1986.

The Code of the County of Arlington County, Virginia. Tallahassee, Fla.: Municipal Code Corp., 1993.

Ashland

Charles Stebbins, Jr., S. J. Doswell, F. W. Tucker, Jr. *The Code of the Town of Ashland, Virginia Together With the Corporate Limits and Rules of the Council.* Ashland: Herald-Progress, 1938. 126 p.

The Code of the Town of Ashland, Virginia, 1959. The General Ordinances of the Town. Charlottesville: Michie City Pub., 1959. 246 p.

Berryville

Charter and Ordinances of the Corporation of Berryville, Codified Under Ordinance of September 16th, 1881. Berryville: Courier Printing, 1889. 34 (i.e. 35) p.

Charter (as Amended) and the General Ordinances of the Town of

Berryville, Virginia. Berryville: Blue Ridge Press, 1908. 37 p.

The Code of the Town of Berryville, Virginia: the Charter and the General Ordinances of the Town. Charlottesville: Michie City Pub., 1964.

The Code of the Town of Berryville, Virginia, 1971: the Charter and the General Ordinances of the Town. Charlottesville: Michie City Pub., 1972. 182 p.

Blacksburg

Building Code for Blacksburg, Virginia. Blacksburg: n.p., 1948. 24 p.

Code of the Town of Blacksburg, Virginia: Adopted, January 13, 1981, Effective March 16, 1981. Tallahassee, Fla.: Municipal Code Corp., 1981.

Blackstone

The Charter and the Code of General Ordinances of the Town of Blackstone, Virginia, 1948. Code Enacted as a Whole January 3, 1949; Effective Date January 20, 1949. Charlottesville: Michie City Pub., 1949. 297 p.

Botetourt County

Code of the County of Botetourt, Virginia. Tallahassee, Fla.: Municipal Code Corp., 1985.

Bristol

Ordinance Regulating the Use and Operation of Automobiles, Motor Cycles and Bicycles. Bristol: McGhee Printing Co., 1918. [3] p.

Ordinances Imposing Taxes on Licenses for the City of Bristol, Virginia, For the Year Beginning January 1, 1948, and Until Otherwise Provided. Bristol: n.p., 1947. 15 p.

License Tax Ordinance for the City of Bristol, Virginia. Adopted December 22, 1949. For the Year Beginning January 1, 1950, and Until Otherwise Provided. Bristol: King Print. Co., 1950. 22 p.

Retailers' Sales Tax Ordinance and Ordinance Providing Rules and Regulations for the Enforcement of the Retailers' Sales Tax Ordinance & Collection of Revenues Thereunder. Adopted May 18, 1950; Effective July 1, 1950. Bristol: Commissioner of the Revenue, 1950. 66 p.

The Code of the City of Bristol, Virginia. Charlottesville: Michie City Pub., 1954. 491 p.

The Code of the City of Bristol, Virginia. The Charter and the General Ordinances. Published by Order of the Council. Charlottesville: Michie City Pub., 1966. vii, 539 p.

Charlottesville

James Alexander. *Revised Ordinances of the Corporation of Charlottesville.* Charlottesville: n.p., 1849.

Charter, Ordinances and by-Laws of the Town of Charlottesville, Va. Charlottesville: Chronicle Book and Job Printing House, 1884. 29 p.

John S. Patton and Fred M. Wills. *Revised Ordinances.* Charlottesville: Daily Progress Print., 1894. 96 p.

The General Ordinances and the Charter of the City of Charlottesville. Charlottesville: City Council, 1898. 136 p.

E. I. Carruthers. *The Code of Charlottesville Containing the Charter as Amended and re-Enacted as a Whole . . . and the General Ordinances of the City in Effect September 1, 1909.* Charlottesville: The Michie Co., 1909. 319 p.

Official Building Code and Builder's Directory, Charlottesville, Va., 1924. Charlottesville: The Michie Co., 1924. 96 p.

Reprint from the Code of the General Ordinances of the City of Charlottesville of Sections 491(1)-492(9); 494(1)-495(23) Inclusive, Regulating Plumbing, Building, and Zoning. Charlottesville: n.p., n.d. 395 p.

The Code of the City of Charlottesville, Virginia: the Charter as Amended and the General Ordinances of the City Enacted as a Whole June 6th, 1932, in Effect July 15th, 1932. Charlottesville: Michie City Pub., 1932. iv, 423 p.

The Code of the City of Charlottesville, Virginia, 1945. The Charter of the City and the General Ordinances of the City. Enacted as a Whole April 16, 1945, Effective May 1, 1945. Charlottesville: Michie City Pub., 1945. 508 p.

Building Code and Plumbing and Sewers. Charlottesville: Michie City Pub., 1945. 345 p.

Zoning, Subdivision Regulations: Chapter 33 [of the City Code]. Charlottesville: n.p., 1949. 38 p.

The Building Code of the City of Charlottesville, Virginia: Adopted August

18th, 1952, Effective January 1st, 1953. Charlottesville: n.p. 1952. 140 p.

Charter of the City of Charlottesville. Revised 1955. Charlottesville: Jarman Printing Co., 1955. 31 p.

The Code of the City of Charlottesville, Virginia, 1959: the Charter and the General Ordinances of the City. Charlottesville: Michie City Pub., 1960. 672 p.

The Code of the City of Charlottesville, Virginia, 1965: the Charter and the General Ordinances of the City. Charlottesville: Michie City Pub., 1966. vi, 715 p.

The Code of the City of Charlottesville, Virginia: the Charter and the General Ordinances. Charlottesville: Michie City Pub., 1976.

Code of the City of Charlottesville, 1990. Tallahassee, Fla.: Municipal Code Corp., 1990.

Chesapeake

The Code of the City of Chesapeake, Virginia: the Charter and the General Ordinances. Tallahassee, Fla.: Municipal Code Corp., 1970.

Code of Ordinances. Tallahassee, Fla.: Municipal Code Corp., 1994.

Chesterfield County

The Code of the County of Chesterfield, Virginia: the General Ordinances and Related Laws. Charlottesville: Michie City Pub., 1978.

Colonial Heights

General and License Ordinances, Town of Colonial Heights, Virginia. Colonial Heights: n.p., 1927. 44 p.

The Code of the City of Colonial Heights, Va.: the Charter and the General Ordinances. Charlottesville: Michie City Pub., 1974.

Covington

Code of Ordinances City of Covington, Virginia: the Charter and General Ordinances of the City, Effective November 11, 1975. Tallahassee, Fla.: Municipal Code Corp., 1975.

Danville

The Charter and Ordinances of the Town of Danville, Va. Danville: Town Council, 1878. 82 p.

The Charter and Ordinances of the City of Danville, Virginia. Danville: J. L. Townes, 1907. 258 p.

Constitutional Provisions, Charter and General Ordinances of the City of Danville, Virginia, 1923. Danville: J. L. Townes, 1923. 284, [18] p.

Constitutional Provisions, Charter and General Ordinances of the City of Danville, Virginia. 1927. Danville: Waddill Printing, 1927. 57, 57a-57c, 58-279, xxii p.

The Code of the City of Danville, Virginia. The Charter as Amended, and the General Ordinances of the City. Enacted as a Whole July 11, 1940, Effective September 1, 1940. Charlottesville: Michie City Pub., 1940. ix, 501 p.

The Code of the City of Danville, Virginia, 1952: the Charter and the General Ordinances of the City. Enacted as a Whole November 10, 1952, Effective January 1, 1953. Charlottesville: Michie City Pub., 1952. vi, 418 p.

Code of the City of Danville, Virginia (1986). Tallahassee, Fla.: Municipal Code Corp., 1986.

Dinwiddie County

Code of the County of Dinwiddie, Virginia. Tallahassee, Fla.: Municipal Code Corp., 1985.

Emporia

Code of Ordinances City of Emporia, Virginia; the Charter and General Ordinances of the City. Adopted June 4, 1971; Effective, July 1, 1971. Tallahassee, Fla.: Municipal Code Corp., 1971.

Fairfax

Code of the City of Fairfax, Virginia: the Charter and the General Ordinances. Tallahassee, Fla: Municipal Code Corp., 1978.

Fairfax County

Plumbing Code. Adopted August 11, 1954. Effective September 6, 1954. Fairfax: n.p., 1954. 92 p.

The Code of the County of Fairfax, Virginia: the General Ordinances of the County. Charlottesville: Michie City Pub., 1961.

The Subdivision Control Ordinance, Chapter 23 of the Code of the County of Fairfax, Virginia: Adopted September 1, 1947: With Amendments to July 18, 1963. Fairfax: n.p., 1962.

The Administrative Code, Fairfax County, 1963. 26 p.

Notice of Re-Adoption of Chapter 19 (The Plumbing Code) of the Code of the County of Fairfax, Virginia. Fairfax: n.p., 1968. 30 p.

Building Code Ordinance: Creating Fire Districts and Regulations Governing the Alterations, Equipment or Removal of Buildings or Structures. Fairfax: n.p., 1971. 113 p.

[Amendments to the Fairfax County Code: Building Code, Electrical Code, Plumbing Code, et al.]. Fairfax: n.p., 1972.

The Zoning Ordinance of the County of Fairfax: Reprinted from Fairfax County Code, Distributed by Division of Administrative Services. N.p., n.d.

The Zoning Ordinance: Chapter 112 of the 1976 Code of the County of Fairfax, Virginia. Fairfax: n.p., n.d.

The Code of the County of Fairfax, Virginia, 1976: the General Ordinances of the County. Washington, D.C.: NIMLO, 1976.

Electrical Code Amendments for the County of Fairfax, Virginia, to be Used With the National Electric Code. Fairfax: Board of Supervisors, 1976. 17 p.

Adoption of Amendment to Chapter 30 (Zoning Ordinance) of the 1961 Code of the County of Fairfax, Virginia, as Amended. Fairfax: n.p., 1977. [24] p.

The Zoning Ordinance chapter 112 of the 1976 Code of the County of Fairfax, Virginia. Fairfax: n.p., 1978.

Tree Preservation and Planting, Fairfax County, Virginia. Fairfax: County of Fairfax, 1978. 63 p.

The Zoning Ordinance; Chapter 112 of the 1976 Code of the County of Fairfax, Virginia. Tallahassee, Fla.: Municipal Code Corp., 1982.

Falls Church

Building Code of the Town of Falls Church, Va. Enacted August 11, 1947. Falls Church: Echo Pub. Co., 1947. 51, [27] p.

Zoning; Chapter 81 of the City Code. Falls Church: n.p., 1971.

The Code of the City of Falls Church, Virginia; the Charter and the General Ordinances. Charlottesville: Michie City Pub., 1973. 689 p.

The Code of the City of Falls Church, Virginia: the Charter and the General Ordinances. Charlottesville: Michie/Bobbs-Merrill, 1981.

Fauquier County

The Code of the County of Fauquier, Virginia. Tallahassee, Fla.: Municipal Code Corp., 1987.

Franklin

Charter and Ordinances of the Town of Franklin, Southampton County, Va. October 12th, 1903. Franklin: J. P. Holland Pub. Co., 1903. 36 p.

Fredericksburg

The General Ordinance of the Corporation of Fredericksburg, Made and Passed by the Mayor and Commonalty of the Town of Fredericksburg, in the Month of December, in the Year Eighteen Hundred and Fifty-Nine. With Several Acts of the General Assembly Relating to Said Corporation. Fredericksburg: Democrat Recorder, 1860. [5], [v]-xii, 46 p.

The General Ordinances of the Corporation of Fredericksburg, Made and Passed by the Mayor and Commonalty of the City of Fredericksburg, Va., and the Act of Assembly Relating Thereto; Together With a Brief Historical Sketch of the City from its Foundation, and a List of Its Mayors and Council. Fredericksburg: True Standard Printing Co., 1883. 1 p. l., [5]-124, [4] p.

Acts of Incorporation and General Ordinance of Fredericksburg, Va. Approved May 19, 1899. Fredericksburg: City Council, 1899. 112 p.

The Code of the City of Fredericksburg, Virginia. The Charter as Amended and the General Ordinances of the City (except as expressly excepted in the adopting Ordinance) Enacted as a Whole May 9, 1944, Effective June 1, 1944. Charlottesville: The Michie Co., 1944. xiii, 283 p.

City Code of Fredericksburg, Virginia, 1952; 1961 Supplement.

Fredericksburg: n.p., 1961. 88 p.

Code of the City of Fredericksburg, Virginia. Fredericksburg: n.p., 1972.

Code of the City of Fredericksburg, Virginia. Tallahassee, Fla.: Municipal Code Corp., 1984.

Code of the City of Fredericksburg, Virginia. Tallahassee, Fla.: Municipal Code Corp., 1991.

Front Royal

Charter and Ordinances of the Town of Front Royal Virginia. Front Royal: Council, 1938. 142 p.

The Code of the Town of Front Royal, Virginia 1951. Charlottesville: Michie City Pub., 1951. 224 p.

Gordonsville

Ordinances of the Town of Gordonsville, Va. Gordonsville: Jeffersonian Book Printing Rooms, 1875. 8 p.

Hampton

Ordinances of the Town of Hampton, Virginia, 1902. Hampton: n.p., 1904. 120 p.

The Code of the City of Hampton, Virginia: the Charter and the General Ordinances of the City. Charlottesville: Michie City Pub., 1964.

Code of the City of Hampton, Virginia, published by Order of the City Council. Tallahassee, Fla.: Municipal Code Corp., 1983.

Hanover County

Code of the County of Hanover, Virginia: General Ordinances of the County, Adopted March 24, 1982; Effective June 1, 1982. Tallahassee, Fla.: Municipal Code Corp., 1982.

Harrisonburg

Charter and Ordinances of the Town of Harrisonburg. Harrisonburg: Rockingham Register Print., 1880. 24 p.

Water and License Ordinances, of the Town of Harrisonburg, Virginia,

1899. Harrisonburg: Spirit Steam Print., 1899. 20 p.

Code of the City of Harrisonburg, Virginia. Adopted July 12, 1935; Effective September 1, 1935 . . . Harrisonburg Code of 1935. Appendix. Harrisonburg: The Shenandoah Press, printers, 1935. 457 p.

Code of the City of Harrisonburg, Virginia. Adopted April 9, 1946; Effective May 1, 1946. Harrisonburg: n.p., 1946. 320 (i.e. 322) p.

The Code of the City of Harrisonburg, Virginia, 1952: the Charter and General Ordinances of the City, Enacted as a Whole, October 30, 1952, Effective, January 1, 1953. Charlottesville: Michie City Pub., 1952. vi, 354 p.

The Code of the City of Harrisonburg, Virginia. The Charter and the General Ordinances [passed on or before June 13, 1972]. Charlottesville: Michie Pub. Co., 1973. 622 p.

The Code of the City of Harrisonburg, Virginia: the Charter and the General Ordinances. Washington, D.C.: PRM Law Publishers, 1979.

Henrico County

The Code of the County of Henrico, Virginia: the General Ordinances of the County. Charlottesville: Michie City Pub., 1960.

The Code of the County of Henrico, Virginia of 1980: the General Ordinances. Charlottesville: Michie/Bobbs-Merrill, 1980.

Herndon

Code of the Town of Herndon, Virginia: the Charter and the General Ordinances. Tallahassee, Fla.: Municipal Code Corp., 1988.

Hopewell

The Code of the City of Hopewell, Virginia, 1963. The Charter and the General Ordinances of the City. Charlottesville: Michie City Pub., 1964. 569 p.

The Code of the City of Hopewell, Virginia, 1981: General Ordinances of the City. Tallahassee, Fla.: Municipal Code Corp., 1982.

James City County

The Code of the County of James City, Virginia: General Ordinances of the County. Tallahassee, Fla.: Municipal Code Corp., 1982.

King William County

Code of the County of King William, Virginia: General Ordinances of the County. Tallahassee, Fla.: Municipal Code Corp., 1987.

Lawrenceville

Charter and Ordinances of the Town of Lawrenceville, Virginia. Lawrenceville: Lawrenceville News Print, 1914. 58 p.

Leesburg

Town Code of Leesburg, Virginia. Tallahassee, Fla.: Municipal Code Corp., 1976.

Lexington

The Charter and General Ordinances of the Town of Lexington, Virginia. Staunton: Stoneburner & Prufer, 1892. 20, viii, [21]-148 p.

The Charter and General Ordinances of the Town of Lexington, Virginia. Staunton: Stoneburner & Prufer, 1914. 22, viii, [21]-136 p.

The Code of the Town of Lexington, Virginia. Charlottesville: The Michie Co., 1932. 369 p.

The Code of the Town of Lexington, Virginia, 1958: the Charter and General Ordinances of the Town. Charlottesville: Michie City Pub., 1959. 442 p.

The Code of the City of Lexington, Virginia: the Charter and the General Ordinances. Charlottesville: Michie City Pub., 1970.

Loudoun County

Codified Ordinances of the County of Loudoun, Virginia. Cleveland, Ohio: Justinian Pub. Co., 1980.

Luray

Water Ordinances and Rates of Luray, Va. Luray: n.p., 1901. 10, [4] p.

Charter and Ordinances of the Town of Luray, Virginia, Adopted November 27th, 1936, Effective January 1st, 1937. Luray: Lauck & Co., 1936. 92 p.

Lynchburg

An Assemblage of the Ordinances of the Corporation. Lynchburg: Pleasants, 1820. 46 p.

G. Ward. *Revised Ordinances of the Corporation of Lynchburg: Preceded by the Acts of Incorporation, and Such Other Acts of the General Assembly, Now in Force, As Materially Concern the Town of Lynchburg.* Lynchburg: Common Council, 1832. 62 p.

Robert J. Davis. *Revised Ordinances of the Corporation of Lynchburg, Together With a Digest of the Acts of the General Assembly, Relating to the Town of Lynchburg.* Lynchburg: Toler Townly & Statham, 1845. 140, [9] p.

Charles W. Christian. *Ordinances of the City of Lynchburg, Revised and Passed by the Council in the Month of December, 1856; To Which Are Prefixed the City Charter, and a Digest of Such Acts of the General Assembly Now in Force As Materially Concern the City of Lynchburg or Its Citizens.* Lynchburg: Virginian job ptg. office, 1857. 217 p.

Charles M[inor] Blackford. *General Ordinances of the City of Lynchburg, Adopted by the Council on the 22d of February, 1867, and All Ordinances Heretofore Passed Under Which Private Rights Have Vested. Also, All Acts of Incorporation of the Town and City, and a Digest of All Acts of the General Assembly Concerning the City or Its Inhabitants.* Lynchburg: Virginian Water-power Press Print, 1867. ii, [3]-214, vii p.

Ja[me]s W[illia]m Morgan. *Ordinances of the City of Lynchburg, Adopted 29 June, 1872. and Amended City Charter, Approved 6 March, 1872.* Lynchburg: Virginian Book and Job Office, 1873, 207 p.

Charles M[inor] Blackford. *The General Ordinances of the City of Lynchburg, Passed 12th August, 1880, and the City Charter, Approved 3d March, 1880; Together With Other Ordinances and Laws Affecting the Rights and Interests of the City of Lynchburg and Its Citizens.* Lynchburg: J. P. Bell, 1880. 167, xxvi p.

Thomas D. Davis. *The Code of the City of Lynchburg, Va., Containing the Charter of 1880, With the Amendments of 1884, 1886, and 1887, and the General Ordinances in Force July 1st, 1887.* Lynchburg: J. P. Bell, 1887. x, 226, xli p.

Henry A. Minor, Jr., and Fred Harper. *The Code of the City of Lynchburg, Containing the Charter as Amended to Date, the Constitutional and Legislative Provisions of the State Relating to Cities, and the General Ordinances of the City Enacted as a Whole March 1st, 1905.* Lynchburg: J. P. Bell, 1905. 272 p.

Contracts, Ordinances and Resolutions Affecting the City of Lynchburg, Va. Lynchburg: J. P. Bell, 1912. 300 p.

Mayo C. Brown. *The Code of the City of Lynchburg, Containing the Charter as Amended to Date, the Constitutional and Legislative Provisions of the State Relating to Cities, and the General Ordinances of the City Enacted as a Whole March 1, 1915.* Lynchburg: Brown-Morrison Co., 1915. 474 p.

Official Building Code and Builders' Directory. Lynchburg: J. P. Bell Co., Inc., 1922. 112 p.

Mayo C. Brown. *The Code of the City of Lynchburg, Virginia. Containing the Constitutional and Legislative Provisions of the State Relating to Cities. The Charter of the City as Amended to Date and the Act Governing the City Manager Plan of City Government and the General Ordinances of the City Enacted as a Whole, 1923.* Lynchburg: J. P. Bell, 1923. 426 p.

The Code of the City of Lynchburg, Virginia; Containing References to the Constitutional and Legislative Provisions of the State Relating Particularly to Cities, the Charter of the City as Amended, and the General Ordinances of the City Enacted as a Whole, 1931. Lynchburg: Mutual Print. Co., 1931. 575 p.

Tax Code of the City of Lynchburg, Virginia. Charlottesville: The Michie Co., 1941. 85 p.

The Code of the City of Lynchburg, Virginia, 1943; the Charter of the City and the General Ordinances of the City (Except as Expressly Excepted in the Adopting Ordinance), Enacted as a Whole January 25, 1943, Effective March 17, 1943. Charlottesville: The Michie Co., 1943. 794 p.

Zoning Ordinance and Building Code of Lynchburg, Virginia. Charlottesville: The Michie Co., 1943. [317]-335, [440]-730 p.

Tax Code of the City of Lynchburg, Virginia, 1941: as Amended to January 1st, 1950. Lynchburg: n.p., 1950. 118 p.

Building Code, City of Lynchburg, Virginia: Revised 1963, Effective January 1, 1964. Lynchburg: n.p., 1963. viii, 408 p.

Code of Ordinances City of Lynchburg, Virginia: the Charter and General Ordinances of the City. Tallahassee, Fla.: Municipal Code Corp., 1981. 3681 p.

Ordinances Imposing Taxes on Licenses and Real and Personal Property in the City of Lynchburg. Lynchburg: n.p., n.d.

Manassas

Town of Manassas, General Laws and Ordinances. Manassas: n.p., 1923. 58 p.

Code of Ordinances, City of Manassas, Virginia: Adopted January 9, 1978, Effective March 1, 1978. Tallahassee, Fla.: Municipal Code Corp., 1977.

Manassas Park

Code, City of Manassas Park, Virginia: Adopted, October 21, 1980: Effective, January 1, 1981. Tallahassee, Fla.: Municipal Code Corp., 1980.

Martinsburg

An Act Establishing the Town of Martinsburg and All Acts Passed Concerning Said Town Together With All the By-Laws of a Permanent Character. Martinsburg, Va.: Samuel Alburtis, 1849. 15 p.

Ordinances and By-Laws of the Corporation of Martinsburg, to which is Appended the Act of Incorporation Passed by the General Assembly of Virginia on the 6th of March, 1856. N.p., n.d. 38 p.

Martinsville

Zoning Ordinance Adopted and Effective February 4th, 1937 as Amended, and Building Code Adopted August 16th, 1937, Effective September 15th, 1937. Martinsville: Service Printing Co., 1937. 72, [3] xii p.

Code of the City of Martinsville, Virginia; Containing the City Charter and General Ordinances of the City; Except Special and Constitutional Ordinances and Resolutions. Adopted as a Whole February 9, 1943; Effective Date February 10, 1943. Martinsville: n.p., 1943. viii, 310 p.

Charter, 1950. Martinsville: n.p., 1950. 30 p.

The Code of the City of Martinsville, Virginia, 1956. The Charter and General Ordinances of the City. Enacted as a Whole, July 23, 1957, Effective September 12, 1957. Charlottesville: Michie City Pub. Co., 1957. vii, 306 p.

Montgomery County

The Code of the County of Montgomery, Virginia: the General Ordinances. Charlottesville: Michie City Pub., 1975.

The Code of the County of Montgomery, Virginia: General Ordinances of the County. Tallahassee, Fla.: Municipal Code Corp., 1987.

Newport News

The Ordinances of the City of Newport News (in force July 1st, 1900): With the Charter as Amended and an Appendix, Containing Acts of the Legislature of Virginia Authorizing the Issuance of Bonds, the Annual Appropriations for 1900-1901, General and School Levies for 1900-1901, License Tax Ordinance for 1900-1901, the Rules of Order of the Common Council of the City, etc. Newport News: Franklin Printing Press, 1900. viii, 283 p.

Samuel R. Buxton. *The Ordinances of the City of Newport News from the Incorporation of the City to September First, Nineteen Hundred and Eight.* Newport News: Franklin Printing Press, 1908. 164, x p.

Charter of the City of Newport News, Virginia; Together With Laws Enacted by the State Legislature Governing Primaries, Creating the Corporation and Circuit Courts, the Appointment of Land Assessors and Setting Time for Such Assessments. Newport News: Franklin Printing Press, 1921. 112 p.

The Building Code of the City of Newport News, Virginia Approved April 28th, 1922. Newport News: n.p., 1922. 157 p.

An Ordinance to Define Ardent Spirits and to Prohibit the Manufacture, Use, Sale, etc. Newport News: Franklin Print. Co., 1924. 53 p.

Allen Carter Jones. *General Ordinances of the City of Newport News, Virginia.* Newport News: Franklin Printing Co., 1927. 163, [1] p.

The Code of the City of Newport News, Virginia. The Charter as Amended and the General Ordinances of the City . . . Enacted as a Whole August 26, 1940; Effective October 1, 1940. Charlottesville: The Michie Co., 1940. 589 p.

Building Code; Recommended by the National Board of Fire Underwriters, New York, Adopted, As Modified by the City of Newport News. Charlottesville: Michie City Pub., 1946. 395 p.

Retirement-Pension Plan Ordinance; Passed by the Council of the City of Newport News, May 2, 1949. N.p., 1949. 20 p.

The Charter and Code of the City of Newport News, Virginia, 1950: Code Enacted as a Whole, April 9, 1951, Effective Date of Code, June 15, 1951. Charlottesville: Michie City Pub., 1951. 30 p.

The Code of the City of Newport News, Virginia: the Charter and the General Ordinances of the City. Charlottesville: Michie City Pub., 1962.

Building Code, City of Newport News, Virginia. Newport News: n.p., 1964. p. 247-277.

Code of Ordinances, City of Newport News, Virginia, Adopted, August 14,

1978, Effective, October 16, 1978. Tallahassee, Fla.: Municipal Code Corp., 1978.

Norfolk

Copy of the Charter of Norfolk Borough. Incorporated the 15th September, 1736. Norfolk: Willett and O'Connor, 1797. 16 p.

A Collection of Acts of Assembly Relative to the Town and Borough of Norfolk, Taken from the Several Revised Codes; Together With the Charter and Sundry Deeds. Norfolk: A. C. Jordan, 1802. 39, [8] p.

Ordinances of the Borough of Norfolk; To Which Are Prefixed the Charter of the Borough, and a Collection of Acts and Parts of Acts of Assembly, Relating to the Corporation. Norfolk: T. G. Broughton, 1829. 281, [1] p.

Ordinances of the Borough of Norfolk Passed Since 1829. Norfolk: T. G. Broughton, 1840. 40 p.

The Ordinances of the Borough of Norfolk; to Which Are Prefixed the Charter of the Borough, and a collection of Acts and parts of Acts of Assembly, Relating to the Corporation. Norfolk, T. G. Broughton, 1845. 325, [2] p.

The Revised Ordinances of the Borough of Norfolk, to Which are Prefixed the Original Charter of the Borough, and the Annexed Charter of 1845, Creating the Borough Into a City. And a Collection of Acts and Parts of Acts of the General Assembly, Relating to the City. Norfolk: Daily News, 1852. 161, [27] p.

The Ordinances of the Borough of Norfolk, to Which is Appended the Charter of the City. Norfolk: Landmark Book and Job Off., 1875. 208 p.

Ordinances of the City of Norfolk, Passed Subsequent to the Revised Edition of 1875, and Prior to July 1st, 1877, Together With Laws of the State. Norfolk: by Authority of Councils, 1877.

The Ordinances of the City of Norfolk and Acts of Assembly of Virginia Relating to the City Government, With an Appendix. 1885. Norfolk: Landmark Steam Print. House, 1885. 239 p.

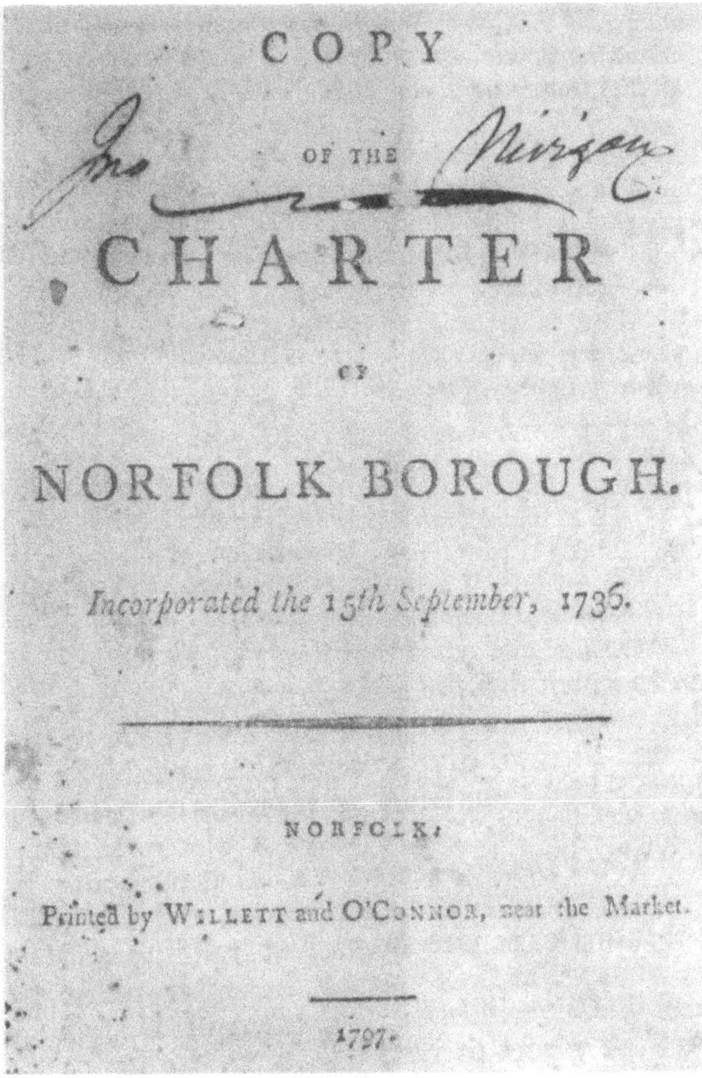

COPY

OF THE

CHARTER

OF

NORFOLK BOROUGH.

Incorporated the 15th September, 1736.

NORFOLK:

Printed by WILLETT and O'CONNOR, near the Market.

1797.

The Ordinances of the City of Norfolk With the Amended Charter and an Appendix, Containing Special Ordinances, Acts of the Assembly of Virginia Relating to the City Government, etc., 1894. Norfolk: W. T. Baron, 1894. viii, 381 p.

H. N. Poulson and R. E. Steed. *The Ordinances of the City of Norfolk, Va. (Date of Enactments Including May 29th, 1902) With the Amended Charter, Acts of Assembly Relating to City Government and an Appendix.* Norfolk: Burke and Gregory, 1902. 932 p.

The Charter of the City of Norfolk, Va., As Adopted March 14, 1906, And As Amended March 12 and March 14, 1908. Norfolk: W. T. Barron & Co., 1908. 125 p.

The Charter of the City of Norfolk, Va., As Adopted March 14, 1906, And As Amended March 12 and March 14, 1908. Norfolk: Tidewater Print. and Blank Book Co., 1908. 131 p.

Charters, Franchises, Ordinances, Resolutions, etc., of Various Companies Composing the Virginia Railway and Power Company, the Bay Shore Terminal Company, and the Norfolk Heat, Light and Power Company. Norfolk: n.p., 1912. 183 p.

The Charter of the City of Norfolk, Va. As Adopted March 14, 1906, And As Amended to and Including March 25, 1914. Norfolk: Donaldson Ackiss Press, 1914. 136 p.

Tentative Draft, Proposed Building Ordinances for the City of Norfolk, Va. Norfolk: W. T. Barron & Co., 1915. 241 p.

Charter of the City of Norfolk. Norfolk Charter of 1918 (As Amended in 1919, Section 2, Clause 10 1/2). Norfolk: W. T. Barron, 1919. 66 p.

Herbert G[reen] Cochran. *The Charter and the General Ordinances of the City of Norfolk. (Passed Prior to January 1, 1920).* Norfolk: n.p., 1920. xviii, 1,026 p.

Edmund S. Ruffin, Jr., and John D. Corbell. *Supplement to the Norfolk City Code, 1920: Including Ordinances of a General Nature Passed Prior to January 1st, 1924.* Norfolk: n.p., 1924. iii, 180 p.

Charter of the City of Norfolk. Norfolk Charter of 1918 (As Amended in 1919, Section 2, Clause 10 1/2 and in 1926, Section 13 and 71). Norfolk: n.p., 1926. 97 p.

The Code of the City of Norfolk, Virginia, 1944. Charlottesville: Michie City Pub., 1945. viii, 691 p.

The Building Code of the City of Norfolk, Virginia, 1948. Norfolk: n.p., 1948. viii, 323 p.

The Charter and Code of the City of Norfolk, Virginia, 1950. Code Enacted as a Whole: March 6, 1951; Effective Date of Code: May 1, 1951. Charlottesville: Michie City Pub., 1951. 876 p.

The Code of the City of Norfolk, Virginia, 1958. Charlottesville: Michie City Pub., 1958.

Code of the City of Norfolk, Virginia, 1979. Tallahassee, Fla.: Municipal Code Corp., 1981.

Norfolk County

Ordinances of Board of Supervisors of Norfolk County. N.p., 1957. 158 p.

Petersburg

Acts of the General Assembly of Virginia Relative to the Jurisdiction and Powers of the Town of Petersburg: to Which Are Added, the Ordinances, Bye-Laws, and Regulations of the Corporation. Petersburg: Edward Pescud, 1824. iv, 100 p.

The Charter and Laws of the City of Petersburg. Petersburg: O. Ellyson, 1852. 94, [1] p.

John C. Armistead. *The Charter and Ordinances of the City of Petersburg.* Petersburg: Jno. B. Ege's Job Print. House, 1869. 128 p.

The Charter and Ordinances of the City of Petersburg. Petersburg: J. B. Ege's Pub. House, 1879. 154 p.

John J. Campbell. *The Code of the City of Petersburg, Virginia, Containing the Charter of 1875, With the Amendments Thereto, and the General Ordinances in Force May 1, 1888. Also, an Appendix, Embracing the Ordinances Vesting Private Rights, the Bond Ordinances of the City, and Those Granting Privileges and Powers to Private Corporations; an Index to the Acts of Assembly Pertaining to the Corporate and Private Interests of Petersburg and Its Citizens; Together With Brief Statistical and Historical Extracts, &c.* Petersburg: Fenn and Owen, 1888. [5]-228, xliv p.

Handbook of Information in Reference to the Southside Railway and Development Company: Containing the Charter and By-Laws of Said Company; the Charters of Sundry Other Companies Now Owned by the Southside Railway and Development Company; All the Ordinances Passed by the Common Council of the City of Petersburg, in Reference to Any of Said

Companies, and Various Deeds, Contracts and Mortgages Relating to the Affairs of the Said Companies. Petersburg: Mitchell Manufacturing Co., 1900. 151 p.

Bernard C. Syme. *Code of the City of Petersburg, Virginia of 1912: Containing Ordinances of a General Nature in Force July 1, 1911, the Charter of 1875, as Amended, Together With an Appendix Embodying Bond Ordinances, Ordinances Vesting Private Rights, etc.* Petersburg: Franklin Press, 1912. 552 p.

Edwin F. Clements. *Code of the City of Petersburg, of 1931. Containing the Constitutional Provisions Relating to Cities. The Act of the State Legislature Governing the City Manager Plan of City Government and the Charter of the City as Amended to Date and the General Ordinances of the City Enacted as a Whole.* Petersburg: Virginia Print. Co., 1931. 650 p.

The Code of the City of Petersburg, Virginia: the Charter as Amended and the General Ordinances of the City, Except as Expressly Excepted in the Adopting Ordinance, Enacted as a Whole, April 15, 1941, Effective May 31, 1941. Charlottesville: The Michie Co., 1941. viii, 600 p.

Code: City of Petersburg, Virginia. Adopted October 5, 1981; Effective January 1, 1982. Tallahassee, Fla.: Municipal Code Corp., 1982. xvii, 3731 p.

Portsmouth

The Revised Ordinances of the City of Portsmouth, Virginia, to Which are Prefixed the Charter of the City and its Amendments, And Also a Collection of the Acts of the General Assembly Relating thereto. Portsmouth: n.p., 1867. 102 p.

Ordinances of the City of Portsmouth, Virginia. Portsmouth: W. A. Fiske, 1905. 165, [1] p.

The Charter of the City of Portsmouth, Va., as Amended by Acts of the General Assembly of Virginia to March 27th, 1914. And the General Ordinances as Revised and Compiled by the Joint Ordinance Committee and as Adopted by the City Council to September 1st, 1914. Portsmouth: W. A. Fiske, 1914. 254 p.

The Charter and Code of the City of Portsmouth, Virginia, 1951. Code Enacted as a Whole August 14, 1951. Effective Date of Code November 1, 1951. Portsmouth: Printcraft Press, 1951. 614 p.

The Code of the City of Portsmouth, Virginia, 1961: the General Ordinances of the City. Charlottesville: Michie City Pub., 1961.

The Code of the City of Portsmouth, Virginia: the Charter and General Ordinances of the City. Tallahassee, Fla.: Municipal Code Corp., 1973.

Prince William County

Code [of the] County of Prince William, Virginia, Adopted December 1981; Effective February 8, 1982. Tallahassee, Fla.: Municipal Code Corp., 1982.

Pulaski

Official Traffic Code and Street Guide Directory of the City of Pulaski, Va. 1934. Pulaski: n.p., 1934. [24] p.

Radford

The Code of the City of Radford, Virginia. Radford: B. D. Smith & Bros., 1914. xxi, 143 p.

Charter of the City of Radford, March 28, 1946. Radford: n.p., 1946. 36, [3] p.

Ordinances Imposing Taxes on Licenses for the City of Radford, Virginia, for the Year Ending December 31, 1948, and Until Otherwise Provided. Radford: n.p., 1948. 43 p.

The Code of the City of Radford, Virginia. Radford: Graphic Arts Dept., Radford News Journal, 1949. 351 p.

The Code of the City of Radford, Virginia: the Charter and the General Ordinances. Charlottesville: The Michie Co., 1976.

Code of Ordinances, City of Radford, Virginia, 1992. Tallahassee, Fla.: Municipal Code Corp., 1992.

Richmond

Ordinances of the Corporation of the City of Richmond and the Acts of Assembly Relating Thereto. Richmond: J. Warrock, 1831. viii, 140 p.

Acts of Assembly Relating to the City of Richmond, and Ordinances of the Common Council, Subsequent to January, 1831. Richmond: J. Warrock, 1839. 80 p.

Charter, Acts of the General Assembly of Virginia, Ordinances of the Common Hall, Concerning the Same, and the By-Laws. Richmond: H. K. Ellyson, 1846. 20 p.

Ordinances Passed by the Council of the City of Richmond, Since the Year 1839. Richmond: John Warrock, 1847. 49, vi p.

Ordinances of the City of Richmond, Revised and Passed by the Council Between April, 1850, and May, 1851. Richmond: P. D. Bernard, 1851. 59 p.

Ordinances of the City of Richmond, Revised and Passed by the Council Between May, 1851, and January, 1852. Richmond: P. D. Bernard, 1852. 61-98 p.

The Charters and Ordinances of the City of Richmond, With the Declaration of Rights, and Constitution of Virginia. Richmond: Ellyson's Steam Presses, 1859. xlvi, 295 p.

The Charter and Ordinances of the City of Richmond, With the Amendments to the Charter. Richmond: V. L. Fore, 1867. xix, 259 p.

The Charter and Ordinances of the City of Richmond. Richmond: V. L. Fore, 1869. 290 p.

The Charter and Ordinances of the City of Richmond: With the Amendments to the Charter. Richmond: V. L. Fore, 1869. 259 p.

The Charter of the City of Richmond: Approved May 24-Amended July 11, 1870; and the City Ordinances, Passed Since the Late Edition of the Ordinances in 1869. Richmond: Evening News Steam Presses, 1871. 95 p.

The Charter and Ordinances of the City of Richmond. Richmond: J. E. Goode, 1875. ix, 349 p.

The Charter and Ordinances of the City of Richmond. Richmond: C. C. Baughman, 1879. viii, 431 p.

The Charter of the Richmond Railway Company. Richmond: Baughman Bros., 1884. 16 p.

Edward H. Fisher. *The Charter and Ordinances of the City of Richmond*. Richmond: Walthall & Bowles, 1885. 301, vi p.

The Charter of the City of Richmond. Richmond: O. E. Flanhart Printing Co., 1898. 45, lv p.

The Charter, the Boundaries, and the General Ordinances of the City of Richmond. Richmond: O. E. Flanhart Printing Co., 1899. 75, [lxxvii]-lxxxix, 577 p.

Certain Resolutions and Ordinances of the Council of the City of

Richmond for the Years Commencing With the Month of July, 1898, and Ending With the Month of June, 1900. Richmond: Ware and Duke, 1900. 193 p.

Franchises Granted by the City Council of Richmond, Virginia. Richmond: Ware & Duke, 1900. 247, [2] p.

Certain Resolutions and Ordinances of the Council of the City of Richmond for the Years Commencing With the Month of July, 1900, and Ending With the Month of June, 1902. Richmond: O. E. Flanhart Printing Co., 1902. 187 p.

The Charter of the City of Richmond. Richmond: n.p., 1906. 188 p.

Building Code of the City of Richmond. Richmond: The City of Richmond, 1908.

Ordinances and Certain Joint Resolutions of the City Council of Richmond. Richmond: C. W. Saunders, n.d.

The Charter and the General Ordinances of the City of Richmond. Richmond: Capitol Printing Co., 1910. 748 p.

Extract from Richmond City Code, 1910. Chapter 15, Concerning the Levying of Taxes. Richmond: C. W. Saunders, 1910. 103-120 p.

Henry P. Beck. *Building Code, City of Richmond, Virginia.* Richmond: C. W. Saunders, 1912. 192 p.

Amendments to the City Charter, 1912. An Act to Amend and Re-Enact Sections 19, 19d, 26, 28, 29, 30, Concerning the Procedure Necessary to Recover and the Liability on Bonds Given by Municipal Officers for the Faithful Discharge of Their Duties, and Creating an Administrative Board. Richmond: C. W. Saunders, 1912. 11 p.

Compilation of Statutes, Ordinances, Resolutions and Other Authority for the Construction, Maintenance and Operation of Street Railways, Electric Light and Power Properties by Virginia Railway & Power Company and Richmond & Henrico Railway Company Within the Corporate Limits of the City of Richmond, Virginia, as They Existed On and After November 5, 1914. Richmond: n.p., 1915. xlvi, 785 p.

The Charter of the City of Richmond. Richmond: Southern Print. Co., 1916. 100 p.

Richmond T. Lacy, Jr. *The Charter of the City of Richmond, as Amended by Act of General Assembly of Virginia, Approved March 6, 1918, Effective*

January 1, 1919. Richmond: William Byrd Press, 1919. 116 p.

Building Code of the City of Richmond, Virginia. Approved January 13th, 1922. Richmond: Old Dominion Press, Inc., 1922. 179 p.

Builders Directory and Building Code, Richmond, Virginia. Richmond: Old Dominion Press, 1922. 259 p.

The Charter of the City of Richmond, as Amended to July 1, 1924. Richmond: C. W. Saunders & Sons, 1924. 106 p.

The Charter of the City of Richmond, as Amended to July 1, 1926. Richmond: Clyde W. Saunders & Sons, 1926. 118 p.

The Charter of the City of Richmond As Amended to July 1, 1927. Richmond: Clyde W. Saunders & Sons, 1927. 122 p.

Fire Prevention Code of the City of Richmond, Virginia, Approved November 21, 1927. Richmond: n.p., 1927. 24 p.

Extract from Richmond City Code, 1924 (As Amended to May 1, 1927) Chapter 10, Concerning the Levying of Taxes and the Assessment of Licenses. Richmond: Williams Print. Co., 1927. 52 p.

The Charter of the City of Richmond As Amended to July 1, 1930 [and The General Ordinances of the City of Richmond As Contained in the Code of 1910, As Amended and Supplemented by the Ordinances of the City Council to September 1, 1924]. Richmond: n.p., 1930. 125, vii, 835 p.

City of Richmond Electrical Code: Issued by Bureau of Electrical Inspection of the Department of Public Safety, City of Richmond. Richmond: City of Richmond, 1930.

Richmond 1930 Traffic Code: City and State Ordinances and Traffic Regulations, Richmond, Va. Richmond: Traffic Code Publishing Co., 1930. 31 p.

Extract From Richmond City Code 1924 (Amended to January 1, 1931) Chapter 10 Concerning the Levying of Taxes and the Assessment of Licenses. N.p., n.d. 84 p.

Ordinances and Resolutions of the Council of the City of Richmond. Richmond: Williams Printing Co., 1934-1952, 10 vols.

The Building Code of the City of Richmond, Virginia: Approved January 13, 1922, Revised to December 1, 1934. Richmond: Clyde W. Saunders, 1934. 190 p.

Extract From Richmond City Code 1924 (Amended to January 1, 1934) Chapter 10 Concerning the Levying of Taxes and the Assessment of Licenses. N.p., n.d. 113 p.

Fire Prevention Code of the City of Richmond, Virginia as Amended to June 6, 1935. Richmond: n.p., 1935. 39 p.

Traffic Guide, Richmond, Virginia. Ordinance of Traffic Rules and Regulations for City of Richmond, 1935-36. Richmond: n.p., 1935. 75 p.

McC. G. Finnigan. *The Charter and The General Ordinances of the City of Richmond.* Richmond: Clyde W. Saunders & Sons, 1937. 125, viii. 1,118 p.

Electrical Code of the City of Richmond, Virginia. Chapter 26, Richmond City Code, 1937. Richmond: n.p., 1937; rept. 1945. 31 p.

The Charter of the City of Richmond As Amended to July 1, 1938. Richmond: n.p., 1939. 134 p.

The Charter of the City of Richmond As Amended to July 1, 1938. [and The General Ordinances of the City of Richmond As Contained in the Code of 1924 As Amended and Supplemented by the Ordinances of the City Council to July 1, 1937.] Richmond: n.p., 1939. 134, x, 1,118 p.

Extract From Richmond City Code 1937 (Amended to April 1, 1944) Chapter 10 Concerning the Levying of Taxes and the Assessment of Licenses. N.p., n.d. 156 p.

Plumbing Code, Richmond, Va. Amended and Reordained Jan. 12, 1945. Richmond: n.p., 1945. 61 p.

Proposed Charter for the City of Richmond. Richmond: Richmond Charter Commission, [1947]. 144 p.

The Charter of the City of Richmond. Richmond: City of Richmond, 1950. 184 p.

An Ordinance — No. 52-130. To Amend the Richmond City Code of 1937 by Inserting Therein a New Chapter, Between Chapter 34 and Chapter 36, Which New Chapter is Designated Chapter 35, Concerning Fire Prevention. Richmond: n.p., 1952. 74 p.

The Code of the City of Richmond, Virginia 1957: the Charter and General Ordinances of the City: Enacted as a Whole, January 27, 1958 Effective, February 1, 1958. Charlottesville: Michie City Pub., 1958. xii, 1,212 p.

The Plumbing Code of the City of Richmond, Virginia. Richmond: n.p.,

1959. 192 p.

The Building Code of the City of Richmond, Virginia. Richmond: Dept. of Safety, Bureau of Building Inspection, 1960. 210 p.

The Code of the City of Richmond, Virginia 1963: the Charter and the General Ordinances of the City. Charlottesville: Michie City Pub., 1963. 2 vols.

The Plumbing Code of the City of Richmond, Virginia. Richmond: n.p., 1963. 183 p.

Richmond City Code: Chapter 38, Water and Gas. Richmond: n.p., 1963. 68 p.

The Richmond City Code of 1963, Chapter 35, Article 8, Sales and Use Tax. Richmond: Office of the Director of Finance, [1966]. 64 p.

The Code of the City of Richmond, Virginia 1968: the Charter and General Ordinances of the City, Enacted as a Whole, September 29, 1969, Effective, October 1, 1969. Charlottesville: Michie City Pub., 1969. 2 vols.

Minimum Property Standards Code: Chapter 24.1 Richmond City Code: City of Richmond. Richmond: City of Richmond, 1969. 52 p.

The Code of the City of Richmond, Virginia, The Charter, the Related Laws and the General Ordinances. Charlottesville: Michie City Pub., 1975. 3 vols.

The Code of the City of Richmond, Virginia. Tallahassee, Fla.: Municipal Code Corp., 1985.

The Code of the City of Richmond, Virginia. Tallahassee, Fla.: Municipal Code Corp., 1993.

Roanoke

Lucian H. Cocke. *The General Ordinances of the City of Roanoke: Together With Other Ordinances and Contracts Affecting the Rights and Interests of the City of Roanoke.* Lynchburg: Bell Printing and Manufacturing Co., 1884. 83 p.

Henry Gibson. *Charter and General Ordinances of the City of Roanoke: Together With Further Acts of the General Assembly Affecting the Corporation and Ordinance Under Which Private Rights Have Vested and Private Liabilities Have Been Imposed.* Lynchburg: Bell Printing and Manufacturing Co., 1890. 137 p.

W. E. Thomas. *Charters and General Ordinances of the City of Roanoke, Virginia: Also Special Ordinances and Curative Acts Pertaining to the Issue of Bonds, Special Ordinances Under Which Private Rights Have Vested or Private Liabilities Have Been Imposed: Together With a Compilation of Miscellaneous Information Pertaining to the City Government*. Roanoke: Stone Print. and Mfg. Co., 1898. x, 412 p.

C. B. Moomaw and C. A. McHugh. *Code of the City of Roanoke, Virginia, Containing Constitutional Provisions Relative to Cities and Towns, Charters of the Town of Big Lick, the Town of Roanoke, and the Charters of the City of Roanoke, Various Amendments Thereto, and a Compilation of All Statutory Provisions Relating to Cities and Towns of the Commonwealth, and the General Ordinances of the City*. Roanoke: Union Printing and Manufacturing Co., 1909. 2 p. l., [7]-583 p.

Building Code, City of Roanoke. Roanoke: Roanoke Printing Co., Inc., 1925. 210 p.

Official Building and Plumbing Code, City of Roanoke. Roanoke: Sibley Advertising Service, 1925. 217 p.

Traffic Code of the City of Roanoke Virginia Effective January 11, 1937. Roanoke: The Stone Printing and Mfg. Co., 1936. x, 37 p.

The Code of the City of Roanoke, Virginia. The Charter as Amended and the General Ordinances of the City . . . Enacted as a Whole June 26, 1939, Effective August 1, 1939. Charlottesville: The Michie Co., 1939. 455 p.

The Code of the City of Roanoke, Virginia, 1956. The Charter and General Ordinances of the City. Charlottesville: Michie City Pub., 1957. 846 p.

Code of the City of Roanoke (1979): Adopted, April 7, 1980, Effective, July 1, 1980. Tallahassee, Fla.: Municipal Code Corp., 1980.

Roanoke County

The Code of the County of Roanoke, Va. The General Ordinances. Charlottesville: Michie City Pub., 1971. 364 p.

Code of the County of Roanoke, Virginia. Tallahassee, Fla.: Municipal Code Corp., 1991.

Rockingham County

The Code of the County of Rockingham, Virginia: the General Ordinances. Charlottesville: Michie City Pub., 1975.

The Code of the County of Rockingham, Virginia. Seattle, Wash.: Book Publishing Co., 1991.

Salem

W. W. Ballard. *Charters and General Ordinances of the Town of Salem, Roanoke County, Virginia.* Salem: Salem Printing and Publishing Co., 1904. 93 p.

W. Frank Chapman. *Charter and General Ordinances of the Town of Salem, Roanoke County, Virginia.* Salem: Salem Publishing Co., 1939. 267 p.

The Code of the City of Salem, Virginia: the Charter and General Ordinances. Charlottesville: Michie City Pub., 1969.

The Code of the City of Salem, Virginia. Tallahassee, Fla.: Municipal Code Corp., 1993.

South Boston

*The Code of the Town of South Boston, Virginia, **1950**. The Charter and General Ordinances of the Town, Enacted as a Whole, August 7, **1950**, Effective September **1**, **1950**.* Charlottesville: The Michie Co., 1950. vi, 241 p.

South Norfolk

*The Code of the City of South Norfolk, Virginia, **1946**. The Charter of the City and the General Ordinances of the City. Enacted as a Whole December **19**, **1946**, Effective February **15**, **1947**.* Charlottesville: Michie City Pub., 1947. vi, 168 p.

Spotsylvania County

Code of the County of Spotsylvania. Tallahassee, Fla.: Municipal Code Corp., 1989.

Staunton

The Ordinances, Resolutions and Orders, of the Common Hall of Staunton, Now in Force. To Which is Prefixed the Act of Incorporation. Staunton: Isaac Collett, 1818. 31 p.

The Charter and General Ordinances of the City of Staunton. Staunton: Stoneburner & Prufer, 1885. vii, 158 p.

The Charter and General Ordinances of the City of Staunton. Staunton: Albert Schultz, 1897. ix, 203 p.

The Code of the City of Staunton, Virginia, Containing the Charter and General Laws and Ordinances. Staunton: Schultz Print. Co., 1910. 279 p.

The Code of the City of Staunton, Virginia, Containing the General Ordinances, the Charter, and the Constitutional and Legislative Provisions of the State Relating to Cities. Staunton: McClure Co., 1938. 450 p.

The Charter and the Code of the City of Staunton, Virginia, 1950: Code Enacted as a Whole: Oct. 12, 1950, Effective Date of Code: Nov. 1, 1950. Staunton: McClure Print. Co., 1950. vii, 376 p.

The Charter and the Code of the City of Staunton, Virginia. Charlottesville: Michie City Pub., 1964. 617 p.

The Code of the City of Staunton, Virginia. Tallahassee, Fla.: Municipal Code Corp., 1985.

Strasburg

Charter and Ordinances of the Town of Strasburg, Va. Strasburg: Council of Strasburg, 1939. 128 p.

Suffolk

Ordinances of the Town of Suffolk, Nansemond County, Virginia; passed January 23, 1867. Suffolk: W. B. Wellons, 1867. 11 p.

Charter and Ordinances of the Town of Suffolk, Virginia. Suffolk: Observer Job Office, 1890. 80 p.

Charter and Ordinances. Approved June 3, 1898. Suffolk: Herald Book and Job Office, 1898. 117 p.

S. M. Lawrence. *Charter and Ordinances. Approved Oct. 4, 1907.* Suffolk: Hammond's Printing Works, 1907. 171 p.

The Code of the City of Suffolk, Virginia. The Charter as Amended and the General Ordinances of the City (Except as Expressly Excepted in the Adopting Ordinance) Enacted as a Whole March 21, 1940. Effective March 22, 1940. Charlottesville: The Michie Co., 1940. iv, 319 p.

City License Taxes, City of Suffolk, Virginia. Ordinances Imposing License Taxes for the Fiscal Year Beginning July 1, 1948. Suffolk: n.p., 1948. 35 p.

The Code of the City of Suffolk, Virginia 1954. Charlottesville: Michie City Pub., 1954. 386 p.

The Code of the City of Suffolk, Virginia: the Charter and the General Ordinances. Charlottesville: The Michie Co., 1978.

Sussex County

Code of Ordinances Sussex County, Virginia. Tallahassee, Fla.: Municipal Code Corp., 1991.

Tazewell

Code of the Town of Tazewell, Virginia. Tallahassee, Fla.: Municipal Code Corp., 1991.

Tazewell County

Code of Tazewell County, Virginia. Tallahassee, Fla.: Municipal Code Corp., 1991.

Vinton

Code Town of Vinton, Virginia: General Ordinances of the Town Adopted, February 16, 1982; Effective, April 19, 1982. Tallahassee, Fla.: Municipal Code Corp., 1982.

Virginia Beach

Code of the City of Virginia Beach, Virginia. Tallahassee, Fla.: Municipal Code Corp., 1981.

Warrenton

Charter and Ordinances of the Town of Warrenton, Virginia. Warrenton: True Index Printers, 1886. 50 p.

Washington County

The Code of the County of Washington, Virginia: the General Ordinances. Tallahassee, Fla.: Municipal Code Corp., 1976.

Waynesboro

The Code of the Town of Waynesboro, Virginia. The Charter as Amended, and the General Ordinances of the Town, Enacted as a Whole August 10, 1936, in Effect September 1, 1936. Waynesboro: News-Virginian Press, 1938. 264 p.

License Tax Ordinance of 1949. Waynesboro: n.p., 1949. 43 p.

Wheeling

Acts Incorporating the Town of Wheeling, and the Ordinances of Said Town, Now in Force. Wheeling, Va.: Gazette Office, 1829. 28, 4 p.

Ordinances of the City of Wheeling: To Which Are Prefixed the Acts of the Legislature of Virginia, Relating to the City. Wheeling, Va.: J. E. Wharton, 1840. 151 p.

Ordinances of the City of Wheeling: To Which Are Prefixed the Acts of the Legislature of Virginia, Relating to the City. Wheeling, Va.: Times & Gazette, 1855, 229 p.

Williamsburg

William M. Willson. *The Code of the City of Williamsburg, 1948. Containing the Charter, as Amended, and the General and Permanent Ordinances. Adopted March 3, 1949, Effective April 14, 1949*. Richmond: Clyde W. Saunders and Sons, Inc., 1949. vi p., 1 l., 336 p.

The Code of the City of Williamsburg Virginia 1958. The Charter and General Ordinances of the City. Enacted as a Whole, June 11, 1959, Effective, June 11, 1959. Charlottesville: Michie City Pub., 1959.

The Code of the City of Williamsburg, Virginia: the Charter and the General Ordinances. Charlottesville: Michie City Pub., 1976. 648 p.

The Code of the City of Williamsburg, Virginia: the Charter and the General Ordinances. Charlottesville: Michie City Pub., 1978. 648 p.

The Code of the City of Williamsburg, Virginia. Tallahassee, Fla.: Municipal Code Corp., 1992. 2506 p.

Winchester

Revised Ordinances of the City of Winchester: Together With the City Charter, and Other Acts of the General Assembly Relating to Cities and Towns. Winchester: Winchester News, 1875. 88, xv p.

License and Tax Ordinances. Winchester: Star Print., 1946. 19 p.

The Code of the City of Winchester, Virginia, 1947. The Charter of the City and the General Ordinances of the City, Enacted as a Whole May 6, 1947, Effective May 6, 1947. Charlottesville: Michie City Pub., 1947. vii, 245 p.

The Code of the City of Winchester, Virginia, 1959: the Charter and General Ordinances of the City. Charlottesville: Michie City Pub., 1959. 396 p.

Code of the City of Winchester, Virginia, 1978: Adopted October 13, 1981, Effective December 31, 1981. Tallahassee, Fla.: Municipal Code Corp., 1981.

Wytheville

The General Ordinances of the Town of Wytheville. Wytheville: D. A. St. Clair, Printer, 1887. vii, 92 p.

H. M. Heuser. *The General Ordinances of the Town of Wytheville, Virginia.* Wytheville: D. A. St. Clair Press, 1911. 82 p.

W. H. Ribble, J. T. Graham, and C. M. Trinkle. *The Water Ordinances of the Town of Wytheville, Virginia.* Wytheville: D. A. St. Clair Press, 1913. 10 p.

York County

Code, County of York, Virginia: General Ordinances of the County. Tallahassee, Fla.: Municipal Code Corp., 1982.

RULES OF COURT

Rebecca G. Bates

I. *Introduction*

THE WORKS INCLUDED in this annotated bibliography are the published rules of various courts of Virginia. A rule of court is a general standing order of the court that is promulgated to regulate the practice or procedure before that court. A general order applies to all practitioners and litigants who appear before that court. General orders of a court differ from specific orders of that court in their application. A specific rule or order of the court applies only to the litigants in a particular case.[1] Rules can be promulgated by an individual court or by the highest court in a particular jurisdiction. A rule that is promulgated by the highest court in the jurisdiction applies to practice or procedure before that court and can also apply to practice or procedure in the lower courts of that jurisdiction.

Courts have the inherent power to make general rules of court;[2] otherwise, they could not govern their own administration and orderly functioning. Without fixed procedures for daily operations, courts could not do their job, and the administration of justice would founder in chaos. However, court-made rules of court, like any judge-made law, are subject to revision or abolition by a statute enacted by the legislature.

II. *The Supreme Court of Virginia*

The extant rules of court of the early courts of Virginia appear to have been issued by each individual court to regulate practice and procedure before that court only. The inherent rule-making power of these early courts does not appear to have been questioned. The colonial General Court of Virginia issued rules to regulate practice and procedure before it.[3] Because the General Court was composed of the

[1] With the understanding that rules are general orders of a particular court, rules of court will hereafter be referred to as general rules, or simply rules. In the legal context, the words rule and order are synonyms, both as nouns and as verbs.

[2] Smith v. Commonwealth, 161 Va. 1112, 1118, 172 S.E. 286 (1934) (Holt, J., dissenting).

[3] E.g. H. R. McIlwaine, comp. *Minutes of the Council and General Court of Colonial Virginia, 1622-1632, 1670-1676*, pp. 601-607 (2d ed. by J. Kukla, 1979).

members of the Council of the Colony, its authority to promulgate rules was unquestionable.

When the Court of Appeals was created in 1779, it was not expressly granted the authority to promulgate rules of practice and procedure. It did, however, promulgate its own rules of court on a sporadic basis without interference from the legislature. In 1792, the Virginia General Assembly began to exercise its authority over the judiciary's rule-making ability by passing legislation that officially extended the power of the Court of Appeals by granting it the power to promulgate rules regarding the forms of writs.[4] In 1849, the General Assembly expanded the Court's authority to include the power to make rules regulating the "practice of all the courts."[5] The Court's power was again expanded by the General Assembly in 1916 and in 1928.[6]

In 1928, the Judicial Council of Virginia was established by the General Assembly. The Judicial Council is composed of five judges, four attorneys, the Chairman of the Committee for Courts of Justice of the Senate, and the Chairman of the Committee for Courts of Justice of the House of Delegates. The Chief Justice of Virginia is the presiding officer of the Judicial Council. The Judicial Council can be the driving force in the rule-making process. In fact, the Judicial Council's primary purpose is to "make a continuous study of the organization and the rules and methods of procedure and practice of the judicial system of the Commonwealth . . . ."[7] The rules of court are often revised based upon the recommendation of the Judicial Council and the advice of its Advisory Committee on Rules of Court.

At the urging of the Virginia State Bar, the Rules of the Supreme Court of Appeals were substantially revised as a code of rules in 1950 and for the first time there were rules promulgated by the appellate court that systematically regulated practice in the trial courts. Prior to the 1950 revision, the Supreme Court of Appeals had recognized its inherent power to promulgate rules regulating procedure and practice for itself.[8] However, at the time of the revision, it was felt that the Court's rule-making power should be further and specifically codified by the General Assembly to make it clear that the Court could create

---

[4] Va. Acts 1792, chap. 11, § 21, Hening's Statutes, vol. 13, p. 411; Va. Code, vol. 1, p. 195, chap. 64, § 23 (1819).

[5] Va. Code, chap. 161, § 4 (1849); Va. Code § 3112 (1887).

[6] Va. Acts 1916, c. 521; Va. Code § 5960a (1928).

[7] Va. Acts 1930, p. 789; Va. Code Ann. § 17-225 (1993 Supp.).

[8] Smith v. Commonwealth, 161 Va. 1112, 1118, 172 S.E. 286 (1934) (Holt, J., dissenting).

a new system of pleading and practice for the lower courts.[9] The preamble to the bill that introduced the proposed rules to the General Assembly did in fact contain an acknowledgment of the Court's inherent power to promulgate rules of practice and procedure, but the acknowledgment was not enacted.[10] Instead, the acknowledgment of the Court's rule-making power was printed in the annotation following Virginia Code section 8-1.1.[11]

The General Assembly at that time declared the supremacy of the new rules over existing statutory provisions that were in conflict with them.[12] This was necessary because of the great number of miscellaneous statutes scattered throughout the Code that were in conflict with the new system of pleading and practice. It would take many years of study and legislative action to amend the Code to remove all of the inconsistencies. By 1971, the conflicts between pre-existing statutes and the 1950 rules had been resolved; thus, the General Assembly revoked this provision. Article VI, section 5, of the 1971 Constitution of Virginia states that the rules of the Supreme Court of Appeals "shall not be in conflict with the general law as . . . established by the General Assembly." The General Assembly later codified its natural and inherent authority to enact laws that "modify, or annul any rules adopted or amended" by the Court.[13]

The General Assembly has also designed a method for the creation of Rules of the Supreme Court of Appeals. The General Assembly's method appears to limit the rule-making power of the Supreme Court by requiring that the Court consult with the chairmen of the Courts of Justice committees and with the executive committees of the judicial conferences. The Courts of Justice committees are entities of the General Assembly, and the judicial conferences are made up of lower court judges. This scheme was originally codified in several sections of the 1977 Supplement to the 1950 Virginia Code.[14]

---

[9] *See* Virginia State Bar Committee to Study the Necessity for Revision of Procedure, Report of the Committee to Study the Necessity for Revision of Procedure in Virginia, p. 15 (1940).

[10] Va. Acts 1950, c. 1.

[11] Va. Code Ann. § 8-1.1 (1950).

[12] Va. Code Ann. § 8-1.2 (1950).

[13] Va. Code Ann. § 8.01-3(D) (1977).

[14] Va. Code Ann. § 16.1-69.32 (1977 Supp.); Va. Code Ann. § 17-116.4 (1977 Supp.).

Rules of court are published in various forms.[15] Some of the earliest entries in this bibliography were originally published in pamphlet form and were later reprinted in periodicals or books. The more comprehensive early works were published as booklets. Because the early entries were reprinted in other publications, the identity of the original publisher is often unclear. In some cases, however, it is clear that the rules of court were published by order of the court itself. The identity of the publishers of the more comprehensive works that appeared in book form is readily apparent. The publishers of the books of rules of court do not appear to be official court publishers, so it seems likely that the rules were seen as a commercial venture by that particular publisher.

The history of the publication of the Rules of the Supreme Court of Appeals, later renamed the Virginia Supreme Court, is a complicated one. The history is complicated in part by the changes in the identity of publishers and the nominal variations of both the title of the Rules and of the Court.

The Rules of the Supreme Court of Appeals of Virginia were originally published in pamphlet form. The pamphlets contained a compilation of individual rules that were promulgated by the Court on a sporadic basis. They were published when new rules were promulgated or when old rules were amended by the Court.

By order of the Court, the pamphlets were later reprinted by the publisher of the Court's decisions; thus, early versions of the Rules of the Supreme Court of Appeals were published at the beginning of each volume of the Court's reports as a separate section. The rules first appeared in Volume One of *Hening and Munford's Reports* under the title "Rules of the Court of Appeals from Its Establishment to the End of May Term, 1806." The rules later appeared in various volumes of *Grattan's Reports* beginning in Volume One in 1845. At that time, the Rules were titled, "Rules of Court."

In Volume 20 of *Grattan's Reports*, the rules were titled "Rules of the Supreme Court of Appeals of the State of Virginia." In 1884, the rules appeared in Volume 77 of the *Virginia Reports*. The rules continued to be published in the *Virginia Reports* on a sporadic basis by order of the Court. In Volume 103, and in succeeding volumes, of the *Virginia Reports*, the title of the rules was shortened to "Rules of Court."

At the urging of the Virginia State Bar, the Rules of Court were substantially revised in 1950. As a result of this revision, the character

[15] Rules of court have been published in England from the seventeenth century onwards. *Sweet and Maxwell's Legal Bibliography*, vol. 1, pp. 280-282, 342-344 (2d ed. 1955).

and format of the rules was substantially changed. The compilation or collection of rules which had existed prior to 1950 was discarded, and the revisors developed a new systematic code of rules. The new code of rules governed practice and procedure in equity and actions at law, pretrial conferences, appellate proceedings, and the integration of the Virginia Bar. The prior compilation of rules had to a certain extent regulated all of these areas, but the new code of rules was more organized and regulated these areas more extensively.

The code format of the rules has endured, but the rules have been revised and amended from time to time. As a result of revisions and amendments, the scope of the rules has been expanded to include regulations regarding foreign attorneys, appeals pursuant to the Administrative Process Act, appeals from the State Corporation Commission, practice and procedure in the Court of Appeals, traffic infractions and fines, pre-payable offenses and fines, appeals from the Workers' Compensation Commission, the unauthorized practice of law, the Virginia Code of Professional Responsibility, the Canons of Judicial Conduct, practice and procedure in the general district courts, and practice and procedure in the juvenile and domestic relations district courts.

By statute, the General Assembly ordered that the revised rules be published in the 1950 Supplement of the Virginia Code of 1950.[16] The rules were published in the 1950 Supplement to Volume Two of the Virginia Code of 1950; Volume Two contained Title 8, "Civil Remedies and Procedure." In the 1957 Replacement Volume of the Virginia Code of 1950, the rules were published as an appendix to Volume Two. They continued to be published as an appendix to Volume Two of the Virginia Code until 1984.

In 1984, the rules were published in a separate volume of the Virginia Code. The rules have continued to be published annually in Volume 11 of the Virginia Code. From 1950 to 1972, the "Rules of the Supreme Court of Appeals of Virginia" were also occasionally published in pamphlet form by the State Division of Purchasing and Printing. The pamphlets were prepared for publication by the Clerk of the Court.

III. *Local Rules*

The lower courts of the Colony also promulgated general rules concerning practice and procedure.[17] That the lower courts issued rules without the interference of the Council or the General Court seems to

---

[16] Va. Code Ann. § 8-1.2 (1950 Supp.).

[17] E.g. "Rules of Lancaster Court in 1671," *Wm. & Mary Qtly.*, 1st ser., vol. 5, p. 264 (1897).

confirm the existence of an inherent judicial rule-making power. Rules of court for the High Court of Chancery were published in 1808.[18]

In 1970, the General Assembly expressly recognized the power of the trial courts to "prescribe such rules as may be reasonably appropriate to promote proper order and decorum, the convenient and efficient use of courthouses and clerks' offices and the orderly management of court dockets." Such local rules cannot apply in any other court than the one promulgating them or be inconsistent with any statute, any rule of the Supreme Court, or any substantive right.[19] In 1977, this statute was amended to omit the power of the lower courts to have any local rule regulating docket calls.[20] The reason for this change was to prevent a state-wide lack of uniformity that was developing in this area of court practice.

IV. *Medical Malpractice Review Panels*

In 1976, the General Assembly created the medical malpractice review panels to review malpractice claims against health care providers.[21] A medical malpractice review panel comprises impartial attorneys and impartial health care providers and the circuit court judge, who serves as the chairman of the panel. The members of the review panel are chosen by the Chief Justice of the Supreme Court of Virginia. Members of the panel are chosen based upon the "nature of the claim and the nature of the practice of the health care provider."[22] The Chief Justice also promulgates "all necessary rules and regulations" for the medical malpractice review panels.[23]

The first code of rules for the review panels was promulgated by the Chief Justice on November 1, 1976. These rules regulate the request for a review panel, the appointment and convening of a review panel, the request for and conduct of an ore tenus hearing, and awards of expenses and costs. The rules also included a form for a subpoena and a form for a subpoena duces tecum. The rules were entitled "Medical Malpractice Rules of Practice," and they were first published in the 1976 Interim Supplement to Volume 2 of the Code of Virginia. In 1977, the rules were published as an appendix to Volume 2 of the

[18] 1 Hen. & M. iv.

[19] Va. Acts 1970, c. 366; Va. Code Ann. § 8-1.3.

[20] Va. Code Ann. § 8.01-4.

[21] Va. Acts 1976, c. 611; Va. Code Ann. §§ 8-911 to 8-922 (1976 Supp.).

[22] Va. Code Ann. § 8-913 (1976 Supp.).

[23] Va. Code Ann. § 8-921 (1976 Supp.).

Code. From 1979 until 1981, the rules were also published in volumes of the *Virginia Reports*. They continued to be published as an appendix to Volume 2 of the Code of Virginia until 1984. In 1984, the rules were published in a separate volume, Volume 11, of the Code. The rules have continued to be published annually in Volume 11 of the Code.

V. *The State Corporation Commission*

The State Corporation Commission was created in 1902 by Article XII of the Constitution of Virginia.[24] The original duties of the State Corporation Commission include issuing charters to domestic corporations, overseeing the operations of domestic corporations, licensing foreign corporations to do business in Virginia, and overseeing and regulating domestic transportation and transmission companies.[25] In conducting its duties, the State Corporation Commission acts as a court of record. Article XII, section 156(c), of the 1902 Constitution states that the Commission shall have the "powers and authority of a court of record" with respect to "all matters pertaining to the public visitation, regulation or control of corporations."[26] In addition, Article XII, section 155, of the 1902 Constitution mandates that "all sessions of the commission shall be public, and a permanent record shall be kept of all its judgments, rules, orders, findings, and decisions."[27] The 1902 Constitution also provides for an appeal of right to the Supreme Court of Appeals for a corporation or an individual who is adversely affected by certain actions of the State Corporation Commission.[28] The Commonwealth is also granted an appeal of right "if allowed by law."[29]

Article XII of the 1902 Constitution grants the Commission the authority to "prescribe its own rules of order and procedure, except so far as the same are specified in this Constitution or any amendment thereof."[30] The Commission's rule-making power was limited, however, by a mandate that the Commission provide notice by publication of the

---

[24] Va. Const., Art. XII (1902).

[25] *Id.* at §§ 156(a)-(b).

[26] *Id.* at § 156(c).

[27] *Id.* at § 155.

[28] *See id.* at § 156(d) for the types of actions that give rise to the appeal of right to the Supreme Court of Appeals.

[29] Va. Const., Art. XII, § 156(d) (1902).

[30] *Id.* at § 155. See also Va. Const., Art. IX, § 3 (1971).

contents before adopting a proposed rule of order or procedure. The Commission was also required to hold a public meeting for the purpose of hearing objections to the proposed rule of order or procedure and publish notice of the hearing. Rules of order or procedure adopted by the Commission must be published in the Commission's annual report.[31]

The provisions of Article XII of the 1902 Constitution were later put into effect by statute.[32] The statutory provisions appear in the Code of 1919. Section 3725 of the 1919 Code mandates that the "Commission shall cause its rules of order and procedure to be entered upon the records of its proceedings and to be printed as well as amendments and additions to the same." The section also mandates that copies of the rules of order and procedure be furnished to the "county and city clerks and to any citizen of this State upon application therefor."[33] The "Rules of Practice and Procedure in Cases and Proceedings before the Commission," as amended to August 31, 1915, are printed in Volume One of the 1919 Code directly following section 3725.

By 1950, the statutes that effectuated the constitutional provisions had undergone several changes. However, the Commission's authority to promulgate rules of order and procedure was kept,[34] and the notice requirements that limit the Commission's rule-making power were also retained.[35] The 1950 statutory provisions relating to the State Corporation Commission were revised and amended by the General Assembly in 1971.[36] The provisions relating to the Commission's rule-making power were retained and recodified in Title 12.1.[37]

The first code of rules of the State Corporation Commission was published in 1904 in the *First Annual Report of the State Corporation Commission*. The rules were adopted by the Commission on October 6, 1903, and were titled "Rules of Practice and Procedure before the State Corporation Commission." Since 1904, the rules have been amended from time to time. As amended, the rules regulate the organization of the Commission itself, the parties to proceedings before the Commission, the pleadings of parties, prehearing procedures, and the

---

[31] *Id.* at § 156(b).

[32] Va. Acts 1902-1904, c. 147.

[33] Va. Code § 3725 (1919).

[34] Va. Code Ann. § 12-49 (1950).

[35] Va. Code Ann. § 12-54 (1950).

[36] Va. Acts 1971, c. 157.

[37] Va. Code Ann. §§ 12.1-25, 12.1-28 (1993).

procedure of the hearing itself. The rules continue to be published annually in each report of the State Corporation Commission. The rules are also published annually in pamphlet form.

VI. *The Workers' Compensation Commission*

The General Assembly passed the Virginia Workmen's Compensation Act in 1918.[38] This statute was enacted "to prevent industrial accidents; to provide medical and surgical care for injured employees; to establish rules of compensation for personal injuries or deaths sustained by employees in the course of employment; [and] to provide methods for insuring the payment of such compensation." The Act provided for the creation of a three-member commission, known as the Industrial Commission, to oversee the administration of the new law. The Commission was empowered to hold hearings to settle compensation disputes between injured employees and their employers. In addition to overseeing the administration of the Virginia Workmen's Compensation Act, the Commission was also empowered with the authority to make rules to carry out the provisions of the Act.

The provisions of the Workmen's Compensation Act of 1918 were later put into effect by statute[39] and were substantially revised in 1968, 1983, and 1991.[40] The Act, as amended, is now known as the Virginia Workers' Compensation Act.[41] It provides that "the Industrial Commission of Virginia shall be continued and shall hereafter be known as the Virginia Workers' Compensation Commission."[42] In addition, the Act provides that all of the powers and duties of the Industrial Commission are "conferred upon and vested in" the Virginia Workers' Compensation Commission. The Act specifically provides the Workers' Compensation Commission with the power to make "rules and regulations for carrying out the provisions" of the new law.[43]

The rules of the Virginia Workers' Compensation Commission were first published by the Michie Company in 1949 in *The Virginia Workers' Compensation Act Annotated.* This work was ordered by the Commonwealth and has been updated and reprinted from time to time.

---

[38] Va. Acts 1918, p. 637.

[39] Va. Code Ann. §§ 65-1 to 65-134 (1950).

[40] Va. Acts 1968, c. 660; Va. Acts 1983, c. 239; Va. Acts 1991, c. 355.

[41] Va. Code Ann. §§ 65.2-100 to 65.2-1310 (1991).

[42] Va. Code Ann. § 65.2-200(A) (1991).

[43] Va. Code Ann. § 65.2-201(A) (1991).

The most recent volume of *The Virginia Workers' Compensation Act Annotated* was published in 1992. In addition to the "Rules of the Virginia Workers' Compensation Commission," the 1992 volume of *The Virginia Workers' Compensation Act Annotated* also contains the full text of Title 65.2 with annotations, some related statutes, and an index. The "Rules of the Virginia Workers' Compensation Commission" regulate the procedure for hearings before the Commission, the review of decisions or awards of the Commission, the award of attorney's fees, and the payment of awards. Publication of *The Virginia Workers' Compensation Act Annotated* has been discontinued by the Commonwealth.

VII. *Conclusion*

The rules of court play an important part in the orderly administration of the legal system. In effect, the rules regulate all areas of the practice of law and consequently shape and define the rights of litigants in some respects. Regulation of behavior and definition of legal rights has long been the province of the common law and the legislature, yet there has always been an understanding that the judiciary possesses an inherent power to regulate the practice of law before it by promulgating rules of court.

BIBLIOGRAPHY

Code of Virginia 1950 Annotated. vol. 11. Charlottesville: The Michie Co., 1984 to present.

> This annual volume publishes the Rules of the Supreme Court of Virginia with an index. Prior to 1984, the Rules of the Supreme Court of Virginia were published as an appendix to Volume Two of the Code, which contained Title 8, "Civil Remedies and Procedure." The Rules of the Supreme Court of Virginia first appeared in the Code in the 1950 Cumulative Supplement to Volume Two.

Griffith, William. *Annual Law Register of the United States.* Burlington, N.J.: David Allinson, 1822; rept. New York: Arno, 1972.

> Vol. 3, pp. 309–383: "Virginia State Law and Regulations": attorneys, courts, rules of the Court of Appeals (May 3, 1811), rules of courts of equity by Creed Taylor (1766-1836).

"Medical Malpractice Rules of Practice." *Code of Virginia 1950 Annotated.* vol. 11. Charlottesville: The Michie Co., 1984 to present.

This annual volume publishes the Medical Malpractice Rules of Practice with an index. Prior to 1984, the Medical Malpractice Rules of Practice were published as an appendix to Volume Two of the Code. The first code of Medical Malpractice Rules of Practice was promulgated by the Chief Justice of the Supreme Court of Virginia in 1976. It was published in the 1976 Interim Supplement to Volume Two of the Code. From 1979 until 1981, these rules were also published in several volumes of the *Virginia Reports.*

"Medical Malpractice Rules of Practice." *Virginia Reports*, vol. 218, pp. 160-172 (1979); vol. 219, pp. 354-366 (1979); vol. 220, pp. 354-364 (1980); vol. 222, pp. 298-300 (1981).

The Medical Malpractice Rules of Practice were first promulgated by the Chief Justice of the Supreme Court of Virginia in 1976. They were published in the *Virginia Reports* from 1979 until 1981. After 1981, the Supreme Court of Virginia ordered that publication of rules of court in the *Virginia Reports* be discontinued.

Rules and Forms for Procedure . . . for Use in Proceedings Under the Uniform Land Registration Act. Richmond: Appeals Press, Inc., 1916.

"Rules and Regulations for Licensing Persons to Practice Law." *Virginia Reports*, vol. 93, pp. v-vi (1897); *Va. L. Reg.*, vol. 2, pp. 910-911 (1897).

"Rules and Regulations Prescribed by the Supreme Court of Appeals of Virginia for Licensing Persons to Practice Law." *Va. L. Reg.*, vol. 2, pp. 219-220 (1896).

"Rules, in Chancery, of the Circuit Superior Courts of Law and Chancery." *Acts of Assembly*. Richmond: Ritchie, 1832.

This work contains rules of procedure, rules for counsel, rules for the clerk, and rules for courtroom procedure.

"Rules of Court." *Grattan's Reports*, vol. 1, pp. xix-xxiii (1845).

This volume of reported cases contains rules promulgated and adopted by the Supreme Court of Appeals of Virginia on January 25, 1845, and March 4, 1845.

"Rules of Court, 1691-1775." *Minutes of the Council and General Court of Colonial Virginia, 1622-1632, 1670-1676.* 2d ed. by Jon Kukla, Richmond: Va. State Library, 1979.

The rules of the General Court of Virginia from 1691 through 1775 are included in an appendix to this work.

"Rules of Court." *Virginia Reports*, vol. 103, p. v (1905); vol. 104, pp. v-vi (1906); vol. 105, p. v (1907); vol. 107, p. iv (1908); vol. 108, pp. iv-vi (1909); vol. 111, p. iv-xiii (1911); vol. 112, p. v (1912); vol. 113, p. iv (1913); vol. 114, p. iv (1913); vol. 115, p. iv (1914); vol. 116, p. iv (1915); vol. 117, p. v (1916); vol. 118, pp. v-x (1916); vol. 120, p. v-xii (1917); vol. 129, pp. v-xii (1921); vol. 138, pp. v-xii (1924); vol. 140, p. ix (1925); vol. 142, pp. xv-xxiii (1926); vol. 148, pp. iv-xiii (1928); vol. 149, pp. v-xiv (1928); vol. 150, p. iv (1928); vol. 152, pp. iv-xv (1929); vol. 153, pp. xv-xxvi (1930); vol. 154, pp. v-xviii (1931); vol. 155, pp. xvii-xxvii (1931); vol. 156, pp. v-xv (1931); vol. 157, pp. xii-xxii (1932); vol. 158, pp. v-xv (1932); vol. 159, pp. v-xiv (1933); vol. 160, pp. v-xiv (1933); vol. 161, pp. v-xiv (1934); vol. 162, pp. v-xv (1934); vol. 163, pp. v-xv (1935); vol. 164, pp. x-xx (1935); vol. 165, pp. xii-xxii (1936); vol. 166, pp. xxi-xxxi (1936); vol. 167, pp. xxviii-xxxviii (1937); vol. 168, pp. xxi-xxxii (1938); vol. 169, pp. xxx-xli (1938); vol. 170, pp. xiv-xxv (1938); vol. 171, pp. lxi-lxxvii (1939); vol. 172, pp. lx-lxxvi (1939); vol. 173, pp. lxvii-lxxxiii (1939); vol. 174, pp. lxvii-lxxxiii (1940); vol. 175, pp. v-xxi (1940); vol. 176, pp. v-xxi (1941); vol. 177, pp. viii-xxiii (1941); vol. 178, pp. xvi- xxxiii (1941); vol. 179, pp. xi-xxvii (1942); vol. 180, pp. xlix-lxv (1942); vol. 181, pp. lxiii-lxxix (1943); vol. 184, pp. lxix-lxxxvii (1946); vol. 185, pp. lxxiii-xci (1947); vol. 186, pp. lxxv-xciii (1948); vol. 187, pp. lxvii-lxxxv (1948); vol. 190, pp. lxxxiii-cxxxv (1950).

The Rules of the Supreme Court of Appeals were published in several volumes of the *Virginia Reports* by order of the Court. Some volumes contain the complete text of the rules; other volumes contain only newly adopted rules. In previous volumes of the *Virginia Reports*, the rules were entitled, "Rules of the Supreme Court of Appeals of the State of Virginia." After the rules were substantially revised in 1950, the rules were regularly published in the Virginia Code by order of the Virginia General Assembly. After 1950, the revised rules also continued to appear in the *Virginia Reports* on a sporadic basis.

"Rules of Lancaster Court in 1671." *Wm. & Mary Qtly.*, 1st ser., vol. 5, p. 264 (1897).

These rules were promulgated by the Lancaster County Court on November 8, 1671. The rules include rules of procedure and rules of courtroom behavior.

"Rules of Practice and Procedure in Cases and Proceedings before the Commission." *Code of Virginia 1919 Annotated.* vol. 1. Richmond: Davis Bottom, 1919.

These rules of order and procedure were promulgated by the State Corporation Commission. The rules published in this work are those of the Commission as amended to August 31, 1915.

"Rules of Practice and Procedure in Cases and Proceedings before the Commission." *Annual Report of the State Corporation Commission of Virginia.* Richmond: J. H. O'Bannon, 1904.

The rules published in this report are rules of order and procedure that were adopted by the State Corporation Commission on October 6, 1903. The rules of the Commission are published annually in each report of the State Corporation Commission. They are also published annually in pamphlet form.

Rules of Practice in the Circuit and County Court of Hampshire County, in the Thirteenth Judicial Circuit of the Commonwealth of Virginia. Romney, Va.: William Harper, 1856.

Rules of Practice in the Circuit Superior Court of Law and Chancery for Jefferson County, in the Seventh District and Thirteenth Judicial Circuit of the Commonwealth of Virginia. Charlestown, Va.: Gallaher, 1834.

"Rules of Practice Settled by the Late High Court of Chancery, and Present Superior Court of Chancery for the Richmond District." *Hening and Munford's Reports,* vol. 1, pp. iv-vii (1808).

This volume of reported cases contains rules promulgated by the High Court of Chancery.

"Rules of the Court of Appeals" in E. Hall, *A Digested Index to the Virginia Reports,* vol. 1, pp. 617-622 (1825).

Rules of court from 1811 to 1823.

"Rules of the Court of Appeals from Its Establishment to the End of May Term, 1806." *Hening and Munford's Reports*, vol. 1, pp. i-iii (1808).

> This volume of reported cases contains rules promulgated by the Court of Appeals from April 29, 1784, to May 5, 1806.

Rules of the Supreme Court of Appeals of the State of Virginia. Richmond: n.p. 1869; *Grattan's Reports*, vol. 20, pp. xxiii-xxvii (1871); Staunton: Yost, 1883; *Va. L. J.*, vol. 7, pp. 705-710 (1883); *Virginia Reports*, vol. 77, pp. v-x (1884); *Virginia Reports*, vol. 95, pp. ix-xvi (1898).

> These rules were promulgated by the Supreme Court of Appeals in 1869. The rules were later revised and adopted in 1871, 1883, and 1898. Each set of revised rules was published with the reported cases of the Supreme Court of Appeals.

"Rules of the Supreme Court of Appeals of Virginia." *Virginia Reports*, vol. 96, p. v (1899); *Virginia Reports*, vol. 100, pp. v-xii (1903).

> By order of the Virginia Supreme Court of Appeals, the rules were published in these two volumes of the *Virginia Reports*. When printed in subsequent volumes of the *Virginia Reports*, the rules are entitled "Rules of Court," *q.v.*

Rules of the Supreme Court of Appeals of Virginia. Richmond: Division of Purchase and Printing, 1950, 1951, 1953, 1957, 1961, 1964, 1966, 1972.

> These pamphlets were prepared for publication by the Clerk of the Supreme Court of Appeals of Virginia. It should be noted that the rules were also published in the Virginia Code and in the *Virginia Reports* during this time period.

"Rules of the Virginia Workers' Compensation Commission." *The Virginia Workers' Compensation Act Annotated.* Charlottesville: The Michie Co., 1949, 1968, 1973, 1980, 1981, 1982, 1991, 1993.

> This work was published by the Michie Company at the request of the Commonwealth. The work contains the full text of the Virginia Workers' Compensation Act with annotations. The work also includes statutes related to the Virginia Workers' Compensation Act. Publication of this work has been discontinued by the Commonwealth.

Taylor, Creed. *The Manual of the Superior Courts of Chancery at Richmond and Lynchburg: Being a Collection of the Rules of the Said Courts; Together with Instructions for the Commissioners Thereof in Chancery*. Richmond: Shepherd, 1829.

These rules were compiled by Creed Taylor (1766-1836), Judge of the Superior Courts of Chancery at Richmond and Lynchburg. The work consists of rules abstracted from decisions of the Supreme Court of Appeals, the late High Court of Chancery, and the Superior Courts of Chancery of Richmond and Lynchburg. The rules date from June 1814 to January 1829. Instructions for commissioners in chancery are also included in this work. The instructions for commissioners are also drawn from court decisions. The instructions include detailed examples of the proper method of accounting and the proper form for a commissioner's report. This work also includes a form for an injunction to "stay personal property in the country."

Taylor, Creed. "Rules of the Superior Courts of Chancery at Richmond and Lynchburg: Together with Instruction for Commissioners in Chancery." In E. Hall, *A Digested Index to the Virginia Reports*, vol. 1, pp. 623-654 (1825).

This is very similar to the preceding pamphlet.

REPORTS OF CASES

W. H. Bryson

I. *Introduction*

COMMON LAW systems of jurisprudence are based on judicial pronouncements of the law. Although legislative statutes may change or restate the law, all legislation operates in the light of the preexisting law. This basic common law, whether it is found or created by the judges, is recorded in the reports of the opinions of the judges in the individual cases that are brought to them for their decision.

A system of common law is grounded upon the statement of the law by the judiciary in contradistinction to statute law enacted by a legislative body and to edicts issued by an administrator. While statutes and edicts are normally general in their scope and application, the statement of the law by a judge arises within the context of a particular dispute between two (usually) individuals. The judge's resolution of the case applies only to the parties before him. However, it is a precedent to guide future judges in future cases. The quantity and quality of precedents that are available will determine the scope and sophistication of the common law.

These individual opinions have been gathered into collections called generically "reports." This genre of legal literature dates back in England to the thirteenth century. However, the systematic and official publication of reports is a recent phenomenon. The courts have always kept a permanent record of the decisions of the judges, but until recently, the reasons for the decisions, where reasons were given, were not officially preserved. It is, of course, the reasoning of the judge rather than the judgment for one individual party or the other that is the foundation of the common law. This is the matter of interest to the lawyers, and it was they who, as a matter of private enterprise, began the compiling of reports of cases.

In imitation of their English legal forebears,[1] Virginia lawyers made and then published reports. This began in the early eighteenth century and continues on today.

[1] The common law of England was brought to Virginia at the beginning, in 1607. W. H. Bryson, "English Common Law in Virginia," *Journal of Legal History*, vol. 6, pp. 249-256 (1985); W. H. Bryson, *Virginia Civil Procedure*, pp. 46-58 (1997).

II. *Private Enterprises*

Before independence from Great Britain in 1776 and the reorganization of the Virginia courts that followed shortly thereafter, there was little incentive to report Virginia court decisions. There were several reasons for this.

First, the colonial courts were composed primarily of laymen, who were supplied with legally-trained clerks. Occasionally, a lawyer was appointed to the bench, but his legal training was not the reason for his nomination.[2] Thus, the colonial courts of Virginia did not, as a general rule, give out opinions or reasons for their judgments, and when they did, they were not learned opinions. The bar, which was trained in the law, was not particularly impressed intellectually by the bench, which was not.

Secondly, the courts were subject to the appellate jurisdiction of the Privy Council, which sat in London; thus not even the General Court, which sat in Williamsburg, was the court of final resort for Virginia.[3]

Thirdly, the published reports of the English courts were widely available in eighteenth century Virginia.[4] Since the law of Virginia was the common law of England and the highest court for Virginia was in England, the English reports were authoritative and sufficient. They served the professional needs of the colonial bar well enough.

Fourthly, the size of the bench and bar of Virginia in the colonial period was too small to make the publication of Virginia reports financially attractive. Thus no law reports of Virginia cases were printed before the very end of the eighteenth century.

Although there were no printed Virginia reports available before 1776, we do know that at least five colonial Virginia lawyers made manuscript reports of cases for their own personal use. They were Sir John Randolph, his son John Randolph, Edward Barradall, William Hopkins, and Thomas Jefferson. Jefferson's reports were printed in 1829, which was after his death. The reports of Sir John Randolph and Edward Barradall were printed in 1909, more for the benefit of historians than practicing lawyers. The manuscript books of Hopkins

---

[2] See generally, P. A. Bruce, *Institutional History of Virginia in the Seventeenth Century*, vol. 1, part 3 (1910); O. P. Chitwood, *Justice in Colonial Virginia* (1905); A. P. Scott, *Criminal Law in Colonial Virginia*, pp. 1-136 (1930).

[3] J. H. Smith, *Appeals to the Privy Council from the American Plantations* (1950).

[4] W. H. Bryson, *Census of Law Books in Colonial Virginia*, pp. xii, 1-17 (1978).

and the younger Randolph have never been printed and are now lost.[5] There were probably others now lost also.

After independence, the Virginia courts were reorganized in two significant ways. The appellate court judges were required to be chosen from the professionally trained bar, and the English Privy Council was replaced with the Court of Appeals of Virginia as the highest court of the Commonwealth.

As was the custom in England, lawyers and judges in Virginia after 1776 continued to make case reports for their own private use. We have manuscript reports from Charles Lee, John Brown, St. George Tucker, David Watson, and David Yancey. John Marshall's manuscript reports are now sadly lost. These manuscripts were used by friends of their makers, and Virginia case authority was much needed by the practicing bar. To meet this great need, Bushrod Washington revised his private manuscript notes of cases and published them in 1798. Washington states in his preface that it was not his original intention to publish them when he made them. Before the first printing of volume one of Washington's reports, Chancellor George Wythe had published a thin volume of his own opinions, but his court, the High Court of Chancery, was not the highest court in Virginia. Also, the quantity and scope of his reports were hardly sufficient to satisfy the needs of the legal community of Virginia.

Washington's reports were well received, and after he gave up the practice of law to accept a seat on the Supreme Court of the United States, his Virginia reports were quickly followed by others. Hening and Munford quite candidly state in the 1808 Preface to volume one of their reports that they compiled them for the purpose of publication. They both had large families to support, and they, no doubt, looked forward to the financial success of their reports of Virginia cases.

One private venture of particular interest was Lucian Minor's condensed reports. In 1848, he wrote an article advocating shorter case reports as the solution to the ever-increasing quantity of law reports.[6] He followed this up in 1857 with a volume of condensed reports of cases that were published by Hening and Munford.[7] However, the idea of

---

[5] W. H. Bryson, "Law Reporting and Legal Records in Virginia, 1607-1800," in J. H. Baker, *Judicial Records, Law Reports, and the Growth of Case Law*, pp. 319-335 (1989); W. H. Bryson, "Virginia Manuscript Law Reports," *Law Library Journal*, vol. 82, pp. 305-311 (1990).

[6] L. Minor, "Law Reports," *Southern Literary Messenger*, vol. 14, pp. 255-260 (1848).

[7] Book notice, *Q.L.J.*, vol. 1, pp. 190-192 (1856).

condensed reports was not well received, and the idea of condensing all of the Virginia reports was discarded.[8]

III. *Official Reporters*

In 1819 the judges of the Court of Appeals petitioned the General Assembly to have an official reporter of their judicial decisions. The reason given for their request was the unacceptable delay in the publication of the *Virginia Reports* by William Munford, who was editing them as a private venture.[9] In the next year, the legislature passed a bill[10] creating the office of reporter, a person who would be selected by the Court of Appeals and serve at the court's pleasure.[11] From this point on, it was the court and not the reporter who designated which cases would be reported.[12] A later act required the official reporter to include the opinions of the General Court as well as the Court of Appeals.[13] These reports were printed by the public printer and sold by the Commonwealth. That the *Virginia Reports* were being sold at a price well above the cost of production was the subject of vigorous editorial comment in the 1880s.[14]

At first, the reporters were compensated by the payment of a royalty based on the number of pages printed. Francis W. Gilmer, the first official reporter, complained that this was an inadequate sum of money considering the labor needed to edit the reports.[15] This was, no doubt, one of the reasons why he edited only one volume of them. However, it was not until 1842 that the reporter was paid a fixed

[8] E. C. Surrency, *History of American Law Publishing*, p. 49 (1990).

[9] Journal Va. House of Delegates, p. 28 (1819); C. Robinson, "Preface," 1 Rob. vi-vii.

[10] 1819-20 Va. Acts, c. 17, p. 16; there were minor amendments in 1820-21 Va. Acts, c. 30, p. 31; and 1828-29 Va. Acts, c. 9, p. 11.

[11] The succession of official reporters is Gilmer, P. Randolph, Leigh, Robinson, Grattan, Matthews, Hansbrough, Burks, T. J. Michie, A. H. Michie, Woltz, Davison, Alford, and Sinclair.

[12] C. Robinson, "Preface," 1 Rob. vi-x.

[13] 1827-28 Va. Acts, c. 25, § 5, p. 21; 1842-43 Va. Acts, c. 39, p. 29.

[14] J. C. Lamb, "Proposed Sale of Virginia Reports," *Va. L. J.*, vol. 8, p. 61 (1884); J. C. Lamb, "The Virginia Reports," *Va. L. J.*, vol. 8, p. 314 (1884); J. C. Lamb, "Publication of State Reports," *Va. L. J.*, vol. 11, p. 700 (1887).

[15] Letter of Dec. 11, 1820, Journal Va. House of Delegates, p. 47 (1820); E. G. Swem, *Bibliography of Virginia*, part II, pp. 1059-1060 (1917).

annual salary by the state.[16] This coincided with the appointment of Conway Robinson as official reporter.

In 1847 and 1871, acts were passed providing for special courts of appeals to alleviate large backlogs of cases pending in the Supreme Court of Appeals.[17] Each of these acts ordered the reporter for the Supreme Court of Appeals to report the opinions of the special courts, but it does not appear that these courts ever functioned. No cases from them were ever reported in the *Virginia Reports*.

In 1854 a Special Court of Appeals was created, and it heard many cases which were then pending in the Supreme Court of Appeals. There was no provision for the reporting of the opinions of the Special Court of Appeals, but John M. Patton, Jr., and Roscoe B. Heath volunteered their services, and they were approved by the court.[18] Patton and Heath's reports were published as a private venture by the reporters. The only official participation was that the judges gave copies of their opinions to the reporters.

The Act that created the Special Court of Appeals in 1924 provided that the Supreme Court of Appeals should designate which opinions should be published in the *Virginia Reports*.[19] Judging by the quantity of opinions from the Special Court of Appeals that were printed in volumes 139 through 151 of the *Virginia Reports*, it appears that they were all designated for publication.

When the intermediary Court of Appeals was created in 1985, it was given an official, salaried reporter.[20]

In 1881 following the death of Peachy R. Grattan, the judges of the Supreme Court of Appeals decided to abandon the older custom of referring to the Virginia reports by the names of the reporter. They ordered that, in the future, they would be called the *Virginia Reports*, and they renamed and renumbered the old state nominative reports as *Virginia Reports*.[21] The reason for this was the vast and confusing

[16] 1841-42 Va. Acts, c. 88, p. 51. The statutes are basically unchanged since 1842 except for an increase in the amount of the reporter's salary. Va. Code Ann. §§ 17-113 through 17-116.

[17] 1847-48 Va. Acts, c. 68, § 11, p. 52; 1871-72 Va. Acts, c. 124, § 8, p. 99.

[18] 1853-54 Va. Acts, c. 17, p. 18; "Preface," 1 Pat. & H. vi.

[19] 1924 Va. Acts, c. 264, p. 393.

[20] 1984 Va. Acts, c. 635, p. 1107.

[21] M. P. Burks, "Preface," 91 Va. xvii. Apparently, this had been unsuccessfully attempted when Gilmer was appointed the first official reporter in 1820; his single volume of cases was produced with a label on the spine naming the book "Virginia Reports," and it was occasionally cited as "1 Va. Rep." C. C. Soule, *The Lawyer's*

accumulation of printed reports from common law jurisdictions around the world. For example, reporters with the surname of Clark(e) edited different reports from Alabama, Bengal, England, Iowa, Michigan, New York, and Pennsylvania. "Jones's reports" could refer to any one of various reports of cases from Alabama, England, Ireland, Missouri, New York, North Carolina, Ontario, or Pennsylvania.[22]

Around 1900, the Virginia Supreme Court of Appeals made the decision to publish in the *Virginia Reports* all, every single one, of its opinions. Since 1887, they had all been printed in West's *South Eastern Reports*. Throughout the nineteenth century, the legal profession had constantly complained of the "excessive" quantity of reported cases.[23] However, the multiplication of reports continued unabated. Obviously, there was a market for more and more. When the West Publishing Company began to publish *all* of the federal and state appellate court opinions in the 1880s, the chorus of complainers got louder and louder.[24] However, the bar believed that they had to have access to as many case reports as possible lest a competitor in the profession get ahead by means of some obscure case magnified into something important. How often have we heard: "Opposing counsel has overlooked the important case of *Smith v. Jones*." How often does a judicial opinion comment that "both counsel have failed to argue the case of *Jones v. Bloggs*, which is squarely on point." It is part of the professional game to cite a case that the others have overlooked. Thus, it was inevitable that totally comprehensive reports would succeed. And succeed they did, regardless of the cost, inconvenience, and difficulties of use. All attempts to limit the reporting of cases have failed.[25]

Lucian Minor was a very learned and well-respected jurist. Why did his efforts to sell condensed reports fail? Why did all attempts to limit the quantity of the printing of seemingly superfluous reports fail?

Reference Manual of Law Books and Citations, p. 61 (1883).

[22] C. C. Soule, *The Lawyer's Reference Manual*, pp. 191-192, 233, 378, 423-424 (1883).

[23] E.g., L. Minor, "Law Reports," *Southern Literary Messenger*, vol. 14, pp. 255-260 (1848).

[24] E.g., R. M. Hughes, "Law Reporting," *Va. State Bar Ass'n Repts.*, vol. 8, pp. 53-62 (1895); *Va. L. Reg.*, vol. 1, pp. 309-317 (1895).

[25] See T. J. Young, Jr., "A Look at American Law Reporting in the 19th Century," *Law Library Journal*, vol. 68, pp. 294-306 (1975).

Why has there been such discontent from the bar over the judges' attempted refusal to allow unpublished opinions to be cited?[26]

The answers to all three of these questions is that a judge is an officer of the state. Whatever a judge says in court in connection with a pending case is an official statement of the law. Whether it is intelligent or not, whether it is right or wrong, it is a precedent, and it is considered to be more authoritative than the opinion of a practicing or academic lawyer. Thus any judicial opinion that favors one's client is appropriate to be cited in support unless it has been expressly overruled by a later opinion or statute. A judicial opinion thus trumps any scholarly opinion to the contrary. Thus the more cases available to the practicing lawyer, the greater is his arsenal of legal arguments.

Of course, judges are human, and they commit error and make mistakes like the rest of us. Their office does not confer any knowledge or wisdom that they did not have before their elevation to the bench. However, the basic premise of judge-declared common law has led us to our present paradox. As to reports of cases, too many are not enough.

IV. *Advance Sheets*

The practicing attorney always wants to have at his fingertips the most recent statement of the law. To satisfy this need, advance sheets are issued as soon as several opinions have been rendered, and thus the lawyer is not forced to wait until enough have been collected to fill an entire permanent volume of reports. The first attempt to supply the Virginia bar with advance sheets was made by William Waller Hening and William Munford in 1807. The first volume of their joint effort at reporting Virginia cases was issued to subscribers in three installments, one after each of the terms of the Supreme Court of Appeals. At the end of the year, they supplied a new title page, preface, table of cases, and index, and the subscriber bound these and the advance sheets together to make the permanent volume. Unfortunately, in the next year, the terms of the court were rearranged, and from a printing standpoint, this system was rendered no longer feasible. However, the idea was good and the lawyers' need remained. In fact in 1819, Munford was criticized for being slow in reporting the decisions of the court, and an official court reporter was appointed to see that the job was done properly and quickly.

[26] See H. J. Stern, "The Enigma of Unpublished Opinions," *A.B.A. Journ.*, vol. 64, pp. 1245-46 (1978); N. H. Andrews, "Reporting Case Law: Unreported Cases, the Definition of a *Ratio* and the Criteria for Reporting Decisions," *Legal Studies*, vol. 5, pp. 205-232 (1985).

REPORTS

OF

CASES

ARGUED AND DETERMINED

IN THE

Supreme Court of Appeals

OF

VIRGINIA:

WITH SELECT CASES,

RELATING CHIEFLY TO POINTS OF PRACTICE,

DECIDED BY THE

Superior Court of Chancery for the Richmond District.

PART I.—VOL. I.

BY WILLIAM W. HENING AND WILLIAM MUNFORD.

RICHMOND:

PRINTED BY SAMUEL PLEASANTS, JUNIOR.

1807.

It was not until the beginning of 1856 that the Virginia bar was again served by any advance reporting of cases. In that year, the first law journal of Virginia, the *Quarterly Law Journal*, was published in Richmond by A. B. Guigon. The major purpose of this venture appears to have been the advance publication of selected Virginia cases. There were also articles and reports from other jurisdictions. This journal was succeeded in format and in purpose by the *Quarterly Law Review* in 1860. This journal, which was edited by A. H. Sands, ceased to appear after the April 1861 issue, being an early casualty of the invasion of Federal troops.

After Virginia had recovered from the war and Reconstruction, a new effort at periodical legal scholarship was launched. In 1877 the *Virginia Law Journal* appeared, and the policy of the two earlier journals of reporting selected cases was reestablished. This journal folded in 1893, but its successor in 1895, the *Virginia Law Register*, continued to function as a selective advance reporter for Virginia cases. From 1895 to 1904, the cases were selected and reported for this journal by M. P. Burks, the official state reporter. The *Virginia Law Register* continued to print opinions of the Virginia Supreme Court of Appeals after 1904, but the quantity constantly declined until the demise of the journal in 1927, no doubt reflecting the competition from other publishers to supply advance sheets for Virginia.

The systematic publication of advance sheets for all of the opinions of the Supreme Court of Appeals began in 1887 when the West Publishing Company inaugurated their *South Eastern Reporter*. In 1899 the short-lived *Virginia Supreme Court Reporter* was begun; this provided advance sheets in only three volumes over a period of three years. In 1907 William Wallace Scott and Maury Baldwin Watts established the series of advance sheets called *Virginia Appeals*. Watts was the sole reporter for volumes two through thirty-five, the last of which appeared in 1926. The official Virginia advance sheets were issued as early as 1944,[27] and they have been published ever since.

V. *Miscellaneous Cases*

The bibliographical notes that follow consider only books that are collections of case reports. Many judicial opinions were printed in law journals, as pamphlets, or as appendices to books. The law journals are dealt with in separate parts of this book. The section that describes accounts of trials does not include appellate opinions and thus does not mention the following items. George Wythe's opinion in *Love v.*

[27] I would like to thank Alan T. Gravitt for supplying me with this date.

Donelson (c. 1800), n.p., n.d., is the only one of Wythe's pamphlet opinions that was not reprinted in the second edition of his *Reports*.[28] A report of the case of *Kamper v. Hawkins*, 1 Va. Cas. 20 (1793), was published by William Tatham in Philadelphia in 1794. There is a sixteen-page pamphlet, which reports the cases of *Bell v. Hill* (1811) and *Chowning v. Allen* (1811) decided by Creed Taylor. Note also *Judge B. R. Wellford's Opinion in the Case of Commonwealth vs. Dismal Swamp Canal Co., 12 March, 1885, Circuit Court of Richmond City* (N.p., n.d.); *In the Circuit Court of the City of Richmond. Henry Lewis et als. vs. The Washington and Ohio Railroad Co. & Als. Opinion of Judge Beverley R. Wellford, Jr.* (N.p., [1880]); and *Decision of Judge Jacob S. Yerger, on the Stay Law. Delivered at the December Term of the Circuit Court of Warren County* (N.p.: Daily Herald, 1866). There was a pamphlet opinion of Judge Brockenbrough Lamb in the case of *Dew v. First and Merchants Nat'l Bank* (1946); it was reprinted in the first volume of his reports at page 218.

W. W. Hening's *New Virginia Justice* published three cases from the Superior Court of Chancery at Richmond, *Purcell v. Purcell*, 4 Hen. & M. 507 (1809), *Woodson v. Gibson* (1806), and *Tinsley v. Sydnor* (1809).[29] The opinion of Judge Henry St. George Tucker of the Superior Court of Chancery at Winchester in the case of *Selden v. Loudoun County Overseers of the Poor* was published as a twenty-six page pamphlet in Leesburg, Virginia, by B. W. Sower in 1830, and it was reprinted as an appendix to volume two of Tucker's *Commentaries on the Laws of Virginia* (2d ed. 1837) and at pages 445-456 in an appendix to volume one of the third edition of that work in 1846.

The judicial opinions of the State Corporation Commission are included in its *Annual Report*. These annual reports were first published in 1904.

REPORTERS

Neill Herbert Alford, Jr.

Neill H. Alford, Jr., was a professor of law at the University of Virginia while he was the official reporter for the Supreme Court of Virginia. His reports are volumes 218 to 228 of the *Virginia Reports* that cover the years 1977 to 1984.

---

[28] Wythe's other pamphlet opinions are described in W. J. Ritz, *American Judicial Proceedings*, pp. 100-105 (1984).

[29] These three opinions are printed as addenda to the last three editions of W. W. Hening, *New Virginia Justice* (1810, 1820, 1825).

Alford's reports are generally typical of the modern style of law reporting. His reports reflect the trend of paring down the number of tables and lists included at the beginning of each volume of the *Virginia Reports*, and conversely expanding the number and size of individual headnotes appearing before each particular case. Volume 221 was the last volume of the Virginia Reports to include a list of "Appeals and Writs of Error Refused"; Volume 222 was the last to include the "Rules of Court" section; and Volume 228 the last to include a list of "Cases Cited in Opinions." The headnotes before each case are extensive and are set out according to subject topic headings. In addition, a short paragraph summarizing the Court's holding precedes each case.

Edward Barradall

Edward Barradall (1704-1743) was a barrister of the Inner Temple who emigrated to Virginia and had a very successful practice in the General Court in Williamsburg. He was Attorney General of Virginia from 1737 until his early death in 1743.[30]

Since the General Court in colonial times was composed of the members of the Council and presided over by the Governor, most of whom were laymen, no reasons were given for their judicial decisions. Therefore, these reports consist of extensive arguments of counsel and the bare final orders of the Court.

The manuscript reports of Edward Barradall,[31] which cover the period 1733 to 1741, were known and used long before they were printed. *Berryman v. Booth*, 2 VCD B42 (1734), in Barradall's reports was cited by Judge Dabney Carr in 1835 in his opinion in *Worsham v. Worsham*, 32 Va. (5 Leigh) 589 at 592 (1835). William Green mentioned that he had consulted *Taylor v. Graves*, 2 VCD B56 (1736), as found in Barradall's reports in his celebrated argument in *Moon v. Stone*, 60 Va. (19 Gratt.) 130 at 320, 321 (1869). Conway Robinson cited seven cases from the manuscript reports of Barradall. They are *Rose v. Cooke*, 2 VCD B192, B229 (1736); *Brooking v. Dudley*, 2 VCD B256 (1737); *Edwards v. Bridger*, 2 VCD B117 (1740); *Micou v. Corbin*, 2 VCD B37 (1733); *Murdock v. Thornton*, 2 VCD B33 (1733); *Spicer v. Pope*, 2 VCD B232 (1736); and *Winston v. Henry*, 2 VCD B213 (1736).[32] They were

[30] R. E. Nance, "Edward Barradall," *Va. Law Reporters* (1977), pp. 71-74.

[31] These manuscripts are discussed in the "Introduction" to R. T. Barton, ed., *Virginia Colonial Decisions*, vol. 1 (1909).

[32] C. Robinson, *Practice in the Courts of Law and Equity in Virginia*, vol. 1, pp. 161, 288, 123, 404, 76, 137, 527 (1832); vol. 2, pp. 98, 121 (1835).

also known to Thomas Jefferson, who used twenty-six cases in his own reports.

J. W. Randolph proposed in 1852 to publish Barradall's reports,[33] but this was not accomplished until 1909: Robert T. Barton, ed., *Virginia Colonial Decisions*, Boston: Boston Book Co., 1909, vol. 2.

William Brockenbrough

William Brockenbrough (1778-1838) was a Richmond lawyer and politician and then judge of the General Court during the period of his law reports.[34] His two volumes of reports of cases in the General Court are usually referred to as the *Virginia Cases*, and they have been designated volumes three and four of the *Virginia Reports*. Most of these reports are of criminal cases. The first volume was edited jointly with his colleague on the bench, Judge Hugh Holmes.[35]

Volume two of the *Virginia Cases*, volume four of the *Virginia Reports*, was edited solely by William Brockenbrough. It was published in Richmond by Peter Cottom in 1826. There was a second edition in Charlottesville by the Michie Company in 1902, and this was photographically reproduced in Richmond by the Virginia Reports Reprint, Inc., in 1979.

After a Preface describing the jurisdiction of the General Court, Judge Brockenbrough gives a "Brief Sketch of the Courts of This Commonwealth." This is followed by a listing of all of the appellate court judges since 1776.

John Brown

John Brown (1750-1810) was the clerk of the Court of Appeals of Virginia from 1785 to 1810. He made notes of legal points decided in the Court of Appeals concentrating on appellate procedure and court costs. This was done no doubt for his own personal future use as clerk of that court. The cases reported date from 1791 to 1799. He was not acting either as an advocate or as a judge, and thus his reports contain no references to printed materials other than Virginia statutes.

---

[33] See the publisher's notice in G. Wythe, *Decisions of Cases*, pp. [v], [xliv] (2d ed. by B. B. Minor, 1852).

[34] D. A. Powers, III, "William Brockenbrough," *Va. Law Reporters*, pp. 7-10 (1977). It is interesting to note that William Brockenbrough's son, John White Brockenbrough (1806-1877), published two volumes of John Marshall's federal circuit court opinions. C. V. Laughlin, "John White Brockenbrough," *Legal Education in Va.*, pp. 99-104 (1982).

[35] This volume is described under Holmes's name.

Occasionally, he notes oral references to other cases that had been recently decided by the Court of Appeals. All of them are earlier than Bushrod Washington's first volume of reports, which was printed in 1798, so that could not have been the source of the information.

The original autograph manuscript of John Brown's reports of Virginia cases in the Court of Appeals is in the Virginia State Library and Archives, MS. 21779c. This manuscript was once owned by William Green. It was first published in the *University of Richmond Law Review*, vol. 11, pp. 711-741 (1977). It was reprinted in W. H. Bryson, ed., *Miscellaneous Virginia Law Reports*, Dobbs Ferry, N.Y.: Oceana Publications, 1992, pp. 27-65.

John Brown made a second volume of notes of cases in the Court of Appeals that was a continuation of the volume noted above. This second volume, which is now lost, may well have covered cases from 1799 until his death in 1810. It was probably a small booklet, as volume one is. On the front cover of the surviving manuscript is written "No. 1" and "See page 18th, 2 Book, for entries of some notes of decisions prior to 1791 — omitted to be entered first, the rough notes being mislaid."

Brown also compiled notes of cases in the General Court from 1788 to 1794; he was clerk of this court from 1781 to 1794. Considering the nature of his surviving reports, it is likely that he ceased to report cases from the General Court when he ceased to be its clerk. This lost volume was used by Conway Robinson in preparing a treatise on Virginia procedure, which was published in 1832. Robinson cited six cases from it: *Graham, adm'x v. Graham, adm'r* (1788), *Jones v. Goode* (1789), *Brownlow v. Custis* (1789), *Bird v. Scott* (1791), *Johnson v. Braxton* (1792), and *Bradley v. Barnett* (1794).[36] Robinson mentioned this now lost manuscript in a letter to Robert T. Barton dated December 20, 1875.[37]

William Hamilton Bryson

W. H. Bryson is a professor of law at the University of Richmond and the editor of the *Virginia Circuit Court Opinions*. Volume one of these trial court opinions was published in 1985. The first three volumes were published by the Dietz Press in Richmond at the editor's expense. In 1986, Aspen Publishers assumed the publication of this series of reports through the foresight of Dabney Oakley. Aspen then

[36] C. Robinson, *Practice in the Courts of Law and Equity in Virginia*, vol. 1, pp. 390, 592, 535-536, 657, 551, 616 (1832).

[37] R. T. Barton, *Practice in the Courts of Law*, p. vi (1st ed. 1877).

published volumes 4 through 24. In 1992, the *Virginia Circuit Court Opinions* was transferred to Butterworth's, the international law publisher founded in the early nineteenth century, and as of January 1995, through a large international corporate publishing merger, this set of reports has been published by The Michie Company.

The cases reported in this reporter are selected by the editor from among the opinions sent to him by the judges and lawyers. As the technical resources available increased over the years, the selection of cases for inclusion also increased. Almost all opinions on the following subjects are reported: corporate law, commercial law, environmental law, mechanic's liens, and civil procedure, the last-mentioned being one of the subjects that the reporter teaches. Few cases in the field of family law are reported because this area is well covered by opinions from the Court of Appeals and because they are usually very fact-specific and thus of lesser precedential value.

Most of the Virginia circuit court judges do not write opinion letters, and some who do decline to share them for publication. However, there are trial court judges from one end of the Commonwealth to the other who are diligent in filling in the gaps in Virginia jurisprudence. These opinions are not received by the reporter in chronological order, and thus they cannot be printed in strict chronological order without an unseemly delay in publication. Therefore, each volume of the *Virginia Circuit Court Opinions* begins with the most recent opinions and has the older ones at the back.

Martin Parks Burks

Martin P. Burks (1851-1928) was a practicing lawyer in Bedford and then professor of law and then law school dean at Washington and Lee University while acting as official reporter of the Commonwealth of Virginia. At this same time, he was an enormously productive legal scholar. He was appointed reporter in 1895 when the readjuster judges were replaced; he resigned in 1917 when he himself became a judge on the Supreme Court of Appeals.[38]

Burks edited volumes 91 through 119 of the *Virginia Reports*, which cover the years 1895 to 1916. These twenty-nine volumes were published in Richmond by J. H. O'Bannon and then by Davis Bottom, who were successively Superintendent of Public Printing. The years of publication were 1896 to 1917.

[38] C. V. Laughlin, "Martin Parks Burks," *Legal Education in Va.*, pp. 117-126 (1982).

Volume 91 has a preface that brings Conway Robinson's history of the Virginia courts and law reporting[39] up to date. Various later volumes are prefaced with rules of court and memorials to deceased Virginia Supreme Court judges and attorneys general.

Daniel Call

Daniel Call (1765-1840) was a Richmond attorney during the period of his reports of Virginia cases. It is interesting to note that his two brothers-in-law were also lawyers and reporters, among their other accomplishments. His first wife's sister married George Wythe, and his second wife's sister was married to John Marshall.[40]

The six volumes of Call's *Reports* have been designated volumes 5 through 10 of the *Virginia Reports*. The first three volumes were printed in Richmond by Thomas Nicolson in 1801, 1802, and 1805. There was a second edition by Joseph Tate of these first three volumes, which was published in Richmond by Peter Cottom and printed by Shepherd and Pollard in 1824. Volumes 4 through 6 were then published in Richmond by Robert I. Smith in 1833. In 1854, Lucian Minor edited a third edition of the first three volumes; this was published in Richmond by A. Morris in 1854. All six volumes were reissued in Charlottesville by the Michie Company in 1902, and this last edition was photographically reproduced in 1979 by the Virginia Reports Reprint, Inc., in Richmond.

The first three volumes report cases in the Court of Appeals of Virginia dating from 1797 to 1803. At the end of volume 3, Call prints several cases from the Court of Appeals from the year 1790, which he copied from the manuscript reports of John Marshall.

In 1833, many years after Call's first three volumes, for that matter nine years after the second edition of them, Daniel Call published an additional three volumes of reports with the intent to fill in the gaps of the then existing *Virginia Reports*. Volume four begins with biographical sketches of all of the judges of the Court of Appeals from 1779 to 1809. The first series of cases is those from the first Court of Appeals, 1779 to 1789. There is also a case from the Court of Admiralty, *Hague v. Stratton*, 4 Call 84 (1786), which was appealed to the Court of Appeals, *Stratton v. Hague*, 4 Call 564 (1790). Note also a case in the General Court, *Hill v. Pride*, 4 Call 107 (1787). The next series of reports in volume 4 is cases dating from 1790 to 1803 that had not been previously printed. Note the case of *Turberville v. Self*, 4 Call

[39] 1 Rob. iii-x.

[40] A. G. Smith, "Daniel Call," *Va. Law Reporters*, pp. 16-18 (1977).

580 (1795), which was extracted from John Marshall's manuscript notes of cases.

Volume 5 and the first part of volume 6 publish opinions from the Court of Appeals from 1804 to 1806 to fill in this gap between the end of Call's third volume and the beginning of the first volume by Hening and Munford. Then another series of previously unprinted cases from 1804 to 1818 is published in volume 6. At the end of this volume are five cases from the federal circuit court for the District of Virginia. These federal cases date from 1793 to 1825 and were reprinted in Robert W. Hughes's reports of opinions in the federal courts and then in *Federal Cases*.

Charles Marshall Davison, Jr.

Charles M. Davison, Jr., (1914-1995) was a professor of law at the University of Virginia while he was the official reporter for the Supreme Court of Virginia. His reports are volumes 208 to 217 of the *Virginia Reports*, which cover the years 1967 to 1977.

John Singleton Diggs

J. Singleton Diggs was born on February 3, 1852, in Cumberland County, Virginia. His father was the Reverend Thomas Diggs, who was originally from Mathews County, and his mother was Elizabeth Ford Diggs of Cumberland County. Before going on the bench, Diggs, practiced law in Lynchburg, and he served in the Senate of Virginia representing the City of Lynchburg and Campbell County from 1881 to 1887. He was then judge of the Corporation Court of the City of Lynchburg from 1888 to 1895.[41] After that, he returned to the practice of law in Lynchburg. He died on November 13, 1927, in Lynchburg at the age of seventy-five and was survived by his wife, Lilly Slaughter Diggs. He was buried in the Presbyterian Cemetery in Lynchburg.

Decisions of Judge J. Singleton Diggs of Corporation Court of Lynchburg, Va., n.p., n.d., contains five opinions of Judge Diggs on points not settled at that time by the Supreme Court of Appeals. These trial court cases date from 1890 to 1893. There are copies of this forty-nine page book in the Alderman Library at the University of Virginia and in the law library at the College of William and Mary. A second edition by W. H. Bryson was published in 1997.

[41] S. D. Martin, *Historical Sketch of the State Courts of Lynchburg*, p. 7 (1951); Journal Va. House of Delegates 1887-88, pp. 172-173.

Francis Walker Gilmer

Francis W. Gilmer (1790-1826) was a practicing lawyer in Richmond when he was appointed the first official reporter for the Virginia Court of Appeals in 1820. In addition to being well known as an attorney, Gilmer had also established a literary reputation as an essayist. Furthermore, he was politically and socially very well connected. Thomas Jefferson knew him from his infancy; two of his closest friends were William Wirt (1772-1834) and Judge Dabney Carr (1773-1837) of Winchester.[42]

In a private letter dated July 3, 1820, Gilmer wrote "My principal recreation this summer will be writing reports and verily I fear the decisions of our Court of Appeals will not rival the Tory opinions of Lord Mansfield in depth or elegance. The judges are too careless both in matter and form. I took up the business for the honor of the profession, and if the legislature will not put it on a more creditable footing, they may go back to the crude and bungling prosing of Munford, which is nearly as bad as his poetry, and worse there could not be."[43] In a public letter dated December 11, 1820, Gilmer pointed out that the labor of editing the reports was not adequately repaid by the statutory scheme of compensation to the reporter.[44] Thus, law reporting not being to Gilmer's taste or purse, he resigned fourteen months after accepting the position.[45]

It is interesting to note that Gilmer's single volume of reports covers a little over a year and is somewhat short. However, this was not the fault of the reporter. As he states in his "Advertisement," which serves as a preface, the judges themselves selected the cases to be reported and wrote down their own opinions. Gilmer's major responsibility was to give a summary of the arguments of counsel.

The single volume of Gilmer's *Reports of Cases* has been designated volume 21 of the Virginia reports. It was published by N. Pollard and printed at the Franklin Press in Richmond in 1821. There was a second edition by the Michie Company of Charlottesville in 1903, and this

[42] Wirt later became Attorney General of the United States, and Carr became a judge on the Court of Appeals of Virginia. *DAB*.

[43] Letter of Francis Walker Gilmer to Peachy Ridgway Gilmer, Richmond, July 3, 1820, in the Virginia Historical Society. I would like to thank E. Lee Shepard for bringing this letter to my attention.

[44] Journal Va. House of Delegates, p. 47 (1820); E. G. Swem, *Bibliography of Virginia*, part II, pp. 1059-1060 (1917).

[45] See M. A. Lofaro, "Francis Walker Gilmer," *Va. Law Reporters*, pp. 33-46 (1977); R. B. Davis, *Francis Walker Gilmer*, p. 330 (1939).

edition was reprinted in 1979 by the Virginia Reports Reprints, Inc., of Richmond.

Peachy Ridgway Grattan

Peachy R. Grattan (1801-1881) was practicing law in Richmond while serving as the official reporter for the Supreme Court of Appeals and the General Court.[46] He edited thirty-three volumes of reports, which are now designated volumes 42 through 74 of the *Virginia Reports*. Grattan's volumes are the last in Virginia that are referred to by the reporter's name, in the older tradition. They cover the years 1844 to 1880. Considering the turbulence of these years in Virginia, it should not be surprising that the history of the publication of Grattan's reports is somewhat complicated compared to the others. The following chart lists the earlier editions.

1 Gratt.	Richmond:	Shepherd & Colin,	1845
	Richmond:	Ritchie & Dunnavant,	1860
	Richmond:	O'Bannon,	1895
2 Gratt.	Richmond:	Shepherd & Colin,	1846
	Richmond:	Ritchie & Dunnavant,	1861
	Richmond:	O'Bannon,	1894
3 Gratt.	Richmond:	Shepherd & Colin,	1847
	Richmond:	Schaffter,	1871
	Richmond:	O'Bannon,	1897
4 Gratt.	Richmond:	Shepherd & Colin,	1848
	Richmond:	Schaffter,	1871
	Richmond:	O'Bannon,	1897
5 Gratt.	Richmond:	Colin,	1849
	Richmond:	Schaffter,	1871
	Richmond:	O'Bannon,	1898
6 Gratt.	Richmond:	Colin, Baptist, Nowlan,	1850
	Richmond:	Schaffter,	1871
	Richmond:	O'Bannon,	1898
7 Gratt.	Richmond:	Colin & Nowlan,	1852

[46] T. M. Blaylock, "Peachy Ridgway Grattan," *Va. Law Reporters*, pp. 65-67 (1977).

	Richmond:	O'Bannon,	1894
8 Gratt.	Richmond:	Colin & Nowlan,	1852
	Richmond:	O'Bannon,	1893
9 Gratt.	Richmond:	Ritchie & Dunnavant,	1854
	Richmond:	O'Bannon,	1893
10 Gratt.	Richmond:	Ritchie & Dunnavant,	1855
	Richmond:	O'Bannon,	1892
11 Gratt.	Richmond:	Ritchie & Dunnavant,	1855
	Richmond:	O'Bannon,	1892
12 Gratt.	Richmond:	Ritchie & Dunnavant,	1856
	Richmond:	O'Bannon,	1891
13 Gratt.	Richmond:	Ritchie & Dunnavant,	1857
	Richmond:	O'Bannon,	1891
14 Gratt.	Richmond:	Ritchie & Dunnavant,	1859
	Richmond:	O'Bannon,	1889
15 Gratt.	Richmond:	Ritchie & Dunnavant,	1860
	Richmond:	O'Bannon,	1889
16 Gratt.	Richmond:	Randolph,	1867
	Richmond:	O'Bannon,	1895
17 Gratt.	Richmond:	Fore,	1867
	Richmond:	O'Bannon,	1896
18 Gratt.	Richmond:	Fergusson & Rady,	1868
	Richmond:	O'Bannon,	1896
19 Gratt.	Richmond:	Schaffter,	1870
	Richmond:	O'Bannon,	1900

Volumes 20 through 33 were published in Richmond by a succession of public printers from 1871 to 1881. The Michie Company of Charlottesville issued a new edition of all 33 volumes in 1900, 1901, and 1902. This latter edition was reprinted in Richmond by the Virginia Reports Reprints, Inc., in 1979.

The first volume of Grattan's reports has a preface containing Rules of Court; so also does volume 20. The Preface to volume 8 comments on the reorganization of the courts under the new state Constitution of 1851. Grattan was somewhat dubious of the new system of electing judges by popular vote. This was the only period in Virginia history during which this ill-advised method of judicial selection was used. The Commonwealth was spared the plague of bad judges in answer, perhaps, to Grattan's appeal to "the guardian providence of God." This same constitution abolished the General Court and gave its jurisdiction to the Supreme Court of Appeals. Thus volume 8 of Grattan's *Reports* published the last cases from this ancient court. Volume 8 is also the last to give summaries of arguments of counsel.[47] The second edition of volume 3, which was reprinted by Schaffter in 1871, does not retain the original pagination or give the star page numbers.

George Woodson Hansbrough

George W. Hansbrough (b. 1831) was born in Culpeper County on August 16, 1831. He was a member of the 1855 law class at the University of Virginia and shortly thereafter was elected Commonwealth's Attorney of Taylor County, Virginia (now West Virginia). After the Civil War, Col. Hansbrough practiced law in Roanoke and the adjacent counties.[48] In 1883, the new readjuster members of the Supreme Court of Appeals refused to reappoint the incumbent law reporter, James M. Matthews, and appointed Hansbrough. When the readjuster judges in their turn were not reelected in 1894,[49] Hansbrough too lost his official position as law reporter.

Hansbrough reports are volumes 76 to 90 of the *Virginia Reports* covering the years 1881 to 1894 for a total of fifteen volumes. They were published in Richmond by a succession of Superintendents of Public Printing. Volumes 76 and 77 were reprinted in 1900 by J. H. O'Bannon. Volumes 76 through 82 were reprinted by the Michie Company variously in 1908, 1909, 1915, and 1921. The prefaces to the volumes include memorials to deceased appellate court judges and rules of court. Volume 90 has an older case printed at the end.

---

[47] See the Preface to volume nine of Grattan's reports.

[48] *South West Virginia and the Valley*, p. 152 (1892).

[49] T. R. Morris, *The Virginia Supreme Court*, p. 23 (1975).

Roscoe Briggs Heath

Roscoe B. Heath (1827-1863) was a Richmond attorney while he co-edited with John M. Patton, Jr., two volumes of opinions from the Special Court of Appeals of Virginia.[50] Heath read law under John Young Mason, Attorney General of the United States, and then attended Harvard Law School, receiving the LL. B. degree in 1848. He later practiced law in partnership with Mason and married his daughter, Elizabeth. Heath was also active in politics and served in the Virginia House of Delegates in 1857. He co-authored with Patton *A General Index to Grattan's Reports*, Richmond: George M. West, 1856.[51]

William Waller Hening

William Waller Hening (1767-1828) was the clerk of the Superior Court of Chancery for the Richmond District while he and William Munford co-edited four volumes of the *Virginia Reports*. Hening was also a prodigious legal scholar and author.[52]

Hening and Munford's *Reports* are now designated volumes 11 through 14 of the *Virginia Reports*. The first volume was issued to subscribers in three installments, one after each term of the Supreme Court of Appeals. This appears to be the first set of advance sheets in Virginia. The first advance issue was printed in Richmond by Samuel Pleasants in 1807, the next in Philadelphia in 1808. The entire volume, or at least a new title page and index, was printed in Flatbush, New York, by Isaac Riley in 1809. In the next year, the terms of the Court were rearranged, making advance sheets no longer feasible from the point of view of printing schedules, and the experiment was discontinued.[53] Volume two was published in Flatbush by Riley in 1809, and volumes three and four in New York City by Riley in 1810 and 1811. All four volumes were reprinted in a new edition by Benjamin Blake Minor in Richmond by J. W. Randolph in 1854. This edition is extremely scarce today because Randolph's warehouse and all of the unsold books in it were destroyed in the Evacuation Fire in 1865.[54] There was a third edition published in Charlottesville by the

---

[50] Patton and Heath's reports are discussed under Patton's name.

[51] R. E. Nance, "Roscoe Briggs Heath," *Va. Law Reporters*, pp. 110-111 (1977).

[52] S. M. Walker, Jr., "William Waller Hening," *Va. Law Reporters*, pp. 19-24 (1977).

[53] Preface to volume 2 of Hening and Munford's *Reports*.

[54] See below, "J. W. Randolph."

Michie Company in 1903. This last edition was reprinted in Richmond by the Virginia Reports Reprint, Inc., in 1979.

In 1857, Lucian Minor[55] published a condensed version of Hening and Munford's *Reports*; it was printed in Richmond by A. Morris. However, the idea of condensed reports was unsuccessful, and the experiment was not continued.[56]

Volumes 1, 2, and 4, in addition to cases from the Supreme Court of Appeals of Virginia, have case reports from the Superior Court of Chancery for the Richmond District by Judge Creed Taylor;[57] these three volumes also print general rules of court. Volume 4 includes a case from the General Court of Virginia, *Commonwealth v. Alexander*, 4 Hen. & M. 522 (1808).

Hugh Holmes

Hugh Holmes (1768-1825) was a Winchester lawyer and politician and then a judge on the General Court of Virginia during the period of his reports.[58] Holmes and Judge William Brockenbrough edited volume one of the reports commonly called "Virginia Cases," later designated volume 3 of the *Virginia Reports*. These reports cover the years 1789 to 1814 and publish cases from the General Court, most of which were criminal cases.

There are several cases reported here of unusual interest. For example, *Kamper v. Hawkins*, 1 Va. Cas. 20 (1793), is of constitutional importance, invoking the doctrine of judicial review of legislative action.[59] The two cases of *Commonwealth v. Swinney*, 1 Va. Cas. 146 and 150 (1806), concern George Wythe Swinney, who is generally believed to have poisoned his illustrious kinsman, George Wythe.[60]

The first volume of Brockenbrough and Holmes's *Virginia Cases* was published in Philadelphia by James Webster in 1815. There was a second edition by J. W. Randolph in Richmond in 1853, and a third

---

[55] For Lucian Minor (1802-1858), see A. J. Rosser, Jr., "Lucian Minor," *Legal Education in Va.*, pp. 435-444 (1982).

[56] E. C. Surrency, *History of American Law Publishing*, p. 49 (1990).

[57] For Creed Taylor (1766-1836), see S. A. Riggs, "Creed Taylor," *Legal Education in Va.*, pp. 589-595 (1982).

[58] H. T. Macrae, Jr., "Hugh Holmes," *Va. Law Reporters*, pp. 11-15 (1977).

[59] See M. V. Nelson, "The Cases of the Judges, Fact or Fiction," *Va. L. Rev.*, vol. 31, pp. 243-255 (1944).

[60] W. E. Hemphill, "Examinations of George Wythe Swinney for Forgery and Murder," *Wm. & Mary Qtly.*, 3d ser., vol. 12, pp. 543-574 (1955).

edition by the Michie Company in Charlottesville in 1902. This last noted edition was reprinted in 1979 by the Virginia Reports Reprint, Inc., in Richmond.

William Hopkins

William Hopkins (d. 1734) practiced law in Williamsburg and compiled a series of reports of cases from the General Court of Virginia dating from at least October 1731 to April 1733. Thomas Jefferson used this now-lost manuscript volume shortly before Independence when it was in the possession of the last colonial Attorney General of Virginia, John Randolph (1727-1784). Jefferson's *Reports* at page 72 includes the case of *Custis v. Fitzhugh* from Hopkins's reports. There are several extracts or fragments of cases abridged from Hopkins's reports in a manuscript book in the Library of Congress entitled "Virginia Reports," which also contains Sir John Randolph's reports.[61]

Hopkins's reports were probably acquired by Sir John Randolph (1693-1737) and passed to his son John, who owned them when Jefferson consulted them. The younger John died in 1784, and they probably then passed to his son Edmund Randolph (1753-1813).

Robert Reid Howison

The reports of Robert R. Howison (1820-1906) date from the time of his law practice in Richmond.[62] Being reports of criminal trials, they are of little precedential value; in fact, it appears from *Shepard's Virginia Citations* that none of them has ever been cited in later cases. However, they are of interest to historians of the criminal law because they describe the trials of criminal cases, which are not usually reported.

The motivation for the publication of this book is not immediately apparent. Perhaps it was to satisfy the interest of the general public in criminal trials. But this little book lacks the crude appeal to the morbid fascination of the lay public for "sex and violence" that characterizes the numerous journalistic accounts of murder trials that were published at this time. It apparently was not for self-promotion as a lawyer; he was only junior counsel for the defendant in one of the cases.

[61] R. T. Barton, *Virginia Colonial Decisions: The Reports by Sir John Randolph and by Edward Barradall*, vol. 1, pp. 1, 12, 184 (1909); T. Jefferson, *Reports of Cases*, preface (1829); C. Robinson, "Of Lawyers in Virginia between 1704 and 1737," *Va. L. J.*, vol. 1, pp. 191, 193 (1877); Sir John Randolph, "Two Old Lawyers," *Va. Historical Reg.*, vol. 1, pp. 119, 122-123 (1848), *Southern Literary Messenger*, vol. 1, pp. 353-354 (1835).

[62] W. H. Bryson, "Robert Reid Howison," *Va. Law Reporters*, pp. 112-117 (1977).

There are eight cases from the Circuit Court of Henrico County and two connected cases from the federal court for the Eastern District of Virginia. These last two cases have been reprinted in 3 Hughes 509 and in *Federal Cases* (No. 14,817). The ten cases, state and federal, date from the years 1850 and 1851. This slim volume has no apparatus at all.

Howison's *Reports of Criminal Trials* was first published in Richmond in 1851 by George M. West & Brother; the printer was MacFarlane & Fergusson. A "photo-reproduction" of this volume was published in New York by H. A. Warren in July, 1937. There was another reprint by Dennis & Co. of Buffalo, New York, in 1950.

James Hughes

James Hughes, a practicing attorney who specialized in land law, reported twenty-two cases from the Virginia Supreme Court for the District of Kentucky;[63] they date from June 1785 to March 1792. (Kentucky became independent of Virginia in 1792.) Harvey Myers, the editor of the second edition, states that "[t]he cases reported in this volume relate wholly to the adjustment of land claims among the original settlers upon that portion of the public domain of Virginia which now constitutes the State of Kentucky."

Hughes's reports have been published in three editions: Lexington, Ky.: John Bradford, 1803; 2d ed. Cincinnati: W. H. Anderson Co., 1869; 3d ed. Louisville: G. Fetter, 1898.

Thomas Jefferson

A set of colonial Virginia reports was made by Thomas Jefferson (1743-1826)[64] when he was a young man engaged in the practice of law in Williamsburg on the eve of Independence. Jefferson extracted four cases from the manuscript of Sir John Randolph, twenty-six from Edward Barradall, and one very short case from William Hopkins. Jefferson followed these in his own manuscript book with eleven cases dating from October 1768 to October 1772.[65]

---

[63] This court was created by the Act of May 1782, c. 48, Hening's Statutes, vol. 11, p. 85.

[64] Jefferson later distinguished himself as "author of the Declaration of American Independence, of the Statute of Virginia for Religious Freedom, and father of the University of Virginia."

[65] G. M. Curtis, III, "Thomas Jefferson," *Va. Law Reporters*, pp. 75-84 (1977).

Jefferson wrote a preface describing his criteria for selecting cases for inclusion in his collection. This suggests that originally he planned to publish these reports. The existence of these manuscript reports was known in 1800.[66] Jefferson also included an Appendix entitled "Whether Christianity is a Part of the Common Law." This essay arose out of the case of *Godwin v. Lunan* (1771), in which George Wythe represented churchwardens seeking to deprive an unworthy rector of his church and Jefferson was junior counsel.[67]

Since the General Court in colonial times was composed of the members of the Council and presided over by the Governor, most of whom were laymen, no reasons were given for their judicial decisions. Therefore, these reports consist of extensive arguments of counsel and the bare final orders of the Court.

Jefferson's *Reports* were made available after his death, by his grandson, Thomas Jefferson Randolph. The first edition of Jefferson's reports was published in Charlottesville in 1829 by F. Carr and Co. and printed by Jefferson Clark. There was a second edition in the *Virginia Reports Annotated*, Charlottesville: The Michie Co., 1903. The second edition was reprinted in 1979 by The Virginia Reports Reprint, Inc. In 1981, William S. Hein and Co. of Buffalo, New York, published a reprint of the first edition with a new introduction by John M. Lindsey.

In addition, the Jefferson manuscripts in the Library of Congress contain four manuscript reports of General Court cases that Jefferson did not include in his published *Reports*. They are *Hunt v. Tucker's Ex'rs, The King v. Dugard, Wormeley v. Wormeley*, and *Blair v. Blair*.[68] The case of *Blair v. Blair* (1773) was printed with a scholarly introduction in Frank L. Dewey, "Thomas Jefferson and a Williamsburg Scandal: The Case of Blair v. Blair," *Virginia Magazine of History and Biography*, vol. 89, pp. 44-63 (1981).

Brockenbrough Lamb

Brockenbrough Lamb (1886-1975) was the judge of the Chancery Court of the City of Richmond from 1942 to 1963. His trial court opinions on the subjects of equity and probate are learned and very useful to the practicing bar. They were published in two volumes by the Trust Department of the First and Merchants National Bank of Richmond, Virginia, in 1955 and 1964. The same bank had previously

[66] F. L. Dewey, *Thomas Jefferson, Lawyer*, p. 20 (1986).

[67] E. Dumbauld, *Thomas Jefferson and the Law*, pp. 75-83 (1978).

[68] F. L. Dewey, *Thomas Jefferson, Lawyer*, pp. 136-137 (1986).

published in pamphlet form Judge Lamb's opinion in the case of *Dew v. First and Merchants National Bank* (1946); this case was later reprinted in volume one at page 218 of Lamb's *Opinions*.

Charles Lee

Charles Lee (1758-1815), who later became the United States Attorney General from 1795 to 1801, compiled a small collection of Virginia cases while he was in practice in Alexandria. He reported cases from many different courts though not many from any single one. There are cases from the Virginia Court of Appeals, the General Court, the High Court of Chancery, the District Court of Fredericksburg, and the federal court for the District of Virginia. They date from April 1784 to 1794 or 1795.

Lee's reports were printed from two sources. The earlier cases, from the beginning through *Anonymous*, were found in a largely unused notebook, which is now in the possession of Colonial Williamsburg, Inc.[69] The later cases, *Alexander v. Murray* to the end, were found at the end of a notebook entitled "Suits pending 1st Jany. 1794."[70] This latter manuscript is not as neat in hand or in grammar as the former; this suggests that we have here only rough notes taken in court. Judging from the presence of a title page in the Williamsburg manuscript, it was apparently intended to be the finished product. However, it is unlikely that Lee ever intended to publish it.

Lee's reports were first published in the *University of Richmond Law Review*, vol. 11, pp. 695-711 (1977). They were reprinted in W. H. Bryson, ed., *Miscellaneous Virginia Law Reports*, Dobbs Ferry, N.Y.: Oceana Publications, 1992, pp. 3-23.

Benjamin Watkins Leigh

Benjamin Watkins Leigh (1781-1849) was a very successful Richmond lawyer, perhaps the most prominent attorney in Virginia, while editing the *Virginia Reports*. He was also active in politics, having, among other things, served as a member of the Virginia Consti-

[69] Another manuscript copy is in the Virginia State Library and Archives, MS. 21779b.

[70] "Register of Law Cases by Charles Lee (1794)," Manuscript Department of the University of Virginia Library, MS. Accession No. 850.

REPORTS OF CASES

ARGUED AND DETERMINED IN

THE COURT OF APPEALS

AND IN

THE GENERAL COURT

OF

VIRGINIA:

BY BENJAMIN WATKINS LEIGH.

VOL. V.

SECOND EDITION.

RICHMOND:
RITCHIE & DUNNAVANT, PRINTERS.
1863.

tutional Convention of 1829 and as a United States Senator from Virginia.[71] Leigh's twelve volumes of reports, which are now referred to as volumes 28 through 39 of the *Virginia Reports*, cover the years 1829 to 1841.

Leigh's *Reports* were originally published in Richmond from 1830 to 1844 by Shepherd and his successor firm of Shepherd & Colin. There was also a second edition. Volumes 1 through 5 were reissued in Richmond by Ritchie & Dunnavant from 1854 to 1863;[72] volumes 6 and 7 in 1867 by Gary & Clemmitt of Richmond;[73] volumes 8 through 12 in Richmond from 1872 through 1875 by R. F. Walker, the Superintendent of Public Printing. Volumes 10 and 11 of the reprint by Walker do not maintain the original pagination or give star page numbers. A third edition was published by the Charlottesville firm, the Michie Company, in the years 1902 and 1903. This last edition was reprinted in Richmond in 1979 by the Virginia Reports Reprint, Inc.

Volumes 1 through 11 publish the opinions of the General Court of Virginia, as well as those of the Court of Appeals. There were no General Court cases in volume 12 because of the spacing of the terms of that court and the date of the resignation of Leigh as official reporter. Volume 3 has a Preface that describes the 1830 reorganization of the Virginia courts.

Leigh resigned as reporter in 1842 at the age of sixty-one. He was succeeded by Conway Robinson (1805-1884), his son-in-law.

John Marshall

John Marshall (1755-1835) reported cases from the time that he was in practice in Richmond, 1781 to 1800. Fifteen of these cases dating from 1790 were printed in Daniel Call's *Reports*, volume 3, pages 506-599, and Marshall's report of *Turberville v. Self*, 8 Va. (4 Call) 580, 590 (1795), was also used by Call.[74] This lost manuscript was last seen by Daniel Call, his brother-in-law, who copied a case into volume four of his own *Reports*, which was first published in 1833.

---

[71] P. M. Grabill, Jr., "Benjamin Watkins Leigh," *Va. Law Reporters*, pp. 49-56 (1977).

[72] 1859-60 Va. Acts, ch. 86, p. 192, ordered the reprinting of 5 Leigh and 1-3 Grattan.

[73] These two volumes were reprinted as required by 1866-67 Va. Acts, ch. 85, p. 546.

[74] C. F. Hobson, ed., *The Papers of John Marshall*, vol. 5, pp. 473-474 (1987); J. W. Wallace, *The Reporters*, p. 590, n. 3 (4th ed. 1882).

James Muscoe Matthews

James M. Matthews (1822-1905) was born in Tappahannock, Virginia, and received his legal education at the College of William and Mary in 1843 and 1844. He later distinguished himself as a chancery lawyer and as a legal scholar. He was practicing law in Richmond at the time of his appointment as law reporter to the Supreme Court of Appeals. He held this office only long enough to produce a single volume of the *Virginia Reports*, volume 75. When the readjusters got control of the state government in 1879, they refused to reappoint any judge who was not a member of their political party, which was dedicated to scaling back the state debt, which was crippling the progress of Virginia. Thus, when the terms of office of the judges of the Supreme Court of Appeals expired in 1882, they were all replaced by judges who were members of the Readjuster Party.[75] The new judges removed Matthews as their reporter and appointed one of their political friends, George W. Hansbrough.

Matthews reports, according to the modern fashion, were not referred to by his name but simply as volume 75 of the *Virginia Reports*. This volume covers cases from the years 1880 to 1882. It was first published in Richmond by R. F. Walker in 1882. There was a second edition in Richmond by J. H. O'Bannon in 1900, and a third edition by the Michie Company in Charlottesville in 1908. There is a memorial to Peachy R. Grattan, Matthews's predecessor, at the beginning of the book.

Addinell Hewson Michie

A. Hewson Michie (1897-1957) succeeded his father, Thomas Johnson Michie, as editor-in-chief of the Michie Company and as official reporter of the *Virginia Reports* in 1937. Hewson Michie received his LL. B. from the University of Virginia in 1922 and then joined the Michie Company as an editorial writer.[76] He edited volumes 168 through 194 of the *Virginia Reports* covering the years 1937 through 1953.

---

[75] T. R. Morris, *The Virginia Supreme Court*, pp. 22-23 (1975); C. C. Pearson, *The Readjuster Movement in Virginia* (1917).

[76] B. P. Chamberlain, "Addinell Hewson Michie," *Va. State Bar Ass'n Repts.*, vol. 69, pp. 191-193 (1958).

Thomas Johnson Michie

Thomas Johnson Michie (1867-1938) was president and editor-in-chief of the Michie Company while he was the official reporter of the *Virginia Reports*. His reports were volumes 120 to 168 of the *Virginia Reports*, covering the period 1917 to 1937. Volumes 139 through 151 also have cases from the Special Court of Appeals[77] dating from 1924 to 1928. He resigned due to ill health and died several months later. He was succeeded by his son, A. Hewson Michie.

T. J. Michie received his law degree from the University of Virginia in 1890, and for several productive years following graduation, he had an editorial position with the law publisher the Edward Thompson Company in Northport, Long Island, New York. In 1896, Michie and his brother founded their own law publishing company in Charlottesville, the Michie Company.[78]

In 1900, the General Assembly authorized the Michie Company to republish the Virginia nominative reports and any other volumes of Virginia reports as they became unavailable from the Commonwealth.[79] As a result, under the supervision of Thomas Johnson Michie, the Michie Company printed a new edition of all of the Virginia reports from Jefferson's reports to the last volume of Grattan's reports. This is the *Virginia Reports . . . Annotated,* which was published in twenty-six volumes from 1900 to 1904. Pursuant to this statutory authorization, the Michie Company also republished volumes 75 and 76 of the *Virginia Reports* in 1908, volume 77 in 1921, volumes 78 and 79 in 1915, and volumes 81 and 82 in 1909. The *Virginia Reports . . . Annotated* were photographically reprinted in 1979 by the Virginia Reports Reprints, Inc., of Richmond.

William Munford

William Munford (1775-1825) was a practicing lawyer in Richmond while he was producing his volumes of the *Virginia Reports*. He was educated in the classics as well as the law, and he published a small volume of poetry as a young man. His translation in verse of Homer's *Iliad* was published after his death; it was said that he worked on it while sitting in court as a reporter. He also was an assistant editor

---

[77] This court was created by 1924 Va. Acts, ch. 264, p. 391.

[78] B. Stedman, "Thomas Johnson Michie," *Va. State Bar Ass'n Repts.*, vol. 50, pp. 241-243 (1939). See also below, "The Michie Company."

[79] 1899-1900 Va. Acts, ch. 510, p. 545.

REPORTS

OF

CASES

ARGUED AND DETERMINED

IN THE

SUPREME COURT OF APPEALS

OF

VIRGINIA.

VOLUME V.

BY WILLIAM MUNFORD.

FREDERICKSBURG, (VA.)
PUBLISHED BY WILLIAM F. GRAY.
1819.

of the Virginia Code of 1819 and the author of an index to Virginia law that was published in the same year.[80]

Munford co-edited four volumes of Virginia reports with William Waller Hening.[81] When Hening dropped out of this venture *circa* 1810, he continued on alone and published six volumes of reports that are now designated as volumes 15 through 20 of the *Virginia Reports*. These reports cover the years 1810 to 1820. The quality and quantity of Munford's reports was unquestionably acceptable; however, the bench and bar grew impatient with the delays in publication. At one point, Munford was three years in arrears. Therefore, the General Assembly was successfully petitioned to provide for a person to serve as an official reporter of opinions.[82] This was accomplished by a statute in 1820.[83] Francis Walker Gilmer was given the position of official reporter, and that put an end to Munford's private publishing venture. The market could not possibly bear two competing sets of Virginia reports.

Munford has an Appendix to volume one, which publishes an earlier unreported opinion. This is *Reed v. Reed* (1805), which was cited and relied on by Judge Roane in his opinion in *Hunter v. Fairfax*, 1 Munf. 218, 225-226 (1810). Volume two begins with a preface describing the new composition of the Supreme Court of Appeals and publishes Judge Tucker's letter of April 2, 1811, resigning from the Court. It is a lengthy, substantive letter expressing criticisms of the General Assembly and the court structure. A general rule of court is printed on page 547. An Appendix to volume three gives two opinions that were accidentally omitted from volume 2. No doubt with an eye on sales, Munford begins volume four with the case of *Hunter v. Martin* (1814), it "being in all respects the most important and interesting case in this volume," rather than printing it in its strict chronological order.[84]

The first three volumes of Munford's reports were published in New York by Isaac Riley in the years 1812, 1814, and 1816. Volume 4 was published in Philadelphia by James Webster and printed by W.

---

[80] P. I. Gordon, "William Munford," *Va. Law Reporters*, pp. 25-32 (1977).

[81] These reports are described above under Hening's name.

[82] Letter from the Court of Appeals to the House of Delegates, Dec. 6, 1819. Journals of the Va. House of Delegates, p. 28 (1819); 1 Rob. vi-vii.

[83] Act of Feb. 24, 1820, 1819-20 Va. Acts, ch. 17, p. 16; note also 1820-21 Va. Acts, ch. 30, p. 31.

[84] John R. Barden has pointed out that there were two editions of 4 Munford printed in the same year by the same publisher; perhaps this was required by additional sales generated by the report of *Hunter v. Martin*.

Brown in 1817; volume 5 was published in Fredericksburg by William F. Gray and printed in Boston by Wells and Lilly in 1819; and volume 6 in Richmond by N. Pollard at the Franklin Office in 1821. All six volumes were reprinted in Charlottesville by the Michie Company in 1903 and 1904. The last-mentioned edition was reproduced photographically in Richmond in 1979 by the Virginia Reports Reprint, Inc.

Opinions of the Workers' Compensation Commission

The Industrial Commission of Virginia was created by statute in 1918 to adjudicate workers' compensation claims. It is a court of record and initially published its judicial opinions in the *Opinions of the Industrial Commission.* In 1991 its name was changed to the Workers' Compensation Commission in order to give it a more descriptive appellation. Therefore, this series of reports was renamed the *Opinions of the Virginia Workers' Compensation Commission* beginning with volume 71.

John Mercer Patton, Jr.

John M. Patton, Jr. (1826-1898) was a practicing member of the Richmond bar when he and Roscoe Briggs Heath (1827-1863) edited the two volumes of reports of the Special Court of Appeals of Virginia.[85] This court was established to alleviate the seven-year backlog of cases that had accumulated unheard in the Supreme Court of Appeals.[86] Patton and Heath were appointed on their own motion to be the approved reporters for this court.[87] Their two volumes of reports include cases from 1855 to 1857. They were published in Richmond by George M. West in 1856 and 1857; a second edition was printed in Charlottesville by the Michie Company in 1902; this second edition was reprinted in Richmond by the Virginia Reports Reprint, Inc., in 1979.

Sir John Randolph

Sir John Randolph (1693-1737) was a prominent lawyer and politician in Williamsburg.[88]

---

[85] J. R. Cottrell, "John Mercer Patton, Jr.," *Va. Law Reporters*, pp. 106-109 (1977).

[86] Act of Feb. 25, 1854, 1853-54 Va. Acts., ch. 17, p. 18.

[87] Patton and Heath, *Reports*, vol. 1, preface (1856).

[88] R. E. Nance, "Sir John Randolph," *Va. Law Reporters*, pp. 68-70 (1977).

His manuscript reports cover the period October 1729 to April 1732.[89]

Since the General Court in colonial times was composed of the members of the Council and presided over by the Governor, most of whom were laymen, no reasons were given for their judicial decisions. Therefore, these reports consist of extensive arguments of counsel and the bare final orders of the Court.

The existence of Sir John Randolph's reports was generally known in Virginia legal circles around 1800.[90] They were used by Thomas Jefferson, who extracted four cases for his own reports. They were published in full in Robert T. Barton, ed., *Virginia Colonial Decisions*, Boston: Boston Book Co., 1909, volume 1.

John Randolph

From later citations, we know that John Randolph (1727-1784), the son of Sir John Randolph (1693-1737), also made reports of cases. The younger John Randolph compiled two volumes of reports in the 1760s and 1770s. He was the last colonial Attorney General of Virginia. Because of his official position and oath, he felt obliged to oppose Independence, though his brother Peyton Randolph (1721-1775) served as the first President of the Continental Congress. John died in England in 1784, but his body was returned to Virginia for burial in Williamsburg.

Unfortunately Randolph's manuscript reports have been lost, but several of the cases reported by him were cited in later cases. *Steger v. Moseley* (1773), "October, 1773, M.S. Rep. by J. Randolph, 2 vol. page 232," was cited in argument by his son, Edmund Randolph (1753-1813),[91] and by Judges Roane and Pendleton in *Wallace v. Taliaferro*, 6 Va. (2 Call) 450, 470, 487 (1800). *Wallace v. Taliaferro* at pages 450, 470, and 488 also cites *Bronaugh v. Cocke* and at page 470 *Smyth v. Lucas*, these last two cases also being found in the younger John Randolph's reports. The case of *Dobson v. Taylor* (1755), which was

---

[89] These manuscripts are discussed in the "Introduction" to R. T. Barton, ed., *Virginia Colonial Decisions*, vol. 1 (1909). Randolph, while a law student in London, compiled reports of king's bench cases dating from 1715 to 1716; E. M. Sowerby, *Catalogue of the Library of Thomas Jefferson*, vol. 2, p. 224, no. 1796 (1952); these were published in 1996.

[90] Letter of Merit Moore Robinson to John Robinson, May 9, 1811, Swem Library at the College of William and Mary (the writer of the letter believed that Edmund Randolph had the book, and he was trying to borrow or copy it). I would like to thank E. Lee Shepard for bringing this letter to my notice.

[91] See generally J. J. Reardon, *Edmund Randolph* (1974).

found at page 77 of John Randolph's reports, was brought to the attention of the Supreme Court of Appeals by Edmund Randolph in the case of *Claiborne v. Henderson* (1809), and it was discussed by the court and printed in a footnote by the reporters.[92]

Peyton Randolph

Peyton Randolph (1779-1828) was the official reporter of the *Virginia Reports* from 1821 until his death in 1828.[93] He edited six volumes of reports, which have been designated volumes 22 to 27 of the *Virginia Reports*. The first five volumes of Randolph's reports were published punctually from 1823 to 1828 by Peter Cottom in Richmond. Volume 6 was published posthumously by Samuel Shepherd in 1829 in Richmond. There was a second edition of volume 6 printed in New York by Joseph Gold in 1832 and a third edition of volume 6 in Richmond by R. F. Walker in 1875. All six volumes were reprinted by the Michie Company in 1904, and the Michie Company edition was reprinted in 1979 by the Virginia Reports Reprints, Inc.

Peyton Randolph was an active member of the Richmond bar. His father was Edmund Randolph (1753-1813), who had been Attorney General of Virginia and the first Attorney General of the United States.[94]

Volume 1 has an appendix, which is the printing of the previously unpublished opinion in *Pickett v. Stewart* (1819), which was cited in *Miller v. Rice*, 1 Rand. 447 (1823).

Volume 5 has an Appendix, No. II, pages 617 through 622, which is a reprint of the case of *Rex v. Ridge*, 4 Price 50, 146 Eng. Rep. 390 (Ex. 1817). This was done upon the request of Judge Cabell in the case of *Whitworth v. Adams*, 5 Rand. 333, 418 (1827), because it was "an express authority, directly on point" in a case of usury, and Judge Cabell thought the English report was not generally available in Virginia.

At the end of volumes 5 and 6 are cases from the General Court of Virginia. This was required by an act of 1828.[95]

The Appendix to volume 6 shows the difficulty of deciding what cases not to report where all cases are not reported. The two connected

---

[92] 13 Va. (3 Hen. & M.) 322 at 335-337, 362, 374-375, 384 (1809).

[93] R. G. Tavenner, "Peyton Randolph," *Va. Law Reporters*, pp. 47-48 (1977).

[94] J. J. Reardon, *Edmund Randolph* (1974).

[95] 1827-28 Va. Acts, ch. 25, § 5, p. 21.

cases in *Shirley v. Long* (1827) at first "were not intended for publication because the court consisted of only three members, and one of the judges dissented from his brethren on one of the important points decided. But as the questions discussed and decided by the two judges are of great importance and reference has been had to them in subsequent cases, it [was later] thought advisable to report them."[96]

Conway Robinson

Conway Robinson (1805-1884) was a Richmond lawyer and legal scholar when he succeeded his father-in-law, Benjamin Watkins Leigh, as the official reporter of Virginia.[97] Robinson edited the two volumes of the *Virginia Reports* that have been designated volumes 40 and 41. They include cases from 1842 to 1844, first the cases from the Supreme Court of Appeals, then those from the General Court. They were first published in Richmond by Shepherd & Colin in 1843 and 1844. There was a second edition printed in Richmond by the Superintendent of Public Printing, R. F. Walker, in 1874 and 1875; volume one of this second edition failed to maintain the original pagination or give the star page numbers. The Michie Company of Charlottesville issued a third edition as a part of its reprint of all of the Virginia nominative reports in 1902; the Michie edition was photographically reproduced in 1979 by the Virginia Reports Reprint, Inc., of Richmond.

Robinson, who was also interested in legal history, wrote a Preface to volume one giving a brief history of the Virginia courts and law reports. The Preface to volume two comments on the delays in hearing appeals and suggests some solutions to the problem. Robinson resigned after a short tenure as a reporter because it took away too much time from his other activities and duties.

William Wallace Scott

W. W. Scott (1845-1929) was born in Orange County, Virginia, on April 10, 1845. He studied law at the University of Virginia from 1865 until 1867, when he received the LL. B. degree. He then practiced law for two years in Lexington and then for ten years in Orange. He founded and published the *Gordonsville Gazette* from 1873 to 1877. He was the Virginia State Librarian for about ten years. In 1903 he resigned that position to become the first Law Librarian of Virginia; he

---

[96] 6 Rand. 735.

[97] R. A. Claybrook, Jr., "Conway Robinson," *Va. Law Reporters*, pp. 57-64 (1977).

served in that office until the date of his death in 1929.[98] He edited with Maury Baldwin Watts the first volume of *Virginia Appeals*, which was a private series of advance sheets for the *Virginia Reports*. This volume covered the period March, 1907, to February, 1908, corresponding to volumes 106 and 107 of the *Virginia Reports*.

Kent Sinclair

Kent Sinclair is professor of law in the University of Virginia and is presently the official reporter for the Supreme Court of Virginia. His reports begin in 1985 with volume 228 of the *Virginia Reports*.

Saint George Tucker

St. George Tucker (1752-1827) read law under George Wythe; he was practicing law in Williamsburg and in Richmond when he began keeping notes of cases. These private reports were continued after he was appointed to the bench of the General Court of Virginia and afterwards to the Court of Appeals. The cases date from 1786 to 1811. From 1788 until 1811, Tucker was a judge and thus was reporting cases argued before him.[99]

In 1825, Daniel Call wrote to Tucker for permission to print a selection of opinions from his manuscript reports. The felicitous result was the publication in 1833 of volumes 4, 5, and 6 of Call's *Reports*; many of the cases were from Tucker's books.[100] The cases in Tucker's reports that involved John Marshall as counsel have been printed in *The Papers of John Marshall*.[101]

St. George Tucker's manuscript reports were relied upon in the following cases. *Blount v. Gee* (1805)[102] was cited in *Dilliard v. Tomlinson*, 15 Va. (1 Munf.) 183 at 197 (1810). *Triplett v. Dunlop*

[98] P. B. Barringer, *University of Virginia*, vol. 1, pp. 461-462 (1904); A. C. Gordon, *Virginian Writers of Fugitive Verse*, p. 129 (1923).

[99] Tucker's manuscript reports are now in the Swem Library of the College of William and Mary. See C. T. Cullen, "St. George Tucker," *Va. Law Reporters*, pp. 96-105 (1977); C. T. Cullen, "St. George Tucker," *Legal Education in Va.*, pp. 657-686 (1982).

[100] D. Call, *Reports*, vol. 4, pp. [v], xxviii (1833); Letter of Daniel Call to St. George Tucker, April 27, 1825, Swem Library, College of William and Mary. I would like to thank Lee Shepard for bringing this letter to my attention.

[101] H. A. Johnson et al., edd., *The Papers of John Marshall* (1974 to date).

[102] Later reported in 9 Va. (5 Call) 481 (1805).

(1806)[103] was cited in his argument by Call in *Templeman v. Steptoe*, 15 Va. (1 Munf.) 339 at 349 (1810). *Sorrell's Case* (1786)[104] and *Bailey's Case* (1798)[105] were cited in *Commonwealth v. Myers*, 3 Va. (1 Va. Cas.) 188 (1811). *Dudley v. Crump* (1786) was cited in his argument by William Green in *Moon v. Stone*, 60 Va. (19 Gratt.) 130 at 321 (1869). *Clayton v. Latham*, "1 Tuck. MSS. 388," was cited by William Green in "Stare Decisis," 14 *Am. L. Rev.* 609 at 645, note 8 (1880). *Dunlop v. Harris* (1804)[106] was cited by Tucker's son, Henry St. G. Tucker in his *Notes on Blackstone's Commentaries* (1826), book 2, page 442, and in his *Commentaries on the Laws of Virginia* (1831), volume 1, book 2, page 336.

Virginia Decisions

Virginia Decisions: A Collection of Virginia Cases Not Officially Reported, Charlottesville: The Michie Co., 1902, 2 vols., was published when the official *Virginia Reports* began to include all of the opinions of the Virginia Supreme Court of Appeals. The publishing philosophy of the West Publishing Company of St. Paul, Minnesota, was to print every single Virginia appellate decision in its *South Eastern Reporter*. This was begun in 1887. In response to this, the Virginia Court abandoned the long-standing policy of selective publication of its opinions. At this same time, the Michie Company published its two volumes of *Virginia Decisions* to fill in the gaps for the benefit of Virginia lawyers who already had a set of the *Virginia Reports* and did not wish to buy the *South Eastern Reporter* in order to get the handful of cases that were not officially reported.

Virginia Decisions reprints Virginia appellate court opinions from 1871 to 1900. The first 179 pages publish twenty-seven cases never before printed; presumably, they were obtained directly from the Supreme Court of Appeals. The next series of opinions, dated 1877 to 1886, had been published in the *Virginia Law Journal*. The remainder of the cases was in print in West's *South Eastern Reporter*. However, the editors of the *Virginia Decisions* overlooked several opinions of the Virginia Court of Appeals printed in the *Quarterly Law Review* (1860-1861) but not officially reported.

---

[103] Later reported *sub nom.* Triplett v. Wilson, 10 Va. (6 Call) 47 (1806).

[104] Later reported in 3 Va. (1 Va. Cas.) 253 (1786).

[105] Later reported in 3 Va. (1 Va. Cas.) 258 (1798).

[106] Later reported in 9 Va. (5 Call) 16 (1804).

Virginia Law Reports

This publication is a photographic reproduction of the slip opinions of the Supreme Court of Virginia and of the Court of Appeals of Virginia. This ongoing series was begun in 1980 with the title *VRR: Virginia Reports Reprint*. In 1984, the title was changed to *Virginia Law Reports* to reflect the addition of the opinions of the newly-created Court of Appeals. These opinions were issued eighteen times a year as soft-bound parts of volumes of the *Virginia Law Reports*, but since the advance sheets for the official reports were not far behind in time, this publication was not reissued in a hard-bound permanent volume. In addition to the opinions of the Virginia appellate courts, the *Virginia Law Reports* included extensive digests of the opinions, indexes, and tables of statutory material cited in the opinions. It was published by Virginia Reports Reprints, Inc., in Midlothian, Virginia. The editor was James R. Wrenn, who practices law in the Richmond metropolitan area. It was discontinued in November 1995.

Virginia Supreme Court Reporter

The *Virginia Supreme Court Reporter* was a privately published series of advance sheets for the *Virginia Reports*. Volume 1 appeared on January 1, 1899, published in seventeen installments, the last being issued on January 1, 1900. Volume 2 was issued in eighteen numbers the next year. The three volumes were published in Richmond by H. Stewart Jones and T. Norment Powell. The third and final volume was edited by Jones and Powell and printed in Richmond by the Everett Waddey Co. They include cases that were later printed in volumes 96 through 100 of the *Virginia Reports*.

Bushrod Washington

Bushrod Washington (1762-1829) was practicing law in Richmond while he was keeping the notes that he reworked into two volumes of reports of cases in the Court of Appeals of Virginia. Bushrod was George Washington's favorite nephew, and Mount Vernon was devised to him. He was the favorite because he was the only one who went into public service.[107]

Washington began keeping notes of cases in the Court of Appeals in 1792. He states in the preface to volume 1 that he did not originally have any thought of publishing them. Considering his general and life-

[107] J. S. McDorman, "Bushrod Washington," *Va. Law Reporters*, pp. 1-6 (1977).

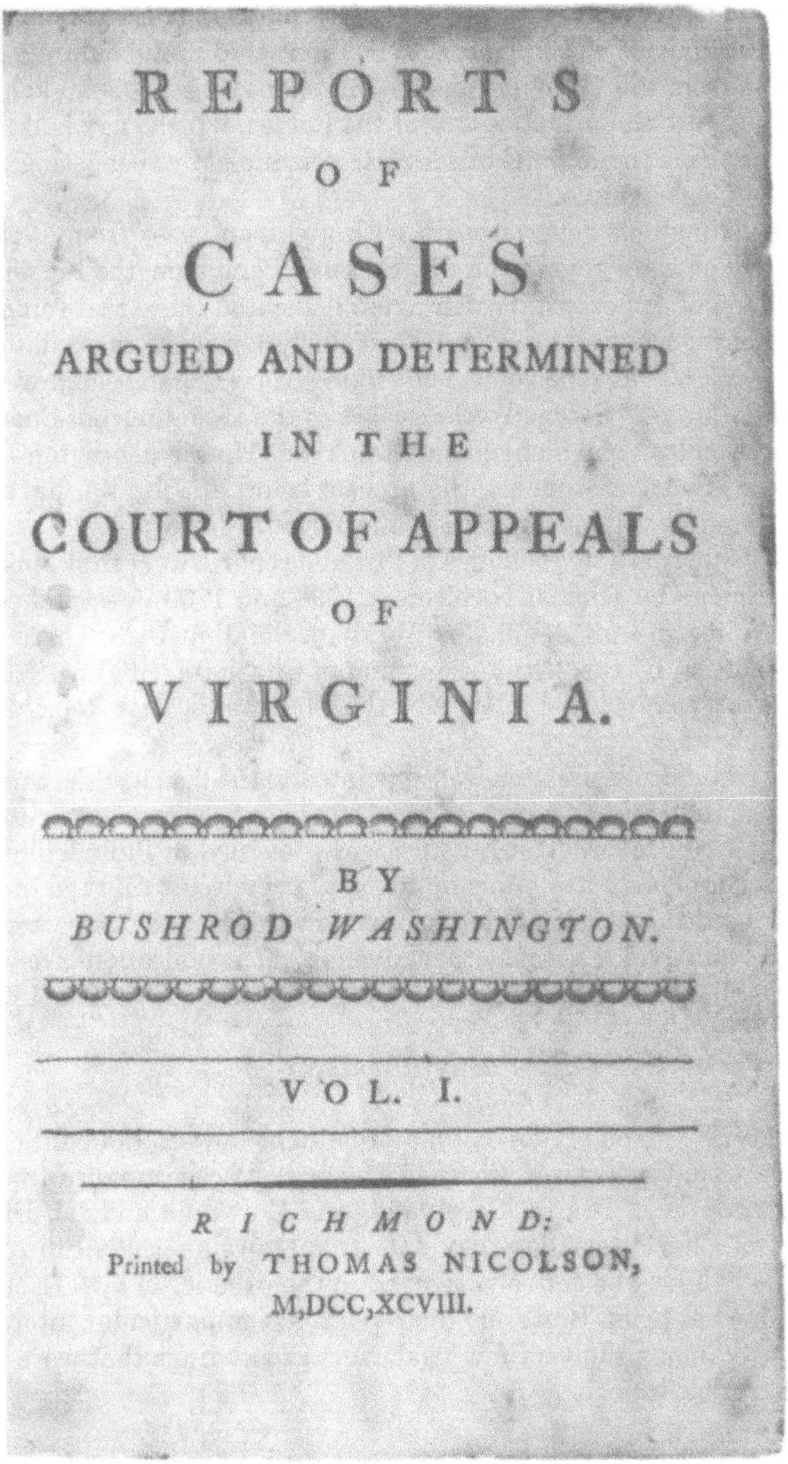

REPORTS
OF
CASES
ARGUED AND DETERMINED
IN THE
COURT OF APPEALS
OF
VIRGINIA.

BY
BUSHROD WASHINGTON.

VOL. I.

RICHMOND:
Printed by THOMAS NICOLSON,
M,DCC,XCVIII.

long modesty of character, this is readily believable. He goes on to say that since no one else appeared to be interested in publishing reports of cases from the Court of Appeals, he revised his notes and checked them against the private notes of the judges, which they had lent to him, and gave them to the printer. He concluded by requesting others to follow his example.

Washington's reports begin with eighteen cases from 1790 and 1791, which were given to him by Edmund Pendleton, the President of the Court of Appeals.[108] (Washington dedicated these two volumes of Virginia reports to Pendleton.) The remainder of the cases date from 1792 to 1796. Only one volume of Virginia reports had been previously printed; this was George Wythe's cases in the High Court of Chancery, the first edition of which appeared in 1795. Thus Washington's cases from the Court of Appeals, the highest court in Virginia, have been designated as volumes 1 and 2 of the *Virginia Reports.*

Washington's two volumes of Virginia reports were first published in Richmond by Thomas Nicolson in 1798 and 1799. A second edition was printed in Philadelphia by Abraham Small in 1823. There was a third edition by the Michie Company of Charlottesville in 1903, and this last was reprinted in 1979 by the Virginia Reports Reprint, Inc., of Richmond.

In 1798, Washington was appointed to the bench of the Supreme Court of the United States, and in 1803 he was assigned to sit in the Third Circuit federal court, which was convened in Philadelphia. He kept scrupulous notes of his opinions in the circuit court in order to guard against inconsistent judgments; toward the end of his career, he was prevailed upon to make them available for publication. They were first published in four volumes in Philadelphia from 1826 to 1829.[109]

David Watson

David Watson (1775-1830), a prominent lawyer and politician in Louisa County, Virginia, compiled a series of case reports from the county courts of Louisa, Goochland, and Fluvanna and the District Court of Charlottesville. They date from November 1799 to August 1809, when he was actively engaged in the practice of law. Each case is somewhat brief. However, the reports are of particular interest as they are among the very few trial court proceedings that were noted down at that time.

[108] See generally, D. J. Mays, *Edmund Pendleton, 1721-1803* (1952).

[109] E. C. Surrency, *A History of American Law Publishing*, pp. 66, 332 (1990).

Watson's manuscript reports are to be found in a small paper booklet in the David Watson Collection in the Library of Congress, MMC 2514, box 2. They are printed in W. H. Bryson, ed., *Miscellaneous Virginia Law Reports*, Dobbs Ferry, N.Y.: Oceana Publications, 1992, pp. 68-108.

Maury Baldwin Watts

Maury Baldwin Watts (1879-1952) was the Executive Secretary and then Clerk of the Supreme Court of Appeals.[110] He edited *Virginia Appeals*, a private venture consisting of advance sheets for the *Virginia Reports*. There were thirty-five volumes covering the years 1907 to 1926. These volumes reported cases later published in volumes 106 to 146 of the *Virginia Reports*. The first volume was issued jointly with William Wallace Scott, the State Law Librarian, and the other thirty-four by Watts alone.

Watts also published monthly advance sheets in one volume entitled *Virginia Special Court of Appeals*. These cases date from September, 1924, to June, 1926, and were later reprinted in the *Virginia Reports*, volumes 139 to 147. The jurisdiction of the ad hoc Special Court of Appeals was expanded in 1924 to enable the Supreme Court of Appeals to deal with an unacceptable backlog.[111]

Richard Alan Williamson

Richard A. Williamson is a professor of law in the College of William and Mary and is the first official reporter for the Court of Appeals of Virginia. The cases reported in volume 1 of his *Reports of Cases* date from 1985, when this intermediary appellate court was established.

The jurisdiction of the Court of Appeals, and thus the scope of the cases in its *Reports*, is limited to appeals from the circuit courts in domestic relations cases, appeals from administrative agencies, and criminal cases unless the death penalty was imposed, and to appeals from the Workers' Compensation Commission.[112]

The Court of Appeals designates for publication only a selection of its opinions, those considered to be of precedential value. However, its unpublished opinions circulate widely among the Virginia bar and are

[110] "Memorial," 195 Va. xcix (1954).

[111] 1924 Va. Acts, ch. 264, p. 391.

[112] Va. Code Ann., §§ 17-116.04, 17-116.05.

available from its clerk's office[113] and the *Virginia Lawyers Weekly*; they are often cited as authority by the trial courts of Virginia.

Charles Killian Woltz

Charles K. Woltz (1914-1996) was a professor of law at the University of Virginia while he was the official reporter for the Supreme Court of Virginia. His reports are volumes 194 to 207 of the *Virginia Reports*, which cover the years 1953 to 1967.

George Wythe

George Wythe (1726-1806) was the judge of the High Court of Chancery of Virginia, and he published a number of his judicial opinions. Wythe was a very learned and scholarly jurist with a distinguished practice in the General Court in Williamsburg on the eve of Independence. When the courts were reorganized after 1776, several of Wythe's former rivals at the bar were appointed to the Court of Appeals of Virginia, which had appellate jurisdiction over his court. While he recognized their appellate authority, he in no way conceded any intellectual superiority. Thus the first edition of his *Reports* was published by himself in order to justify several of his decisions that were reversed, in his opinion, erroneously. He published his judicial decrees and followed them by learned notes in justification. However, he was able to acknowledge his own errors where he agreed with the reversal.[114]

And thus the first volume of Virginia case reports came into existence. The first edition of Wythe's *Decisions of Cases* was published in Richmond by Thomas Nicolson in 1795. After the publication of this book, Wythe published several new opinions in the form of pamphlets.[115] Because the second edition of Wythe's reports incorporates these pamphlets and does not follow the pagination of the first edition, it is the second edition that is always cited and, in this exceptional case, properly so.

The second edition of Wythe's reports is a *tour de force* by Benjamin Blake Minor (1818-1905), a well-known lawyer and scholar.

---

[113] Va. Code Ann. § 17-116.010.

[114] E. L. Shepard, "George Wythe," *Va. Law Reporters*, pp. 90-95 (1977); E. L. Shepard, "George Wythe," *Legal Education in Va.*, pp. 749-755 (1982).

[115] These pamphlets are noted in W. J. Ritz, *American Judicial Proceedings First Printed Before 1801*, pp. 100-102, 104-105 (1984). The pamphlet report of *Love v. Donelson* (c. 1800) was not reprinted in Minor's edition of Wythe's *Reports*.

It begins with a dedication to Judge John Robertson, who was Wythe's successor as judge of the Circuit Court of Chancery for the Richmond Circuit. There is an extensive "Memoir of the Author" by Henry Clay (1777-1852), who read law with George Wythe. At the end of the second edition of Wythe's reports is an extensive and scholarly Appendix by William Green (1806-1880) discussing later cases *in pari materia* to those reported by George Wythe. The subjects discussed are "Lapse — Joint Tenants — Tenants in Common" and "Foreclosure of Mortgages — Account of Rents and Profits," and there is a section on miscellaneous subjects. This second edition of Wythe's reports was published in Richmond by J. W. Randolph in 1852. The second edition was reprinted in Charlottesville by the Michie Company in 1903. The Michie Company edition was photographically reissued in Richmond by the Virginia Reports Reprint, Inc., in 1979.

David Yancey

David Yancey (d. c. 1808), was a practicing lawyer in Louisa County, Virginia. Yancey's brief collection of cases is all from the nearby District Court of Charlottesville, where he also appeared on behalf of his clients. The cases date from April 1804 to April 1806. This collection of cases was made from his observations in the courtroom, no doubt while waiting for his own cases to be called. Some of the information, however, was given to him by others.

Yancey's manuscript reports are found in a small paper booklet that is now in the David Watson Collection in the Library of Congress, MMC 2514, box 2. Yancey was a close personal friend and a close neighbor of Watson in Louisa County. They practiced law in the same part of Virginia, and therefore it is not surprising that Watson possessed these reports made by his friend and brother at the bar.

They are printed in W. H. Bryson, ed., *Miscellaneous Virginia Law Reports*, Dobbs Ferry, N.Y.: Oceana Publications, 1992, pp. 110-131.

OFFICIAL COURT RECORDS IN PRINT

Rebecca G. Bates

THE WORKS explored in this annotated bibliography are the official accounts of court proceedings recorded by the clerk of a particular court. These official accounts assume two different forms. The first form of official accounts of court proceedings is the minute book. The minute book is an abbreviated or shorthand account of the court's daily activities. In fact, the minute book can be viewed as the clerk's own note-taking mechanism. It appears that the clerk made concise notes of the proceedings in the minute book during the court's session and later used these notes to create a more formal record of the court's activities. The formal record of the court's proceedings can be found in the order book, which is the second form of official court records. The order book contains a brief account of the action or issue before the court, the court's findings, and the court's order.

Both the minute book and the order book differ, in form and in content, from the traditional accounts of cases that are found in official reports of opinions. The difference can best be explained by examining the purpose or use of the three forms of records. As was indicated above, the minute book and the order book are simply official accounts of the proceedings of a particular court. It appears that the sole purpose of these official accounts was to keep a permanent record of the court's activities on file in the clerk's office for the future reference of the parties involved in or concerned with the court's proceedings. They record results as opposed to reasons. While one can undoubtedly glean some understanding of the substantive law from the accounts of proceedings in the minute book or order book, neither one of these records would be of much help to a legal practitioner because they do not contain an account of the court's rationale. An account of the court's rationale in a particular case can be found in a reporter; thus, a legal practitioner would look to this form of law book for an exposition of the substantive law.

This bibliography contains entries from different courts of different eras. The majority of entries are minute books or order books from the county courts of Colonial Virginia. All of the entries are complete transcriptions of the official court records. There are many books and periodicals that contain extracts from official court record books. Extracts from court records were made primarily for genealogical purposes; thus, the integrity of the records is not maintained. The extracts, therefore, are not very useful to lawyers or legal historians. For this reason, the books and periodicals that contain extracts of court records are not included in this bibliography. It should also be noted that the original minute books and order books that are extant are not included in this bibliography of official court records in print because the original materials are in manuscript form.

In 1606, King James I granted the Virginia Company a charter that established a Council to govern the Colony of Virginia in accordance with the laws of England. The thirteen-member Council performed the legislative, executive, and judicial functions of the government. During the early years of the Colony, the Council performed all three of these functions at the same time. Sometime in the 1620s, the Council began to separate its legislative and executive functions from its judicial function by holding court at a different session of the Council. Because sessions were held four times a year, the court was named the Quarter Court. By 1661, the court was meeting less than four times a year; thus, it was renamed the General Court. The General Court, like the Quarter Court and the court of the Council before it, was the highest appellate court in the Colony and heard cases from the lower courts of the Colony. It was also within the jurisdiction of the General Court and its predecessors to try felonies and treason.[1]

The early records of the Council reflect the fact that it performed all three of its governmental functions at the same time. Accounts of the executive, legislative, and judicial proceedings of the Council are recorded together according to the activity of the Council at a particular session. Records of proceedings from the 1620s and later periods reflect the development of the Quarter Court, and the later General Court, as a separate entity.

Many of the Council's records, and the records of the Quarter Court and General Court as well, were unfortunately destroyed during the Civil War. The majority of the records were housed in the state office building in Richmond, which was burned during the Confederates' evacuation of the city in 1865. The few extant records that survived the Evacuation Fire did so because they were on loan from the archives.[2]

---

[1] See generally, P. A. Bruce, *Institutional History of Virginia in the Seventeenth Century*, vol. 1, part 3 (1910); O. P. Chitwood, *Justice in Colonial Virginia* (1905); A. P. Scott, *Criminal Law in Colonial Virginia*, pp. 1-136 (1930).

[2] H. R. McIlwaine, comp., *Minutes of the Council and General Court of Colonial Virginia, 1622-1632, 1670-1676*. Richmond: Va. State Library, 1924; 2d ed. by Jon Kukla, Richmond: Va. State Library, 1979.

In 1696, the king's Commissioner of the Customs recommended that a Court of Vice-Admiralty be established for each colony. The Court of Vice-Admiralty for the Colony of Virginia was duly established in 1698. The Courts of Vice-Admiralty had jurisdiction over maritime actions heard in the colony. When the Crown's government of the Colonies collapsed in 1775, the Court of Vice-Admiralty for the Colony of Virginia ceased to exist. All of the known extant records of the Court of Vice-Admiralty of Colonial Virginia are in print in a thin volume of 115 pages.[3]

The county courts of Virginia were created by the General Assembly in 1634. At that time the Colony of Virginia was divided into eight counties. Other county courts were established for each newly formed county. The county court had jurisdiction over civil causes in law and equity and could also try misdemeanors and felonies committed by slaves. Cases involving freemen accused of felonies were certified in the county court to be tried in the General Court in Williamsburg.

Many of the county court records are extant. Some of the original manuscripts are still housed in the county clerk's office. Other manuscripts have been sent to the Virginia State Archives for safe keeping. Most of the records have been photocopied or reproduced on microfilm.

Many of the original manuscripts of early court records have survived and have been copied or reproduced on microfilm; thus, the original manuscripts or copies of them are available to anyone who desires to study them.[4] It may be difficult, however, for a layman to study the original manuscripts because of their physical condition or because of the style of writing used by the clerks. The audience for the original manuscripts is therefore limited to scholars and historians. By editing, indexing, and publishing the early court records, the editors and publishers of the works listed in this bibliography have expanded the audience to include the general public. In fact, it appears that the purpose or goal of the editors and publishers of the early court records was to make the documents available and accessible to a larger audience. Many of the editors of the records were professional historians or scholars. Some of the works included in this bibliography

[3] G. Reese, ed., *Proceedings in the Court of Vice-Admiralty of Virginia 1698-1775*. Richmond: Va. State Library, 1983.

[4] They are listed in S. S. Ray, L. H. Hart, III, and J. C. Kolbe, *A Preliminary Guide to Pre-1904 County Records in the Archives Branch, Virginia State Library and Archives* (1994); L. H. Hart, III, and J. C. Kolbe, *A Preliminary Guide to Pre-1904 Municipal Records in the Archives Branch, Virginia State Library and Archives* (1987).

were published by or for a historical society. Other works were published by the Virginia State Library.

The early records of Virginia's courts are of obvious value to the genealogist who is tracing the roots of some family tree. The sheer volume of extracts from the minute books and order books that are printed in genealogical publications is evidence of the historical value of these records. The legal profession itself has, however, largely overlooked and devalued these early records because the minute books and record books appear to be of no use to an attorney who is in the business of representing a client. Despite the fact that the early records of the court's proceedings do not contain an exposition of the court's reasoning in any particular case, the minute books and order books are nevertheless important to the practicing attorney. The minute books and order books are filled with accounts of the problems that arise in everyday life and of the role that the law plays in the resolution of those problems; thus, the early court records are a reminder to the practicing attorney of the importance of the law in our society. As for the legal historian, these primary legal sources are the foundation for meaningful scholarship.

BIBLIOGRAPHY

Ames, Susie M[ay], ed. *County Court Records of Accomack-Northampton, Virginia, 1632-1640*. Preface by Francis S. Philbrick; American Legal Records, vol. 7. Washington, D.C.: Am. Hist. Assn. 1954.

Susie M. Ames (1888-1969) was a professor of history at Randolph-Macon Woman's College. After retiring from teaching, she returned to her native Northampton County and became actively involved in the Eastern Shore's historical society. Ames's continuing interest in history led her to transcribe and edit the records of the Accomack-Northampton County Court from 1632 to 1645. Ames introduces this work with an extensive historical background of the Eastern Shore of Virginia. This work was favorably reviewed by Christopher Crittenden of the North Carolina Department of Archives and History. Crittenden noted that Ames had done a "superb work of editing." Crittenden also noted that the introduction written by Ames "seems to provide all the information that could be desired." *Am. Hist. Rev.*, vol. 62, p. 249 (1956). This work was also reviewed by John Melville Jennings of the Virginia Historical Society. Jennings recognized that the records were "edited with impeccable craftsmanship." *Wm. & Mary Qtly.*, 3d ser., vol. 12, pp. 358-360 (1955).

Ames, Susie M[ay], ed. *County Court Records of Accomack-Northampton, Virginia, 1640-1645.* Virginia Historical Society Documents, vol. 10. Charlottesville: Univ. Press of Va., 1973.

> This work is a continuation of Ames's first volume of records. This volume was published after Ames's death as a tribute to her contributions as a Virginia historian. The introduction of this work contains brief biographical sketches of the officials who presided over the County Court from 1640 to 1645.

"At a Court Held for Fairfax County XXIst January 1771." *Historical Soc. of Fairfax County, Va. Bull.*, vol. 12 (1971-1973).

> This work is a complete transcription of the Minute Book of the Fairfax County Court for the year 1771.

Crumrine, Boyd, ed. *Virginia Court Records in Southwestern Pennsylvania: Records of the District of West Augusta and Ohio and Yohogania Counties, Virginia, 1775-1780.* Baltimore: Genealogical Pub. Co., 1974; rept. Baltimore: Genealogical Pub. Co., 1981.

> This work contains full transcriptions of the records of the courts of West Augusta, Ohio, and Yohogania Counties. These counties were originally part of Virginia, but were later ceded to Pennsylvania. This work also contains a brief account of the boundary dispute between Virginia and Pennsylvania. The records were originally printed in the *Annals of the Carnegie Museum*, vols. 1-3 (1902-1905). The text of the records without Crumrine's introduction was reprinted by Richard W. Loveless, Columbus, Ohio: Ohio St. Univ., 1970.

Hoffer, Peter Charles, and William B. Scott, eds. *Criminal Proceedings in Colonial Virginia: [Records of] Fines, Examination of Criminals, Trial of Slaves, etc. from March 1710 [1711] to [1754] [Richmond County, Virginia].* American Legal Records, vol. 10. Washington, D.C.: Am. Hist. Assn., 1984.

> This work contains a lengthy introduction that provides an historical background for the court records.

"Lower Norfolk County Records." *Va. Mag. Hist. Biog.*, vol. 39, pp. 1-20, 118-125, 239-249 (1931), vol. 40, pp. 35-43, 133-146, 236-240, 355-361 (1932), vol. 41, pp. 50-58, 117-122, 244-250, 335-345 (1933).

This works contains a transcription of the records of the Court of Lower Norfolk County from May 15, 1637, to March 30, 1640.

McIlwaine, H[enry] R[ead], comp. *Minutes of the Council and General Court of Colonial Virginia, 1622-1632, 1670-1676*. Richmond: Va. State Library, 1924; 2d ed. by Jon Kukla, Richmond: Va. State Library, 1979.

The appendix of the second edition of this work contains an inventory of the General Court records that survived the Civil War. The records were inventoried by Conway Robinson (1805-1884), the Clerk of the Court, in 1829. Other appendices of the second edition include: extracts from Minutes of the Council and General Court, 1642-1645; extracts from the records of the General Court, 1664; the Rules of Court from 1691 to 1775; and Jefferson's Manuscript Memoranda of Colonial Virginia Records. The Jefferson Manuscript Memoranda are notes taken from the original records. Some of these records have been printed in *Va. Mag. Hist. Biog.*, vols. 3, 4, 19-31. This work was reviewed by J. Franklin Jameson, the Managing Editor of the *American Historical Review*, in *Am. Hist. Rev.*, vol. 30, pp. 152-153 (1924).

Rawlings, Mary, ed. "Albemarle County Court, Order Book, 1744-45." Intro. by Jack Dalton. *Papers of the Albemarle County Historical Society*, vol. 5, pp. 5-35 (1945).

This is a transcription of pp. 1-10 of the Order Book followed by some miscellaneous extracts.

Reese, George, ed. *Proceedings in the Court of Vice-Admiralty of Virginia 1698-1775*. Richmond: Va. State Library, 1983.

This work is a bound collection of three separate works. The three works combine to encompass all of the known records of the Court of Vice-Admiralty of Virginia from the time of the Court's creation in 1698 until its demise in 1775. The transcription of the records is accompanied by a narrative account of the historical events surrounding the Court's proceedings. Parts two and three of the collection are reprinted from *Va. Mag. Hist. Biog.*, vol. 88, pp. 301-337 (1980), vol. 89, pp. 405-424 (1981).

Wingfield, Marshall, ed. *An Old Virginia Court: Being a Transcript of the Records of the First Court of Franklin County, Virginia, 1786-1789*. Memphis: West Tenn. Historical Soc., 1948.

Dr. Marshall Wingfield (1893-1961) was a native of Franklin County, Virginia, and a pastor of the First Congregational Church in Memphis, Tennessee; he was also an avid historian. This work includes biographies of the justices of the first court of Franklin County, stories of famous cases, and a glossary of legal terms.

ACCOUNTS OF TRIALS

Ellen Firsching Brown

THIS BIBLIOGRAPHY lists books written about trials in Virginia. In addition to trials in Virginia state courts, those in the federal courts sitting in Virginia are included because the federal courts used the procedure of the individual state in which they sat until the promulgation of the *Federal Rules of Criminal Procedure* in 1945. The entries are arranged alphabetically according to the last name of the defendant.

It does not include periodical articles or reprints of them or reports of cases, since these are dealt with elsewhere. Nor does it consider newspaper accounts of trials or appellate court records and briefs. Many criminal trials and civil cases of local interest will have been commented on contemporaneously in the local newspapers since the courts are traditional sources of journalistic grist. The researcher can easily find these. The appellate courts require the records and briefs of cases to be presented in a printed format, and these are very useful to supplement the courts' formal opinions. They have been preserved in the archives of the Virginia Supreme Court and in the libraries of the law schools in Virginia. Moreover, miscellaneous items have washed ashore into the Virginia State Library, the Virginia Historical Society, and many local public libraries.

These publications can serve as valuable tools for scholars researching American state and federal trials and court procedures. Though many of these trials are dealt with in the case reporters, these books offer significantly different information from what is available in the traditional report of an appellate case. The following brief description of the nature of these publications explains their significance.

Notably, most of the works included in this listing are most appropriately referred to as booklets or pamphlets. In many instances, they were published by the defendants themselves or their family members to tell their sides of the stories and to vindicate the defendants' names. Equally as interesting are those published commercially, usually by a newspaper publisher, in order to provide the public with all the gory details of a particular trial. Apparently, those dealing with the more sensationalized trials served a market similar to that of today's talk shows and tabloids. Though the listing here deals exclusively with Virginia trials, hundreds of these pamphlets are available from all around the country.[1]

Though most of the pamphlets are very sensational or one-sided, they typically provide a broader perspective on these trials than could be reflected by a court opinion or a mere transcript. These booklets provide valuable information not available in these other sources, including evidence excluded from the jury's consideration or discovered after the trial, and personal information on the jurors, witnesses, and court personnel. With this information, the researcher is able to understand the "politics" behind the trials and how it impacted upon the final determination. Through an understanding of what actually took place throughout the trial, the reader acquires an invaluable sense of the history of trial practice. For a more personal or human view of some trials, the publishers included detailed biographies of or autobiographies by the defendants. In most of the murder trials, the author or publisher included a description of the defendant's last days and execution. Such information certainly adds a worthwhile perspective not available from traditional sources. The more recent publications typically offer a sociological perspective of the trial by offering information about the community where the trial and crime took place and how this impacted upon the trial and vice versa.

Many of the more popular or infamous trials included here have been the subject of many books. In this bibliography, only those volumes that dealt primarily with the trial have been included. The books that dealt with these events in a historical context tended not to shed any additional light on the trial and were, in fact, typically derived directly from the sources included here.

Perhaps it is worthy to note the dearth of entries dealing with modern trials. The difference should probably be attributed to modern forms of mass media, namely radio and television. Modern coverage of sensational trials brings the public right into the courtroom, either through actual recording or re-enactment in a television movie-of-the-week. However, despite the barrage of media coverage, a few non-newspaper printed versions of these stories do manage to get published. Despite the differences between the original booklets and today's mass media coverage, the lesson remains the same; Americans are fascinated with scandals and horror stories, especially ones dealing with real crimes and trials.

[1] T. M. McDade, *The Annals of Murder: A Bibliography of Books and Pamphlets on American Murders from Colonial Times to 1900* (1961); J. D. Lawson, *American State Trials; A Collection of the Important and Interesting Criminal Trials Which Have Taken Place in the United States* (1914-1936), 17 vols.

Whether our interest and the mass coverage of these trials is appropriate or worthwhile is a separate issue. An argument can certainly be made that the extra-judicial reports of these trials serve a valuable purpose in that they expose the public to the criminal justice system, or they reflect society in some significant way. However, lawmakers are questioning the propriety of allowing criminals to profit from their wrongdoing by selling the rights to their stories. Several states have passed so-called "Son-of-Sam" laws, which require the proceeds from these publication deals be put into a fund for the benefit of the victim or the victim's family. The policy at stake is whether we should allow criminals to profit from their crimes. Regardless of the constitutionality of these statutes,[2] they seem to reflect a growing distaste for the commercialization of sensational trials and personal tragedies.

In summary, each of the documents listed in this bibliography offers valuable information on the history of the trial practice in Virginia. Consulting them for scholarly or entertainment purposes, the reader comes away with a sense of how courtroom drama actually unfolds.

BIBLIOGRAPHY

A. H. Robins Company

Mintz, Morton. *At Any Cost: Corporate Greed, Women, and the Dalkon Shield.* New York: Pantheon Books, 1985. 308 p.

> This was a product liability case involving thousands of claimants injured by the dalkon shields that were manufactured by the A. H. Robins Co. The author is a reporter for the *Washington Post.*

Perry, Susan L., and James L. Dawson. *Nightmare: Women and the Dalkon Shield.* New York: Macmillan Pub. Co., 1985. 261 p.

> "This book attempts to tell the story of the dalkon shield from . . . the perspective of the thousands of women who suffered. . . ."

[2] In *Simon & Schuster, Inc. v. Members of the New York State Crime Victims Board,* 502 U.S. 105, 112 S. Ct. 501 (1991), the United States Supreme Court held invalid a law that required proceeds from books and publications by criminals describing their crimes to be placed in escrow for five years to satisfy the claims of victims of those crimes.

Engelmayer, Sheldon D., and Robert J. Wagman. *Lord's Justice.* Garden City, N.Y.: Anchor Press/Doubleday, 1985. 300 p.

Bacigal, Ronald J[oseph]. *The Limits of Litigation: The Dalkon Shield Controversy.* Durham, N.C.: Carolina Academic Press, 1990. 143 p.

This work details the complex Dalkon Shield litigation in the United States District Court for the Eastern District of Virginia. This book focuses "upon the judicial role played by Judge [Robert R.] Merhige and Federal District Judge Miles W. Lord of Minnesota." It has a detailed bibliography of the subject. The author is a professor of law at the University of Richmond.

Sobol, Richard B. *Bending the Law: The Story of the Dalkon Shield Bankruptcy.* Chicago: Univ. of Chicago Pr., 1991. 408 p.

The author is a civil rights litigator.

J. Sidna Allen
Claude S. Allen
Floyd Allen

114 Va. 826 (1913)

James, Edgar. *The Allen Outlaws: A Complete History of Their Lives and Exploits Concluding With the Hillsville Courthouse Tragedy.* Baltimore: Phoenix Publishing Co., 1912. 191 p.

Note also N. C. Manson, Jr., "Judge Thornton Lemmon Massie," *Va. State Bar Assn. Repts.*, vol. 25, pp. 73-75 (1912); "Report of the Special Committee on the Massie-Foster Memorial," *Va. State Bar Assn. Repts.*, vol. 37, pp. 141-143 (1925); Samuel S. Hurt, "Gentlemen, I Ain't A-Goin," *Virginia Record*, vol. 86, no. 12, pp. 5-15 (Dec. 1964); Louise Jones Du Bose, "The Fatal Doom of the Allens of Carroll County." *Virginia Record*, vol. 86, no. 12, pp. 16-31 (Dec. 1964); M. Clifford Harrison, "Murder in the Courtroom: Sensational Newspaper Accounts Distorted the Hillsville Massacre," *Virginia Cavalcade*, vol. 17, no. 1, pp. 43-47 (Summer 1967).

James, Edgar. *The Allen Outlaws and Their Career of Crime in the Mountains of Virginia.* Baltimore: Phoenix Publishing Co., 1912. 191 p.; Baltimore: Phoenix Publishing Co., 1912. 64 p.

Reynolds, J. J. *The Allen Gang: Outlaws of the Blue Ridge.* Baltimore: I. & M. Ottenheimer, 1912, 182 p.

"Gentlemen, I Aint A-Goin' ": The Hillsville Tragedy from the Morning of the Tragedy, Through the Courts, to the Cemetery. Wytheville: n.p., 1913. 73.

Payne, Edwin Chancellor. *The Hillsville Tragedy: Story of the Allen Clan.* Chicago: M. A. Donohue & Co., 1913. 126 p.

Payne, Edwin Chancellor. *The Hillsville Tragedy: Complete Story of the Allen Clan.* rev. ed. Chicago: M. A. Donohue & Co., 1913. 134 p.

Allen, J. Sidna. *Memoirs of J. Sidna Allen; Being a True Narrative of his Life and Early Manhood, the History of the Allen Family, What Happened at Hillsville and His Life at the Penitentiary.* Madison, N.C., Alwith Pub. Co., 1929. 142 p.; Madison, N.C., Alwith Pub. Co., 1929. 140 p.; Winston-Salem, N.C.: Clay Printing Co., 1929. 133 p.; Mt. Airy, N.C.: Reliable Print. Co., 1956. 141 p.; Mt. Airy, N.C.: Rufus L. Gardner, 1956. 142 p.

> J. Sidna Allen (1866-1941) wrote this autobiography after being pardoned by the Governor of Virginia for his part in the Hillsville "tragedy." He wrote this text to tell his family's side to the story with a brief description of his trial in Wythe County for the slaying of Judge Thornton L. Massie (1866-1912) and others.

Parker, G[eorge] M[artin] N[athaniel]. *The Mountain Massacre.* Bluefield, W. Va.: Callers to Country Life, 1930. 97 p.

> This book is an emotional and hostile reaction to the publication of the *Memoirs of J. Sidna Allen* (1929).

Cooley, E[lmer] J[ackson]. *The Inside Story of the World Famous Courtroom Tragedy.* Charlottesville: The Michie Co., n.d. 84 p.

Gardner, Rufus L. *The Courthouse Tragedy Hillsville, Va.* Mt. Airy, N.C.: Reliable Printing Co., 1962. 140 p.; "4th ed.," Mt. Airy, N.C.: Reliable Printing Co., 1962. 141 p.

> "This book is based on newspaper articles, courthouse records, and last statements by Claude Allen and his father Floyd Allen, who requested before being electrocuted that this information be passed on to the public."

Ebenezer Thompson Baird

The Case of Dr. E. T. Baird in the Hustings Court of the City of Richmond, Va. Richmond: Whittet & Shepperson, 1877. 24 p.

> Baird (1821-1887), the secretary of the Presbyterian Committee of Publication, was tried for embezzlement. After the case of the prosecution against the defendant collapsed, the jury found him not guilty without retiring to deliberate. (Under modern rules of procedure, the court would have stricken the evidence and dismissed the case without a formal submission to the jury.)

Philip Pendleton Barbour
William Smith

[Payne, John]. *Payne's Vindication, Addressed to the People of Virginia.* Printed and Published for John Payne, of Orange County, Va., 1838. 36 p.

> John Payne printed this brochure to present his version of the facts of two lawsuits that he filed and lost: *Payne v. Barbour* and *Payne v. Smith.* He sued two attorneys, one of whom, Philip Pendleton Barbour (1783-1841), was currently sitting on the United States Supreme Court, for legal malpractice. Payne's character was called into question by the *Fredericksburg Arena,* and he wrote this book "to tell the unvarnished truth-supported in every instance by such documentary evidence as cannot but convince you that [he was] deeply injured, and wantonly subjected to much unnecessary suffering." It is in narrative style and incorporates documents presented in court in the two trials, including depositions.

Henry Clay Beattie, Jr.

A Full and Complete History of the Great Beattie Case: Most Highly Sensational Tragedy of the Century A Thrilling Story of a Man's Double Life, a Trusting Wife's Sufferings and Death and a Young Girl's Betrayal. Baltimore: Phoenix Publishing Co., 1911. 128 p.; 2d ed., Baltimore: I. & M. Ottenheimer, 1911. 128 p.

> This journalistic text provides a detailed account of the much sensationalized trial and conviction in Chesterfield County of Henry Clay Beattie, Jr., (1884-1911) for the murder of his wife. Note also Ben Pope, "The Beattie Case," *Virginia Record,* vol.

77, no. 6, pp. 4-7, 26, no. 7, pp. 16-18, 36-38, 45, no. 8, pp. 40-41, 49, 52-53 (June–Aug. 1955).

[Smith, Hiram M., Jr.] *This Story of the Trial of Henry Clay Beattie was Reprinted from the Virginia Trooper by Popular Demand.* N.p., n.d.

This is a reprint of "An Amateur Murder – The Celebrated Beattie Case," *The Virginia Trooper*, vol. 6, no. 6, pp. 17-21; no. 7, pp. 15-34; no. 8, pp. 11-18 (Jan.–Mar., 1953). The author was the grandson of Harry M. Smith, Jr., chief counsel for the defense, whose notes on the case were used in the preparation of this article.

John Brown

The Life, Trial and Execution of Captain John Brown . . . with a Full Account of the Attempted Insurrection at Harper's Ferry, Compiled from Official and Authentic Sources. New York: Robert M. De Witt, 1859. 108 p.

Note also George E. Caskie, "Trial of John Brown," *Va. State Bar Ass'n Repts.*, vol. 22, pp. 256-278 (1909).

Glasgow, J. Ewing. *The Harper's Ferry Insurrection . . . The Trial and Execution of Captain John Brown.* Edinburgh: Myles Macphail, 1860. 47 p.

The John Brown Invasion . . . With Full Details of the Capture, Trial, and Execution of the Invaders. Boston: James Campbell, 1860. 112 p.

Redpath, James. *The Public Life of Capt. John Brown, by James Redpath, With an Autobiography of His Childhood and Youth.* Boston: Thayer and Eldridge, 1860. 407 p.

This text was written by an associate of Brown's, with the approval of his widow. It purports to provide an accurate account of Brown's life and trial for, *inter alia*, conspiring to make an insurrection and open war against the Commonwealth of Virginia. It includes a detailed description of the trial in Charlestown, Virginia, including the charge to the grand jury, description of the empaneled jury, and the evidence presented.

Aaron Burr
25 Fed. Cas. 2 (C.C. D. Va. 1807)

Message From the President of the United States Transmitting a Copy of the Proceedings and of the Evidence Exhibited on the Arraignment of Aaron Burr and Others. Washington, D.C.: A. & C. Way, 1807. 222 p.

> Note also Robert K. Faulkner, "John Marshall and the Burr Trial," *Jour. of Am. Hist.*, vol. 53, pp. 247-258 (1966); James Alston Cabell, "The Trial of Aaron Burr," *Proc. N.Y. State Bar Ass'n*, vol. 23, pp. 56-86 (1900); William Wirt Henry, "The Trial of Aaron Burr," *Va. L. Reg.*, vol. 3, pp. 477-501 (1897), *Va. State Bar Ass'n Repts.*, vol. 10, pp. 239-269 (1897); Richmond: Whittet & Shepperson, [1960], pp. 9-42; Louis A. Sigaud, "Tried and Not Found Wanting," *Tyler's Qtly.*, vol. 31, pp. 225-252 (1950).

Carpenter, T. *The Trial of Aaron Burr.* Washington, D.C.: Westcott & Co., 1807, 1808. 147, 465, 418 p.

> This is a short hand report.

The Examination of Col. Aaron Burr. Richmond: S. Grantland, 1807. 47 p.

> This gives the courtroom examination of Aaron Burr (1756-1836) and his answer.

Thomson, William. *A Compendious View of the Trial of Aaron Burr.* Richmond: S. Grantland, 1807. 155 p.; Petersburg: Somervell & Conrad, 1808.

Robertson, David. *Reports of the Trials of Colonel Aaron Burr.* Philadelphia: Hopkins and Earle, 1808, 2 vols., 596, 539 p.; rept. New York: Da Capo Press, 1969, 2 vols., 596, 539 p. [*Trial of Aaron Burr for Treason*]. New York: James Cockcroft & Co., 1875, 2 vols., 677, 556 p.; Jersey City: Frederick D. Linn & Co., 1879, 2 vols., 677, 556 p.

> This publication constitutes a report taken by short hand of all the testimony and the documents presented at the two politically charged trials in Richmond of Burr for treason and misdemeanor.

Coombs, J. J. *The Trial of Aaron Burr for High Treason.* Washington, D.C.: Morrison, 1864; rept. New York: Notable Trials Library, 1992.

Brady, Joseph P[lunkett]. *The Trial of Aaron Burr.* New York: The Neale Publishing Co., 1913. 89 p.

> Brady, the Clerk of the United States District Court for the Eastern District of Virginia, prepared this version of Aaron Burr's trial based on the original records of the federal court at Richmond. It includes photocopies of many of the original documents.

Beirne, Francis F[oulke]. *Shout Treason: the Trial of Aaron Burr.* New York: Hastings House, 1959. 298 p.

E. A. Burson

Burson, Zach L. *Trial and Acquittal of E. A. Burson, and Speech of Honorable Thos. N. Williams at Abingdon, Virginia, May 1890.* Bristol, Tenn.: J. L. King, 1890. 130 p.

> This book was published by the father of the defendant so that the record of his son's trial would be properly preserved and so that the "testimony introduced in the trial, and the very able argument of Hon. Thos. N. Williams, of Lynchburg, Va., made in behalf of [the author's] son in the case, may be so arranged and presented as the same occurred on the trial, so that it may be open for the public to inspect and peruse." It consists of transcripts of witnesses' testimony and closing remarks of the defense attorney. The trial was in the Circuit Court of Washington County, during the May term 1890 at Abingdon.

James Thomson Callender

25 Fed. Cas. 239 (C.C. D. Va. 1800)

Trial of James Thompson Callender, for Sedition, on Tuesday the Third Day of June, 1800, in the Middle Circuit Court at Richmond, in the District of Virginia. N.p., 1804. 75 p.

> This pamphlet is a copy of the transcript of the trial "taken from the *Virginia Gazette*, from the 18th July, 1800, till the 19th August, 1800, both inclusive, examined and corrected by David Robertson."

C. J. Campbell

Investigation by the Committee for Courts of Justice of the House of Delegates of Charges Preferred Against C. J. Campbell, Judge of the County Court of Amherst. Richmond: Clyde W. Saunders, [1903]. 860, 233 p.

> This is a printed transcript of the impeachment proceedings of Judge Campbell for various offenses and his trial for felonious assault upon a preacher who had insulted him. Note also *Va. Senate Journal 1902-04*, pp. 331-335, 444-452, 490, 568-574, 649, 677.

Jose Demes Garcia Castillano
Manuel Philip Garcia

Lyford, William G[ilman]. *An Account of the Apprehension, Trial, Conviction, and Condemnation of Manuel Philip Garcia and Jose Demes Garcia Castillano, Who Were Executed on Friday the 1st of June, 1821, in the Rear of the Town of Portsmouth, in Virginia, for a Most Horrid Murder of Butchery, Committed on Peter Lagoardette, in the Borough of Norfolk on the 20th of March Preceding. Together with an Appendix, Containing Their Confessions, &c.* Norfolk: C. Hall, 1821. 24 p.

> This pamphlet was commercially published to provide the public with an accurate account of the testimony offered at the trial.

Abel Clemmons

Cruel Murder!! A True Account of the Life and Character of Abel Clemmens, Who Was Executed at Morgantown, Virginia, on Monday the 30th of June 1806, for the Murder of His Wife and Eight Children. Morgantown, Va.: J. Campbell, n.d.

A Succinct Narrative of the Life and Character of Abel Clemmens, Who Was Executed at Morgantown, Virginia, on Monday the 30th of June 1806, for the Murder of His Wife and Eight Children. Morgantown, Va.: J. Campbell, 1806.

AN

ACCOUNT

OF THE

APPREHENSION, TRIAL, CONVICTION, AND CONDEMNATION

OF

MANUEL PHILIP GARCIA

AND

JOSE DEMAS GARCIA CASTILLANO,

Who were executed on Friday the 1st of June, 1821, in the rear of the town of Portsmouth, in Virginia, for a most horrid murder and butchery, committed on

PETER LAGOARDETTE,

IN THE BOROUGH OF NORFOLK ON THE 20th OF MARCH PRECEDING.

TOGETHER WITH AN

APPENDIX,

CONTAINING THEIR CONFESSIONS, &c.

Norfolk.

PUBLISHED BY C. HALL,

And sold by most of the Booksellers in the United States.

June, 1821.

Thomas Judson Cluverius
81 Va. 787 (1886)

Booker, George A. *The Virginia Tragedy. Trial and Conviction of Thomas J. Cluverius, for the Murder of Lillian Madison, March 13, 1885.* Richmond: Johns & Goolsby, 1885.

> This book also discusses the "Jeter Philips Case" at pages 151-164 (Philips v. Commonwealth, 19 Gratt. 485 (1868)). Note also "The Cluverius Case," *Va. L. J.*, vol. 9, pp. 507-509 (1885); G[eorge] Watson James, Jr., "The Famous Cluverius – Lillian Madison Murder Case," *Virginia Trooper*, vol. 5, no. 11, pp. 15-31, no. 12, pp. 4-23, vol. 6, no. 1, pp. 5-26, no. 2, pp. 6-27, no. 3, pp. 13-49, no. 4, pp. 14-35 (June-Nov. 1952); Ben Pope, "The Cluverius Case," *Virginia Record*, vol. 78, no. 1, pp. 32-33, 73-77 (Jan. 1956).

"Cousin Tommie!" (T. J. Cluverius): A Parody. Richmond: C. F. Johnston, 1885. 8 p.

> This is a poem.

Cluverius, Thomas J[udson]. *Cluverius: My Life, Trial and Conviction.* Richmond: S. J. Dudley, 1887. 112 p.; 2d ed., Richmond: S. J. Dudley, 1887. 128 p.

> This autobiography was published as a commercial venture. The defendant wrote the book in order to tell his story in his own way and to acknowledge the sacrifices his family made on his behalf. It includes the story of his childhood, history of acquaintance with Fannie Lillian Madison (1863-1885), account of his arrest and trial, the text of Judge Hinton's dissenting opinion from the decision of the Supreme Court of Appeals, the text of Cluverius's petition for executive clemency, and the details of his prison life.

Leigh, Phillip. *Lillian's Marriage and Murder. "Cluverius Did Not Kill Her" The Sequel Told.* Richmond: Patrick Keenan, 1887. 29 p.

> This narrative details evidence the author obtained pertaining to the innocence of T. J. Cluverius (1861-1887) in Lillian Madison's murder. Leigh's story centers on a confession by another man and the testimony of a man claiming to be Lillian's secret husband. Leigh wrote this narrative to clear the name of

T. J. Cluverius because Leigh was not able to do so prior to the execution.

William D. Coleman
66 Va. (25 Gratt.) 865 (1874)

Coleman, William D. *The Case of William D. Coleman.* Baltimore: J. H. Foster, 1878. 110 p.

This case involved the embezzlement of public funds and the alleged perjury and insanity of Joseph Mayo, Jr. See also *Va. Journals of the House of Delegates, 1883-84,* pp. 157-158.

James Thomas DeJarnette
75 Va. 867 (1881)

Grissom, Eugene. *Report of the Trial of James Thomas DeJarnette, for Homicide, with an Appendix.* Raleigh, N.C.: n.p., 1881. 66 p.

This booklet, which was published by a psychiatrist, describes DeJarnette's trial for the murder of his sister. He was originally convicted of the crime by the Hustings Court of the City of Danville but was acquitted upon a retrial on the basis of an insanity defense. The work discusses in detail the insanity defense. It is a reprint of an article in the *North Carolina Medical Journal,* vol. 7, pp. 319-366 (1881), with a seventeen-page appendix of testimony given at trial.

William Dandridge Epes

Brunet, J. M. H. *The Trial of William Dandridge Epes, for the Murder of Francis Adolphus Muir, Dinwiddie County, Virginia.* Petersburg: J. M. H. Brunet, 1849. 76 p.

This booklet, prepared by a reporter, includes the testimony submitted in the case, the speeches of counsel, the prisoner's confessions, and an account of his execution.

Jones, Richard L[yon]. *The Muir-Epes Murder of 1846, Dinwiddie County, Virginia, A History.* Richmond: Dietz Press, 1993. 178 p.

TRIAL

OF

WILLIAM DANDRIDGE EPES,

FOR THE

MURDER OF FRANCIS ADOLPHUS MUIR,

DINWIDDIE COUNTY, VIRGINIA.

WILLIAM DANDRIDGE EPES.

Petersburg, Va:
J. M. H. BRUNET, REPORTER.
1849.

Larry Flynt
521 F. Supp. 1204 (W.D. Va. 1981)
797 F.2d 1270 (4th Cir. 1986)
805 F.2d 484 (4th Cir. 1986)
485 U.S. 46 (1987)

Smolla, Rodney A[lan]. *Jerry Falwell v. Larry Flynt: The First Amendment on Trial*. New York: St. Martin's Press, 1988. 336 p.; rept. Urbana, Ill.: Univ. of Ill. Press, 1990, 336 p.; 2d ed. Urbana, Ill.: Univ. of Ill. Press, 1990. 352 p.; rept. New York: Notable Trials Library, 1991. 336 p.

> This book describes in the Falwell-Flynt libel trial, which began in the United States District Court for the Western District of Virginia and ended up in the United States Supreme Court. Professor Smolla participated in the trial of this case through the preparation of an *amicus curiae* brief in the United States Supreme Court. "The book is intended to be as much an exercise in American Studies as Constitutional Law, for the case was as much a cultural battle as a legal battle, a case in which we as a culture put the First Amendment itself on trial."

James Grant

Pollard, Edward A[lfred]. *Memoir of the Assassination of Henry Rives Pollard*. Lynchburg: Schaffter & Bryant, 1869. 32 p.

> This pamphlet was prepared by the decedent's brother. It was in response to the acquittal of James Grant, who was tried for murder in the Hustings Court of the City of Richmond in February 1869. It includes a narrative of the "assassination," the argument of the prosecuting attorney, and the judge's charge to the jury. Note also Robert Grant Willis, "The Ghost of 1008 East Clay Street," *Richmond Qtly.*, vol. 9, no. 3, pp. 32-35 (Winter, 1987).

Samuel Hardy
110 Va. 910 (1910)

Jones, J. Bunyan. *History of the Case of the Commonwealth vs. Samuel Hardy for the Murder of Tiberius Gracchus Jones at Holland, Nansemond County, Va. October 26th, 1908*. Norfolk: Hampton Roads Paper Co., 1910. 285 p.

> This book is "a summary of the court records, together with a review of the press comment, and the personal observations of his brother," the author.

Elizabeth Haysom
Jens Soering

Englade, Ken. *Beyond Reason: A True Story of a Shocking Double Murder, a Brilliant and Beautiful Socialite and a Deadly Psychotic Obsession.* New York: St. Martin's Press, 1990. 353 p.; 2d ed. New York: St. Martin's Paperbacks, 1990. 375 p.

> This journalistic book tells the sensational story of the murder of Derek and Nancy Haysom in Bedford County and the subsequent trial and conviction of their daughter Elizabeth, who pleaded guilty, and of Jens Soering, her lover.

Thomas Hellier

The Vain Prodigal Life, and Tragical Penitent Death of Thomas Hellier . . . Who for Murdering His Master, Mistress, and a Maid, Was Executed According to Law at Westover in Charles City. London: Crouch, 1680.

> Portions of this pamphlet were reprinted in T. H. Breen, James H. Lewis, and Keith Schlesinger. "Motive for Murder: A Servant's Life in Virginia, 1678," *Wm. & Mary Qtly.*, 3d ser., vol. 40, pp. 106-120 (1983).

William F. Hooe

The Interesting Trial of William F. Hooe, for the Murder of William Simpson. New York: M'Cleland, 1826.

Full Report of the Trial of William F. Hooe for the Murder of William Simpson. Alexandria: D.C. Pittman, 1826.

James H. Johnson

The Trial of James H. Johnson, at the March Term, 1859, of the Circuit Court of Rappahannock County, Va., Charged with the Poisoning of His Wife. N.p., n.d.

Lyndon LaRouche
896 F.2d 815 (4th Cir. 1990)

Spannaus, Edward, comp. *Railroad! U.S.A. v. Lyndon LaRouche, et al.* Washington, D.C.: Comm'n to Investigate Human Rights Violations, 1989. 623 p.

The compiler of this paperback book was one of LaRouche's co-defendants, and the publisher was one of LaRouche's organizations. The purpose of this book is to exonerate LaRouche, his associates, and his organizations. The trial took place in the federal District Court in Alexandria, Virginia.

Ambrose Sharpe Lee

Case of A. S. Lee and Trial in the County Court of Mecklenburg, Va. N.p., [1884]. 32 p.

The defendant in *Commonwealth v. Lee* published this account of his case. It includes the testimony of certain witnesses, the instructions to the jury, and a statement of the "not guilty" verdict in the second trial and certain other relevant correspondence and newspaper articles concerning the trial. Sharpe Lee (1829-1901) was acquitted of the charges of malicious and unlawful cutting with intent to kill. The defendant Lee published this volume, "without comment," to allow the public to decide whether the prosecution against him was "well or ill-founded."

James Samuel McCue
103 Va. 870 (1905)

Chesterman, Evan R[agland], and Jo[seph] F[rancis] Geisinger. *History of the McCue Case: Full Particulars of the Crime, Inquest, Trial and Conviction With Argument of Counsel.* Richmond: Williams Printing, Co., 1904. 174 p.

This account of the McCue murder trial was written jointly by reporters from the *News Leader* and the *Times Dispatch.* It includes a full description of the trial in Charlottesville and responds to allegations that the press withheld information from the public during the McCue trial. It includes a section of biographies of the attorneys in the case.

[Lindsay, James Hubert]. *The McCue Murder: Complete Story of the Crime and the Famous Trial of the Ex-Mayor of Charlottesville, Virginia.* Charlottesville: Progress Pub. Co., [1904]. 192 p.

> This commercially prepared narrative describes the investigation and trial "in true detail" including selection of the venire, speeches of counsel, motions, evidence presented, jury instructions, opinions of the Virginia press on the verdict, and condensed biographies of the most prominent persons involved in the case. The text also includes a summary of four other Virginia murder convictions based on circumstantial evidence, those of Young, Epes, Phillips, and Cluverius.

Alexander Mahood

Report of the Special Committee of the House of Delegates, to Investigate the Charges against Hon. Alexander Mahood, Judge of the 14th Judicial Circuit of Virginia, Together with the Testimony Taken by the Committee. Richmond: C. A. Schaffter, 1871. 51 p.

> This is the committee report and transcript of the evidence against Judge Mahood, who was accused with being drunk while sitting on the bench as a circuit court judge. The House of Delegates refused to impeach him. Note also *Va. Journals of the House of Delegates 1870-71*, pp. 146, 183, 231, 308, 346.

William R. Myers
Samuel S. Myers
William S. Burr

An Authenticated Report of the Trial of Myers and Others, for the Murder of Dudley Marvin Hoyt. With the Eloquent Speeches of Counsel, and "the Letters" in Full, with Explanatory Notes, Which Furnish a Clear and Complete History of the Case. Drawn up by the Editor of the Richmond Southern Standard. New York: Richards and Company, [1846]. 48 p.

> This booklet presents a description of all aspects of the trial, including a summary of the evidence presented, testimony of the witnesses and letters admitted into evidence.

Speech of James Lyons, in Defence of William R. Myers, Samuel S. Myers, and William S. Burr, Charged with the Murder of D. Marvin Hoyt. Richmond: Bernard, 1847.

The Letters and Correspondence of Mrs. Virginia Myers, (Which Have Never Before Been Published or Even Read in Court,) to Dudley Marvin Hoyt, Who Was Murdered at Richmond, Sept. 28th, 1846, By Wm. Myers, and Two Others. Together With a Denial of the Truth of Mrs. Myers' Letter of Explanation of November Last, From Alta Vista. Likewise Added a Short Biography of D. M. Hoyt, by a Relative of the Deceased. Philadelphia: n.p., 1847. 63 p.

> This pamphlet consists primarily of correspondence written by Mrs. Myers to the decedent. It was published, apparently by a relative of the decedent, "for the purpose of denying the foul charge of Dudley Marvin Hoyt having basely seduced Mrs. Virginia Myers." Her husband and two others were discharged without trial for Hoyt's murder.

Francis S. O'Reilly

O'Reilly, Francis S. *The Evidence in the Case of Commonwealth Against Francis S. O'Reilly, for Stabbing James Madison Pleasants, on the 31st of October, 1818.* Richmond: Franklin Press, [1819]. 8 p.

> This booklet concerns O'Reilly's trial in Powhatan County and includes a summary of witness and victim testimony. It was prepared by the defendant to provide a true statement of the case to distribute to friends, not the general public.

James Jeter Phillips
60 Va. (19 Gratt.) 485 (1868)

The Drinker's Farm Tragedy. Trial and Conviction of James Jeter Phillips for the Murder of His Wife. Richmond: J. Wall Turner, 1868. 96 p.

> This book was a commercial venture by a Richmond book seller. It includes an account of the discovery of the body, the arrest of Phillips, his trials, and eventual conviction for first-degree murder. Note also G[eorge] Watson James, Jr., "The Jeter Phillips Murder Case or The Drinkers Farm Tragedy," *Virginia Trooper*, vol. 7, no. 8, pp. 2-28; no. 9, pp. 5-37; no. 10, pp. 12-37; no. 11, pp. 22-32; no. 12, pp. 27-35 (March-July, 1954).

John E. Poindexter
74 Va. (33 Gratt.) 766 (1880)

An Account of the Curtis Homicide and Trials of John E. Poindexter. Richmond: Dispatch Steam Presses, 1879. 54 p.

This text consists of a description of the inquest and both trials of John Poindexter, including testimony of witnesses, description of the venire, and jury instructions.

Thomas Ritchie

A Full Report, Embracing All the Evidence and Arguments in the Case of the Commonwealth of Virginia vs. Thomas Ritchie, Jr., Tried at the Spring Term of the Chesterfield Superior Court, 1846. New York: Burgess, Stringer and Co., 1846. 91 p.

This is a report of the trial of Thomas Ritchie (1820-1854), who killed a rival journalist, John Hampden Pleasants (1797-1846), in a duel. Ritchie was acquitted by the jury. This book includes copies of newspaper articles and transcripts of the testimony presented at trial. The counsel and witnesses were afforded the opportunity to see the text of this publication and correct any inaccuracies. There is also an appendix describing the action of the court in relation to the other parties, P. J. Archer, W. Greenhow, and William Scott. For the background of this trial, see Barbara J. Griffin, "Thomas Ritchie and the Code Duello," *Va. Mag. Hist. Biog.*, vol. 92, pp. 71-95 (1984).

George Wythe Swinney
3 Va. (1 Va. Cas.) 146, 150 (1806)

Boyd, Julian P[arks]. *The Murder of George Wythe*. Philadelphia: Philobiblon Club, 1949. 46 p.; rept. in *Wm & Mary Qtly.*, 3d ser., vol. 12, pp. 513-542 (1955); rept. Williamsburg: Inst. of Early Am. Hist. and Culture, 1955, pp. 3-32.

This short book was originally privately published by a scholarly bibliographical society. The text includes biographical information of George Wythe (1726-1806), an account of his murder, and a brief summary of the trial in which the accused, George Wythe Swinney, his great-nephew, was acquitted. Note also W[illiam] Edwin Hemphill, "Examinations of George Wythe Swinney for Forgery and Murder: A Documentary Essay," *Wm. & Mary Qtly.*, 3d ser., vol. 12, pp. 543-574 (1955); rept. Williamsburg: Inst. of Early Am. Hist. and Culture, 1955, pp. 33-64.

Maria Black Thorn

Murdock, William C. *Trial, Conviction, and Confession of Maria Black Thorn*. Norfolk: n.p., 1855.

Preston S. Turley

The Trial, Conviction, Sentence, Confession, and Execut S. Turley, for the Murder of His Wife, Mary Susan Turley, in Kanawha County, Virginia. Charleston, Va.: Kanawha Valley Star, 1858.

Nat Turner

Gray, Thomas R[uffin]. *The Confessions of Nat Turner*. Baltimore: Thomas R. Gray, 1831. 23 p.; Richmond: Thomas R. Gray, 1832. 24 p.; Petersburg: John B. Ege, 1881. 23 p.; New York: AMS Press, 1975. 23 p.

> This pamphlet publishes the confession and other statements made by Nat Turner (d. 1831) and the court proceedings and judgment of the Court of Southampton County. Turner and his followers murdered thirteen men, eighteen women, and twenty-four children.

Tragle, Henry Irving. *The Southampton Slave Revolt of 1831. A Compilation of Source Material*. Amherst, Mass.: Univ. of Mass. Press, 1971. 489 p.

> This publication includes copies of selected newspaper accounts of the insurrection, a verbatim record of the trials, and previously printed accounts. The author's motivation was to "resurrect the major segments of the record" and to "assemble in a manner which will permit comparison and cross reference, some of the published materials relating to the man and the event."

Abner Vance
4 Va. (2 Va. Cas.) 132, 162 (1818, 1819)

Barrett, Theodosia Wells. *A Frontier Murder*. Bristol, Tenn.: Service Printing Co., n.d. 29 p.

This modern pamphlet gives the background and later history of the trials and convictions in Russell County and in Washington County of Abner Vance for the murder of Lewis Horton. Vance was hanged just before a pardon was delivered and was cut down still alive, but he died six hours later.

Odell Waller

178 Va. 294 (1941)

Sherman, Richard B[eatty]. *The Case of Odell Waller and Virginia Justice, 1940-1942*. Knoxville: Univ. of Tenn. Press, 1992. 264 p.

This book tells the story of Odell Waller (1917-1942), a black sharecropper, who murdered his white landlord and was sentenced to death. It includes a description of the murder, the trial, and the campaign to save Waller's life.

Thomas Wells

S., A. B. *Report of the Trials of Capt. Thomas Wells Before the County Court of Nottoway . . . Charged with . . . Shooting with Intent to Kill Peter Randolph, Esq., Judge of the 5th Circuit, and Col. Wm. C. Greenhill*. Petersburg: Marvel W. Dunnavant, 1816. 94 p.

This volume was prepared by a practitioner at the bar of Nottoway County, an "idle spectator" at Wells's trial for feloniously and maliciously shooting with the intent to kill Peter Randolph, a judge of the Fifth Circuit. It offers summaries of the evidence presented and the events of the trial based on the author's personal notes, which were published on account of urging by unnamed persons.

Jane Williams
John Williams

Particulars of the Dreadful Tragedy in Richmond, on the Morning of the 19th July, 1852: Being a Full Account of the Awful Murder of the Winston Family . . . the Evidence of the Final Trials of the Murderess and Murderer, Jane and John Williams. Richmond: Hammersley, 1852.

Vincent Witcher
Addison Witcher
Samuel Swanson
John A. Smith
Vincent O. Smith

The Evidence in the Case of the Commonwealth versus Vincent Witcher, Addison Witcher, Samuel Swanson, John A. Smith and Vincent O. Smith, Charged with the Murder of Ralph A., Wm. C., and James R. Clement, on the 25th of February, 1860. Lynchburg: n.p., 1860.

INDEXES, DIGESTS, AND ENCYCLOPEDIAS

Michael L. Loy

I. *Introduction*

THE KEY to data retrieval is indexing. The value of any book containing information is enhanced or limited by the indexes to it. Law books are largely reference books.[1] One rarely uses a law book by reading it straight through beginning at the first page and proceeding thence to the last page. One normally reads portions here and there from time to time as needed to aid one's own legal research and writing. This is equally true of reports of cases, compilations of statutes, periodical collections of legal essays, and legal treatises. Thus the key to the usefulness of all law books is their apparatus, their tables and indexes. Any law book of any significance will be well endowed with such apparatus.[2] Moreover, there are free-standing indexes and digests that constitute the apparatus to several law books and to entire classes of law books. These books are absolutely indispensable to serious legal research.

The modern "word searches" of electronic legal data bases are no more than individual on-the-spot indexing, which requires the same creativity and legal experience that goes into the making of a traditional printed index. An inexperienced or amateurish or ignorant word search will be as useless as a badly-made printed legal index, and it will be just as expensive of time and money.

An index is a serious intellectual enterprise, and there is an extensive literature on the principles of indexing. Professional indexers are well paid for their efforts and expertise, and a good index is indeed "a thing of beauty [and] a joy forever."

There are those who believe that "on line word searches" of written materials in computer format will replace indexes. This belief is erroneous because the "on line search" will be no better than the indexing skill of the searcher, and few of us are trained in the subtleties of indexing. Furthermore, a word search will not find synonyms.

---

[1] Only books on the philosophy of the law, jurisprudence, fall outside of this comment.

[2] Note that tables of contents can be used as analytical indexes.

The giving of synonyms along with analytical subdivisions is the essence of a good legal index. The creation of a good legal index requires substantive legal work, which is hard work. If legal indexes are discontinued, the legal profession will sustain the loss of a significant type of research tool, one for which on line word searching is a poor substitute.

Through the evolutionary process of legal scholarship and law book production, the terms "dictionary," "index," "citator," "digest," "case finder," "encyclopedia," "treatise," and "institutes" have emerged as a means of defining the publications encompassing the types of information required by practitioners of the law. One should not expect these terms to be so precise that creative compilers and publishers would be thwarted from creating works that do not exactly fit one of the definitions. Thus, it is not surprising that, beginning in the earliest times, distinctions between indexes, digests, and encyclopedias have become blurred. It is equally unsurprising that Virginia law publications also are not immune to such blurred distinctions.[3] In fact, the older Virginia publications exhibit a remarkable variety of approaches to solving the problems of making the primary legal sources available to the researcher. The creativity defies easy description, and the reader must consider individually the utility of each approach, many of which are unique. Comparatively, the legal reference works currently in print follow a somewhat standard pattern of organization and presentation.

This bibliography deals with free-standing printed legal apparatuses: indexes, citators, digests, and encyclopedias of Virginia law. All well-produced law books have their own indexes; these are beyond the scope of this bibliography. Digests of cases and statutes are regularly included in some newsletters; these are considered in the bibliographies of legal periodicals. However, periodicals which are purely digests are included here.

II. *Indexes*

An index is an alphabetical list of references to other material. Legal indexes are "[t]itles or subjects . . . in brief form suggestive of subject matter, all in alphabetical order, and so prepared and arranged as to point out the page, or volume . . . where the discussion of a par-

[3] In addition to the works discussed here, note that John Tayloe Lomax's *Digest of the Laws Respecting Real Property* (1839) is actually a treatise though it is more modestly entitled a digest.

ticular point or bit of subject matter may be found."[4]

A. *Indexes of Reports*

Virginia's first two indexes of reports were presented to the bar in the year 1856. One of these indexes was compiled by Alexander Barclay Guigon. Entitled *A General Index of Grattan's Virginia Reports, from First to Eleventh Volume, Inclusive,* this work was compiled by Guigon while he was serving as the editor of the *Quarterly Law Journal.* Virginia's other index of reports appearing in 1856, compiled by John Mercer Patton, Jr., and Roscoe Briggs Heath, is entitled *A General Index to Grattan's Reports, from Second to Eleventh Volume, Inclusive* and was printed by a rival publisher. It is interesting to note that both Guigon's and Patton's and Heath's indexes focus on Grattan's *Reports,* the last of the nominative reports. They fill the gap since the publication of Benjamin Tate's *Analytical Digested Index* (1847).

In the year 1881, Virginia's third and fourth indexes of reports were published. One by Henry Augustus Converse, entitled *Indexes to the Virginia and West Virginia Reports,* was published posthumously. Having moved from Pennsylvania to Harrisonburg, Virginia, fifteen months prior to his death, Converse regarded his work as a supplement to William Lawrence Royall's *Digest of the Decisions of the Supreme Court of Appeals of Virginia Contained in Grattan's Reports, Vols. I to XXI,* published in 1873.[5] Arranged alphabetically, Converse's work completely adheres to the definition of an index.

Also published in the year 1881 was William Bruce Martin's *An Index to the Virginia Reports.* It is interesting to note that Martin, perhaps responding to confusion within the law publishing circle regarding the difference between an index and a digest, stated in the preface to his first edition that his work was "an index, not a digest."[6] True to his word, the work is an index as the format is alphabetical, without subheadings, and cites cases at the end of each index entry. Despite an episode of ill health, Martin's index of reports consists of five editions with the last edition published in 1903.

From 1881 until 1902, Martin's index dominated the field of indexes to reports. However, in 1902, the Michie Company published *An Index-Digest to Volumes 92 to 99 of Virginia Reports and Volumes*

---

[4] *Ballentine's Law Dictionary,* p. 610 (3d ed. 1969).

[5] H. A. Converse, *Indexes to the Virginia and West Virginia Reports,* Preface (1881).

[6] W. B. Martin, *Index to the Virginia Reports,* Preface (1881).

A

GENERAL INDEX

OF

Grattan's Virginia Reports,

FROM

FIRST TO ELEVENTH VOLUME INCLUSIVE,

BY

A. B. GUIGON,

OF THE

RICHMOND BAR.

J. W. RANDOLPH:
121 MAIN STREET, RICHMOND.
1859.

1 and 2 of Virginia Decisions. Compiled by Thomas Johnson Michie, this work was originally intended to assist Michie and his assistants in preparing their publication, *Virginia Reports, Annotated*, a new edition of the Virginia nominative law reports. Sensing the bar's need for an index to the volumes of *Virginia Reports* and *Virginia Decisions* not already indexed, Michie published this work, the company's first and last index. Despite its title, the work is arranged and functions as an index.

Another index to reports to date is the *Index to the Virginia Law Register*, published in 1907. Compiled by James H. Guthrie, a member of the Lynchburg bar, the work indexes the first ten volumes of the *Virginia Law Register* from May 1895 to April 1905. Specifically, Guthrie's work provides an index to the "Leading Articles," "Table of Cases Reported in Full," and "Table of Cases Digested," as well as a "General Index." In Guthrie's opinion, "the list of 'Leading Articles' is alone worth the price of the book. Apart from the value of these articles . . . one is enabled to review the procession of so many of those Worthies, who have answered the 'last roll call' and passed 'over the river' "; among those mentioned are John W. Brockenbrough, Conway Robinson, and John B. Minor.[7]

The most recent index to appear in the field of Virginia legal bibliography is the *Virginia Circuit Court Opinions Cumulative Index* compiled by Lucinda Harrison-Cox. This work includes a table of trial court cases reported, as well as a subject matter index. Except for *Shepard's Virginia Citations*, it is the only reference work that analyzes or refers to the published judicial opinions of the Virginia trial court judges.

In addition to these subject matter indexes, most of the digests and encyclopedias of Virginia law include tables of cases cited. These are invaluable aids when one has a case name but no citation to a reporter. Furthermore, the annotations to the *Code of Virginia* are in effect a digest to the appellate case decisions; the annotations constitute a case digest arranged according to the order of the sections of the *Constitution of Virginia* and the *Code of Virginia*.

B. *Indexes of Statutes*

Indexes to statutes are not as much needed today as they were before the appearance of pocket parts and annual indexes to the *Code of Virginia*. However, before 1950, when searching for a legislative enactment, one had to consult the indexes to the current code and to all

[7] J. H. Guthrie, *Index to the Virginia Law Register* (1907).

subsequent volumes of the *Acts of Assembly*. These cumulative indexes to statutes were very useful and commercially viable. Moreover, the indexes to the older codes could always be improved upon if one were willing to do the work.

Like indexes of reports, indexes of statutes do not enjoy an elaborate or lengthy history. Similar to digests of statutes, however, the publication of indexes of statutes generally follows soon after a new or revised Code of Virginia is enacted. Thus, it is not surprising that the first index was published in 1883 soon after the appearance of Virginia's new Code of 1873.

Entitled *Index to the Acts of General Assembly of Virginia, of a General Nature, Passed Since the Code of 1873*, this work was compiled by John Terrill Lovell, a member of the Front Royal bar. Unlike previously discussed indexes and digests, this work is not hard-bound and consists of only thirty-two pages. Nevertheless, stylistically, the alphabetical arrangement and function adhere to the definition of an index.

Twelve years later, Overton Howard compiled the *Index to the Code of Virginia of 1887*, published in 1895. Like Lovell's *Index*, this index was published in response to Virginia's enactment of a new Code in 1887. Stylistically, this work is an index in every sense of the word. Interestingly, Howard states in his preface that because his work was not the first index of statutes, he was able to reap the benefits of refinement. Thus, he considered his work better than his predecessor's.[8]

Continuing with indexes to the Code of Virginia, in 1914, Samuel Need Hurst compiled and published the *Index and Directory of Virginia Law*. In his work, Hurst indexed the Code of Virginia from 1887 to 1914 as well as the Constitution of Virginia. Further, he indexed volumes 1 to 19 of the *Virginia Law Register* and provided Rules of Practice, Canons of Ethics, and an Official Directory of Virginia courts and officers. As discussed below, it was clearly influential.

Prior to 1906, original laws of Virginia were enrolled upon single sheets of parchment, rolled into bundles, and placed in tin tubes for storage. However, in 1906, the General Assembly directed that the bills be properly analyzed, cleaned, bound, labeled, and indexed. This task fell to the Clerk of the House of Delegates and Keeper of the Rolls, John William Williams.

In fulfilling his task, Williams compiled two works. The first work was the *Index to Enrolled Bills of the General Assembly of Virginia, 1776 to 1862, Original Parchments*, published in 1908. The second

[8] O. Howard, *Index to the Code of Virginia of 1887*, Preface (1895).

work was the *Index to Enrolled Bills of the General Assembly of Virginia, 1776 to 1910.* Although these works may not meet the traditional definition of indexes to statutes, they do provide an inventory-like index to the enrolled bills. This indexing is continued by the *Index of Acts of the General Assembly*, which brings the work of Williams's second index up to the present. In addition, the work of each session of the General Assembly is indexed by the *Digest of Acts of Assembly.*

Generally known as "Swem's Index," the *Virginia Historical Index* was compiled by Earl Gregg Swem, the celebrated librarian, and published in 1934 to 1936. This two-volume set indexes Hening's *Statutes at Large of Virginia.* This is a useful tool because Hening's original indexes to each separate volume are poor and there was no cumulative index.[9]

Clearly, Virginia has a brief history of indexes as compared to digests. One explanation might be that indexes are not thought to be as important or commercially lucrative as digests.

C. *Indexes of Periodicals*

The Virginia legal periodicals are indexed in the six-volume *Index to Legal Periodical Literature* (1888-1939), its rival and successor, the *Index to Legal Periodicals*, and the *Current Law Index*, all of which are national in coverage. In addition, there are several separate indexes to two Virginia publications. James H. Guthrie published an index to the *Virginia Law Register* up to 1907, and Hurst's *Index and Directory to Virginia Law* (1914) includes an index to the first nineteen volumes of this same publication. Also the *Virginia Law Review* has four separate volumes of cumulative indexes covering the first fifty volumes of that journal.

III. *Citators*

A citator is a type of index that lists later citations to a particular case or statute. It is an enormously useful tool for legal research. It enables the user to find later cases on the same points of law as a case or statute already known. It guards against citing a case that has been later overruled or questioned or a statute that has been amended or repealed or declared unconstitutional.

---

[9] J. J. Casey, *Personal Names in Hening's Statutes at Large of Virginia, and Shepherd's Continuation* (1896, rept. 1967), was compiled for the benefit of genealogists, it is of little use to lawyers though it may be of value to legal historians.

The most complete citator for the Virginia practitioner is *Shepard's Virginia Citations*. Beginning in 1873, Frank Shepard printed citations to Illinois cases on gummed paper and sold them to attorneys to paste into the margins of their bound reporters, updating the cases published in those volumes.[10] Unlike traditional indexes, to use this work, one must first know the volume and page number of the case under consideration. It includes the Virginia trial court opinions as well as the appellate court cases and statutes. The case citations are presented chronologically; the citations to the statutes are arranged according to the sections of the Constitution and the Code. *Shepard's Virginia Citations* is a sophisticated index and research tool.[11]

In 1895, Abram C. Eby published his *Citations to the Code of Virginia*. These digests of cases arranged according to the order of the *Code of Virginia of 1887* serve as a citator as well as annotations to the Code in force at that time.

Volumes 23A and 23B of *Michie's Jurisprudence of Virginia and West Virginia* constitute a two-volume citator to appellate case opinions. This citator is arranged alphabetically by the names of the cases; *Shepard's Virginia Citations* is arranged chronologically.

IV. *Digests*

Digests are collections of summaries of primary sources. They can be presented in many different ways, but, most frequently, they are arranged by subject matter. Legal digests are "[l]aw books arranged in alphabetical order of titles and presenting in analytical distribution summaries and syllabi of cases."[12] Two types of digests emerged: digests of reports and digests of statutes. Each type is discussed below.

The digest is an ancient form of legal literature, the earliest known today being the one compiled by Alfenus Varus in the first century A.D.[13] The most famous digest of all times is the *Digesta* that was promulgated in 533 by Justinian.

In England, law books in this category were called abridgments. The first abridgment of the law has been attributed to Nicholas

---

[10] M. L. Cohen, R. C. Berring, and K. C. Olson, *How to Find the Law*, p. 55 (9th ed. 1989); see generally F. R. Shapiro, "Origins of Bibliometrics, Citation Indexing, and Citation Analysis: the Neglected Legal Literature," *Journ. of the Am. Soc. for Information Sciences*, vol. 43, pp. 337-339 (1992).

[11] M. R. Doubles and F. Farmer, *Manual of Legal Bibliography*, pp. 129-144 (1947).

[12] *Ballentine's Law Dictionary*, p. 348 (3d ed. 1969).

[13] A. Watson, *Law Making in the Later Roman Republic*, pp. 162-167 (1974).

Statham; it was published around 1495. It was a modest beginning and was soon superseded by the monumental abridgment of Sir Anthony Fitzherbert, which was first printed in 1516. English legal scholars continued to produce more and more elaborate abridgments until the nineteenth century. (John Comyns and William Cruise used the word digest to label their books.) The last "abridgment" was compiled by Charles Petersdorff; it was issued in a second edition in 1861 to 1864 with a supplement in 1870.[14]

A. *Digests of Reports*

Although judicial opinions were unofficially reported from as early as 1729 and the first were printed in 1795, it was not until 90 years later that a member of the Virginia law profession compiled and published a work intended to provide the bar with quick access to points of law without having to labor through volumes of reports.[15] In the year 1819, William Munford, a noted Virginia lawyer and former reporter of the decisions of the Supreme Court of Virginia, compiled the first digest of Virginia case law. Entitled *A General Index to the Virginia Law Authorities*, Munford's work extracts reported case decisions from *Washington* to *Hening and Munford*. Apparently Munford had almost finished a second volume to his *Index*; however, this work was never published.[16] Stylistically, despite being modestly entitled an index, the work is arranged and reads like a digest, not an index.

By the year 1825, the decisions of the Court of Appeals of Virginia numbered eighteen volumes. Recognizing this large amount thwarted easy access to points of law and precedencts, Everard Hall, a member of the bar, "furnish[ed] the profession with a book of easy reference"[17] entitled *A Digested Index to the Virginia Reports, Containing All the Points Argued and Determined in the Court of Appeals of Virginia, From Washington to Second Randolph, Inclusive*. Published in the year of Munford's death, Hall acknowledged the completeness of Munford's *Index* in his preface.[18] Ten years later, in 1835, Hall published the sec-

[14] P. H. Winfield, *The Chief Sources of English Legal History*, pp. 200-251 (1925); J. D. Cowley, *A Bibliography of Abridgments, Digests, Dictionaries, and Indexes of English Law to the Year 1800* (1932); J. H. Baker, *An Introduction to English Legal History*, pp. 211-214 (3d ed. 1990).

[15] W. Munford, *General Index*, p. iv (1819).

[16] P. I. Gordon, "William Munford," *Va. Law Reporters*, pp. 24, 31 (1977).

[17] E. Hall, *Digested Index*, p. iii (1825).

[18] *Id.*

A

DIGESTED INDEX

CONTAINING

THE POINTS ARGUED AND DETERMINED

IN

THE COURT OF APPEALS

OF

VIRGINIA,

FROM THIRD RANDOLPH TO THIRD LEIGH, INCLUSIVE,

WITH

A TABLE OF THE NAMES OF THE CASES REPORTED,

WITH REFERENCES TO THE PRINCIPLES,

WITH NOTES.

TO WHICH IS ADDED,

A LIST OF THE ACTS OF ASSEMBLY

To be given in charge to Grand Juries, and a specification of the offences therein contained.

BY EVERARD HALL,

COUNSELLOR AT LAW.

VOL. II.

RICHMOND:

PRINTED FOR THE AUTHOR.

SAMUEL SHEPHERD & CO. PRINTERS.

1835.

ond volume of this work. Stylistically similar to Munford's *Index*, Hall's *Digested Index* is arranged and functions as a digest, not an index.

In the year 1847, Benjamin Tate, a member of the bar, noted that the number of volumes filled by reports of cases from the Court of Appeals and General Court had swelled to forty-three. Thus, mirroring Everard Hall's effort to provide the profession with easy access to case decisions, Tate compiled two volumes of *An Analytical Digested Index to the Reported Cases of the Court of Appeals and General Court of Virginia; From Washington to Second Grattan, Inclusive*. In his work, Tate stressed that his work was different from Munford's and Hall's in that his did not reference from one part to another.[19] Nevertheless, the result is that, like Munford's and Hall's works, Tate's *Digested Index* is a digest, not an index.

Unfortunately, because of the turmoil caused by the Civil War and ensuing Reconstruction period, the next digest of reports was not published until 1873. This was a work entitled *A Digest of the Decisions of the Supreme Court of Appeals of Virginia Contained in Grattan's Reports, Vols. I-XXI* compiled by William Lawrence Royall, a member of the Richmond bar. A great-nephew of Chief Justice Marshall, Royall enlisted in the Confederate Army in 1862 at the age of seventeen, and was wounded and taken prisoner in 1864. Following the war, Royall studied law with the legal scholar, William Green, and later practiced law with General Bradley T. Johnson. He was later one of the major figures of the heated readjuster-funder controversy involving the Virginia state debt. Royal represented the Northern bond holders.[20] Stylistically, Royall's *Digest* is a digest in every respect. Moreover, it is the first digest properly entitled as such. Although Royall planned to compile another volume, there was no later publication.[21]

Beginning in 1897 and continuing until 1902, attorney Samuel Need Hurst compiled and published an eight-volume collection entitled *A Complete Alphabetical, Analytical, Chronological Annotated Digest of All the Reported Decisions of the Supreme Court of Appeals of Virginia*. Recognizing that the *Virginia Reports* had increased to ninety-two volumes, and unhappy with the inconvenience of having to go first to an index and then to the reports, Hurst embarked on a

---

[19] B. Tate, *Analytical Digested Index*, Preface (1847).

[20] W. L. Royall, *Some Reminiscences* (1909).

[21] W. L. Royall, *Digest of the Decisions of the Supreme Court of Appeals of Virginia*, p. vi (1873).

prolific publishing journey.[22]

During the years of publishing his *Digest*, Hurst refined the art of digesting. In his first volume, he simply listed expositions of case law chronologically. Later, he incorporated a format that included general headings and sub-headings, and adopted a format of using catchlines to each section or paragraph in heavy-faced type "so as to readily catch the eye."[23] Although Hurst intended to publish a ninth volume in 1910, he did not do so. Nevertheless, the evolution of Hurst's *Digest* significantly influenced those digests which followed by other compilers.

Between publishing volumes two and three of his *Digest*, Hurst also published *A Complete Annotated Criminal Digest* in 1900. This work digests all criminal case law decisions of the Supreme Court of Appeals of Virginia and West Virginia. This work is divided into two parts with the decisions of each state digested separately. Not surprisingly, this work mirrors stylistically the alphabetical and chronological format of his eight-volume *Digest*.

As for Hurst's ready acceptance of format changes, he likely adopted such format changes based on the format of national digests, which emerged between 1879 and 1897.[24] Thus, these national digests' sophisticated formats and regular publishing schedules likely influenced Virginia digests as we know them today.

Heralding a change in law publishing, in 1905, Thomas Johnson Michie began a new chapter in the history of Virginia digests of reports. In that year, the Michie Company of Charlottesville, Virginia, began publishing *The Encyclopedic Digest of Virginia and West Virginia*. This publication provided practitioners with a regularly published and updated digest of Virginia and West Virginia law.

Similar to Hurst's and the national digests, Michie's *Encyclopedic Digest* is an easily accessible, alphabetical publication with a significant amount of case law exposition. Obviously a successful publication, the *Encyclopedic Digest* consists of twenty-eight volumes and continued until 1928 when it was replaced by *Michie's Digest*.

In 1907, while Michie was publishing the *Encyclopedic Digest*, Josiah Dickenson Hank, Jr., a member of the Norfolk bar and former

---

[22] S. N. Hurst, *A Complete Alphabetical, Analytical, Chronological Annotated Digest of All the Reported Decisions of the Supreme Court of Appeals of Virginia*, p. v (1897).

[23] S. N. Hurst, *A Complete Alphabetical, Analytical, Chronological Annotated Digest of All the Reported Decisions of the Supreme Court of Appeals of Virginia*, Preface (1897).

[24] Specifically, the *American Reports Digest, American Decisions Digest, American Reports and Decisions Digest, American State Reports Digest*, and the West Publishing Company's annual and monthly digests.

Attorney General of Virginia, compiled *Annotations to Volumes 75-105 Virginia Reports Inclusive*. Unlike any previous digest of reports, Hank's *Annotations* are arranged in sequential, chronological order, beginning with 75 Va. 1. Substantively, Hank's work is similar to a traditional digest as it provides syllabi and a complete history of the cases. Stylistically, however, his work is not arranged alphabetically and does not provide easy reference to points of law. Although not an index, neither is his work an encyclopedia.

Fifteen years later, in 1922, Fred P. Caldwell presented the bar with volume 1 of his six-volume *Virginia and West Virginia Judicial Dictionary-Digest: Words and Phrases*. Touted as a work that "combines the features of a Digest, a Law Dictionary, a Word-Index and a book on Words and Phrases,"[25] Caldwell's *Dictionary-Digest* is a digest in every sense of the definition.

In 1929, *Michie's Digest of Virginia and West Virginia Reports* replaced Michie's *Encyclopedic Digest*. Compiled by Addinell Hewson Michie, each volume contains an extensive index compiled by Thomas Johnson Michie. The major difference between the former *Encyclopedic Digest* and Michie's new *Digest* is that the new publication added federal cases decided pursuant to the laws of Virginia and West Virginia.

For the next six years, the Michie Company dominated the Virginia digest publishing market. However, in 1935, Michie found itself in stiff competition with the West Publishing Company from St. Paul, Minnesota; this competition continues today. Although the West Publishing Company began publishing national reporter digests as early as 1888, it was not until 1935 that West entered into the Virginias with the *South Eastern Digest*. Today, West's *Digest* covers all cases reported in the *Virginia Reports, South Eastern Reporter*, and various other reports of southeastern states, and provides cumulative pocket service.

Perhaps because West published more often and more routinely than did the Michie Company, in 1943, yet another blow was delivered to *Michie's Digest*. In that year, West began publishing the *Virginia and West Virginia Digest* and it continues in publication today. This digest covers all the cases covered in the *South Eastern Digest* as well as Virginia and West Virginia cases decided in the federal courts.

Without a doubt, West's *Virginia and West Virginia Digest* significantly affected the Michie Company. Likely the impact is reflected in the fact that the last bound volume of *Michie's Digest* was published the very year West began publishing the *Virginia and West*

[25] F. P. Caldwell, *Virginia and West Virginia Judicial Dictionary-Digest*, p. iii (1922).

Virginia Digest. Although Michie continued providing pocket part service to its *Digest*, the publication ended in 1952 as Michie turned its attention to its current publication, *Michie's Jurisprudence*, described later in this essay as an encyclopedia.[26]

The arrival of West's *Virginia and West Virginia Digest* in 1943 and the departure of *Michie's Digest* in 1952 mark an important historical milestone in Virginia law publishing. For the first time in the history of digests of reports in Virginia, Virginia lawyers began relying upon a publication that was neither compiled by a local practitioner nor published by a local publisher, except for the book by Caldwell. Obviously aided by the advent of modern transportation and communication, the business of compiling and publishing digests had evolved into a sophisticated business enterprise, national in scope.

The emergence of the West Publishing Company as a dominant publisher of law reference books in Virginia did not, however, portend the end of local compilations and publishing. Quite the contrary, numerous works exist that are equally sophisticated but not as voluminous as West's digests. One such publication is the *Law Letter*.

Another looseleaf digest, *Virginia Researcher*, was a commercial venture of the National Legal Research Group based in Charlottesville. Published from 1982 until 1989, this work mirrored the *Law Letter* both stylistically and substantively, digesting case law of the same courts as did the *Law Letter*.

Yet another looseleaf digest is the *Circuit Court Report*. Published by Court Report Publications from 1982 to 1989, this publication, arranged alphabetically, digests monthly civil jury trials for the Richmond metropolitan area.

Perhaps one of the shortest lived publications was *briefCases*, a commercial venture of J. C. Avery & Associates, Inc., Richmond. A weekly digest of Virginia's latest court opinions, *briefCases* was published from January 14, 1991, until September 27, 1991. Looseleaf and alphabetically arranged, the publication ceased because of the lack of subscribers.

Whereas looseleaf publications serve somewhat as broad current events digests, practitioners often require information specific to certain areas of law. Consequently, as practitioners' needs are becoming more precise, digests are becoming more sophisticated.

Responding to practitioners' sophisticated needs, Brien A. Roche's "case finders" address specific areas of law. In his *Virginia Torts Case Finder*, published in 1984 and 1990, and his *Virginia Domestic*

---

[26] In 1948, four years prior to the final publication of Michie's *Digest*, the Michie Company began publishing an encyclopedic work known as *Michie's Jurisprudence*.

Relations Case Finder, published in 1986 and 1991, Roche first paraphrases the statutory tort law and then provides case law illustrations, focusing in detail on relevant legal principles. Unlike traditional digests, however, both case finders are arranged topically rather than alphabetically. Nevertheless, functionally, Roche's works provide easy access to appellate case law decisions. Thus, Roche's case finders more closely resemble digests than any other type of law publication.

Rivaling the specificity of Roche's case finders is Ronald J. Bacigal's and Thomas F. Guernsey's work entitled *Admissibility of Evidence in Virginia: A Manual for Virginia Trial Lawyers*. First published in 1990, this work compiles statutory and case law regarding the admissibility of evidence in Virginia. Stylistically, the work's alphabetical format and easy access to the law clearly permit it to be called a digest.

Although lacking case law illustration found in Professors Bacigal's and Guernsey's work, Charles E. Friend's rival work, *The Lawyer's Pocket Guide to Virginia Evidence Law*, also focuses upon evidence law. Published in 1990, Friend's work is arranged topically, not alphabetically. However, *The Lawyer's Pocket Guide* is more appropriately termed a digest than an index because of its relatively simple arrangement and easy access to case law.

Despite the process of sophistication, as reflected in Roche's and others' contemporary works, blurred distinctions between law publications are just as prevalent today as they were in 1819 when William Munford entitled his digest a *General Index*. The only difference may be that today's compilers are more creative when entitling their works than were their predecessors more than 170 years ago.

Finally, unlike any of the digests previously discussed, John Paul Jones's *Case Decisions By the Virginia Commissioner of Motor Vehicles Under the Virginia Vehicle Dealer Licensing Act*, published in 1987, is a digest-like, looseleaf work that digests key abstracts and summarizes case decisions under the Virginia Motor Vehicles Dealer Licensing Act. Published as a project of the Administrative Law Committee of the Virginia Bar Association, it reflects the sophistication to which digests of statutes have evolved.

As the law continues to grow in new directions, one can predict that case law digests will become even more specialized than they are today. Indeed, today's newsletters, such as those published by the Virginia Bar Association, and *Virginia Lawyer's Weekly*, which digest particularized topics of law, might well be the new digests.[27] Thus, the specialization of practitioners and sophistication of creative compilers and publishers will continue to blur distinctions that have evolved throughout the history of case law digests in Virginia.

B. *Digests of Statutes*

Although not as abundant as digests of reports, digests of statutes have a significantly longer and equally important history. Like digests of reports, digests of statutes are meant to supply easy access to the statutory law. Although generally published in response to new or significantly revised codes, like digests of reports, digests of statutes have experienced an evolution of sophistication.

The earliest digest of statutes pertaining to Virginia law was compiled in 1694. Likely compiled or orchestrated by Philip Ludwell, a Virginian and governor of North Carolina, this work is known as "An Abridgment of the Laws of Virginia."[28] Arranged topically and alphabetically, this work was prepared as a manuscript, evidently intended for publication. There is no evidence, however, that this intention was ever carried out.

Perhaps because of the lack of printers in colonial Virginia, or English indifference to unofficial publications from within the colonies, it was not until 1704 that the next such work appeared. In 1704, *An Abridgement of the Laws in Force in Her Majesty's Plantations of Virginia, Jamaica, Barbadoes, Maryland, New-England, New-York, Carolina, &c.* was published in London for several booksellers. As evidenced from its title, the work clearly reflects England's governance of her colonies. Compiling all the law up to the date of publication, this work is arranged similar to "An Abridgment of the Laws of Virginia." With the portion relating to Virginia contained in eighty-six pages, the work digests the law alphabetically. Formatted with general headings, the entries thereunder are in chronological order, noting first the year of the particular law's enactment, followed with a brief paraphrase of the law.

The next abridgment was published fourteen years later, in 1722. Entitled *An Abridgement of the Publick Laws of Virginia in Force and Use June 10, 1720*, this work, like its predecessor, was also published

[27] Newsletter publications of the Virginia State Bar Association having digests include *Family Law Section Newsletter*, *Antitrust, Franchise and Trade Regulation Newsletter*, and *Litigation News*. These and the others are listed in the bibliography of twentieth-century legal periodicals.

[28] This was first printed in the *Virginia Magazine of History and Biography* in 1902.

in London. Although the publisher and compiler are unknown, it has been attributed to Robert Beverley, a Virginia historian. Dedicated to Virginia's Governor Spotswood, the work is without "special topical or alphabetical arrangement," yet it clearly functions as a digest.

As the number of Virginia colonists increased, so did the need for local publications. Thus, in 1737, one year after the first printer arrived in Virginia, *An Exact Abridgement of All the Public Acts of Assembly of Virginia in Force & Use* was published in Williamsburg. Compiled by John Mercer, this abridgment is likely the first Virginia digest published in America. The first edition compiled all public acts in force as of 1736. In between the first and second editions of this work, Mercer compiled *A Continuation of the Abridgment of All the Public Acts of Assembly of Virginia,* published in Williamsburg in 1739. Twenty years later, in 1759, Mercer compiled his second edition of *An Exact Abridgement of All the Public Acts of Assembly of Virginia in Force & Use.* It is interesting to note that the second edition was printed in Glasgow, Scotland.

Mercer's *Abridgment,* second edition, is a Virginia historian's treasure. In digesting all the public acts in force since March 23, 1660, and in force as of January 1, 1758, this work also provides an excellent historical record of Assemblies' meetings. It is interesting to note that this work was the last "abridgment," that term having been replaced with the term "digest."

In 1819, the Revised Code of Virginia was adopted. Four years later, in 1823, Joseph Tate published a digest of statutes in hope that his work would prove useful to the bar.[29] Entitled *A Digest of the Laws of Virginia, Which Are of a Permanent Character and General Operation; Illustrated by Judicial Decisions: To Which Is Added, An Index of the Names of the Cases in the Virginia Reporters,* Tate digests statutes alphabetically and illustrates their application with footnoted case decisions. His second edition was published posthumously in 1841.

Five years later, in 1846, responding to the thirty subsequent sessions of the General Assembly since Tate's second edition, Chapman Johnson and Robert Gourmain Scott compiled the *Revision and Digest of the Criminal Code of Virginia.* By acts of the General Assembly in 1834, 1836, and 1841, Johnson was appointed to publish a concise revision of Virginia's criminal law. He toiled at this task from 1836 until 1841, at which time he was prevented from continuing due to ill health. In 1846, the General Assembly, again by Act, appointed Scott to continue Johnson's mission. Scott completed the revision that same year.

---

[29] J. Tate, *Digest of the Laws of Virginia,* Preface (1823).

DIGEST

OF THE

LAWS OF VIRGINIA,

OF A

CRIMINAL NATURE,

ILLUSTRATED

BY JUDICIAL DECISIONS.

BY

JAMES M. MATTHEWS,

Attorney at Law.

RICHMOND:

WEST & JOHNSTON, PUBLISHERS, 145 MAIN STREET.

PRINTED BY C. H. WYNNE.

1861.

In 1849, a new Code of Virginia was enacted. By 1856, many of the Code's chapters had been replaced. Responding to these changes, and intending to assist the bar, James Muscoe Matthews compiled a two-volume collection entitled *A Digest of the Laws of Virginia of a Civil Nature*, published in 1856.[30] With a format similar to that of Joseph Tate's digest, Matthews's collection provided a detailed, alphabetized digest of statutory law ranging from Aliens and Indians to County Roads and Bridges. Five years later, Matthews presented the bar with another work also aimed at providing easy access to the law. This work, however, focused on Virginia's criminal law.

Entitled *A Digest of the Laws of Virginia of a Criminal Nature*, this work consists of at least three editions and a supplement, spanning 1861 to 1890. Stylistically, the first and second editions are arranged alphabetically addressing statutory law and illustrated with case exposition in footnotes. The third edition, however, is not arranged alphabetically. Instead, the third edition, published in 1890, encompasses and parallels, stylistically, the 1887 Code of Virginia. It is interesting to note that the second edition was published in 1871 because the supply of copies of the first edition were destroyed by the "great conflagration in Richmond at the close of the Civil War."[31]

In 1878, simultaneous with Matthews's supplement to his *Criminal Digest*, James E. Goode compiled and published *The New Criminal Procedure of the State of Virginia: With Full Annotations and a Complete Index*. Although he asserts that his work is "neither a compendium nor a digest," Goode's work reads like a digest.[32] Formatted according to the new criminal procedure to take effect on July 1, 1879, it paraphrases the criminal law of 1878 and references, as applicable, the new Act in the side margins. He then lists illustrative cases in footnotes. His goal was to publish this work before the new criminal procedures took effect so that the practitioners would be ready to apply current law.

The year 1886 saw the publication of a digest unlike previous digests. Wyndham Robertson Meredith's *Digest of Acts and Extracts from Acts in Relation to the Public Debt of Virginia, with References to, and a List of Decisions Thereof*. In this work, Meredith, a staunch advocate for decreasing Virginia's public debt, focuses on the law regarding the restructuring or "readjusting" of Virginia's public debt following the Civil War and Reconstruction period. Published by the

[30] J. M. Matthews, *A Digest of the Laws of Virginia of a Civil Nature*, Preface (1856).

[31] J. M. Matthews, *Digest of the Laws of Virginia of a Criminal Nature*, Preface (1871).

[32] J. E. Goode, *New Criminal Procedure of the State of Virginia: With Full Annotations and a Complete Index*, Introduction, p. vii (1878).

Sinking Fund Commissioners, Meredith's *Digest* is arranged alphabetically; however, the format does not lend itself to easy reference. Cases pertaining to the public debt of Virginia are listed at the back of the book. The readjustment of the state debt was a hot political issue at that time.

Returning to Virginia's criminal and civil law, Virginia enacted a new Code in 1873 and another one in 1887. Not surprisingly, confusion existed within the bar as to the status of certain laws. Thus, in 1888, Conway Whittle Sams compiled a digest comparing selected statutes of the new Code of 1887 with the former Code of 1873, placing special emphasis on those statutes referred to in Minor's *Institutes of Common and Statute Law*. Entitled *A Brief Comparison of the Most Important Statutes of the Codes of Virginia of 1873 and 1887*, Sams's work is not alphabetically formatted. Rather, the work parallels, topically, the Code of 1887. Although this work does not meet the strict definition of a digest, it surely is not an index. Substantively, however, it is more of a digest than an index.

In 1919, Virginia once again adopted a new Code. Three years later, Samuel Need Hurst presented the bar with a two-volume work that encompassed the new Code as well as the common law. This work, which, by its title, further blurred the distinction between digests, indexes and encyclopedias, is entitled *A Complete Encyclopedia of Virginia Law*.

Published in 1922, Hurst's *Encyclopedia* is arranged alphabetically with each major heading providing a general definition of statutory law and common law followed by subtopics and paragraph expositions of case law. Because of the work's format, brevity of entries, paraphrasing of the law, and case law illustrations, Hurst's *Encyclopedia* more closely resembles a digest of statutes than an encyclopedia.

In 1926, Howard Burton Lee compiled *The Criminal Trial in the Virginias* while serving as the Attorney General of West Virginia. It is interesting to note that, reflecting the restraints of Prohibition, one chapter addresses "Moonshine Stills." Similar to Matthews's digests and Goode's *Criminal Procedure*, Lee's work apparently parallels the Code of 1919, digesting statutory law and then illustrating with case law. Lee followed this work with a second edition in 1940.

Ten years after Lee's second edition, Virginia adopted yet another new Code in 1950. However, the next digest presented to the bar is the current *Digest of Acts of the General Assembly of Virginia*, published at least since 1980 by the Virginia Code Commission and the Division of Legislative Services. This is a looseleaf digest, published in an annual volume. The format parallels the title and section number of the Code of Virginia; it is the only digest of statutory law in the most recent volume of the *Acts of Assembly*.

Today's digests of statutes, like digests of reports, not only encapsulate the broad statutory law but also respond to the particularized needs of specialized practitioners. Consequently, as the law and practitioners' needs become more particularized, it is likely that digests of statutes will evolve into tailor-made publications digesting specific aspects of statutory law.

V. *Encyclopedias*

An encyclopedia is a collection of essays or articles arranged alphabetically. Abridgments and digests of the law evolved into encyclopedias of the law as the compilers reworked the individual items of the digests into a more literary paragraph and chapter form. Thus, the articles of an encyclopedia are more logical and easier to read than a section of a digest, and the user gets a clearer perspective on the topic.

One of the typical characteristics of legal encyclopedias is that they usually do not give any analysis or editorial comment. The encyclopedias normally string together the pronouncements of the courts and the legislatures without addition. This distinguishes them from articles, treatises, and institutes of the law. These latter forms of legal writing allow the author to express his or her own opinions on the law, both what it is and what it should be. However, there is often a blurring of this distinction between encyclopedias and treatises.

In theory and in etymology, an encyclopedia of the law is intended to cover all aspects of the circle of the law; it is meant to encircle the law. An encyclopedia is "a work that contains information on all branches of knowledge or treats comprehensively a particular branch of knowledge usually in articles arranged alphabetically by subject."[33] A treatise, however, is "a systematic exposition or argument in writing including a methodical discussion of the facts and principles involved and conclusions reached."[34]

It is only fitting that Virginia's sole legal encyclopedia, *Michie's Jurisprudence*, is compiled and published by the Michie Company, one of Virginia's oldest and best-known law publishing companies. Published since 1948, this work is tailored exclusively to the Virginia and West Virginia practitioner and focuses on the similarities and conflicts of both states' law. With articles arranged alphabetically, *Michie's Jurisprudence* provides practitioners with easy access to

[33] *Webster's New Collegiate Dictionary*, p. 375 (1976).

[34] *Id.* at p. 1244.

points of law. This encyclopedia evolved out of *Michie's Digest* and is not much more than a digest in that the editors do not give any independent analysis of the law under discussion.

In this publication, the Michie Company employs a few of West's techniques. For example, *Michie's Jurisprudence* is regularly updated, informing practitioners of the most recent legal developments by means of replacement volumes and annual pocket supplements. Thus, having successfully carved out a niche in Virginia and West Virginia law publishing, *Michie's Jurisprudence* is without a rival.

VI. *Conclusion*

Law publishing in Virginia has enjoyed a long history, dating from the colonial period. As primary legal authority accumulated, the need for apparatus to it increased. Thus in Virginia, since statutes in print accumulated long before case decisions, abridgments and indexes to statutes appeared first. In the colonial period, the Virginia legal profession relied on English case authority and thus on English books of apparatus.[35] After Independence in 1776 and, more significantly, after the Virginia bench was professionalized and Virginia case law began to appear in print, indexes and digests to the Virginia law reports became possible and then became necessary.

In the nineteenth century and earlier, the compilers of these books were practicing attorneys. Their motivation was financial in that there might be some quick reward in the form of royalties. Furthermore, there would more likely be a sustained long-term dividend in the form of enhancement of one's professional reputation leading to future legal employment. Although individual lawyers have continued to the present day to produce legal reference books, the majority of such works in the twentieth century, and certainly the larger and more elaborate ones, have been, and are being, produced by the salaried staffs of the Michie Company in Charlottesville and the West Publishing Company in Saint Paul, Minnesota.

What, then, is the value of the older legal reference books that are considered by this bibliography? The older works form the basis of the newer ones; the older ones are incorporated into and thus superseded by the newer ones. Furthermore, some people believe that all of these apparatuses will be superseded by electronic word searches.

There are two responses to the computer buffs, one of which is also the response to the modernists. We will respond to the computer people first and then give the joint response to both groups.

[35] See W. H. Bryson, *Census of Law Books in Colonial Virginia* (1978).

First, for all of the many advantages of the computer word processor, it has not improved upon the codex form of the book. Here the computer is a retrograde, a throwback, to the volumen or scroll form of the book, which was superseded in the sixth century by the codex, the present form of the book.[36] The reader of a codex, or of several at the same time, can consult many different pages at the same time. Moreover, the user of a codex can conveniently flip through it in a manner denied to the user of a volumen or of a computer word processor. Thus, the word processor, however valuable it may be for its own unique virtues, will not supersede or supplant the printed book in its codex form.

In addition, the computer data bases are far from adequate. As for Virginia, they do not include any code except the current one.

Secondly, even though the earlier reference books may have been superseded, some of them present unique systems of classifications and subclassifications of the law. Naturally, some of these systems are more subtle and sophisticated than others, but each gives the individual insight of its author, which may be useful to the present. These indexes, digests, and encyclopedias can give a glimpse of the law as a logical system because the parts of each section are logically, or systematically, subdivided, even though the sections are often presented alphabetically. The subdivisions illustrate a crude classification and definition of the law.[37]

The enormous bulk of the written sources of the law forces the creation of epitomes, digests, indexes, and other apparatuses. Otherwise, the law would remain inaccessible. The creation of these works forces the compiler to systematize it or some part of it. This systemization is the definition of the law. The creation of categories forces the creation of definitions. The definition of the law is the creation of the law. The opposite of definition is chaos and anarchy. Anarchy is not law. This may appear to the reader to be a circular argument, but to the writer, it attempts to describe an historical process that is a spiral, an upward spiral of progress through trial and error, through consideration and reconsideration, through definition and redefinition.

---

[36] C. H. Roberts and T. C. Skeat, *The Birth of the Codex*, p. 75 (1983).

[37] For good discussions of the subject of the classification of the law, see J. E. Herget, *American Jurisprudence 1870-1970*, pp. 63-81, 353-361 (1990); D. J. Seipp, "The Structure of English Common Law in the Seventeenth Century," in W. M. Gordon and T. D. Fergus, *Legal History in the Making*, pp. 61-83 (1991); J. W. Cairns, "Eighteenth Century Professorial Classifications of English Common Law," *McGill Law Journ.*, vol. 33, pp. 225-244 (1987).

BIBLIOGRAPHY

I. *Indexes, Digests, and Encyclopedias of Virginia Law*

"An Abridgment of the Laws of Virginia." *Virginia Magazine of History and Biography*, vol. 9, pp. 273–88, 369–84 (1902), vol. 10, pp. 49–64, 145–60, 241–54 (1902); rept. Richmond: Va. Historical Soc., 1903.

This work is the earliest known abridgment of Virginia law. It was compiled in 1694 and consists of 112 manuscript pages. Arranged topically and alphabetically, the manuscript was evidently intended for publication; however, there is no evidence that this intention was ever carried out. The manuscript was likely compiled or orchestrated by Philip Ludwell (1638–1716), a Virginian and governor of North Carolina.

An Abridgement of the Publick Laws of Virginia in Force and Use June 10, 1720. London: n.p., 1722.

The third earliest abridgment of Virginia laws, this work is dedicated to Virginia's Governor Alexander Spotswood and has been attributed to Robert Beverley, a Virginian historian. The format is random rather than alphabetical or topical. At the end of the work is "An Alphabet to the Laws."

Attorney General's Criminal Law Digest. Richmond: Office of the Attorney General, 1984 to 1987, 4 vols.

This is a quarterly digest of criminal opinions issued by the Attorney General of Virginia. It was replaced by *The Law Digest.*

Bacigal, Ronald J[oseph], and Thomas F[ranklin] Guernsey. *Admissibility of Evidence in Virginia: A Manual for Virginia Trial Lawyers.* Norcross, Ga.: The Harrison Co., 1990; 2d ed. by Ronald J. Bacigal, Joseph S. Tate, and Thomas F. Guernsey, Norcross, Ga.: The Harrison Co., 1998.

This work compiles statutory and case law on the law of evidence in Virginia. It is kept up to date with annual pocket supplements.

briefCases. Richmond: J. C. Avery & Associates, Inc., 1991.

This work was a private venture endorsed by the Virginia Trial Lawyers Association. Published weekly from January 14, 1991, until September 27, 1991, the work summarized, alphabetically by subject matter, Virginia's latest court opinions. This looseleaf work ceased publication because the number of subscribers did not outweigh the production costs.

Bryson, W[illiam] Hamilton, Lucinda Harrison-Cox, Stephanie Ploszay Karn, and Rosemary Golden Seltzer. *An Index of Printed Virginia Trial Court Opinions Between 1850 and 1928.* Richmond: Va. Ass'n of Law Libraries, 1995.

This index analyses the reports printed in *The Quarterly Law Journal* (1856–1859), *The Quarterly Law Review* (1860–1861), *The Virginia Law Journal* (1877–1893), *The Virginia Law Register* (1895–1928), Howison's *Reports*, and Diggs' *Reports.*

Caldwell, Fred P. *The Virginia and West Virginia Judicial Dictionary-Digest: Words and Phrases.* Cincinnati: W. H. Anderson Co., 1922–1923, 6 vols.

This work is formatted alphabetically, providing definitions of words, phrases and maxims interpreted or applied in Virginia and West Virginia case law. Applicable case exposition follows each definition.

Chichester, Cassius M[oncure]. *Virginia Legislation of 1942. A Digest.* Richmond: Richmond Press, Inc., [1942].

This digest was printed for distribution by the Virginia State Bar Association.

Circuit Court Report. Richmond: Court Report Publications, Jan. 1982 to Oct. 1989, 8 vols.

This looseleaf publication was a monthly digest of civil jury trials in personal injury cases in the Richmond metropolitan area. The primary interest of this service was in the monetary amounts of settlements, verdicts, and judgments. Volumes 4 through 8 were edited by Mary Bruner.

The Civil Digest. Richmond: Office of the Attorney General, Jan. 1973 to April, 1987, 15 vols.

This is a monthly digest of civil opinions issued by the Attorney General of Virginia relative to problems of interest to officials of Virginia state and local governments. It was replaced by *The Law Digest*.

Clarke, Joseph M., II. *Virginia Criminal Law Case Finder*. Charlottesville: The Michie Co., 1987; 2d ed., Charlottesville: The Michie Co., 1991; 3d ed., Charlottesville: The Michie Co., 1995, 2 vols.; 4th ed., Charlottesville: Lexis Law Publishing, 1999, 2 vols.

This digest of appellate court opinions is kept up to date by means of pocket supplements.

Converse, Henry A[ugustus]. *Indexes to the Virginia and West Virginia Reports*. Ed. by Howard R. Bayne. Richmond: West, Johnston & Co., 1881.

Having moved to Harrisonburg from Pennsylvania, Converse (1839–1880) was a member of the Harrisonburg bar for only fifteen months before his death. The substantially completed manuscript of this work was found after his death. The preface to the published work has a memoir to the author written by his brother, James B. Converse. In his work, Converse notes the fine quality of Benjamin Tate's index. Arranged alphabetically, this work was regarded by Converse as a supplement to William Royall's digest, which was published in 1873.

Digest of Virginia Legislation. Richmond: Div. of Purchase and Printing, 1934 to present.

This annual publication summarizes all of the amendments to the Code of Virginia enacted during the preceding year. It was originally prepared by the Virginia Division of Statutory Research and Drafting and is now the product of the Virginia Division of Legislative Services. The current title is *Digest of Acts*.

Diggs, Isaac, and Ben T[emple] Barret. *Virginia Corporation Digest. A Collection of the Case and Statute Law of Virginia on Corporations, Including Railroad, Municipal and Other Corporations, With Notes and References*. Richmond: C. E. Picot Printing Co., 1907.

Eby, Abram C. *Citations to the Code of Virginia*. Richmond: J. W. Randolph & Co., 1895.

This work annotates the *Code of Virginia*. Arranged in chronological order under each section of the Code, the work provides principle cases that define and illustrate the principles of the statute. Eby, a member of the Richmond bar, digested case law from the U.S. Supreme Court, the Supreme Court of Appeals of Virginia, and the former General Court of Virginia.

Friend, Charles E. *Lawyer's Pocket Guide to Virginia Evidence Law*. Williamsburg: Barrister Press, 1990.

Formatted into thirteen chapters, non-alphabetical, the work is designed to provide easy access to basic evidence information and applicable cases.

Goode, James E. *New Criminal Procedure of the State of Virginia: With Full Annotations and a Complete Index*. Richmond: Goode, 1878.

The preface asserts the book is neither a compendium nor a digest. Formatted topically, the work addresses the new Criminal Procedure Act of 1879 by stating the criminal law of Virginia with statutory law referenced in the side margins and case law exposition in footnotes. The work was published before the new criminal procedures went into effect on July 1, 1879.

Guernsey, Thomas F[ranklin], Anthony J. Bocchino, and David A. Sonenshein. *Virginia Evidence with Objections*. Notre Dame, Ind.: National Institute for Trial Advocacy, 1995.

This is a small pocket book designed for handy reference during the course of a trial. It has a few references to Virginia cases.

Guigon, A[lexander] B[arclay]. *A General Index of Grattan's Virginia Reports, from First to Eleventh Volume, Inclusive*. Richmond: J. W. Randolph, 1859.

This work was first issued in parts and is often found bound with the *Quarterly Law Journal* (1856–1859), which was initiated by the same publisher, J. W. Randolph (1815–1893). Randolph's intent was to provide a complete digest of Grattan's *Reports* (the current official reporter), which would continue Benjamin Tate's digest, which was published in 1847. Guigon (1831–1878) served as the editor of the *Quar-*

terly Law Journal from its beginning in April, 1856, until its demise in October, 1859.

Guild, June Purcell. *Black Laws of Virginia: A Summary of the Legislative Acts of Virginia Concerning Negroes from Earliest Times to the Present.* Richmond: Whittet & Shepperson, 1936; rept. Westport, Conn.: Negro Universities Press, 1969; rept. Lovettsville, Va.: Willow Bend Books, 1996.

This is a digest of statutes.

Guthrie, James H. *Index to the Virginia Law Register.* Lynchburg: J. P. Bell, 1907.

A member of the Lynchburg bar, Guthrie indexes, alphabetically, the first ten volumes of the *Virginia Law Register* from May 1895 to April 1905, inclusive. The work is divided into four parts: an index to Leading Articles; Table of Cases Reported in Full; Table of Cases Digested; and a General Index.

Hall, Everard. *A Digested Index to the Virginia Reports, Containing All the Points Argued and Determined in the Court of Appeals of Virginia, From Washington to Second Randolph, Inclusive.* Vol. 1, Richmond: Peter Cottom, 1825; vol. 2, Richmond: Samuel Shepherd & Co., 1835.

This work is formatted alphabetically with general headings, followed by a brief index of the sub-headings and then numbered paragraphs exposing case law. It includes rules of the various Virginia courts. Reading more like a digest than an index, the work encompasses reports from Washington to Second Randolph, all matters in William Munford's *General Index to Virginia Law Authorities,* and the first and second volumes of Randolph's Reports. This work was published as the number of volumes of decisions of the Court of Appeals had increased to eighteen.

Hank, J[osiah] D[ickenson], Jr. *Annotations to Volumes 75–105 Virginia Reports Both Inclusive.* Charlottesville: The Michie Co., 1907.

Unlike the traditional digest format, this work is arranged in sequential, chronological order. The work begins with 75 Virginia 1 and digests the volumes thereafter. Following the heading denoting the report number is the case name. In a note to each case, the work collected all the Virginia and West Virginia decisions referring to the case report. The note gave a complete history of the case, which, quite similar to "Shepardized" cases, set forth the propositions in connection with which it had been criticized, and show if it had been affirmed, explained, criticized, distinguished, or overruled. The work makes reference to appropriate statutes and sections of the Virginia Constitution of 1902. Hank (1875–1924) was an Assistant Attorney General of Virginia and a member of the Norfolk bar. An obituary of Hank is printed in *Va. State Bar Ass'n Repts.*, vol. 36, pp. 93–94 (1924).

Harlow, B[enjamin] F[ranklin], comp. *Delinquent and Forfeited Lands: Acts of the Legislatures of Virginia and West Virginia, Constitutional Provisions, and Decisions of the Court of Appeals Respecting Same.* Lewisburg, W. Va.: Harlow & Argabrite, 1877.

Harrison[-Cox], Lucinda D[enise]. *Virginia Circuit Court Opinions Cumulative Index.* Rockville, Md.: Aspen Publishers, 1988, 1991; Orford, N.H.: Butterworth, 1994, 1995; Charlottesville: The Michie Co., 1996 to present.

These indexes include tables of cases reported and subject indexes to the Virginia trial court opinions.

Hogg, William Edward. *Virginia Criminal Law.* Richmond: Richmond Press, Inc., 1939.

This is a digest of criminal law cases.

Howard, Overton. *Howard's Index to the Code of Virginia of 1887.* Richmond: West, Johnston & Co., 1895.

Formatted alphabetically, Howard considered his index better than his predecessors' because theirs was the first effort and his work had the benefit of refinement. This work was reviewed in *Wm. & Mary Qtly.*, 1st ser., vol. 4, p. 287 (1896).

Hurst, Sam[uel] N[eed]. *A Complete Annotated Criminal Digest.* Pulaski City, Va.: Hurst & Co., 1900.

This work digests all criminal case law decisions of the Supreme Court of Appeals of Virginia and West Virginia from the first organization of the old General Court of Virginia down to the time of publishing. Dedicated to Charles A.

Graves (1850–1928), Professor of Law at the University of Virginia, the work's format mirrors the alphabetical and chronological plan of *Hurst's Digest*. The work is divided into two parts with the decisions of each state digested separately. Each part contains an alphabetical listing of cases with corresponding pages of the digest, listed under the subjects where found, with parallel citations to the *South Eastern Reports*.

Hurst, Sam[uel] N[eed], and Randal M. Brown. *A Complete Alphabetical, Analytical, Chronological Annotated Digest of All the Reported Decisions of the Supreme Court of Appeals of Virginia*. Vols. 1–5, Pulaski City, Va.: Hurst & Co., 1897–1900; vols. 6–8, supp., index, Luray, Va.: Hurst & Co., 1901–1902, 8 vols., supp., index.

In his preface, Hurst states that this work was prepared because the Virginia Reports had swelled to 92 volumes and it was inconvenient to first search in an index and then the reports. Volume 1, pages 1–81, provides a history of the Supreme Court of Appeals of Virginia, law reporting in the state, and biographical sketches of the judges of the Courts of Appeals from 1779 to 1897. Formatted with general headings and subheadings, the cases are arranged chronologically. Volume 2 is formatted with subheadings and paragraphs with catchlines printed in bold faced type "so as to readily catch the eye." Volume three includes a memorial to the Honorable Randal M. Brown (1846–1898), judge of the Fifteenth Judicial Circuit of Virginia, who assisted Hurst with volumes 1 and 2. Brown died during the creation of volume three. Between volumes 2 and 3, Hurst published *A Complete Criminal Digest* and apologized for the third volume's delay. Upon recommendations of the *Virginia Law Register*, volume 4 provides one principal case with similar cases digested in a note immediately following. In the 1902 supplement, Hurst planned to provide another supplement in 1910 but never did.

Hurst, Sam[uel] N[eed]. *A Complete Encyclopedia of Virginia Law*. Pulaski and Richmond: Hurst & Co., 1922, 2 vols.

The compiler considers his work the first encyclopedia of Virginia law. Asserting the work was influenced by Minor's *Institutes* and the style of the *American and English Encyclopedia of Laws*, the format is alphabetical, providing a general definition and subtopic index of statutory and common law. Despite Hurst's claim that this work is an encyclopedia, the work more closely resembles a digest of statutory law.

Hurst, Sam[uel] N[eed]. *Index and Directory of Virginia Law.* Pulaski, Va.: Hurst & Co., 1914.

> This work indexes, alphabetically, the *Virginia Law Register,* vols. 1–19; Codes of Virginia of 1887 and of 1914; and the Constitution of Virginia. Further, the work provides a directory of annotations in the "Trinity Series," *L.R.A., Virginia Reports Annotated,* and *Virginia Law Register* and, it includes Rules of Practice, Canons of Ethics, Court Calendar, and an Official Directory.

Index of Acts of the General Assembly of the Commonwealth of Virginia. Richmond: Dept. of Purchases & Supply, 1959–1990, 7 vols.

> These seven volumes are cumulative indexes to the *Acts of Assembly* for the years covered by each volume. The first volume begins with the year 1912, and thus these volumes continue Williams's *Index to Enrolled Bills* up to the present.

Johnson, Chapman, and Robert G[ourmain] Scott. *Revision and Digest of the Criminal Code of Virginia.* Richmond: Shepherd & Colin, 1846.

> As a result of thirty sessions of the General Assembly since Joseph Tate's second edition of *Digest of the Laws of Virginia* in 1841, the General Assembly, by acts in 1834, 1836, 1841, and 1846, appointed Johnson (1779–1849) and Scott (1794–1869) to revise and digest the criminal code. Johnson worked on the revision from 1836 to 1841, but was prevented from completing the revision because of ill health and other causes. His work was delivered in 1846 to Scott, who then completed the revision that same year.

Jones, Anna L. *An Abridgment of the Virginia Laws Concerning Education.* Lynchburg: J. P. Bell Co., 1915.

Jones, John Paul. *Digest [of] Case Decisions By the Virginia Commissioner of Motor Vehicles Under the Virginia Vehicle Dealer Licensing Act.* Richmond: Virginia Bar Association, 1987.

> The compiler is a professor of law at the University of Richmond. This looseleaf publication, a project of the Administrative Law Committee of the Virginia Bar Association, digests key abstracts and summarizes case decisions under the Virginia Motor Vehicle Dealer Licensing

Act, Virginia Code, §§ 46.1-515 to 46.1-550.5. The Act regulates relationships between motor vehicle manufacturers or distributors and their dealers in Virginia.

Lamb, James C[hristian]. *Fraudulent Conveyances: A Collection of the Virginia Decisions*. Richmond: Ware, Duke & Taylor, 1890.

This is a seventeen-page pamphlet summarizing the cases on fraudulent conveyances.

The Law Digest. Richmond: Office of the Attorney General, May 1987 to present.

This is a monthly newsletter and digest of the official opinions of the Attorney General of Virginia. It replaced *The Civil Digest* and *The Criminal Law Digest*.

Lee, Howard B[urton]. *The Criminal Trial in the Virginias*. Charleston, W. Va.: Jarrett Printing Co., 1926; 2d ed., Charlottesville: The Michie Co., 1940, 2 vols.

The first edition was written while Lee (b. 1879) was serving as the Attorney General of West Virginia. Although the format is not alphabetical, the work is arranged with bold faced print and appears to follow the Virginia Code. The arrangement encapsulates statutory law and then provides case expositions. The first edition is composed of thirty-two chapters. Reflecting the restraints of Prohibition, one chapter addresses "Moonshine Stills." The second edition was published because West Virginia had adopted a new code and Virginia had significantly amended its code. The two volumes of the second edition are formatted into thirty-nine chapters, minus the chapter on Moonshine Stills, but adding topics such as Indictment, Appellate Jurisdiction, and Dying Declarations.

Lovell, John Terrill. *Index to the Acts of the General Assembly of Virginia, of a General Nature, Passed Since the Code of 1873*. Front Royal: Warren Sentinel, 1883.

This pamphlet consists of 32 pages, including the title page. The work is formatted alphabetically, listing chronologically the acts following the general topic heading. Lovell (1832–1900) was a member of the Front Royal bar.

Martin, William B[ruce]. *An Index to the Virginia Reports.* Richmond: J. W. Randolph & English, 1881; 2d ed., Richmond: J. W. Randolph & English, 1889; 3d ed., Richmond: J. W. Randolph & English, 1896; 4th ed., Richmond: J. P. Bell, 1901; 5th ed., Richmond: J. P. Bell, 1903.

> The first edition indexes Virginia Reports from Jefferson to 33rd Grattan. The second edition, a continuation of the first edition, indexes Virginia Reports from volumes 75 to 84. The third edition indexes Virginia Reports from Jefferson to volume 91 of the Virginia Reports. Alphabetically indexing the reported decisions of Virginia's Supreme Court of Appeals, the General Court, and the High Court of Chancery, the first editions index the decisions of the Special Court of Appeals reported in the two volumes of reports by John Mercer Patton, Jr., and Roscoe Briggs Heath. In the prefaces to the first and third editions, Martin states, "[t]his is an index, not a digest." In the third edition, published five years after writing the preface, Martin states that he had been unable to compile a Table of Cases because of illness. Instead, Richard McIlwaine, Jr., of the Norfolk Bar, compiled the Table of Cases. William B. Martin (1846–1921) practiced law in Norfolk and was later judge of the Court of Law and Chancery of the City of Norfolk.

Matthews, James M[uscoe]. *Digest of the Laws of Virginia of a Civil Nature.* Richmond: J. W. Randolph, 1856, 1857, 2 vols.

> This work is formatted alphabetically into sixty-eight chapters. Volume 1 includes "A to E" and volume 2 "E to W." The second volume was published within months of the first volume. The work references the corresponding chapter of the Code of 1849 and is a detailed digest of statutory law, followed by case law exposition in footnotes. Addressing topics such as Aliens & Indians, Bastards, Attorneys at Law, County Roads and Bridges, Courthouses, Clerk's Offices and Jails, the work reflects the needs of rural attorneys and court officials regarding law reference materials. The work was favorably reviewed in *Quarterly Law Journal*, vol. 1, pp. 75–76, 189–190 (1856).

Matthews, James M[uscoe]. *Digest of the Laws of Virginia of a Criminal Nature.* Richmond: West & Johnston, 1861; 2d ed., Richmond: J. W. Randolph & English, 1871; supp., Richmond: J. W. Randolph & English, 1878; 3d ed., Richmond: J. W. Randolph & English, 1890.

> The first and second editions are formatted alphabetically,

referencing the corresponding chapter of the Code of 1849. The digest first addresses statutory law and illustrates with case expositions in footnotes. The second edition was published because the supply of copies of the first edition was destroyed by the great conflagration in Richmond in April 1865, at the close of the Civil War. An Addendum, at the end of the work, encompasses the Acts of 1870–1871. The third edition is not alphabetized as the format corresponds directly to the criminal part of the Code of 1887. During the Civil War, Matthews (1822–1905) compiled annual editions of *Private Laws of the Confederate States of America* pertaining to the most recently passed laws; these works were published in Richmond by R. M. Smith.

Mercer, John. *A Continuation of the Abridgment of All the Public Acts of Assembly of Virginia.* Williamsburg: William Parks, 1739.

This work continues the 1737 edition of *An Exact Abridgment of All the Public Acts of Assembly of Virginia in Force and Use.*

Mercer, John. *An Exact Abridgment of All the Public Acts of Assembly of Virginia in Force and Use.* Williamsburg: William Parks, 1737; 2d ed., Glasgow: Bryce and Paterson, 1759.

The first edition is the fourth earliest abridgment of Virginia laws. Both editions are alphabetical in format. The second edition consists of all the public acts in force on January 1, 1758.

Meredith, Wyndham Robertson. *Digest of Acts and Extracts from Acts in Relation to the Public Debt of Virginia, with References to, and a List of Decisions Thereon.* Richmond: Goode, 1886.

Published by the Sinking Fund Commissioners, the work consists of 147 pages. Although arranged alphabetically, the format does not lend itself to easy reference. Cases regarding the public debt of Virginia are listed at the back of the book.

Michie, A[ddinell] Hewson. *Michie's Digest of Virginia and West Virginia Reports.* Charlottesville: The Michie Co., 1929–1938, 11 vols., 2 supps.

Indexed by Thomas Johnson Michie (1867–1938), unlike *Michie's Encyclopedic Digest, Michie's Digest* includes federal cases decided pursuant to the laws of Virginia and West

> Virginia. It is formatted much like Michie's earlier *Encyclopedic Digest*; the preface refers to the work as an encyclopedia and digest because of its organization of principle, illustration, and case law. The work digests, alphabetically, case law up to and including volume 151 of the *Virginia Reports*; volume 105 of the *West Virginia Reports*; and, volume 22 of the *Federal Reporter, Second Series*.

Michie, A[ddinell] Hewson. *Michie's Digest of Virginia and West Virginia Reports: Permanent Supplement*. Charlottesville: The Michie Co., 1941–1943, 6 vols.

> A continuation of *Michie's Digest*, this work was supplemented with pocket parts until 1952. Unlike *Michie's Digest*, however, volume 1 thanks the West Publishing Company for permission to use copyrighted headnotes appearing in the National Reporter System. Formatted alphabetically, the work provides brief paraphrases of law as decided in Virginia and West Virginia courts.

Michie, Thomas Johnson. *An Index-Digest to Volumes 92 to 99 of Virginia Reports and Volumes 1 and 2 of Virginia Decisions*. Charlottesville: The Michie Co., 1902.

> Originally undertaken to aid his assistants and himself in preparing annotations for *Virginia Reports, Annotated*, which was then passing through the press, Michie decided to make an index-digest to the volumes of *Virginia Reports* and *Virginia Decisions* not already digested by others. The format is arranged alphabetically, with bold faced general topics followed by subtopics that provide a catchline and applicable case.

Michie, Thomas Johnson. *The Encyclopedic Digest of Virginia and West Virginia Reports*. Charlottesville: The Michie Co., 1905–1919, 17 vols.; table of cases; cumulative supplement; Charlottesville: The Michie Co., 1922–1923, 6 vols.; supp., 1925, 2 vols.; supp., 1927; supp., table of cases, 1928.

> A. Hewson Michie (1897–1957) assisted with the 1925 supplement and was later the editorial supervisor of *Michie's Digest of Virginia and West Virginia Reports*.

Michie's Jurisprudence of Virginia and West Virginia. Charlottesville: The Michie Co., 1948 to present.

Undoubtedly referring to *Michie's Digest*, the preface to volume 1 states the work "is a completely new publication." The Michie Company believed the digest format no longer met the needs of the law professional. Consequently, the compilers assert that the work evaluates and comments on cases and statutes, points out and resolves conflicts, and provides reference to law review articles, legal periodicals, and textbooks. Formatted alphabetically and regularly updated, the work is an encyclopedia of Virginia and West Virginia law. There are several volumes of apparatus: a subject index, a table of cases cited, a citator, and words and phrases judicially defined. The first Editorial Supervisor was George P. Smith, Jr., with Consulting Editors, Prof. Garrard Glenn (1878–1949) and Kenneth Redden. The work is dedicated to the memory of Thomas Johnson Michie, III (1867–1938), a founder of the Michie Publishing Company.

Minor, Lucian. *Reports of Cases*. Richmond: A. Morris, 1857.

All the cases reported by Hening and Munford are condensed and annotated. Even though it was favorably reviewed in *Quarterly Law Journal*, vol. 1, pp. 190–192 (1856), the remaining volumes in the proposed series were never made. Condensed reports are unsound in concept and unsuccessful in practice, and this volume was not well received by the bar. C. C. Soule, *The Lawyer's Reference Manual*, p. 61 (1883).

Munford, William. *A General Index to the Virginian Law Authorities*. Richmond: Warrock, 1819.

Although William Munford (1775–1825) labels his work a general index or abridgment, the work functions and is arranged more like a digest than an index. Formatted alphabetically, with general headings and numbered paragraphs containing case exposition, the book digests reports from Washington to Munford. He intended to compile another digest but apparently did not do so.

Muse, William Taylor. *Virginia Annotations to the Restatement of the Law of Torts*. St. Paul, Minn.: A.L.I., 1944.

Patton, John M[ercer], Jr., and Roscoe B[riggs] Heath. *A General Index to Grattan's Reports, from Second to Eleventh Volume Inclusive*. Richmond: Geo. M. West, 1856.

This index was issued with and as a part of the first volume of

> Patton and Heath's *Reports*. It is sometimes found bound with it, sometimes not.

Rashkind, Alan Brody, and Gerard P. Rowe. *Virginia Insurance Case Finder*. Charlottesville: The Michie Co., 1994.

> This digest of cases on insurance law includes cases from the Supreme Court of Virginia since 1925 and from the United States Court of Appeals for the Fourth Circuit since 1965. There is an index and a table of cases.

Renehan, James J[oseph]. *Virginia Legal Deskbook: The Common Sense Approach*. Richmond: Common Sense, Inc., 1991 to present.

> This annual publication contains an index to statutory law arranged alphabetically, based upon common name usage of the particular law. The work also includes reference tables and directories to penalties, courts, government offices, and law libraries.

Roche, Brien A. *Virginia Domestic Relations Case Finder*. Charlottesville: The Michie Co., 1986, supp.; 2d ed., Charlottesville: The Michie Co., 1991; 3d ed., Charlottesville: The Michie Co., 1996.

> Although not arranged alphabetically, the format first articulates statutory law and follows with brief expositions of applicable appellate case law, beginning with the most recent case. The first edition, arranged into eight chapters, contains a 1990 supplementary pocket part. Roche is a member of the Virginia and District of Columbia Bars.

Roche, Brien A. *Virginia Torts Case Finder*. Charlottesville: The Michie Co., 1984; 2d ed., Charlottesville: The Michie Co., 1990; 3d ed., Charlottesville: The Michie Co., 1994; 4th ed. Charlottesville: Lexis Law Publishing, 1999.

> Although not arranged alphabetically, the format articulates statutory law and follows with case expositions, and contains twenty-two chapters that encapsulate, in detail, relevant legal principles ranging from Pedestrians to Products Liability to Damages to Defenses. The work includes only appellate court cases. There are annual pocket supplements.

Royall, William L[awrence]. *A Digest of the Decisions of the Supreme Court of Appeals of Virginia Contained in Grattan's Reports,*

Vols. I to XXI. New York: Diossy & Co., 1873.

Formatted alphabetically, Royall (1844–1912) used "particular" and "general" headings. In 1873, General Bradley T. Johnson (1829–1903) invited Royall to become his law partner, and Royall dedicated this book to him. He planned to do another volume but did not do so.

Sams, C[onway] Whittle. *A Brief Comparison of the Most Important Statutes of the Codes of Virginia of 1873 and 1887.* Richmond: West, Johnston & Co., J. W. Randolph & English, 1888.

The work compares selected statutes of the new Code of 1887 with the former Code of 1873, placing special emphasis on those statutes referred to in Minor's *Institutes of Common and Statute Law*. The format is not alphabetized and corresponds, topically, to the Code of 1887. Substantively, the work is more than an index but less than a digest. There is an index at the end of the book.

Shepard's Virginia Case Names Citator. Colorado Springs: Shepard's/McGraw-Hill, Inc., 1985 to present.

This is a name index of Virginia Supreme Court cases from 1920 to 1985.

Shepard's Virginia Citations. Colorado Springs: Shepard's/McGraw-Hill, Inc., 1900 to present.

Functioning as an index to later citations to a particular case or statute, this work is arranged according to the volume and page number of the reporter in which the case appears and according to sections of the *Code of Virginia*. There are permanent hard bound volumes and monthly supplementary pamphlets. The predecessor to this series was a system of gummed labels that were published as early as 1892; the gummed labels were replaced in 1900 with the book form of the citator.

Sketches of the Acts and Joint Resolutions of the General Assembly of Virginia, 1859–60. N.p., n.d.

A copy is bound with volume one of *Quarterly Law Review* in the Virginia State Law Library.

Sweeny, Peter M. *Virginia Workers' Compensation Case Finder*. Charlottesville: The Michie Co., 1990; 2d ed., Charlottesville: Lexis Law Publishing, 1998.

> This work is kept up to date by means of pocket supplements.

Swem, Earl Gregg. *Virginia Historical Index*. Roanoke: Stone, 1934–36, 2 vols.; rept. Gloucester, Mass.: Peter Smith, 1965, 2 vols.

> This work indexes W. W. Hening's *Statutes at Large of Virginia*, the *Calendar of Virginia State Papers*, and various history journals.

Tate, Benjamin. *An Analytical Digested Index of the Reported Cases of the Court of Appeals and General Court of Virginia; From Washington to Second Grattan, Inclusive*. Richmond: Drinker & Morris, 1847, 2 vols.

> This work digests forty-three volumes of reports of cases decided by the Court of Appeals and the General Court of Virginia. Tate distinguishes his work from those of Everard Hall and William Munford in that this "digested index," although formatted alphabetically, does not cross-reference within the work. Volume one covers "A–M" and volume two "N–W." In 1855, William Green (1806–1880), the well-known legal scholar and practitioner at the bar, wrote to J. W. Randolph (1815–1893) calling Tate's digested index "a book of *less* than no value at all."

Tate, Joseph, *A Digest of the Laws of Virginia, Which Are of a Permanent Character and General Operation; Illustrated by Judicial Decisions: To Which Is Added, An Index of the Names of the Cases in the Virginia Reporters*. Richmond: Shepherd & Pollard, 1823; 2d ed., Richmond: Smith & Palmer, 1841.

> The work's first edition digests the *Revised Code of 1819*. The second edition encompasses the subsequent amendments and alterations to the *Revised Code of 1819*, and most decisions in the ninth volume of Leigh's *Reports*. The second edition was published posthumously. In both editions, the alphabetical format digests statutes and then footnotes applicable cases. The work includes a Table of Cases and Index to Names of the Cases used within the digest.

Torrence, [William] Clayton. *Virginia Wills and Administrations*

1632–1800 An Index. Richmond: William Byrd Pr., 1931; rept. Baltimore: Genealogical Pub. Co., 1965, 1972, 1977, 1978.

> This is an index of wills and inventories of decedents' estates recorded in Virginia local courts. This book was compiled by Torrence (1884–1953), a noted librarian and genealogist, to aid historical research.

Tyler, D[avid] Gardiner, Jr. *Index to the Opinions of the Attorney General of Virginia Included in the Annual Reports July 1, 1930 [to] June 30, 1947.* Richmond: Div. of Purchase and Printing, 1949.

> Tyler was Assistant Attorney General of Virginia.

Virginia and West Virginia Digest. St. Paul, Minn.: West Publishing Co., 1943 to present.

> This work digests, alphabetically, cases within Virginia Reports, West Virginia Reports and the South Eastern Reporter as well as Virginia and West Virginia cases decided in the Supreme Court of the United States, Circuit Courts of Appeals, and Federal District Courts.

Virginia Code Research Guide. Rochester, N.Y.: Lawyers Co-operative Pub. Co., 1989.

> This is an index to citations to Virginia statutory law in the various publications of the Lawyers Co-operative Publishing Co. It is updated by pocket supplements.

Virginia Law Review Cumulative Index. Charlottesville: Virginia Law Review Ass'n, 1934, 1948, 1957, 1967.

> These four volumes index the first fifty volumes of the *Virginia Law Review*. This law journal is also indexed by the *Index to Legal Periodicals.*

The Virginia Lawyers Weekly Research Library. Richmond: Va. Lawyers Weekly, 1990 to date.

Vol. 1: Bankruptcy
Vol. 2: Business
Vol. 3: Criminal
Vol. 4: Employment
Vol. 5: Family Law

Vol. 6: Litigation
Vol. 7: Municipal & Administrative
Vol. 8: Real Estate & Property
Vol. 9: Trial Reports
Vol. 10: Workers' Compensation

These are subject digests of Virginia cases from all levels of courts. Each volume has its own subject index and index of cases. These digests are reprinted from the *Virginia Lawyers Weekly*. It is a looseleaf service that is supplemented twice a year.

The Virginia Prosecutor. Richmond: Office of the Attorney General, Dec. 1971 to present.

This is a monthly digest of criminal opinions issued by the Attorney General of Virginia.

The Virginia Researcher. Charlottesville: National Legal Research Group, 1970–1988, 7 vols.

This was a monthly looseleaf publication that digested recent Virginia case law of the Supreme Court of Virginia, Court of Appeals of Virginia, U.S. Fourth Circuit Court of Appeals, and the U.S. District Courts of Virginia. The format digested case law according to the appropriate court. Within the digest of each court, headings are alphabetized, followed by the case digested.

Watts, M[aury] B[aldwin]. *Virginia Law Digest*. Richmond: M. B. Watts, Jan. 1928 to Dec. 1933, 6 vols.

This is a brief digest of the decisions of the Virginia Supreme Court of Appeals and the Special Court of Appeals published monthly under the auspices of the Virginia State Bar Association.

Williams, John W[illiam]. *Index to Enrolled Bills of the General Assembly of Virginia, 1776 to 1862, Original Parchments*. Richmond: Davis Bottom, 1908.

Williams (1869–1934) was the Clerk of the House of Delegates and Keeper of the Rolls. The original laws were enrolled upon single sheets of parchment and rolled into bundles and placed in tin tubes for preservation. In 1906, the General Assembly directed that they be properly analyzed, cleaned, bound, labeled and indexed.

Williams, John W[illiam]. *Index to Enrolled Bills of the General Assembly of Virginia, 1776 to 1910.* Richmond: Davis Bottom, 1911.

Workers' Compensation Commission of Virginia. *Cumulative Index-Digest, Volumes 65–71 (1989–1992).* Richmond: Workers' Compensation Commission, [1993].

> This is volume 72 of the *Opinions of the Workers' Compensation Commission.*

Young, John Hardin, Myron H. Bright, Ronald L. Carlson. *Virginia Objections at Trial.* Clearwater, Fla.: Butterworth, 1993; 2d ed. by John Hardin Young, Kenneth W. Curtis, Myron H. Bright, Ronald L. Carlson, [Charlottesville]: Lexis Law Publishing, 1998.

II. *General Digests and Indexes Containing References to Virginia Law*

An Abridgement of the Laws in Force and Use in Her Majesty's Plantations of Virginia, Jamaica, Barbadoes, Maryland, New-England, New-York, Carolina, &c. London: John Nicholson, 1704.

> This work is the second earliest abridgment of Virginia laws. The portion relating to Virginia contains eighty-six pages. Printed for John Nicholson, the work alphabetically digests the law under general headings. Entries under each heading are arranged in chronological order, noting first the year of the law's enactment, followed by a brief paraphrase of the law. This work is arranged in a similar format to Virginia's earliest abridgment, "An Abridgment of the Laws of Virginia," compiled in 1694.

American Digest. St. Paul, Minn.: West Publishing Co., 1888 to present.

> This work is an annual volume prepared by the editorial staff of the National Reporter System, which digests all decisions of the U.S. Supreme Court, U.S. circuit and district courts, and courts of last resort of all states and territories, as reported in the National Reporter System. Between 1897 and 1908, the name changed from *The American Digest* to *American Digest Continuations.* Between 1908 and 1917, the name changed to *American Digest, Key-Number System.* Between 1917 and 1928, the name changed to *Current Digest.* Between 1928 and 1937, the name changed to *General Digest,*

the present title of the work. Every ten years, the *General Digest* for that time period is compiled into the *Decennial Digests.*

Browne, Irving. *Digest of Decisions of the Courts of Last Resort of the Several States Contained in the American Reports for Volumes XXV to XLVIII, Inclusive.* San Francisco: Bancroft-Whitney, 1885.

This is a digest of the *American Reports,* a sixty-volume, national compilation that includes selected Virginia cases. The preface states that "[s]ome books are to be tasted; others to be swallowed and some few to be chewed and *digested.*"

Browne, Irving. *Index-Digest of the American Reports, Volumes 49 to 60, Inclusive.* San Francisco: Bancroft-Whitney, 1888.

This work indexes the final eleven volumes of the *American Reports.* Unlike his earlier digest, this work lacks exposition of case law, and is printed on considerably thicker paper. The work includes a table of cases to volumes 1 to 60.

Brunner, Albert J. *Digest of the Cases Reported in the American Decisions and the Editor's Notes Thereto, From Volume Sixty-One to One Hundred.* San Francisco: Bancroft-Whitney, 1888, vol. 3.

This is a digest of the *American Decisions,* a one-hundred-volume, national compilation that includes selected Virginia cases. Volumes 1 and 2 of the digest were compiled by A. C. Freeman.

Catterall, Helen Honor Tunnicliff. *Judicial Cases Concerning American Slavery and the Negro.* Washington, D.C.: Carnegie Inst., 1926-1937, 5 vols.; rept. New York: Octagon, 1968, 5 vols.

Virginia cases are digested in vol. 1, pp. 76-265.

Century Edition of The American Digest. St. Paul, Minn.: West Publishing Co., 1897–1904, 50 vols.

This work is a complete digest of all reported American cases from the earliest times to 1896; it adopts the digesting system developed in the first ten volumes of *The American Digest.*

Church, W. S. *Digest of the Decisions of the Courts of Last Resort of the Several States, From the Year 1892 to the Year 1896 Contained in the American State Reports, Volumes 25 to 48, Inclusive.* San

Francisco: Bancroft-Whitney, 1896.

> Generally known as *Church's Digest*, this work digests volumes 25 to 48 of the *American State Reports*, a 140-volume, national compilation that includes selected Virginia cases. The work was styled after *Rapalje's Digest*.

Decennial Edition of The American Digest: 1897 to 1906. St. Paul, Minn.: West Publishing Co., 1908, 25 vols.

> The first of the *Decennial Digests*, this work is a complete digest of all decisions of the state and federal courts as reported in the National Reporter System and the state reports during the period 1897 to 1906. The *Tenth Decennial Digest* is the current work.

Eighth Decennial Digest, American Digest System: 1966 to 1976. St. Paul, Minn.: West Publishing Co., 1977–1979, 50 vols.

> This work is a complete digest of all decisions of the state and federal courts as reported in the National Reporter System and the state reports during the period 1966 to 1976. The *Tenth Decennial Digest* is the current work.

Fifth Decennial Digest, American Digest System: 1936 to 1946. St. Paul, Minn.: West Publishing Co., 1947–1950, 52 vols.

> A complete digest of all decisions of the state and federal courts as reported in the National Reporter System and the state reports during the period 1936 to 1946. The *Tenth Decennial Digest* is the current work.

Fourth Decennial Digest, American Digest System: 1926 to 1936. St. Paul, Minn.: West Publishing Co., 1937–1938, 34 vols.

> A complete digest of all decisions of the state and federal courts as reported in the National Reporter System and the state reports during the period 1926 to 1936. The *Tenth Decennial Digest* is the current work.

Freeman, A. C. *Digest of American Decisions and Index to the Notes Thereto*. San Francisco: A. L. Bancroft, 1882–1885, 2 vols.

> This work digests volumes 1 to 30 and 31 to 60 of the *American Decisions*, a one-hundred-volume, national compil-

ation that includes selected Virginia cases. Volume 3 of the digest, compiled by A. J. Brunner, digests volumes 61 to 100.

Freeman, A. C. *Index to the American Decisions: Volumes One to Twenty Inclusive, 1760 to 1830*. San Francisco: A. L. Bancroft, 1880.

This work is an Index and Table of Cases in volumes 1 to 20 of the *American Decisions*.

Green, Edmund Samson. *Digest of the Decisions of the Courts of Last Resort of the Several States, From the Year 1887 to the Year 1904 Contained in the American State Reports, Volumes 1 to 96, Inclusive*. Vols. 1–3, San Francisco: Bancroft-Whitney, 1904, supp. (vol. 4), Bancroft-Whitney, 1909, supp. (vol. 5), Bancroft-Whitney, 1912, 5 vols.

This work is generally known as *Green's Digest*. Although W. Mack, W. S. Church, and E. Magee had already digested volumes 1 to 72, Green digests the complete 140 volumes of *American State Reports*, a national compilation that includes selected Virginia cases.

Mack, William. *Digest of the Decisions of the Courts of Last Resort of the Several States, From the Year 1887 to the Year 1892 Contained in the American State Reports, Volumes 1 to 24, Inclusive*. San Francisco: Bancroft-Whitney, 1892.

This work digests volumes 1 to 24 of the *American State Reports*, a 140-volume, national compilation that includes selected Virginia cases. The work is styled after *Rapalje's Digest*.

Magee, E. De Los. *Digest of the Decisions of the Courts of Last Resort of the Several States, From the Year 1896 to the Year 1900 Contained in the American State Reports, Volumes 49 to 72, Inclusive*. San Francisco: Bancroft-Whitney, 1900.

This work digests volumes 49 to 72 of the *American State Reports*, a 140-volume, national compilation that includes selected Virginia cases. The work is styled after *Rapalje's Digest*.

Ninth Decennial Digest, American Digest System: Part One, 1976 to 1981, Part Two, 1981 to 1986. St. Paul, Minn.: West Publishing Co., 1982–1988, 85 vols.

Part One consists of thirty-eight volumes. Part Two consists of forty-seven volumes. This work is a complete digest of all decisions of the state and federal courts as reported in the National Reporter System and the state reports during the period 1976 to 1986. The *Tenth Decennial Digest* is the current work.

Rapalje, Stewart. *Digest of the Decisions of the Courts of Last Resort of the Several States for the Earliest Period to the Year 1888 Contained in the One Hundred and Sixty Volumes of The American Decisions and the American Reports.* San Francisco: Bancroft-Whitney, 1891, 3 vols.

This work digests the 160 volumes of *American Reports* and *American Decisions* into one work.

Second Decennial Edition of The American Digest: 1906 to 1916. St. Paul, Minn.: West Publishing Co., 1917–1923, 24 vols.

This is a complete digest of all decisions of the state and federal courts as reported in the National Reporter System and the state reports during the period 1906 to 1916. The *Tenth Decennial Digest* is the current work.

Seventh Decennial Digest, American Digest System: 1956 to 1966. St. Paul, Minn.: West Publishing Co., 1967–1968, 38 vols.

This is a complete digest of all decisions of the state and federal courts as reported in the National Reporter System and the state reports during the period 1956 to 1966. The *Tenth Decennial Digest* is the current work.

Shepard's Southeastern Reporter Citations. Colorado Springs: Shepard's/McGraw-Hill, 1921 to present.

This citator analyzes all of the Virginia cases that are printed in the *Southeastern Reporter*.

Sixth Decennial Digest, American Digest System: 1946 to 1956. St. Paul, Minn.: West Publishing Co., 1957–1958, 36 vols.

This is a complete digest of all decisions of the state and federal courts as reported in the National Reporter System and the state reports during the period 1946 to 1956. The *Tenth Decennial Digest* is the current work.

South Eastern Digest. St. Paul, Minn.: West Publishing Co., 1935 to present.

This digest covers all cases reported in *Virginia Reports, South Eastern Reporter*, and various reports of the states of the upper South from earliest times. Arranged alphabetically, this work is supplemented with cumulative pocket service.

Table of Cases and Index to the Notes in the 160 Volumes of American Decisions and American Reports. San Francisco: Bancroft-Whitney, 1888.

This work was compiled and sent to owners of the *American Decisions* and *American Reports* with the compliments of the publisher as a forerunner of *Rapalje's Digest*.

Tenth Decennial Digest, American Digest System: Part One, 1986 to 1991, Part Two, 1991 to 1996. St. Paul, Minn.: West Publishing Co., 1992 to present.

Part One consists of twenty-three volumes. Currently in progress, this work will be a complete digest of all decisions of the state and federal courts as reported in the National Reporter System and the state reports during the period 1992 to 2002.

Third Decennial Edition of The American Digest: 1916 to 1926. St. Paul, Minn.: West Publishing Co., 1928–1929, 28 vols.

This is a complete digest of all decisions of the state and federal courts as reported in the National Reporter System and the state reports during the period 1916 to 1926. The *Tenth Decennial Digest* is the current work. Perhaps because of the stock market crash, there was a five year interval between this publication and the *Second Decennial Edition of The American Digest: 1906 to 1916*.

Thompson, Isaac Grant. *Digest of Decisions of the Courts of Last Resort of the Several States Contained in the American Reports for Volumes I to XXIV, Inclusive*. San Francisco: Bancroft-Whitney, 1879.

This work digests the first twenty-four volumes of the *American Reports*, a sixty-volume, national compilation, that includes selected Virginia cases.

FORM BOOKS

W. H. Bryson

THE IMPORTANCE and usefulness of legal form books and of legal forms in general is often overlooked by legal scholars. However, the legal practitioner is keenly aware of their utility and practical significance. But what practitioners as well as the academic lawyers too often take for granted is the legal acumen and experience behind a successful, effective, and valid legal form. A good legal form must take the existing law and rephrase it into a practical document that accomplishes the client's goal. Drafting a good form is as difficult as drafting a statute. This is so because a legal form must anticipate future possibilities and problems as well as account for the present state of the law. The quality of a legal form depends upon the legal skill of the person who made it.

One can set out to create a general or generic document to be used as a form for future cases. However, most persons will start with a document that was created for a particular client and alter it to suit the needs of a later client, thus using the earlier as the form for the later. Where the earlier one has proved successful in court, then it can be presented as a judicially-approved precedent.[1] Thus, while the accepted document, the form, must be altered to suit the new need, the fewer the alterations the better, because the more that is retained, the closer it will be to the legal precedent. This leads to ultra-conservatism in the modernizing and redrafting of forms. Of course, forms need to be updated to reflect changes in the law. However, changes that are not so dictated are to be avoided in order to continue the precedential value of the form as far as possible. Thus archaic words continue in forms lest they have some meaning or purpose not readily apparent to the would-be revisor. The practicing attorney will not stray from an old form without some good reason lest the client suffer some unforeseen consequence. There might be some good reason for the language that might appear to be clumsy, archaic, or tautologous. Perhaps the words give, devise, and bequeath are not perfect synonyms. Why risk malpractice to make a legal document read better? "If it ain't broke, don't fix it."

Forms and form books are also created in a more abstract way

[1] Appellate court opinions frequently approve or disapprove jury instructions; the ones that are approved then get copied into the commercial form books.

by law writers and commercial law publishers. Individual forms[2] and books of legal forms are available for wills, contracts, conveyances, commercial documents, pleadings, interrogatories, and many other instruments.

Forms thus created then get collected and published in a variety of places. They may be interspersed in the text of a treatise. The first book on English law, Ranulf de Glanvill's *Tractatus de Legibus* (c. 1188) included numerous forms for writs and process, and prepared forms have been published in Anglo-American legal literature ever since.[3] They have appeared, and still appear, as separate pre-printed forms, as incorporated in the body of treatises,[4] as appendices to treatises, and as free-standing books of forms. Today there are many collections of legal forms that are published in computer-readable formats that can be easily retrieved and edited for the particular occasion of need and then printed out "in hard copy."[5] However, it is still useful also to have a printed book version of the forms in order to know which form to retrieve from the machine; this is because the form books have indexes.

A form that has been judicially approved, as have many jury instructions and insurance contract clauses, will have the weight of authority. However, a legal form that has been suggested[6] or mandated by statute[7] or by rule of court,[8] and there are many, cannot be ignored.

This bibliography lists only books of forms that relate exclusively to Virginia law. Furthermore, it does not include books that are treatises with forms interspersed in the text or books with forms added as appendices.[9]

---

[2] Standard forms for leases, other conveyances, powers of attorney, wills, and notes, for example, can be bought in many stationery shops and office supply stores. Printed blank checks supplied by banks are legal forms.

[3] E. C. Surrency, *History of American Law Publishing*, pp. 138-141 (1990).

[4] E.g. G. Webb, *Justice of Peace* (1736), the first legal treatise printed in Virginia.

[5] E.g. J. P. Harris, *Virginia Personal Injury Forms* (1994).

[6] E.g. *Virginia Model Jury Instructions*, which was composed by a committee of judicial, practicing, and academic lawyers.

[7] E.g. Garnishment Summons, Va. Code Ann. § 8.01-512.3.

[8] E.g. Praecipe, Va. Rule 1:15(b) App.; Subpoena, Va. Rule 2:4; Proof of Service, Va. Rule 2:5.

[9] See the articles on "Criminal Law Books" and "Law Treatises."

John B. Dabney.— 14th May. 1817

THE

NEW AMERICAN

CLERK'S MAGAZINE,

AND

YOUNG CONVEYANCER'S

POCKET COMPANION,

CONTAINING

ALL THE NECESSARY FORMS OF

ARTICLES OF AGREEMENT,
BONDS,
BILLS,
RECOGNISANCES,
LEASES AND RELEASES,
LETTERS OR POWERS OF ATTORNEY,
LETTERS OF LICENSE,
AWARDS,
BILLS OF SALE,
GIFTS,
GRANTS,
ASSIGNMENTS,
MORTGAGES,
SURRENDERS,
JOINTURES,
COVENANTS,
COPARTNERSHIPS, &c.

WITH NECESSARY DIRECTIONS FOR

MAKING DISTRESSES FOR RENT, &c.

As the Law between Landlord & Tenant now stands.

THE WHOLE MADE CONFORMABLE TO

THE LAWS OF THE UNITED STATES,

AND ADAPTED, MORE PARTICULARLY TO

THE STATE OF VIRGINIA.

BY A GENTLEMAN OF THE BAR.

ALEXANDRIA.

PRINTED FOR R. GRAY, BY S. SNOWDEN & J. D. SIMMS.

1814.

BIBLIOGRAPHY

Abbott, Earl L[eighton], and Erwin S. Solomon. *Instructions for Virginia and West Virginia.* 2d ed., Charlottesville: The Michie Co., 1962, 3 vols.; 3d ed., Charlottesville: The Michie Co., 1987, 3 vols.

E. L. Abbott (1905-1973) was a circuit court judge from Clifton Forge; E. S. Solomon was a member of the Virginia House of Delegates from Bath County. The first edition of this form book was compiled by H. Casparian. It is kept up to date with cumulative pocket parts.

Bacigal, Ronald J[oseph]. *Virginia Criminal Procedure Forms.* Norcross, Ga.: The Harrison Co., 1984; 2d ed., Norcross, Ga.: The Harrison Co., 1989; 3d ed., Norcross, Ga.: The Harrison Co., 1995; 4th ed., Norcross, Ga.: The Harrison Co., 2000.

R. J. Bacigal is a professor of law at the University of Richmond. This book contains a large number of sample forms pertaining to Virginia criminal procedure. Some of them are official forms, which are provided in printed format by the Office of the Executive Secretary of the Virginia Supreme Court.

Barton, R[obert] T[homas]. *Pleading & Practice in the Courts of Chancery.* 3d ed. by Robert T. Barton, Jr., Charlottesville: The Michie Co., 1926, vol. 2.

Volume 2 is a separate form book which accompanies the third edition of the treatise.

Bowden, Thomas L. *Virginia Legal and Business Forms.* Rochester, N.Y.: Lawyers Cooperative Pub., 1995, 4 vols.

This is a looseleaf publication.

Casparian, Harry. *Instructions: The Law and Approved Forms for Virginia & West Virginia.* Charlottesville: The Michie Co., 1931, 2 vols.

H. Casparian was associate editor-in-chief of the Michie Company. Later editions were edited by Judge Earl L. Abbott, E. S. Solomon, and the editorial staff of the Michie Company.

Doubles, M[alcolm] Ray, Emanuel Emroch, and Robert R[eynold] Merhige, Jr. *Virginia Jury Instructions.* St. Paul, Minn.: West

FORMS OF PLEADINGS

IN

CIVIL AND CRIMINAL CASES,

AND OF

DEEDS, WILLS, &c.,

AND PROCEEDINGS IN BANKRUPTCY.

BY

WILLIAM B. MATTHEWS,

Attorney at Law.

J. W. RANDOLPH & ENGLISH,

1318 MAIN STREET, RICHMOND, VIRGINIA.

1873.

Publishing Co., 1964; 2d ed. by Emanuel Emroch, L. Paul Byrne, and Michael J[oseph] Herbert, St. Paul, Minn.: West Publishing Co., 1990; 3d ed. by Michael J[oseph] Herbert and Ronald J[oseph] Bacigal, St. Paul, Minn.: West Group, 1998.

This collection is kept up to date through annual pocket parts.

Edmonds, John W., III. *Virginia Uniform Commercial Code Forms Annotated.* St. Paul, Minn.: West Publishing Co., 1968, 2 vols.

This form book was kept up to date with annual pocket supplements until 1977.

Gregory, George C[raghead]. *Forms for Virginia and West Virginia.* Albany: J. B. Lyon Co., 1906; 2d ed. by Manley P. Caldwell, Charlottesville: The Michie Co., 1925; 3d ed. by Henry B. Gordon, Charlottesville: The Michie Co., 1935, 3 vols.; 4th ed. by Henry B. Gordon and Stewart McReynolds, Charlottesville: The Michie Co., 1951, 4 vols.

Gregory, George C[raghead]. *Forms of Common Law Declarations for Use in State and Federal Courts.* Albany: J. B. Lyon Co., 1906.

G. C. Gregory (1878-1956) lived in Richmond.

A Handbook of Standard Procedures and Model Orders in Certain Cases for Judges and Clerks of Courts of Record. Richmond: Supreme Court of Virginia, Office of the Executive Secretary, 1966, 1985, 1987.

This looseleaf manual was prepared with the goal of presenting to the trial judges and clerks of courts of record a ready reference to standard procedures in the trial of civil, criminal, and condemnation cases.

Harris, John P., III. *Virginia Personal Injury Forms.* Charlottesville: The Michie Co., 1994.

This book of forms is accompanied by a diskette containing the same forms for easy editing and reproduction.

Hening, William W[aller]. *The American Pleader and Lawyer's Guide.* vol. 1, New York: Isaac Riley, 1811; vol. 2, Richmond: Peter Cottom, 1826.

THE

VIRGINIA SCRIVENER,

BEING A COLLECTION OF FORMS OF

BONDS, CONTRACTS, CONVEYANCING,

AND OTHER INSTRUMENTS OF WRITING,

CAREFULLY SELECTED FROM THE MOST APPROVED AUTHORS, AND ACCOMPANIED BY PLAIN AND WELL ESTABLISHED EXPLANATORY RULES OF LAW:

TOGETHER WITH THE MODE OF AUTHENTICATING DEEDS FOR RECORD IN ALL THE STATES OF THE UNION:

ADAPTED TO THE USE OF THE PEOPLE OF VIRGINIA.

PREPARED BY A GENTLEMAN OF THE BAR OF STAUNTON.

TO WHICH ARE PREFIXED THE

CONSTITUTION OF THE U. STATES,

AND

THE BILL OF RIGHTS,

AND NEW

CONSTITUTION OF VIRGINIA.

KENTON HARPER, PUBLISHER,

STAUNTON, VA.

1833.

Hurst, Sam[uel] N[eed]. *The Virginia Form Book*. Pulaski City, Va.: Hurst & Co., 1905.

S. N. Hurst (b. 1867) was a lawyer, teacher, and preacher in southwest Virginia.

Johnston, Frederick. *A New and Complete Book of Forms: Intended as a Guide to Clerks of Court in Virginia*. Richmond: Whittet & Shepperson, 1887.

F. Johnston (1812-1893) was clerk of the Roanoke County courts.

Matthews, William B[aynham]. *Forms of Pleading in Civil and Criminal Cases and of Deeds, Wills, &c*. Richmond: J. W. Randolph & English, 1873.

W. B. Matthews (1850-1914) was practicing law in Richmond when he compiled this form book; he moved his practice to Washington, D.C., in 1888.

[Michie, Thomas Johnson]. *The Virginia Scrivener*. Staunton: Kenton Harper, 1833.

T. J. Michie (1796-1873), who practiced law in Staunton, compiled this form book for the use of laymen.

The New American Clerk's Magazine, and Young Conveyancer's Pocket Companion . . . Adapted More Particularly to the State of Virginia. Alexandria: R. & J. Gray, 1803; 2d ed., Alexandria: R. Gray, 1814.

[Patteson, W. N.]. *Patteson's Hand Book of Forms*. Wytheville: D. A. St. Clair, 1869.

W. N. Patteson was a practicing attorney in Wytheville when he published this form book.

Phillips, Louis C[harles]. *The Law of Instructions to Juries in Virginia with a Collection of Forms in Civil and Criminal Cases Approved by the Supreme Court of Appeals of Virginia*. Newport News: James E. Abbe, 1908.

L. C. Phillips (1871-1918) was a practicing lawyer in Newport

News. This book was printed in Albany, N.Y., by J. B. Lyon Co.

The Pocket Lawyer, or Self-conveyancer: Containing All the Most Useful Forms. 5th ed., Wheeling, Va.: A. & E. Picket, 1831.

Redden, Kenneth Robert, George P. Smith, Jr., and Vernon Meredith Geddy, Jr. *The Law Student's Form Manual.* Charlottesville: The Michie Co., 1951.

This publication provides the law student with examples of forms that are used daily in the commercial and legal world. This manual is not conclusive and is intended only as a study aid.

Robinson, Conway. *Forms Adapted to the Practice in Virginia.* Vol. 1. Richmond: Shepherd & Colin, 1841.

This volume follows the organization of Conway Robinson's *Practice in the Courts of Law and Equity in Virginia* (1832-1839) and was intended as a form book to accompany that treatise. Only volume 1 of this form book was ever published.

Robinson, John. *A Collection of Forms Used by the Clerks of the Courts of Law and Equity in Virginia.* 2d ed., by Conway Robinson, Richmond: Shepherd & Pollard, 1826.

Conway Robinson (1805-1884) was the son of John Robinson; when this book was published, the son was acting as deputy clerk to his father. This is the second edition to the 1809 collection of forms by John Robinson.

Robinson, John. *A Collection of the Most Useful and Approved Forms of Process, Judgments and Orders Used in the County Courts and Late District Courts of Law in Virginia.* Richmond: Seaton Grantland, 1809.

John Robinson (1773-1850) was clerk of the District Court of Law at Richmond and clerk of the Superior Court of Law for Henrico County.

Sands, Alexander H[amilton]. *Practical Forms.* Richmond: Woodhouse & Parham, 1867; 2d ed., J. W. Randolph & English, 1872.

A. H. Sands (1828-1887) practiced law in Richmond. This book

A

COLLECTION OF FORMS

USED BY THE CLERKS

OF THE

COURTS OF LAW AND EQUITY

IN

VIRGINIA.

TO WHICH ARE ADDED,

MANY PRECEDENTS OF DECLARATIONS,
INDICTMENTS AND INFORMATIONS,

AND

SOME USEFUL FORMS OF CONVEYANCES.

BY JOHN ROBINSON.

Clerk of the Superior Court of Law for Henrico County.

THE SECOND EDITION.

In which the various forms have been adapted to the laws now in force; many new forms inserted; and references given to numerous decisions of the General Court and Court of Appeals of Virginia, relating chiefly to questions of practice.

BY CONWAY ROBINSON,

Deputy Clerk of the same Court.

RICHMOND:

SHEPHERD & POLLARD, *Printers.*

1826.

is the successor to Sands's editions of B. Tate's *American Form Book*.

Tate, Benjamin. *The American Form Book*. Richmond: Drinker & Morris, 1845; 2d ed., Richmond: Drinker & Morris, 1847; 3d ed., Richmond: Morris & Brother, 1850; 4th ed. by A. H. Sands, Richmond: A. Morris, 1853; 5th ed. by A. H. Sands, Richmond: A. Morris, 1854; 6th ed. by A. H. Sands, Richmond: A. Morris, 1857, 2 vols.

Virginia Forms. Charlottesville: The Michie Co., vol. 1, "Civil Litigation," ed. by W. Clyde Gouldman, II, and Amy Morris Hess, 1st ed. 1978, 2d ed. 1989; vol. 2, "Civil Litigation," ed. by Barbara Goshorn Gallo, 1st ed. 1982, 2d ed. 1991; vol. 3, "Commercial Transactions, Criminal Procedure, Medical Malpractice," ed. by Frank J. Gallo and Barbara G. Gallo, 1st ed. 1984, 2d ed. 1988, 3d ed. 1993; vol. 4, "Civil Matters," ed. by Barbara G. Gallo, 1st ed. 1984, 2d ed. 1990; vol. 5, "Real Estate Transactions," ed. by Barbara G. Gallo, 1st ed. 1988, 2d ed. 1992.

This set of form books is kept up to date with annual pocket supplements.

Virginia Legal Forms for the Transaction of Business. Martinsburg, Va.: Gazette Office, 1854.

Virginia Model Jury Instructions: Civil. Charlottesville: The Michie Co., 1980 to date, 2 vols.

This is a looseleaf service.

Virginia Model Jury Instructions: Criminal. Charlottesville: The Michie Co., 1979 to date, 2 vols.

This is a looseleaf service.

Wagner, Laura L., and Robert J. Wagner. *Virginia Litigation Forms and Analysis*. Rochester, N.Y.: Lawyers Cooperative Pub., 1994 to date, 3 vols.

This is a looseleaf publication.

Will and Trust Forms. Chicago: Schiff, Hardin & Waite, 1983.

This is a looseleaf form book distributed by the Dominion Trust Company of Roanoke.

Will and Trust Forms for Attorneys. Richmond: First & Merchants National Bank, 1978.

This is a looseleaf form book.

LAW TREATISES PRINTED BEFORE 1950

A. Gray Collins, III

THIS BIBLIOGRAPHY catalogs secondary legal literature not included in another section of this book.[1] It includes historical as well as current, practical legal scholarship. However, books written for law students that would have been of less value to practicing lawyers are listed in the section on legal education. The term treatise is used here in a sense that is far broader than that used by Professor Brian Simpson, who follows the narrow definition of Plucknett.[2] This is desirable in order to prevent a number of items from falling through the cracks of the scheme of classification of this book.

The scope of this annotated bibliography is limited to books and pamphlets on Virginia law printed before 1950. The date of 1950 was chosen as the terminus ad quem because the Code of Virginia was substantially revised in that year. After the Code of 1950 was published, looseleaf services came into existence and books and continuing legal education pamphlets explaining or clarifying the law became much more numerous due to major innovations in printing and publishing.[3] This time limitation thus gives a manageable amount of material to work with.

To make the bibliography more helpful to Virginia lawyers and legal historians, only books that deal with Virginia law exclusively or primarily are included. Remembering that West Virginia was once a part of Virginia and that West Virginia has adopted much of the Virginia law,[4] this bibliography includes books that cover both West

[1] Note the sections on periodicals, indexes, form books, accounts of trials, legal education, and criminal law books. The criminal law books are noted here with cross-references.

[2] Simpson limits the term legal treatise to refer only to analytical, expository commentaries on the substantive law. A. W. B. Simpson, "The Rise and Fall of the Legal Treatise: Legal Principles and the Forms of Legal Literature," *Univ. of Chicago Law Rev.*, vol. 48, pp. 632-679 (1981).

[3] Note, however, that the Michie Company used pocket parts as early as 1938 for their book entitled *The Law of Automobiles in Virginia and West Virginia*. It is interesting to note that in 1921 a suggestion was made for the publication of a looseleaf code, but it was never done. W. W. Ackerly, "A Loose-Leaf Code for Virginia," *Va. L. Reg.*, n.s., vol. 7, pp. 345-346 (1921).

[4] The common and statute law of Virginia before 1863 is the common law of West Virginia. W. Va. Code Ann. § 2-1-1.

Virginia and Virginia.

The majority of the authors of these books were law professors. The law school that produced the most authors was the University of Virginia, which happens to be the second oldest law school in Virginia; Washington and Lee produced the second most authors. Only those lecture notes that were rewritten and extended in book form and not merely printed from the professor's notes are included in this bibliography.[5]

Not all the authors were law teachers; many of the authors were lawyers and judges. Howard and Whitfield were medical doctors and professors of forensic medicine. In order to enhance the value of this bibliography for legal historians, works of historical scholarship by historians are also included.

The most frequently treated area of the law was the criminal law.[6] The next two are the procedures of the courts, both common law and equity, and the law of property, both real and personal.

BIBLIOGRAPHY

Barton, R[obert] T[homas]. *Pleading and Practice in the Courts of Chancery*. Richmond: J. W. Randolph & English, 1881, 1883, 2 vols.; 2d ed., Lynchburg: J. P. Bell, 1899, 2 vols.; 3d ed. by Robert T. Barton, Jr., Charlottesville: The Michie Co., 1926, 2 vols.

> This treatise is founded on Conway Robinson's *Practice* (1832), and includes a table of contents, an index of cases, and an index. The review in *Va. L. J.*, vol. 5, pp. 601–602 (1881), commends the work to the bench and bar of the two Virginias; the review in *Va. L. Reg.*, vol. 5, pp. 279–280 (1899), states that this is "the standard law book, especially for the Virginia and West Virginia lawyer." An obituary of Barton is printed in *Va. St. Bar Ass'n Repts.*, vol. 30, pp. 91–94 (1918).

Barton, R[obert] T[homas]. *The Practice in the Courts of Law in Civil Cases, Founded on Conway Robinson's Practice (1832)*. Richmond: J. W. Randolph & English, 1877; 2d ed., Richmond: J. W. Randolph, 1891, 2 vols.; 3d ed., Richmond: Bell Book and Stationery Co., 1901, 2 vols.

> This treatise includes a table of cases and a general index. In

[5] See below, the bibliography to the essay on "Legal Education" for the others.

[6] There is a separate bibliography for these books, but they are included here also, though without annotations.

the preface, Barton (1842–1917) includes a letter from Conway Robinson (1805–1884), giving Barton permission to update his book. The preface also states that this book is different from Robinson's book because of the multitude of changes by Barton. The treatise was written to help the practitioner when dealing with a civil case at common law. The review in *Va. L. J.*, vol. 1, pp. 511–512 (1877), states that "no Virginia lawyer can afford to be without the book."

Brenaman, J[acob] N[eff]. *A History of Virginia Conventions.* Richmond: J. L. Hill, 1902.

Brenaman was Assistant Secretary of the Constitutional Convention of 1901–1902.

Burks, Martin P[arks]. *Demurrer.* Lynchburg: J. P. Bell Co., 1908.

For a biographical sketch of Burks, see W. H. Bryson, ed., *Legal Education in Virginia,* pp. 117–126 (1982).

Burks, Martin P[arks]. *Demurrer to Evidence.* Charlottesville: The Michie Co., n.d.

Burks, M[artin] P[arks]. *Notes on the Property Rights of Married Women in Virginia.* Lynchburg: J. P. Bell Co., 1893; 2d ed., Lynchburg: J. P. Bell Co., 1894.

Burks (1851–1928) claimed that this work was originally only done for himself, but that other lawyers persuaded him to publish it. The book includes a table of cases and statutes at the end of the book. Martin P. Burks was a teacher at Washington and Lee Law School and later a judge of the Supreme Court of Appeals of Virginia. W. M. Lile (1859–1935) commended this book to the practitioner in the *Va. L. Reg.*, vol. 1, p. 76 (1895), and stated that the conclusions in this book were affirmed by two subsequent court cases, *Grant v. Sutton,* 90 Va. 771 (1894), and *Hutchings v. Commercial Bank,* 91 Va. 68 (1895).

Burks, Martin P[arks]. *Pleading and Practice in Actions at Common Law.* Charlottesville: The Michie Co., 1913; 2d ed. by C. H. Morrissett, Charlottesville: Surber-Arundale, 1921; 3d ed. by Clayton E. Williams and Martin P. Burks, III, Charlottesville: The Michie Co., 1934; 4th ed. by T. Munford Boyd, Charlottesville: The Michie Co., 1952; last pocket supplement, Charlottesville: The Michie Co., 1961.

Contained in the first edition are cases and forms that illustrate how to plead a case in Virginia. The second edition deals with the statutory changes and court decisions since 1912, while the third edition expands the West Virginia cases, and adds several new chapters dealing with declaratory judgments. Burks wanted this to be a handbook to help practitioners in Virginia law. Later, when Burks was on the Supreme Court of Appeals of Virginia, one of his former students at Washington and Lee Law School, C. H. Morrissett (1892–1976), edited the second edition. The first edition was only printed by the Michie Company, but was sold by W. C. Stuart in Lexington.

Chichester, Cassius M[oncure]. *Notes on Draftsmanship of Bills in Virginia.* Richmond: Div. of Purchase and Printing, 1947.

This is a very brief publication. For a biographical sketch of Chichester (1882–1950), see W. H. Bryson, ed., *Legal Education in Virginia*, pp. 137–141 (1982).

Chitwood, Oliver Perry. *Justice in Colonial Virginia.* Baltimore: Johns Hopkins Press, 1905; rept. in *West Va. Law Quart.*, vol. 32, pp. 83-101, 192-225, 269-312 (1926); rept. New York: Da Capo, 1971.

This is a scholarly history book on the courts of colonial Virginia. The evolution of the courts and the courts' jurisdiction are described in the book. The last page gives a list of manuscripts used. A reference is made in the preface to J. A. C. Chandler (1872–1934) of Richmond College for his assistance in researching. Lyon Gardiner Tyler (1853–1935) states in a review of this book, *A.H.R.*, vol. 11, pp. 406-408 (1906), that "Dr. Chitwood's work is a valuable contribution to the study of our antiquities and beginnings."

Chumbley, George Lewis. *Colonial Justice in Virginia: the Development of a Judicial System, Typical Laws and Cases of the Period.* Richmond: The Dietz Press, 1938.

This treatise describes the development of the colonial court system. Also described are the colonial laws on Imprisonment for debt, chapter VIII; Labor, chapter IX; Gambling, chapter X; and Punishment, chapter XI. The book includes a bibliography and an index. It was reviewed in *A.H.R.*, vol. 45, pp. 406-408 (1940), by Richard B. Morris (1904–1989), who stated that "[s]ubject to qualifications, the author has treated the materials at hand systematically and thoroughly, and his

> conclusions are carefully documented." George P. Coleman (1870–1948) states in *Va. Mag. Hist. Biog.*, vol. 47, pp. 86-87 (1939), that "[t]his is a book much needed by the ever increasing number of students of Virginia colonial history, and is remarkably well and attractively written." Wesley Frank Craven in *J. of Southern Hist.*, vol. 5, pp. 255-257 (1939), states "Mr. Chumbley's work is slight and disappointing." Dudley W. Woodbridge (1896–1969) states in *Wm. & Mary Qtly.*, 2d ser., vol. 19, pp. 536-537 (1939), that "[t]he title as a whole is not exhaustively enough treated, and hence the book will be of little use to the scholar, even though of value to the casual reader."

Cohen, Alfred E[ugene]. *Divorce and Alimony in Virginia and West Virginia With Forms.* Charlottesville: The Michie Co., 1949; 2d ed. by Arthur Warren Phelps, Charlottesville: The Michie Co., 1963.

> This book was superseded by Arthur Warren Phelps. *Domestic Relations in Virginia With Forms.* Charlottesville: The Michie Co., 1977.

Cox, Lucian B[aum]. *A Manual for Title Examiners in Virginia.* Richmond: Richmond Press, Inc., 1939; 2d ed., Charlottesville: The Michie Co., 1947.

> This treatise pulls together the cases and statutes that concern title examiners. The first edition was written in response to the (unofficial) Code of 1936, while the second edition was upgraded to reflect the changes in the new (unofficial) Code of 1942. A table of contents and an index are included in the book. Cox (b. 1879) states with appropriate modesty that this is not a treatise on property law. It was superseded and replaced by S. F. Parham, *A Virginia Title Examiner's Manual* (1973).

Daniel, John Warwick. *The Law and Practice of Attachment, under the Code of Virginia; and of Bail and Injunction in Analogous Cases Wherein Attachment Is Not Available with a Variety of All Necessary Forms.* Lynchburg: Schaffter & Bryant, 1869.

> This treatise contains a general index, a table of Virginia reports, a table of Virginia cases cited, and an index of English and American cases cited. The appendix contains forms for use in Virginia. Daniel (1842–1910) wrote this treatise because no other manual was in existence for Virginia which explained this area of the law. Also, Daniel states that he had

to use foreign and other American cases to illustrate the law in Virginia. Daniel, the Lame Lion of Lynchburg, practiced law in Lynchburg and was a United States Senator. An obituary of Daniel is printed in *Va. St. Bar Ass'n Repts.*, vol. 23, pp. 73–80 (1910).

Davis, J[ohn] A[nthony] G[ardner]. *A Treatise on Criminal Law with an Exposition of the Office and Authority of Justices of the Peace in Virginia.* Philadelphia: C. S. Sherman & Co., 1838.

See Criminal Law Books Section.

Eckenrode, Hamilton James. *Separation of Church and State in Virginia.* Richmond: Davis Bottom, 1910; rept. New York: Da Capo, 1971.

This book is a legal history of the church in Virginia before, during, and after the American Revolution. Eckenrode (1881–1952) was an archivist and wrote this treatise as a special report of the Virginia Department of Archives and History.

Embrey, Alvin T[homas]. *Waters of the State.* Richmond: Old Dominion Pr., 1931.

This treatise deals with the property laws that govern the waters in and around Virginia. It includes maps of all the Virginia waters. Embrey (1874–1957) practiced law in Fredericksburg; he specialized in water power resources.

Fuller, Hugh N[elson]. *Criminal Justice in Virginia.* Charlottesville: The Century Co., 1931.

See Criminal Law Books Section.

Graves, Charles A[lfred]. *Notes on Real Property.* N.p., 1880; Indianapolis: Bobbs–Merrill Co., n.d.; Indianapolis: Bobbs–Merrill Co., 1912.

This treatise deals with the subject of real property. The use of statutes along with cases is the main focus. This book includes a table of contents and a general index, but no preface or introduction. Graves (1850–1928) was a professor of law at Washington and Lee University and then at the University of Virginia Law School; he wrote this book to help

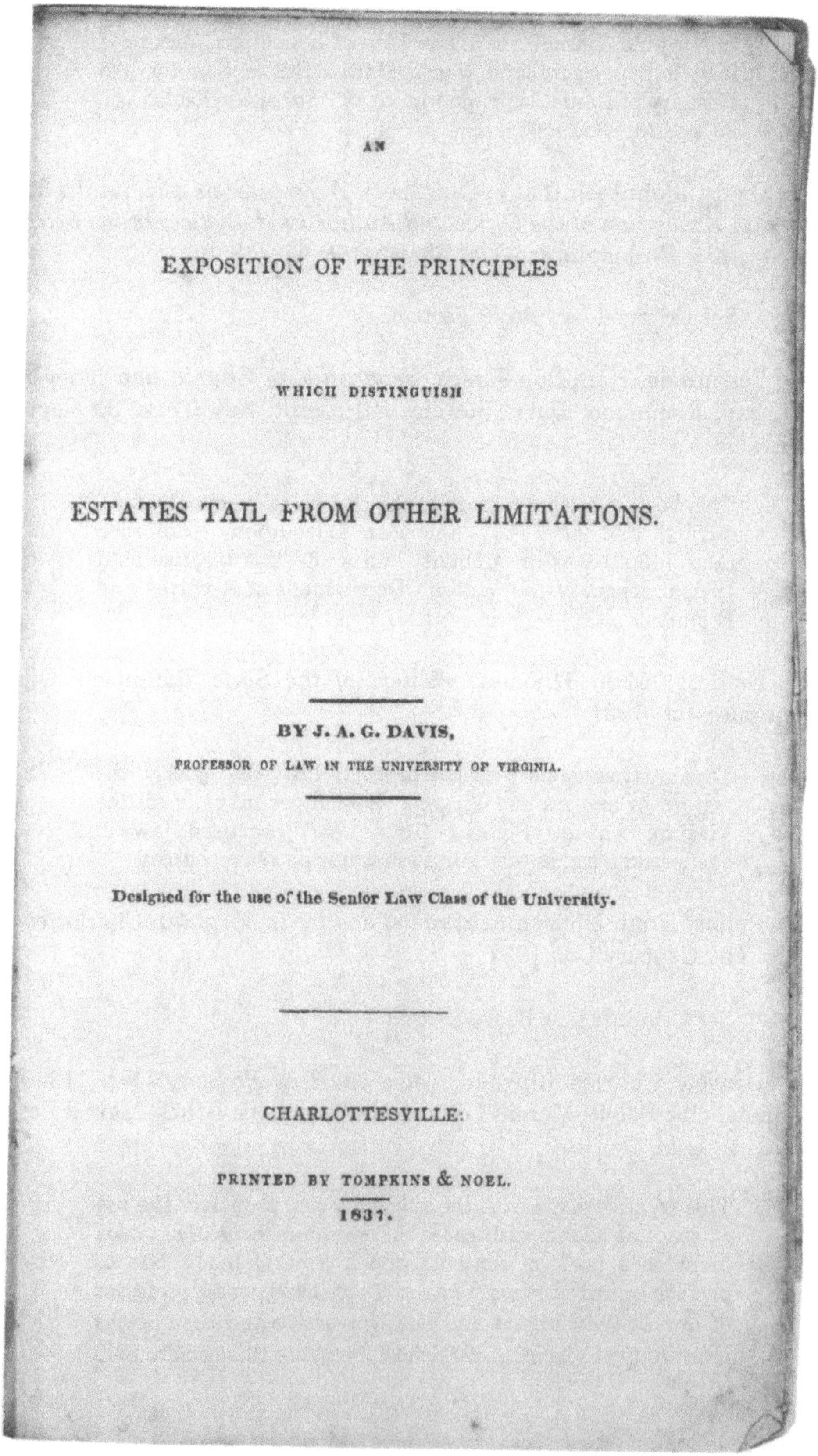

AN

EXPOSITION OF THE PRINCIPLES

WHICH DISTINGUISH

ESTATES TAIL FROM OTHER LIMITATIONS.

BY J. A. G. DAVIS,

PROFESSOR OF LAW IN THE UNIVERSITY OF VIRGINIA.

Designed for the use of the Senior Law Class of the University.

CHARLOTTESVILLE:

PRINTED BY TOMPKINS & NOEL.

1837.

his students.

Graves, Charles A[lfred]. *Summary of Title to Personal Property.* Lynchburg: J. P. Bell Co., 1897.

This book is based on articles in volumes one and two of the *Virginia Law Register*. Graves deals with personal property law of the United States, and particularly with Virginia law; the book was written for his law students at Washington and Lee University. There is a table of contents, a table of cases cited, and an index.

Hank, J[osiah] D[ickenson, Jr.]. *Virginia Law Made Plain.* Kansas City, Mo.: Bankers Law Pub. Co., 1923.

This short volume is only slightly fuller in coverage than a law dictionary. It has a few forms at the end. An obituary of Hank (1875–1924), who was the Assistant Attorney General of Virginia from 1917 to 1924, is printed in *Va. St. Bar Ass'n Repts.*, vol. 36, pp. 93–94 (1924).

Harrison, Fairfax. *Virginia Land Grants: A Study of Conveyancing in Relation to Colonial Politics.* Richmond: Old Dominion Press, 1925.

This is a history book on Virginia land grants during the colonial period. There is an introduction, table of contents, and an index. Also, there are extensive and comprehensive endnotes.

Harrison, T[homas] W[alter]. *Wills and Administration.* Ed. by Burr P. Harrison, Charlottesville: The Michie Co., 1927, 2 vols.; 2d ed. by George P. Smith, Jr., Charlottesville: The Michie Co., 1960–1963, 3 vols.; 3d ed. by George P. Smith, Jr., Charlottesville: The Michie Co., 1985–1990, 4 vols.

This general treatise is kept up to date with annual pocket supplements.

Hawes, Herbert Bouldin, and Joel W[est] Flood. *Prohibition Index–Manual, Virginia and West Virginia.* Charlottesville: The Michie Co., 1930.

Hening, William Waller. *The New Virginia Justice.* Richmond: T. Nicolson, 1795; Richmond: Aug. Davis, 1799; "2d ed.," Richmond: Johnson & Warner, 1810; "3d ed.," Richmond: J. & G. Cochran, 1820;

"4th ed." [*The Virginia Justice*], Richmond: Shepherd & Pollard, 1825.

> See Criminal Law Books Section.

Hogg, Charles Eggar. *Equity Procedure Embodying the Principles of Pleading and Practice Applicable to Courts of Equity and Containing Many Precedents of General Practical Utility Designed to Meet the Demands of Practice in Virginia and West Virginia and for the General Use in Other States.* Cincinnati: The W. H. Anderson Co., 1903, 2 vols.; 2d ed. by Leo Carlin, Cincinnati: The W. H. Anderson Co., 1921, 2 vols.; [*Hogg's Equity Procedure A Treatise on Practice and Procedure in the Courts of Chancery of Virginia and West Virginia with Approved Forms*]. 3d ed. by Lewis H. Miller, Cincinnati: The W. H. Anderson Co., 1943, 2 vols.

> All editions of this treatise contain a preface, a table of contents, a table of cases, an index, and forms. The second edition's title included the words "Being a Thorough Revision of Hogg's Equity Procedure," yet the treatise was not considered to be a second edition by its author, Leo Carlin. Carlin was a professor of law at West Virginia University. The third edition was written by Lewis H. Miller, who was a judge of the Fifth Judicial Circuit in Ripley, West Virginia. Miller stated in his preface that the reasons for his rewrite were the new Code of West Virginia and, for all practical purposes, a new Code of Virginia.

Howard, Henry. *Outlines of Medical Jurisprudence.* Charlottesville: Magruder & Noel, 1842; 3d ed., Charlottesville: Noel, 1845; 4th ed. [*Synopsis of Medical Jurisprudence*], Charlottesville: Allen, 1849; 5th ed., Charlottesville: James Alexander, 1851.

> This book is based on Professor Howard's lectures on forensic medicine at the School of Medicine of the University of Virginia.

Howard, Overton. *The Life of the Law or Universal Principles of Law.* Richmond: J. W. Randolph & English, 1889.

> This book gives some general comments on the state of the law.

Hulvey, Charles Newton, and William Hamlin Wandel. *Life Insurance in Virginia.* [Charlottesville]: Institute for Research in the

A SYNOPSIS

OF

MEDICAL JURISPRUDENCE,

FROM

THE LATEST AND BEST AUTHORITIES

FORMING THE BASIS OF LECTURES ON THE SCIENCE,

BY

HENRY HOWARD, M. D.,

Professor of the Pathology and Practice of Medicine, Obstetrics, and Medical Jurisprudence,

IN THE

UNIVERSITY OF VIRGINIA.

FOURTH EDITION.

CHARLOTTESVILLE:

PRINTED BY O. S. ALLEN & CO.

1849.

Social Sciences, 1929.

Chapter 5: "The Law of Life Insurance in Virginia."

Hulvey, Charles Newton, and William Hamlin Wandel. *Workmen's Compensation and Automobile Liability Insurance in Virginia.* New York: The Century Co., 1931.

This book discusses the workers' compensation laws in Virginia.

Hurst, Samuel N[eed]. *A New Guide for Justices of the Peace in Virginia.* Richmond: J. L. Hill, 1893; 2d ed., Pulaski City, Va.: Hurst & Co., 1904.

See Criminal Law Books Section.

Hutchinson, John A[lexander]. *Land Titles in Virginia and West Virginia.* Cincinnati: Robert Clarke & Co., 1887.

Joynes, William T[homas]. *An Essay Upon the Act of the General Assembly of Virginia, Passed April 3, 1838, Entitled "An Act Amending the Statute of Limitations," and Founded on the English Statute of 9 Geo. IV, c. 14, with a Preliminary Inquiry into the Law of New Promises, Under the "Statute of Limitations."* Richmond: Drinker & Morris, 1844.

This book looks at the history of the Statute of Limitations, and how the amendment of 1838 changed the Statute. It contains much case authority from both England and America.

Karraker, Cyrus Harreld. *The Seventeenth-Century Sheriff: A Comparative Study of the Sheriff in England and the Chesapeake Colonies, 1607-1689.* Chapel Hill: Univ. of North Carolina Press, 1930; rept. Plainview, N.Y.: Books for Libraries, 1973.

This learned treatise includes a preface, table of contents, bibliography, index, and appendix of illustrative documents. Karraker was an associate professor of history at Birmingham–Southern College. The treatise covers Virginia and Maryland during the colonial period. It was a dissertation presented to the University of Pennsylvania for the degree of doctor of philosophy. Reviewed in *A.H.R.*, vol. 36, pp. 429-430

(1931), Harold Hulme states that "[t]here is an excellent bibliography and an index, which omits too much to be called adequate." Hulme concludes that "[t]here are, however, few slips to mar an otherwise excellent piece of work which should help considerably to stimulate the production of more comparative studies on English and American institutions."

Kittle, Warren B[rance]. *The Law of Rule Days in Virginia and West Virginia, Including the Subject of Judgments by Default With Forms*. Cincinnati: The W. H. Anderson Co., 1914.

Statutes along with forms for Virginia and West Virginia are contained in this treatise. There is no introduction or preface to the book. Warren B. Kittle was a judge for the Nineteenth Judicial Circuit of West Virginia.

The Law of Automobiles in Virginia and West Virginia. 2d ed., Charlottesville: The Michie Co., 1938; 3d ed., Charlottesville: The Michie Co., 1947, 3 vols.

This treatise discusses the principal cases and statutes dealing with automobiles in Virginia and West Virginia. This second edition begins the idea of the pocket supplement to keep the volume current with the most recent changes in the law. The third edition includes forms. These books are later versions of Vartanian's *The Law of Automobiles in Virginia and West Virginia*.

Lile, W[illiam] M[inor]. *Lectures on Equity Pleading and Practice: With Forms and the New Federal Equity Rules Prepared for the Use of the Students of the Law School of the University of Virginia*. [Charlottesville]: George W. Olivier, 1916; 2d ed., [Charlottesville]: George W. Olivier, 1922; 3d ed. by Edwin B. Meade, Charlottesville: The Michie Co., 1952.

Lile (1859–1935) had his lectures printed for his students at the University of Virginia Law School. It includes a discussion on the forms needed and the rules of equity in the federal system. Lile was a professor and dean at the University of Virginia Law School from 1893 to 1935. For a biographical sketch of Lile, see W. H. Bryson, ed., *Legal Education in Virginia*, pp. 353–357 (1982).

Lomax, John Tayloe. *Digest of the Laws Respecting Real Property*. Philadelphia: John S. Littell, 1839, 3 vols.; 2d ed., Richmond: Adolphus

Morris, 1855, 3 vols.

> This is more a treatise than a digest and deals with property laws for the whole United States; however, there is a concentration on Virginia property law. This book is based on Cruise's *Digest of Laws of England, Respecting Real Property*, but Lomax (1781–1862) wrote this book because England and the United States, while similar, had developed differences in the law since the Revolution. The second edition was printed because a new Virginia code was adopted in 1849. For a biographical sketch of Lomax, see W. H. Bryson, ed., *Legal Education in Virginia*, pp. 359–366 (1982).

Lomax, John Tayloe. *A Treatise on the Law of Executors and Administrators, Generally in Use in the United States; and Adapted More Particularly to the Practice of Virginia*. Philadelphia: John S. Littell, 1841, 2 vols.; 2d ed., Richmond: Morris, 1857, 2 vols.

> Lomax was a professor at the University of Virginia Law School and later one of the judges of the General Court. This book deals with more than Virginia; however, there is a concentration on Virginia law. The second edition was written in response to the adoption of a new code in Virginia in 1849.

Massie, Eugene C[arter]. *The Torrens System: a Manual of the Uniform Land Registration Act in Virginia, To Which is Appended the Annotated Act, Proposed Rules of Court, and a Complete System of Forms*. Richmond: Everett Waddey Co., 1916.

> Massie (1861–1924) was an enthusiastic supporter of land registration to supplant the traditional system of land recordation. Even though he convinced the General Assembly to adopt the Torrens system of land registration (1916 Va. Acts., c. 62, p. 70), it has never been put into practice in Virginia. An obituary of Massie is printed in *Va. St. Bar Ass'n Repts.*, vol. 36, pp. 99–105 (1924).

Matthews, James M[uscoe]. *A Guide to Commissioners in Chancery with Practical Forms for the Discharge of Their Duties, Adapted to the New Code of Virginia*. Richmond: J. W. Randolph, 1850; 2d ed., Richmond: J. W. Randolph & English, 1871.

> The first edition is written in response to the new Code of 1849. Matthews (1822–1905) was a practicing lawyer and the reporter to the Supreme Court of Appeals of Virginia.

Matthews, W[illiam] B[aynham]. *Guide for Executors and Administrators in Virginia.* Richmond: J. W. Randolph & English, 1872.

This is a handbook to help executors and administrators in proving wills and administering estates in Virginia. W. B. Matthews (1850–1914) was the son of James M. Matthews (1822–1905).

Mayo, Joseph. *A Guide to Magistrates.* Richmond: Smith, 1849; new ed., Richmond: Colin, Baptist & Nowlan, 1850; Richmond: Nash & Woodhouse, 1853; 2d ed., Richmond: A. Morris, 1860; 3d ed., by H. W. Flournoy and J. Thompson Brown, Richmond: James E. Goode, 1892.

See Criminal Law Books Section.

Minor, James F[ontaine]. *The Workmen's Compensation Laws of Virginia and West Virginia.* Charlottesville: The Michie Co., 1919.

J. F. Minor (1876–1961) practiced law in Richmond. This book is a manual for practitioners.

[Minor, John Barbee]. *Equity Pleading: Extracts from Minor's Institutes Volume IV, Part II.* Lynchburg: J. P. Bell, 1907.

This is a reprint from Minor's encyclopedic work; see below.

Minor, John B[arbee]. *Exposition of the Law of Crimes and Punishments.* Richmond: Anderson Bros., 1894.

See Criminal Law Books Section.

Minor, John B[arbee]. *Institutes of Common and Statute Law.* Richmond: vol. 1: 1st ed. 1875, 2d ed. 1876, 3d ed. 1882, 4th ed. 1891; vol. 2: 1st ed. 1875, 2d ed. 1877, 3d ed. 1882, 4th ed. 1892; vol. 3: "2d ed." 1895; vol. 4: 1st ed. 1878, 1879, 2d ed. 1883, 3d ed. 1892, 4th ed. 1893. 4 vols. in 6.

Minor (1813–1895) was a professor at the University of Virginia Law School. This encyclopedic work was written from his class lectures and published for his students as well as for practicing lawyers. The treatise was recommended despite minor blemishes by William Green (1806–1880) in *Va. L. J.*, vol. 1, pp. 314-317 (1877). Also, it was reviewed in *Va. L. J.*, vol. 3, p. 255 (1879), where it was again commended to practitioners, and in *Va. L. J.*, vol. 6, pp. 643–644 (1882), where it is stated that the treatise is "a necessity to the Virginia lawyer" and it is "difficult to over-estimate the value to the student." For a biographical sketch of Minor, see W. H. Bryson, ed., *Legal Education in Virginia*, pp. 417–430 (1982).

Minor, Raleigh Colston. *The Law of Real Property*. Charlottesville: Anderson Bros., 1908, 2 vols.; 2d ed. by Frederick Deane Goodwin Ribble, Charlottesville: The Michie Co., 1928, 2 vols.

This treatise is based on John B. Minor's *Institutes*. At the time of this work, R. C. Minor (1869–1923) was a professor of law at the University of Virginia, and when Ribble (1898–1970) wrote the second edition, Ribble also was a professor of law at the University of Virginia. Both editions include a table of cases, a table of contents, and an index. For a biographical sketch of Minor, see W. H. Bryson, ed., *Legal Education in Virginia*, pp. 445–449 (1982).

Minor, Raleigh C[olston]. *The Law of Tax Titles in Virginia*. Charlottesville: Anderson Bros., 1898.

This treatise contains a table of cases, table of contents, and an index. Minor states that the reason for writing this treatise is that the subject had not been written on before. When Minor wrote this work, he was an adjunct professor of law at the University of Virginia.

Nelson, Margaret Virginia. *A Study of Judicial Review in Virginia, 1789-1928*. New York: Columbia Univ. Press, 1947; rept. New York: AMS Press, 1967.

This is a history book on the Virginia courts. Appendix B is a series of charts entitled "Judicial Review in Virginia, 1789-1928" showing the development of the Virginia court system. This scholarly treatise was reviewed by John W. Eggleston (1886–1976), a Justice of the Supreme Court of Appeals of Virginia, in *Va. L. Rev.*, vol. 34, pp. 248–252 (1948); he states that "the excellent quality of the work outweighs the minor defects."

Patterson, A[rchibald] W[illiams]. *The Code Duello with Special Reference to the State of Virginia*. Richmond: Richmond Press, Inc., 1927.

This refers to cases on dueling and the 1810 Act (now Va. Code Ann., § 8.01-45 (1950): actions for insulting words). An obituary of Patterson (1858–1940) is printed in *Va. St. Bar Ass'n Repts.*, vol. 52, pp. 142–143 (1940).

Pollard, John Garland, and Christopher B[rowne] Garnett. *A Guide to Magistrates and Constables . . . to Which is Added a Guide to Notaries Public by Carroll G. Walter*. Richmond: Everett Waddey Co., 1906.

See Criminal Law Books Section.

Pulliam, David L[loyd]. *The Constitutional Conventions of Virginia from the Foundation of the Commonwealth to the Present Time.* Richmond: J. T. West, 1901.

This book contains a preface and a table of contents. Pulliam (1852–1931) discusses the conventions of 1776, 1788, 1829–30, 1850–51, 1867–68, and 1901. Pulliam states that he wrote the book because another Constitutional Convention was due. Included in the discussions are biographical sketches of the people who attended the conventions. Pulliam practiced law in Richmond.

Robinson, Conway. *The Practice in the Courts of Law and Equity in Virginia.* Richmond: Samuel Shepherd & Co., 1832, 1835, 1839, 3 vols.

These volumes were not all printed at one time; Robinson (1805–1884) wrote one volume at a time to determine whether another volume was needed. This work is often found cited as "Rob. Old Pr." It was reviewed by Lucian Minor (1802–1858) in *Southern Literary Messenger*, vol. 2, pp. 50-51 (1835), where Minor found the index to be frustrating but concluded "[h]is book is one which we would advise every lawyer, in Virginia at least, to buy."

Sams, C[onway] Whittle. *A Treatise on the Law of Attachment and Bail in Virginia and West Virginia.* Richmond: J. W. Randolph, 1896.

The treatise is divided into two parts, one on Virginia law and one on West Virginia law. Sams (1864–1935) intended the work to be a practical handbook for the practitioner. The book has a table of contents, a table of cases, and an index for each part.

THE

PRACTICE

IN THE

COURTS OF LAW AND EQUITY

IN

VIRGINIA.

BY CONWAY ROBINSON.

VOLUME I.

CONTAINING

PRACTICE IN THE COURTS OF LAW IN CIVIL CASES.

RICHMOND:

PRINTED BY SAMUEL SHEPHERD & CO.

And sold by Robert I. Smith.

1832.

Sands, Alexander H[amilton]. *History of a Suit in Equity, as Prosecuted and Defended in the Virginia State Courts and in the United States Circuit Courts.* Richmond: A. Morris, 1854; 2d ed., Richmond: J. W. Randolph & English, 1882.

> This book shows the process of a suit in equity from the beginning to the final decree and execution thereof. The book has a chapter on evidence in equity. It contains a table of contents, an index, and an appendix on the rules of equity procedure. The review in *Va. L. J.*, vol. 6, pp. 383–384 (1882), states that "the Bench and Bar of Virginia are indebted to Mr. Sands." In the *Quart. L. J.*, vol. 1, p. 189 (1856), the book is favorably reviewed, and the review states "[w]e are pleased to hear that it has been adopted as a text book at William and Mary College and as a book of reference at the University of Virginia."

Scott, Arthur P[earson]. *Criminal Law in Colonial Virginia.* Chicago: Univ. of Chicago Press, 1930.

> This is a scholarly history book on colonial Virginia law. The reviewer in *Va. L. Rev.*, vol. 17, pp. 410–412 (1931), states that "one gets a very good picture of colonial history from the book. It is full of enlightening disclosures, some of which are rather shocking." Richard B. Morris (1904–1989) in *A.H.R.*, vol. 36, pp. 605-606 (1931), states "[t]he volume is an important contribution to the legal history of the colonies. A valuable bibliography is appended, but the index is inadequate." Dudley W. Woodbridge (1896–1969) concluded in *Wm. & Mary Qtly.*, 2d ser., vol. 11, pp. 169-172 (1931), that "[t]he book should be of interest to laymen of an historical turn of mind and to sociologists and criminologists." In the *Mississippi Valley Historical Rev.*, vol. 17, pp. 664-665 (1931), Cyrus H. Karraker found too many errors that should have been found in the proofreading, but states "[t]his study, strangely enough, is almost a pioneer in the field of colonial law."

Smith, A. Meade. *Commissioners in Chancery in Virginia; Comprising a Digest of the Statute Law Governing Commissioners Under the Code of Virginia, 1887.* Richmond: West, Johnston and Co., 1888.

> Smith, a member of the Norfolk bar, wrote this book to show the differences between England, where the institution had been abolished, and the United States. The book distinguishes the duties of the three types of commissioners in Virginia,

commissioners acting under a decree of reference, commissioners of accounts, and commissioners in chancery generally.

Smith, Charles S[amuel], Jr. *Smith's Justices' Guide.* Charlottesville: The Michie Co., 1929.

See Criminal Law Books Section.

Smith, Margaret Vowell. *A Few Notes upon the History of the Constitution or Form of Government of Virginia from the Foundation of the Colony to the Present Time.* Glens Falls, N.Y.: Glens Falls Publishing Co., 1901.

This is a very sketchy work.

Staples, Abram Penn. *Notes on Virginia Corporation Law.* Charlottesville: The Michie Co., 1909.

For a biographical sketch of Staples (1858–1913), see W. H. Bryson, ed., *Legal Education in Virginia,* pp. 585–588 (1982).

Starke, Richard. *The Office and Authority of a Justice of Peace.* Williamsburg: Alexander Purdie & John Dixon, 1774.

See Criminal Law Books Section.

Stauffer, William Henry. *Taxation in Virginia.* New York: The Century Co., 1931.

This treatise contains a preface and a foreword by C. H. Morrissett (1892–1976), the Virginia State Tax Commissioner. Also there is a table of contents and an index. It has many charts and tables dealing with valuation of land and expenditures by the local and state governments. Stauffer was a research professor at the University of Virginia and an economist at the State Department of Taxation.

Tucker, Henry St. George. *Commentaries on the Laws of Virginia.* Winchester: The Winchester Virginian, 1831, 2 vols.; 2d ed., Winchester: The Republican, 1836, 1837, 2 vols.; 3d ed. Richmond: Colin & Shepherd, 1846, 2 vols.

This treatise is a compilation of course lectures at the Winchester Law School; it was widely used by practitioners and by students at other law schools until the publisher's stock was destroyed in the Evacuation Fire of 1865. W. H. Bryson, ed., *Essays on Legal Education in Nineteenth Century Virginia, passim* (1998). Tucker (1780–1848) was the chancellor of the Fourth Judicial Circuit when he wrote this work. For a biographical sketch of Tucker, see W. H. Bryson, ed., *Legal Education in Virginia*, pp. 601–613 (1982).

Tucker, Henry St. George. *Notes on Blackstone's Commentaries for the Use of Students*. Winchester: Samuel H. Davis, 1826.

This treatise is a compilation of lectures on Blackstone's *Commentaries* at the Winchester Law School and the precursor of the previous work.

Tucker, [Nathaniel] B[everley]. *The Principles of Pleading*. Boston: Little and Brown, 1846.

Tucker (1784–1851) stated that he wrote this treatise because the old forms were confusing and had a mystique about them. The appendix contains a discussion of fraud in law. Tucker was the law professor at the College of William and Mary. For a biographical sketch of Tucker, see W. H. Bryson, ed., *Legal Education in Virginia*, pp. 643–656 (1982).

Vartanian, P[arounak] H[atch]. *The Law of Automobiles in Virginia and West Virginia*. Charlottesville: The Michie Co., 1928.

This treatise discusses the principal cases and statutes dealing with automobiles in Virginia and West Virginia. It includes a table of contents, a table of cases, and an index, but no forms.

Vartanian, P[arounak] H[atch]. *The Law of Corporations in Virginia*. Charlottesville: The Michie Co., 1929.

Walter, Carroll G[ibson]. *A Treatise on the Office and Work of Notaries Public in Virginia With Forms and Precedents*. Richmond: Everett Waddey Co., 1906.

This treatise was published bound at the end of Pollard and Garnett's *Guide to Magistrates and Constables*, see above, but it is a free standing work otherwise, with forms and an index.

Webb, George. *The Office and Authority of a Justice of Peace.* Williamsburg: William Parks, 1736; rept. Holmes Beach, Fla.: Wm. W. Gaunt & Sons, Inc., 1969.

> See Criminal Law Books Section.

Whitfield, Ja[me]s M. *Medical Jurisprudence: A Manual for Students and Practitioners.* Richmond: Central Pub. Co., Inc., 1925.

> This treatise is based on Whitfield's lectures at the Medical College of Virginia. While there is no table of contents, the book is divided into the following sections: contracts, wills, dying declarations, death, phenomena of death, sudden deaths, examination of a dead body, personal identity, wounds, burns and scalds, blood, death from asphyxia, death by electricity, pregnancy, abortion, infanticide, rape, insanity, and toxicology. Whitfield was the Coroner of the City of Richmond and a lecturer on medical jurisprudence at the Medical College of Virginia.

Williams, Ashby. *Corporation Laws of Virginia.* Roanoke: Stone Printing and Mfg. Co., 1909.

> This is an edition of the Virginia statutes governing corporations with extensive annotations and many forms for corporate law practice.

THE

Office and Authority

OF A

Justice of Peace.

AND ALSO

The Duty of Sheriffs, Coroners, Church-wardens, Surveiors of Highways, Constables, and Officers of Militia.

Together with

Precedents of Warrants, Judgments, Executions, and other legal Process, issuable by Magistrates within their respective Jurisdictions, in Cases Civil or Criminal.

AND

The Method of Judicial Proceedings, before Justices of Peace, in Matters within their Cognisance out of Sessions.

Collected from the Common and Statute Laws of *England*, and Acts of Assembly, now in Force; And adapted to the Constitution and Practice of *Virginia*.

By GEORGE WEBB, *Gent. One of His Majesty's Justices of Peace of the County of* New-Kent.

WILLIAMSBURG:

Printed by WILLIAM PARKS. M,DCC,XXXVI.

CRIMINAL LAW BOOKS

Anne P. Cataline

THE EARLIEST TYPE of criminal law book published in Virginia was the manual for justices of the peace. Justices of the peace were also known as magistrates or commissioners (of the peace). To best understand the significance of the manuals published for the justices of the peace, it is imperative to understand why they were written. This comprehension will only come from a history of the justices in Virginia.

The laws of Virginia began with the settlement at Jamestown as an English colony, which was governed according to the laws of England. This was required by the letters patent given to the Virginia Company by King James I in 1606.[1] The first settlement expanded into plantations, each of which was governed by a commander.[2] It was the responsibility of each of these commanders to hold monthly courts. The jurisdiction of these monthly courts was limited by the amounts in controversy, which could not exceed the value of one hundred pounds of tobacco. Commanders could also hear petty criminal cases.

In 1634, the commanders of the plantations were succeeded by commissioners of the monthly court.[3] Each commissioner or justice of the peace was appointed by the Governor with the approval of the Council. As Virginia grew and counties were added, new courts were created and new commissioners were appointed and their authority grew. In 1643, the frequency of the meetings was reduced from twelve times a year to six, and the monthly courts were renamed county courts.[4]

In addition to petty criminal cases and civil actions, the commissioners of the county courts were also involved with the administrative matters of the counties. All bridges, roads, and ferries were constructed and maintained and taverns were supervised by the authority of the commissioners. They performed the functions of the

[1] See generally A. P. Scott, *Criminal Law in Colonial Virginia*, pp. 3-38 (1930); W. H. Bryson, *Virginia Civil Procedure*, pp. 48-57 (3d ed. 1997).

[2] The meaning of plantation in the seventeenth century was a settlement; it was considered a place where people were planted, rather than a seating of a single planter. R. Goodwin, *Williamsburg in Virginia*, p. 3 (4th ed. 1941).

[3] Hening's Statutes, vol. 1, p. 224.

[4] Act of Mar. 1643, sect. 56, Hening's Statutes, vol. 1, p. 272; see generally A. G. Roeber, *Faithful Magistrates and Republican Lawyers*, pp. 41-50 (1981); O. P. Chitwood, *Justice in Colonial Virginia*, pp. 74-95 (1905).

present-day county boards of supervisors. Administration of property and land titles also fell under the responsibility of the commissioners. Since church courts did not exist in Virginia, the commissioners were required to oversee the probate and administration of wills and matters of divorce. It was demanded of the justices that they be "the most able, honest, and judicious persons of the county."[5] To be learned in the law was not required and in fact most of the justices had no formal education. This one fact alone broadcasts the need for manuals.

During the first years of Virginia, the commanders and then the justices had no local informational source to aid them in the exercise of their position in the court. Since they followed the laws of England and the county courts were modeled on the English quarter sessions, they used manuals written for the magistrates in England. In 1666, An act of the General Assembly required all of the county courts to purchase copies of Michael Dalton's *Country Justice* for "the use of" the county.[6]

The first manual published in Virginia was written by George Webb in 1736. This book rephrases the English law as explained by Dalton and other English legal authors in accordance with the contemporary law of the Virginia colony. It explains the laws of England, noting the changes that were applicable to Virginia.

Over the next two hundred years manuals for justices appeared regularly. The appearance of these works usually has a direct correlation with significant recent changes in the laws of Virginia, both substantive and procedural.

A second manual, written by Richard Starke and published posthumously in 1774,[7] was quickly out of date due to Independence from Great Britain, a new state constitution, and the new Code of Virginia of 1792, which made major changes in the criminal law. The General Assembly in 1789 and 1796 made significant changes in the law of punishments following some of the earlier recommendations of Thomas Jefferson, who was very much influenced by Beccaria. Many medieval aspects of the criminal law were removed, such as unduly cruel punishments, the death penalty for minor offenses, forfeiture of felons' goods, and corruption of blood.[8]

[5] Act of Mar. 23, 1662, sect. 31, Hening's Statutes, vol. 2, p. 69.

[6] Act of Oct. 1666, sect. 20, Hening's Statutes, vol. 2, p. 246.

[7] Note "Stark's Free School and 'Justices of the Peace'," *Wm. & Mary Qtly.*, 1st ser., vol. 4, pp. 197-200 (1896).

[8] Act of Dec. 9, 1789, sect. 13, Hening's Statutes, vol. 13, p. 40; Act of Dec. 15, 1796, *Shepherd's Statutes*, vol. 2, pp. 5-16; see generally K. Preyer, "Crime, the Criminal Law and reform in Post-Revolutionary Virginia," *Law and History Rev.*, vol. 1, pp. 53-85

A clear turning point in the history of legal publications in Virginia was W. W. Hening's first edition of *The New Virginia Justice* in 1795. Hening's work is distinctive for several reasons. It was an encompassing work that provided guidance and direction for the justices of the peace in criminal matters and also gave them direction in civil and administrative matters. This is a marked difference from the English texts. Justices in England had jurisdiction only over criminal cases, whereas the Virginia justices had both criminal and civil jurisdiction, as well as administrative duties. Hening provided four editions of this work and a final fifth edition entitled *The Virginia Justice.* Its wide use is documented in the order placed for this last edition in 1825. By Executive Order of the state of Virginia, three thousand copies were requested.[9] One explanation for its wide use is that it was the only work available on Virginia criminal law and procedure.

John Anthony Gardner Davis published *A Treatise on Criminal Law . . . Including Forms of Practice* in 1838. In his preface, Davis concedes the plan he chose in writing the text was novel. Davis was referring to the attempt to deal with the substantive criminal law in Virginia in a text to be used as a manual for the justices. However, it can just as appropriately refer to the treatise format he adopted when compiling the work. As a justice for Albemarle County in 1835, Davis personally saw the need for such a text. Even though a mere thirty-six years old when he undertook the project, he was well qualified for the task. Davis had been a law professor at the University of Virginia since the age of twenty-eight and was respected for his clear and concise analytical skills.[10]

The next treatise published was written by a former student of Davis, John B. Minor. In 1858, *A Synopsis of the Law of Crimes and Punishments* was published. This work was a compilation of the law lectures that Minor gave at the University of Virginia. Students of Minor remarked that the manner and clarity of his lectures were "unsurpassed."[11] A second edition was published in 1869. Minor developed an unusual style of writing, best described as an outline form. He used a series of numbers and letters along with indentation

---

(1983).

[9] Copies were to be distributed to every magistrate in Virginia. 1825 Va. Acts, p. 25, chap. 26; W. W. Hening, *A View of the Conduct of the Executive of Virginia* (1825); S. M. Walker, Jr., "William Waller Hening," *Va. Law Reporters*, pp. 19-24 (1977).

[10] E. L. Shepard, "John Anthony Gardner Davis," *Legal Education in Va.*, pp. 181-185 (1982).

[11] H. B. Fitzsimmons, "John Barbee Minor," *Legal Education in Va.*, pp. 417-430 (1982).

THE

NEW VIRGINIA JUSTICE,

COMPRISING THE

OFFICE AND AUTHORITY

OF A

JUSTICE OF THE PEACE,

IN THE

COMMONWEALTH of VIRGINIA.

TOGETHER

WITH A VARIETY OF USEFUL PRECEDENTS
ADOPTED TO THE LAWS NOW IN FORCE.

To which is added,

An APPENDIX containing all the moſt approved forms of
CONVEYANCING, commonly uſed in this country,
Such as Deeds, of Bargain and Sale, of
Leaſe and Releaſe, of Truſt, Mort-
gages, &c.—Alſo the duties of
a Juſtice of the Peace ariſ-
ing under the laws of
the United States.

BY WILLIAM WALLER HENING,
ATTORNEY AT LAW.

RICHMOND: PRINTED BY T. NICOLSON, 1795.

to aid the student in determining which principles were the most important. This same style of printing was used in his *Exposition of the Law of Crimes and Punishments*. The latter book was published in 1894 and was a revision of the *Synopsis*.

In 1809 the new circuit court system was integrated into the Virginia judiciary.[12] After the establishment of this system of courts with closer appellate supervision over the county courts, the powers of the justices gradually began to decline.[13] By 1852, a constitutional change required all justices be elected, paid officials.[14] In 1870, a new constitution removed the justices from the county counts and abolished their administrative duties, which were thenceforth to be performed by the county boards of supervisors.[15] Being stripped of administrative duties, the power and prestige of the lay justices experienced further decline.

Just prior to the constitutional change instituting the new county court system, Joseph Mayo published his guide for the justices in 1849. Several editions were issued, the final one in 1892. This was the sole guide published until S. N. Hurst's work in 1893. Except for the 1860 edition, each new edition was published in conjunction with major changes in the law. The 1852 edition follows the constitutional change establishing the new court system and the 1892 edition was necessary to bring the work up to date under the Code of 1887.

The demise of the lay justice was nearly complete during Reconstruction when he was replaced by a new county court under the authority of a professional judge.[16] This new county court further reduced the justices' power, sharing concurrent jurisdiction over minor offenses and claims in value of twenty to one hundred dollars.[17] The revision of this new system in 1902 did not revive the former powers of the justices. They remained elected officials, paid on a fee basis, and shared concurrent jurisdiction with the circuit courts.

[12] Va. Code, vol. 1, p. 226, chap. 69 (1819).

[13] For comments on the county courts and the justices of the peace from 1800 to 1850, see H. Conrad, "The Old County Court System of Virginia: Its Place in History," *Va. State Bar Ass'n Repts.*, vol. 21, pp. 321, 334-339 (1908); W. R. Staples, "History of the Old County Court System of Virginia Prior to 1861," *Va. State Bar Ass'n Repts.*, vol. 7, pp. 127, 141-142 (1894).

[14] Va. Const., Art. 6, §§ 27-28 (1851); 1852 Va. Acts, p. 64, chap. 71.

[15] Va. Const., Art. 6, § 13, Art. 7, § 2 (1870); A. O. Porter, *County Government in Virginia*, pp. 244-245 (1947).

[16] Va. Const., Art. 6, § 13 (1870).

[17] W. R. Furr, II, "The Justice of the Peace in Virginia: A Neglected Aspect of the Judiciary," *Va. L. Rev.*, vol. 52, pp. 151, 157-158 (1966).

It is noteworthy how the officials were paid. It was not a set annual salary, but rather, the justices were paid on a case by case basis, which was the medieval English method of funding the government, including the judiciary. To be compensated in a civil action, the justice must have found for the plaintiff, and in a criminal action, he received only half his normal compensation if he failed to convict.[18] It is thus readily apparent that the justices had an interest in the outcome of the action. This interest became a question of procedural due process addressed by the United States Supreme Court in 1927.[19] In Virginia, a conviction was upheld despite this pecuniary interest of the justice since the Virginia court system allowed for a *de novo* review of the conviction in the circuit court; where a timely appeal was made to the circuit court, a conviction was upheld.[20] During this period, a new manual appeared. The publication of *Smith's Justices' Guide* in 1929 was a response to the need of an update of the laws and duties of the justices.

Despite the judicial approval of the fee basis system in Virginia, the General Assembly did institute changes in response to the critics of the program. In 1936, the Assembly enacted into law the system of salaried trial justices.[21] Under this legislation, only the power to admit to bail and to issue warrants was reserved for the justices.[22] Little substantive change occurred over the next thirty years even with the adoption of the Code of 1950.[23]

By the 1960s, questions were posed regarding the effect of a justice system administered by individuals not required to be experienced in the law.[24] A response to this was the publication of the *Virginia Justices of the Peace Manual* in 1967, published by the Association of Justices of the Peace. If the Association was attempting to thwart the mounting criticisms of the system, it failed. In 1973, the justice of the peace system was abolished in Virginia and replaced by a magistrates

[18] *Id.* at p. 162.

[19] Tumey v. Ohio, 273 U.S. 510 (1927), holding a direct pecuniary interest by the justice disqualifies him from judgment. Subsequently, courts interpreted this holding narrowly given the facts in *Tumey*.

[20] Brooks v. Town of Potomac, 149 Va. 427, 141 S.E. 249 (1928).

[21] The Trial Justice Act of 1936, 1936 Va. Acts, p. 615, chap. 385.

[22] W. R. Furr, II, "The Justice of the Peace in Virginia," *Va. L. Rev.*, vol. 52, pp. 151, 165-168 (1966).

[23] Compare Va. Code Ann. § 39-1 *et seq.* (1953) with The Trial Justice Act of 1936.

[24] See W. R. Furr, II, "The Justice of the Peace in Virginia," *Va. L. Rev.*, vol. 52, pp. 151, 176-179 (1966).

system.[25]

To underscore how few treatises were written on the substantive criminal law, the next treatise after those of John B. Minor appeared in 1984. Professor Roger Groot's *Criminal Offenses and Defenses in Virginia* discusses the substantive criminal law since the nineteenth century. In an effort to compile all this material into a useful text, the author lists alphabetically the types of offenses that may occur and the punishment that may result. This is a format similar to that used by the old manuals for justices of the peace. An explanation of the law is given as well as citations to the code and applicable cases. To read Groot coupled with Davis would well inform anyone on the substantive criminal law in the history of Virginia.

Even though the three texts by Davis, Minor, and Groot and a fourth one by J. L. Costello provide a wealth of information, it may be puzzling that so few treatises were written. Certainly the justices' manuals filled some of the void, but 1894 to 1984 is an extremely long time without some substantive new work. Perhaps there were no significant changes in the criminal law. Perhaps it was the new case method of law studies. This method was based on the premise that to begin the study of law with a textbook was starting backward. This method posited that the better learning experience for the student was to deduct the rule of law that dictated the outcome of each case. Only after this deductive process had occurred was the student able to understand fully a text stating the substantive law. No longer was a student required to study law from "institutes and authoritative treatises"[26] as their original sources. Virginia's publication of criminal law treatises supports this explanation.

For ninety years after Minor's, no other general treatise[27] on the criminal law was presented. This bears a direct correlation with the national trend. Francis Wharton's *A Treatise on the Criminal Law of the United States* went unchallenged for nearly one hundred years.[28] As the case method of law study gained in popularity, the need for treatises diminished. This may explain the drought in the creation of criminal law treatises in Virginia. But this is not to say legal writing ceased in Virginia, for during this dry spell on the substantive law,

[25] 1973 Va. Acts, p. 1234, chap. 545; Va. Code Ann. § 19.2-26 *et seq.*

[26] H. F. Stone, "Introduction," in F. C. Hicks, *Men and Books Famous in the Law*, p. 10 (1921).

[27] Note that H. B. Lee's book was not a treatise but merely a digest.

[28] Wharton's treatise, which was first published in 1846, received wide acclaim with multiple editions up to 1932. E. C. Surrency, *A History of American Law Publishing*, p. 146 (1990).

manuals for justices were still prepared and treatises on criminal procedure began to appear in Virginia.

In the 1960s, the United States Supreme Court forced major changes in the federal and state laws of criminal procedure. This was done in order to control abusive police practices. It was accomplished by declaring the use of improperly obtained statements and objects to be an unconstitutional deprivation of rights if admitted as evidence to convict of a crime. This was a huge change in the criminal law, and new books were needed to explain the practical ramifications.

Professor Ronald Bacigal's *Virginia Criminal Procedure* takes the reader through the subject from arrest to appeal and gives special attention to federal constitutional law. This discussion of constitutional law provides guidance for police actions taken prior to the formal arrest. Originally published in 1983, it remains current through its annual supplements.

Defending Criminal Cases in Virginia, authored by Professor Richard Williamson, is sponsored jointly by the Virginia State Bar and the Virginia Bar Association; it may be characterized as a handbook. This looseleaf book explains the procedures to be followed coupled with explanation and analysis.

This bibliography also includes manuals for magistrates in Virginia. These appeared after the justice of the peace system was abolished in 1973. The manuals prepared by Professor Bacigal and by the Supreme Court of Virginia were written to educate the magistrates in the proper performance of the their jobs, just like the manuals for the justices of the peace. The magistrates' manuals provide a clear and concise text on the criminal law along with explanations of its application. Both manuals come in looseleaf binder form so that as changes in the law are made, they are quickly noted in the manuals.

Several books have been written that cover narrow areas of the criminal law, such as bootlegging, duelling, and forensic medicine. Books on penal institutions have been included here in order to complete the picture of the criminal law.

The purpose of this bibliography is to offer assistance to legal researchers and historians. Its scope is restricted to works about Virginia law and more specifically the criminal law in Virginia.[29] The earliest works to systematically characterize these legal doctrines are the manuals prepared for the justices of the peace. The offshoot of these texts are the criminal law treatises that first appeared in the nineteenth century. By consulting these books, one can embark on a time line journey of the developing criminal law in Virginia to

[29] Accounts of individual criminal trials are included in "Accounts of Trials," see above.

understand how it evolved into its current form.

BIBLIOGRAPHY

Attorney General's Criminal Law Digest. Richmond: Office of the Attorney General, 1984 to 1987, 4 vols.

> This is a quarterly digest of criminal opinions issued by the Attorney General of Virginia. It was replaced by *The Law Digest.*

Bacigal, Ronald J[oseph]. *Virginia Criminal Procedure.* Norcross, Ga.: The Harrison Co., 1983; 2d ed., Norcross, Ga.: The Harrison Co., 1989; 3d ed., Norcross, Ga.: The Harrison Co., 1994; 4th ed., Norcross, Ga.: The Harrison Co., 1999.

> This guide takes the practitioner from arrest to appeal, with explanation of the points of law along the way. There is a focus on Virginia law with special attention paid to the federal constitutional law. Pocket part supplements are published annually. It was reviewed by Charles E. Friend, *Va. Bar Ass'n J.*, vol. 9, no. 4, p. 26 (Fall, 1983), and Murray J. Janus, *U. of Richmond Law Rev.*, vol. 17, pp. 881-883 (1983).

Bacigal, Ronald J[oseph]. *Virginia Criminal Procedure Forms.* Norcross, Ga.: The Harrison Co., 1984; 2d ed., Norcross, Ga.: The Harrison Co., 1989; 3d ed., Norcross, Ga.: The Harrison Co., 1995; 4th ed., Norcross, Ga.: The Harrison Co., 2000.

> This book contains a large number of sample forms pertaining to Virginia criminal procedure. Some of them are official forms, which are provided in printed format by the Office of the Executive Secretary of the Virginia Supreme Court.

Bacigal, Ronald J[oseph]. *Virginia Magistrates' Manual.* Richmond: Division of Justice and Crime Prevention, 1974.

> This guide was prepared for the magistrates in office in 1974, after the abolition of the justice of the peace system, with the purpose of educating them in the proper performance of their office. The applicable forms are included.

Berry, Calvin W. *Arrest, Search, and Seizure.* Charlottesville: The Michie Co., 1973.

This book analyzes current Virginia and federal law.

Berry, Calvin W. *Criminal Practice in Municipal and County Courts.* Charlottesville: The Michie Co., 1964.

Burks, Martin P[arks]. *Criminal Procedure: Notes to Beale's Criminal Pleading and Practice.* N.p., 1911.

This short book was printed for the use of law students.

Burton, Peter J. *Police Court Pictures at Richmond, Virginia.* Richmond: C. N. Williams, 1892.

This is a book of humorous sketches and anecdotes.

Clarke, Joseph M., II. *Virginia Criminal Law Case Finder.* Charlottesville: The Michie Co., 1987; 2d ed., Charlottesville: The Michie Co., 1991; 3d ed., Charlottesville: Michie, 1995, 2 vols.

This digest is kept up to date by means of pocket supplements.

Clayton, Michael F., and Preston T. Scott. *Juvenile Justice in Virginia.* Charlottesville: The Michie Co., 1982.

Costello, John L. *Virginia Criminal Law and Procedure.* Charlottesville: The Michie Co., 1991; 2d ed., Charlottesville: The Michie Co., 1995.

Davis, J[ohn] A[nthony] G[ardner]. *A Treatise on Criminal Law, with an Exposition of the Office and Authority of Justices of the Peace in Virginia; Including Forms of Practice.* Philadelphia: C. Sherman and Co., 1838.

The first treatise on the criminal law of Virginia. A "novel" approach by the author to combine legal study with the practical application of these principles. Davis (1802-1840) was a practicing attorney, professor of law at the University of Virginia, and a justice of the peace for Albemarle County. He was able to rely on this background to provide a comprehensive treatise on the criminal law.

Fuller, Hugh N[elson]. *Criminal Justice in Virginia.* New York: The Century Co., 1931.

This is a descriptive and statistical study of the Virginia criminal justice system.

Furr, Warwick R[ex], II. *Virginia Justices of the Peace Manual.* Charlottesville: Association of Justices of the Peace, 1967.

This was a guide for the justices sponsored by the Association of Justices of the Peace of Virginia. For an extensive discussion of justices of the peace, see W. R. Furr, II, "The Justice of the Peace in Virginia: A Neglected Aspect of the Judiciary," *Va. L. Rev.*, vol. 52, pp. 151-188 (1966).

Geimer, William S., and Roger D[ouglas] Groot. *Trial of Capital Murder Cases in Virginia.* Charlottesville: Committee on Continuing Legal Education of the Virginia Law Foundation, 1991 to present.

This is a looseleaf handbook.

Goode, James E. *New Criminal Procedure of the State of Virginia: With Full Annotations and a Complete Index.* Richmond: Goode, 1878.

Groot, Roger D[ouglas]. *Criminal Offenses and Defenses in Virginia.* Norcross, Ga.: The Harrison Co., 1984; 2d ed., Norcross, Ga.: The Harrison Co., 1989; 3d ed., Norcross, Ga.: The Harrison Co., 1994; 4th ed., Norcross, Ga.: The Harrison Co., 1998.

The author compiles all the substantive criminal law from the nineteenth century through the current acts of the General Assembly; it includes an outline of crimes and defenses and the relevant appellate case law interpreting them. This book is kept up to date by means of annual pocket supplements.

Gwathmey, John H[astings]. *Justice John: Tales from the Courtroom of the Virginia Judge.* Richmond: Dietz Printing Co., 1934.

This book is a humorous and sentimental portrait of John Jeter Crutchfield (1844-1920), who was the police court judge in the City of Richmond from 1888 to 1920.

Hawes, Herbert Bouldin, and Joel W[est] Flood. *Prohibition Index-Manual, Virginia and West Virginia.* Charlottesville: The Michie Co., 1930.

Hening, William Waller. *The New Virginia Justice.* Richmond: T. Nicolson, 1795; Richmond: Aug. Davis, 1799; "2d ed.," Richmond:

Johnson & Warner, 1810; "3d ed.," Richmond: J. & G. Cochran, 1820; "4th ed." (*The Virginia Justice*), Richmond: Shepherd & Pollard, 1825.

> This is an encompassing guide for the justices explaining the law and its application in Virginia. It also provides a guide regarding laws arising under the laws of the United States and their application in Virginia. It includes a glossary of legal terms and many forms. 1825 Va. Acts, p. 25, chap. 26, provided for the Commonwealth to buy copies of the last edition to be given to each magistrate in Virginia. This was the opportunity for political skullduggery resulting in a serious financial loss to Hening. See S. M. Walker, Jr., "William Waller Hening," *Law Reporters in Virginia Before 1880*, pp. 19-24 (1977).

Hoffer, Frank William, Delbert Martin Mann, and Floyd Nelson House. *The Jails of Virginia: A Study of the Local Penal System*. New York: D. Appleton-Century Co., 1933.

Hoffer, Peter Charles, and William B. Scott, eds. *Criminal Proceedings in Colonial Virginia: [Records of] Fines, Examination of Criminals, Trial of Slaves, etc. from March 1710 [1711] to [1754] [Richmond County, Virginia]*. American Legal Records, vol. 10. Washington, D.C.: Am. Hist. Assn., 1984.

> This work contains a lengthy introduction that provides a historical background for the court records.

Hogg, William Edward. *Virginia Criminal Law*. Richmond: Richmond Press, Inc., 1939.

> This is a digest of criminal law cases.

Howard, Henry. *Outlines of Medical Jurisprudence*. Charlottesville: Magruder & Noel, 1842; 3d ed. Charlottesville: Noel, 1845; 4th ed. [*Synopsis of Medical Jurisprudence*] Charlottesville: Allen, 1849; 5th ed. Charlottesville: James Alexander, 1851.

> This book was based on Professor Howard's lectures on forensic medicine at the Medical School of the University of Virginia.

Howison, Robert R[eid]. *Reports of Criminal Trials*. Richmond: George M. West & Brother, 1851; New York: H. A. Warren, 1937;

Buffalo, N.Y.: Dennis & Co., 1950.

> See Reports Section.

Hurst, Sam[uel] N[eed]. *A Complete Annotated Criminal Digest.* Pulaski City, Va.: Hurst and Co., 1900.

> See Indexes, Digests Section.

Hurst, Sam[ue]l N[eed]. *A New Guide for Justices of the Peace in Virginia.* Richmond: J. L. Hill, 1893; 2d ed., Pulaski City, Va.: Hurst & Co., 1904.

> This guide was written in conjunction with the Virginia Code of 1887 to bring the justices up to date. A second edition was published following the Constitution of 1902.

Johnson, Chapman, and Robert G[ourmain] Scott. *Revision and Digest of the Criminal Code of Virginia.* Richmond: Shepherd & Colin, 1846.

> See Indexes, Digests Section.

Jordan, Louis F[enimore]. *Memoirs of a Criminal Lawyer or Trying the Criminal Case.* Staunton: The Beverley Press, Inc., 1935.

> Jordan began the practice of law in 1917; he practiced in the City of Waynesboro.

Karraker, Cyrus Harreld. *The Seventeenth-Century Sheriff: A Comparative Study of the Sheriff in England and the Chesapeake Colonies, 1607-1689.* Chapel Hill: Univ. of North Carolina Press, 1930; rept. Plainview, N.Y.: Books for Libraries, 1973.

> This work of legal history has an appendix of illustrative documents; it was reviewed in *A.H.R.*, vol. 36, pp. 429-430 (1931).

Keve, Paul W. *The History of Corrections in Virginia.* Charlottesville: Univ. Press of Va., 1986.

> This is a scholarly history of prisons and penal institutions in Virginia.

A

NEW GUIDE

FOR

JUSTICES OF THE PEACE OF VIRGINIA;

ALSO

COMMONWEALTH'S ATTORNEYS, AND OTHER COUNTY AND DISTRICT OFFICERS OF THE STATE,

IN THE DISCHARGE OF THEIR RESPECTIVE DUTIES,

TOGETHER WITH

USEFUL FORMS

FOR THE PRACTICAL PERFORMANCE OF THE SAME;

AS WELL AS A

MANUAL

FOR

ATTORNEYS AT LAW,

AS TO

CRIMINAL LAW AND PRACTICE, AND ALL MATTERS OF A CIVIL OR CRIMINAL NATURE COGNIZABLE BY OR APPERTAINING TO THE COURTS OF A SINGLE JUSTICE.

BY

SAM N. HURST,

Author of "Hurst's Annotated Virginia Digest;" "Hurst's Annotated Pocket Code of Virginia;" "Hurst's Annotated Virginia Constitution;" &c.

Second Edition, Revised and Subjects Treated Alphabetically.

PULASKI CITY, VIRGINIA:
HURST & COMPANY, LAW PUBLISHERS.
1904.

Lee, Howard B[urton]. *The Criminal Trial in the Virginias.* Charleston, W. Va.: Jarrett Printing Co., 1926; 2d ed., Charlottesville: The Michie Co., 1940, 2 vols.

> This is accurately described by the author as "a ready reference volume for trial work, and a digest with citations." There are also numerous forms for the criminal law practice in Virginia and West Virginia. Lee was Attorney General of West Virginia.

Matthews, James M[uscoe]. *Digest of the Laws of Virginia of a Criminal Nature.* Richmond: West & Johnston, 1861; 2d ed., Richmond: J. W. Randolph & English, 1871; supp., Richmond: J. W. Randolph & English, 1878; 3d ed., Richmond: J. W. Randolph & English, 1890.

> See Indexes, Digests Section.

Mayo, Joseph. *A Guide to Magistrates: With Practical Forms.* Richmond: Smith, 1849; new ed., Richmond: Colin, Baptist & Nowlan, 1850; Richmond: Nash & Woodhouse, 1853; 2d ed., Richmond: A. Morris, 1860; 3d ed. by H. W. Flournoy & J. Thompson Brown, Richmond: James E. Goode, 1892.

> This guide offered the justices analysis of and citations to Virginia case law; it includes forms for the justices' use in discharging their duties. Copies were bought by the Commonwealth for distribution to all clerks of court, justices of the peace, and coroners: 1859-60 Va. Acts, ch. 87, p. 192; 1861 Va. Acts, ch. 33, p. 57. The 1892 edition was revised and adapted by Flournoy and Brown after Mayo's death, but it was their intention only to make revisions necessary to bring the work current with the present state of the law under the Code of 1887. It was reviewed in *Q.L.J.*, vol. 1, p. 287 (1856).

Minor, John B[arbee]. *Exposition of the Law of Crimes and Punishments.* Richmond: Anderson Bros., 1894.

> Even though the title has changed, this is actually an enlargement of *A Synopsis of the Law of the Crimes and Punishments in Virginia* and some may even consider it the completed edition. Comparing this to *Synopsis*, the chapter headings are the same and the unusual outline format is used. Unlike *Synopsis*, this work includes a general index and an index of cases.

Minor, John B[arbee]. *A Synopsis of the Law of Crimes and Punishments in Virginia.* Philadelphia: William S. Young, 1858; 2d ed., Richmond: Hazlewood, 1869.

> The author intended this work to be used by the law students of the University of Virginia. It is a syllabus of the lectures the author gave as part of his classroom instruction in the study of the criminal law. The reader should take notice of the unusual format adopted by Minor. He planned the printing of the text so that certain principles are numbered, lettered, and indented to aid the student in distinguishing the principles of major importance from those of lesser importance.

Patterson, A[rchibald] W[illiams]. *The Code Duello with Special Reference to the State of Virginia.* Richmond: Richmond Press, Inc., 1927.

> This refers to cases on dueling and the 1810 Va. Act (now Va. Code Ann., § 8.01-45 (1950): action for insulting words).

Pollard, John Garland, and Christopher B[rowne] Garnett. *A Guide to Magistrates and Constables.* Richmond: Everett Waddey Co., 1906.

> This book includes the full texts of the relevant statutes and numerous forms.

Rankin, Hugh F[ranklin]. *Criminal Trial Proceedings in the General Court of Colonial Virginia.* Williamsburg: Colonial Williamsburg, 1965.

Redden, Kenneth R[obert], and Dulcey Fowler. *The Judicial Administration of Criminal Justice in Virginia.* Charlottesville: n.p., 1974.

Schwarz, Philip J[ames]. *Twice Condemned: Slaves and the Criminal Laws of Virginia, 1705-1865.* [Baton Rouge, La.]: Louisiana State Univ. Pr., 1988; rept., Union, N.J.: Lawbook Exchange, Ltd., 1998.

> Portions of this book were also published in *Va. Mag. Hist. Biog.*, vol. 90, pp. 283-309 (1982). This is a work of painstaking research; however, as to the interpretation of it, "Schwarz insists that every crime by a slave was an act of

> rebellion . . . . [which] does not correspond well to human experience." D. J. Bodenhamer, book review, *Law and Hist. Rev.*, vol. 10, p. 195 (1992).

Scott, Arthur P[earson]. *Criminal Law in Colonial Virginia.* Chicago: Univ. of Chicago Press, 1930.

Smith, Charles S[amuel], Jr. *Smith's Justices' Guide.* Charlottesville: The Michie Co., 1929.

> This is a guide to justices of the peace intended to revise Mayo's *Guide to Magistrates.* It is a simple explanation of the Code as reflected in the statutory changes of 1919 and 1928. Applicable forms are included throughout the text.

Starke, Richard. *The Office and Authority of a Justice of Peace.* Williamsburg: Alexander Purdie & John Dixon, 1774.

> The duties of the justices are explained and precedents are provided; also this book discusses the duties of sheriffs and other public officials. It was published posthumously by the friends of the author. See "Stark's Free School and `Justice of the Peace'." *Wm. & Mary Qtly.*, 1st ser., vol. 4, pp. 197-200 (1896).

Virginia Circuit Court Judges Benchbook: Criminal. Charlottesville: The Michie Co., 1991 to present.

> This is a looseleaf handbook.

Virginia Magistrates' Manual. Richmond: Executive Secretary of the Supreme Court of Va., 1981.

> This is a looseleaf publication that provides the magistrates with information on the orientation and disposition of their duties. To date there have been ten revisions of this text.

Virginia Model Jury Instructions: Criminal. Charlottesville: The Michie Co., 1979 to present, 2 vols.

> This is a looseleaf service.

The Virginia Prosecutor. Richmond: Office of the Attorney General, Dec. 1971 to present.

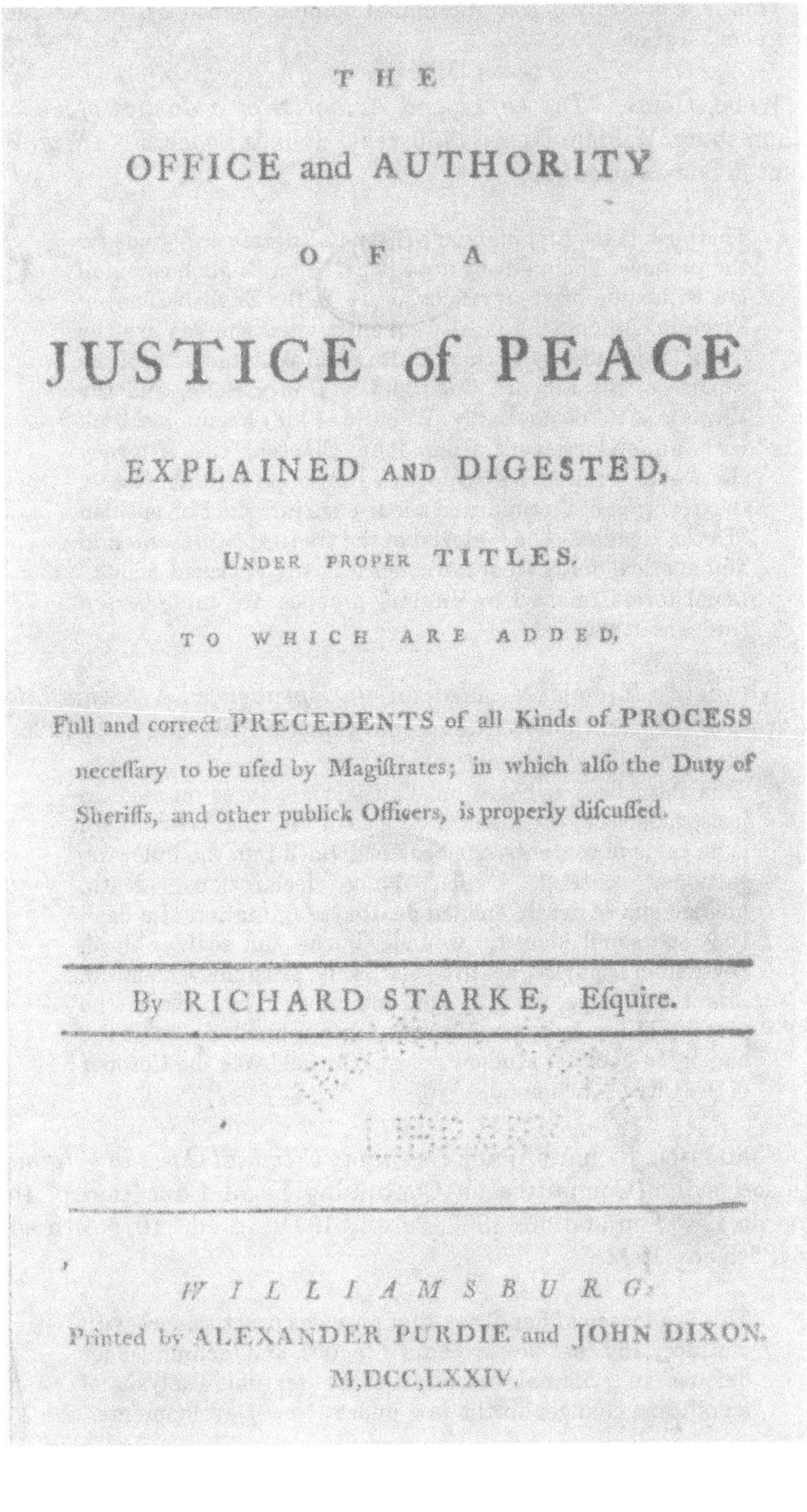

THE

OFFICE and AUTHORITY

OF A

JUSTICE of PEACE

EXPLAINED AND DIGESTED,

UNDER PROPER TITLES.

TO WHICH ARE ADDED,

Full and correct PRECEDENTS of all Kinds of PROCESS neceſſary to be uſed by Magiſtrates; in which alſo the Duty of Sheriffs, and other publick Officers, is properly diſcuſſed.

By RICHARD STARKE, Eſquire.

WILLIAMSBURG:

Printed by ALEXANDER PURDIE and JOHN DIXON.

M,DCC,LXXIV.

This is a monthly digest of criminal opinions issued by the Attorney General of Virginia.

Webb, George. *The Office and Authority of a Justice of Peace.* Williamsburg: William Parks, 1736; rept. Holmes Beach, Fla.: Wm. W. Gaunt & Sons, Inc., 1969.

> This book is the first manual written in Virginia as a guide for the justices. The analysis used is based on English common law with appropriate revisions for use in the English colony of Virginia. Among the most frequently cited sources are the books for justices by Michael Dalton and William Nelson, the reports of Sir Edward Coke and of Henry Rolle, and the Virginia Acts of Assembly. Webb (d. 1758) begins his book with an endorsement from John Clayton, the Attorney General of Virginia, a four-page dedication to William Gooch, the Governor of Virginia, and a four-page introduction entitled "To the Reader." The material of the treatise is presented in alphabetical form from "Accessories" to "Wrecked Ships." Legal forms tailored to Virginia practice are interspersed throughout the text.

Whitfield, Ja[me]s M. *Medical Jurisprudence: A Manual for Students and Practitioners.* Richmond: Central Pub. Co., Inc., 1925.

> This short book is based on Whitfield's lectures on medical jurisprudence at the Medical College of Virginia. While there is no table of contents, the book is divided into the following sections: contracts, wills, dying declarations, death, phenomena of death, sudden deaths, examination of a dead body, personal identity, wounds, burns and scalds, blood, death from asphyxia, death by electricity, pregnancy, abortion, infanticide, rape, insanity, and toxicology. The book has no preface, index or forms, but does contain blank pages at the end of the book for student notes. Whitfield was the Coroner of the City of Richmond.

Williamson, Richard A[lan]. *Defending Criminal Cases in Virginia.* Charlottesville: Committee on Continuing Legal Education of the Virginia Law Foundation, 1966; 2d ed., 1971; 3d ed., 1975; 4th ed., 1981; 5th ed., 1992.

> This is a looseleaf handbook that provides practitioners with statutory and case law procedure, tactics, and techniques for defense in criminal cases. It offers textual analysis of significant changes in the law under "New Developments."

The different editions coincide with significant revisions in the law. There are frequent supplements, which give all relevant statutory changes that have occurred since the last edition. It was reviewed by Murray J. Janus, *Va. Bar Ass'n J.*, vol. 8, no. 1, p. 27 (Winter 1982).

NINETEENTH-CENTURY LAW JOURNALS

E. Lee Shepard

A DEFINITE MARK of the increasing sophistication of any professional group is the encouragement and support its members provide for the publication of a serial devoted to their special field.[1] Several preconditions must be met to insure even moderate success for such a venture. The professional group must be large enough and successful enough to support a specialized journal, both intellectually and financially; the economic climate must be favorable for the inauguration and maintenance of a new publishing venture; and there must be a sense among the members of the profession of their need as individuals and as a group for the technical expertise provided for a mass audience by such a publication. This latter condition would seem to be dependent upon a burgeoning sense of group self-awareness, a "professional consciousness," which fosters both a concern for the public image of the group and a desire to upgrade the practical abilities and knowledge of its rank and file.[2]

I. *Law Quarterly Journal*

Ironically, the lion's share of the credit for establishing the first legal periodicals in Virginia belongs to a person who was not even an attorney. Joseph Williamson Randolph (1815-1893) was a Chesterfield County native. At age fourteen, he had been apprenticed to Richmond book seller John W. Nash and, by the mid-1830s, he had prospered so well as to have established his own successful business in the capital city.[3] He was operating a bindery, publishing house, and bookstore at 121 Main Street when, in 1855, he circulated through the Richmond legal community a prospectus concerning the publication of "A Quarterly Law Journal."[4]

---

[1] This essay was first published as "The First Law Journals in Virginia," in *Law Library Journal*, vol. 79, pp. 33-52 (1987), and is reprinted with permission.

[2] E. L. Shepard, "Lawyers Look at Themselves: Professional Consciousness and the Virginia Bar, 1770-1850," *Am. J. Legal Hist.*, vol. 25, pp. 1, 3 (1981).

[3] See below, "J. W. Randolph."

[4] J. W. Randolph, *A Quarterly Law Journal: Edited by a Member of the Richmond Bar* (1855) (broadside collection, Virginia Historical Society, Richmond, Virginia).

THE

QUARTERLY

LAW JOURNAL.

EDITED BY

A. B. GUIGON,

OF THE RICHMOND BAR.

VOLUME II.

J. W. RANDOLPH, PUBLISHER,
121 MAIN STREET, RICHMOND, VIRGINIA.

RICHMOND:
MACFARLANE & FERGUSSON, PRINTERS.
1857.

Randolph advanced his proposal for what would become the Richmond-based *Quarterly Law Journal* at a time when lawyers were beginning actively to support the publication of legal periodicals. Tired of the limiting nature of literary journals, general magazines, and reviews, lawyers throughout the nation looked for other outlets for their contributions and patronage.[5]

Support for magazines devoted strictly to the law, though never overwhelming in the early nineteenth century, seemed strongest in the North. John E. Hall published the *American Law Journal* in Philadelphia for nine years (1808-1817), and Willard Phillips produced the *American Jurist and Law Magazine* in Boston for fourteen (1829-1843).[6] Several efforts in Pennsylvania proved moderately successful before the Civil War, most notably the Philadelphia *Legal Intelligencer*,[7] and a professor of law at Cincinnati College could boast of the ten-year existence of his *Western Law Journal* (1843-1853).[8]

In the South, on the other hand, support lagged well behind the ambitious plans of some prominent attorneys. Three attempts to begin law journals in southern states – North Carolina, South Carolina, and

[5] The *Southern Literary Messenger*, published in Richmond from 1834 to 1864, provided an important outlet for the writings of Southern attorneys in the antebellum era. For some examples, see "Memoir of the Ambitious Lawyer," *Sou. Literary Messenger*, vol. 1, p. 645 (1835); "Bar Associations," *Sou. Literary Messenger*, vol. 4, p. 581 (1838); "Study of the Law," *Sou. Literary Messenger*, vol. 2, p. 25 (1837); "Recollections of a Retired Lawyer," *Sou. Literary Messenger*, vol. 5, p. 97 (1839); C. Robinson, "Slavery and the Constitution," *Sou. Literary Messenger*, vol. 6, p. 89 (1840); B. B. Minor, "The Legal Profession: Lawyers and Lawyers' Fees in the 'Old Dominion'," *Sou. Literary Messenger*, vol. 13, p. 611 (1847); L. Minor, "Law Reports," *Sou. Literary Messenger*, vol. 14, p. 255 (1848). The *Southern Review*, based in Charleston, South Carolina, served a similar purpose.

[6] F. L. Mott, *A History of American Magazines*, vol. 1, pp. 154-156 (1930).

[7] *Id.*, vol. 2, p. 93, n. 212 (1938).

[8] *Id.*, vol. 1, p. 452 & n. 5. See also the bibliographical note on "contemporary law journals" in J. Horton, *James Kent: A Study in Conservatism, 1763-1847*, pp. 331-333 (1939); M. Bloomfield, *American Lawyers in a Changing Society, 1776-1876*, pp. 142-144 (1976). Despite their limited success, most of the state and regional law journals in the North left much to be desired. A Philadelphia legal scholar remarked to a Virginia correspondent, for instance, that the short-lived *Pennsylvania Law Journal* was: "a sort of penny trumpet for the use of all the country judges throughout this big state to blast themselves into fame; each one of them being willing to pay for printing the blatterations of his 150 co-judges for the sake of seeing his own seven or eight yards of nonsense brought out into like legibility. It is in short a mere repertory of Common Pleas decisions, supported by that first great love of our countrymen, the love of being everlastingly before the public in some form, and a willingness to appear there as dullheads and mountebanks rather than not appear at all." Letter from John William Wallace to William Green (Dec. 24, 1847) (William Green Papers, available at Virginia Historical Society).

Louisiana – all proved to be short-lived.[9] Consequently, J. W. Randolph adroitly traded on the Northern supremacy in the publishing of legal literature when seeking support for his *Quarterly Law Journal*. "The want of such a work, containing material of peculiar interest and importance to the Bar of Virginia and of other States," declared Randolph, "has been long felt and frequently expressed, and more than one publisher has been solicited to undertake its publication." Stressing that the bars of Massachusetts, New York, and Pennsylvania already had specialized serials available to them – and that members were supporting such publications financially – Randolph asked, "Why should not the barristers of Virginia and of the South have theirs? A journal which they may call their own, and in the pages of which they will find law more peculiarly affecting their actual daily practice?"

Randolph initially planned to furnish reports from the federal courts in Richmond and the Virginia Court of Appeals ("before they can be published by the State Reporter"), a significant aid to attorneys anxious to acquire the most recent decisions in the absence of advance sheets. He also intended to supply a complete digest of *Grattan's Reports*, which would succeed Benjamin Tate's *Analytical Digested Index of the Reported Cases from the Court of Appeals and General Court of Virginia* (1847). Each number of his proposed journal would contain, in addition, a chapter from the *Reports of the Revisors of the Code of Virginia*, compiled by Conway Robinson and John Mercer Patton, with the revisors' notes "and such alterations of the Code of Virginia as have been made by statutory enactments since the year 1849. . . . The importance of these Reports is well known by members of the profession who have had occasion to consult them, as shedding light upon the provisions of the Code." Lastly, Randolph announced that the remainder of the journal would be filled with "the usual matter of such publications; – the latest reports of new and important decisions, essays on interesting legal subjects, and occasional biographies of those distinguished members of the bar, now deceased, who in their day and generation, won for it merited distinction and honor. . . ." He promised contributions by such prominent Virginia legalists as William Green, Professor John B. Minor of the University

[9] The *Carolina Law Repository* of Raleigh ran through two volumes, March 1813 to September 1816; the *Carolina Law Journal* was published in Columbia, South Carolina, from July 1830 to April 1831; the *Louisiana Law Journal* of New Orleans appeared quarterly from May 1841 to April 1842. On the second of these, see Leverette, "The Carolina Law Journal of 1830," *S. C. Law Qtly.*, vol. 12, p. 193 (1960).

of Virginia, William T. Joynes, J. M. Matthews, and Alexander H. Sands.[10]

One of these intended contributors, William Green, responded to Randolph's overture and offered some important advice on how he should proceed. Green, himself an able practitioner at the bar of the Court of Appeals and an acknowledged legal scholar, first suggested a broadening of the scope of the journal by including reported cases from sister states, lest it have no attraction outside Virginia. If reports of Virginia cases were to be published, Green proposed that they contain supplementary annotations not to be included in the official reporter's version. He also recommended that in important cases, counsel be urged to provide their full arguments for publication. Green strongly opposed a continuation of Tate's *Index* ("a book of *less* than no value at all")[11] and the reprinting of the Revisors' Reports ("Most of the gentlemen, who can be reasonably expected to patronize the Law Journal have already got the Revisors' Reports in bound volumes. It would be irksome to them to get duplicates at such an expense."). Finally, Green suggested a feature that he claimed would be interesting, popular, and valuable, one that would "*judge the Judges*. . . . [A] manly and able review of the decisions of our courts, conducted with perfect candour, and entire respect for the integrity of the Judges would be of great public advantage," he argued. Such a venture in the new journal, however, could only prove successful, Green told Randolph, "if you could find gentlemen of spirit enough" to serve as editors.[12]

Randolph heeded much of Green's advice. He did, indeed, find a "gentleman of spirit" to edit the journal: Alexander Barclay Guigon (1831-1878). Guigon, a relatively unknown Richmonder, practiced in the local courts in and around the capital city but only qualified in the Court of Appeals in April, 1859, near the end of his editorial career. He was early admired by his brother attorneys, however, for his scholarly abilities.[13] Under his hand, and with the supervisory talents of J. W. Randolph, the first number of the *Quarterly Law Journal* appeared in January, 1856.

---

[10] *Id.*; W. H. Bryson, "Advance Sheets in Virginia," *Virginia Law Reporters*, pp. 129-130 (1977). Randolph's plan followed the general pattern of law journals of the day, though in some respects he seems more ambitious. See M. Bloomfield, *supra*, at pp. 142-144.

[11] Letter from William Green to J. W. Randolph (Sept. 26, 1855) (William Green Papers, available at Virginia Historical Society).

[12] *Id.*

[13] P. A. Bruce, *History of Virginia*, vol. 4, pp. 237-238 (1924).

The American legal periodicals of that time, it must be remembered, primarily comprised *reports* of cases rather than *reviews* of the law and thus differed significantly from periodicals of that genre today. Though the bulk of each issue of the *Journal* would be filled with case reports, Guigon had ambitious plans for his publication. "The columns of the Journal," he declared in the first number, "will always be open to fair criticisms of judicial decisions and conduct, and to such propositions for modifications of the laws and the present judicial system as they seem to require."[14] This encouragement of contributions by fellow attorneys was tinged with a healthy measure of realism, for "the cordial and profuse offers of assistance with which [the editor] was cheered at the commencement of the work, [have] in the main proved, as usual, delusive."[15]

The first issue carried articles on "Legislative Tinkering"[16] (the amendment of the Code and statute law by poorly qualified legislators) and "The Usury Laws" in Virginia.[17] Several essays were reprinted from the *London Law Magazine*. Primarily, the issue contained case reports from such divergent tribunals as the English common law and chancery courts, the New York Supreme Court, the United States district and circuit courts for Virginia, and the Virginia Court of Appeals. This number set the basic tone for the entire run of the *Journal*.

Initially, Guigon borrowed heavily from British law journals and court reports. He also attempted to reprint important American case law that came to his attention and that had, or seemed to have, particular relevance for his Southern audience. The early numbers of the *Journal* abound with railroad and industrial litigation, commercial law, and, not surprisingly, cases involving slavery and emancipation.[18] Guigon himself routinely took the legislature to task for producing inadequate or ill-advised laws and chastised members of the judiciary

---

[14] "Introductory," *Q.L.J.*, vol. 1, p. 2 (1856).

[15] *Id.* Fellow editors encouraged Guigon to expect and rely upon the aid of judges and practitioners. See "Notices of New Books," *Am. L. Reg.*, vol. 4, p. 447 (1856).

[16] "Legislative Tinkering," *Q.L.J.*, vol. 1, p. 7 (1856).

[17] "The Usury Laws," *Q.L.J.*, vol. 1, p. 3 (1856). Feature articles in this and subsequent journals examined herein are listed in W. H. Bryson, *A Bibliography of Virginia Legal History Before 1900* (1997). Articles reprinted from out-of-state sources, however, are not included there.

[18] See, e.g., "Liability of Railroad Companies for Injuries &c.," *Q.L.J.*, vol. 1, p. 289 (1856); "Company's Liability for Slave Employee," *Q.L.J.*, vol. 2, p. 257 (1857); "Liability of Master for Servants' Acts," *Q.L.J.*, vol. 1, p. 103 (1856); "Mail Robbery by Slave," *Q.L.J.*, vol. 4, p. 163 (1859).

in a firm but respectful manner for rendering faulty decisions. In an essay on how lightly Virginia law treated duelling, he noted sardonically that this was "another instance of the remarkable foresight which distinguishes Virginia legislation."[19] Commenting on the provisions of the *Revised Code of 1849* concerning imprisonment for debt, Guigon castigated both the revisors and the *Code* in general:

> Too many of its provisions seem to have been enacted merely under the influence of a restless desire for change; and a servile spirit of imitation after untried experiments, recently inaugurated in England and at the North. Many of these changes were undesired by the community, or the legal profession; and scarcely one has, in practice, obtained the approbation of the bar, the bench, or the public. Complaint, ridicule, and denunciation have been lavishly heaped upon the unlucky compilation; and no one dares to stand forth as its champion or advocate.[20]

Such forthright, and perhaps injudicious, commentary did not win Guigon friends within Virginia's legal establishment.

Despite his occasionally caustic approach, Guigon did earn laurels, at least initially, as editor of the *Journal*. The periodical itself was received most cordially throughout Virginia and elsewhere in the South. "The work is what we had a right to expect,"[21] remarked a dispassionate writer in the *Richmond Enquirer*. The *Wheeling Intelligencer* hailed the "advent of the Journal as an epoch in the jurisprudence of the South."[22] The *Valley Whig* in Fincastle proclaimed that the *Journal* "should be in the hands of every member of the bar,"[23] while the *Norfolk Herald* crowed, "It is a work superior in every respect to any of the Northern law periodicals with which we are deluged, and should take precedence of them."[24] Even the editors of Philadelphia's *American Law Register* labeled the first number "certainly attractive to any educated and well read professional man, as containing sound

---

[19] "Editorial Miscellany: Duelling Protected by Virginia Laws," *Q.L.J.*, vol. 2, pp. 98, 99 (1857).

[20] "Imprisonment for Debt," *Q.L.J.*, vol. 2, pp. 209, 214 (1857). For an example of Guigon's criticism of members of the bench, see "Seal – Scroll – Demurrer – Pleading: Smith use &c. v. Neely," *Q.L.J.*, vol. 2, pp. 299, 302-303 (1857).

[21] Quoted in J. W. Randolph, *Law Catalogue for 1856*, at p. 15 (1856).

[22] *Id.*

[23] *Id.*

[24] *Id.*

and discriminating leading articles, carefully selected and well decided cases which have been adjudicated both abroad and at home."[25]

Guigon was not quite so sanguine. He depended heavily upon expected contributions to fill the hundred pages of each issue. In volume 1, number 2, issued in April 1856, he lamented that "with one or two exceptions, we have been disappointed, and our duties have been performed with very little assistance. . . . [W]e earnestly desire our friends to furnish us with such important cases as come within their practice."[26] But contributions were still slow to appear. In volume 1, number 3, Edward Cantwell of Raleigh sent an essay on "The Law of Limitation in North Carolina,"[27] and in volume 3, William Green supplied several articles on his special forte, equity.[28] Guigon began reporting cases himself from the local Richmond courts but still relied primarily on reports from other localities, especially Britain and the northeastern United States.

One Virginia correspondent did remain particularly faithful to Guigon. William H. Cook, a practicing attorney of Carroll County, regularly reported cases decided by Judge A. S. Fulton in the circuit courts of Carroll, Floyd, Grayson, and Wythe counties, and in the District Court of Appeals held at Wytheville. Beginning with the October 1856 number, Cook's reports began to appear with increasing frequency until they comprised the vast majority of Virginia cases included in the *Journal*.[29] Pressured by the lack of materials from other jurisdictions, Guigon was forced to print all or most of Cook's reports. An embarrassing slant in the *Journal*'s contents toward litigation in the courts of southwest Virginia resulted. While the opinions of Judge Fulton and his occasional substitute Judge Samuel V. Fulkerson were sound, the cases reported were not always of "landmark" status. Consequently, the reputation of the *Journal* suffered.

[25] *Am. L. Reg.*, vol. 4, p. 447 (1856).

[26] "Editorial Miscellany," *Q.L.J.*, vol. 1, p. 184 (1856).

[27] E. Cantwell, "The Law of Limitations in North Carolina," *Q.L.J.*, vol. 1, p. 193 (1856).

[28] "On Construing Statutes by Equity," *Q.L.J.*, vol. 3, p. 150 (1858); "Lien of the Fieri Facias," *Q.L.J.*, vol. 3, p. 277 (1858). For other contributions, see "Lien of the Fieri Facias," *Q.L.J.*, vol. 3, p. 14 (1858) (signed "W. H."); "The Dignity of Debts," *Q.L.J.*, vol. 3, p. 117 (1858) (signed "C."); "On the Present Value of Dower Rights - Vested and Contingent," *Q.L.J.*, vol. 4, p. 1 (1859) (signed "E. F. P."); "Tenant by the Curtesy," *Q.L.J.*, vol. 4, p. 115 (1859) (signed "G.").

[29] See, e.g., Cook's reporting of cases in *Q.L.J.*, vol. 1, pp. 327-34; *Q.L.J.*, vol. 3 *passim*; *Q.L.J.*, vol. 4 *passim*.

Guigon valiantly attempted to remedy the situation. Thanking Cook for his courtesy and dependability, the editor at the same time begged attorneys in other sections of the state "to furnish us reports of cases actually determined in the District and Circuit Courts, [for then] our pages would be much more valuable to the profession."[30] In another instance, he urged the need for case reports in which issues involving the *Revised Code* were concerned "because there are numerous questions daily arising under the Code which may not be settled for years by the supreme tribunal of the State, and it is of the utmost importance to the profession that an early judicial exposition of these points should be made."[31] Still, the contributions and reports only trickled in.

With the completion of the first volume of the *Journal*, Guigon had mixed feelings: he was pleased with the moderate success of the publication, but he was disappointed in the lack of response and assistance actually afforded by his fellow attorneys. "[W]e do not find," he wrote:

> in the members of our bar at the South, the younger ones especially, that inclination to reduce their thoughts and studies to writing, upon which we had largely calculated. It cannot be from want of leisure, as our daily experience for the last few years witnesseth, and we are reluctant to attribute it to a want of inclination or capacity for labor, or to a falling off of that *esprit de corps*, for which the bar of the South and especially of Virginia has been, in former days, so honorably distinguished. . . . [W]e lament it as one of the evidences of a departure from that high standard of legal enterprise and attainment, which the past furnishes.[32]

There were other problems. Though vocally supported by some of the most prominent men in Virginia's legal profession, Guigon had great difficulty in securing their financial backing, especially in getting subscribers to pay their bills.[33] At the end of the second year of publication, Guigon and Randolph both felt severe doubts about continuing the venture. But they took the gamble and persisted.[34] The *Journal*, however, was obviously suffering. The number of pages in

---

[30] *Q.L.J.*, vol. 2, p. 400 (1857).

[31] *Q.L.J.*, vol. 2, p. 110 (1857).

[32] "Editorial Miscellany," *Q.L.J.*, vol. 1, pp. 361, 362 (1856).

[33] *Q.L.J.*, vol. 2, inside front covers (1857).

[34] *Q.L.J.*, vol. 3, p. 94 (1858).

each issue dwindled; by January 1859 there were only about eighty pages per quarterly release. Commentaries and reviews became even more sporadic, and reports dominated. The last number, October 1859, was given over wholly to case reports. Not a word was printed about the imminent termination of the *Journal*. Guigon gave no hint as to the ultimate causes of his suspension of the *Journal*, yet we may suspect his utter frustration at the lack of financial support and written contributions. Perhaps he had expected more than his fellow practitioners at the time could give him.

II. *Quarterly Law Review*

If Alexander Guigon had had his fill of legal editing, J. W. Randolph had not yet surrendered his publishing ambitions. With the demise of the *Quarterly Law Journal*, Randolph immediately set to work fashioning a successor. As editor he chose Alexander Hamilton Sands (1828-1887), a fascinating Williamsburg native who had long mixed very successfully the dual occupations of practicing attorney and Baptist minister. A confidant of Conway Robinson, Nathaniel P. Howard, William Green, and others, Sands already had published several volumes that considerably aided the legal profession. His *History of a Suit in Equity* (first published in 1854) served as the basic procedural guide to equity practice in Virginia for law students and attorneys.[35]

By April 1860 a Richmond-based Virginia law journal was back in production – the *Quarterly Law Review*. In general format it differed little from its predecessor. The great bulk of each issue was devoted to case reports from Virginia superior courts and from those of other states. Recent English cases also were reprinted, and a "Book Notices" section closed each issue. Support within the legal community seems to have remained rather half-hearted. But with regular contributions by such articulate and knowledgeable practitioners as William Green,[36] the *Review* began to capture the spirit of a modern legal publication.

The life of the *Review* was destined to be short. The crisis of secession dealt a death-blow to the struggling young journal. The January 1861 issue appeared several months late, which Sands attributed to:

---

[35] G. B. Taylor, *Virginia Baptist Ministers*, pp. 39-40 (4th ser. 1913); "Book Notices," *Q.L.J.*, vol. 1, p. 189 (1856).

[36] Green wrote two articles with identical titles. W. Green, "Vendor's Responsibility for Quality of Chattels Personal," *Q. L. Rev.*, vol. 1, pp. 10, 101 (1860).

> the extraordinary crisis through which the country is now passing. "*Inter arma silent leges*" seems to be the motto adopted by the Virginia tribunals of justice; and though we have doubted very much the policy of carrying it so far as it has been carried, we must yet yield somewhat to the prevailing current. After a lull in the storm, we hope for a renewal of the more quiet pursuits of peace.[37]

The lull was not to come, however. With this notice Virginia's earliest venture into the regular publishing of legal literature – the godchild of J. W. Randolph – passed into history.

Brief as the existence of the *Quarterly Law Journal* and the *Quarterly Law Review* was, it represented the most long-lived publishing enterprise in legal literature in the antebellum South. These volumes set important precedents for future law publications in Virginia and in the South at large.

If the Civil War itself put an end to the earliest ventures in serialized legal publication in Virginia, its effects similarly delayed any resurgence of interest in such an enterprise for at least a decade. Attorneys and judges in the Old Dominion had more pressing concerns with which to deal in the wake of the Confederacy's defeat.[38]

III. *Virginia Law Journal*

By the mid-1870s, with the heavy hand of Reconstruction essentially lifted from Virginia, thoughts of a regular legal periodical again surfaced in Richmond. Attorneys and brothers George L. Christian and Frank Wood Christian proposed to launch a new venture in 1877. They envisioned the *Virginia Law Journal* as eminently "useful to the profession" if it could prove to be more than "a mere vehicle for the reports of decisions, but that one of its most valuable functions shall be to reflect the legal thought of the State as to the condition, practical working, administration and reform of the law."[39]

Even before embarking upon publication, the Christians secured the services of several important Virginia legal figures, including William Green, William A. Maury, John W. Daniel, and Judge E. H. Fitzhugh, to provide "original articles, on legal subjects of immediate

[37] *Q. L. Rev.*, vol. 2, p. 68 (1861).

[38] W. H. Bryson and E. L. Shepard, "The Virginia Bar, 1870-1900," in *The New High Priests: Lawyers in Post-Civil War America*, p. 171 (G. W. Gawalt ed. 1984).

[39] *Va. L. J*, vol. 1, p. [iii] (1877). For biographical information on Frank Christian, see *Va. State Bar Ass'n Repts.*, vol. 21, p. 112 (1908); on George Christian, see *Va. State Bar Ass'n Repts.*, vol. 36, p. 88 (1924).

and practical interest."[40] They intended also to print reports of cases argued in the Virginia Court of Appeals: important cases would be printed in full; others would be condensed, some of which "would probably never reach the profession through any other channel."[41] To publish this ambitious serial, the editors turned to none other than J. W. Randolph, now associated with another Richmond publisher/bookseller in the firm of J. W. Randolph & English.[42]

The first volume of the *Virginia Law Journal* delivered what its editors had promised. The January 1877 issue carried a learned article by William Green,[43] case reports bearing lengthy explanatory notes by the editors or reporters,[44] "miscellany" (including a report on the attempt of Mrs. Belva Lockwood to secure admission to practice before the U. S. Supreme Court),[45] and the rules of practice before the Virginia Supreme Court as amended since 20 *Grattan*.[46] Later volumes conformed to this same auspicious format, while adding reports from U. S. circuit court, supreme tribunals of other states, and even the Virginia circuit courts, as well as extensive treatises on special aspects of legal practice. The editors issued the *Journal* monthly rather than quarterly in an attempt to make it a vehicle for communicating rapidly developing case law, as well as current legal thinking, to Virginia's practitioners.

In the middle of the first volume, the editors addressed their brothers in the profession, sounding two familiar, changeless themes: practicality and the need for support and assistance. "We have from the highest sources letters of commendation and encouragement," they announced proudly, indicating that many of their readers concurred in the belief that they could make this journal a success "and a work of great practical use" to the bar.[47]

---

[40] *Va. L. J.*, vol. 1, p. [iii] (1877).

[41] *Id.*

[42] *Id.* at [ii]. To place the *Journal* in the context of postwar legal periodicals, see L. M. Friedman, *A History of American Law*, pp. 546-548 (1973); F. L. Mott, *supra*, vol. 3, p. 144 (1938).

[43] W. Green, "Res Judicata," *Va. L. J.*, vol. 1, p. 1 (1877).

[44] *Va. L. J.*, vol. 1, p. 21 (1877).

[45] "Miscellany," *Va. L. J.*, vol. 1, p. 58 (1877) (Lockwood's application was denied).

[46] "Special Court of Appeals of Virginia," *Va. L. J.*, vol. 1, p. 109 (1877).

[47] "Miscellany," *Va. L. J.*, vol. 1, p. 444 (1877).

> We wish this Journal to be the medium of communication among our profession in this section, and therefore, we invite contributions from you on such subjects as you have investigated, and which will be interesting to others in the profession. . . . This is the only Law Periodical, save one, in the South that we are advised of, and we hope you will sustain it as a Southern work.[48]

Comparing the *Virginia Law Journal* with sister publications of the period, in both the North and South, one is struck at once by the definite similarity in content and format and yet a lack of the sophistication that marked some of the established or more ambitious Northern publications. The *Journal* certainly served the needs of the Virginia profession, however, to which its survival through the next decade and a half would attest. The first volumes devoted space to numerous important issues, including the "waiver of homestead" constitutionality debate,[49] partnerships,[50] and the legislative funding of Virginia's state debt.[51] The editors even provided space for articles on Virginia's legal past.[52]

While on the one hand eschewing politics, George Christian and his brother found that they could not refrain from occasional diatribes on Virginia or national affairs. Endorsement of a candidate for the office of Virginia attorney general seemed reasonable for the *Journal*; but old wounds left from the war and Reconstruction occasionally

[48] *Id. The Southern Law Review* of Nashville (later moved to St. Louis) began in 1872 and in 1883 merged with the *American Law Review* in New York.

[49] "Transfer of 'Homestead' Exemption: Richardson v. Butler Reviewed," *Va. L. J.*, vol. 1, p. 261 (1877); "The Claim of Homestead Against the State," *Va. L. J.*, vol. 1, p. 319 (1877); "Waiver of Homestead," *Va. L. J.*, vol. 1, p. 383 (1877); C. Patteson, "Waiver of Homestead," *Va. L. J.*, vol. 1, p. 513 (1877); "Waiver of Homestead," *Va. L. J.*, vol. 1, p. 592 (1877); J. S. Wise, "Can the Homestead Exemption Be Claimed Against Liabilities for Tort?" *Va. L. J.*, vol. 2, p. 449 (1878).

[50] W. Green, "Power of a Partner," *Va. L. J.*, vol. 1, p. 127 (1877); "Notice of Dissolution by a Retiring Partner," *Va. L. J.*, vol. 1, p. 577 (1877); "The Obligation of Retiring Partners to Partnership Creditors," *Va. L. J.*, vol. 2, p. 647 (1878) (reprinted from the *Albany Law Journal*).

[51] P. R. Grattan, "War Interest on the State Debt," *Va. L. J.*, vol. 2, p. 65 (1878); W. L. Royall, "Constitutionality of the Funding Bill," *Va. L. J.*, vol. 2, p. 129 (1878); W. Green, "The Funding Act," *Va. L. J.*, vol. 2, p. 193 (1878); W. H. Burroughs, "Can States Be Compelled to Pay Their Debts?" *Va. L. J.*, vol. 3, pp. 129-148 (1879).

[52] C. Robinson, "Of Lawyers in Virginia Between 1704 and 1737," *Va. L. J.*, vol. 1, p. 191 (1877); W. L. Royall, "Virginia Colonial Money, and Tobacco's Part Therein – Tobacco Warehouses, &c.," *Va. L. J.*, vol. 1, p. 447 (1877).

brought forth the editors' vituperation. In remarking on the repealed bankruptcy law, one of the Christian brothers wrote that the

> history of the administration of [Judge John C.] *Underwood's* Court in Virginia would be one of the most remarkable and interesting that could be written.
>
> We wish Mr. [A. M.] Keiley, or some one else who is competent, would undertake to write a history of Richmond *since the war*, including the administration of this court. We think it would shew to the world that we have been the most conservative and *long suffering* people in the universe.[53]

Aside from these infrequent editorial excursions into the Virginia political scene, the pages of the *Virginia Law Journal* remained largely filled with the matter of practical legal professionalism as the decade of the 1880s opened. George Christian became sole editor in 1879, convinced that he could make the *Journal* "not only *useful*, but *attractive* to the profession . . . if our friends will . . . take that interest in our work that it seems to us they should take."[54] He continued to provide lengthy, well-researched notes to cases and to some articles, drew heavily from other periodicals for both essays and decisions, and enjoyed poking fun at the profession through his "miscellany." Correspondents from throughout Virginia sent occasional essays,[55] while some brought their professional rivalries from the courtroom into the pages of the *Journal*.[56] The editor focused on matters of judicial administration,[57] while additional space was filled with anecdotes and reminiscences of renowned lawyers and jurists of Virginia's past.[58] The

---

53 "Miscellany," *Va. L. J.*, vol. 2, p. 383 (1878).

54 *Va. L. J.*, vol. 3, at p. vi (1879).

55 E.g., S. C. Graham, "Uncommunicated Threats," *Va. L. J.*, vol. 3, p. 65 (1879); W. D. Dabney, "The Virginia Married Woman's Act," *Va. L. J.*, vol. 3, p. 193 (1879); W. Green, "Editions of the Code," *Va. L. J.*, vol. 3, p. 709 (1879).

56 See "Brown v. Burton's Executors et als.," *Va. L. J.*, vol. 3, p. 416 (1879); W. L. Royall, "The Case of Brown v. Burton," *Va. L. J.*, vol. 3, pp. 390-411 (1879); B. T. C[rump], "Brown v. Burton: Tenancy in Common and Survivorship," *Va. L. J.*, vol. 3, p. 517 (1879).

57 "The Judicial Term of Office in Virginia," *Va. L. J.*, vol. 4, pp. 1-15 (1880); "County Judges," *Va. L. J.*, vol. 4, p. 129 (1880).

58 *Va. L. J.*, vol. 5, pp. 76, 141 (1881) (anecdotes of Chapman Johnson); *id.* at p. 273 ("A Stoical Criminal").

deaths of prominent contemporary professionals likewise elicited tributes in the *Journal*.[59]

In December 1880, the *Journal* announced the appointment of Professor Samuel D. Davies of Richmond College as full editor.[60] Davies, elected professor of law at Richmond in 1877, already had been a contributor to the *Journal*.[61] Though his tenure as editor was brief, ending in 1882 when he left the college, his contribution presaged a crucial future development – the association of legal periodicals with academic law schools.

Far more important for the ultimate destiny of the *Virginia Law Journal* was the publication in 1879 of the *Northwestern Reporter*, which would be the first element in the West Publishing Company's National Reporter System.[62] This was followed in 1887 by the inauguration of the *Southeastern Reporter* by the same firm. With this new systematic release of advance sheets of all opinions of the Court of Appeals of Virginia, much of the raison d'etre of publications like the *Journal*, which subsisted almost wholly upon the printing of recent case reports, vanished. Unable to adapt because they continued to be edited by practitioners and case reporters with limited time and resources for developing essays on legal theory and practice, these pioneering legal periodicals would gradually fade from the scene.[63]

The days of the *Virginia Law Journal*'s passing, however, still lay well into the future. The opening of volume 6 in 1882 saw law reporter James M. Matthews take the helm as editor.[64] He was followed within a year by attorneys James C. Lamb and Benjamin T. Christian of Richmond. Lamb was a graduate of the Law School of the University of Virginia, while Christian, for several years deputy clerk of the Virginia Supreme Court of Appeals, had studied both at Virginia and

[59] *Va. L. J.*, vol. 5, p. 467 (1881) (tribute to Judge Robert Stanard); W. R. Aylett, "Patrick Henry Aylett," *Va. L. J.*, vol. 4, p. 517 (1880) (memorial by the deceased's brother); *Va. L. J.*, vol. 4, p. 575 (1880) (tribute to Judge William Green); *Va. L. J.*, vol. 4, p. 635 (1880) (resolutions of the Culpeper bar on the death of William Green); "William Green, LL. D.," *Va. L. J.*, vol. 5, p. 7 (1881).

[60] *Va. L. J.*, vol. 4, p. 765 (1880); J. A. V. Berry, "Samuel David Davies," *Legal Education in Virginia*, p. 175 (1982).

[61] S. D. Davies, "What is Municipal Law?" *Va. L. J.*, vol. 3, p. 645 (1879); S. D. Davies, "Has an Insolvent Testator the Power of Preference among Creditors of Different Classes?" *Va. L. J.*, vol. 4, p. 581 (1880).

[62] L. M. Friedman, *supra*, at p. 356.

[63] *Id.* at p. 546; *Va. Law Reporters*, at pp. 129-130.

[64] *Va. L. J.*, vol. 6, p. 60 (1882).

under Davies at Richmond College.[65] Under these energetic young men, the *Journal* turned, with the American bar as a whole, to consider critical issues of professionalism.[66] Following Christian's sudden death in August 1883, the prolific Lamb assumed the editorship, addressing such pertinent concerns as the state debt coupon cases[67] and judicial election, compensation, and administration.[68]

Lamb detected the dwindling role of law journals of the traditional cast and strove to introduce some new and potentially useful departments into the *Journal*. In volume 8 he inaugurated a section on "New Laws of Virginia,"[69] and followed it up with a proposed column of "Queries and Answers." The latter was to

> afford an opportunity and a place for propounding and answering questions of law and of practice which are of practical importance to the profession. . . . Questions of novelty and difficulty, which seem at first sight to be governed by no rule or precedent, are constantly arising and must continue to arise as long as human affairs are mutable and judicial decision and construction uncertain.[70]

The idea, unfortunately, did not catch on, and the *Journal* continued to be composed primarily of the "Digest of Recent Decisions."

---

[65] *Va. L. J.*, vol. 7, p. 59 (1883); on Christian (d. 1883), see *id.* at p. 570; on Lamb (1853-1903), *see* Leake and Montague, "James Christian Lamb," *Va. State Bar Ass'n Repts.*, vol. 16, p. 75 (1903).

[66] J. P. Bishop, "The Elements of Distinguishing the Successful from the Ordinary Legal Practitioner and What They Suggest," *Va. L. J.*, vol. 7, p. 321 (1883) (reprinted from the *Am. L. Rev.*; *Va. L. J.*, vol. 7, p. 638 (1883)) on the "dignity of the profession," reprinted from the *Legal Adviser*); J. M. Shirley, "The Future of Our Profession," *Va. L. J.*, vol. 7, p. 645 (1883).

[67] "The `Coupon Killers'," *Va. L. J.*, vol. 7, p. 513 (1883).

[68] *Va. L. J.*, vol. 7, p. 315 (1883) (on "judicial prolixity"); *Va. L. J.*, vol. 8, p. 252 (1884) (on "judicial compensation"); *Va. L. J.*, vol. 8, p. 314 (1884) (on "the circuit bench"); *Va. L. J.*, vol. 8, p. 446 (1884) (on testing the *nisi prius* courts); *Va. L. J.*, vol. 8, p. 761 (1884) (on law journal editors' responsibility to "look after" the judges). For a listing of Lamb's articles in the *Journal*, see W. H. Bryson, *Bibliography*, at pp. 125-127.

[69] "New Laws of Virginia," *Va. L. J.*, vol. 8, p. 184 (1884).

[70] "Miscellany," *Va. L. J.*, vol. 8, pp. 252, 253 (1884). For the disappointing response to the latter, see "Queries and Answers," *Va. L. J.*, vol. 8, p. 505 (1884); "Queries and Answers," *Va. L. J.*, vol. 8, p. 701 (1884); "Queries and Answers," *Va. L. J.*, vol. 8, p. 760 (1884).

As early as 1878 the *Journal* had called for the formation of a bar association in Virginia.[71] The founding of the Richmond Bar Association in 1885 gave new impetus to the drive for a statewide organization of attorneys. Lamb, treasurer of the Richmond association, covered the activities of the emerging local group in some detail in the pages of the *Journal* and renewed the publication's call to Virginia lawyers.[72] In early 1888 the Richmond bar proposed a statewide organizational meeting to be held in July at Virginia Beach. There, a sizable number of attorneys from across the Commonwealth met to form the Virginia State Bar Association.[73] Lamb himself served on the committee charged with drafting a constitution and bylaws. The Association published a report of the convention proceedings, printed by Everett Waddey of Richmond, which included the constitution, bylaws, names of officers and standing committees, a roll of members, and a proposed code of ethics.[74] The next year a report of the Association's first annual meeting commenced a series that only ceased publication in 1974. Each volume contained proceedings of the yearly session, committee reports, speeches, and papers delivered at the meeting.[75] Later volumes added obituary notices of and memorials to Virginia attorneys who had died during each previous year.

James Lamb anticipated, with some justification, that the *Virginia Law Journal* would play a large role in the State Bar Association's activities. No doubt he expected that soon the *Journal* would become the organization's official organ. This was not to be the case. A move to place the publications of the Association in the hands of the *Journal*'s editor stirred a lengthy debate in 1891 and the resolution went down to defeat in a close vote.[76] The State Bar continued publication of its yearly reports and failed to take advantage of the opportunity afforded by the *Journal*'s broad, statewide distribution.

The *Journal* struggled on, providing a vehicle for the dissemination of case reports and legal learning to the practicing bar in Virginia and

---

[71] "Miscellany," *Va. L. J.*, vol. 2, p. 704 (1878).

[72] "Editorial," *Va. L. J.*, vol. 9, p. 754 (1885); "Editorial," *Va. L. J.*, vol. 12, p. 422 (1888); "Editorial," *Va. L. J.*, vol. 12, p. 550 (1888); "Code of Ethics," *Va. L. J.*, vol. 13, p. 327 (1889) (formulated by the Richmond Bar Association).

[73] J. O. Peters, *Tale of the Century: A History of the Bar Association of the City of Richmond, 1885-1985*, pp. 23-26 (1985). See also Bryson and Shepard, *supra*, pp. 176-177.

[74] *Va. State Bar Ass'n Repts.*, vol. 1, p. 14 (1888).

[75] *Va. State Bar Ass'n Repts.*, vol. 2, *passim* (1889).

[76] *Va. State Bar Ass'n Repts.*, vol. 4, pp. 19-25 (1891).

serving as the chief medium of communication among lawyers across the state. Lamb resigned the editorship in late 1888, to be replaced by Richmond attorney Philip B. Sheild.[77] Sheild observed the necessity for change and began to issue the *Journal* in weekly installments, to "enable us to lay before our subscribers *every decision of the Supreme Court of Appeals within a week after it is rendered.*"[78] Weekly issues of twenty to thirty pages retained the usual features – book notices, editorials, and articles – but rapidly became filled almost exclusively with case reports. Only when the high court stood in vacation did the editors trot out articles and filler reserved for that particular season.[79] Within two years, Sheild would give way to Henry Magruder Tyler, a brother of Governor John Hoge Tyler. In taking the helm of the *Journal*, Tyler announced, "No other legal publication is issued in the State; it is a State institution."[80]

These later volumes of the *Journal*, under the editorships of Sheild and Tyler, became the arena in which a heated debate over legal reform and code revision came to be aired. Chief among the participants were Sergeant S. P. Patteson, chairman of the State Bar Association's Special Committee on Law Reform, and William B. Pettit, chairman of the Standing Committee on Law Reform.[81] Arguing both the merits and the disadvantages of merging law and equity and of simplifying procedure, these men attracted attention far beyond the borders of the Old Dominion and even drew articles from America's famous codifier, David Dudley Field.[82] Concern surfaced, too, in the pages of the *Journal*, over the matter of standards of admission to the bar and judicial administration of the admitting system.[83] Despite the treatment of these pertinent issues, however, the *Journal* failed to

[77] For biographical information on Sheild (1860-1922), see *Va. State Bar Ass'n Repts.*, vol. 35, pp. 104-105 (1923).

[78] *Va. L. J.*, vol. 12, p. 806 (1888).

[79] See, e.g., "Law Reform," *Va. L. J.*, vol. 13, p. 461 (1889).

[80] "Editorial," *Va. L. J.*, vol. 15, p. 72 (1891).

[81] "Editorial," *Va. L. J.*, vol. 13, p. 586.

[82] D. D. Field, "Codification – Mr. Field's Answer to Mr. Carter," *Va. L. J.*, vol. 14, p. 1 (1890); Letter from David Dudley Field to S. S. P. Patteson, *Va. L. J.*, vol. 16, p. 148 (1892). For a discussion of the law reform debate, see Bryson and Shepard, *supra*, p. 177-180; for a complete list of the Patteson-Pettit articles in the *Journal*, see W. H. Bryson, *Bibliography*, pp. 163, 166. Their debate continued in the pages of volumes 4 to 7 of *Va. State Bar Ass'n Repts.* (1891-1894).

[83] "Editorial," *Va. L. J.*, vol. 13, p. 531 (1889); *Va. L. J.*, vol. 13, p. 722 (1889) (letter to the editor from Samuel D. Davies).

secure adequate financial support. Tyler surrendered the editorship to Daniel Jenifer Barton, an 1891 graduate of the Law School at the University of Virginia, in late 1892. Barton was able to continue only until September 1893, when the *Journal* ceased publication.[84]

The lessons of the *Virginia Law Journal*'s final days were clear. A lawyer in active practice could not handle the publication of a privately sponsored state journal, nor were the attendant remunerations sufficient to allow him to withdraw from his other legal business to continue the task. Likewise, the dependence upon case reports in the absence of a regular stream of contributors could not serve as an effective guarantee of a legal publication's success. As the new century loomed, a fresh formula had to be discovered to establish a successful legal periodical in Virginia.

Yet, by its very existence, the *Virginia Law Journal* had been influential by helping to bring the legal profession in Virginia together and directing its focus toward critical issues of professional concern. Moreover, considering that only thirty legal periodicals existed across the United States by 1885, and about ten more twenty years later,[85] the sixteen-year career of the *Virginia Law Journal* takes on national significance.[86]

IV. *Virginia Law Register*

The Virginia bar did not want long for a regularly published legal periodical. Within two years of the demise of the *Virginia Law Journal*, a triumvirate composed of Judge Edward C. Burks of Bedford, Professor Charles A. Graves of the Washington and Lee University Law School, and William Minor Lile of the University of Virginia Law School issued the first volume of the *Virginia Law Register*.[87] This was a momentous coalition: a practicing attorney and two law professors. Together they emphasized that among more than twelve hundred Virginia attorneys

---

[84] "Editorial," *Va. L. J.*, vol. 16, p. 662 (1892).

[85] F. L. Mott, *supra*, vol. 4, p. 346 (1957).

[86] *Id.*, vol. 3, p. 144, n. 31 (1938).

[87] Biographical sketches for each of these men are included in the following: for Burks, see *Va. State Bar Ass'n Repts.*, vol. 10, p. 127 (1897), and *Va. L. Reg.*, vol. 3, p. 323 (1897-1898); for Graves, see C. V. Laughlin, "Charles Alfred Graves," *Legal Education in Va.*, p. 253; for Lile, see W. H. Bryson, "William Minor Lile," *id.* p. 353. The first issue of the *Register* appeared in May 1895. Laughlin, *supra*, p. 255.

> there exists no regular medium of communication. Cases of great moment are decided by our Court of Appeals, the precise bearing and extent of which, often difficult to determine, each lawyer is left to ascertain for himself. By reason of the limited right of appeal with us, important questions of practice and of general law remain unsettled, and different views prevail in the different circuits respecting them.[88]

The editors promised to draw every practitioner's attention

> to the new decisions and new statutes of his own State, without delay, and by which diverse views on important topics of the law may be brought together and compared. . . . . [The editorial policy would] naturally be to give preference to subjects of local professional interest, over those of a broader and more philosophical nature. The especial efforts of the editors will be to make [the *Register*'s] influence felt and its practical utility recognized as a *vade mecum* by those who are daily engaged in the practice and administration of the law in Virginia.
>
> We shall observe critically the outgivings of our Court of Appeals and comment upon the opinions with freedom and candor, not always with kindness.[89]

They also wisely harbored "no disposition to rival or supplant, but rather to supplement, that very excellent publication, the *Southeastern Reporter*."[90] After pledging to attend to the needs of the younger members of the profession and to offer "cordial sympathy and support . . . [to the Virginia State Bar Association] in all its laudable measures, especially in its aims to maintain a high standard of legal ethics and professional integrity,"[91] the editors sounded the customary call for contributors:

> It is a familiar experience in every lawyer's practice to investigate laboriously nice and difficult questions of law and to allow the result to remain pigeon-holed in his own office – not so much from lack of inclination to share it with his professional brethren, as from want of proper encouragement and the opportunity to do so.[92]

[88] "Miscellaneous Notes," *Va. L. Reg.*, vol. 1, p. 71 (1895).

[89] *Id.*

[90] *Id.* at 72.

[91] *Id.*

[92] *Id.*

That gap, they trusted, would now be adequately filled.

The first issue of the *Virginia Law Register* carried articles by Judge R. G. H. Kean[93] and Professor J. R. Tucker of the Law School at Washington and Lee,[94] as well as reports of cases in the Virginia Supreme Court of Appeals, which were followed by succinct editorial comment.[95] In the second issue, distributed in June 1895, Graves instituted a feature, "For the Juniors," which, although "intended primarily for the younger members of the bar, we trust . . . may not be without interest and even some benefit to the seniors."[96] The strong contributions continued unabated with each succeeding monthly release, to which were added obituary notices and tributes to deceased members of the bench and bar. In many respects, these first issues had the look and feel of a modern law journal. At the close of the first volume, the publishers, J. P. Bell Company in Lynchburg, acknowledged the support of a healthy list of subscribers, but at the same time urged others to "think about it seriously *now*, and if you conclude that the undertaking is worthy to be sustained, send in your subscription at once."[97]

With the opening of volume 2, the editors again sounded a light-hearted call for contributions: "send us brief, crisp notes on practical subjects, either of law, pure and simple, or of collateral professional interest. If nothing else occurs to you, abuse something or somebody."[98] They also provided a synopsis of acts recently passed by the Virginia legislature, contributed by William P. McRae of the Petersburg bar[99] and began reporting major decisions from the United States Supreme Court in advance of their regular appearance in the federal reports.

The section for junior members of the bar lasted only as long as Graves's connection with the *Register*, which terminated in May 1897. Burks died two months later, leaving Lile to carry on alone. Under the professor's direction, the *Register* witnessed a gradual decline in

---

[93] R. G. H. Kean, "Licenses by Cities and Towns to Use Streets," *Va. L. Reg.*, vol. 1, p. 1 (1895).

[94] J. R. Tucker, "The Deeds of Trust Puzzle: A Legal Paradox," *Va. L. Reg.*, vol. 1, p. 4 (1895).

[95] *Va. L. Reg.*, vol. 1, pp. 24, 35, 45 (1895). "Arguments of counsel . . . cannot be reported in the Register for want of space." *Va. L. Reg.*, vol. 1, p. 14 note (1895).

[96] "Miscellaneous Notes," 1 *Va. L. Reg.*, vol. 1, p. 148 (1895).

[97] "Notes by the Publishers," *Va. L. Reg.*, vol. 1, p. 940 (1896).

[98] "Miscellaneous Notes," *Va. L. Reg.*, vol. 2, pp. 45, 46 (1896).

[99] W. P. McRae, "Acts of the General Assembly, 1895-96 - Synopsis," *Va. L. Reg.*, vol. 2, p. 131 (1896).

lengthy Virginia case reports, replaced by a digest of recent decisions consisting primarily of the state reporter's headnotes.[100] The periodical's filler notes concentrated on matters of professional integrity and self-awareness, as well as control of admissions to the bar.

Professor Lile announced his retirement from the editorship at the close of volume 8. "The conduct of a local law journal," he observed

> means not only editorial supervision and the preparation of editorial matter (in themselves delightful recreation for any enthusiastic lawyer), but much labor in the revision of careless copy supplied by others, the correction of proofs, and the conduct of an extensive correspondence. . . . But howsoever laborious, the conduct of the journal has been a grateful task and is now laid aside with genuine regret.[101]

Succeeding Lile as editor was George Bryan of the Richmond bar, who had signed on as an associate editor of the *Register* in October 1901.[102]

Bryan, interestingly, shifted gears immediately, with a conscious look backward. "The future policy of the *Register* will be a conservative one,"[103] he announced, adding that he planned to begin "publication *seriatim* of all the decisions of the Supreme Court of Appeals of Virginia. . . . We also expect to publish the syllabi of all of the decisions of the Supreme Court of Appeals of West Virginia, which concern the Constitution, statutes and practice of her mother state."[104] Quickly, the capital city attorney learned the folly of his decision. Within six months, he chose to return to the publication only of selected cases from the Virginia Supreme Court: "The *Virginia Law Register* does not purport to be a mere reporter. Its functions are rather those of comment, annotation and suggestion," he acknowledged.[105]

"The pressure of other demands" forced George Bryan quickly to relinquish the editorship in June 1904.[106] He was succeeded by another

[100] See, e.g., *Va. L. Reg.*, vol. 3, p. 665 (1898).

[101] *Va. L. Reg.*, vol. 8, p. 902 (1903).

[102] *Va. L. Reg.*, vol. 7, p. 276 (1901). For an obituary of Bryan, see *Va. State Bar Ass'n Repts.*, vol. 42, p. 194 (1930).

[103] *Va. L. Reg.*, vol. 9, p. 55 (1903).

[104] *Id.*, pp. 55-56.

[105] *Va. L. Reg.*, vol. 9, p. 822 (1904).

[106] *Va. L. Reg.*, vol. 10, p. 162 (1904).

Richmonder, John Garland Pollard, later attorney general and governor of Virginia. Pollard and his two associates observed that

> the new and voluminous [state] Constitution, the vast deluge of statutes following, the many important questions which must be decided while the state is adjusting herself to her new conditions, all combine to furnish the *Register* a broad and rich field of usefulness. Just at this time there is much for the Virginia bar to learn; and perhaps as much to unlearn. In such times a law journal can be exceedingly helpful.[107]

The new editor in particular promised to direct special attention to the "rules, regulations, and decisions issued from the State Corporation Commission. This new department of government is of the greatest importance, and its powers, as yet, little understood and appreciated."[108] The succeeding volumes contain from one to three articles per monthly issue, case reports, editorial remarks, reports of decisions outside Virginia, head titles of Virginia cases not fully reported, miscellany, correspondence, book reviews, and notices.

Pollard restated the guiding principles of his editorship the following year. "The present editors of the *Register*," he announced,

> consider it their special mission to collect and present to their readers those questions of law peculiar to Virginia statutes and practice which are daily arising in the trial courts. It is true that the decisions in such cases cannot have the weight accorded to the decisions of the courts of last resort, but they are valuable not only on account of the well-known ability of many of our trial judges, but because they are suggestive of points which the lawyer may raise in the conduct of his practice.[109]

Moreover, the editors hoped to "be able to call attention to, and thus promote, such legislation as will perfect our statutes and make the administration of justice more speedy and sure."[110]

A change of great significance for the future of the *Register* took place in February 1906. Ownership of the periodical transferred from

---

[107] *Id.*, p. 163.

[108] *Id.* The new Virginia Constitution, drafted by the Convention of 1901-1902, went into effect on July 10, 1902. See also B. W. White, "John Garland Pollard," *Legal Education in Va.*, p. 511.

[109] *Va. L. Reg.*, vol. 11, p. 54 (1905).

[110] *Id.*, p. 55.

the J. P. Bell Company to the well-known legal publishers, the Michie Company of Charlottesville.[111] Under this new management, Richard T. W. Duke, Jr., formerly judge of the Corporation Court of the City of Charlottesville, was induced to assume the post of editor-in-chief of the *Register*. "As one busily engaged in the active practice of the profession," Duke confessed, "I should have for a long time hesitated before undertaking this work if I had not known that in it I should have the assistance of the able corps of law writers who have now for some years been engaged by The Michie Company in their work of annotating the State, Railway and Corporation Reports."[112] Duke and his able coterie of associates set to work fashioning the *Register* into one of the best law journals of the period.[113]

During R. T. W. Duke's lengthy tenure, a major development in Virginia law publishing occurred, which augured the ultimate doom of the periodical. In March 1913 students and faculty at the University of Virginia School of Law met to form the Virginia Law Review Association. The first issue of their publication, the *Virginia Law Review*, consciously modeled after the design of the *Review* founded at Harvard Law School in the 1880s, contained leading articles, notes and summaries of recent decisions written by students, and book reviews. Several years later a Virginia section, focusing specifically on issues of interest to practitioners in the Old Dominion, was added.[114] As in states throughout the nation, so too in Virginia,

> [t]he university law review proved an apt vehicle for speculative writing on the law. It was the perfect outlet for shorter works by the new class of teaching scholars. The law review could justify itself as a training device for students and as a scholarly journal; it did not have to meet the immediate demands of the market place.[115]

---

[111] *Va. L. Reg.*, vol. 11, p. 843 (1906); see below; "The Michie Company."

[112] *Va. L. Reg.*, vol. 12, p. 68 (1906). For an obituary of Duke, see *Va. L. Reg.* (n.s.), vol. 11, pp. 757-760 (1926).

[113] Such is the assessment in F. L. Mott, *History of American Magazines*, vol. 4, p. 347, n. 5 (1957). For an editorial history of the *Register*, which lists the various assistant editors, see "O! Tempore, O! Mores – The Curtain Falls," *Va. L. Reg.* (n.s.), vol. 13, pp. 759, 760-761 (1928).

[114] J. Ritchie, *The First Hundred Years: A Short History of the School of Law of the University of Virginia for the Period 1826-1926*, p. 92 (1978).

[115] L. M. Friedman, *supra*, p. 547.

Suddenly the *Virginia Law Register* discovered intense, albeit friendly, new competition right at its own back door. The *Virginia Law Review*, with a ready supply of student writers, also offered a prestigious outlet for law professors and other legal writers in the Commonwealth; the various reporter series, each with its own plan for the systematic distribution of advance sheets, brought important case law rapidly into the hands of practitioners; and the *Reports of the Virginia State Bar Association* served as a regular, if infrequent, vehicle for communication within the profession. The time had come when a private law journal, edited by attorneys engaged in active practice, dependent upon a variable pool of contributors, and largely directed toward the dissemination of case reports, could no longer survive in Virginia. These journals always had led a precarious existence, yet had provided an immeasurably valuable ingredient in the rise of professionalism in the bar of old Virginia. As did only a few such publications in the South, they had influenced attorneys throughout the region and gained the respect of sister journals across the country. For many years they had provided the only regular outlet in the Commonwealth for legal scholarship, the promotion of professionalism, and the debate over legal reform.

The *Virginia Law Register* struggled on for another decade. After the death of R. T. W. Duke in March 1926, one of his able associates, Beirne Stedman, assumed the editorship. But Stedman and the Michie Company soon acknowledged the inevitable. They entered an agreement with the Virginia Law Review Association, transferring their subscribers to the *Review* and calling upon all their readers to support this "very excellent publication of the University of Virginia Law School."[116] The era of the first law journals in Virginia had ended.

BIBLIOGRAPHY

Quarterly Law Journal. Richmond: J. W. Randolph, 1856-1859, 4 vols.; rept. [Buffalo, N.Y.: Dennis & Co., n.d.], 4 vols.

Quarterly Law Review. Richmond: J. W. Randolph, 1860-1861, 2 vols.; rept. Buffalo, N.Y.: Dennis & Co., 1965, 2 vols. in 1.

Virginia Law Journal. 1877-1893, 17 vols.; rept. n.p., n.d., 17 vols.

[116] "O! Tempore, O! Mores – The Curtain Falls," *supra*, p. 759.

Virginia Law Register. Lynchburg: J. P. Bell Co., 1895-1906, vols. 1-10 and Index vol.; Charlottesville: Michie Co., 1905-1928, vols. 11-20, and new series, 13 vols; rept. Taiwan, n.p., n.d., 34 vols.

TWENTIETH-CENTURY LEGAL PERIODICALS

James N. Jorgensen

I. *Introduction*

THIS ESSAY discusses Virginia legal periodicals printed after 1900.[1] Annual publications are included as well as those that were or are issued more frequently.

Periodicals have played an important role in the Virginia legal community, serving as a medium for scholarly legal commentary and debate, for keeping practitioners abreast of developments in the law, and for providing information on current events and activities in the legal community. Although the fundamental purposes of the legal periodical have remained somewhat constant, the number and circulation of Virginia legal periodicals have expanded greatly and, as a result, so has their role in the Virginia legal community. A chronological examination of legal periodicals in twentieth-century Virginia reveals that the role of the legal periodical has significantly increased from the publication of the Virginia Bar Association *Reports* and the *Virginia Law Register* at the turn of the century to the present, when dozens of legal periodicals are published monthly, many targeted to a very specific audience in the legal community.

The twentieth-century legal periodicals published in Virginia can be classified as commercial ventures, bar association publications, and academic journals. The broad outline of twentieth-century law periodical activity is that the early commercial ventures lost ground to the law school journals in the first quarter of this century, and, in the last quarter of the century, even though academic publications increased significantly, there has been a phenomenal surge of bar association periodical and newsletter publishing.

II. *Commercial Ventures*

The first law journals that were published in Virginia, and elsewhere in America for that matter, were commercial ventures.[2] The

---

[1] An earlier version of this essay was published in *Law Library Journal*, vol. 86, pp. 541-558 (1994), and is reprinted with permission.

[2] See above, "Nineteenth Century Law Journals."

publishers hoped to make a profit from supplying the legal community with various types of legal information. In 1900, there was one such journal in Virginia, the *Virginia Law Register*. The only other legal periodicals of any description were the annual proceedings of the Virginia State Bar Association and the ephemeral and highly elusive newsletter, *Pro Querente*.

The *Virginia Law Register* catered to the bar and the bench by providing a forum for legal scholarship and debate in the form of essays that were both academic and practical in approach. It published the most important recent judicial opinions of the Virginia Supreme Court of Appeals; often these "advance" reports were accompanied by editorial notes and comments. Also reported were selected cases from the federal courts and occasionally those of other states and from England. There were also miscellaneous notes, notices of bar activities, legal news, book reviews, letters to the editor, and facetiae. Profitability was pursued by providing something for everyone.

This journal ceased publishing in 1928. Although it was a valuable source of information in the beginning, it succumbed to competition from more specialized publications. The *Virginia Law Review* was founded by the law students at the University of Virginia in 1913 to publish articles of legal scholarship. There was also another rivalry. The West Publishing Company of St. Paul, Minnesota, was supplying the Virginia bar with advance reports of Virginia judicial opinions in its *South Eastern Reporter*, and *Virginia Appeals*, which was edited by Maury Baldwin Watts, also furnished advance sheets for the Virginia appellate court opinions from 1907 to 1926.[3]

It was not until 1941 that the next successful commercial legal publication was begun. This was the *Virginia Bar Weekly*, which was a legal newspaper of general circulation. It was forced to suspend publication in January 1944 because of the wartime shortage of newsprint. Then there was the *Virginia Researcher*, which was begun in 1970. It was a monthly publication for sale by the Research Group, Inc., of Charlottesville. In 1986, the *Virginia Lawyers Weekly*, was founded; it is owned by Lawyers Weekly Publications and is published weekly in Richmond. This newspaper has become a valuable fixture in Virginia with its news reporting and slip opinion services.

The financial success of this latter venture was made possible by the recent phenomenal growth in the size of the Virginia state bar. This increase in the number of lawyers in the Commonwealth is due in part to the change in the Virginia economy following the Second World War; this change was from being primarily agricultural to primarily

[3] W. H. Bryson, "Advance Sheets in Virginia," *Va. Law Reporters*, pp. 129-130 (1977).

commercial and industrial. Furthermore, the size of the general population of the state has grown significantly. However, the main cause has been the enormous growth of both the state and the federal government; northern Virginia is now primarily a suburb of the nation's capital city. The number of lawyers who work for or against government has skyrocketed in the last few decades.

III. *Bar Publications*

In 1888, the newly-formed Virginia State Bar Association published its first volume of proceedings. This annual publication continued unaltered in form until 1975, when it was replaced by the *Virginia Bar Association Journal*, a quarterly publication of scholarly articles and official reports of the Association. The original publication of the Bar Association was truly a scholarly journal in that it published the Presidential Address and the Annual Address, which were delivered at the annual general meetings of the Association. These two papers were intended to be scholarly presentations on topical legal issues; indeed, the first pair of addresses were impressive discussions of the issue of law reform by codification.[4] Later papers were given by prominent judges, practitioners, and academics.[5] Many of the committee reports were more academic than one might have anticipated.[6] The reports of the activities of the Virginia State Bar Association and the memorials to decreased members are important sources of information about the bar, its members, and its activities.

The annual reports of the Bar Association of the City of Richmond go back to 1886, the year after its founding. This publication, however, was more a newsletter and presentation of reports of activities than a scholarly journal, even though, at the beginning, the president of the Association reported on recent legislation of interest to the bar.

The Virginia State Bar, which was created by statute in 1938,[7] publishes annual reports, and other organizations of the legal

---

[4] W. J. Robertson, "Address," and J. C. Carter, "Provinces of the Written and the Unwritten Law," *Va. State Bar Ass'n Repts.*, vol. 2, pp. 85-137 (1889).

[5] *E.g.*, R. A. Pryor, "Influence of Virginia in the Formation of the Federal Constitution," *id.*, vol. 8, p. 175-195 (1895); W. Wilson, "Leaderless Government," *id.*, vol. 10, pp. 271-292 (1897); W. H. Taft, "The Administration of Justice – Its Speeding and Cheapening," *id.*, vol. 21, pp. 233-246 (1908); R. Pound, "The Judicial Office in America," *id.*, vol. 41, pp. 406-421 (1929).

[6] *E.g.*, J. S. Bryan, "Report of Committee on Library and Legal Literature," *id.*, vol. 11, pp. 55-70 (1898), *id.*, vol. 12, pp. 58-72 (1899); this was a bibliographical essay on the various editions of the Code of Virginia from 1612 to 1898.

[7] 1938 Va. Acts, ch. 410.

profession in Virginia do so as well. However, since about 1975, there has been a phenomenal proliferation of legal periodical literature emanating from various well-established and newly-organized legal groups. This has been in the form of scholarly publications, newsletters, and reports of seminars and activities. It reflects two developments. First, there has been a huge increase in the size, sophistication, and specialization of the bar. In 1940, there were a total of 2,776 active and associate members of the Virginia State Bar. In 1950, there were 3,626 members; in 1960, 5,079; in 1970, 8,335; in 1980, 15,123; and in 1990, there were over 22,000.[8] Second, there has been a general abandonment of Virginia state law by the Virginia academic community and its publications.

Within the past twenty-five years, the bar of Virginia has subdivided into numerous geographic, legal specialty, and social interest groups, and the old, established bar groups have set up specialty sections under their general umbrellas. This trend was possible because of the increase in the size of the bar; it was desirable because of the increase in the specialization of many lawyers' practice. The result has been an explosion of newsletters to keep members informed of news and recent legislative and judicial activity. For example, from 1980 through 1983, twelve newsletters and annual seminar proceedings were founded by the various sections, committees, and groups sponsored by the Virginia State Bar, which was then under the leadership of Samuel N. Clifton, the executive director, and presidents William M. Baskin, James C. Roberts, and William B. Poff. Some of these publications are somewhat superficial; others perform the functions of purveying the news, recording official actions, and presenting scholarly articles. Among the more notable examples of the latter type are the *Virginia Bar Association Journal*, which is edited by Charles E. Friend, a well-known legal scholar, and the *Journal of Civil Litigation*, which evolved from a newsletter into a scholarly journal under the leadership of Professor W. Clark Williams.[9] These efforts are the first steps to filling the academic void that was created when the law school journals abandoned the service of the Virginia legal community.

These publications are sponsored by and financially subsidized by the various bar groups. Most are distributed free to their members as one of the services provided and as one of the benefits of membership.

---

[8] *Annual Report of the Virginia State Bar*, p. i (1940); *id.*, p. 14 (1950); *id.*, p. 15 (1960); *id.*, p. 11 (1970); *id.*, p. 8 (1980); *Virginia Lawyer*, vol. 39, no. 3, p. 8 (Sept. 1990).

[9] R. W. West, "A History of the Virginia Association of Defense Attorneys, 1968-1993," *Journal of Civil Litigation*, vol. 5, pp. 287, 289-291 (1993).

IV. *Academic Journals*

The first academic journal in Virginia was the *Virginia Law Review*, which was founded by the law students of the University of Virginia in 1913. It was modeled on the *Harvard Law Review*, the first of its kind. It was originally funded through subscriptions and payments from advertising.[10] The academic journals are now financially subsidized by their law schools.

The *Washington and Lee Law Review* was founded in 1939. It began with a Board of Student Editors and a Board of Faculty Editors. Faculty control ended in 1968 when the faculty editors were replaced by a single faculty advisor.

In May of 1949, students at the Marshall-Wythe School of Law at the College of William and Mary began publication of the *William and Mary Review of Virginia Law*. The forerunner to the *William and Mary Law Review*, this intramural law review featured legal analysis focused on Virginia law. It was replaced by the *William and Mary Law Review* in 1956. The fundamental difference between the *William and Mary Review of Virginia Law* and the *William and Mary Law Review* is that the former featured articles written by Marshall-Wythe law students, while the latter features articles by members of every branch of the legal profession, including comments by Marshall-Wythe law students.

The purposes of a law school journal are twofold. An academic law review provides a vehicle for the scholarly study and exposition of the law. It provides a forum for new ideas as well as the exposition of the present state of the law. Here is the opportunity for debate, calls for reform, historical explanation, and philosophical speculation. Secondly, such a publication provides an important educational experience for the students of the law school. Publications also enhance the visibility and prestige of their sponsoring institutions. Because of the opportunity for recognition and because of the educational value, all of the Virginia law schools have established academic legal journals as soon as they were financially able to do so.

The exception was the University of Richmond, where the dean of the law school was hostile to the idea of a student-run law review. Before the *University of Richmond Law Review* was founded, the T. C. Williams School of Law at the University of Richmond had a very modest occasional publication entitled *University of Richmond Law Notes*, which was originally a law faculty-edited journal for faculty contributions only. In 1968, the law students, with strong alumni

---

[10] J. Ritchie, *The First Hundred Years: A Short History of the School of Law of the University of Virginia*, pp. 92-94 (1978); R. C. Coleman, "The Plan and History of the Virginia Law Review," *The Centennial of the University of Virginia*, pp. 159-162 (1922).

support, forced Dean William T. Muse to allow a student-run law review to come into existence in order to bring their school's offerings into line with those of the other law schools in the state. This new law review had the support of the faculty. The reason for the dean's reluctance is unclear. It may have been the weak financial position of the law school and of the university at that time.[11] It may have been due to Muse's reluctance to part with any power and with the control of the publication of the *Law Notes*.[12] It may have been due to the illness of the dean, who was suffering from cancer at that time; this was unknown to the student body and to the general public[13] at the time, and this may account for his pathological reluctance to relinquish any control or accept new ideas at this difficult period of his life. He died in 1971.

The two newest law schools in Virginia, those at George Mason University and at Regent University, had law journals from their inception. The most recent development is for a law school to sponsor several journals.

Until recent times, these academic journals served the bench and bar of Virginia with relevant scholarly commentary on state law. But now they have largely abandoned this function in their school's pursuit of reputations as "national" law schools, again, in imitation of the Harvard Law School. The result is the phenomenon, which is nationwide, of law professors who largely ignore state law. There is a plethora of information and commentary on federal and general American law but little academic discussion of legal problems and issues of Virginia state law.[14] The marginal utility of the only scholarly article on a point of state law is likely to be far greater than that of the fiftieth one on any subject.

Another national trend in the United States is an increasing separation of the academic and the practicing legal communities. The academics are writing more for other scholars and less for the practitioners of the law. Unfortunately, the practitioner does not have

---

[11] D. J. Mays, *The Pursuit of Excellence: A History of the University of Richmond Law School*, pp. 73-74 (1970). However, it is to be noted that in 1968 the University of Richmond could field a costly Division I football team, but it could not provide the law faculty with a secretary.

[12] "The University of Richmond Law Review: The First Twenty-Five Volumes," *U. Rich. L. Rev.*, vol. 25, pp. xiii at xiv-xv (1991).

[13] J. A. V. Berry, "William Taylor Muse," *Legal Education in Va.*, pp. 477-483 (1982).

[14] One issue of each annual volume of the *University of Richmond Law Review* is devoted to recent developments in Virginia law. This is by far the most popular part of that law review.

the leisure or the inclination to read and ruminate upon the philosophic emanations of the legal academy. The legal humanists began the academic trend away from the consideration of practical legal problems several centuries ago. Now the academic community of the common law countries is beginning to turn its back on the bench and the bar; it is set on a course of irrelevancy from the practitioners' point of view. It is to be remembered that it was the *mos italicus* of the Bartolists, not the *mos gallicus* of the humanists, that led to the *usus modernus*.[15]

Legal philosophy is important, but the academy should also serve the practicing branches of the legal profession. On the other hand, the philosophers must maintain contact with the practitioners because where practice and theory seriously and fundamentally differ, it is the theory that should be reconsidered first. Not only do the bench and bar need the services of the legal scholar, but the jurist needs to maintain contact with the practitioner and the daily reality of the law.

To remedy the lack of legal commentary on Virginia law, Virginia bar organizations of all descriptions have begun publishing a wide assortment of periodicals, reports, and newsletters. A few of these are general, but most are limited to some specific branch of Virginia law. The vast majority of them are being edited by practicing lawyers and are full of digests of recent judicial opinions, comments on recent legislation, and notes of legal happenings. Only a few have articles of legal scholarship that place recent developments within the broader framework.

V. *Conclusion*

Not only do the scholars and practitioners of the law need each other, but they also need the law librarians. And so we implore present and future librarians to preserve the items here described, especially the ephemeral ones, for the use of present and future generations of researchers. On numerous occasions, we have searched in vain for a periodical. Too often have we been told that a particular publication was "ephemeral" and neither catalogued nor preserved. One cannot expect the practicing lawyers to care for the printed materials sent to them, but this is, we believe, the duty of librarians. And who is to say what is ephemeral and what is eternal? Who can say what will be of value to an historian two hundred years from now?[16]

---

[15] P. Stein, "Legal Humanism and Legal Science," *The Character and Influence of the Roman Civil Law*, pp. 91-100 (1988).

[16] For a sad example of such a loss, note that the records of the first thirty-two years of the Richmond Bar Association have been lost. J. O. Peters, *Tale of the Century: A*

BIBLIOGRAPHY

Administrative Law News. Richmond: Administrative Law Section of the Virginia State Bar, 1981 to present.

> *Administrative Law News* is published at various frequencies to provide useful information to administrative law practitioners. Featured in each issue of this publication are updates on the legislative activity of the Virginia General Assembly, articles of interest to the members of the Administrative Law Section, a message from the editor, and synopses of recent case law affecting administrative law.

Administrative, Franchise and Trade Regulation Newsletter. Richmond: Antitrust Section of the Virginia State Bar, 1981 to present.

> This publication features updates on recent case law, state and national legislative activity, and Attorney General's opinions affecting antitrust, franchise, and trade regulation in Virginia.

Advanced Business Law Seminar. Richmond: Virginia State Bar and the Virginia State Bar Association, 1970 to present.

> Published annually by the Joint Committee on Continuing Legal Education of the Virginia State Bar Association and Virginia State Bar, this publication contains the substance of each presentation offered at the annual advanced business seminar. This seminar treats different topics of particular interest to the Virginia practitioner who is involved in business law, including commercial real estate development, commercial law, reorganization and bankruptcy, and environmental law for the business practitioner.

Advanced Estate Planning and Administration Seminar. Richmond: Section on Wills, Trusts and Estates, Virginia State Bar and the Virginia Bar Association, 1980 to present.

> This publication is issued annually to inform the practitioner of recent trends and developments in this particular area of law. The presentations offered at the seminar are contained in this annual publication in outline form.

History of the Bar Association of the City of Richmond 1885-1985, p. vii (1985).

Annual Report of the Attorney General. Richmond: Attorney General's Office, 1836 to present.

> This report contains the full texts of all official opinions of the Attorney General of Virginia.

[*Annual Report*]. Richmond: Bar Association of the City of Richmond, 1885 to ?

> These reports include the association's constitution, by laws, code of ethics, minimum fee schedules, lists of members and officers, committee reports, reports of recent legislation, and lists of the books in the bar library. The Virginia State Library has five dating from 1886 to 1909.

Annual Report of the Virginia State Bar. Richmond: Virginia State Bar, 1939 to 1987.

> Published annually by the Virginia State Bar, this publication reports the minutes of the annual Virginia State Bar meeting. In addition, reports of the President, Executive Director, Treasurer, and of each section and committee are included. Opinions on the unauthorized practice of law are published here.

Annual Tax Conference. Williamsburg: College of William and Mary, 1955 to present.

> The papers of the second to the seventh conferences were not published.

Annual Trusts and Estates Seminar: Recent Developments and Current Issues in Estate Planning and Administration. Richmond: Virginia Law Foundation and Trusts and Estate Section of Virginia State Bar, 1982 to present.

> This periodical is published annually for the benefit of Virginia practitioners with an interest in trusts and estates. This particular seminar provides practitioners with recent developments and changes in trusts and estates law. The substance of presentations offered at the seminar are contained in this publication in outline form.

Attorney General's Criminal Law Digest. Richmond: Office of the Attorney General, 1984 to 1987, 4 vols.

> This is a quarterly digest of criminal opinions issued by the Attorney General of Virginia. It was replaced by *The Law Digest*.

The Bar Bulletin. Norfolk: Norfolk and Portsmouth Bar Ass'n, ? to present.

> This is a monthly newsletter for the membership of the Norfolk and Portsmouth Bar Association. It has been published for the last ten to fifteen years.

The Barrister. Charlottesville: University of Virginia School of Law, 1956 to present.

> This law school annual publishes photographs of all law faculty and students. Also, there are notes of law school organizations and clubs.

Basic Business Law Seminar. Richmond: Virginia Law Foundation, 1983 to present.

> Co-sponsored by the Committee on Continuing Legal Education of the Virginia Law Foundation and the Business Law Section of the Virginia State Bar, this annual publication includes different topics of particular interest to the Virginia practitioner who is involved in business law. Presented in outline form, this seminar report includes topics such as corporate representation, servicing business clients, and current issues in business law.

Bill of Particulars. Charlottesville: Local Government Attorneys of Virginia, 1975 to present.

> This monthly publication gives short news items and digests of judicial opinions and attorney general opinions of interest to city and county attorneys. It is sponsored by the Local Government Attorneys of Virginia and published by the National Research Group.

Circuit Court Report. Richmond: Court Report Publications, Jan. 1982 to Oct. 1989, 8 vols.

This looseleaf publication was a monthly digest of civil jury trials in personal injury cases in the Richmond metropolitan area. The primary interest of this commercial venture was in the monetary amounts of settlements, verdicts, and judgments. Volumes 4 through 8 were edited by Mary Bruner.

The Civil Digest. Richmond: Office of the Attorney General, Jan. 1973 to April 1987, 15 vols.

This is a monthly digest of civil opinions issued by the Attorney General of Virginia relative to problems of interest to officials of Virginia state and local governments. It was replaced by *The Law Digest.*

The Colonial Lawyer. Williamsburg: Marshall-Wythe School of Law, 1967 to 1991, 20 vols.

This publication was issued semiannually, originally, as a student in-house publication about the law school; it was suspended for several years and then reissued as a substantive legal periodical.

Construction Law News. Richmond: Construction Law Section of the Virginia State Bar, 1981 to present.

Published twice annually by the Construction Law Section of the Virginia State Bar, this publication targets Virginia practitioners who practice construction law. It features Virginia legislation and case law that affects construction contracts.

Corporate Counsel News. Richmond: Corporate Counsel Section of the Virginia State Bar, 1990 to present.

Published at various frequencies for corporate counsel practicing in the Commonwealth, *Corporate Counsel News* features articles, case synopses, and legislative updates affecting the practice of corporate law in Virginia.

Developments in Mental Health Law. Charlottesville: Institute of Law, Psychiatry, and Public Policy, 1980 to present.

Published twice annually by the University of Virginia's Institute of Law, Psychiatry, and Public Policy, this periodical is published with the support of funds from the Virginia Department of Mental Health, Mental Retardation and

> Substance Abuse Services. It features contributions from University of Virginia law and graduate students as well as Virginia law practitioners. Case law in federal and Virginia courts as well as legislative activity is updated in each issue.

Dicta: a Compilation of the Virginia Law Weekly Dicta. Charlottesville: University of Virginia School of Law, 1949 to 1976, 27 vols.

> This annual publication by the law students of the University of Virginia reprinted a regular editorial feature from the *Virginia Law Weekly* entitled "Dicta." Each volume is a collection of brief essays on a particular topic that appeared weekly during the previous academic year. Volume 25 was not published.

Digest of Virginia Legislation. Richmond: Div. of Purchase and Printing, 1934 to present.

> This annual publication summarizes all of the amendments to the Code of Virginia enacted during the preceding year. It was originally prepared by the Virginia Division of Statutory Research and Drafting and is now the product of the Virginia Division of Legislative Services. The current title is *Digest of Acts*.

Education and Practice. Richmond: Section on Education of Lawyers of the Virginia State Bar, 1993 to present.

> This is a newsletter for the members of the Section on Education of Lawyers of the Virginia State Bar.

Environmental Law News. Richmond: Environmental Law Section of the Virginia State Bar, 1988 to present.

> The fundamental objective of this quarterly publication is to inform the Virginia environmental law practitioner of recent developments in environmental law in Virginia and the nation. Edited by Washington and Lee University law students, it features articles of general interest, Virginia legislative committee reports, and recent case reports from the district courts, courts of appeals, and the Fourth Circuit in each issue.

Environmental Practice News. Williamsburg: Environmental Law Society of Marshall-Wythe School of Law, 1975 to present.

This periodical is published by law students of the Marshall-Wythe School of Law at the College of William and Mary at variable frequencies since its inception in 1975. Distributed to law schools, Virginia practitioners, City and Commonwealth's Attorneys, and conservation organizations, this periodical focuses on case law and legislative activity affecting the environment and its protection.

Fairfax Bar Journal. Fairfax: Fairfax Bar Association, 1979 to present.

This publication is a monthly newsletter.

Family Law Section Newsletter. Richmond: Family Law Section of the Virginia State Bar, Winter 1980 to present.

Family Law Section Newsletter is published quarterly for lawyers who have an interest in family law practice and want to keep informed of recent trends and new developments. Featured in each issue of this newsletter are the legislative update, the editor's message, case notes, and family law articles penned by members of the Virginia bar. Peter N. Swisher, professor of law at the University of Richmond, edited the newsletter from the Winter of 1982 issue through the Summer 1990 publication. Richard E. Crouch, a family law practitioner in Arlington, has edited the newsletter since Spring 1991.

Family Law Seminar. Richmond: Family Law Section of the Virginia State Bar and Virginia Law Foundation, 1982 to present.

Focused on recent developments in the field of family law, this annual publication contains all of the presentations offered at the seminar in outline form. Recent developments and tough issues in family law are featured in this publication.

The Fee Simple. Richmond: Real Property Section of the Virginia State Bar, 1980 to present.

Serving the second largest section of the Virginia State Bar (behind the Litigation Section), *The Fee Simple* is published quarterly for practitioners with an interest in real property issues. Feature articles, recent case opinions and synopses, and legislative updates highlight each issue of this publication.

General Practice Plus. Richmond: General Practice Section of the Virginia State Bar, 1987 to present.

This periodical, which is published at variable frequencies, focuses on matters of interest to general practitioners of the Commonwealth. It includes articles of interest to the general practitioner including management of a firm, effective billing, and legal ethics and opinion summaries.

George Mason Independent Law Journal. Arlington: George Mason Independent Law Journal Ass'n, Winter 1992 to present.

This semiannual journal was founded by the students of George Mason School of Law when their Law School ceased to support the student edited *George Mason University Law Review.*

George Mason University Civil Rights Law Journal. Arlington: George Mason University School of Law, 1990 to present.

This student-edited journal is published semiannually.

George Mason University Law Review. Arlington: George Mason Law Review Association, Winter 1978 to 1992, 14 vols.

Originally the *ISL Law Review,* this publication became the *GMU Law Review* in 1978 when the International School of Law merged with George Mason University. The name of the journal was changed to the *George Mason University Law Review* in 1982. This law review is published on a quarterly basis at George Mason University Law School. It has lead articles, case notes, and comments.

Health Law News. Richmond: Virginia State Bar Section on Health Law, November 1984 to present.

Originally published as the *Health Law Section Newsletter,* this publication changed its name to *Health Law News* in February of 1988. It includes feature articles, legislative updates of Congress and the Virginia General Assembly, and synopses of recent case law opinions concerning health law.

Intellectual Property News. Richmond: Intellectual Property Law Section of the Virginia State Bar, 1989 to present.

> *Intellectual Property News*, published at various frequencies, provides practical information to those attorneys who practice intellectual property law in Virginia. Featured in each edition are lead articles, the section's administrative news, such as notices of upcoming events and social functions, and recent case synopses affecting intellectual property law practitioners.

International Practice News. Richmond: International Practice Section of the Virginia State Bar, 1981 to present.

> The purpose of this publication is to provide current, important developments relating to international law and practice, section news, and other information believed to be of interest to Virginia's legal and business community. Included in each issue are judicial and administrative decisions affecting international law and practice, letters to the editor, and legislative activity updates.

The Journal. Richmond: Virginia Trial Lawyers Association, March 1989 to present.

> Published quarterly to educate and promote professionalism among trial attorneys, *The Journal* focuses on recent trends in Virginia trial practice. The magazine features articles written by members of the Virginia bar and edited by a board of editors who are members of the Virginia Trial Lawyers Association and who primarily practice in the fields of personal injury representing plaintiffs and criminal law representing defendants.

Journal of Christian Jurisprudence. Virginia Beach: Regent University, 1980 to present.

> Published annually to prepare its students for the practice of law, Regent University's *Journal of Christian Jurisprudence* contains articles concerning the Biblical perspective on various areas of jurisprudence and targets both the legal and non-legal communities of the Commonwealth. Originally, this journal was published by the former O. W. Coburn School of Law at Oral Roberts University in Tulsa, Oklahoma, under the same name. When the latter law school moved to CBN University in the City of Virginia Beach in 1986, this journal moved also. CBN University changed its name to Regent University in 1992.

The Journal of Civil Litigation. Richmond: Virginia Association of Defense Attorneys, Summer 1988 to present.

> This quarterly features a different format from that of its predecessor, *VADA Quarterly*. *The Journal of Civil Litigation* consists of three sections: "articles," which includes scholarly articles on topics of interest to VADA members; "opinions," which reports judicial opinions and memoranda affecting civil litigators in Virginia; and "miscellany," which includes VADA administrative news, such as a listing of new membership, VADA convention news, and any special updates concerning the VADA membership.

Journal of the John Bassett Moore Society of International Law. Charlottesville: John Bassett Moore Society of International Law Association, 1960 to 1961, 2 vols.

> This student-edited publication was not an official publication of the University of Virginia. However, it was edited by University of Virginia law students. Published two times per year, this journal dealt with comparative law, public international law, and private international law. This journal was continued as the *Virginia Journal of International Law*.

The Journal of Law and Politics. Charlottesville: University of Virginia, Fall 1983 to present.

> Although this journal is not an official publication of the University of Virginia, it is edited by the University's law and graduate students. Published quarterly by the Journal of Law and Politics, Inc., with funding provided in part by the Law School Foundation and the Student Activities Fund, this publication is devoted to analyzing the interaction of law and politics.

Journal of Local Government Law. Richmond: Municipal and Local Government Section of the Virginia State Bar, 1986 to present.

> Published at various frequencies for the legal, political, and business communities of Virginia, this publication focuses on issues affecting local government law. Legislative updates, synopses of recent case decisions, and the section's administrative affairs are featured in each issue of this periodical.

The Law Digest. Richmond: Office of the Attorney General, May 1987, to present.

This is a monthly newsletter and digest of the official opinions of the Attorney General of Virginia. It replaced *The Civil Digest* and *The Criminal Law Digest.*

Lex Claudia. Richmond: Virginia Women Attorneys Association, 1984 to present.

Named for the Roman law that abolished the ancient guardianship of adult women by their male relatives, *Lex Claudia* centers on legal matters of interest to women in general and women attorneys practicing in the Commonwealth of Virginia in particular. This publication is published sporadically and edited by volunteers.

Litigation News. Richmond: Litigation Section of the Virginia State Bar, 1983 to present.

This publication focuses on litigation issues confronted by Virginia litigators. Included in each issue are short articles and updates on different types of actions in court (e.g. personal injury, contracts, and workers' compensation), section news, and letters to the editor.

Michie Mouth. Charlottesville: The Michie Co., 1979 to 1996.

This in-house newsletter was published six times a year by and for the employees of the Michie Company. See below, "The Michie Company."

News & Views. Richmond: The Virginia Bar Association, 1988 to 1998.

Published quarterly by The Virginia Bar Association, *News & Views* focused on keeping members of the association informed on upcoming events, such as social events, conventions, and seminars. Articles, legislative updates, and recent case synopses are also included in this publication.

Petitions Denied in the Supreme Court of Appeals of Virginia. Current Summaries of Facts and Issues of Cases in Which Petitions for Appeals [Were] Denied. Richmond: Va. State Bar Assn., 1956-1960, 4 vols.

This publication was the labor of the Committee on Library, Legal Records and Legal Literature and its successor, the Committee on Publications. It has tables of cases and cumulative indexes. There were also selected opinions of the State Tax Commissioner. It was discontinued in 1960 for financial reasons.

Pro Querente "P.Q." A Journal Devoted to the Lawyer, Merchant, Manufacturer, and Jobber. Richmond: Pro Querente Co., 1899 to ?

This ephemeral publication contained a few notes of recent court decisions and a few legal notices, but the major part of it was a list of lawyers recommended for debt collections work. There were also paid notices of Richmond attorneys and merchants. The Virginia State Library has three issues from January, May, and July 1901.

Proceedings of the . . . Annual Seminar. Richmond: Virginia Trial Lawyers Association. 1960 to 1977, 18 vols.

This was a publication of the proceedings, including reports and papers, of the annual meetings of the state-wide trial lawyers' association.

Real Estate Practice Seminar. Richmond: Virginia Law Foundation and the Real Property Section of the Virginia State Bar, 1983 to present.

Published annually by the Virginia Law Foundation in conjunction with the Real Property Section of the Virginia State Bar, this periodical contains all of the presentations offered at the real estate practice seminar in outline form. Topics that are of particular interest to attorneys who practice real estate law are selected for this seminar.

Recent Developments in the Law Seminar. Richmond: Virginia State Bar and Virginia Law Foundation, 1975 to present.

This publication is presented annually by the Committee on Continuing Legal Education of the Virginia Law Foundation in conjunction with the Virginia State Bar. As the name would suggest, this publication focuses on recent developments in the law. Issues involving civil litigation, real estate, legal ethics, criminal litigation, taxation, and family law are all featured in this periodical.

Regent University Law Review. Virginia Beach: Regent University, 1991 to present.

> This journal is published semiannually by the law students of Regent University. It includes lead articles and student-written notes and comments.

Report of the Virginia State Bar Association. Richmond: The Virginia Bar Association, 1888 to 1975, 85 volumes; vol. 1 was reprinted: Richmond: Richmond Press, 1937.

> Published annually by the Virginia Bar Association, this publication informed bar association members of the annual bar meeting events and bar membership news. Volumes 33 to 85 were issued under the title of *Proceedings of the Virginia State Bar Association*; it was supplanted by the *Virginia Bar Association Journal*. This publication offered the Annual Address, which was delivered by a distinguished legal scholar, the Presidential Address, and other scholarly papers, committee reports, and obituaries of deceased members.

Resolutions. Richmond: Dept. of Dispute Resolution Services, 1992 to present.

> This quarterly newsletter is published by a department of the Office of the Executive Secretary of the Supreme Court of Virginia. It is the successor to the *Virginia Dispute Resolution Center Newsletter*.

The Richmond Bar. Richmond: The Bar Association of the City of Richmond, 1988 to present.

> Published to inform the members of the Bar Association of the City of Richmond, *Richmond Bar* features announcements, notices, membership surveys, and a calendar of upcoming events. Short articles and a column, "From Your President," are included in each issue as well.

Richmond Law. Richmond: The T. C. Williams School of Law, University of Richmond, Winter 1988 to present.

> This periodical, published twice annually, is targeted at alumni, faculty, and other friends of the School of Law. Short articles, "class notes" (including changes in employment, professional recognition, births, marriages, and deaths),

"Notes from the Dean's Office," and the "Faculty Forum" are featured in each issue.

Senior Lawyer News. Richmond: Senior Lawyers Section of the Virginia State Bar, 1988 to present.

> *Senior Lawyer News* is published for Virginia attorneys who are the age of fifty-five or older. Issues unique to senior attorneys such as retirement, pension plans, and Medicaid are featured in each issue.

State of the Judiciary Report. Richmond: Supreme Court of Virginia, 1975 to present.

> This is the annual report of the Supreme Court of Virginia. It contains lists of all of the judges in Virginia and much statistical information about the state courts.

The Supreme Court Economic Review. Fairfax: George Mason Univ. Pr., 1993 to present.

> This annual publication is sponsored by the Law and Economics Center and the School of Law of George Mason University.

Trusts and Estates Newsletter. Richmond: Trusts and Estates Section of the Virginia State Bar, 1982 to present.

> Published at various frequencies, *Trusts and Estates Newsletter* focuses on the planning of estates and trusts in Virginia. Section news, feature articles, and legislative updates are all a part of this publication.

University of Richmond Law Notes. Richmond: The T. C. Williams School of Law, Spring 1958 to Spring 1967, 2 vols.

> The forerunner to the *University of Richmond Law Review*, the *University of Richmond Law Notes* was published on an annual basis and featured articles discussing practical problems of current interest to the Virginia practitioner. J. Westwood Smithers, a member of the University of Richmond law faculty, edited the *Law Notes* from its inception until 1963, when it became a student-edited publication.

University of Richmond Law Review. Richmond: University of Richmond Law Review Association, Spring 1968 to present.

> This student-edited law review is published quarterly as a practical resource for the Virginia practitioner. The most popular issue of the *Law Review* is the annual Summer Survey of Virginia Law, which features articles that discuss and analyze recent decisions of Virginia and federal courts in addition to developments in the Virginia General Assembly; this feature was first published in 1985.

UVA Lawyer. Charlottesville: University of Virginia Law School Alumni Association, 1987 to present.

> This is a newsletter published by and for the law alumni of the University of Virginia. It contains articles as well as news of the law school. It was first published three times a year; it is now issued semiannually.

Vabwa News. Richmond: Virginia Association of Black Women Attorneys, Fall 1990 to present.

> This quarterly newsletter contains short articles and items of news of interest to the members of the Virginia Association of Black Women Attorneys.

VADA Newsletter. Richmond: Virginia Association of Defense Attorneys, May 1976 to June 1982, 7 vols.

> This newsletter was published on a quarterly basis by the Virginia Association of Defense Attorneys. In addition to articles of interest to Virginia defense attorneys, this publication featured VADA administrative news such as the "Treasurer's Report," the "President's Page," and "Minutes from VADA Meetings." Reports of civil cases and opinions and letters to the editor were staples of the *VADA Newsletter*. It was continued by the *VADA Quarterly*, which in turn was succeeded by *The Journal of Civil Litigation*.

VADA Quarterly. Richmond: Virginia Association of Defense Attorneys, June 1982 to Summer 1988, 5 vols. (vols. 8-12).

> The change in title from *VADA Newsletter* to *VADA Quarterly* reflected the expanded functions of the periodical. In addition to reporting recent opinions from various courts, *VADA Quarterly* also included articles on topics of interest to VADA members. VADA administrative features continued to include

the "Treasurer's Report," the "President's Page," and "Minutes from VADA Meetings." *VADA Quarterly* was continued as *The Journal of Civil Litigation* in the Summer 1988 issue.

VBA News Journal. Richmond: Virginia Bar Association, September 1998 to present.

This publication, which is the successor to the *Virginia Bar Association Journal* and *News and Views*, is published eight times per year for the membership of the Virginia Bar Association. It has short practice-oriented articles and news of the Association and its members.

Virginia Association of Defense Attorneys Bulletin. Richmond: Va. Ass'n of Defense Attorneys, June 1990 to present.

This newsletter is published eight time a year and distributed to the members of the Virginia Association of Defense Attorneys. Its primary purpose is to digest the most recent Virginia Supreme Court decisions, and the publication dates of each issue are scheduled to be shortly after the monthly rendering of that court's decisions.

Virginia Bar Association Journal. Richmond: Virginia Bar Association, 1975 to 1998, 24 vols.

Published quarterly by the Virginia Bar Association, this journal was edited by Charles E. Friend. Featured in this publication are articles on Virginia law, a young lawyers section, a report on bar association proceedings, and the "President's Page." It supplanted the *Virginia Bar Association Proceedings*.

Virginia Bar News. Richmond: Virginia State Bar, 1953 to 1988, 36 vols.

Published monthly by the Virginia State Bar, *Virginia Bar News* informed Virginia practitioners on local bar activities. Articles on judges and lawyers in the news, law-related advertisements and classifieds, professional notices, disciplinary orders, and ethics opinions were included in this journal.

Virginia Bar Weekly. Richmond: Daily Record Co., Inc., 1941 to 1944, 3 vols.

This legal newspaper was published from January 21, 1941, to January 4, 1944, "for Virginia's busy practicing attorneys" edited by Esther Sutro Weinberg, a member of the Virginia bar. It had items of legal news, but its primary function was to digest recent opinions of the Virginia Supreme Court of Appeals, Virginia circuit courts, and federal courts sitting in Virginia. It suspended publication because of the shortage of newsprint during the war.

Virginia Business Law. Richmond: Business Law Section of the Virginia State Bar, 1987 to present.

Published twice annually, this publication includes a "Chairman's Report" (a message from the Chairman of the Business Section of the Virginia State Bar) and "Editor's Notes." In addition, feature articles penned by members of the Virginia bar and recent U.C.C., bankruptcy, and Virginia cases are reported in each issue.

Virginia Dispute Resolution Center Newsletter. Richmond: Virginia Dispute Resolution Center. 1988 to 1992.

This publication was funded by the Virginia Law Foundation. It was a joint project of the Virginia State Bar and the Virginia Bar Association. Feature articles on dispute resolution, book and video reviews, and legislative updates were all included in this newsletter. It was superseded in 1992 by *Resolutions.*

Virginia Environmental Law Journal. Charlottesville: Virginia Environmental Law Journal Association, Spring 1989 to present.

Although not an official University of Virginia publication, this quarterly is edited by University of Virginia law students. Originally the *Virginia Journal of Natural Resources Law*, the name of this publication was changed to the *Virginia Environmental Law Journal* to convey to readers and potential contributing authors the comprehensive scope of the journal. It has lead articles, case notes, and comments treating local, regional, national, and international environmental issues.

Virginia Journal of International Law. Charlottesville: Virginia Journal of International Law Association, 1963 to present.

Originally published as the *Journal of the John Bassett Moore Society of International Law*, this quarterly is edited by

University of Virginia law students. The title of this publication was changed to the *Virginia Journal of International Law* to demonstrate the periodical's changed emphasis from public international law to private, or commercial, problems of international law. Unlike its predecessor, the *Virginia Journal of International Law* often publishes student-written material.

Virginia Journal of Natural Resources Law. Charlottesville: Virginia Journal of Natural Resources Law Association, Summer 1980 to Fall 1988, 8 vols.

The forerunner of the *Virginia Environmental Law Journal*, this publication was issued twice annually by law students of the University of Virginia.

Virginia Journal of Social Policy and the Law. Charlottesville: University of Virginia School of Law, 1993 to present.

This is published semi-annually by the law students of the University of Virginia. It "provides a forum for examining contending legal, judicial, and political perspectives relating to the interaction of law and social policy."

Virginia Land Use Digest. Lynchburg: Cenva Publishing Co., October 1990 to present.

Virginia Land Use Digest is an attempt to provide a single forum to address land use and zoning issues. Published at variable frequencies, this periodical has been edited by William W. Hibbert, former Executive Director of the Central Virginia Planning District Commission, from its inception. General Assembly activity, recent case law, and Attorney General opinions are featured in each issue. In addition, feature articles deal with legal issues affecting land use planners and developers.

Virginia Law Digest. Richmond: Maury Baldwin Watts, Jan. 1928 to Dec. 1933, 6 vols.

This is a brief digest of the decisions of the Virginia Supreme Court of Appeals and the Special Court of Appeals published monthly under the auspices of the Virginia State Bar Association.

Virginia Law Register. Lynchburg: J. P. Bell Co., May 1895 to 1905, vols. 1-10 and Index vol.; Charlottesville: Michie Co., 1905 to

April 1928, vols. 11-20, and new series, 13 vols; rept. Taiwan, n.p., n.d., 34 vols.

> The old series was edited by E. C. Burks. This monthly periodical was published to aid the Virginia practitioner through the use of four featured sections: full reports of leading cases, table of cases reported in full, table of cases digested, and the general index. The new series was published in a different format from its predecessor; it featured editorials, book reviews, leading articles and notes of cases. R. T. W. Duke was the editor of the new series. Burks and Duke were prominent and distinguished practicing lawyers.

Virginia Law Review. Charlottesville: Virginia Law Review Association, October 1913 to present.

> The *Virginia Law Review* is an official publication of the University of Virginia. It is published monthly during the school year for a total of eight issues annually. This publication is edited by University of Virginia law students and features lead articles and case notes. From 1920 to 1955, the *Virginia Law Review* published a "Virginia Section" in each issue to inform the practitioner of recent case law, legislative activity, and developments in Virginia law. It published an annual survey of Virginia law from 1955 to 1985.

Virginia Law School Report. Charlottesville: The University of Virginia School of Law, 1977 to present.

> This is a publication for the law alumni of the University of Virginia. It was first published three times a year; it is now issued semiannually.

Virginia Law Weekly. Charlottesville: University of Virginia School of Law, May 27, 1948, to present.

> This newspaper is a weekly publication by and for the law students of the University of Virginia. It is not issued during holidays and examination periods.

Virginia Lawyer. Richmond: Virginia State Bar, 1988 to present.

> Beginning with volume 37, no. 1 (July 1988), this periodical shares volume numbering and alternates issues with *Virginia Lawyer Register*, which replaced the *Virginia Bar News*. *Virginia Lawyer*, with *Virginia Lawyer Register*, is the official publication of the Virginia State Bar. In addition to lead

articles written by members of the bar, *Virginia Lawyer* features professional notices, placement services, legal ethics opinions, monthly classified advertisements, and news concerning Virginia judges and lawyers.

Virginia Lawyer Register. Richmond: Virginia State Bar, 1988 to present.

This periodical is published alternately with the *Virginia Lawyer* and reports recent disciplinary actions, a calendar of events for bar members, classified advertisements, placements services, local bar elections, and news. *Virginia Lawyer Register* releases an annual *Professional Guidelines for the Virginia Lawyer*, which includes recent disciplinary opinions and professional ethical guidelines for the Virginia practitioner.

Virginia Lawyers Weekly. Richmond: Virginia Lawyers Weekly, June 9, 1989, to present.

A commercial weekly newspaper, *Virginia Lawyers Weekly* reports developments in the Virginia legal community. Features in each issue include "This Week's Opinions" (digests of opinions of courts affecting the practice of law in Virginia), "Local Bar News," "Professional Announcements," and "Lawyers in the News."

Virginia Poverty Law Review. Richmond: Virginia Poverty Law Center, July 1980 to present.

Published on a monthly basis, the *Virginia Poverty Law Review* is written for the legal services community of the Commonwealth of Virginia. In addition to announcements and a calendar of events of interest to Virginia practitioners, this law review reports recent case law on housing, family, employment, and consumer issues.

The Virginia Prosecutor. Richmond: Office of the Attorney General, Dec. 1971 to present.

This is a monthly digest of criminal opinions issued by the Attorney General of Virginia.

The Virginia Researcher. Charlottesville: The Research Group, Inc., 1970 to 1988, 7 vols.

A publication issued monthly by The Research Group, Inc., *Virginia Researcher* provided synopses of recent Virginia and federal case law. The earlier volumes had short articles.

Virginia Tax Newsletter. Richmond: Taxation Section of the Virginia State Bar, 1989 to present.

Focused on issues of taxation, this publication features reports on section meetings, announcements, lead articles, legislative updates, and synopses of recent case law.

Virginia Tax Review. Charlottesville: Virginia Tax Review Association, Spring 1981 to present.

Exclusively devoted to taxation issues, this student-edited law review was the first of its kind in the United States. It is published quarterly; it is not an official publication of the University of Virginia.

Virginia Trial Lawyers Association Law Letter. Richmond: Virginia Trial Lawyers Association, 1962 to present.

This newsletter is published seven times a year and is accompanied by a packet of recent case synopses from the following courts: federal district court, the Fourth Circuit Court of Appeals, the Virginia Supreme Court, Virginia Circuit Courts, the Virginia Court of Appeals, and the Workers' Compensation Commission. In addition, a report from the Workers' Compensation Commission is included as well as a bulletin outlining the activities of the Virginia General Assembly entitled "Lawflash."

Washington and Lee Law Review. Lexington, Virginia: Washington and Lee Law Review Association, Fall 1939 to present.

This student-edited law review is published quarterly, featuring the summer issue, an annual review of securities and commodities law, and the spring issue, which contains a comprehensive review of the decisions of the United States Court of Appeals for the Fourth Circuit for the past year.

The William and Mary Bill of Rights Journal. Williamsburg: Marshall-Wythe School of Law, College of William and Mary, 1992 to present.

This is a law student publication that is issued twice yearly.

William and Mary Journal of Environmental Law. Williamsburg: Marshall-Wythe School of Law, College of William and Mary, c. 1975 to present.

> This semiannual law student publication was founded as a newsletter; beginning with volume 15 in 1990, it has published scholarly articles.

William and Mary Law Review. Williamsburg: Marshall-Wythe School of Law, 1957 to present.

> The purpose of this student-edited quarterly is to offer opportunity for publication by members of every branch of the legal profession as well as provide an opportunity for student legal composition and expression.

The William & Mary Lawyer: the Annual Report of the Marshall-Wythe School of Law. Williamsburg: Marshall-Wythe School of Law, 1987 to present.

> This publication is the annual report of the law alumni association of the College of William and Mary.

William and Mary Review of Virginia Law. Williamsburg: Department of Jurisprudence, the College of William and Mary, May 1949 to July 1956, 2 vols.

> The primary objective of this annual student-edited publication was to provide an opportunity for student legal commentary. The forerunner of the *William and Mary Law Review,* this intramural law review featured case comments and notes. In 1956, the law review conducted a survey of Virginia case law.

LEGAL EDUCATION

W. H. Bryson

I. *Before 1779*

A. *Introduction*

THE ENGLISH INNS OF COURT in London had ceased to perform their educational functions by the middle of the seventeenth century.[1] For the next hundred years or so, there was no formal or organized instruction of the English common law. Lawyers, both barristers and solicitors in England and in America, learned their profession as best they could in unstructured situations. They learned by serving as apprentices or clerks to practicing lawyers, by the independent reading of law books, and by observation in the courtroom itself.[2]

Although the four Inns of Court in the eighteenth century no longer gave an education, they did give the professional degree of barrister. (A barrister was deemed to be of the social degree of an esquire; this is the origin of the American custom of lawyers, including women, using the title of esquire.) The Inns of Court thrived in the eighteenth century because they controlled the admission of barristers to the practice of law, pretended to supervise the general conduct of the bar, and provided office space, a library, and a social club for their members. In this period, there was no examination prerequisite to being called to the bar. All that was required was membership in the inn for a period of time and the payment of various fees; in fact, fees could be substituted for the traditional eating of dinners that marked the passing of time. When a person was called to the bar of his inn, he was thereby entitled to argue in the high courts of justice in Westminster, to practice in any of the courts of the colony of Virginia,

---

[1] An earlier version of this essay was first published as the introduction to the author's *Legal Education in Virginia 1779-1979: A Biographical Approach* (1982) and is reprinted here with the permission of the University Press of Virginia.

[2] W. S. Holdsworth, *History of English Law*, vol. 6, pp. 481-99; vol. 12, pp. 77-89 (1924) [hereinafter cited as Holdsworth, *H.E.L.*]; W. C. Richardson, *History of the Inns of Court*, pp. 167-210 (1975); W. S. Holdsworth, "The Disappearance of the Educational System of the Inns of Court," *U. Pa. L. Rev.*, vol. 69, pp. 201-22 (1921); J. H. Baker, *The Third University of England*, p. 21 (1990); A. M. Smith, *Virginia Lawyers, 1680-1776: the Birth of an American Profession*, pp. 146-63, Ph. D. diss., Johns Hopkins Univ., 1967 [hereinafter cited as Smith, *Virginia Lawyers*].

and to style himself esquire.[3] There was no meaningful examination for admission to the English bar until 1871.[4]

The lower branch of the English legal profession, the attorneys at law and solicitors, had no professional organization until the eighteenth century. Before they began to organize themselves, however, an act of Parliament in 1729 required that they be examined by a judge before they could practice as attorneys or solicitors. Before 1836, however, the examination was normally a mere sham.[5]

It is the common law of England that is the law or the basis of the law in Virginia. The original instructions to the Virginia Company required litigation to be settled "as near to the common laws of England and the equity thereof as may be."[6] In 1632 when commissioners were appointed to hold the monthly courts (later renamed the county courts) for Warwick, Warrosquyoke (Isle of Wight), Elizabeth City, and Accomack, their commissions required them to execute the office of justice of the peace and to act "as near as may be according to the laws of the realm of England."[7] When the statutes of Virginia were recodified in 1662, the common law of England was acknowledged to be in force.[8] When independence from Great Britain was declared in 1776, a statute was enacted that stated that the general common law of England remained in force, and this provision has been continued in substance by every Virginia code since.[9] Because

---

[3] Holdsworth, *H.E.L.*, vol. 12, pp. 15-17, 22-23; A. Z. Reed, *Training for the Public Profession of the Law*, pp. 15-16, 68 (1921) [hereinafter cited as Reed]; Act of May 1732, c. 13, § 12, Hening's Statutes, vol. 4, p. 362; Smith, *Virginia Lawyers*, pp. 300-01.

[4] Holdsworth, *H.E.L.*, vol. 15, p. 239.

[5] Stat. 2 Geo. II [1729], c. 23; H. Kirk, *Portrait of a Profession: A History of the Solicitor's Profession, 1100 to the Present Day*, pp. 52-54 (1976); R. Robson, *The Attorney in Eighteenth-Century England*, pp. 53, 54, 62, 159-61 (1959).

[6] Articles, Instructions, and Orders (Nov. 20, 1606), Hening's Statutes, vol. 1, p. 68; note also the second Virginia Charter (1609), art. 23, Hening's Statutes, vol. 1, p. 96. "The English planters carr[ied] along with them those English liberties that [were] incident to their persons." M. Hale, *The Prerogatives of the King, Selden Soc.*, vol. 92, pp. 43-44 (D. E. C. Yale ed. 1976); see generally W. H. Bryson, *Virginia Civil Procedure*, pp. 46-57 (1997); A. E. D. Howard, *The Road from Runnymede: Magna Carta and Constitutionalism in America* (1968).

[7] Act of Sept. 1632, c. 18, Hening's Statutes, vol. 1, p. 186.

[8] Act of Mar. 1662, preamble, Hening's Statutes, vol. 2, p. 186.

[9] Act of May 1776, c. 5, § 6, Hening's Statutes, vol. 9, p. 127; Va. Rev. Code, vol. 1, p. 135, c. 38 (1819); Va. Code, p. 98, c. 16, § 1 (1849); Va. Code, § 2 (1887); Va. Code, § 2 (1919); Va. Code Ann., § 1-10 (Repl. Vol. 1973); T. Jefferson, *Notes on the State of Va.*, pp. 179-80 (1803).

of this tie going back to the first settling of Virginia, Virginians have always been interested in the English methods of legal education.

B. *APPRENTICESHIP*

In the late seventeenth and early eighteenth centuries, in England and in Virginia, the law was learned primarily through an apprenticeship with a practicing lawyer. The apprentice performed legal and menial chores for his master. One of the more important of these was copying forms, pleadings, and whatever. The apprentice thus did the work of a legal secretary and at the same time gained an intimate knowledge of the contents of the various writs and pleadings. He carried his master's books and notes into court and there observed the legal proceedings and his master's handling of the case. He had the use of his master's law library, and the master had an obligation to teach his apprentice the art of practicing law.

Although some lawyers would take on several apprentices at a time, the normal practice was to have only one at a time. The personal one-on-one teaching opportunity could be far more effective than the impersonal mass-production education of a school. The student observed very closely every stage of every case in his master's office. The lawyer would explain every legal step taken. As the student progressed, he would be given more responsibility for the legal research and the out-of-court preparation of the cases of his master's clients. He learned by handling actual cases under the watchful eye of a practicing lawyer. For these opportunities, the apprentice or his family paid a fee to the lawyer who gave of his time and resources to educate the younger man.[10]

The term apprentice was not used at the time, for it applied to a person learning a trade; the correct appellation was clerk or pupil. A person who had already been called to the bar but wished to work under the supervision of an older lawyer was said to devil for him; this position was similar to that of the modern associate in a firm of lawyers. It is to be kept in mind that the law is a profession that one practices; it is not a trade or occupation of which one can become a master, having learned all there is to know about it. One can become a master mason or a master scrivener, but one cannot become a master lawyer. A lawyer is constantly learning more about his business, and he is always improving his professional abilities, or else he is in a state of atrophy.

---

[10] Smith, *Virginia Lawyers*, pp. 181-204; for a list of some Virginia law clerks and masters, see *id.*, p. 377; Holdsworth, *H.E.L.*, vol. 12, pp. 85-91.

The weaknesses of learning the law by means of an apprenticeship are obvious, and in fact it was seldom that the reality measured up to the theory. The master might not be a good lawyer, or he might have a very narrow or meager practice so that the student would be exposed only to a small part of the law; in other words there might be a totally insufficient curriculum. The lawyer might be a bad teacher, or he might be too busy, or he might be unconcerned to teach; in every case he was not a professional teacher. Moreover, the master's law library might be inadequate.

A law student in 1837, William B. Clarke, wrote, "It is true I have access to a large library, but my reading for one year will require but few authors, and I believe the only advantage a student can derive from being in a lawyer's office is to see practice." Clarke proceeded to comment on the "mistaken notion that our eminent lawyers are the best instructors, their business is so extensive that they could not find time to devote to their students if they had the inclination."[11]

Thomas Jefferson had a very low opinion of apprenticeships because of the tendency of the lawyers to busy their students with repetitious drudgery that kept them away from their studies.[12] George Wythe had bitter memories of the sterile clerkship that he served under his uncle, Stephen Dewey, a lawyer in Prince George county. However, Wythe did not follow this bad example. After Wythe became established at the bar, he always had several young men studying under him, among them Jefferson. Wythe was exemplary as a master; he was concerned to teach his students rather than to exact clerical chores from them, and he never charged them fees.[13]

In Virginia there was no definite period of apprenticeship required, but the usual time was four or five years. Also, the amount of the fee varied greatly. Frequently, the master was the boy's father or close

[11] Letter of William B. Clarke to Robert Beverley, Apr. 12, 1837, Virginia Historical Society MSS1B4678a975. These opinions were also expressed by Henry St. George Tucker in his *Introductory Lecture*, p. 20 (1841).

[12] Letter of Thomas Jefferson to Thomas Turpin, Feb. 5, 1769, J. P. Boyd, ed., *Papers of Thomas Jefferson*, vol. 1, p. 24 (1950); letter of Thomas Jefferson to John Garland Jefferson, June 11, 1790, *id.*, vol. 15, pp. 480-82 (1961). This was also the experience of Littleton Waller Tazewell when he was sent to study law in 1795 under Edmund Randolph (L. R. Heaton, "Littleton Waller Tazewell's Sketch of His Own Family," pp. 187-88, M.A. thesis, Coll. of William and Mary, 1967).

[13] A. T. Dill, *George Wythe*, pp. 8-9, 20-21, 42-43, 78 (1979); B. B. Minor, "Memoir of the Author," Wythe's Reports, pp. xii, xiv, xxxii (1852); E. L. Shepard, "George Wythe," *Va. Law Reporters*, pp. 90-95 (1977); Smith, *Virginia Lawyers*, pp. 190-93, 377; W. E. Hemphill, *George Wythe, the Colonial Briton*, pp. 36-38, 114-15, 119-24, Ph. D. diss., Univ. of Va., 1937.

relative, in which case no fee was involved.[14] Edmund Pendleton, for instance, taught his nephew, Edmund Pendleton, Jr., his cousin and legal ward, John Taylor of Caroline, and his cousin, John Penn.[15] Henry Tazewell studied law under the supervision of his uncle John Tazewell, and Littleton Waller Tazewell studied for a year and a half under John Wickham, his uncle by marriage.[16] Edmund Randolph studied under his father, John Randolph, who was attorney general of the colony of Virginia.[17]

C. *READING LAW*

From the standpoint of education, the most important aspect of an apprenticeship was access to the master's law library and his guidance in reading the law. So all-important was this to the student that then, and still today, studying law as an apprentice or clerk is referred to as reading law. Reading law was also frequently done independently of an apprenticeship, as Jefferson advised Philip Turpin in 1769.[18]

In addition to reading, independently or not, there was commonplacing, a form of note-taking that had been developed in England well before the founding of Virginia. As a lawyer or student read a book, he would enter in his commonplace book under the various heads the comments on the points of law that he found in the book he was reading. Treatises, reports, and statutes could be common-placed, though statute law was relatively unimportant until the nineteenth century. To begin a commonplace book, a person would take a large blank book and write at the top of each page, in alphabetical order, the major divisions of the common law. Then the individual points of law would be added on the appropriate page. A person might begin a commonplace book as a student and continue to add to it throughout his career at the bar. The end result was a small, general, personal digest or abridgment. Both Thomas Jefferson and John Marshall kept

[14] Smith, *Virginia Lawyers*, pp. 188-90, 196-97; Reed, pp. 82-83.

[15] D. J. Mays, *Edmund Pendleton*, vol. 1, pp. 138-41, 243-44 (1952).

[16] L. R. Heaton, "Littleton Waller Tazewell's Sketch of His Own Family," pp. 71, 190-92, M.A. thesis, Coll. of William and Mary, 1967; *DAB*, s. vv. "Tazewell, Henry," and "Tazewell, Littleton Waller."

[17] J. J. Reardon, *Edmund Randolph*, p. 14 (1974).

[18] See above.

commonplace books.[19]

It was the responsibility of the practicing lawyer to direct the reading of his pupil or clerk. This duty was more often than not shirked both in England and in Virginia. Lewis Burwell wrote in 1734, when he was reading law on his own, that "for want of advice and proper books, I am afraid I shall make a very indifferent lawyer." He had already read *Coke upon Littleton*.[20]

Books were written, however, to guide the reading of law students. One of the earliest of these, J. Doddridge, *Lawyer's Light*; or, a *True Direction for the Study of the Law* (1629), was owned by a lawyer, John Mercer. This book gave to the law student only general advice and a list of principles and maxims. Robert Carter owned a copy of W. Fulbecke's *Direction of, or Preparative to, the Study of the Law*. This work went through at least three editions in the first part of the seventeenth century. Fulbecke advised the law student to keep a commonplace book and listed the various English law books in print. He pointed out the matter but not the method of study. W. Phillips, *Studii Legalis Ratio; or, Directions for the Study of the Law*, went through four editions in the late seventeenth century. There were at least two copies in Virginia; they were in the libraries of Arthur Spicer, J.P., and William Byrd, II, a member of the General Court.[21]

Phillips gave a list of English law books and then a course of study. He advised beginning with two law dictionaries: Cowell's *Interpreter* and Rastell's *Terms of the Law*. The student was then directed to study *Coke upon Littleton* and the more recent reports of cases, followed by the older reports. Finally, Phillips recommended the "ancient authors" of the English law so that the student would have a historical background to his understanding of the law.

All the significant English law books were present in eighteenth-century Virginia libraries, as were plenty of insignificant ones.[22] It is clear that any law book could have been borrowed from a neighbor or ordered from England. The colonial Virginians even owned legal

[19] See G. Chinard, ed., *The Commonplace Book of Thomas Jefferson* (1926); letter of Thomas Jefferson to Thomas Cooper, Feb. 10, 1814, A. E. Bergh and A. A. Lipscomb, eds., *Writings of Thomas Jefferson*, vol. 14, pp. 85-97 (1904); H. A. Johnson et al., eds., *Papers of John Marshall*, vol. 1, pp. 37-87 (1974). See also the commonplace book that James D. Riddle began in 1815 when he was studying law in Richmond (Virginia Historical Society MSS5:4R4315:1).

[20] W. H. Bryson, "A Letter of Lewis Burwell to James Burrough, July 8, 1734," *Va. Mag. Hist. Biog.*, vol. 81, pp. 405-14 (1973).

[21] W. H. Bryson, *Census of Law Books in Colonial Va.*, pp. 47, 50, 68 (1978).

[22] Bryson, *Census, passim*.

bibliographies and catalogs so they could keep up with the availability of English law books.[23]

The most popular legal title in colonial Virginia was *Coke upon Littleton*.[24] Sir Thomas Littleton wrote a learned treatise on the law of real property in the fifteenth century; in the early seventeenth century, Sir Edward Coke brought it up to date and enlarged it. Coke's version went through many editions, and by the end of the eighteenth century, the original work had acquired several layers of footnotes and was as much venerated because of Coke's commentary as it was for Littleton's authorship.[25] It was and is authoritative, erudite, complicated, and thoroughly turgid. It was frequently the first law book that a law student was assigned[26] even though it was quite difficult and more elementary introductions were available by the mid-eighteenth century. Sooner or later, however, *Coke upon Littleton* had to be mastered. The first assault on it was usually unsatisfactory at whatever stage it was read. Jefferson during his initial study of this work wrote to a friend, "I do wish the Devil had old Coke, for I am sure I was never so tired of an old dull scoundrel in my life."[27]

The legal dictionaries, J. Cowell, *Interpreter*, and J. Rastell, *Terms of the Law*, that were mentioned by Phillips both went through many editions in England; there were six copies of the former and fifteen copies of the latter present in colonial Virginia. The English law reports were also widely read throughout the colony; the most popular were those by Coke, Croke, and Hobart. The works of Glanvill, Bracton, Fortescue, and Saint Germain could also be found. Thomas Wood's *Institutes of the Laws of England* (1720), which was written for

[23] *Id.*, pp. 33, 40 (T. Bassett, *Catalogue of the Common and Statute Law Books of This Realm*), p. 81 (J. Worrall, *Bibliotheca Legum*). Jefferson and St. George Tucker also owned copies of Worrall's catalog (E. M. Sowerby, *Catalogue of the Library of Thomas Jefferson*, vol. 5, p. 56 (1953) [hereinafter cited as Sowerby]; H. A. Johnson, *Imported Eighteenth Century Law Treatises in American Libraries*, p. 58 (1978).

[24] Bryson, *Census*, pp. xvii, 41-42; Sowerby, vol. 2, p. 217.

[25] W. H. Maxwell and L. F. Maxwell, *A Legal Bibliography*, vol. 1, pp. 449-52, 454-58 (1955); W. S. Holdsworth, *Some Makers of English Law*, pp. 56-58, 111-32 (1938).

[26] Letter of Lewis Burwell to James Burrough, July 8, 1734, *Va. Mag. Hist. Biog.*, vol. 81, p. 413 (1973); letter of Chapman Johnson to David Watson, Oct. 27, 1800, *Va. Mag. Hist. Biog.*, vol. 29, p. 274 (1921); letter of Thomas Jefferson to Dabney Terrell, Feb. 26, 1821, H. A. Washington, ed., *Writings of Thomas Jefferson*, vol. 7, p. 207 (1854); letter, *Va. Gazette*, Dec. 30, 1773, p. 1.

[27] Letter of Thomas Jefferson to John Page, Dec. 25, 1762, J. P. Boyd, ed., *Papers of Thomas Jefferson*, vol. 1, p. 5 (1950); Smith, *Virginia Lawyers*, pp. 206-08; D. Malone, *Jefferson the Virginian*, pp. 70-73 (1948); E. Dumbauld, *Thomas Jefferson and the Law*, pp. 8, 11-12 (1978).

students, was also popular in Virginia.[28]

D. *ATTENDANCE AT THE INNS OF COURT*

A goodly number of Virginians sent their sons to England to study law in the Inns of Court. This often was preceded by study in Cambridge or Oxford. Secondary education, of course, was available in both Virginia and England. The study of law in one of the English Inns of Court meant an apprenticeship to a practicing lawyer in London with residence in the inn. Apprenticeship in England was similar to that in Virginia; however, the choice of a master was far broader, and the cultural life of London was greater than that of Williamsburg or Norfolk. London was much more expensive, but a Virginia lawyer who was a member of an inn of court had a great deal of professional and social prestige that was lacking to the Virginia-educated attorney. In fact, many Virginians who were members of an inn had no intention of ever practicing law but joined for purely social purposes.

From 1674 to 1776 there were at least sixty Virginians who were members of one of the English Inns of Court. The Middle Temple was by far the favorite of the Virginians. Of these sixty men, all but three returned to Virginia, but only twenty engaged in the practice of law once they got home. Of these sixty, only twenty were actually formally called to the bar, but some of these twenty never practiced. The essence of membership in an English inn was that it was a prestigious place to do a legal apprenticeship.[29]

E. *Admission to the Bar*

The end of the period of law studies and of preparation was marked in England by the barrister's being called to the bar of his inn or by the solicitor's being licensed by a judge. In Virginia the first control over the admission to practice law was adopted in 1643 when an act of Assembly required lawyers to be licensed and sworn by each court in which they practiced.[30] In 1645, however, the practice of law

[28] See Bryson, *Census, passim*. Jefferson also owned most of these works (Sowerby, vol. 2, pp. 211-15, 231-33, 329, 331, 336-37; vol. 3, p. 119).

[29] Smith, *Virginia Lawyers*, pp. 143-46, 163-78, 366-76. St. George Tucker's name must be subtracted from Smith's list; Tucker was enrolled in the Inner Temple by his father, but he went to Williamsburg instead (C. T. Cullen, "St. George Tucker," *Va. Law Reporters*, pp. 96-98 (1977)).

[30] Act of Mar. 1643, c. 61, Hening's Statutes, vol. 1, p. 275; see generally Smith, *Virginia Lawyers*, pp. 280-299.

as a profession was made illegal.[31] It was soon found to be "inconvenient" not to have a legal profession in the colony, and so in 1656, this prohibition was repealed, and each court was again allowed to license attorneys to practice before it.[32] Two years later the pendulum swung back, and lawyers were again forbidden to accept fees for their services.[33] This prohibition on professional lawyers lasted until 1680. In that year, because the courts were "many times hindered and troubled in their judicial proceedings by the impertinent discourses of many busy and ignorant men who will pretend to assist their friend in his business and to clear the matter more plainly to the court, although never desired or requested thereunto by the person whom they pretend to assist, and many times to the destruction of his cause and the great trouble and hindrance of the court," it was enacted that no one could appear as an attorney at law unless he had been licensed by the governor, and licensed lawyers were once again allowed to receive fees for their services.[34] In 1682 the act of 1680 was "found inconvenient" and repealed.[35] Thus, lawyers were allowed to practice freely without any approval needed or restrictions imposed.

This lack of official regulation resulted in ignorant and dishonest persons holding themselves out as lawyers to the prejudice of the general public. Therefore, by executive order of the Council of State in 1715, it was decreed that no one could practice law in Virginia without the approval of the governor and Council.[36] (It is to be remembered that the Council of State constituted the upper house of the colonial legislature and that the governor and the Council of State sat judicially as the General Court, the highest court of the colony.)

The first examination for admission to the Virginia bar was required in 1732.[37] It is interesting to note that this step was taken only three years after English attorneys and solicitors were required

[31] Act of Nov. 1645, c. 7, Hening's Statutes, vol. 1, p. 302; Act of Mar. 1646, c. 8, Hening's Statutes, vol. 1, p. 313, Act of Nov. 1647, c. 15, Hening's Statutes, vol. 1, p. 349.

[32] Act of Dec. 1656, c. 6, Hening's Statutes, vol. 1, p. 419.

[33] Act of Mar. 1658, c. 112, Hening's Statutes, vol. 1, pp. 482-83.

[34] Act of June 1680, c. 6, Hening's Statutes, vol. 1, pp. 478-79.

[35] Act of Nov. 1682, c. 6, Hening's Statutes, vol. 2, p. 498.

[36] Order of Sept. 6, 1715, H. R. McIlwaine, ed., *Executive Journals of the Council of Colonial Virginia*, vol. 3, p. 411 (1928); Smith, *Virginia Lawyers*, pp. 286-89.

[37] Act of May 1732, c. 13, §§ 8-12, Hening's Statutes, vol. 4, pp. 360-62.

to submit to a qualifying examination.[38] It is doubly interesting that the Virginia act did not apply to those who had been formally called to the bar in England or to those who had been or were to be admitted to practice before the General Court in Williamsburg.

This act thus divided the colonial Virginia legal profession into an upper order and a lower order. The division, however, was quite different from that in England, where the profession was and is divided according to the legal services performed. In Virginia the distinction was drawn by the level of court in which the lawyer practiced. In colonial Virginia a lawyer practiced as both barrister and solicitor, but either in the General Court at Williamsburg or in the county courts. In England a lawyer practiced in any court but only as a barrister or as a solicitor. In both England and Virginia at this time, only the lower level of the practice was subjected to an entrance examination.

The Virginia act of 1732 required a candidate for admission to the county court bar to petition the governor and Council "setting forth his qualifications."[39] The petitioner was then referred to one or more practicing lawyers to be examined. The successful candidate was licensed by the governor and Council and then sworn and admitted in every county court in which he wished to practice.

Ten years later, in 1742, the act of 1732 was found not "to answer the good design and intention thereof" and was repealed.[40] The act of 1732 was not popular with the weaker county court lawyers, and it was they who managed to have it repealed.[41] However, their triumph was short-lived, and in 1745 county court lawyers were again made subject to a bar examination.[42] This new act was similar to that of 1732. After 1745 the governor and Council as such were no longer involved, but the same gentlemen sitting as the General Court appointed examiners from among the General Court bar or themselves. The candidate, along with his petition and a fee of twenty shillings, presented a certificate of good character from a judge in a county in which he intended to practice. The examiners themselves issued the license to the successful

---

[38] See above.

[39] See above.

[40] Act of May 1742, c. 7, Hening's Statutes, vol. 5, p. 171.

[41] D. J. Mays, *Edmund Pendleton*, vol. 1, pp. 27-28 (1952).

[42] Act of Feb. 1745, c. 7, §§ 1-9, Hening's Statutes, vol. 5, pp. 345-48. This statute was continued in force by Act of Oct. 1748, c. 47, Hening's Statutes, vol. 6, pp. 140-43; Act of Mar. 1761, c. 8, Hening's Statutes, vol. 7, pp. 397-401; Act of Nov. 1766, c. 10, Hening's Statutes, vol. 8, p. 198; Act of Nov. 1769, c. 31, Hening's Statutes, vol. 8, pp. 385-86.

applicant. The attorney was then sworn and admitted in every county court before which he wished to appear professionally.

The examinations were not too difficult, but they were more than an empty formality. For the period 1734 to 1742, there were twenty-five examinations; the attorney general of the colony was usually appointed an examiner.[43] Edmund Pendleton recounted that in April 1741 he was licensed to practice law after having been "strictly examined by Mr. Barradall."[44] In 1760 Patrick Henry was examined by John Randolph and George Wythe. Henry had read law for less than a year, and he had a rough time during the examination. His license was signed, however, because his industry and general intelligence were obvious to the examiners.[45] In the 1790s William Wirt was subjected to a "minute scrutiny" of his knowledge of the law.[46]

The ambivalence of the seventeenth-century General Assembly toward professional lawyers no doubt reflects the poor quality of the Virginia bar at that time. It is not likely that there were many well-trained attorneys in Virginia then. In the eighteenth century, however, the prosperity of the colony was well established, and Virginians had the means to acquire sufficient education before embarking on the practice of law. The reputation of the county court bar in the eighteenth century was consequently high. It presented good prospects of earning a decent living or of supplementing one's agricultural income. Good men were attracted to the profession, and the ignorant were excluded by means of the examination and admission procedures.

Admission to the General Court bar was not subject to official regulation during the colonial period. An aspiring lawyer would be formally introduced to the court by a practicing member of the General Court bar, and the court would admit him and administer the oaths. Thus, the bar of the General Court was a self-perpetuating professional elite. Normally, a lawyer would be admitted to the bar of the highest court in the colony after having distinguished himself at the county court level, as, for example, was Edmund Pendleton. However, if one were well-connected, like Thomas Jefferson, who was a cousin of Attorney General John Randolph and a student of the eminent George Wythe, one might begin his legal career in the General Court. A barrister of an English Inn of Court had an immediate entree to the

[43] Smith, *Virginia Lawyers*, p. 380.

[44] D. J. Mays, ed., *Letters and Papers of Edmund Pendleton*, vol. 2, p. 605 (1967); see also R. E. Nance, "Edward Barradall," *Va. Law Reporters*, pp. 71-74 (1977).

[45] R. D. Meade, *Patrick Henry*, vol. 1, pp. 93-98 (1957).

[46] Letter of William Wirt to Mr. Carnes, Nov. 1792, J. P. Kennedy, *Memoirs of the Life of William Wirt*, vol. 1, p. 55 (1850).

General Court bar.[47] The upper bar in the eighteenth century was brilliant and justly famous; it was these distinguished gentlemen who led the movement for Independence in Virginia.

In 1776 the statute requiring the examination of new lawyers expired by its own terms. The General Assembly was too preoccupied with more important matters to pass a new statute, and the governor and Council assumed the authority to license attorneys. From 1778 to 1782, they referred candidates to two eminent attorneys each for examination and then licensed those who were successful.[48] It was during this period, in 1780, that Thomas Jefferson as governor of Virginia signed John Marshall's license to practice law.[49] Later legal rivalries and disagreements between President Jefferson and Chief Justice Marshall give this fact a noteworthy irony.

In 1782 an act was passed reviving the late colonial method of bar examination and admission.[50] Four years later, in 1786, the law was altered to require the license to be granted after an examination by three judges of the Court of Chancery or the General Court, which were the superior courts at that time. The candidate could not present himself for examination without presenting a certificate of good character from the judge of the county in which he lived. The admission to the bar was accompanied by an appropriate oath.[51] The act of 1786 applied to all lawyers and to all courts. This method of examination by superior court judges continued to be used until 1896.[52] By having different people administer the bar examination, a great disparity in the rigor of the exercise resulted. Furthermore, the custom arose that after one judge had examined an applicant and signed his license to

[47] Smith, *Virginia Lawyers*, pp. 303-05.

[48] H. R. McIlwaine et al., eds., *Journals of the Council of the State of Virginia*, vol. 2, pp. 183, 187, 244, 306, 319, 324, 371 (1932); vol. 3, pp. 46-47, 56, 59, 70, 108, 137, 145, 162, 165 (1952).

[49] A. J. Beveridge, *Life of John Marshall*, vol. 1, p. 161 (1919); C. T. Cullen, "New Light on John Marshall's Legal Education and Admission to the Bar," *Am. J. Legal Hist.*, vol. 15, pp. 345-51 (1972).

[50] Act of Oct. 1782, c. 48, Hening's Statutes, vol. 11, pp. 182-83.

[51] Act of Oct. 1786, c. 56, Hening's Statutes, vol. 12, p. 339; R. M. Hughes, "Historical Evolution of the Board of Law Examiners and Its Influence on Legal Education," *A.B.A. Repts.*, vol. 39, pp. 846-54 (1914); J. H. Corbitt, "Admission to the Bar in Virginia," *Va. State Bar Ass'n Repts.*, vol. 40, p. 286 (1928).

[52] Va. Rev. Code, pp. 102-03, c. 71, §§ 1-2 (1792); S. Shepherd, ed., *Statutes at Large of Va.*, vol. 1, p. 13 (1835); Va. Rev. Code, vol. 1, pp. 267-68, c. 76, §§ 1, 2 (1819); Va. Code, c. 164, §§ 1, 3 (1849), Va. Acts 1866-67, p. 485, c. 15; Va. Acts 1874, p. 249, c. 215; Va. Code, §§ 3191, 3193 (1887); Va. Acts 1895-96, p. 49, c. 41. Only two judges were required to examine after 1866.

practice law, the other two judges would sign the license without any further examination as a matter of courtesy to the first judge.[53]

In 1819 lawyers licensed in contiguous states were allowed to qualify in Virginia without further examination.[54] And in 1842 graduates of a Virginia university or college law school were exempted from the bar examination.[55] However, Prof. John B. Minor of the University of Virginia law department had this "diploma privilege" repealed in 1849. He did not believe in coddling his students or in favoritism; he also wanted to advertise the University of Virginia by letting the judges see how well trained his own students were.[56]

F. *LAW FOR THE LAYMAN*

Returning to the study of law in colonial Virginia, we see that the law was also the object of the attention of planters who did not ever intend to practice law. The ambition of the settlers from England "was to produce in the wilderness of Virginia the county life of England. . . . They were trying to be country gentlemen in the English manner."[57] They were concerned to give their children liberal educations as far as their means would allow, and their reading kept them in touch with English ideas on education.

In 1693 John Locke wrote the following much-read passage.

> It would be strange to suppose an English gentleman should be ignorant of the law of his country. This, whatever station he is in, is so requisite that, from a justice of the peace to a minister of state, I know no place he can well fill without it.. ..And to that purpose [service to his country], I think the right way for a gentleman to study our law, which he does not design for his calling, is to take a view of our English constitution and government in the ancient books of the common law, and some more modern writers, who out of them have given an account of this government. And having got a true idea of that, then to read our history and with it join in

[53] For example, Robert Reid Howison, who was licensed in 1841 (R. R. Howison, "Twice Forty Years of American Life," pp. 162-63, photocopy of MS. autobiography in the Swem Library, Coll. of William and Mary; W. H. Bryson, "Robert Reid Howison," *Va. Law Reporters*, p. 113 (1977)).

[54] Va. Rev. Code, vol. 1, p. 268, c. 76, § 4 (1819); Va. Code, c. 164, § 2 (1849). In 1887 anyone licensed in any other state could practice in Virginia (Va. Code, § 3192 (1887)).

[55] Va. Acts 1841-42, p. 22, c. 27.

[56] Reed, pp. 249-50; *Report of the Revisors of the Code of Va.*, vol. 2, p. 824 (1849).

[57] L. B. Wright, *First Gentlemen of Virginia*, p. 2 (1970).

> every king's reign the laws then made. This will give an insight into the reason of our statutes and show the true ground upon which they came to be made and what weight they ought to have.[58]

At least four copies of Locke's book on education were present in eighteenth-century Virginia.[59]

Gilbert Burnet, writing in the early eighteenth century, stated succinctly the value of some knowledge of the law to the country gentleman. "A competent measure of the knowledge of the law is a good foundation for distinguishing a gentleman; but I am in doubt whether his being for some time in the inns of court will contribute much to this if he is not a studious person. . . . A competent skill in this [i.e., the law] makes a man very useful in his country, both in conducting his own affairs and in giving good advice to those about him: it will enable him to be a good justice of peace and to settle matters by arbitration so as to prevent lawsuits; and, which ought to be the top of an English gentleman's ambition, to be an able parliament man."[60]

J. Clarke in his *Essay upon Study* (1731) expressed similar opinions. "The proper business of gentlemen as such is, I presume, to serve their country in the making or execution of the laws; as likewise in preventing the breach and violation of them, by preserving the peace and good order of the world about them. . . ." In Clarke's view, "the studies of most use to a gentlemen . . . are . . . logic, eloquence, morality and history, especially of his own country, with some knowledge of its laws and trade." "As for morality, or the law of nature and nations, the knowledge thereof is very useful and necessary for a gentleman, whether he be concerned in the making or execution of laws, and especially in preventing of law suits by the arbitration of differences

[58] J. Locke, *Some Thoughts Concerning Education,* § 187 (1693); *id.*, § 186 advises the reading of works on international law and legal philosophy by Grotius and Pufendorf. The works of these two jurists were very popular in Virginia (see Bryson, *Census*, pp. 27-29).

[59] They were owned by Thomas Jefferson (Sowerby, vol. 1, p. 503); William Key in 1764 (*Wm. & Mary Qtly.*, 1st ser., vol. 9, p. 167 (1901)); Samuel Peachy in 1750 (*Wm. & Mary Qtly.*, 1st ser., vol. 3, p. 133 (1894)); *Va. Mag. Hist. Biog.*, vol. 33, p. 40 (1925); Daniel Parke Custis in 1759 (*Va. Mag. Hist. Biog.*, vol. 17, p. 410 (1909)); and John Parke Custis in 1782, probably the same copy as that owned by D. P. Custis (*Tyler's Qtly.*, vol. 8, p. 103 (1928)). Also, copies were for sale in Williamsburg in 1775 (*Wm. & Mary Qtly.*, 1st ser., vol. 15, p. 111 (1906)).

[60] G. Burnet, *History of His Own Time,* vol. 6, p. 201 (1823); this passage was first published in 1734. Thomas Jefferson owned a copy and John Carter, secretary of Virginia, was a subscriber (Sowerby, vol. 1, p. 161); Robert "Councillor" Carter owned a copy in 1772 (H. D. Farish, ed., *Journal and Letters of Philip Vickers Fithian,* p. 290 (1943); *Wm. & Mary Qtly.*, 1st ser., vol. 10, p. 241 (1902)).

amongst neighbors. . . . I shall say no more upon this head than that a gentleman can hardly read Grotius, Pufendorf, and Barbeyrac too much."[61]

It was generally agreed in England and in Virginia that a knowledge of the law was desirable for that class of society from which were drawn the county court judges, the justices of the peace, who were not professional lawyers.[62] The colonial Virginian, as did his English model and counterpart, viewed the study of law as a part of a gentleman's liberal education. Law books were, therefore, present in the libraries of small as well as large landholders throughout Virginia.[63] The advice of the English writers and the dictates of common sense were followed.

Thomas Wood, writing in 1720, approached the study of law primarily from a vocational point of view. His *Institute of the Laws of England* was a textbook for those reading the law in preparation for careers as barristers or solicitors. But Wood was also trying to reach the young gentlemen in the universities. In his preface he wrote, "My intention, by this institute, is not only to help the students in the inns of court and chancery, but moreover to recommend the study of the English laws to our young nobility and gentry and to the youth in our universities."[64]

G. *WILLIAM BLACKSTONE*

William Blackstone, building upon the ideas of Locke and Wood and the others, carried these theories to culmination. It was Blackstone who first introduced the study of the English common law into the university curriculum. Two independent preliminary steps were taken in 1752. In that year, Charles Viner made a will leaving his money to Oxford University to establish a professorship of English law.[65] Sir

---

[61] J. Clarke, *An Essay Upon Study*, pp. 224, 226, 232-33 (1731); Robert "Councillor" Carter owned a copy of this book in 1772 (H. D. Farish, ed., *Journal and Letters of Philip Vickers Fithian*, p. 291 (1943); *Wm. & Mary Qtly.*, 1st ser., vol. 11, p. 23 (1902)).

[62] Smith, *Virginia Lawyers*, pp. 59-75; G. C. Brauer, Jr., *The Education of a Gentleman, 1660-1775*, pp. 44, 80-82 (1959); letter, *Virginia Gazette*, Oct. 10, 1745, p. 1.

[63] Bryson, *Census, passim*; see also below, "Private Law Libraries Before 1776."

[64] T. Wood, *Institute of the Laws of England*, vol. 1, p. viii (1720). There were many copies of this popular work in colonial Virginia (Bryson, *Census*, pp. xvi, xvii, 81).

[65] Holdsworth, *H.E.L.*, vol. 12, pp. 92-95, 164-68. Viner rewrote his will in 1755. See also H. G. Hanbury, *Vinerian Chair and Legal Education*, pp. 10-51 (1958); D. J. Ibbetson, "Charles Viner and his Chair: Legal Education in Eighteenth-Century Oxford," in J. A. Bush and A. Wijffels, *Learning the Law: Teaching and the*

William Murray (later Lord Mansfield) recommended in 1752 that Blackstone be appointed to the chair of Roman law at Oxford; after his recommendation was refused, Murray then urged Blackstone to teach English law at Oxford.[66]

On November 6, 1753, Blackstone delivered his first lecture on English law at Oxford; he inaugurated his famous course as a private lecturer in the university. In 1756 Viner died, leaving his entire fortune to Oxford to establish a chair of English law. The estate was quickly settled, and in 1758 Blackstone was elected first Vinerian Professor of English Law.

Blackstone along with Locke, Burnet, and many others believed that the study of law should be included in a gentleman's liberal education. In his introductory lecture on the study of the law, he wrote, "I think it an undeniable position that a competent knowledge of the laws of that society in which we live is the proper accomplishment of every gentleman and scholar; an highly useful, I had almost said essential, part of liberal and polite education."[67] Blackstone, citing Locke, argued that the country gentleman needed an understanding of the law in order to manage his estates effectively and to draft his own will. Gentlemen would also be called upon to serve the public as jurors, justices of the peace, and legislators.[68] Therefore, it was most appropriate to teach English law in the eighteenth-century university, where young gentlemen were sent to receive their education.

Blackstone further believed that the study of law in the university setting was invaluable to the future practitioner of the law. A person who studied law as an apprentice to a practicing lawyer learned only the forms and practices of the law but received little or no instruction in the theory or reason of the law. "If practice be the whole he is taught, practice must also be the whole he will ever know: if he be uninstructed in the elements and first principles upon which the rule of practice is founded, the least variation from established precedents will totally distract and bewilder him."[69] For Blackstone, the apprenticeship approach to the learning of law was superficial and inadequate

Transmission of Law in England 1150-1900, pp. 315-328 (1999).

[66] Holdsworth, *H.E.L.*, vol. 12, p. 91; see generally D. A. Lockmiller, *Sir William Blackstone*, pp. 37-52, 133-82 (1938); L. C. Warden, *Life of Blackstone*, pp. 139-71, 252-348 (1938).

[67] W. Blackstone, *Commentaries on the Laws of England*, vol. 1, pp. 5-6 (1765).

[68] *Id.*, vol. 1, pp. 7-10 (1765); J. Locke, *Some Thoughts Concerning Education*, § 187 (1693); see above.

[69] W. Blackstone, *Commentaries*, vol. 1, p. 32 (1765).

(except for a genius like Lord Hardwicke). He saw that the academic study of English law had vocational as well as liberal purposes. This was Blackstone's contribution.

Blackstone's university lectures were well received by the students; however, petty academic jealousies and bickering made his life in Oxford miserable. He resigned in 1766 and several years later was made a high court judge.[70] Fortunately, his lectures were published, giving them the wide audience they deserved. His *Commentaries on the Laws of England* first appeared between 1765 and 1769. These four volumes were intended to introduce students to the common law of England, but they were so clearly and concisely written that the practicing bar was unanimously delighted, and they instantly became a work of authority. Their popularity was as great in Virginia as it was in England. Here was an encyclopedia of English law that could be carried on circuit from county court to county court in a saddlebag. The demand in America for sets was so great that an edition was published in Philadelphia in 1771; many Virginians subscribed to this edition.[71] Blackstone's *Commentaries* became the first law book that many a law student read.

Henry St. George Tucker compared Coke and Blackstone as text writers for law students. "It is indeed a matter of no little surprise that in a former generation so little good sense was displayed in the course recommended to the students of the law. The first work which was put into their hands was the first Institute of Lord Coke which, as Mr. Blackstone very justly observes, has very little indeed of the institutional method to recommend it." This book's "learning is profound indeed, but it does not cover the whole ground, and the student moreover is plunged at once into the abstrusest doctrines, without a previous knowledge of the matters on which they depend. Hale's *Analysis and History of the Common Law* advanced an important step towards the great work which was to be accomplished by Mr. Blackstone." Blackstone "has indeed brought order out of chaos and placed the study of the law in the rank of the sciences by system and classification."[72]

---

[70] Holdsworth, *H.E.L.*, vol. 12, pp. 95, 706.

[71] "Subscribers in Virginia to Blackstone's Commentaries," *Wm. & Mary Qtly.*, 2d ser., vol. 1, pp. 183-85 (1921), lists 89 individuals and 66 sets ordered by booksellers; the count is 82 individuals and 97 sets for resale, according to Smith, *Virginia Lawyers*, p. 212. See also Bryson, *Census*, pp. x, xvi, 34; Sowerby, vol. 2, pp. 228-30; H. A. Johnson, *Imported Eighteenth Century Law Treatises in American Libraries*, pp. 6-7 (1978) (re St. George Tucker).

[72] H. St. G. Tucker, *Introductory Lecture*, pp. 14-16 (1841).

NOTES

ON

BLACKSTONE'S COMMENTARIES,

FOR THE

USE OF STUDENTS.

[Henry St. George Tucker]

HAUD NOMINE DIGNUS.

WINCHESTER:

PRINTED BY SAMUEL H. DAVIS.

1826.

Perhaps the *Commentaries* of the Oxford professor inspired the letter to the editor that appeared in the *Virginia Gazette* on December 30, 1773. This letter advocated the establishment of a professorship of law at the College of William and Mary. Its author, an anonymous county justice of the peace, explained:

> I had not long acted in the capacity of a judge before I discovered great confusion, want of argument, of reasoning, and, I conceived, of law, too, in the pleadings of some of our lawyers. . . . At first I apprehended it might have been the peculiar fate of my own county to be unassisted by able lawyers; but since I find we are not altogether singular in that respect, I have been led to reflect on the cause of this inconvenience, and the means of removing it hereafter. When a young gentleman has resolved to study the law, he applies to some attorney for his advice, assists him in copying a few declarations, reads the first book of Coke upon Littleton, and the Virginia laws [i.e., statutes], and then applies for a license, and begins to practice a profession, the grounds and first principles of which he is perhaps utterly unacquainted with. He is involved in difficulties at his first setting out, which he is unable to remove by referring to authors, and, in one continued scene of error, plods on to the last, nor gives himself the least trouble to investigate the reason of what he reads. . . . By establishing a professorship in the law, many of those gentlemen, who are obliged to struggle with the greatest difficulties through want of proper books and proper instructions, would repair to a place where they might enjoy the most ample means of pursuing their studies with success, where the road to truth, instead of an inexplorable wilderness, would be opened to them, and where they might unravel the mysteries, and reconcile the seeming absurdities, of the profession they were studying under the auspices of an able professor. . . .
>
> If the candidates for the bar were obliged to go through a regular course of lectures on the civil and municipal laws at the college [of William and Mary], and to attend the General Court when sitting, where they might imbibe proper ideas of the practice of the law, at the same time that they received the greatest instruction from the learned arguments and judicious determinations there, I am persuaded our gentlemen of the bar would appear to much greater advantage than at present. . . .
>
> The plan that I would propose, therefore, is . . . that a professor of law be appointed, who shall read a regular and complete course of lectures on the law once in a year, and that no persons but those who have attended the lectures of such

> professor for two years, and have attended the General Court whilst sitting, during that period, shall be admitted to practice as counsel, or as attorneys, in any of the county courts in this colony . . . and upon examination should be found qualified for it.

The author of this letter pointed out the major defect of a legal apprenticeship. This traditional method of legal education taught only the mere mechanics of the practice of the law. It completely ignored or neglected the theories, reasons, origins, purposes, and policies of the law. It is a well-written and a logical letter; it was certainly read by the bench and bar of Virginia in 1773.

This was not the first suggestion that law be taught at William and Mary. On October 10, 1745, a letter had been published in the *Virginia Gazette* urging that law be taught there so that the justices and lawyers would be trained in the English and colonial law that they administered. The extensive and thoughtful proposal in the *Virginia Gazette* in 1773, however, was more likely the suggestion that led to the next step in the development of legal education in Virginia. This step was taken six years later, in 1779.

II. *1779 to 1861*

A. *College of William and Mary, 1779-1834*

In 1779 the third professorship of English law to be established anywhere was inaugurated in Williamsburg at the College of William and Mary. This was the first law school in the United States, and the first law professor there was the eminent George Wythe.[73]

George Wythe was born in Virginia in 1726 or 1727. He entered the practice of law at an early age and rapidly rose to prominence as a practitioner before the General Court in Williamsburg. He was scholarly and distinguished and very successful at the bar. In addition he was civic-minded, serving many years in the House of Burgesses and on the board of visitors of the College of William and Mary. He was an ardent patriot and a signer of the Declaration of Independence. In 1777 Wythe was elected Speaker of the House of Delegates, but he resigned in 1778 to become a judge on the newly-established High

---

[73] F. B. Devitt, Jr., "William and Mary: America's First Law School," *Wm. & Mary L. Rev.*, vol. 2, p. 424-36 (1960); R. M. Hughes, "William and Mary, the First American Law School," *Wm. & Mary Qtly.*, 2d ser., vol. 2, pp. 40-48 (1922); J. E. Morpurgo, *Their Majesties Royall Colledge, William and Mary*, pp. 189-98 (1976). The first professorship of English law was at Oxford University; the second was at Trinity College, Dublin.

Court of Chancery.[74]

Not only was Wythe a lawyer, legislator, and judge, but he also had the temperament of a teacher. His natural bent for teaching led him to accept many young men as apprentices in his law office; among them were Thomas Jefferson, St. George Tucker, and James Innes.[75] Another of Wythe's noteworthy law clerks was James Madison, who later became president of William and Mary and bishop of Virginia. Wythe also taught some of the local youths nonlegal subjects. He instructed the young Littleton Waller Tazewell in Greek, Latin, and mathematics and Peter Carr in similar subjects.When his second wife died in 1787, Wythe attempted to operate a grammar school, but added to his judicial and law duties, it proved too much for him, and he quickly gave it up.[76]

In 1779 Thomas Jefferson, then governor of Virginia, was elected to the board of visitors of William and Mary, and he and James Madison, president of the college, reformed the college curriculum. The modernization effected by Jefferson and Madison resulted in suppressing the professorships of Hebrew and theology and the grammar school and in creating, inter alia, the new professorship of law and police. Jefferson had attempted to make these changes by an act of Assembly, but the dissenters from the Church of England killed the bill because they did not want William and Mary, which was then an Episcopal college, to be strengthened in any way. Therefore, Jefferson had to make his reforms by acting through the college's board of visitors.[77] In 1779 Jefferson and Madison called their former law teacher, Chancellor Wythe, to the new professorship of law. It is difficult to conceive that anyone more acceptable, more appropriate, more competent, or more scholarly could have been found; no one else was considered.

The title of Wythe's chair, law and police, was unusual. The word *police* did not refer to enforcement of the criminal law but was a transliteration of the Greek word for *state*. In the context of the

---

[74] A. T. Dill, *George Wythe* (1979); E. L. Shepard, "George Wythe," *Va. Law Reporters*, pp. 90-95 (1977).

[75] Smith, *Virginia Lawyers*, p. 377.

[76] A. T. Dill, *George Wythe*, pp. 41-52, 55-56, 65-66 (1979). For Wythe's classical erudition, see R. J. Hoffman, "Classics in the Courts of the United States, 1790-1800," *Am. J. Legal Hist.*, vol. 22, pp. 55-85 (1978).

[77] R. T. Honeywell, *Educational Work of Thomas Jefferson*, pp. 54-56 (1964); P. A. Bruce, *History of the University of Virginia*, vol. 1, pp. 65-72 (1920). For the closing of the grammar school, see Bracken v. William and Mary, 5 Va. (1 Call) 161 (1797); J. W. Bridge, "The Rev. John Bracken v. the Visitors of William and Mary College," *Wm. & Mary L. Rev.*, vol. 20, p. 415 (1979).

William and Mary curriculum, it meant government or political science. Thus Wythe was to teach law as a vocational science and as a liberal arts subject.

That Virginia was the location of the first American chair of law is not a mere coincidence. The lawyers in the other populous colonies were strongly and openly loyal to Great Britain during the Revolutionary period, and those lawyers who were not forced to leave the United States found themselves discredited in the eyes of the general public. In Virginia, on the other hand, the leaders of the Revolution were the lawyers Jefferson, Henry, Wythe, Pendleton, and others. When Jefferson proposed a law professorship to teach republican legal and political theories, there was enthusiastic approval.

Wythe lectured to his students twice a week; once or twice a month he held a moot court, and every Saturday he presided over a mock legislature. His course of lectures was based on Blackstone's *Commentaries*, the natural model, but they included also his own thoughts on American constitutional law. After the government of Virginia was moved to Richmond in 1780, Wythe held his moot courts and model legislature in the old Capitol in Williamsburg in the very chambers the General Assembly had recently abandoned. He continued to use the courtroom in the Capitol for his real cases as chancellor as well as for his moot courts.[78]

His moot court exercises were popular with the students, and the citizens of Williamsburg used to come and sit as spectators. Wythe's innovation of bringing the moot court to the university gave his students an understanding of the procedures and practices of the law. His mock legislature prepared them for the role of statesman, which he and Jefferson expected them in the course of time to assume.[79] It has been suggested that this latter purpose was the sole one of the early law schools.[80] However, the presence and popularity of the moot court shows that Wythe intended to give his students professional training as well, as he had done formerly as master to his legal apprentices.[81]

[78] C. T. Cullen, "New Light on John Marshall's Legal Education," *Am. J. Legal Hist.*, vol. 16, pp. 345-51 (1972); H. A. Johnson et al., eds., *Papers of John Marshall*, vol. 1, pp. 37-41 (1974); Reed, pp. 116-19; letter of John Tyler to Thomas Jefferson, Nov. 12, 1810, L. G. Tyler, *Letters and Times of the Tylers*, vol. 1, pp. 249-50 (1884). Tyler hoped that Jefferson would publish Wythe's lectures.

[79] Letter of Thomas Jefferson to James Madison, July 26, 1780, J. P. Boyd, ed., *Papers of Thomas Jefferson*, vol. 3, p. 507 (1951).

[80] A. J. Harno, *Legal Education in the United States*, p. 27 (1953).

[81] See F. B. Devitt, Jr., "William and Mary: America's First Law School," *Wm. & Mary L. Rev.*, vol. 2, pp. 424, 427, 429-31 (1960).

Also, his law school students usually applied for admission to the bar immediately upon completion of his course and without reading in the office of any practicing lawyer.

Wythe's lectures were a success from the start. In July 1780 Jefferson wrote: "Our new institution at the college has had a success which has gained it universal applause. Wythe's school is numerous."[82] The later careers of his students are further evidence of his teaching abilities. Among those who sat at his feet were John Marshall, Spencer Roane, and James Breckenridge.

In 1788 the courts of Virginia were reorganized, and Chancellor Wythe was required to move his residence to Richmond. This forced his resignation in 1789 of the professorship in Williamsburg after a decade of lecturing. On March 7, 1790, Wythe was succeeded as professor of law and police by one of his former students, St. George Tucker, who was granted an annual salary of £120. He had been elected judge of the General Court in 1788 and was prominent in Virginia legal circles.[83]

Tucker began teaching law at William and Mary in September 1790. He used Blackstone's *Commentaries* as the basis of his lectures and supplemented it by discourses on federal and state constitutional law and on Virginia property law. In 1803 Tucker published an edition of Blackstone's *Commentaries* with notes to American cases and statutes and with appendixes on American constitutional law. This edition immediately became popular and remained so for decades afterwards, earning Tucker the title of "the American Blackstone." Tucker's law school lectures were also very successful; as evidence of this, he had from thirty to forty students in his 1798-99 course.[84]

Tucker's course was slightly more structured than Wythe's, and there was less emphasis on political science. One of Tucker's law students wrote a letter in 1801 to a friend, saying: "You may remember that a notion formerly prevailed here that a student of law should make the study of his profession subservient to that of politics. This opinion, however, seems not to prevail here this course but has yielded to one perhaps much more rational. The general opinion at this time appears to be that students of law should devote their time partly to legal acquirements, partly to the pursuit of general science [i.e., the

[82] Letter of Thomas Jefferson to James Madison, July 26, 1780, J. P. Boyd, ed., *Papers of Thomas Jefferson*, vol. 3, p. 507 (1951).

[83] "Election of St. George Tucker as Professor of Law," *Wm. & Mary Qtly.*, 1st ser., vol. 18, p. 220 (1910); see generally M. H. Coleman, *Saint George Tucker* (1938).

[84] C. T. Cullen, *St. George Tucker and the Law in Virginia, 1772-1804* (1987); letter of Benjamin Howard to David Watson, Jan. 30, 1799, *Va. Mag. Hist. Biog.*, vol. 30, p. 249 (1922).

liberal arts], and but partially to the science of government."[85]

It was during Tucker's professorship that the first earned law degree was granted in America. In 1793 the bachelor of law degree was conferred on William H. Cabell. (Cabell later distinguished himself further as governor of Virginia and as a justice of the Virginia Supreme Court of Appeals.)

In 1802 Judge Tucker and the board of visitors had serious disagreements over the administration of the college, and Tucker resigned.[86] For the next thirty years or so, William and Mary was in a serious decline that affected all parts of the college, including the law department. There was a succession of law professors, who also sat as judges during their professorships; they were respectable but undistinguished people. Not much is known of them or of their teaching.

B. *Reading Law*

Even though law was being taught at William and Mary and additional law schools would be founded in the first third of the nineteenth century, the apprenticeship and the independent reading of the law remained the usual methods of legal education in Virginia. Prominent lawyers were often solicited for their advice on the books to be read in preparation for a career at the bar. Thomas Jefferson, William Wirt, John B. Minor, and no doubt many others produced reading lists of their favorite legal authors.

Thomas Jefferson, for example, wrote to John Garland Jefferson on June 11, 1790, suggesting that he study for the bar only by reading. He began by disparaging apprenticeships. "It is a general practice to study the law in the office of some lawyer. This indeed gives to the student the advantage of his instruction. But I have ever seen that the services expected in return have been more than the instructions have been worth. All that is necessary for a student is access to a library and directions in what order the books are to be read." Jefferson then set forth three lists of books for his young cousin; the first was of works on municipal law, the second on legal history and political theory, and the third on English and American political history. The law was to be read in the morning, legal history in the early afternoon, and the rest in the evening. The first list was headed by *Coke upon Littleton*, followed by

[85] Letter of Joseph C. Cabell to David Watson, Apr. 6, 1801, *Va. Mag. Hist. Biog.*, vol. 29, p. 278 (1921). Note also, letter of St. George Tucker to John Ambler, Dec. 16, 1801, Ambler Family Papers, Virginia Historical Society MSS1Am167c77, which was kindly shown me by E. Lee Shepard.

[86] C. T. Cullen, "St. George Tucker," *Va. Law Reporters*, p. 102 (1977).

the remaining three of Coke's *Institutes*. Then Jefferson listed the reports of Coke, Vaughan, Salkeld, Lord Raymond, Strange, and Burrow. The student was then to proceed to the study of equity, beginning with Kames's *Principles of Equity* and proceeding to the reports of Vernon, Peere Williams, *Precedents in Chancery*, Atkyns, and Vesey. The final books on the first list were Hawkins's *Pleas of the Crown*, a standard work on criminal law, Blackstone's *Commentaries*, and the Virginia statutes.

The second list began with Dalrymple's history of feudal property and continued with Hale's *History of the Common Law* and the tracts by Gilbert on devises, uses, tenures, rents, distresses, ejectments, executions, and evidence. It also included Sayer's *Law of Costs*, Lambarde's manual for justices of the peace, Bacon's "Pleas and Pleadings," Cunningham's *Law of Bills of Exchange*, Molloy's *De Jure Maritimo*, and works by Locke, Montesquieu, Adam Smith, Beccaria, James, and Vattel. Jefferson estimated that this course of reading would require between two and three years to complete.[87]

Jefferson in 1814 sent to John Minor an updated copy of a letter he had written to Bernard Moore "near fifty years ago." Jefferson recommended a course of study in the liberal arts as a prelude to reading law; he emphasized Latin, French, mathematics, and science, then ethics, literature, political science, and history. The latter subjects were to be studied concurrently with the law. The following legal works were to be read and commonplaced in order: Coke's *Institutes*, the seventeenth-century English law reports, Matthew Bacon's *New Abridgment of the Law*, the modern reports of common law cases, the various law tracts by Baron Gilbert, then the Virginia statutes and reports. The student was then to study equity by reading Kames's *Principles of Equity* (3d ed.), reports of equity cases, and Fonblanque's *Treatise of Equity*. The final book to be read was St. George Tucker's edition of Blackstone's *Commentaries*, which Jefferson described as "the last perfect digest of both branches of law."[88] This letter gained general circulation in Virginia in 1848 when it was published in the *Southern Literary Messenger*.[89]

In 1821 Jefferson wrote to Dabney Terrell giving him a list of books to read in preparation for a career at the bar. He advised the

[87] Letter of Thomas Jefferson to John Garland Jefferson, June 11, 1790, J. P. Boyd, ed., *Papers of Thomas Jefferson*, vol. 16, pp. 480-82 (1961).

[88] Letter of Thomas Jefferson to John Minor, Aug. 30, 1814, P. L. Ford, ed., *Writings of Thomas Jefferson*, vol. 9, pp. 480-85 (1898); M. L. Cohen, "Thomas Jefferson Recommends a Course of Law Study," *U. Pa. L. Rev.*, vol. 119, pp. 823-44 (1971).

[89] *Southern Literary Messenger*, vol. 14, pp. 187-90 (1848).

young Terrell to begin with Coke's *Institutes*, "a complete body of the law as it stood in the reign of the first James, an epoch the more interesting to us, as we separated at that point from English legislation, and acknowledge no subsequent statutory alterations." He was then assigned the common law reports and Bacon's *Abridgment*. Then equity was to be studied by reading the two-column *General Abridgment of Cases in Equity*. Passing over the more recent reports of cases, Blackstone's *Commentaries* was to be read. Blackstone was to be supplemented by reading R. Wooddeson's lectures on the law of England, Fonblanque's edition of Francis's *Maxims of Equity*, and R. W. Bridgman's digest of cases in equity. Jefferson wrote that "this course comprehends about twenty-six octavo volumes, and reading four or five hours a day would employ about two years." But Jefferson went on to recommend that Terrell read the reports of modern cases, the law tracts of Baron Gilbert, Bracton, Justinian's *Institutes*, and Reeves's *History of the English Law*. The lawyer should also have a passing understanding of admiralty, ecclesiastical, and international law. To this end the law student should read C. Molloy, *De Jure Maritimo et Navali*; A. Browne, *Compendious View of the Civil Law and the Law of the Admiralty; Jura Ecclesiastica*; and Gerard de Rayneval, *Institutions du Droit de la Nature et des Gens*. In addition to this course of law reading, Jefferson wrote, "there will still be six or eight hours for reading history, politics, ethics, physics, oratory, poetry, criticism, etc., as necessary as law to form an accomplished lawyer."[90]

William Wirt wrote in 1813 to Francis W. Gilmer suggesting that in his course of reading law, he should keep a commonplace book. He advised Gilmer to begin with St. George Tucker's edition of Blackstone's *Commentaries*, then to consult J. Chitty's *Treatise on Pleading* and M. Bacon's *Abridgment*, and finally to read the most recent reports of cases, English, American, and Virginian.[91]

Several months before he died, Wirt again responded with a letter of advice to a law student. This time he declined to give a simple list of law books to read but instead emphasized the need for a broad liberal education, particularly in the areas of English composition and rhetoric, logic, history, and economics. He urged the student to "read the legal and political arguments of Chief Justice Marshall, and those of Alexander Hamilton." He did mention, however, almost in passing,

---

[90] Letter of Thomas Jefferson to Dabney Terrall, Feb. 26, 1821, H. A. Washington, *Writings of Thomas Jefferson*, vol. 7, pp. 206-09 (1854).

[91] Letter of William Wirt to Francis Walker Gilmer, Nov. 16, 1813, J. P. Kennedy, *William Wirt*, vol. 1, pp. 323-25 (1850); E. Lee Shepard kindly supplied this information. For Gilmer's career, see R. B. Davis, *Francis Walker Gilmer* (1939), and M. A. Lofaro, "Francis Walker Gilmer," *Va. Law Reporters*, pp. 33-46 (1977).

Coke upon Littleton, Coke's *Reports*, Plowden's *Reports*, Fearne on *Contingent Remainders*, and Blackstone's *Commentaries*.[92]

In 1850 William Wirt Henry asked Prof. John B. Minor of Charlottesville for advice on a course of reading for the bar. The then youthful teacher responded quickly. He recommended that Henry make himself familiar with European political history, feudalism, and political science as a preliminary to the study of law. The order of law reading was first international law, then constitutional law, and lastly municipal law. Sufficient international law could be found in Kent's *Commentaries; The Federalist Papers* and James Madison's *Report* of 1799-1800 would be enough constitutional law.

"Coming now to municipal law, I think your studies should embrace in succession Blackstone's *Commentaries*, Kent's *Commentaries*, and Tucker's *Commentaries*, which with the statute law would probably . . . occupy you for a year." Since Kent's views of the federal Constitution were not generally accepted in Virginia, Minor advised Henry to reread Madison's essay and A. P. Upshur's *A Brief Enquiry into the True Nature and Character of Our Federal Government* (1840). Minor continued: "Should time permit, it would be of great service to you to read Reeves's *History of the English Law*, Hale's *History of the Common Law*, Gilbert's *Tenures*, Sullivan's *Lectures*, Campbell's *Lives of the Chancellors and [Lives] of the Chief Justices of England*, and Smith's *Leading Cases*. The latter, indeed, you ought, at all events, to read at intervals, as soon as you have completed and mastered Blackstone."[93] It is to be noted that Minor, like Jefferson and Wirt, fully appreciated the importance of a liberal education and legal history to the practicing lawyer.

The legal education of Robert Reid Howison of Fredericksburg furnishes an interesting example of the combination of methods. Howison in July 1838, at the age of eighteen, began reading law books in his spare time in the evenings. In the fall of 1840, Howison entered the proprietary law school that Judge John T. Lomax operated in the basement of his house in Fredericksburg. When Lomax had completed his course of lectures in the early spring of 1841, Howison then spent three weeks in the office of the clerk of the court in Fredericksburg copying documents for his master. He was examined and admitted to the bar and, in June 1841, moved to Richmond to begin the practice of

[92] "Letter [Dec. 20, 1833] from Mr. Wirt to a Law Student," *Southern Literary Messenger*, vol. 1, pp. 33-36 (1834).

[93] Letter of John Barbee Minor to William Wirt Henry, Aug. 7, 1850, W. H. Bryson, *Essays on Legal Education in Nineteenth Century Virginia*, pp. 151-56 (1998).

law.[94]

C. *PROPRIETARY LAW SCHOOLS*

The first half of the nineteenth century saw an interesting novelty in legal education in Virginia. This was the expansion of legal apprenticeships into formal proprietary law schools. It began with the establishment of a private law school in Richmond in 1810 by Chancellor Creed Taylor.[95] Taylor had learned the law by reading under a lawyer who was the clerk of Cumberland County. In 1806 Taylor was elected chancellor of the Richmond district of the High Court of Chancery to succeed George Wythe. In 1810 he began teaching law in Richmond. Four years later, Lynchburg was added to his jurisdiction, and he moved his residence to Needham in Cumberland County, near Farmville, which is equidistant between Richmond and Lynchburg. In 1821 Taylor reestablished his law school in Needham.

Taylor's method of instruction was unique in Virginia and appears to have been his invention. He did not lecture. Instead, Taylor assigned books to be read, and when the student passed an examination on these books, he then moved into a moot court program. The moot courts were conducted at both the trial and appellate levels; Taylor, of course, presided.

Taylor required his students to read first these seven books:

Coke upon Littleton
Blackstone's *Commentaries* (Tucker ed.)
Runnington, *Action of Ejectment*
Chitty, *Treatise on Pleading*
Chitty, *Bills of Exchange*
Peake, *Evidence*
Noy's *Maxims*

When the student had passed an examination based on these books, he was admitted to the common law side of the moot court. Then, as he participated in the moot court exercises, he was to be reading:

---

94 W. H. Bryson, "Robert Reid Howison," *Va. Law Reporters*, pp. 112-13 (1977).

95 Letter of S. Myers et al. to Creed Taylor, Feb. 20, 1810, and letter of Creed Taylor to S. Myers et al., Feb. 22, 1810, Creed Taylor Papers, Special Collections Dept., Alderman Library, Univ. of Va.; "A Law School," Richmond *Enquirer*, Jan. 18, 1821, p. 1. Susan A. Riggs kindly supplied this information.

Fonblanque, *Equity*
Maddock, *Practice of Chancery*
Mitford or Cooper on equity pleading
Francis, *Maxims*

When Chancellor Taylor was convinced that these works had been mastered, the student was allowed to participate in the equity division of the moot court. All cases were carried to appeals. After the equity works were read, the student was given a list of standard books on substantive topics:

Fearne, *Contingent Remainders*
Newland, *Contracts in Equity*
Sugden, *Vendors and Purchasers*
Roberts, *Fraudulent Conveyances*
Toller, *Executors and Administrators*
Kyd, *Law of Awards*
Abbott, *Law Relative to Merchant Ships and Seamen*

The Virginia statutes and reports were also to be read. Taylor estimated that his course could be completed in eighteen months. This course was designed only as an introduction to the law. After joining the bar, the lawyer was to read works on international law, admiralty, criminal law, and federal law. The Bible, too, was to be studied "because, for its morality, history, and law, it is not equalled by any other work extant."[96]

In 1822 Taylor summarized in print the proceedings of the first year of his revived law school moot court in a curious little volume entitled *Journal of the Law School and of the Moot Court Attached to It at Needham in Virginia*. It included an extensive appendix of forms. Taylor intended to publish additional volumes, but he never did.

Creed Taylor followed Wythe in reviving the medieval moot court and in conducting it at the nisi prius stage of litigation. However, while Wythe used the moot court as a minor adjunct to his lectures, Taylor used it in conjunction with independent reading, making the mock court the major element of the law course. A good master would give his apprentice books to read and teach him to draft legal documents, but Taylor went a step further and gave his students the opportunity to practice arguing before a judge. Taylor's 1821 session was very successful; he had nineteen students. Very little is known about this law school past that year, however. It probably declined gradually but

[96] C. Taylor, *Journal of the Law School*, pp. iii-vii, 9-14 (1822).

steadily; in any event, it was no longer in existence in 1830. Certainly the competition from the University of Virginia's law department, established in 1826, hastened its demise.

The next Virginia law school was established in 1824 in Winchester by Judge Henry St. George Tucker. Tucker had studied law at William and Mary where his father, St. George Tucker, was the law professor. At the conclusion of his law course in Williamsburg, he left home and entered the practice of law in Winchester. In 1824 he was made the equity judge for the Winchester and Clarksburg districts. In order to supplement his greatly reduced income, he opened a private law school.[97]

Henry Tucker's primary purpose was to teach his students to practice law. However, he followed in the steps of Wythe and of his father when he said in his introductory lecture, "Spare no pains to improve and enlarge the mind which is to be devoted to the important concerns of the administration of justice and perhaps at a future day to the duties of a lawgiver."[98]

Henry Tucker used his father's edition of Blackstone's *Commentaries* as his text. He lectured three days a week on the text, but he gave daily quizzes to his students on their reading of it. In addition, in 1826 he published a thick volume of his own annotations to Blackstone's treatise. Tucker's *Notes on Blackstone's Commentaries for the Use of Students* (Winchester, 1826) gave the current Virginia and federal law on each point covered by Blackstone. This book contained the material that Tucker added in class to the text of the English teacher. Tucker did not lecture on those sections that dealt with English political theory but stuck to the common law.[99]

Tucker's law school was a great success. He had eleven students in his first session, 1824-25, ten the next, then over thirty; in the 1827-28 course, he had thirty-four, and thirty-one the following year. Among them were students from Georgia, South Carolina, Louisiana, Alabama, Ohio, and Massachusetts. (Tucker was widely known because of his own service in Congress from 1815 to 1819.) Some of Tucker's students participated in a moot court exercise in the summer

---

[97] J. R. Tucker, "Judges Tucker of the Court of Appeals of Virginia," *Va. L. Reg.*, vol. 1, pp. 796-812 (1896); *DAB*, s.v. "Tucker, Henry St. George."

[98] H. St. G. Tucker, "Introductory Lecture," *Notes on Blackstone's Commentaries*, p. 13 (1826); this was repeated in H. St. G. Tucker, *Introductory Lecture*, pp. 23-24 (1841).

[99] H. St. G. Tucker, "Introductory Lecture," *Notes on Blackstone's Commentaries*, p. 11 (1826).

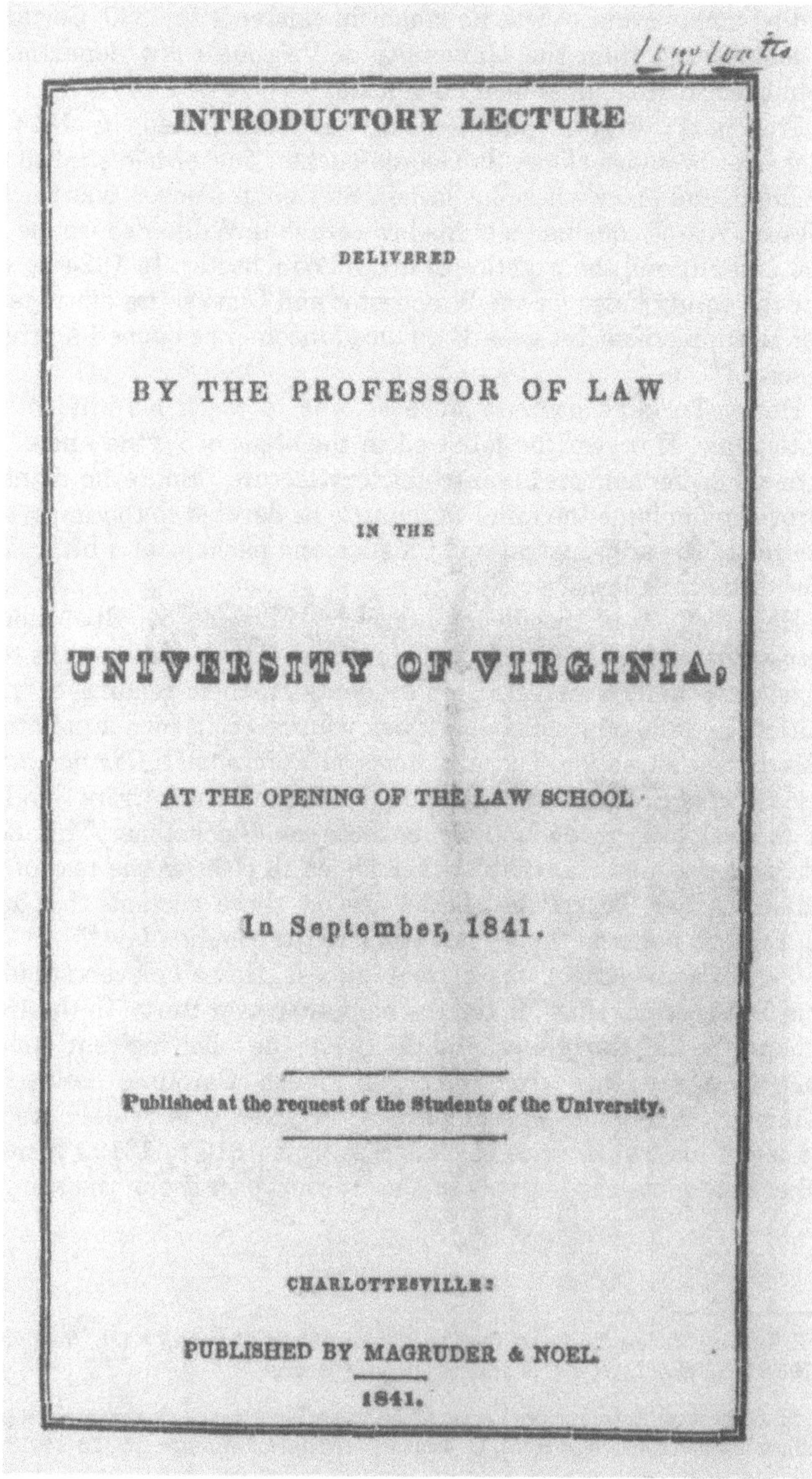

INTRODUCTORY LECTURE

DELIVERED

BY THE PROFESSOR OF LAW

IN THE

UNIVERSITY OF VIRGINIA,

AT THE OPENING OF THE LAW SCHOOL

In September, 1841.

Published at the request of the Students of the University.

CHARLOTTESVILLE:

PUBLISHED BY MAGRUDER & NOEL.

1841.

of 1828.[100]

In 1831 Henry Tucker was elected to the Virginia Court of Appeals, making it necessary for him to move to Richmond and to close his law school. In this same year, he completed the revision and editing of his law lectures, and they appeared under the title of *Commentaries on the Laws of Virginia, Comprising the Substance of a Course of Lectures Delivered to the Winchester Law School.* The debt to Blackstone is not hidden, but this two-volume work displays the experience and labors of Henry Tucker. Tucker's *Commentaries* was the first encyclopedia of Virginia law; it went through three editions between 1831 and 1846.

In 1826 the University of Virginia law department was established with John Tayloe Lomax as its first law professor. We shall return to the University of Virginia after we have considered the other proprietary law schools.

In 1830 Professor Lomax resigned his chair at the University of Virginia to become the circuit superior judge in Fredericksburg. The main reason for this move was financial. A year later Lomax opened a private law school in the basement of his house on Hanover Street in Fredericksburg.[101] He had had four years of law teaching experience at the University of Virginia, and he had corresponded with Henry Tucker on the subject of organizing a proprietary law school. Tucker sent him a copy of his recently published *Commentaries.*[102]

Although one of his students in 1840 described his courses as "lectures,"[103] Lomax's initial method of instruction in this private law school was to be strictly Socratic. Indeed, in his prospectus for the school, Lomax declared that reading lectures to students was "a most ineffectual and unsatisfactory mode of instruction in a science so extensive and so abstruse as the law." Instead of lecturing, Lomax intended to instruct by means of "text books with examinations and explanations." He would assign Chitty's edition of Blackstone's *Commentaries* (being the cheapest edition), Cruise's *Digest* (New York edition of 1827), H. St. G. Tucker's *Commentaries*, and Kent's

[100] Letters of Henry St. G. Tucker to St. George Tucker, Dec. 19, 1824, Mar. 21, Nov. 20, 1825, Nov. 5, 1826, Tucker-Coleman Papers, Special Collections Dept., Swem Library, College of William and Mary; "Law School of H. St. G. Tucker in Winchester," *Wm. & Mary Qtly.*, 2d ser., vol. 10, pp. 310-11 (1930).

[101] *DAB*, s.v. "Lomax, John Tayloe"; E. W. P. Lomax, "John Tayloe Lomax," *Green Bag*, vol. 9, pp. 373-78 (1897).

[102] Letter of Henry St. George Tucker to Briscoe Gerard Baldwin, May 5, 1831, W. H. Bryson, *Essays on Legal Education in Nineteenth Century Virginia*, p. 59 (1998).

[103] R. R. Howison, "Twice Forty Years in American Life," photocopy of MS. in Swem Library, Coll. of William and Mary, p. 155.

Commentaries. The students were to be given daily assignments and daily "exercises." His prospectus stated that the students "will be rigidly examined upon the matter which has been thus assigned for their studies, and in the course of the examination, such additional references and explanations will be supplied as will best illustrate the subject in hand." Thus Lomax's teaching was to be a Socratic exchange based on secondary treatises; this would be supplemented by whatever further explanations the students needed in order to understand the law. His announced aim was "to facilitate the acquisition of a knowledge of forensic law as practiced in America and principally in Virginia."[104] Not much else is known about the Fredericksburg Law School. There were at least thirteen students there during the 1840-41 session.[105] It was in existence as late as 1844.

Also in 1831, a private law school was opened in Staunton by Briscoe Gerard Baldwin. Baldwin had read law under his brother-in-law, Judge William Daniel, Sr., before setting up a law practice in Staunton. Baldwin rapidly rose to the top of the widely respected Staunton bar, and he also became prominent in Virginia politics. After consultation with Henry St. George Tucker, Baldwin commenced his law school on October 3, 1831.[106]

Baldwin was critical of practicing attorneys who accepted clerks into their offices but did not take the time to teach them. He announced that he would experiment with a new teaching method. He divided his school into a junior and a senior class. The junior class was given a program of reading elementary legal treatises, and the senior class was given lectures; there were daily Socratic examinations for both classes. Baldwin's students were allowed to enroll in either or both classes simultaneously. His lectures were directed primarily to the procedures and remedies of the law; the substance of the law was to be learned from reading. He prescribed books for advanced study on jurisprudence, constitutional law, and the Roman-based civil law. Dr. Joseph Addison Waddell was engaged to give a lecture on "medical jurisprudence."[107] This law school was quite successful, but the pressure of business and age forced Baldwin to give it up sometime before 1839.

In the year 1839, Judge Lucas Powell Thompson opened a law

---

[104] J. T. Lomax, *Circular* (Aug. 4, 1831).

[105] E. L. Shepard, "John Tayloe Lomax," *Legal Education in Va.*, pp. 358-366, 766-767 (1982).

[106] Letter of Henry St. George Tucker to Briscoe Gerard Baldwin, June 5, 1831, W. H. Bryson, *Essays on Legal Education in Nineteenth Century Virginia*, pp. 61-63 (1998).

[107] B. G. Baldwin, *Introductory Lecture* (1931); A. R. Rouse, *The Reads and Their Relatives*, p. 623 (1930).

school in Staunton to fill the gap left when Baldwin's school closed. Judge Thompson did not believe that he had the time to prepare original lectures, nor did he see any point in reading aloud to a class that which they could read for themselves. Therefore, his announced teaching method was to assign books to read and then to examine the students on their reading. He recommended that Blackstone, Wooddeson, Kent, and the Bible be studied. Then he quizzed his students in class on these works.[108] Using this method, he pointed out, "[t]he instructor by a minute and strict catechetical examination is enabled to fix and deepen upon the mind the impression of that which is already superficially or imperfectly understood, by apposite and well-timed hints, suggestions or illustrations, to explain what is dark or perplexing, and to remove difficulties, and to conduct step by step, and by easy and natural gradations, from principle to principle, until he compasses such a knowledge of the outlines as to qualify him to be his own teacher, which is the most any system of instruction can accomplish."[109]

Unlike many others who were educated by reading law under a practicing attorney, normally a narrow education, Thompson had an appreciation of the place of law in society. He believed that "the science of law and government should in some measure, and in some degree, be the study of every free citizen." However, he knew that a lawyer must also understand the law in "its theory, and its practice, its general principles, and its minute details."[110]

In 1849 John White Brockenbrough inaugurated a very successful law school in Lexington. This was the year in which Thompson closed his Staunton Law School. Brockenbrough had studied law in Tucker's Winchester Law School, and after a very successful practice in Lexington, he was appointed United States district judge for the Western district of Virginia in 1846. Three years later, Judge Brockenbrough founded the Lexington Law School in order to fill the gap in legal education west of the Blue Ridge Mountains left by the closing of the Staunton Law School and in order to provide additional income for his large family.[111]

Although Brockenbrough had studied under Henry Tucker, he followed the teaching methods of Lomax and Thompson, which he

[108] L. P. Thompson, *Introductory Lecture*, pp. 11-12 (1839).

[109] *Id.*, p. 13.

[110] *Id.*, pp. 7-8.

[111] M. W. Paxton, *A Judge's School: The Story of John White Brockenbrough* (1971); A. M. Dobie, "Federal District Judges in Virginia Before the Civil War," *Federal Rules Decisions*, vol. 12, pp. 451, 477-80 (1952).

termed the "catechetical system of instruction." Brockenbrough examined his students in class on their assigned reading and then discoursed on those parts with which the students were having difficulty or where the text was out of date. The school was divided into two classes, beginners and those who had previously read some law. Each class met every other day, and a student could enroll in either or both. The course lasted five months, at the end of which there was a moot court at the trial level.[112] The Lexington Law School was highly successful from its beginning. Between 1849 and 1861 when war forced its closing, this school educated more than two hundred lawyers.[113]

These six proprietary law schools constitute a fascinating period in the history of legal education in Virginia. Each did not hesitate to experiment with new teaching methods or combinations of old ones that met the needs of the teachers and the students. The teachers were in correspondence with each other or were at least fully aware of what the others had done. Creed Taylor abandoned the apprenticeship and university lecture methods and used independent reading and the moot court as his method of instruction. Henry Tucker followed the methods of William and Mary and of his father by lecturing and giving Socratic quizzes augmented by a moot court. Baldwin followed Tucker. Lomax, Thompson, and Brockenbrough did not deliver formal lectures but used what we today call the Socratic method. To this Brockenbrough added a moot court.

The positive aspects of the proprietary law schools were their freedom to experiment with new teaching methods and the practical experience that the teachers brought to the classroom. The judges were in daily contact with the practice of the law and could draw on this for their instruction of the students. On the other hand, it is to be remembered that they were only part-time teachers and had to divide their time between their students and their courts or clients. Thus they did not have time to be immersed completely in the academic side of the law. Only Tucker and Lomax found the time to write.

It is interesting to note that all of these men, except for Baldwin, were judges. Judges were notoriously poorly paid then, and teaching law was a method of supplementing their income without becoming involved in any potential conflicts of interest. Students were attracted to these teaching judges because of their high legal reputations. Many of their students also probably anticipated practicing before them later on.

---

[112] J. W. Brockenbrough, *Introductory Address*, pp. 8-9 (1849); J. W. Brockenbrough, *Introductory Lecture*, pp. 12-16 (1858).

[113] O. Crenshaw, *General Lee's College*, pp. 324-28 (1969).

As to the period during which these private schools flourished, it is to be noted that the College of William and Mary was in a state of decline. When in 1804 the eminent St. George Tucker resigned his professorship of law, William and Mary was facing serious competition from Hampden-Sydney College near Farmville and from Washington College in Lexington. Even though these two institutions did not teach law, the loss of other students to them weakened William and Mary. The ties of the college with the Episcopal church and student disturbances were also detrimental. Moreover, the law department began to feel new competition. In 1810 the first proprietary law school, that of Creed Taylor, was established. In 1811 the first Virginian was enrolled at the Litchfield Law School in Connecticut.[114] William and Mary had a series of less than noteworthy law professors until 1834 when Beverley Tucker was given the chair of law and police, which was formerly held by his father. It was the period from 1810 to 1834 in which four of the six proprietary law schools were established.

D. *University of Virginia*

Returning now to the organization of the University of Virginia law school, we can see that when Jefferson retired from politics in 1809, he devoted the rest of his long life to the cause of education. He returned to his plans of 1779, but now he thought in terms of a new university. Jefferson's educational plans for the Commonwealth of Virginia were characteristically grandiose and ahead of his time, but he succeeded in part in that he founded the University of Virginia. This institution opened its doors in 1825.

Jefferson's original plan for the University of Virginia included a law school that would teach common and statute law, equity, federal law, civil and mercantile law, jurisprudence and international law, and the principles of government and political science.[115] It is noteworthy that, as in the original William and Mary law school curriculum, political science was included along with the technical aspects of the law.

Of all the positions at the new university, the chair of law was the most difficult to fill. This was not because Jefferson insisted that the

[114] S. H. Fisher, *Litchfield Law School*, p. 23 (1933). From 1811 to 1832, there were twenty-two law students from Virginia at Litchfield; it was a steady trickle of one or two each year (A. J. Morrison, "Virginia and North Carolina at the Litchfield Law School," *Tyler's Qtly.*, vol. 2, pp. 157-58 (1921)).

[115] P. A. Bruce, *History of the University of Virginia*, vol. 1, p. 323 (1920); R. J. Honeywell, *The Educational Work of Thomas Jefferson*, pp. 120-23 (1964).

professor of law be of his political and constitutional persuasion,[116] for there were many eminent lawyers who fervently supported Jeffersonian ideas. Rather, it was the problem of the insufficient salary that accompanied the appointment. It was difficult to find a sufficiently prestigious lawyer who would be willing to give up a good income and the hope of a political or judicial office in order to become a teacher. Many including Henry St. George Tucker and William Wirt refused offers. Finally in 1826, the second year of the university, John Tayloe Lomax, a bright young Fredericksburg lawyer, accepted the position. He was successful as a teacher, but four years later, he resigned because of the low salary and the offer of a judgeship.[117]

The University of Virginia started out with a broad legal curriculum that had a liberal arts flavor. Two years were required to take all the law courses, and the law students were encouraged to enroll in other departments also. However, in 1829, three years after the death of Jefferson, pressure from the students resulted in a revision of the law curriculum so that they could take all of the basic law courses in a single year and begin practice that much sooner.[118]

John A. G. Davis replaced Lomax in 1830, and the University of Virginia law school continued to flourish. Davis unfortunately was shot and killed during a student riot in 1840. A noted Richmond lawyer, Nathaniel Pope Howard, was recruited on short notice to teach law the next academic year. In 1841 Henry St. George Tucker decided to retire from the Virginia Court of Appeals, and he accepted the professorship of law in Charlottesville. This was felicitous for the University of Virginia in that he was the most highly respected jurist in the Commonwealth at that time, and he was an experienced teacher, having been the proprietor of the Winchester Law School from 1824 to 1831. He is credited with introducing the honor system to the University of Virginia and the moot court to its law school. Tucker, an old man, had to resign because of ill health in 1845; he died three years later.[119]

The universally eminent Henry St. G. Tucker was succeeded by a young man, John Barbee Minor, the brother-in-law of Professor John A. G. Davis. By the end of his fifty-year tenure as professor of law, Minor had completely eclipsed the reputations of all of his

[116] P. A. Bruce, *History of the University of Virginia*, vol. 1, p. 323 (1920); R. J. Honeywell, *The Educational Work of Thomas Jefferson*, pp. 120-23 (1964).

[117] P. A. Bruce, *History of the University of Virginia*, vol. 2, pp. 24-32, 169-71 (1920).

[118] *Id.*, vol. 2, pp. 101-05.

[119] *Id.*, vol. 3, pp. 45-48, 66-68.

predecessors. From his initial appointment in 1845, Minor was a success. He was a very hardworking man, and his lectures were enthusiastically received. By 1851 the law department was the most successful division of the University of Virginia, and in that year a third year was added to the law curriculum and a full-time adjunct professor of law, James Philemon Holcombe, was added to the faculty. Minor believed in a law curriculum that included academic as well as professional studies. He taught by delivering original lectures; these were later published under the title of *Institutes of Common and Statute Law*. This remarkable work served as the encyclopedia of Virginia law until 1948. The whole body of Virginia law was compacted into six learned volumes. Minor was a supporter of the moot court and allowed nothing to interfere with those exercises.

E. *College of William and Mary, 1834-1861*

The William and Mary law department meanwhile was rescued from the doldrums by the arrival in 1834 of Nathaniel Beverley Tucker as professor of law and police. Beverley Tucker was the son of St. George Tucker, the younger brother of Henry St. George Tucker, and the half-brother of John Randolph of Roanoke, whom he idolized. Beverley Tucker continued the broad academic approach to the education of lawyers. He was well qualified to deliver his lectures on the technical aspects of the law, having been a successful lawyer and judge, but he enjoyed more those lectures on politics and constitutional law. He was self-conscious of the fact that his father had been one of the leaders of the movement for independence in Virginia and that his half-brother had been prominent in Congress. He was a prolific writer and speaker on the subject of states' rights. His vibrant activity gave an excitement to his classes, and this contributed to the revival of the College of William and Mary at that time. He died in 1851.[120]

William and Mary continued to flourish until the Civil War. Tucker was succeeded in 1852 by Judge George Parker Scarburgh, who was in turn succeeded by Lucian Minor in 1855. Lucian Minor was an older brother of John B. Minor, the professor of law at the University of Virginia. It is interesting to note that Lucian Minor was the first professor of law and police at William and Mary who was not a judge or a former judge. He died in 1858 and was followed by Charles Morris. In 1859 there was a disastrous fire, and all classes were suspended during the academic year 1859-60 while the college building was being

---

[120] N. B. Tucker, *A Lecture on the Study of the Law; Being an Introduction to a Course of Lectures* (1834); reprinted in *Southern Literary Messenger*, vol. 1, pp. 145-54 (1834); R. J. Brugger, *Beverley Tucker: Heart over Head in the Old South* (1978).

reconstructed.

In 1861 Lincoln's armies invaded Virginia. Professor Morris along with the rest of the faculty and students at William and Mary joined the Confederate army and went off to war. Judge Brockenbrough closed his law school in Lexington in order to serve the Confederacy as judge of the Western District of Virginia. Professor Holcombe left the University of Virginia to join the Confederate Congress, and Professor John B. Minor remained in Charlottesville to teach a handful of students who were too young to fight.

III. *1865 to 1895*

The thirty years from 1865 to 1895 were a period of rebuilding as opposed to the previous period of innovation. Virginia at the end of the war was a physical and financial wreck, and so were its universities.

During the war, Pennsylvania troops had burned the newly rebuilt William and Mary College academic building; a good part of the college endowment, which had been patriotically invested in Confederate bonds, was gone too. The College was reopened after the war, but the law department could not be revived. Not until 1922 would law again be taught at William and Mary.[121]

A. *UNIVERSITY OF VIRGINIA*

Jefferson's University of Virginia had better luck. Federal troops did not get to Charlottesville until the very end of the war, and Professor Minor and two colleagues succeeded in their appeal to the Union general to throw a guard around the University when his troops marched through the town.[122] Furthermore, the University of Virginia, being a state-supported institution, did not have to rely so heavily on a private endowment as did William and Mary. As a result, the university was a much stronger institution in 1861 than was William and Mary.

Minor's success had not been forgotten during the war, and at the close of the hostilities, law students immediately returned to the University of Virginia in great numbers. In 1866 Stephen O. Southall was added to the law faculty. He was a good teacher, but he died suddenly in 1884. He was replaced by James H. Gilmore. A summer

[121] Report of the President to the Board of Visitors, July 5, 1865, *Wm. & Mary Qtly.*, 2d ser., vol. 8, pp. 290-96 (1928); R. M. Hughes, "William and Mary, the First American Law School," *Wm. & Mary Qtly.*, 2d ser., vol. 2, pp. 40, 43 (1922).

[122] P. A. Bruce, *History of the University of Virginia*, vol. 3, pp. 331-40 (1921).

law course was begun in 1870. Minor, Southall, and Gilmore taught by lecturing. Although there were regular quizzes, these were designed only to encourage the students to read their daily assignments. The moot court continued, but the prime pedagogical method was the lecture.

The curriculum at Virginia was designed by Minor to take two years, but many of the students could afford only a single year of legal education, and so the lectures were arranged so that a student could attend them all in a single year. The students were always urged to stay in school a second year, if that was at all possible. Whether they did or did not, Minor was a strict grader, and less than twenty percent of his students were awarded law degrees. This was the subject of dissension, but it must be remembered that the degree was not a prerequisite to the practice of law at that time.

Minor's reputation continued to increase, after the war, and by the time of his death in 1895, he was nationally prominent. To him as much as, if not more so than, anyone else in the nineteenth century is due the credit for the good name of the University of Virginia and of its law school. He died in 1895, shortly after his fiftieth anniversary as a law professor. Professor Gilmore retired the next year. The passing of John B. Minor marked the end of an era for the University of Virginia law school and for legal education in Virginia.[123]

B. *Washington and Lee University*

As soon as the Civil War was over, John W. Brockenbrough announced the reopening of his law school in Lexington. Brockenbrough was no longer a judge, so he resumed the practice and teaching of law.

Before the war, Brockenbrough had held his school in the Franklin Hall in the Town of Lexington. After the war, his revived law school was allowed to use the facilities of Washington College, of which he was the rector of the board of trustees. In fact, Washington College was in debt to Brockenbrough because he was greatly instrumental in persuading General Robert E. Lee to accept the presidency of the college in 1865, assuring the future of that institution. From 1866 to 1870, Brockenbrough's law school had an informal affiliation with Washington College, but the law students were not allowed to use the college library or other buildings. This four-year period saw a decline

[123] *Id.*, vol. 4, pp. 1-5; J. Ritchie, *The First Hundred Years*, pp. 30-51 (1978).

in the number of law students.[124]

In 1870 General Lee died, and the name of the institution was changed to Washington and Lee University. In that same year, in order to strengthen the law program, the law school became a formal department of the university and its teachers members of the university faculty. Brockenbrough therefore resigned from the board of trustees to avoid the conflict of interest. Also in 1870, John Randolph Tucker was hired as a professor of law in addition to Brockenbrough. Ran Tucker was the son of Henry St. George Tucker, who owned the Winchester Law School and later taught at the University of Virginia.

Brockenbrough and Tucker were remunerated for teaching law by splitting the students' fees between themselves. They both also had private law practices. However, only Tucker arranged with the university to receive a minimum income from the institution. The number of law students at Washington and Lee continued to decline, and in 1873 the fees were not sufficient for both professors. Tucker, having had the foresight to contract for a minimum salary, was the one to remain, and Brockenbrough for financial reasons was forced to resign, to his great chagrin. Brockenbrough died four years later still bitter over the turn of events.

In 1873 Charles Alfred Graves, a recent law graduate, was appointed assistant professor of law to take the place of Brockenbrough. Two years later, Tucker resigned to serve in Congress. From 1875 until 1889, Graves was the sole teacher of law at Washington and Lee. Several local attorneys gave a few lectures, but their teaching was minimal. Although the University of Virginia law school was in a state of prosperity, Washington and Lee was finding it very difficult to attract law students at this time. The board of trustees came close to terminating the law department altogether, but Graves managed to dissuade them. Even though the numbers were small, by 1885 the fees from the law students were sufficient to cover their professor's salary. At this time, the law school was divided into junior and senior years, which the students could take together in a single year or separately in two years.

In 1889 Ran Tucker returned to the law school at Washington and Lee after having distinguished himself in Congress. He resumed the leadership of the school and was now able to attract a goodly number of students. Tucker was given the title of dean in 1893; he died in 1897. In 1897 Graves was made dean but resigned in 1899 to accept a professorship of law at the University of Virginia. The years 1889 to 1899 are referred to in the annals of Washington and Lee as "the

---

[124] M. W. Paxton, *A Judge's School* (1971); O. Crenshaw, *General Lee's College*, pp. 329-32 (1969).

golden years of Randy and Charlie." For the first time, the law school was in a state of financial stability. The enrollment and academic standards increased. A two-year residency was now required to receive the law degree, and a third professorship was added to the law school.[125]

C. *Richmond College*

In 1870 Richmond College instituted a law department. All of the law courses were taught in the late afternoon or in the evening so that the students, many of whom were impoverished by the Civil War and Reconstruction, could support themselves while studying law. It is surprising that no law school had existed before in Richmond except the activities of Creed Taylor in the 1810s. Perhaps this is to be explained by the fact that Richmond is equidistant between William and Mary and the University of Virginia. Moreover, there was a distinguished bar in Richmond, and an apprentice could easily find there a good master with a good law library.

The original law faculty of Richmond College was composed of three distinguished lawyers: William Green, James D. Halyburton, and J. L. M. Curry. Green was the most erudite practicing lawyer in Virginia; he was a scholar by temperament, and in 1870 he was more highly regarded than John B. Minor or Conway Robinson.[126] Judge James D. Halyburton had been the United States district judge for the Eastern District of Virginia from 1843 until 1861, and he served as the Confederate judge for eastern Virginia from 1861 until the end of the war. He then went into the private practice of the law in Richmond.[127] Curry, a native of Georgia, was a graduate of the Harvard Law School. He had been very active in politics and had served in the United States Congress and in the Confederate Congress. After the war he devoted his life to education in the South. In 1868 he settled in Richmond to teach English and history at Richmond College. When the law school was opened in 1870, he taught the courses in constitutional and international law.[128] After two years of law teaching, however, all three of these men resigned, Green and Halyburton for reasons of old age

[125] O. Crenshaw, *General Lee's College*, pp. 333-44 (1969). Charles V. Laughlin very kindly supplied much of this information.

[126] P. Slaughter, *A Brief Sketch of the Life of William Green* (1883); *DAB*.

[127] A. M. Dobie, "Federal District Judges in Virginia Before the Civil War," *Federal Rules Decisions*, vol. 12, pp. 451, 473 (1952).

[128] E. A. Alderman and A. C. Gordon, *J. L. M. Curry* (1911); J. P. Rice, *J. L. M. Curry, Southerner, Statesman, and Educator* (1949).

and ill health, Curry in order to pursue a career in education as general agent of the Peabody and Slater funds.

The prestige and efforts of these three men were successful in establishing the new law school in Richmond. William Green in particular set the tone of the new institution. It was he who was chosen to deliver the inaugural lecture. He urged his students to have a love of excellence and to pursue not money or mere success but the ideals of truth and justice.[129]

From 1872 to 1874, the law classes at Richmond College were taught by William A. Maury and James Neeson. From 1870 to 1874, the law classes varied in size from ten to sixteen students. This was not considered sufficient to justify the continuation of the law department, and it was suspended for three years. During these same four years, the law classes at Washington and Lee were about the same size, but at the University of Virginia, the law classes had between 70 and 137 students.

In 1877 law classes were resumed at Richmond by Professor Samuel D. Davies. He taught until 1882, when the poor financial situation again forced the closing of the law school. After a period of eight years, it became clear that it would take more than student fees to finance legal education at Richmond College. Therefore, in 1890, the family of the late T. C. Williams, Sr., a wealthy Richmond businessman, endowed a professorship in law with $25,000. The first T. C. Williams Professor of Law was Roger Gregory. With this gift, the Richmond College law school was put on a sound financial footing, and it has increased in quantity and in quality ever since. Roger Gregory retired from teaching in 1906 and died in 1920.[130]

From its founding in 1870 throughout the period to 1895 and beyond, all of the law professors at Richmond College were practicing attorneys. The lecture was the sole method of instruction, and classes were held in the evening to accommodate the faculty and the students. The period 1870 to 1895 was one of beginning and competence; excellence was yet to be achieved.

IV. *After 1895*

The period from 1895 to the present has been one of steady growth both in quantity and in quality for legal education in Virginia. There

[129] W. Green, *Address to the Law Class of Richmond College* (1870); D. J. Mays, *The Pursuit of Excellence: A History of the University of Richmond Law School*, pp. 3-13 (1970).

[130] D. J. Mays, *The Pursuit of Excellence*, pp. 13-18 (1970); R. E. Alley, *History of the University of Richmond*, pp. 51-52, 60-62 (1977).

were lean times during the two world wars, but peace brought the immediate revival of all of the Virginia law schools.

A. *UNIVERSITY OF VIRGINIA*

The University of Virginia School of Law added a third law professor in 1893 when William Minor Lile was hired. When John B. Minor died in 1895, he was replaced by Walter D. Dabney, and in the next year, Raleigh C. Minor replaced Gilmore, whose resignation had been accepted. Raleigh Minor, the son of John B. Minor, had been a junior instructor at the law school since 1893. In 1895 the course offerings were enlarged and rearranged so that the students could get credit in the first year for courses taken then without having to wait for the examinations on those courses at the end of the second year.[131] The law faculty petitioned the board of visitors in 1897 to allow them to require two years of law study before granting a law degree, but this was not allowed until the 1901-02 session.[132] In 1900 the Association of American Law Schools was founded, but the University of Virginia declined the invitation to be a charter member and did not join until 1916.

In 1904 the administration of the University of Virginia was reformed, and E. A. Alderman was appointed the first president of the university. (Before 1904 the university had been administered by the faculty.) Alderman appointed Lile as the first dean of the law school. The law school continued to prosper and to expand. In 1907 a fourth law professor was added to the faculty, Armistead M. Dobie, and two years later the law course was increased to three years. In 1911 the law school moved into a building of its own, and the new edifice was appropriately named after John B. Minor. After World War I was over, Professor Dobie was given a leave of absence to pursue graduate law studies at Harvard Law School. He returned to Charlottesville in 1922 with an S.J.D. degree and with the convert's enthusiasm for the Langdell method of legal education.[133]

This revolutionary method of legal education had been developed in the latter quarter of the nineteenth century by Dean Christopher C.

---

[131] "Re-arrangement of the Law Course at the University of Virginia," *Va. L. Reg.*, vol. 1, p. 150 (1895).

[132] P. A. Bruce, *History of the University of Virginia*, vol. 4, pp. 289-90 (1921). "The Law Course at the University of Virginia," *Va. L. Reg.*, vol. 3, p. 670 (1898), assumed incorrectly that this improvement would be made immediately by the visitors.

[133] P. A. Bruce, *History of the University of Virginia*, vol. 5, pp. 38, 170-77 (1922); J. Ritchie, *The First Hundred Years*, pp. 66-100 (1978).

Langdell at the Harvard Law School. Langdell believed that the common law was basically judge-made law and that the students should study law "scientifically," by going directly to the sources of the law and not by reading commentaries on the law. Primary sources should be preferred to secondary sources. Therefore, law students should study cases exclusively, but only good cases. Thus Langdell prepared casebooks of unedited appellate court decisions, and these were all that his students used in their law studies. If the student was to avoid secondary literature, then logically any lecture or even comments from the classroom law teacher must also be avoided. This required the use of the Socratic dialogue in the classroom. The case method cannot function independently of the Socratic method. The law student extracted from the carefully chosen leading cases in the casebooks the points of law to be learned. He thereby acquired a method of legal research for future use in his practice of law. The classroom discussion assured that a method of legal reasoning was acquired. Langdell taught methodology, not law. It has been said that if you give a man a fish, you feed him for a day, but if you teach him how to fish, you feed him for his lifetime.

There were many problems with Langdell's method of teaching, and they were quickly pointed out. Dean J. R. Tucker at Washington and Lee and Dean W. M. Lile at the University of Virginia both expressly declined to follow the new Harvard system. Socratic teaching is much slower than lecturing, and since the case method requires immersion therein, the law school curriculum must be greatly reduced. Langdell did not provide practical or tactical training, and by concentrating on judicial opinions, his system was narrowly professional and ignored the social and philosophical aspects of the law. Langdell did not deal with statutory law or with any local state law. He taught only general principles. Yet in spite of these obvious drawbacks, it soon was recognized that they were all vastly outweighed by the teaching of legal methodology. Langdell's casebook-Socratic system of legal education steadily spread throughout the United States and is today generally accepted. The starkness of the original method of teaching has been greatly modified; statutory law is taught, problems are used as teaching tools, moot courts and drafting exercises have been retained. But the basic Langdell theory of studying law at its primary source so as to develop a method of dealing with legal problems remains as vigorous as ever.[134]

[134] A. E. Sutherland, *The Law at Harvard*, pp. 174-78 (1967); C. Warren, *History of the Harvard Law School*, vol. 2, pp. 419-27 (1970); A. Z. Reed, *Training for the Public Profession of the Law*, pp. 369-85 (1921); A. J. Harno, *Legal Education in the U.S.*, pp. 53-70 (1953).

Dobie brought the Langdell method back with him to the University of Virginia in 1922, and it slowly caught on there. In 1932 Dobie succeeded Lile as dean, and the Langdell way of teaching became generally accepted in Charlottesville.

In 1928 Garrard Glenn was enticed away from his practice in New York City to teach at the University of Virginia. Glenn had been very successful in the practice of law, but his temperament was that of a scholar. While in Charlottesville, he published extensively in the fields of creditors' rights and equity. Glenn is said to have set the pace for the University of Virginia School of Law in the twentieth century. His presence on the faculty attracted other good teachers, and his high standards as a scholar were emulated by his colleagues.

Following World War II, the law school at the University of Virginia took the step of greatly increasing its course offering by hiring a substantial number of part-time lecturers. These persons are for the most part lawyers practicing in Charlottesville, Richmond, and Washington, D.C.; they teach advanced courses, such as aviation law and labor law, and practical courses like trial tactics and estate management. They add a new dimension to the basic and traditional courses taught by the permanent, full-time faculty. In 1946 the University of Virginia began its graduate law program, which grants the LL. M. and S.J.D. degrees.

B. *WASHINGTON AND LEE UNIVERSITY*

The year 1896 saw the beginning of the present period of growth and general prosperity for the Washington and Lee law school. In that year, a third professor, John W. Davis, was appointed to the law faculty; this provided the much-needed opportunity to expand the law curriculum. In 1897, Dean J. R. Tucker died and Davis resigned to return to practice; two years later, Dean Charles A. Graves resigned to accept a professorship at the University of Virginia. The next dean was Henry St. George Tucker, the son of the first Dean Tucker. In 1900 the president of the university died, and Dean Tucker aspired to succeed to the presidency. When he was not elected, he resigned his position as law dean and professor in protest. Professor William R. Vance was elected dean in 1902, but he resigned the next year to accept a law professorship at Columbian University in Washington, D.C. In 1902 Professor Martin P. Burks was made dean, and he held this post until 1917. J. R. Long was appointed professor in 1902 and A. P. Staples in 1904; these two plus Burks were the law faculty until 1913 when Staples died. In 1917 Burks resigned as dean to become a justice of the Virginia Supreme Court of Appeals; the new dean was Joseph R. Long.

Fortunately, this unusual instability in the faculty did not affect the student body significantly. In 1900 the law school in Lexington moved into a new building designed for its exclusive use. It was named for John Randolph Tucker.

In 1916 E. Merrick Dodd was brought to the Washington and Lee law school to demonstrate the Langdell casebook method of legal education, on the recommendation of Dean Burks. Dodd had graduated from the Harvard Law School in 1913 and had practiced law in Boston from then until his appointment to the law faculty. Although World War I forced Dodd to leave Lexington after only one year of teaching, he had been a success, and the Langdell system began to be adopted by the other law teachers at Washington and Lee. In 1923 the board of trustees eased Long out of the deanship and replaced him with William H. Moreland so that the case method of instruction would be used throughout the law school.

A new era for the Washington and Lee law school began with the end of World War I. As of 1920, the attendance required for the LL. B. degree was expanded to three years, and the law school became a member of the Association of American Law Schools. There were five full-time law professors, and the case method was in use in the classroom. It was the beginning of the period of the "Old Guard," also known as the "famous five." This group consisted of Professors William H. Moreland (who taught at Washington and Lee from 1914 to 1944), Clayton E. Williams (1919-68), Raymon T. Johnson (1925-48), Charles P. Light (1926-76), and Charles R. McDowell (1927-68). These five outstanding teachers dominated the law school from 1923, when Moreland became dean, until 1968 when Light retired as dean. From 1927 to 1937, they were the entire law faculty, and because of their seniority, experience, and prestige, they controlled the law school until the 1960s. Under them the Washington and Lee law school flourished.[135]

C. *UNIVERSITY OF RICHMOND*

The University of Richmond law school began a period of growth with the appointment of a second part-time law professor in 1895. This new man on the faculty was John B. Minor, Jr., the son of the famous law teacher at the University of Virginia. The law school at Richmond

[135] Professor Charles V. Laughlin kindly supplied much of this information; see also O. Crenshaw, *General Lee's College*, pp. 342-46 (1969); O. Crenshaw, "The School of Law, 1849-1949: A Century Revisited," *Wash. & Lee L. Rev.*, vol. 6, pp. 12, 30-34 (1949); C. E. Williams, "Development of the Law Curriculum," *Alumni Mag., Wash. & Lee Univ.*, pp. 11-15 (Mar.-Apr. 1936).

continued to grow, and E. M. Long was added to the faculty in 1898.

It is, however, the year 1905 that marks the dawn of the modern period of law teaching at the University of Richmond. This was the date of the appointment of Professor Walter Scott McNeill. McNeill received his B.A. from Richmond College, his Ph. D. in economics from the University of Berlin, and his LL. B. from Harvard Law School. In 1905, refusing an offer to teach at Princeton, McNeill returned to his alma mater to teach law. McNeill, a product of the Harvard Law School, brought Langdell's case method of legal education to the University of Richmond. He was the first law professor to use the Langdell system in Virginia. McNeill was an outstanding teacher.

In 1906 Professor Roger Gregory retired. He was succeeded by A. J. Montague, whose term as Governor of Virginia had just expired. Montague was given the titles of T. C. Williams Professor of Law and dean of the law school. He was the first person to have the title of dean. He resigned in 1909 to reenter the political world, and both titles of T. C. Williams Professor and dean were suppressed. McNeill became the unofficial administrator of the law school.

John Randolph Tucker, Jr., joined the law faculty in 1909; he taught at Richmond until 1925. He was the son of Henry St. George Tucker, the law professor and dean at Washington and Lee. It is interesting to note that the law professor at the University of Richmond represented his family's fifth generation of law professors in Virginia.[136]

The University of Richmond moved from downtown Richmond to a new campus in the western suburbs in 1914, and the law school moved along with the rest of the university. During World War I, however, the new campus became too cramped for space, and the law school moved back into one of the old university buildings, the Columbia Building, at the corner of Grace and Lombardy Streets. For the first time, the law school had a building of its own. In 1954 a new law school building was constructed on the new campus.

In 1920 to acknowledge the further financial generosity of the Williams family, the name of the school was changed to the T. C. Williams School of Law. The conclusion of World War I also marked the beginning of significant academic improvements in the law school. In 1922 the morning division of the law school was opened, as was the

[136] The first was St. George Tucker at William and Mary (1790-1804); his son Henry St. George Tucker taught at the University of Virginia (1841-45); his son John Randolph Tucker taught at Washington and Lee (1870-75, 1889-97); his son Henry St. George Tucker also taught at Washington and Lee (1897-1902); and his son John Randolph Tucker taught at the University of Richmond (1909-25). B. R. Tucker, *Tales of the Tuckers*, pp. 1-8, 12-17, 65-73, 146-52 (1942).

summer session. The curriculum was increased to require three years of study for the law degree. Two years of undergraduate education were required for admission to the law school as of 1924. The University of Richmond joined the Association of American Law Schools in 1930. The year 1930 was also a year of transition in that it marked the end of McNeill's vital and constructive service to the law school and the commencement of the deanship of Professor M. Ray Doubles.[137]

D. *COLLEGE OF WILLIAM AND MARY*

The College of William and Mary reactivated its law school in 1922 after a sixty-one-year period of dormancy. In 1906 the college had become a state-supported institution; J. A. C. Chandler had become its president in 1919 with the understanding that the college would regain its former prestige. Part of Chandler's mission was to restore the law school. In this goal, he was aided by Robert M. Hughes, Oscar L. Shewmake, and many other friends of the college.[138]

On January 14, 1922, the law school at William and Mary was formally reopened. It was officially known as the School of Jurisprudence and for administrative purposes was within the Marshall-Wythe School of Government and Citizenship. There was also a close connection between these two schools and the School of Economics and Business Administration. These three departments were academically independent of each other, but they shared faculty and other personnel. The first two law professors were William A. Hamilton and Oscar L. Shewmake; they actually started teaching law in September 1921 in the government department in anticipation of the reactivation of the law school. In 1922 John Garland Pollard was added to the law faculty, and in 1924 Peter Paul Peebles was granted the first law degree of the modern period.

The law school got off to a slow start; until about 1930 there were very few students. In 1925 P. P. Peebles joined the faculty, and Dudley W. Woodbridge followed in 1927. By 1929 the original three law teachers had resigned or retired, and Theodore S. Cox was appointed to the faculty in 1930. Two years later Cox was made dean of the School of Jurisprudence, the first person to hold this title. By 1932 Peebles, Woodbridge, and Cox had put the law school onto a sound footing, and from then until the present, it has continued to grow and

[137] D. J. Mays, *The Pursuit of Excellence*, pp. 17-65 (1970); R. E. Alley, *History of the University of Richmond*, pp. 110, 143, 170-71, 193-95, 210, 220-21, 243-45 (1977).

[138] See *infra*, "College of William and Mary Law Library."

expand its horizons.

In 1932 when Cox was made dean, the law school was separated from the government department. By 1934 the Brafferton building was given to the law school for classes. In 1953 the name of the law school was changed to the Marshall-Wythe School of Law to honor its most distinguished alumnus and professor.

The early curriculum of the modern law school emphasized the liberal arts aspect of law. Legal history and jurisprudence were among the first offerings. This no doubt reflects the fact that the law school was reorganized through the department of government. The law curriculum has steadily expanded, and today it includes a program in tax law leading to the degree of master of law and taxation.[139]

E. *Virginia Union University*

Virginia Union University in Richmond opened a law school in 1922 to give local blacks the opportunity for legal education without having to go to Howard University in Washington, D.C., or even farther from home. The law school at Virginia Union University was initiated and developed by Professor Peter James Henry, who taught civics and history. Henry had received an LL. B. from Howard University and was a member of the Virginia State Bar. He was joined by Professor Clarence McDonald Maloney, who had a law degree from Dalhousie University and taught history at Virginia Union University. As the law program developed, they were joined by six other black lawyers who taught law on a part-time basis.

The law department of Virginia Union University offered a four-year evening course leading to the LL. B. The only entrance requirement was a high school diploma or its equivalency, and the program was open to women as well as to men. The classes were held in Pickford Hall on Tuesday and Thursday evenings from seven until nine.

This law school got off to a good start, but there was not a sufficient demand to keep it going for very long. It closed in 1931. From 1922 to 1931, there were twenty-three graduates and sixteen students who enrolled but did not complete the course. Of the twenty-three graduates, only six passed the Virginia bar examination. Of these six, four were members of the first graduating class; this suggests that after the initial year, the quality of the student body went down. In addition to the small number of students, the economic depression, no doubt, also contributed to the demise of the school. Furthermore, the

---

139 *William and Mary Alumni Gazette*, vol. 1, no. 3, pp. 1, 4 (May 31, 1934); vol. 8, no. 2, pp. 6-7, 22-24 (Dec. 1940).

university was unprepared at that time to offer good legal education; the law school was the weakest department of the university. The law school was a well-intended undertaking, but it was ambitious beyond the resources of the university and the needs of the community.[140]

F. *GEORGE MASON UNIVERSITY*

In 1978 the International School of Law moved across the Potomac River from Washington, D.C., to Arlington, Virginia, and merged with George Mason University. The International School of Law was a proprietary law school. When the accreditation committee of the American Bar Association tightened its rules on recognition of proprietary law school degrees, this merger was forced on a rather reluctant state supported university in Fairfax. A large amount of political pressure was put on the General Assembly to effectuate this in order to have a publicly supported law school in northern Virginia.

G. *REGENT UNIVERSITY*

In 1986 the O. W. Coburn School of Law at Oral Roberts University in Tulsa, Oklahoma, was closed, its library was given to CBN University in the City of Virginia Beach, and several law professors followed.[141] CBN University was renamed Regent University in 1990. This law school, like its parent university, emphasizes the religious aspect of the law from a Christian perspective.

H. *PROPRIETARY LAW SCHOOLS*

Proprietary legal education revived, after a long break, in Norfolk in the 1910s. At this time, the nearest law school was in Richmond, and there was a need in Norfolk for inexpensive legal education. To meet this need, the Norfolk Law School was established and maintained by a series of prominent Norfolk attorneys. It was a night law school and was held in the offices of the various lawyers who taught in it. It was sometimes called the Norfolk Night Law School and also Grant's Law School. At times there was a single instructor, but in

[140] John M. Ellison kindly supplied much of this information. Note also M. M. Fisher, ed., *Virginia Union University and Some of Her Achievements*, pp. 8, 12, 16, 52 (1924); *Virginia Union Bull.*, vol. 31, pp. 176, 183, 192, 200, 211, 222, 231, 234, 236 (Jan.-Feb. 1931).

[141] Richmond *Times-Dispatch*, Nov. 2, 1985, pp. B-1, B-4; July 14, 1988, p. B-5; *National Law Journal*, Dec. 2, 1985, vol. 8, no. 2, p. 4; *Christianity Today*, Feb. 7, 1986, vol. 30, p. 48.

the thirties, at least, the teaching assignments were divided among several men. Although somewhat amorphous, the Norfolk Law School was kept going until the middle of the 1930s.

In 1911 and for the next several years, Eugene A. Bilisoly conducted the Norfolk Law School. After Bilisoly stopped teaching, Ernest S. Merrill took over. Merrill was teaching alone between 1920 and 1924; at this time he was conducting a law course which took two years. In the late 1920s and in the 1930s, the Norfolk Law School was run by Walter Grant, and the teaching was done by him, John C. Davis, Ernest S. Merrill, and D. Lawrence Groner, Jr. During this later period, classes were held three times a week for three hours each evening. Just before the bar examinations, refresher classes were held nightly, principally by J. C. Davis. The Norfolk Law School produced a number of prominent attorneys and judges in the Norfolk area.[142]

In 1924 Marcus G. James founded a business college called Norfolk College, located at Granby Street and Brooke Avenue. Among the departments of this institution was a school of law which offered courses preparing its students to take the Virginia bar examination. These law courses were taught by L. W. Sherritt in 1927, and for the year 1930-31, they were being taught by A. C. Philpotts, W. B. Tilley, and W. Shepherd Drewry. William M. Phipps was an instructor in 1932 and 1933. This law school appears to have been in operation as late as 1947. It was defunct before 1952; there is no connection between it and the present Norfolk College.[143]

In Richmond there were two proprietary evening law schools which operated in the twentieth century. William Parham Martin was the owner and "dean" of the Smithdeal-Massey College of Law, which was in operation from about 1947 to about 1959.[144] The teachers were local practicing attorneys. Martin owned the law school, but he had an arrangement whereby he used the name and building of the Smithdeal-Massey Business College, a highly respected secretarial school in Richmond. At least seventy-five of Martin's graduates applied to take the Virginia state bar examination; this was allowed under the theory that they were reading law under Martin. This institution catered mainly to returning veterans of the Second World War who wanted to

[142] Samuel Goldblatt, Herman A. Sacks, James A. Howard, and L. S. Parsons very kindly supplied this information; see also "Eugene A. Bilisoly," *Va. State Bar Ass'n Repts.*, vol. 50, p. 215 (1938).

[143] This information was kindly given by Judge Richard B. Kellam, Philip B. West, L. L. Underwood, Jr., and Frances Ripley; see also Norfolk *Virginian Pilot*, July 10, 1927, pt. 1, p. 4.

[144] See Richmond *Times-Dispatch*, June 8, 1970, p. B-2 (obituary of W. P. Martin); *Va. State Bar Ass'n Repts.*, vol. 58, pp. 57-58 (1947); vol. 61, pp. 77-80 (1950).

go to law school under the G.I. Bill but could not be accommodated by the established law schools. Many of the graduates of the Smithdeal-Massey law school passed the bar, and the school was a great financial success.

The Virginia College of Commerce and Law was chartered in 1937 as a nonprofit organization, but it was closely associated with the Richmond Business College, which had been founded in 1922. It was an evening course which prepared its students to take the Virginia bar examination. From 1948 to 1954, approximately fifty of its graduates applied to take the bar examination. A. Clair Sager was its first dean and taught law from 1937 to about 1943; after World War II, Gordon B. Ambler and then W. Griffith Purcell acted as dean.[145] This law school, along with the other proprietary efforts, ended soon after 1952 when the law was changed so that its students were no longer eligible to take the Virginia bar examination.[146]

In 1980, the District of Columbia Law School, which had been founded in 1977, moved to Alexandria, Virginia, and changed its name to the Northern Virginia Law School. It was a private weekend law school controlled by Alfred Avins. This law school had provisional accreditation from the Virginia Council of Higher Education from 1982 to 1986, but it was never accredited by any other body.[147]

The Appalachian School of Law in Grundy, Buchanan County, Virginia, was opened in 1997.

These private law schools were operated not by judges as before the Civil War but by lawyers and persons in the business of making legal education lucrative. In addition to these schools, the various business colleges in the state taught business law to their students, who were not studying to become attorneys. In the twentieth century, the colleges and universities in Virginia as throughout the nation added to their liberal arts courses classes in constitutional law and commercial law and introductory classes in law. They thus continued the idea of John Locke and others that law should be part of a liberal education.

I. *ADMISSION TO THE BAR*

In 1888 the Virginia State Bar Association was established with one of its original stated goals being to require higher qualifications for

---

[145] See Richmond *News Leader*, Feb. 19, 1953, p. 20.

[146] Va. Acts 1952, pp. 867-68, c. 553.

[147] Richmond *Times-Dispatch*, Aug. 7, 1986, p. B-5, col. 4; Avins v. Virginia Council of Higher Education, 11 Va. Cir. 191 (1988); Avins v. Harrison, 14 Va. Cir. 66 (1988).

the admission to the practice of law in Virginia. This would result in forcing greater study of law on the part of aspirants to the legal profession, and it would indirectly encourage the study of law in a proper law school and discourage reading law under an attorney. A standing committee on legal education and admission to the bar was erected at the first meeting of the association. It was noted that "the tests prescribed for determining fitness for admission to the bar in Virginia are a mocking farce." The committee was therefore directed to draft an act making the examination for admission to the bar a rigorous experience.[148]

The draft act, which required a bar examination to be conducted by three attorneys who were to be appointed by the local circuit judge, was presented to the General Assembly, but it was defeated. The reason for the failure of the bill seems to have been a feeling that anyone who can get clients should have the right to practice law.[149] This philosophy was directly counter to that of the association, which was trying to raise the level of the practice of law by excluding those who lacked knowledge, intelligence, or integrity.

In 1895 the committee on legal education and admission to the bar presented to the Virginia State Bar Association two proposed bills. The first would have set up boards of bar examiners; the second would transfer the examination of applicants from the circuit judges to the justices of the Supreme Court of Appeals. Although the committee favored the first, the association voted to recommend the second.[150] In 1896 the General Assembly finally acted, and an act was passed requiring the Supreme Court of Appeals to license future members of the Virginia bar after an examination pursuant to regulations to be promulgated.[151] Rules for a written bar examination were promptly published,[152] and the first meaningful bar exam was given on January

[148] *Va. State Bar Ass'n Repts.*, vol. 1, pp. 6, 7, 12, 15 (1888); note also *Va. L. J.*, vol. 13, p. 531 (1889). Reports that the good and the ignorant were being licensed indiscriminately are in J. L. Anderson and W. M. Lile, "Report of the Committee on Legal Education and Admission to the Bar," *Va. State Bar Ass'n Repts.*, vol. 7, pp. 49-50 (1894); "Examination for Admission to the Bar in Virginia – The Past – The Future," *Va. L. Reg.*, vol. 2, pp. 310, 312 (1896).

[149] *Va. State Bar Ass'n Repts.*, vol. 2, pp. 52-54 (1889); vol. 3, pp. 22-23 (1890). The bill was resubmitted to the General Assembly in 1894 and was again defeated (*Id.*, vol. 6, pp. 44-46, 273-75 (1893); vol. 7, pp. 16-22, 49 (1894)).

[150] *Id.*, vol. 8, pp. 26-40, 62-68 (1895).

[151] Va. Acts 1895-96, p. 49, c. 41.

[152] *Va. L. Reg.*, vol. 2, p. 219 (1896); vol. 2, p. 910 (1897); 93 Va. v (1897). They were applauded in *Va. L. Reg.*, vol. 2, pp. 310-12 (1896), and *Va. State Bar Ass'n Repts.*, vol. 9, pp. 39-43 (1896); J. H. Corbitt, "Admission to the Bar in Virginia," *Id.*, vol. 40, p. 286

8, 1897.[153] In 1910 the Virginia Board of Bar Examiners was created to relieve the court of this time-consuming responsibility.[154]

The year 1934 saw the first requirement of any academic study before taking the Virginia bar examination. William M. Lile, chairman of the committee on legal education, had recommended in 1901 that no one be allowed to practice law who had not studied law for at least two years.[155] This proposal, however, was not heeded at the time. This cudgel of professional betterment was taken up in 1927 by F. D. G. Ribble, Lile's successor at the University of Virginia and on the committee. In that year, the committee recommended that two years of college work and two years of law study be a prerequisite to taking the bar examination.[156] From then until 1934, the Virginia State Bar Association worked diligently to secure the passage of an act to that effect, undaunted by its initial failure.[157] The act of 1934 required every applicant either to have a degree from a law school which was approved by the American Bar Association or to have two years of undergraduate education.[158] Unsatisfied, the bar association got this act amended in 1936 to require two years of reading law in addition to the two years of college if the applicant did not have a law degree.[159]

At the close of World War II, the two proprietary Richmond night law schools came into prominence because of the demand of the returning armed forces for legal education in Virginia. The students of these schools were being allowed to take the Virginia state bar examination under the provision of the statute that was designed for law students who were reading law with a practicing attorney; the proprietors were licensed attorneys at law. The Virginia State Bar Association, in an effort to maintain the high quality of the Virginia bar, moved against these proprietary law schools and succeeded in

(1928).

[153] The examination was later published in *Va. L. Reg.*, vol. 2, p. 774 (1897); for other bar examinations, see the Bibliography, Part IV, below.

[154] Va. Acts 1910, p. 238, c. 152.

[155] W. M. Lile, "Report of the Committee on Legal Education," *Va. State Bar Ass'n Repts.*, vol. 14, pp. 62-67 (1901).

[156] *Id.*, vol. 39, pp. 72-76 (1927).

[157] *Id.*, vol. 40, pp. 61-68 (1928); vol. 41, pp. 161-66 (1929); vol. 43, pp. 73-74, 89-94 (1931); vol. 44, pp. 16, 48-54, 96-102 (1932); vol. 45, pp. 26-27, 44-46, 56-58 (1933); J. H. Corbitt, "Admission to the Bar in Virginia," *Id.*, vol. 40, p. 286 (1928).

[158] Va. Acts 1934, p. 411, c. 266.

[159] Va. Acts 1936, p. 79, c. 53; *Va. State Bar Ass'n Repts.*, vol. 46, pp. 45-52 (1934); vol. 47, pp. 41-42, 100-08 (1935); vol. 50, pp. 136-38 (1938).

amending the relevant statute.[160] As of 1952, if an applicant is not a graduate of an ABA-approved law school, he must have completed a three-year college course and have read law for three years with an attorney who has been approved by the Board of Bar Examiners and is also a full-time practitioner.[161] These new qualifications for the law reader's master removed the proprietary law schools from the Virginia legal scene. It is interesting to note that today Virginia is one of the very few remaining states to allow persons to qualify to practice after reading law without attending any law school.

The reintroduction of a strict bar examination in 1896 and the subsequent academic requirements for the practice of law were a very important part of the improvements in Virginia legal education in the twentieth century. There has been in Virginia no diploma privilege whereby graduates of law schools are exempt from the bar exam and admitted to practice on the sole basis of their law school diplomas. Such direct power of law schools over the practice of law invites in return direct or indirect public interference with the administration of the law schools, particularly with matters of curriculum and teaching methodology. It would be a great loss to legal education if the academic freedom of law faculties were thus diminished by people outside the law school. The present informal contacts between the bar and the schools is sufficient to keep the schools informed of the thinking of the practitioners and judges; more would be harmful.

The functions of the law school and the bar examiners are not directly the same. This is demonstrated by the fact that many subjects taught in law school are not included on the bar exam. The bar examination is directed toward assuring a minimum competency in the basics of law practice. The law schools strive to educate their students so that they will be of maximum competency. The law schools emphasize legal methodology, and a good law school examination is a learning experience. The bar exam, on the other hand, recognizes only the memorization of legal doctrine.

V. *Conclusion*

In general, by 1895 Virginia had recovered from the Civil War and from Reconstruction. More and more law students could afford to attend law school, and by that time studying law in a school was recognized to be vastly preferable to reading in a law office, even

[160] *Id.*, vol. 58, pp. 57-58 (1947); vol. 61, pp. 77-80 (1950); vol. 62, pp. 89-91 (1951); vol. 62, pp. 77-80 (1952).

[161] Va. Acts 1952, pp. 867-68, c. 553; Va. Code Ann., § 54-62 (Repl. Vol. 1978).

though it was much more expensive. The increase in students' fees made possible the hiring of more law professors. The economics of a larger law school was instantly felt. It was possible to enlarge the curriculum and the law libraries, and this was vital because the reach of the law was expanding dramatically. Before 1900 there was no need for such courses as tax law, labor law, antitrust law, administrative law, or workers' compensation; constitutional law was relatively unimportant, as was criminal procedure. The more persons there were on the law faculties, the greater was the opportunity for a teacher to develop an expertise in one or two of the multiplying branches of the law and to do research and writing.

The twentieth century has also seen a decrease in the number of part-time students and part-time teachers. The part-time student does not receive as good a legal education as he might because he does not have sufficient time to study his assignments outside of class. At the end of his workday, he cannot have as much energy as he did at the beginning of it; evening law classes are a burden even for the highly motivated student. Furthermore, the time for any contemplation of the law is not there.

In actual numbers, there are more part-time law instructors today than there were in 1895, but the percentage is less. In 1895 and earlier, it was necessary for many law professors to supplement their inadequate university salaries by practicing law on the side. Perhaps they thought of themselves as practitioners who were teaching on the side. In any case, they could not give their undivided attention to their schools, students, and research. After 1895 it became less necessary and then unnecessary for law teachers to practice law also, and most law schools gave up part-time teachers as soon as they could. After World War II, however, a new phenomenon occurred in the law schools. This was the hiring of great numbers of local lawyers to teach highly specialized and very technical law courses. Actually this had been done on a very limited scale since about 1870, but before about 1895, the part-time teachers had frequently taught basic, required courses. It is not good to have them teach the basic law curriculum because they are not generally available during the day for conferences with the individual students. Nor do they serve on faculty committees or aid in the administration of the law school.

In modern times, however, the part-time law teacher adds a unique dimension to legal education. He brings to the law school practical legal experience, but more importantly, he brings an expertise in his field of practice. Usually, it is a special knowledge not otherwise present in the faculty. These outside specialists provide great depth to the curriculum.

There can be, however, too much of a good thing. Legal education in Virginia is a part of the American picture and is affected very much by national thinking. Not everything new is good, nor is every change necessarily an improvement. Some twentieth-century trends should be followed only in moderation.

The growth in the law school student bodies is a problem as well as a blessing. As the law schools increase in size, the contact between the student and the teacher diminishes. The much-talked-about student-teacher ratio is a false measure. A law school does not divide the students up among the faculty so that each student sees only one teacher and each professor teaches only a certain small group of students. Each teacher should teach each student. In a law school of four hundred students and twenty teachers, the true figure is four hundred to one, not twenty to one.

A further problem in large schools is that where there is a large faculty, the teachers are so busy keeping in touch with each other that they have little time left for their students. The intellectual cross-fertilization of ideas within a law faculty is a good thing, and it keeps a teacher from becoming stale or jaded. But if it interferes too much with the student-teacher contact, then it defeats the primary purpose of the institution.

Another of the curses of bigness in a law school is the problem of administration. First, too much of the professor's time is taken up with administration; this keeps him away from teaching. Second, the professional administrators, deans, and others, can too easily lose touch with the students and even with the teaching purposes of their law school. It happens occasionally that academic decisions are more influenced by the money-raising functions of the dean's office than the pedagogical purposes of the law school. Not only can law school deans and university presidents lose contact with their students, but they can also get out of touch with their teaching faculties. So far no Virginia law school has come to this unhappy stage of development.

Many, many people have contributed to the new ideas and improvements of legal education over the centuries. The great professors have used and built upon the contributions of the lesser, and vice versa. Perhaps the celebrities could not have succeeded had not others prepared the way before them. The lesser figures have made and do make significant achievements, though public acclaim is awarded to others. Almost all of the Virginia law teachers have been useful and important as instructors.

Also many methods of legal education have been used over the years. Each has its strengths and its weaknesses. The study of the past is instructive and useful in showing both the good and the bad goals and methods. There has always been progress, slow but constant improvement, in law teaching goals and techniques.

BIBLIOGRAPHY

I. General

[Burks, Martin Parks]. "Suggestion to Young Lawyers on Studying Law." *Va. L. Reg.*, n.s., vol. 6, pp. 101-05 (1920).

> The author was a judge on the Virginia Supreme Court of Appeals and a former law professor and dean.

Cohen, Morris L[eo]. "Thomas Jefferson Recommends a Course of Law Study." *Univ. of Pa. Law Rev.*, vol. 119, pp. 823-44 (1971).

> This gives the text and comment on a letter from Jefferson dated Monticello, August 30, 1814. This letter is also printed in P. L. Ford, ed., *Writings of Thomas Jefferson*, vol. 9, pp. 480-85 (1898), and in *Southern Literary Messenger*, vol. 14, pp. 187-90 (1848).

Education and Practice. Richmond: Section on Education of Lawyers of the Virginia State Bar, 1993 to present.

> This is a newsletter for the members of the Section on Education of Lawyers of the Virginia State Bar.

Jefferson, Th[omas]. "The Study of the Law." *Southern Literary Messenger*, vol. 14, pp. 187-90 (1848).

> This is a letter dated Monticello, August 30, 1814. This letter is also printed in P. L. Ford, ed., *Writings of Thomas Jefferson*, vol. 9, pp. 480-85 (1898), and in *Univ. of Pa. Law Rev.*, vol. 119, pp. 823-44 (1971).

[Shield, Philip B.]. "Legal Education and Admission to the Bar." *Va. L. J.*, vol. 13, pp. 531-45 (1889).

[Wirt, William]. "Advice to a Law Student: A Letter of William Wirt in the Hampton L. Carson Collection of the Free Library of Philadelphia." ed. by Howell J. Heaney. *Am. Jour. Leg. Hist.*, vol. 2, pp. 256-58 (1958).

This letter is dated July 22, 1822.

Wirt, William. "Letter from Mr. Wirt to a Law Student." *Southern Literary Messenger*, vol. 1, pp. 33-36 (1834).

This letter is dated December 20, 1833.

II. Law Schools and Law Teachers

Aiken, Ada Holcombe. "Prof. J. P. Holcombe." *Alumni Bull. U. Va.*, 1st ser., vol. 3, pp. 83-86 (1897).

Baker, Liva. "George Wythe: First Professor of Law and Police at the College of William and Mary." *Virginia Cavalcade*, vol. 22, no. 4, pp. 31-35 (1973).

The Barrister. Charlottesville: University of Virginia School of Law, 1956 to present.

This law school annual publishes photographs of all law faculty and students. Also, there are notes of law school organizations and clubs.

Brock, Robert Kincaid. *Needham Law School, 1821-1842, Cumberland County Virginia, Founded and Conducted by Chancellor Creed Taylor*. Farmville: Herald, 1935. Rept. from the Farmville *Herald*, March 29, 1935, and *Today and Yesterday*. Farmville: Herald, 1935, pp. 219-24.

Bryson, W[illiam] Hamilton. *Legal Education in Virginia 1779-1979: A Biographical Approach*. Charlottesville: Univ. Press of Va., 1982.

This book includes biographical sketches of all Virginia law professors who were deceased before 1979, the bicentennial of Wythe's first law lectures; it lists the students at the antebellum proprietary law schools, which lists were complied by E. Lee Shepard.

Carrington, Paul D. "The Revolutionary Idea of University Legal Education," *Wm. & Mary Law Rev.*, vol. 31, pp. 527-74 (1990).

Catalogue of the Alumni of the Lexington Law School and of its

Successor, the Law Department of Washington and Lee University 1849-1881. Lynchburg: Virginian Steam Print., 1881.

> This book also contains a biographical sketch of John W. Brockenbrough and copies of the law school examinations for the year 1881.

Catalogue of the Officers and Alumni of Washington and Lee University, Lexington, Virginia, 1749-1888. Baltimore: Murphy, 1888.

> This lists all law alumni and faculty and the alumni of Brockenbrough's Lexington Law School, 1849-1866.

Cohen, Edwin S[amuel]. *A Lawyer's Life: Deep in the Heart of Taxes.* Arlington: Tax Analysts, 1994.

> This is the autobiography of a law professor at the University of Virginia.

The Colonial Lawyer. Williamsburg: Marshall-Wythe School of Law, 1967 to 1991, 20 vols.

> This publication was issued semiannually, originally, as a student in-house publication about the law school; it was suspended for several years and then reissued as a substantive legal periodical.

Crenshaw, Ollinger. *General Lee's College: The Rise and Growth of Washington and Lee University.* New York: Random House, 1969.

> Chapter 24: "The School of Law."

Crenshaw, Ollinger. "The School of Law, 1849-1949: A Century Revisited." *Wash. & Lee L. Rev.*, vol. 6, pp. 12-34 (1949).

Cullen, Charles T[homas]. *St. George Tucker and Law in Virginia, 1772-1804.* New York: Garland Pub., Inc., 1987.

Devitt, Fred B., Jr. "William & Mary: America's First Law School." *Wm. & Mary L. Rev.*, vol. 2, pp. 424-36 (1960).

Directory of Alumni of the Law School — The University of Virginia. Charlottesville: Univ. of Virginia Law School Alumni Assn., 1972.

This lists law faculty and law students from 1826 to 1972.

Dobie, Armistead M[ason]. "A Private Law School in Old Virginia." *Va. L. Rev.*, vol. 16, pp. 815-18 (1930).

Creed Taylor's law school was at Needham, Cumberland County.

Dworkin, Ira Bernard. "America's First Law School: The College of William and Mary." *A.B.A. Jour.*, vol. 37, pp. 348-50 (1951).

"Election of St. George Tucker as Professor of Law." *Wm. & Mary Quart.*, 1st ser., vol. 18, p. 220 (1910).

"The First Chair of Law and Police." *Wm. & Mary Quart.*, 1st ser., vol. 4, pp. 264-65 (1896).

Hughes, Robert M[orton]. "William and Mary, the First American Law School." *Wm. & Mary Quart.*, 2d ser., vol. 2, pp. 40-48 (1922).

Kean, R[obert] G[arlick] H[ill]. "Prof. John B. Minor's Jubilee." *Va. L. Reg.*, vol. 1, pp. 235-36 (1895).

Kemp, Verbon Eric, comp. *The Alumni Directory and Service Record of Washington and Lee University*. Lexington: The Alumni, Inc., 1926.

This gives lists all law alumni and faculty.

"Law School of H. St. G. Tucker in Winchester." *Wm. & Mary Quart.*, 2d ser., vol. 10, pp. 310-11 (1930).

This gives lists of law students from 1827 to 1829.

[Lile, William Minor]. "Changes in Virginia Law Schools." *Va. L. Reg.*, vol. 5, p. 199 (1899).

Lile, William Minor. "The Honor System." 2 *Am. Law Sch. Rev.*, vol. 2, pp. 456-64 (1910).

This describes the honor system as practiced in University of Virginia law school.

[Lile, William Minor]. "The Law Course at the University of Virginia — Action of the Board of Visitors." *Va. L. Reg.*, vol. 3, pp. 670-71 (1898).

Lile, William Minor. "The Law School of the University of Virginia." *Alumni Bull. U. Va.*, 3d ser., vol. 14, no. 3, pp. 86-99 (1921).

Lile, W[illiam] M[inor]. "Work of the Virginia Law Schools for 1897-8." *Va. L. Reg.*, vol. 4, pp. 199-200 (1898).

Mays, David J[ohn]. *The Pursuit of Excellence: A History of the University of Richmond Law School.* Richmond: Univ. of Richmond, 1970.

Meador, Daniel J[ohn]. "The Graduate Degree Program for Judges at the University of Virginia." *Judges' Journal,* vol. 22, no. 2, pp. 18-22, 54-56 (Spring 1983).

Meador, Daniel John. *Hardy Cross Dillard: Writings and Speeches.* Charlottesville: Univ. of Va. Law School Foundation, 1995.

Minor, Lucian. *Discourse on the Life and Character of the Late John A. G. Davis, Professor of Law in the University of Virginia.* Richmond: Shepherd & Colin, 1847.

Paxton, M[atthew] W[hite], Jr. *A Judge's School: The Story of John White Brockenbrough.* Lexington: Washington and Lee Univ., 1971.

"Re-arrangement of the Law Course at the University of Virginia." *Va. L. Reg.*, vol. 1, pp. 150-51 (1895).

Reed, Thomas W. "Professors at William and Mary College: Charles Morris." *Tyler's Qtly.*, vol. 4, pp. 130-33 (1923).

Morris was Professor of Law from 1859 to 1861.

Richmond Law. Richmond: The T. C. Williams School of Law, University of Richmond, Winter 1988 to present.

This periodical, published twice annually, is targeted at alumni, faculty, and other friends of the School of Law. Short articles, "class notes" (including changes in employment, professional recognition, births, marriages, and deaths),

"Notes from the Dean's Office," and the "Faculty Forum" are featured in each issue.

Ritchie, John. *The First Hundred Years: A Short History of the School of Law of the University of Virginia for the Period 1826-1926.* Charlottesville: Univ. Press of Va., 1978.

Sears, Otis Burgess. "An Early School of Law." *Alumni Bull. U. Va.*, n.s., vol. 4, pp. 324-28 (1904).

Creed Taylor's private law school was at his home in Needham, Cumberland County, Virginia.

Seiken, Jeff, and Liz Marshall. "Tragedy on the Lawn: The Murder of Professor John A. G. Davis." *Va. Cavalcade*, vol. 34, no. 1, pp. 40-47 (Summer 1984).

Davis taught law at the University of Virginia from 1830 to 1840.

Shepard, E[dwin] Lee. "Learning the Law: Private Law Schools in Antebellum Virginia." *Va. Cavalcade*, vol. 37, no. 4, pp. 148-57 (Spring 1988).

Sokol, Ronald P. "In Forma Pauperis Appeals: the University of Virginia Experiment with a Neglected Asset." *J. Legal Ed.*, vol. 18, pp. 96-100 (1965).

Swindler, William F[inley], "William and Mary Marks Bicentennial of its First Chair of Law." *A.B.A. Jour.*, vol. 64, pp. 1872-77 (1978).

Taylor, Creed. *Journal of the Law School and of the Moot Court Attached to It; at Needham, in Virginia: with an Appendix, Comprising a Variety of Precedents Adapted to the Proceedings of the Courts, Agreeably to the Revised Code, of 1819; and of the Pleadings in Law and Equity, with Complete Records Thereof.* Vol. 1. Richmond: J. & G. Cochran, 1822; rept. Buffalo, N.Y.: Dennis & Co., 1955.

Moots were at the trial court level; this book includes legal forms; note that only one volume was ever published.

Trimble, Marsha. "Attending the Lectures of Law: A Perspective on the 19th-Century Law School Experience." *UVA Lawyer*, vol. 20, No. 2, pp. 34-47 (1996).

UVA Lawyer. Charlottesville: Univ. of Va. Law School Alumni Ass'n, 1987 to present.

> This is a newsletter published by and for the law alumni of the University of Virginia. It contains articles as well as news of the law school. It was first published three times a year; it is now issued semiannually.

Virginia Law School Report. Charlottesville: Univ. of Va. School of Law, 1977 to present.

> This is a publication for the law alumni of the University of Virginia. It was first published three times a year; it is now issued semiannually.

Virginia Law Weekly. Charlottesville: University of Virginia School of Law, May 27, 1948, to present.

> This newspaper is a weekly publication by and for the law students of the University of Virginia. It is not issued during holidays and examinations periods.

Walker, George K. "Third-Year Practice Rules in Virginia: Notes for the Practitioner." *Univ. of Richmond L. Rev.*, vol. 11, pp. 69-85 (1976).

The William & Mary Lawyer: the Annual Report of the Marshall Wythe School of Law. Williamsburg: Marshall-Wythe School of Law, 1987 to present.

> This publication is the annual report of the law alumni association of the College of William and Mary.

[Wilson, Thomas Carlyle, Jr.]. *Washington and Lee University Alumni Directory 1749-1949*. Lexington, Va.: Washington and Lee Univ., 1949.

> This lists all law alumni including those of Brockenbrough's law school.

"Work of the Virginia Law Schools for 1896-97." *Va. L. Reg.*, vol. 3, pp. 230-31 (1897).

III. Law Lectures and Books for Law Students

[Baldwin, Briscoe Gerard]. *Introductory Lecture Delivered by General Briscoe G. Baldwin Before His Law School in Staunton.* Staunton: K. Harper, 1831.

Brockenbrough, John W[hite]. *Introductory Address to the Law Class of Lexington Delivered in the Franklin Hall, October 31, 1849.* Lexington, Va.: Gazette Office, 1849; rept. from the *Valley Star*, Nov. 22, 1849.

Brockenbrough, John W[hite]. *Introductory Lecture Delivered in the Franklin Hall, Lexington, Va.* Richmond: Ritchie, Dunnavant and Co., 1858.

Bryson, W[illiam] Hamilton, ed. *Essays on Legal Education in Nineteenth Century Virginia.* Buffalo, N.Y.: William S. Hein & Co., Inc., 1998.

> Creed Taylor, Introductory Lecture (1822)
> Henry St. George Tucker, "Introductory Lecture" (1826)
> Robert M. T. Hunter Letter to John T. Lomax (1829)
> John Tayloe Lomax Letter to R. M. T. Hunter (1829)
> Henry St. George Tucker Letters to Briscoe G. Baldwin (1831)
> Briscoe Gerard Baldwin, "Introductory Lecture" (1831)
> John Tayloe Lomax, "Circular" (1831)
> "The Law School of Judge Lomax" (1832)
> N. B. Tucker, "Lecture on the Study of the Law" (1834)
> N. B. Tucker, "Valedictory Lecture" (1835)
> Benjamin W. Leigh Letter to T. R. Johnston (1836)
> Lucas Powell Thompson, "Introductory Lecture" (1839)
> Henry St. George Tucker, "Introductory Lecture" (1841)
> John Barbee Minor Letter to William Wirt Henry (1850)
> John White Brockenbrough, "Introductory Lecture" (1858)
> Daniel Bedinger Lucas Letter to William Lucas (1857)
> Stephen Osborne Southall, "Inaugural Address" (1867)
> William Green, "Address" (1870)

Burks, Martin P[arks]. *Abstract of Lectures on Conveyancing: Prepared for the Law Class of Washington and Lee University.* Lexington, Va.: W. C. Stuart, 1906.

Burks, Martin P[arks]. *Criminal Procedure: Notes to Beale's Criminal Pleading and Practice.* N.p., 1911.

Burks, Martin P[arks]. *Notes on Employers' Liability Laws.* Lexington, Va.: Boley Book Store, n.d.

[Burks, Martin Parks]. *Notes on Equity Procedure: Prepared for the Washington and Lee University Law Class.* N.p., n.d.

Burks, Martin P[arks]. *Notes on Pleading and Practice: Printed for the Use of Students.* Richmond: Chas. E. Picot, 1905.

Burks, Martin P[arks]. *Parol Evidence Rule.* Charlottesville: The Michie Co., n.d.

The Code of Virginia (Pleading and Practice) An Abridgment of the Virginia Code of 1924 for the Student of Virginia Pleading and Practice. Charlottesville: The Michie Co., 1927.

> This is a reprint of pages 1505 to 1821 of the *Code of Virginia* with a new title page and the Tax Bill added as an appendix.

Dabney, W[alter] D[avis]. *Outlines of Federal Jurisdiction and Law Procedure, Prepared as a Basis of Lectures to Law Students at the University of Virginia.* [Charlottesville]: Geo. W. Olivier, 1897.

Davis, John Anthony Gardner. *An Exposition of the Principles Which Distinguish Estates Tail from Other Limitations.* Charlottesville: Tompkins & Noel, 1837.

Doubles, M[alcolm] Ray, and Frances Farmer. *Manual of Legal Bibliography.* Charlottesville: The Michie Casebook Co., 1947.

Gilmore, James Houston. *Notes of a Course of Lectures on Mercantile Law.* Charlottesville: Blakey, 1891.

Gilmore, James H[ouston]. *Notes on Adams' Equity, in a Course of Lectures.* Charlottesville: Blakey, 1891.

[Graves, Charles Alfred]. *Answers to Questions on Evidence.* N.p., n.d., 42 p.

Graves, Charles A[lfred]. *Common Law Pleading.* Charlottesville:

INTRODUCTORY ADDRESS

TO THE LAW CLASS OF LEXINGTON

DELIVERED IN THE

FRANKLIN HALL;

OCTOBER 31, 1849

BY

JUDGE JOHN W. BROCKENBROUGH

LEXINGTON:

PRINTED AT THE "GAZETTE OFFICE."

1849

The Michie Co., 1915.

Graves, Charles A[lfred]. *Notes on Pleading: With References to Andrews' Stephen on Pleading.* Richmond: Whittet & Shepperson, 1900; Richmond: Whittet & Shepperson, 1905.

Graves, Charles A[lfred]. *Notes on Torts.* N.p., n.d., 16 p.; Charlottesville: The Michie Co., n.d., 31 p.

Graves, C[harles] A[lfred]. *Notes to Clark on Contracts.* N.p., n.d., 44 p.; Charlottesville: The Michie Co., 1910, 43 p.; Richmond: Whittet & Shepperson, n.d., 43 p.

Graves, Charles A[lfred]. *Questions on Evidence.* Charlottesville: The Michie Co., 1907; Charlottesville: The Michie Co., 1916.

Graves, Charles A[lfred]. *Questions on Pleading and Practice.* Richmond: Whittet & Shepperson, 1900; Richmond: Chas. E. Picot, 1905; Charlottesville: The Michie Co., 1914.

Graves, Charles A[lfred]. *Summary of the Law of Real Property for the Use of Students in Connection with the Second Book of Blackstone's Commentaries.* Lexington, Va.: Press of Rockbridge County News, 1894.

Green, William. *Address to the Law Class of Richmond College.* Richmond: Fergusson & Rady, 1870; rept. in David J. Mays. *The Pursuit of Excellence.* Richmond: Univ. of Richmond, 1970.

Keith, Thomas Randolph, comp. *Law Examinations, Embracing Examination Papers from the Year 1869 to 1894.* 4th ed., Charlottesville: Anderson Bros., 1894.

Lile, W[illiam] M[inor]. *Lectures on Equity Pleading and Practice: with Forms and the New Federal Equity Rules Prepared for the Use of the Students of the Law School of the University of Virginia.* [Charlottesville]: George W. Olivier, 1916; 2d ed., [Charlottesville]: George W. Olivier, 1922; 3d ed. by Edwin B. Meade, Charlottesville: The Michie Co., 1952.

The title varies slightly with the different editions.

Lile, W[illiam] M[inor]. *Notes of Lectures on Private Corporations in Connection with Clark on Corporations.* N.p., 1921, 46 p.

Lile, W[illiam] M[inor]. *Notes on Bigelow's Bills, Notes and Cheques (2d ed.) Prepared for the Use of the Students of the Law School of the University of Virginia.* N.p., 1914, 71 p.; 2d ed., n.p., 1918, 91 p.; 3d ed., [Charlottesville]: G. W. Olivier, 1922.

Lile, W[illiam] M[inor]. *Notes on Equity Jurisprudence to Accompany Merwin's Equity Prepared for the Use of the Students of the Law School of the University of Virginia.* N.p., 1909, 137 p.; N.p., 1913, 190 p.; [Charlottesville]: Anderson Brothers, 1921, 314 p.; [Charlottesville]: G. W. Olivier, 1922.

The title varies slightly with the different editions.

Lile, W[illia]m M[inor]. *Notes on Equity Pleading and Practice.* N.p., n.d., 28 p.

This pamphlet was written to accompany lectures based on J. B. Minor's *Institutes*, vol. 4.

Lile, W[illiam] M[inor]. *Notes on Municipal Corporations Prepared for the Use of the Students in the Law Department of the University of Virginia.* Richmond: Whittet & Shepperson, 1900; 2d ed., Richmond: Whittet & Shepperson, 1905; 3d ed., Charlottesville: The Michie Co., 1910; "3d ed.", [Charlottesville]: G. W. Olivier, 1922.

Lile, W[illiam] M[inor]. *Notes on Private Corporations Prepared for the Use of the Students in the Law Department of the University of Virginia.* Richmond: Whittet & Shepperson, 1900.

Lile, W[illiam] M[inor]. *Notes on Statutes. For Use of the Students of the Law School of the University of Virginia.* N.p., 1911.

Lile, W[illiam] M[inor]. *Notes to Volume I of Minor's Institutes and on Corporations Prepared for the Use of the Law Class of the University of Virginia.* Lynchburg: J. P. Bell Co., 1894; Charlottesville: The Michie Co., 1899.

Lile, William Minor. *Notes to Volume III, Minor's Institutes. Prepared for the Use of the Students of the Junior Law Class at the University of Virginia.* Charlottesville: The Michie Co., 1901, 67 p.; Charlottesville: Charlottesville Printing Co., Old Dominion Pr., n.d., 84 p.

Lile, W[illiam] M[inor]. *Some Practical Hints for the Beginner in the Making of a Brief.* N.p., 1911, 18 p.; N.p., 1914; N.p., 1915, 40 p. *Study of Cases: Head-Noting, Supplementary to Wambaugh's Study of Cases: Some Practical Hints for the Beginner in the Making of a Brief.* Charlottesville: Surber-Arundale Co., 1921, 52 p.; "3d ed.", Charlottesville: Va. Law Rev. Ass'n, 1927, 53 p.

Long, Joseph R[agland]. *Notes of Lectures Introductory to the Study of Law.* Charlottesville: The Michie Co., 1910.

Long, Joseph R[agland]. *Notes of Lectures on the Law of Domestic Relations.* Lynchburg: J. P. Bell, 1903.

Long, Joseph R[agland]. *Notes of Lectures on the Law of Wills and Administrations.* Charlottesville: The Michie Co., 1910.

Long, Joseph R[agland]. *Outline of the Jurisdiction and Procedure of the Federal Courts.* Charlottesville: The Michie Co., 1910; 2d ed., Charlottesville: The Michie Co., 1911; 3d ed., Chicago: Callaghan and Co., 1917.

Minor, John B[arbee]. *Abstract of Vattel's International Law, Federalist, and Constitution of the United States.* Charlottesville: Anderson Bros., 1894.

Minor, John B[arbee]. *A Synopsis of the Law of Crimes and Punishments in Virginia.* Philadelphia: William S. Young, 1858; 2d ed., Richmond: Hazlewood, 1869.

Minor, R[aleigh] C[olston]. *Analytical Abstract of Greenleaf on Evidence and Prof. Gilmore's Notes on Greenleaf.* Charlottesville: Anderson Bros., 1894.

Minor, Raleigh Colston. *Lecture Introductory to the Study of Common Law Pleading.* N.p., n.d.; 2d ed., Charlottesville: Anderson Bros., 1898.

Notes on Domestic Relations for the Use of Students in the Law School of Washington and Lee University. N.p., n.d.

[*Notes on*] *Negotiable Paper.* N.p., n.d., 142 p.

Other topics in this 142-page book are "Corporations" and

"Conflict of Laws." It is in the same format as *Notes on Domestic Relations* and was, no doubt, written for the use of the law students at Washington and Lee University. The precise title given here is speculative.

An Outline of the Principal Proceedings in an Action. Printed for the Use of the Law Class of Richmond College. N.p., n.d.

Practice Cases in Criminal Procedure. N.p., n.d. 22 p.

[Sheffey, Hugh White]. *Washington and Lee University, June 1st, 1878: Head Notes of Lecture Delivered by Hugh W. Sheffey, Lecturer on Wills and Probate Practice.* N.p., n.d. 8 p.

This was a farewell lecture.

Simonton, Charles H[enry]. *The Federal Courts: Their Organization, Jurisdiction and Procedure. Lectures before the Richmond Law School, Richmond College, Virginia.* Richmond: B. F. Johnson, 1896. 120 p.

Simonton (1829-1904) was a United States Circuit Judge.

Southall, Stephen O[sborne]. *Inaugural Address Delivered to the Law Class of the University of Virginia.* Richmond: Enquirer, 1867; Charlottesville: Chronicle Steam Printing House, 1883.

The date of this lecture was October 4, 1866.

[Thompson, Lucas Powell]. *Introductory Lecture, Delivered by Judge Lucas P. Thompson, Before His Law School in Staunton, December 3, 1839.* Staunton: Kenton Harper, 1839.

Tucker, Henry St. George. *Commentaries on the Laws of Virginia, Comprising the Substance of a Course of Lectures Delivered to the Winchester Law School.* Winchester: The Winchester Virginian, 1831, 2 vols.; 2d ed., Winchester: The Republican, 1836, 1837, 2 vols.; 3d ed., Richmond: Colin & Shepherd, 1846, 2 vols.

Tucker, Henry St. George. *A Few Lectures on Natural Law.* Charlottesville: James Alexander, 1844.

Tucker, Henry St. George. *Introductory Lecture Delivered by the*

Professor of Law in the University of Virginia, at the Opening of the Law School in September, 1841. Charlottesville: Magruder & Noel, 1841.

Tucker, Henry St. George. *Lectures on Constitutional Law for the Use of the Law Class at the University of Virginia.* Richmond: Shepherd and Colin, 1843.

Tucker, Henry St. George. *Lectures on Government.* Charlottesville: J. Alexander, 1844.

[Tucker, Henry St. George]. *Notes on Blackstone's Commentaries for the Use of Students.* Winchester: Samuel H. Davis, 1826.

[Tucker, John Randolph]. *Appendix to Notes on Domestic Relations.* N.p., n.d.

[Tucker, John Randolph]. *Doctrine of Notice.* N.p., n.d.

[Tucker, John Randolph]. *Frauds.* N.p., n.d.

[Tucker, John Randolph]. *Married Women's Act of Virginia.* N.p., n.d.

[Tucker, John Randolph]. *Notes and References on Woolsey's International Law.* N.p., n.d.

Tucker, J[ohn] R[andolph]. *Notes of Equity Pleadings.* N.p., n.d.

[Tucker, John Randolph]. *Notes of Lectures on Corporation.* N.p., n.d.

Tucker, J[ohn] R[andolph]. *Notes of Lectures on Political Science.* N.p., n.d.

[Tucker, John Randolph]. *Notes on Insurance.* N.p., n.d.

Tucker, J[ohn] R[andolph]. *Notes on Lectures on Natural Law.* N.p., n.d.

INAUGURAL ADDRESS,

DELIVERED TO

THE LAW CLASS

OF THE

University of Virginia,

BY

STEPHEN O. SOUTHALL,

PROFESSOR IN THE DEPARTMENT OF EQUITY, MERCANTILE, INTERNATIONAL AND CONSTITUTIONAL LAW AND GOVERNMENT,

IN THE

SCHOOL OF LAW

IN THE

UNIVERSITY OF VIRGINIA.

OCTOBER 4TH, 1866.

RICHMOND:
"ENQUIRER" PRINT.
1867.

[Tucker, John Randolph]. *Notes on Negotiable Paper*. N.p., n.d.

[Tucker, John Randolph]. *Notes on Schouler's Domestic Relations*. N.p., n.d.

Tucker, J[ohn] R[andolph]. *Woolsey on International Law. Notes of Lectures*. N.p., n.d.

[Tucker, Nathaniel Beverley]. *A Lecture on the Study of the Law; Being an Introduction to a Course of Lectures on That Subject, in the College of William and Mary*. Richmond: White, 1834; rept. in *Southern Literary Messenger*, vol. 1, pp. 145-54 (1834); rept. in Michael H. Hoeflich, ed. *The Gladsome Light of Jurisprudence*. Westport, Conn.: Greenwood Press, 1988, pp. 118-33.

[Tucker, Nathaniel Beverley]. "Professor Beverley Tucker's Valedictory Address to His Class." *Southern Literary Messenger*, vol. 1, pp. 597-602 (1835).

IV. **Bar Examinations**

A. **General**

"Bar Examinations in Virginia." *Va. L. Reg.*, vol. 3, pp. 152-53 (1897).

"Examination for Admission to the Bar in Virginia — The Past — The Future." *Va. L. Reg.*, vol. 2, pp. 310-12 (1896).

Hughes, Robert Morton. "The Historical Evolution of the Board of Law Examiners and Its Influence on Legal Education." *Reports of the American Bar Association*, vol. 39, pp. 846-63 (1914).

Hylton, J[oseph] Gordon. "The Written Bar Examination and the Development of the Modern Legal Profession in Virginia." *Richmond Law*, vol. 4, no. 2, pp. 4-7 (Summer, 1991).

"Rules and Regulations for Licensing Persons to Practice Law." *Virginia Reports*, vol. 93, p. v-vi (1897); *Va. L. Reg.*, vol. 2, pp. 910-11 (1897).

"Rules and Regulations Prescribed by the Supreme Court of

LECTURES

ON

CONSTITUTIONAL LAW,

FOR THE USE OF THE

LAW CLASS

AT THE

UNIVERSITY OF VIRGINIA.

BY HENRY ST. GEORGE TUCKER,

PROFESSOR.

RICHMOND:
PRINTED BY SHEPHERD AND COLIN.

1843.

Appeals of Virginia for Licensing Persons to Practice Law." *Va. L. Reg.*, vol. 2, pp. 219-20 (1896).

B. Examination Questions and Admittees

"Questions Propounded by the Court of Appeals to Applicants for License to Practice Law, January 8, 1897." *Va. L. Reg.*, vol. 2, pp. 774-77 (1897).

"The Recent Bar Examination at Wytheville." *Va. L. Reg.*, vol. 3, pp. 315-17 (1897).

"The Bar Examination at Staunton." *Va. L. Reg.*, vol. 3, pp. 465-68 (1897).

"Questions Propounded to Applicants for License to Practice Law, on the Examination Held July 1, 1898, at Wytheville, Va." *Va. L. Reg.*, vol. 4, pp. 270-76 (1898).

"The Bar Examination at Staunton." *Va. L. Reg.*, vol. 4, pp. 404-07 (1898).

"Questions Propounded on the Bar Examination at Richmond, January 6, 1899." *Va. L. Reg.*, vol. 4, pp. 707-09 (1899).

"Questions Propounded by the Virginia Court of Appeals to Applicants for License to Practice Law, July 7, 1899." *Va. L. Reg.*, vol. 5, pp. 273-77 (1899).

"Questions Propounded by the Supreme Court of Appeals of Virginia to Applicants for Admission to the Bar, September 8, 1899." *Va. L. Reg.*, vol. 5, pp. 422-24 (1899).

"Questions Propounded by the Court of Appeals, on the Bar Examination, at Richmond, January 12, 1900." *Va. L. Reg.*, vol. 5, pp. 723-27 (1900).

"The Bar Examination at Wytheville [July 6, 1900]." *Va. L. Reg.*, vol. 6, pp. 198-202 (1900).

"Questions Propounded to Candidates for Admission to the Bar at Staunton, September 7, 1900." *Va. L. Reg.*, vol. 6, pp. 431-33 (1900).

"The Recent Bar Examination at Richmond — Questions Propounded." *Va. L. Reg.*, vol. 6, pp. 717-19 (1901).

> This examination was criticized and defended in *Va. L. Reg.*, vol. 6, pp. 788-89, 797 (1901).

"Questions Propounded at the Bar Examination Held at Wytheville, Va., July 5, 1901." *Va. L. Reg.*, vol. 7, pp. 229-32 (1901).

> This examination was criticized in *Va. L. Reg.*, vol. 7, pp. 216-17 (1901).

"Questions Propounded at the Staunton Bar Examination." *Va. L. Reg.*, vol. 7, pp. 446-49 (1901).

"Questions Propounded on the Bar Examination at Richmond, January 10, 1902." *Va. L. Reg.*, vol. 7, pp. 662-65 (1902).

"Questions Propounded to Applicants for License to Practice Law at Bar Examination Held at Wytheville, on Tuesday, June 24, 1392 [sic]." *Va. L. Reg.*, vol. 8, pp. 228-32 (1902).

"Questions Propounded by the Court of Appeals on the Bar Examination at Richmond, January, 1903." *Va. L. Reg.*, vol. 8, pp. 700-03 (1903).

"Questions Propounded by the Court of Appeals on the Bar Examination at Wytheville, June, 1903." *Va. L. Reg.*, vol. 9, pp. 259-62 (1903).

"Questions Propounded at the Examination of Candidates for Admission to the Bar, Held by the Supreme Court of Appeals of Virginia at Richmond, Virginia, January 8, 1904." *Va. L. Reg.*, vol. 9, pp. 836-39 (1904).

"Bar Examination. Wytheville, Va., June 24, 1904." *Va. L. Reg.*, vol. 10, pp. 275-80 (1904).

"State Bar Examination, Richmond, Va., January 6, 1905." *Va. L. Reg.*, vol. 10, pp. 947-50 (1905).

"Bar Examination, Wytheville, Virginia, June 24, 1905." *Va. L. Reg.*, vol. 11, pp. 346-51 (1905).

"Bar Examination. Richmond, Virginia, January 12th, 1906." *Va. L. Reg.*, vol. 11, pp. 853-56 (1906).

"Bar Examination. Wytheville, Virginia, June 22, 1906." *Va. L. Reg.*, vol. 12, pp. 265-69 (1906).

"Bar Examination. Richmond, Virginia, January 11, 1907." *Va. L. Reg.*, vol. 12, pp. 841-45 (1907).

"Bar Examination. Wytheville, Virginia, June 21, 1907." *Va. L. Reg.*, vol. 13, pp. 328-32 (1907).

"Bar Examination. Richmond, Virginia, November 15, 1907." *Va. L. Reg.*, vol. 13, pp. 650-54 (1907).

"Bar Examination. Wytheville, Virginia, June 19, 1908." *Va. L. Reg.*, vol. 14, pp. 231-35 (1908).

"Bar Examination. Richmond, Virginia, November 13, 1908." *Va. L. Reg.*, vol. 14, pp. 651-53 (1908).

"Bar Examination. Wytheville, Virginia, June 18, 1909." *Va. L. Reg.*, vol. 15, pp. 246-52 (1909).

> This examination was defended in *Va. L. Reg.*, vol. 15, pp. 323-24 (1909).

"Bar Examination. Richmond, Virginia, November 12, 1909." *Va. L. Reg.*, vol. 15, pp. 648-53 (1909).

"Bar Examination. Roanoke, Virginia, June 23rd, 1910." *Va. L. Reg.*, vol. 16, pp. 232-38 (1910).

"Virginia Board of Law Examiners, Richmond, Va., November 2, 1910." *Va. L. Reg.*, vol. 16, pp. 630-33 (1910).

"Virginia Board of Law Examiners, Roanoke, Va., June 28, 1911." *Va. L. Reg.*, vol. 17, pp. 329-33 (1911).

"State Bar Examination and Successful Applicants. Virginia Board of Law Examiners. Richmond, Va., November 1, 1911." *Va. L. Reg.*, vol. 17, pp. 651-55 (1911).

"Virginia Board of Law Examiners, Roanoke, Va., June 26, 1912." *Va. L. Reg.*, vol. 18, pp. 310-14 (1912).

> This examination was criticized in *Va. L. Reg.*, vol. 18, pp. 463-65 (1912), and defended in *Va. L. Reg.*, vol. 18, pp. 384-86, 394-96, 465-66 (1912).

"Virginia Board of Law Examiners, Richmond, Va., November 6, 1912." *Va. L. Reg.*, vol. 18, pp. 635-38 (1912).

"Virginia Board of Law Examiners, Richmond, Va., January 15, 1913." *Va. L. Reg.*, vol. 18, pp. 793-96 (1913).

> This examination was criticized in *Va. L. Reg.*, vol. 18, pp. 859-61 (1913).

"Virginia Board of Law Examiners, Roanoke, Va., June 25th, 1913." *Va. L. Reg.*, vol. 19, pp. 312-18 (1913).

> This examination was criticized in *Va. L. Reg.*, vol. 19, pp. 301-02 (1913).

"Virginia Board of Law Examiners. Richmond, Va., November 5, 1913." *Va. L. Reg.*, vol. 19, pp. 635-38 (1913).

"Virginia Board of Law Examiners, Roanoke, Va., June 24, 1914." *Va. L. Reg.*, vol. 20, pp. 313-18 (1914).

"Virginia Board of Law Examiners, Richmond, Va., December 9, 1914." *Va. L. Reg.*, vol. 20, pp. 713-18 (1915).

"Virginia Board of Law Examiners, Roanoke, Va., June 23-24, 1915." *Va. L. Reg.*, n.s., vol. 1, pp. 311-18 (1915).

"Virginia Board of Law Examiners, Roanoke, Va., June 27-28, 1916." *Va. L. Reg.*, n.s., vol. 2, pp. 310-16 (1916).

"Bar Examination, Richmond, Va., December 12-13, 1916." *Va. L. Reg.*, n.s., vol. 3, pp. 300-08 (1917).

[Bar Examination] "Roanoke, Va., June 26-27, 1917." *Va. L. Reg.*, n.s., vol. 3, pp. 308-18 (1917).

"Questions on Bar Examination Held at Roanoke, Va., June 28-29, 1921." *Va. L. Reg.*, n.s., vol. 7, pp. 313-19 (1921).

"Questions on Bar Examination Held at Richmond, Va., Dec. 13-14, 1921." *Va. L. Reg.*, n.s., vol. 7, pp, 868-77 (1922).

Boyd, T[homas] Munford, Ellsworth Wiltshire, and T. Nelson Parker, edd. *Virginia Bar Examinations Annotated.* Richmond: Appeals Press, Inc., 1925. 294 pp.

> This book reprints by subject matter bar examination questions from 1910 to 1925. There is a supplement containing questions from 1925 to 1930. The annotations, which are only to the questions from 1917 to 1925, give the sources of the questions.

ACADEMIC LAW LIBRARIES

Marsha Trimble

I. *Introduction*

THE HISTORY of Virginia's academic law libraries is inextricably bound with the founding and growth of its law schools. For many years the personalities and reputations of the men who taught law courses were critical to the success of the programs. Through the nineteenth century Virginia's law professors employed the lecture and textbook methods of instruction, and independent legal research scarcely figured into any program. In this respect Virginia's schools were typical.

Unlike several major libraries in other states, however, Virginia's law school libraries, were not beneficiaries of significant private book collections. From early colonial times, a number of Virginia's eminent bibliophiles collected legal treatises, reports, and rare legislative documents from American and European sources.[1] In his discussion of early colonists' reading interests, Louis B. Wright wrote:

> The preponderance of lawbooks, even in the smaller collections, suggests the litigiousness which accompanied the struggle for landed possessions in the colony. . . .But farther-reaching than the mere present usefulness of legal works was the tradition of law which they helped fix in Virginia.[2]

It is not surprising that the state had the nation's first university-affiliated course in law and some of its most prominent early law teachers and lawyers. Thomas Jefferson, who was responsible for establishing two of the law schools and providing the nexus of the library at the University of Virginia, was also Virginia's most celebrated private book collector with a special interest in law. Despite the influence some of these men had on legal education, their personal collections of law books do not figure into this history. Virginia did not have the tradition of creating public libraries that Pennsylvania and

---

[1] For descriptions of these collections, see L. B. Wright, *The First Gentlemen of Virginia: Intellectual Qualities of the Early Colonial Ruling Class*, pp. 117-154 (1964); R. B. Davis, *Intellectual Life in Jefferson's Virginia 1790-1830*, pp. 71-118 (1972); "Private Law Libraries Before 1776," *infra*; "Private Law Libraries After 1776," *infra*.

[2] Wright, p. 132.

the New England states had. And many families fell into economic difficulties. For these and other reasons, few of the early private collections became part of the academic law libraries as they did so often in the Northeast.[3] The collections examined here were largely built by successions of professors, librarians, and alumni with the aid of institutional and private funds.

Toward the close of the nineteenth century, the creation of the American Bar Association, the development of a radical new approach to legal education, and the explosive growth of legal publishing reverberated through the nation's law schools and their libraries. Virginia's schools reacted more slowly than some others but were nonetheless dramatically affected by these changes. The state's academic law libraries have significantly benefitted from the standards of professional organizations and the leadership of the nation's major law libraries.

This essay will explore the development of the libraries that began in the eighteenth century at the College of William and Mary,[4] and in the nineteenth century at the University of Virginia, Washington and Lee University, and the University of Richmond. In the late twentieth century new law schools opened at George Mason University and Regent University, and the creation and development of their libraries will be briefly described.

II. *Law Programs Created by Jefferson*

A. *The College of William and Mary*

In 1779 Virginia's Governor Thomas Jefferson persuaded the College of William and Mary to create the first American professorship in law. He had in mind his own law teacher, George Wythe, whom the College appointed to the post. Jefferson had studied law for several years under Wythe's direction and had access to Wythe's personal library. His studies began with the daunting primer, Coke's *Institutes*. None of Wythe's reading lists have survived, but in later years Jefferson drew up several lists of recommended reading for would-be lawyers, and those lists suggest the extensiveness of his own background in law, equity, history and political theory. Unlike most other law students of his day, Jefferson undertook on his own a close reading and analysis of English case law. He explained the value of this research to a young friend: "In reading the reporters, enter in a

[3] Davis, pp. 86-89, 96, 108.

[4] For further information, see "William and Mary Law Library," *infra*.

common-place book every case of value, condensed into the narrowest compass possible which will admit of presenting distinctly the principles of the case. This operation is doubly useful, inasmuch as it obliges the student to seek out the pith of the case, and habituates him to a condensation of thought. . . ."[5]

The curriculum established by Wythe at William and Mary and adopted later at the University of Virginia was a considerably compressed version of Jefferson's experience. The majority of nineteenth century law students had marginal educational backgrounds, although at William and Mary a bachelor of arts degree was a prerequisite to law. More importantly, a high percentage of law students were unable or unwilling to devote more than one year to their legal training. Wythe chose as his basic text, Blackstone's *Commentaries on the Laws of England,* a modern and far more accessible introduction to English common law than Coke's *Institutes.* The *Commentaries,* or in later years, American editions of the work, were taught to beginning law students in every Virginia law school until the end of the nineteenth century. Wythe furthermore encouraged students to read widely from his law library. He required them to argue cases in a moot court and draft bills in a moot legislature, thus introducing practical legal training in the university setting. Wythe's impact on early American law and politics was immeasurable. Besides Jefferson, his students included, Henry Clay, John Marshall, James Monroe, and St. George Tucker.[6]

Wythe left the William and Mary law professorship in 1790 and was succeeded by St. George Tucker. Tucker's program was similar to his teacher's although he omitted the practical instruction. So dependent upon his own law library was Tucker that he chose to deliver his lectures in his home, despite complaints from college authorities. He tried carrying his most important legal texts to the college for a few terms, but gave up when he found that he could not predict what a given lecture and discussion might prompt him to consult. Apparently the college had few or no law books at the time. Having his own library, Tucker probably did not urge the administration to make that investment. St. George Tucker left an invaluable legacy to legal education in his own edition of Blackstone's *Com-*

[5] M. L. Cohen, "Commentary: Thomas Jefferson Recommends a Course of Law Study," *University of Pennsylvania L. Rev.*, vol. 119, p. 842 (1971); D. Malone, *Jefferson the Virginian*, pp. 68-74 (1948).

[6] P. D. Carrington, "The Revolutionary Idea of University Legal Education," *William and Mary L. Rev.*, vol. 31, pp. 527, 535-538 (1990); Davis, p. 94. For a biographical sketch of Wythe and other law professors discussed in this article, see W. H. Bryson, *Legal Education in Va.* (1982).

mentaries and in his five descendants who taught at one or more of Virginia's law schools over the next hundred years. But the value he placed on having an adequate law library at hand for teaching was apparently not shared by his successors.[7]

Seven professors, including Nathaniel Beverley Tucker, followed Wythe and St. George Tucker at William and Mary. The constant change in faculty and shortage of funds surely had a deleterious effect on the development of a law library, but in the early 1820s the collection started to grow and had reached three hundred volumes by 1829.[8] During the 1850s when George Scarburgh was law professor, the college catalog announced that "the Law Library, belonging to the College, is kept in the law lecture room, and the student is allowed constant access to it."[9] In February 1859, however, the college building was destroyed by fire, and those books were lost. Law classes continued for two more years, until the beginning of the Civil War caused the college to close its doors.[10]

B. *THE UNIVERSITY OF VIRGINIA*

Forty years after the William and Mary law professorship had been established Jefferson was working patiently and skillfully behind the scenes to persuade the General Assembly to approve a public education program which would include a state university. A charter for the university was finally granted in 1819. Until the end of his life seven years later, Jefferson struggled with the legislature for approval of his architectural designs and sufficient funds to build and open the university. His grand vision for an institution which would be a national leader in education rivaling those in New York and Massachusetts was not shared by the majority of legislators.[11]

---

[7] C. T. Cullen, *St. George Tucker and Law in Virginia, 1772-1804*, pp. 116-141 (1987). One of Tucker's students, Joseph Carrington Cabell, preserved a list of the professor's recommended law books, the works of the standard English and European legal and political writers read at the time in America. See H. T. Colbourn, "The Reading of Joseph Carrington Cabell: 'A List of Books . . .' " in *Studies in Bibliography*, vol. 13, pp. 180-181 (1960).

[8] *Report of the Committee of Schools and Colleges*, pp. 25-26 (1824); Report of the Faculty to the Visitors of William and Mary College, 1829, College Papers, Swem Library, College of William and Mary.

[9] *Catalogue and Course of Studies of William and Mary College*, p. 19 (1855).

[10] S. H. Godson, et al., *The College of William and Mary: A History*, pp. 287-290 (1993).

[11] D. Malone, *The Sage of Monticello*, pp. 382-388 (1981).

In addition to designing the buildings and masterminding the educational program at the university, Jefferson also drew up the catalogue of books for its library. Few people in the country were better read or better qualified for establishing a university library. Over the course of his life Jefferson had assembled three personal libraries. His first library comprised principally of law books was lost in a fire when he was in his twenties. He planned to donate the second library of about 6500 volumes to the university he would create. When the United States Capitol building burned in the War of 1812, however, Jefferson saw the government's urgent need for books and sold his collection to form the nucleus of the new Library of Congress.[12] Between the time he sold his library to Congress and his death, he had acquired about a thousand more books.[13] Jefferson located the university's library in the grandest room of the Rotunda, the centerpiece of his design. In his final year he contacted booksellers, ensured that the General Assembly designated $50,000 for the initial purchases, and, according to local lore, inspected the unpacking of a few boxes of books on his last visit to the University.[14]

Meanwhile a desperate search was on for a suitable professor of law. Many prominent lawyers had refused the low-salaried position, and the university had been open a year before John Tayloe Lomax accepted and began teaching in 1826. During the four years of his tenure Lomax lectured from several basic texts including Blackstone.[15] It is not known whether Lomax provided additional recommended reading lists, but the founder of the university had ordered for its library 370 titles in law and 170 in government and political economy.[16]

Before the end of the 1820s the first of many complaints were heard that the library was not purchasing current publications. After his death Jefferson's third library, comprised primarily of contemporary books and intended for the university, was instead sold by his executors to settle the estate's debts. Lomax wrote a member of the Board of Visitors that the lack of recent reports meant that "instruction

[12] E. M. Sowerby, *Catalogue of the Library of Thomas Jefferson* (1952); W. D. Johnston, *History of the Library of Congress*, vol. 1, pp. 68-104 (1904).

[13] Malone, pp. 169-184.

[14] P. A. Bruce, *History of the University of Virginia, 1819-1919*, vol. 2, pp. 38-42 (1920); H. Clemons, *The University of Virginia Library 1825-1850*, pp. 5-11 (1954).

[15] Bruce, vol. 2, pp. 31, 32, 103.

[16] Davis, pp. 91-92. They are listed in *Catalogue of the Library of the University of Virginia* (1828).

upon some of the most important and interesting subjects must fail."[17] The situation improved in 1836 when the library received its first large bequest, six hundred books and $1,500 from the estate of James Madison. Many of the books were on constitutional law and had been purchased by Jefferson at Madison's request while the former was in France. The books were a valuable asset to the fledgling law col-lection, and the endowment funded new acquisitions in all disciplines.[18]

Lomax was followed by John A. G. Davis, and then Henry St. George Tucker, each of whom varied the required texts but did not appreciably change the method of instruction. More significant changes were made by John B. Minor who was appointed in 1845 and taught until his death in 1895. Over the years Minor became the most prominent and influential figure in legal education in the South.

Like Wythe, Minor advocated a thorough and exhaustive study of the theory of law coupled with a structured, detailed moot court experience so that graduates would be competent to practice law on their own. Perusal of Minor's detailed outline of common law, eventually published as *Institutes of Common and Statute Law*, reveals the thoroughness of his scholarship and analysis. He delivered minutely detailed lectures, occasionally asking students questions requiring yes-or-no answers. A former student wrote, "The draft of his lectures from the beginning was remarkable for a rigorously logical and scientific arrangement in imitation of the searching methods of Hale and Blackstone. . . .All the principles of modern law were diligently and confidently traced by him to the common law."[19]

In 1875 Minor complained about the dearth of expenditures for law books, writing that no money had been spent in six or seven years.[20] But never in his tenure did he mention the law library in the university's catalog or his own brochure descriptions of the course of law study. Indeed Virginia's law collection grew very little from 1826 to 1895. Because of the enormous success of his course and the number of students he attracted to the university, it would seem that Minor could have substantially developed the law collection Jefferson began if that had been a significant priority for him.

[17] Clemons, p. 22.

[18] *Id.*, pp. 24-25.

[19] T. J. Michie, "John Barbee Minor," *Green Bag*, vol. 7, p. 403 (1895); Bruce, vol. 3, p. 69.

[20] "Notes for Law Classes," Box 51, Minor-Wilson Family Papers, Alderman Library, Univ. of Va.

III. *Post-Civil War Expansion in Legal Education*

After the Civil War the College of William and Mary rebuilt and reopened, but the law class was dropped from the curriculum. The law course at the University of Virginia, which was taught throughout the war, began to attract more students from a wider area. At almost the same time in Lexington and Richmond, new, university-affiliated law classes were initiated. The challenges of rebuilding the war-ravaged state and the changing economy were creating a greater need for lawyers.

A. *Washington and Lee University*

In Lexington, Judge John White Brockenbrough had been running a successful proprietary law school annually, except for the war years, since 1849. After the war Brockenbrough, a trustee of Lexington's Washington College, persuaded General Robert E. Lee to accept the presidency of the college. As part of his plan to expand the college to a university, Lee was instrumental in drawing Brockenbrough's law program into loose affiliation with the institution in 1866. In 1870 it became part of Washington and Lee University. John Randolph Tucker, son of Henry St. George Tucker, was hired to teach with Brockenbrough, and together they made a plea to the college president for book funds since at that time there was no law library at all. For the next several years the entire program was in a state of transition as first Brockenbrough and then Tucker resigned, leaving a young newcomer, Charles A. Graves, to carry on with the help of occasional lecturers. Graves had been a student of Brockenbrough and Tucker and followed their teaching methods, requiring a careful reading of legal theory in respected texts and demonstrating the application of theory in important cases.[21] As one student put it:

> the textbooks which give the principles are not the real authority for the law; that is to be found in the application of these principles by the courts, and collected in their reports. Professor Graves, by patient and systematic work, has looked up [for his students] the leading cases on all the most important subjects.[22]

---

[21] O. Crenshaw, *General Lee's College: The Rise and Growth of Washington and Lee University*, pp. 329-337 (1969).

[22] *Id.*, p. 338.

In spite of Graves's dedication and perseverance, the law department struggled, with fewer than twenty students during some of the 1870s and 1880s.[23]

Washington and Lee's law program espoused a strong states' rights doctrine which brought it to the attention of a like-minded, wealthy Philadelphia railroad lawyer, Vincent L. Bradford. After the university awarded him an honorary degree, Bradford reciprocated with an annual donation to Washington and Lee's law library.[24] This fund gave a tremendous boost to the collection. In his 1876 report to the president, Graves described a skeleton library of 592 volumes which included standard text books, full sets of the United States, New York and Virginia reports, and recent English reports.[25] Over the next few years, he reported spending some of the Bradford money for more English reports, but each year he indicated that he saved some of the fund.[26] Upon his death in 1884, Bradford left half of his estate to Washington and Lee with provisions for a professorship, an annual fund for law book purchases, and $75 for a librarian's salary. In addition Bradford left his own law books to the law school and asked that the library be named after him.[27]

In the late 1880s John Randolph Tucker, having attained a national reputation after a number of terms in Congress, returned to teach law with his former colleague. Enrollment climbed rapidly to 63 students by 1892. Tucker and Graves taught together for less than ten years before Tucker's death in 1897, and two years later Graves moved to the University of Virginia. However, the prosperity of the school, its alumni, and friends had reached the point that Tucker's son and successor as dean, Harry, was able to move the law school to a new building dedicated to his father.[28]

B. *RICHMOND COLLEGE*

In the meantime the trustees of Richmond College had decided in 1870 to add a course of law study to its humanities program, believing that the state's capital was the perfect location for attracting and

[23] *Id.*, p. 337.

[24] *Id.*, pp. 335-336.

[25] Dean's Report to the President, 1876, Trustees' Papers, Leyburn Library, Washington and Lee University.

[26] Dean's Reports, 1880, 1882, and 1883.

[27] Memorandum re Bradford Law Fund and Professorship (n.d.), Trustees' Papers.

[28] Crenshaw, pp. 339-343.

training law students. The three professors who opened the school were former judges, William Green and J. D. Halyburton, and Richmond College literature professor, J. L. M. Curry, who was also a former lawyer and Congressman. Green was largely self-taught but an erudite legal scholar, and it was unfortunate for Richmond College that ill health forced his resignation after only two years. Over his lifetime Green built a personal library of 10,000 heavily annotated books. His collection, unparalleled in the state, was tragically auctioned piecemeal after his death.[29]

The Richmond law faculty lectured in the evenings and pursued their other careers by day. Ideally the students could observe the state courts and legislature or do research in the state law library during the daytime, but in reality they held down jobs of their own. Over the next two decades low enrollments and a poor economy forced the law school to close twice for extended periods. Samuel Davies who taught for a minuscule salary along with Curry in the early 1880s, commented when he resigned that his "experience is only a repetition of that which has heretofore attended the enterprise—failure to attract sufficient patronage to make the school self-sustaining, and this state of things will doubtless continue as long as Professor Minor remains at the University of Virginia."[30]

In 1890, however, a major benefactor appeared. The bequest of $25,000 came from one of Richmond's wealthiest businessmen, T. C. Williams. This gift, the first of many from the Williams family, endowed a professorship in law and put the school on a more stable footing. The first person to hold the chair was Roger Gregory, a well-respected former lawyer, judge and legislator. At about the same time Mrs. Harriet M. Purcell of Loudoun County donated the library of her brother Henry Heaton, a gift of about 700 volumes which became the nucleus of the law school's library. This collection was shelved in "the Law Alcove" in Jeter Hall, where law lectures were given. State and federal reports were added annually.[31]

As the end of the nineteenth century approached, each of Virginia's law schools was on relatively firm footing, but none of the school's libraries could be considered adequate for serious legal research. The

[29] D. J. Mays, *The Pursuit of Excellence: A History of the University of Richmond Law School*, pp. 4-11 (1970); R. A. Brock, comp., *Catalogue of the Choice and Extensive Law and Miscellaneous Library of the Late Hon. William Green, LL. D.* (1880).

[30] Mays, pp. 13-15; R. E. Alley, *History of the University of Richmond, 1830-1971*, p. 61 (1977).

[31] Mays, pp. 15-16; *Catalogue of Richmond College*, pp. 12, 22 (1890-91); pp. 33, 35 (1894-95).

nineteenth century had posed many financial difficulties for the state and for the three schools, but libraries simply were not important enough to their leaders to receive a significant portion of the funds which were available. Most private law collections had been passed on to descendants or widely scattered by auction; thus few of them enriched academic study. However, it was thanks to beneficent donors that Washington and Lee and Richmond had libraries worth mentioning. By 1895 it was estimated that the University of Virginia's Board of Visitors had spent less than a thousand dollars on its law library since classes began in 1826.[32] After seventy years the collection was limited to a few thousand volumes.[33]

Also of major significance to the slow growth of law book collections was the teaching method. Students were expected to master the relatively few treatises they were assigned, and the professor's doctrinal lectures were based upon his own or other scholar's interpretations of case or statutory law. Alfred Reed, in his historical study of legal education, wrote that "the student was encouraged and obliged to take the lecturer's or textwriter's word that the principles had been correctly derived from the decisions."[34] As long as the professors' needs were met by the reports, statutes, and treatises available to him, there was little reason to enlarge the library.

IV. *Changes in Legal Education and Law Publishing*

In the 1870s Christopher Columbus Langdell, dean at the Harvard Law School, began to introduce a new method of instruction which eventually caused virtually all law professors to reconsider their own teaching and to place a higher value on the importance of the law library in the educational program. Rather than understanding the doctrine in case law by listening to him lecture on it, Langdell's students were required to read the cases and, through class discussions with him, ferret out the legal principles for themselves. In Reed's words, "American law became for the student not a field to be surveyed broadly, but a thicket, within which a partial clearing, pointing in the

---

[32] Bruce, vol. 5, p. 174.

[33] By contrast, Harvard Law School which opened in 1817 had 60,000 volumes by 1900. *Catalogue of the Library of the Law School of Harvard University*, p. v (1909). At about the turn of the century, Yale Law School had approximately 15,000 volumes. F. C. Hicks, *Yale Law School: 1895-1915*, p. 52 (1938). Columbia had 30,000 volumes. *Columbia University Law School Bulletin*, 1899-1900. And the University of Pennsylvania had over 9,000 volumes. *University of Pennsylvania The Law School Announcement*, 1943-44, p. 17.

[34] A. Z. Reed, *Training for the Public Profession of the Law*, p. 377 (1921).

right direction, is made. The young practitioner is then equipped with a 'trained mind,' as with a trusty axe, and commissioned to spend the rest of his life chopping his way through the tangle."[35] This radical change in instruction drew criticism from the outset and continues to do so, but by World War I most law schools had adopted the new method. Harvard also set a higher standard for legal education by requiring a bachelor's degree (or a special examination) for law school admission and a three-year course of study because Langdell and his colleagues believed both were essential for success with the case method of learning law.[36]

Virginia's law schools were slow to adopt the case method, but its academic law libraries benefitted from the new value placed on the library and its use in legal education. In a much-quoted published speech, Langdell wrote:

> My associates, and myself, therefore, have constantly acted upon the view that law is a science, and that a well-equipped university is the true place for teaching and learning that science. Accordingly the law library has been the object of our greatest and most constant solicitude. . . .We have also constantly inculcated the idea that the library is the proper workshop of professors and students alike; that it is to us all that the laboratories of the university are to the chemists and physicists. . . .[37]

Langdell's revolution in teaching coincided with a dramatic increase in the amount of United States case law. By the 1880s there were nearly four thousand volumes of reports from the federal and state courts. Access to cases was growing chaotic, and several commercial publishers attempted to remedy this situation. Within a few years the West Publishing Company's National Reporter System had become a standard component of law libraries. Another expanding area of American publishing was the legal periodical, of which there were more than thirty soon after the turn of the century.

---

[35] *Id.*, 380.

[36] R. A. Cosgrove, *Our Lady the Common Law: An Anglo-American Legal Community, 1870-1930*, pp. 25-38 (1987). For other discussions of the impact of Langdell's work, see R. Stevens, *Law School: Legal Education in America for the 1850s to the 1980s*, pp. 35-72 (1983), and Reed, pp. 343-388.

[37] [C. C.] Langdell, "Harvard Celebration Speeches," *Law Qtly. Rev.*, vol. 9, p. 124 (1887).

Meanwhile two professional organizations launched movements to impose minimum standards on schools responsible for training members of the bar. By 1896 the American Bar Association (ABA), created in 1878, was recommending a high school diploma for law school entrance and three years of legal study for bar admission. This increased to three years of study the following year. In 1900 an outgrowth of the ABA, the Association of American Law Schools (AALS), was formed by thirty-five leading law schools. (Virginia's three law schools were invited to the organizational meeting, and Richmond and Washington and Lee sent delegates. All three declined to become charter members.)[38] Both national organizations worked for many years separately and in tandem to establish guidelines and to set minimum standards for legal education. Many schools fell far short of the level of preparation and law training required by Harvard and other accepted leaders.[39]

In 1906 the American Association of Law Libraries (AALL) was established. Made up primarily of librarians from state and court libraries, as well as twelve librarians from midwestern and northeastern law schools, the organization's immediate purpose was to assist members in providing order and access to the rapidly expanding legal literature in their care.[40] Through its annual meetings and quarterly publication, *Law Library Journal*, AALL attempted to establish standards for the new profession in law librarianship, but credibility with the legal profession came slowly. It was not until the late 1930s that AALS began to work jointly with AALL to establish library standards.

At its founding in 1900 the AALS had stipulated that each member school should "own or have convenient access to" the United States Supreme Court reports and the reports of the state in which it was located.[41] After much debate the standard rose by 1924 to "not less than five thousand volumes well selected and properly housed and

[38] *Report of the Twentieth Annual Meeting of the American Bar Association*, pp. 349-382 (1897); *Report of the Twenty-third Annual Meeting of the American Bar Association*, pp. 569-570 (1900) (hereafter cited as *ABA Reports*); *Minutes of the First Annual Meeting of the Association of American Law Schools*, pp. 3-4 (1901).

[39] Stevens, pp. 92-111.

[40] President's Address and List of Members, *Law Library Journal*, vol. 1, pp. 3-6, 26-28 (1908).

[41] "Association of American Law Schools Articles of Association," *ABA Report*, p. 572 (1900).

administered."[42] Three years later the volume count was increased to 7500, and, for the first time, the organization specified seven categories of critical materials the library must own: its own state's reports, statutes, and related digests; published reports and current statutes of half the states; U.S. Supreme Court decisions, federal statutes, and digests; the complete National Reporter System; "general digests, encyclopedias, and treatises of accepted worth;" at least six complete legal periodicals; and the English reprinted reports.[43] In 1932 the minimum volume count rose to 10,000, and schools were required to spend at least $10,000 on books during a five-year period, and no less than $1,500 annually.[44] Toward the end of the decade the organization's committee on libraries debated whether members should be required to hire librarians. Smaller schools or those with tight budgets insisted that a faculty member could take sufficient care of the library.[45] But by 1940 the organization was requiring schools to hire "a qualified librarian whose principal activities are devoted to the development and maintenance of an effective library service."[46]

Librarians have been critical of the AALS for its conservative standards and the retarded pace it held in establishing them.[47] Nevertheless, meeting the minimum standards was of vital concern to Virginia's smaller schools as one-by-one they decided to joined AALS.

V. *The Libraries Begin to Grow*

A. *The University of Virginia*

The first glimmer of progress for the University of Virginia's law library occurred when William Minor Lile was hired in 1893 as a colleague and subsequent replacement for his uncle, John B. Minor. The first year Lile was on the faculty the library was removed from the general collection in the Rotunda to a room adjacent to the law lecture

---

[42] *Proceedings of the Twelfth Annual Meeting of the Association of American Law Schools*, pp. 37-40 (1912); *Handbook of the Association of American Law Schools and Proceedings of the Twenty-second Annual Meeting*, p. 35 (1924) (hereafter cited as *Handbook*).

[43] *Handbook*, p. 7 (1927).

[44] *Handbook*, p. 176 (1932).

[45] H. C. Horack, "The Small Law Library and the Librarian," *Law Library Journal*, vol. 30, pp. 6-12 (1937).

[46] *Handbook*, p. 370 (1937).

[47] See, for example, C. A. Brock, "Law Libraries and Librarians: A Revisionist History," *Law Library Journal*, vol. 67, pp. 325-326 (1974).

room in the Rotunda Annex. The move proved fortuitous a year later when the Rotunda and Annex were consumed by fire. The law library, on the basement level, was rescued by law professor Raleigh C. Minor, John's son. A year later this collection was described for the first time in the catalogue:

> The department is provided with an excellent law library, to which considerable additions have recently been made, containing several thousand volumes of well-selected reports and text-books, English and American. Its location has been chosen with especial reference to the convenience of the student. And, while he is not encouraged to venture for himself into either cases or text-books, save for the purpose of verifying or clearing up some proposition of the lecture, or for the preparation of opinions or briefs, the student is especially incited to familiarize himself with the bibliography of the law and the use of the books. To this subject, in addition to the instruction incidentally given, several lectures are especially devoted.[48]

This instruction in legal bibliography was given by Lile himself, and by 1912 he taught a semester long course to all beginning law students. Lile was a lifelong, adamant opponent to the case method, but possibly his experience as a struggling young lawyer made him a strong advocate of teaching students how to find law.

At the same time he was teaching students how to use the library, Lile was relentlessly pleading with the administration to increase its funding. Under his leadership the collection grew to ten thousand volumes when the law school's own building, Minor Hall, was completed in 1911. Five years later Virginia decided to join AALS.

Each year since 1896 a student had been employed to care for the library. After Lile's persistent urging the first librarian, Ella W. Johnson, was appointed the year Minor Hall opened, and she was followed a year later by Catherine R. Lipop, who served until 1945. Lipop was not a trained librarian, but a few years after she was hired, she took a summer course in library methods and attended her first AALL meeting.[49] By the mid-1920s the catalogue announced that appropriations from the university, supplemented by endowments, adequately provided for yearly acquisitions. The collection of twenty thousand volumes included all English and American reports, the National Reporter System, digests, leading encyclopedias, a large collection of

---

[48] *University of Virginia Announcements of the Law Department*, p. 2 (1895-96).

[49] Dean's Report to the President, 1918, Deans' Papers, University of Virginia Law Library.

textbooks and all current legal periodicals.[50] With only very primitive author and subject cataloguing, locating material grew increasingly difficult and would soon reach a crisis point.

B. *WASHINGTON AND LEE UNIVERSITY*

The law school of Washington and Lee moved into Tucker Memorial Hall in 1900, the year after Martin P. Burks joined the faculty. Initially Tucker Hall had two rooms for the Vincent L. Bradford law library, a stack area and a reading room which held reference works and periodicals. Burks, who soon became dean, worked diligently to improve the library, which by 1911 would contain over five thousand volumes.[51] In his 1908 report to the president he pointed out that the Bradford fund alone could not cover the library's acquisition needs, for it was barely sufficient to pay current serial subscription costs. He asked for $500 more for reports and textbooks.[52] The library served an important function for Burks and his colleagues, as the textbook/lecture method of teaching was being broadened to include use of illustrative cases, interspersed with class discussions. Since 1896 students had been strongly encouraged to take the law course in two years, and 1906 they were required to do so. More library research was expected of students, and in that same year they were given the twenty-four hour, wholly unlimited access to the library which holds to this day.[53] The Law Bulletin of 1911 stated:

> The library is always open, and the students have unrestricted access to the books, and are encouraged to use them as much as possible. They thus soon become familiar with the books they are to use in actual practice. This use of law books—the true "laboratory method" of study—is believed to be one of the most valuable features of the instruction offered in this institution. The librarian [a student] will render such aid as the students may need in their search for authorities and in the use of the books; and one of the

[50] General volume counts from 1911 to 1926 are given in J. Ritchie, *The First Hundred Years: A Short History of the School of Law of the University of Virginia . . . 1826-1929*, p. 119 (1978). On July 1, 1937, there were 30,533 volumes: H. Clemons, *A Survey of Research Materials in Virginia Libraries 1936-37*, pp. 56-58 (1941).

[51] *Washington and Lee University Law Bulletin*, p. 7 (Apr. 1911).

[52] Dean's Report, 1908, Trustees' Papers.

[53] C. E. Williams, "Development of the Law Curriculum," *Alumni Mag., Washington and Lee Univ.*, pp. 12-13 (Mar.-Apr. 1936).

> members of the faculty is usually at hand to give such further assistance as may be necessary.[54]

Washington and Lee joined AALS in 1920. Subsequently successive deans utilized the association's library standards as a prod for increases in library funding. Through the 1920s they repeatedly requested more money for books, re-binding, shelving and most importantly a librarian. While the library had grown enough to fill the second floor of Tucker Hall, annual expenditures for the library remained below the AALS minimum by the early 1930s. Students tended the library, although a librarian from Harvard spent a week in 1928 appraising the collection and helping to organize and catalogue it.[55] Then in 1934 the entire library was lost when Tucker Hall was devastated by fire. Fortunately insurance funds, a Carnegie Corporation grant, and general funds from the university were pooled to replace the collection, albeit without the guidance of a librarian, soon after Tucker Hall was rebuilt in 1936. The collection numbered 13,000 by 1940 when Theodore A. Smedley was hired, the first of several young professors who were asked to teach a course or two and also manage the library.[56] It was not until 1949 that Wanda Lee Spears was hired to assume primary duty as librarian and to teach legal bibliography and brief-making.[57]

C. *RICHMOND COLLEGE*

Despite the boost the T. C. Williams endowment gave to Richmond College's law school, thereafter named for Williams, difficulties in hiring and retaining faculty persisted. Roger Gregory taught from 1890 to 1895 and was followed by young John B. Minor, Jr., who had trained a few years under his father. The continued use of peripatetic lecturers and the short terms served by permanent faculty deterred applicants. Enrollment remained very low until Walter S. McNeill was hired in 1905. Harvard-trained McNeill brought the case method to legal education in Virginia. His revitalization of the instructional program increased the student body and prompted the purchase of 950 volumes

---

[54] *Washington and Lee Univ. Law Bull.*, p. 7 (Apr. 1911).

[55] *Washington and Lee Univ. Bull. President's Rept.*, p. 33 (1923); pp. 41-42 (1924); pp. 40-43 (1925); pp. 35-36 (1928); pp. 38-39 (1930); pp. 42-48 (1931).

[56] *Washington and Lee Univ. Bull. School of Law*, pp. 8-11 (Mar. 1940).

[57] *Washington and Lee Univ. Bull. School of Law*, pp. 8, 27-28 (May 1949).

for the library in 1910.[58] Too big for an alcove, the law library now occupied a room adjoining the main lecture room. The catalogue of 1910 announced the recent purchase and explained:

> Under the "Case System" constant reference has to be made to Digests and Reports for decisions of the Courts bearing upon given points, and the purchase of these works is designed to strengthen the library in this direction. The College now subscribes to the National Reporter System.[59]

Major changes occurred in the 1920s when the school began offering daytime as well as evening classes, and expanded its space with funds provided by T. C. Williams, Jr. The law school had remained at the college's original location at Grace and Lombardy Streets when the other departments moved to a new campus west of Richmond. After the renovation, the school tripled the size of its library, chiefly with English and state reports, in order to meet minimum standards for election to membership in AALS in 1930. That year Madeline R. Bigger served as law librarian, followed a year later by new faculty member (later dean) William T. Muse, whose responsibility was to oversee student library workers. With the help of a federal work fund, "needy" students catalogued and rearranged the library in 1933. In 1939 Frances Farmer became the part-time librarian. She had worked as secretary to the law school dean, Ray Doubles, since she began law school in 1931. After she received library training under Miles O. Price, librarian at Columbia University School of Law, she divided her time between the T. C. Williams' dean's office and its law library. Thanks to several bequests of books through the 1930s the collection had grown to 17,000 by 1940 when a library committee was formulating lists of books, especially treatises, the library needed.[60]

D. *The College of William and Mary*

Around 1920 William and Mary's President J. A. C. Chandler attempted to raise endowment and building funds for the Marshall-Wythe School of Government and Citizenship. Though the fund-raising

---

[58] Mays, pp. 19-25.

[59] *Catalogue of Richmond College*, p. 75 (1910-11).

[60] *Univ. of Richmond President's Annual Rept.*, pp. 4, 20 (1930); p. 26 (1931); p. 24 (1933); pp. 28, 40 (1939); pp. 36-37 (1940).

campaign had limited success, the school opened in 1922. Led by John Garland Pollard, an outstanding Virginia lawyer, the school's purpose was "to train students for political leadership and public service" through a fundamental grounding in constitutional law. The name of the school exposed the college leadership's ambivalent feelings about renewing a law program: despite their pride in having had the first law chair in the country, they had reasonable doubts that the legislature would give adequate support to a second state-funded law school. The school did offer a law degree program, although for about the first twenty years of its existence, most of the students were undergraduates and only twenty-eight law degrees were awarded.[61]

Nonetheless a librarian, John Latané Lewis, was hired in 1932 to care for a collection of about sixty-five hundred law books housed on the third floor of the college library. Serving a tiny law program with an uncertain future, the law library remained small, and its inadequacy was partially responsible for the delay in AALS membership until 1936. Five years later an AALS representative reported that the school had an outstanding faculty but "lamentably low" salaries and a deficient library collection.[62] These problems would haunt the law program and the library would barely meet the minimum standards for decades, but from the time Lewis was hired, there would always be a law librarian responsible for the collection.

As the twentieth century neared the halfway point, each of the law schools could claim progress for its library, but none could be classified more than merely adequate, if that. The size of the collections varied roughly according to the size of the educational programs they served, and the libraries at Washington and Lee and University of Virginia had surely benefitted from the aggressive interest of their deans. Nonetheless, all of the libraries aimed to meet the needs of the student and the practitioner. Even the University of Virginia, with the largest library of the four could not support in-depth scholarly research. It would be a number of years before Richmond and Washington and Lee took seriously the AALS requirement for a permanent, full-time librarian to care for their collections. None of the libraries had been properly and fully catalogued by professionals, so research in some areas was next to impossible for occasional or first-time patrons. And not since Thomas Jefferson had anyone at any of these libraries given extensive, informed attention to collection development beyond bare necessities.

---

[61] Godson, pp. 568-72.

[62] *Id.*, pp. 572-573, 651.

VI. *Mid-Century and Beyond*

During World War II a Joint Committees on Cooperation between the Association of American Law Schools and the American Association of Law Libraries worked at length to provide more explicit guidelines for libraries. (Washington and Lee's Theodore Smedley and University of Virginia's Frances Farmer participated in this joint effort.) In a report published in the 1943 AALS handbook, the joint committee interpreted, or qualified, standards for the librarian, the administration of the library, the physical facility, and the collection. This effort, spearheaded by William R. Roalfe, law librarian at Duke University, finally led to higher standards adopted by AALS in 1952. Written primarily for the smaller schools trying to gain admission into AALS, the standards were nevertheless highly controversial. The recommendation regarding the librarian exemplifies the committee's efforts to please as many members as possible: "A member school shall have a full-time librarian . . .[with] either a sound knowledge of the practical problems of a law school library, or legal education, and preferably both. It is preferable, but not mandatory, that such librarian be a member of the law school faculty."[63] By 1968 the librarian was required to have degrees in both law and library science,[64] after almost seventy years an acknowledgement of the peculiar dual qualifications necessary for this faculty position.

Transitions in collection development around mid-century placed increasingly higher demands on the librarian. Between the world wars but more markedly after the second war, social and political changes were reflected in the curricula and libraries of many law schools. In the 1930s the legal realist movement turned Langdell's concept of law-as-science on its head. The realists asserted that law, rather than objective doctrine to be discovered, is reflective of the particular society and value system in which it operates. This new approach gradually caused legal scholars to recognize and explore the interconnection of law and social sciences. By the 1960s the interdisciplinary outlook extended to medicine and other sciences, as well as to arts and humanities. And gradually through the century but more precipitously after 1950, foreign, comparative, and international law became more prominent in the curriculum. Some libraries, which had previously maintained the narrow, skeletal focus outlined by the AALS guidelines, were suddenly faced with new and costly areas of research to support.

---

[63] *Proceedings of the Annual Meeting of the Association of American Law Schools*, p. 171 (1952) (hereafter cited as *Proceedings*).

[64] *Proceedings*, p. 235 (1968).

Higher budgets and a thoroughly professional staff were crucial elements to achieving these sorts of collection developments.

A. *THE UNIVERSITY OF VIRGINIA*

Dramatic changes sparked by alumni interest occurred at the University of Virginia during World War II. An alumni committee echoed the faculty's position that the collection of 38,000 volumes now housed in a new law building, Clark Hall, needed to be fully organized and catalogued. They also wanted to begin an intensive acquisition program to fill in significant gaps. The legislature provided a special fund for the cataloging project, and the alumni donated $48,000 for acquisitions. Frances Farmer was hired in 1942 to organize and supervise this major transformation.[65]

Farmer had earned her B.A. and LL. B. at the University of Richmond, finishing first in her law class. But after her graduation in 1933, during the Depression, she had not been able to find a job in a law firm. Dean M. Ray Doubles had encouraged her to take library training and the job at Virginia.

Following the advice of her consultant and mentor, Miles Price, Farmer successfully supervised the classification of the core library of 38,000 volumes plus over 17,000 new acquisitions in two and a half years.[66] Additions acquired by purchase or trade included states' official reports and session laws, as well as Commonwealth reports and statutes. Significant numbers of treatises and periodicals were added, and acquisitions began to supplement a collection of international law donated by John Bassett Moore in the 1930s.[67]

In an article describing this whirlwind project, Farmer gratefully acknowledged by name the alumni who made the work possible, and she urged other librarians to seek assistance from their graduates.[68] Farmer became the librarian when Lipop retired in 1945, and the cataloguing project was the first of countless progressive steps she made on the library's behalf with the generous support of the alumni. The collection topped 100,000 volumes in 1953, shortly after the school began to offer master's degrees in law. As the collection grew, Farmer oversaw additions to Clark Hall. In the early seventies she raised

[65] F. Farmer, "The Revival of the University of Virginia Law Library in Wartime," *Law Library Journal*, vol. 38, p. 30 (1945).

[66] Miles O. Price to William H. White, July 10, 1944, Annual Reports of the Law Librarian, University of Virginia Law Library.

[67] Farmer, pp. 30-37.

[68] *Id.*, p. 35.

funds, consulted on planning, and supervised the move of the nearly 300,000-volume collection to a new library named for alumnus Arthur J. Morris. Throughout her tenure, Farmer demonstrated her interest in progress and innovation in legal research, serving as a spokesperson for online database research shortly before retirement at age 67.[69]

Under the leadership of Larry B. Wenger, librarian since 1976, the library has grown to over 600,000 volumes with a budget of over $2.5 million. Its special strengths include international, oceans, and historic preservation law; foreign and comparative military law; interdisciplinary subjects, especially economics, medicine and psychology; rare seventeenth through nineteenth-century English and American material; the law school archives; and twentieth-century legal manuscripts. The library now ranks in the top twelve of academic United States law libraries.

B. *WASHINGTON AND LEE UNIVERSITY*

The alumni association of Washington and Lee also played an active role in financing and acquiring materials for its law library. Assistance was especially needed in the early 1950s since after Wanda Lee Spears left in 1952, the law librarian was once again part of the teaching faculty. The alumni library committee regarded the stiffer AALS standards carefully. Voicing a desire to rank above the minimum, the committee annually circulated lists of books and periodicals required to complete sets and implored the university to increase the library's financial allocation.[70] In 1958 an assistant librarian, Louise P. Moore, was hired to devote full attention to organizing and cataloging "prime materials."[71] Moore was promoted to librarian the following year, and she led the library through the 1960s when the diminution of shelf space became a serious problem. Upon the advice of consultant Miles Price, dormitory basement space was converted to library storage but provided only temporary relief. The library then acquired an annex in a former dean's home.

---

[69] Proceedings of the Conference of Virginia Law Librarians, November 21-22, 1975, Law Library Files, Univ. of Va. Law Library; M. Trimble, "Answering the Challenge: Frances Farmer, Law Librarian," *UVA Lawyer*, vol. 19, no. 2, pp. 43-50 (Spring 1995); [obit.], Richmond *Times-Dispatch*, Sept. 15, 1993, pp. B2, B3; H. C. Dillard and B. P. Chamberlain, "Frances Farmer," *Va. Law Rev.*, vol. 63, pp. 349-354 (1977); L. N. Gasaway, "Women as Directors of Academic Law Libraries" in L. N. Gasaway and M. C. Chiorazzi, *Law Librarianship: Historical Perspectives*, pp. 522-524 (1996).

[70] *Washington and Lee Law Ass'n Annual Rept.*, pp. 10-12 (1953); pp. 16-17 (1954); pp. 15-17 (1955).

[71] *Washington and Lee Law School Ass'n Annual Rept.*, p. 31 (1958).

The next major developments for the library occurred under the leadership of Dean Roy Steinheimer, whose ambition to raise the school to national rank resulted in a large increase in the library's funding. In the early 1970s under Librarian Peyton Neal's leadership the library was finally entirely catalogued. With the move to a new building in 1976 the collection finally had room to expand; since 1970 it has mushroomed from 45,000 to 320,000 volumes. Washington and Lee now ranks high among small, private law schools in the country. Its library, directed by Sarah K. Wiant since 1978, now operates on a budget of $1.7 million and supports the needs of its academic program as well as in-depth research in international, international environmental, and securities law. In 1992 the library opened a new wing named for alumnus Justice Lewis F. Powell housing his extensive collection of Supreme Court and other professional papers, along with other manuscript collections and the law school's archives.

C. *THE COLLEGE OF WILLIAM AND MARY*

In 1951 when AALS was debating raising the minimum standards for members' libraries, Joseph McCormack spoke for the Marshall-Wythe School opposing the change, saying that "in the judgment of our dean, this is a matter of life and death for our little law school."[72] McCormack presented the association a memorandum from Marshall-Wythe Librarian Chester Baker to Dean Dudley Woodbridge. Baker estimated that the school of less than one hundred students would have to spend $31,000 to purchase the four thousand books they would need to meet the minimum volume count. The librarian also gave this description of the library: "only one reading room, poor lighting, poorly ventilated, insufficient tables for the [minimum required] four square feet of table space for forty per cent of law students, no separate office for law librarian, or for staff to process its material."[73] The AALS plan was revised to allow libraries two to three years to comply, and William and Mary voted in favor of the new library standards, which were adopted in 1952.[74]

In 1953 William and Mary's law program was elevated from department status to the Marshall-Wythe School of Law. A master's degree program in tax law was created and an endowed chair in tax established. The name change was accompanied by a consolidation of the law lecture rooms, offices, and library under one roof carried out

[72] *Proceedings*, p. 71 (1951).

[73] *Id.*, pp. 72-75.

[74] *Proceedings*, pp. 42, 50-53 (1952).

with the help of private donations.[75] At that time efforts were made to increase the size of the library by about 4,000 volumes to meet the AALS minimum of 20,000. Enrollment remained low, and the school's status continued uncertain, but newsletters circulated to alumni beginning in the 1950s indicate that librarian Anna B. Johnson was making a concerted effort to improve the library, especially its collection of state materials and legal periodicals.[76]

Not long after moving to the abandoned college library in 1968, the law school was seriously threatened with losing its ABA accreditation. Identified as having "the most inadequate physical plant of any ABA approved law school in the country," it was cited for its deficient library and low faculty salaries. With the help of the governor, the college president persuaded the General Assembly to allocate sufficient funds for a new building. A dynamic new dean, William B. Spong, was hired in 1976 to see through the building construction, as well as to increase the size of the faculty and their salaries. Student enrollment jumped from 54 in 1960 to 515 by 1984.[77]

A new law librarian, Caroline C. Heriot, was also hired in 1976. A woman with previous experience in setting up new libraries and with a vision for the role of Marshall-Wythe's library in its educational program, she made a rapid transformation before her premature death in 1981. During her tenure the collection was catalogued, endowment funds were increased, and the treatise collection was developed. So successful was she that Dean Spong was reportedly fond of quipping that Marshall-Wythe was "a law school attached to a law library."[78] Her successors, Edmund P. Edmonds and James S. Heller have continued to build on Heriot's progress. Constitutional law has remained a focus of the Marshall-Wythe faculty and library, but the 300,000-volume collection also supports scholarship in tax, environmental law, and jurisprudence. The school now enjoys a solid reputation and secure support of the state legislature, and the library with an annual budget of about $1.5 million carries on Heriot's legacy as a source of pride for Marshall-Wythe.

---

[75] Godson, p. 784; Dudley W. Woodbridge, "A Short History of the Marshall-Wythe School of Law," (n.d.) Swem Library, Coll. of William and Mary.

[76] Law School News Letters, 1957-1962, Marshall-Wythe Law Library.

[77] Godson, p. 843.

[78] Memorial statement for Caroline A. Heriot presented by Walter Leslie Williams, Jr., (n.d.) Marshall-Wythe Law Library.

D. *THE UNIVERSITY OF RICHMOND*

After World War II, the T. C. Williams School of Law hired its first full-time librarian, Virginia Ivey. Her successor, Ellen Morris Keene, was in charge of the collection when it was moved from Columbia Hall to the new building on the University of Richmond campus in 1953. The next year Dean Muse proudly reported that "for the first time in our history the library is adequately fulfilling its mission as the core of the educational program of the school."[79] But by 1969 he reported that the library's small size ranked it near the bottom nationally.[80]

Through the 1960s and early 1970s the full-time librarian worked with a small staff of part-time assistants, keeping the library open relatively limited hours. By 1970 the volume count barely exceeded 40,000 and the annual budget was $15,000. When the school received its AALS inspection in 1973, the library was found to be pitifully deficient. The inspection report advised the school to invest $400,000 above the annual budget over the next four years to catch up to minimum standards. The report also recommended hiring a qualified assistant librarian and suggested a larger salary for the head librarian, more travel funds for librarians, and adequate work space for library services.[81] Five years later a consultant from Duke University detailed areas of the collection still needing improvement. In the late 1970s, the re-cataloguing of the collection finally began under the direction of a trained cataloguer, eventually aided by the Ohio College Library Center (OCLC) computerized system in the main university library.

Under the leadership of Susan B. English and her successor, Steven D. Hinckley, the library collection has grown from 70,000 volumes in 1977 to well over 200,000 with an annual budget of $1.3 million. Sufficient staff was hired as the collection grew, and the library has recently spread into an addition which provides 49,000 more square feet of space.[82] For most of its history as a practitioner's collection, the library now fulfills its mission to support the educational program, in addition to in-depth research in environmental law and the field of law and medicine.

---

[79] *Univ. of Richmond President's Annual Rept.*, p. 32 (1954).

[80] *Id.*, p. 45 (1969).

[81] Librarian's Annual Report, 1973, University of Richmond Law Library.

[82] Joyce M. Janto memorandum to Steven D. Hinckley, Dec. 2, 1994, University of Richmond Law Library.

VII. *Creation and Development of Two New Libraries*

A. *GEORGE MASON UNIVERSITY*

George Mason University, which wanted to open a law school in the early 1970s, finally got approval from the General Assembly in 1979 to purchase a struggling law program, the International School of Law. That school had started in 1972 and was located in a former department store building in Arlington, which George Mason's Foundation bought without the legislature's help. From 1980 to 1986 the young school strove to attain its ABA accreditation which was threatened by financial problems and an inadequate physical facility. Since that time, under the leadership of a new dean, Henry Manne, the accredited school is on a stronger footing.[83]

George Mason had acquired a library of five thousand volumes from International in 1975 and, by 1979 when the school was purchased, had increased the book collection to 110,000 volumes, primarily through the Exchange and Gift Division of the Law Library of Congress. Judge Oliver Murdock donated a substantial international law collection. Since the original library space was considered inadequate by the ABA, renovation of the area secured its approval of the school in 1986. An increase in the library budget paved the way for AALS membership. Now a collection of 265,000 volumes with a budget of $1.1 million, the library, directed by Philip Berwick, supports a curriculum strong in law and economics, patent law, banking, ethics and philosophy.[84]

B. *REGENT UNIVERSITY*

CBN University, located in Virginia Beach, acquired the O. W. Coburn School of Law from Oral Roberts University in late 1985. In an unusual move, CBN, now called Regent University, accepted twenty-three second and third year law students, a 190,000-volume law library transferred in refrigerated tractor trailers, and five law professors from the Oklahoma university. Coburn had had accreditation difficulties with the ABA, and similar problems have continued at Regent, although the organization's inspectors have approved the library. Recently the school's trustees allocated funds to double the library facility and substantially boost the collection to 290,000 volumes. A recent gift has connected this school, one of the nation's youngest, with Transylvania University Law School, one

---

[83] *Legal Times*, p. 1 (Apr. 27, 1987); *Washington Post*, p. B1 (Nov. 4, 1987); *American Lawyer*, p. 60 (Dec. 1991).

[84] Telefax communication from Librarian Philip Berwick to the author, Jan. 26, 1995.

of the earliest. Regent received 1,000 law books from Transylvania, whose law school closed at the beginning of the Civil War. Other strengths of the collection include legal history, jurisprudence, and constitutional law.[85]

VIII. *Conclusion*

Thus did the present Virginia academic law libraries grow out of small alcoves in the general libraries of impoverished nineteenth century universities. In the early days, they were cared for by a law professor in his spare time, perhaps with the aid of a student assistant. Acquisition budgets were at first minimal; indeed most of the budgets for the entire universities were small, for it was a period when professors were paid directly and proportionately out of student fees if there were any students at all. Thus, donations, rather than purchases, of law books were of major significance in the growth of the law libraries. In the twentieth century, the colleges and universities in Virginia participated in the economic growth of the nation, and this has been reflected in the increased growth and professionalization of their law libraries.

As Virginia's academic law libraries move into the twenty-first century, all of them are working in a network information environment. In addition to their own online catalogs, they provide access to remote libraries' catalogs and databases of library holdings, such as Online Computer Library Center (OCLC). LEXIS and WESTLAW are just two of a growing number of online research databases. Many libraries are now providing a great deal of information in the CD-ROM format. In addition, more and more faculty and students are capable of conducting research at home via the Internet. All of these changes are challenging law librarians to rethink their role in providing access to legal material. Nevertheless, while wild predictions of the paperless library abound, today's librarians are acutely aware that their responsibilities for several decades will cover the enormous gamut of materials from the crumbling reports purchased from the West Publishing Company in the 1890s to the database service someone will offer them tomorrow.

---

[85] *American Lawyer*, p. 85 (Mar. 1987); *Christianity Today*, vol. 38, no. 1, p. 40 (Jan. 10, 1994); telefax communication from Acting Librarian Charles Oates to the author, Jan. 30, 1995.

FULL TIME ACADEMIC LAW LIBRARIANS

The College of William and Mary

John Latané Lewis	1932-1946
Charles Harper Anderson	1946-1947
Virginia Blanche Till	1947-1949
Chester Stoyle Baker, Jr.	1950-1959
Anna Boothe Johnson	1960-1971
J. Madison Whitehead	1971-1976
Caroline Chandler Heriot	1976-1981
Edmund P. Edmonds	1981-1988
James Stephen Heller	1988-

The University of Richmond

Virginia Ivey	1949-1952?
Ellen Morris Keene	1953-1959
José M. Cabanillas	1959-1966
Jack S. Shackelton	1966-1975
Peter A. Frey	1975-1979
Leigh Morris	1979-1981
Susan B. English	1981-1990
Steven D. Hinckley	1990-1996
Timothy L. Coggins	1997-

The University of Virginia

Ella W. Johnson	1911-1912
Catherine R. Lipop	1912-1945
Frances Farmer	1945-1976
Larry B. Wenger	1976-

Washington and Lee University

Theodore Allyn Smedley	1939-1942
Catherine McDowell	1947-1949
Wanda Lee Spears	1949-1952
Erson McGruder Faris	1952-1957
James William Horne Stewart	1957-1958
Louise Pendleton Moore	1958-1972
Jill Perry Huntley	1967-1968
Peyton Ring Neal, Jr.	1972-1978
Sarah Kirsten Wiant	1978-

COLLEGE OF WILLIAM AND MARY LAW LIBRARY

James S. Heller

I. *Introduction*

THE DEVELOPMENT of the College of William and Mary's Marshall-Wythe School of Law and its law library spans more than two centuries. As in most institutions, the history of the law library tracks closely the development of the law school.[1]

This history breaks down into four distinct stages, which reflect the relative success of the study of law as a whole at the College. The founding stage, beginning in 1779 and ending with the commencement of hostilities during the Civil War, represents a slow period of gradual growth for the young law program. The next stage of decline encompasses over a half century between the closing of the College during the Civil War and the formal re-institution of the study of law at William and Mary in the early 1920s. A third stage reemerged in the early 1920s but struggled through the 1970s. During this revival era, the law library suffered continually from inadequate financial resources, dismal facilities, and deficient staffing. The modern era began in 1980, following completion of the present law building. The last fifteen years has been a period of maturation and growth, and ultimately great success, for both the law school and the law library.

II. *The Founding Stage*

The antebellum history of the study of law and the law library at the College is limited, since "[d]isastrous conflagrations consumed the library collections on three different occasions, in 1705, 1859, and 1862."[2] A few scattered bits of information have survived, but we have, unfortunately, only a hazy picture of the early law school and its

---

[1] An earlier version of this essay appeared in L. N. Gasaway and M. G. Chiorazzi, edd., *Law Librarianship: Historical Perspectives*, pp. 43–76 (1996); it is reprinted with permission. The author would like to thank his two research assistants for their work on this paper. Scott Boak provided invaluable assistance researching and providing a first draft of the history from the founding stage through 1975; David Elliott offered research support for the period 1976 through 1995.

[2] J. M. Jennings, *The Library of the College of William and Mary in Virginia, 1693-1793*, p. viii (1968) [hereinafter Jennings].

library. Many conclusions about the law program and the law library up to the Civil War, and then well into the twentieth century, must be inferred from other pieces of information.

The College of William and Mary was chartered by King William III and Queen Mary II of England in 1693. From its inception, the College provided Virginia's elite with a sound education in the liberal arts. For almost a century, however, the study of law in Virginia remained within the parameters of England's legal education system. Lawyers-to-be were educated independently, either through apprenticeships with practicing lawyers or through the Inns of Court in England. Legal education changed forever in 1758, however, when Sir William Blackstone occupied the Vinerian Chair at Oxford University, the first professorship of English law. The creation of this professorship signified the beginning of formal legal education. But formal, academic study of law on this side of the Atlantic was not achieved until after the American Revolution.

The Revolution severed most ties with England and created a dearth of available legal training in the new nation. "Before the Revolution young men aspiring to the bar either had to serve as a lawyer's apprentice or cross the Atlantic to the Inns of Court. Independence brought new constitutions and new laws that made the Inns of Court professionally obsolete."[3] The only viable manner of study was an apprenticeship under an established American lawyer, who were few in number.[4]

Thomas Jefferson saw the need for legal reorganization in the colonies[5] and began to remedy the situation in his home state of Virginia. He chose to enact his reforms at his alma mater, the College of William and Mary. In 1779, at Jefferson's urging, the College's Board of Visitors resolved to create a professorship of Law and Police. On December 28, 1779, the Board named Jefferson's mentor, George Wythe, to that position.

Even before the commencement of formal legal training under Wythe, the College began to acquire some materials on the subject of law. But there was no separate law library, nor would there be for nearly 200 years. The law collection developed slowly, and usually

[3] S. H. Godson, et al., *The College of William and Mary*, p. 192 (1993) [hereinafter Godson].

[4] W. H. Bryson, *Legal Education in Va.*, pp. 8-9 [hereinafter Bryson]; also see above "Legal Education."

[5] "The specific effort to change the curriculum and the governance of the College took place within this context of far broader efforts to reshape the legal system in Virginia." Godson, p. 130.

haphazardly. The College at that time "levied a matriculation fee of ten shillings a student for the support of the [main] library and allocated two thirds of the total proceeds annually to the purchase of books."[6] While it is unclear how much, if any, of this early funding went to the purchase of law-related materials, we know that the College's "plans for importing `the best modern books' foundered on the shoals of inadequate financing,"[7] a pattern that would continue for far too long. It is also known that in the early 1770s the Flat Hat Club, an undergraduate fraternity that sought to develop the library collection, prepared a list of valuable and useful books to add to the College's main library, and that the first of the six headings of recommended books was titled "moral philosophy and civil law."[8]

During its first full year of operation in 1780, at least eight students were associated with the law curriculum at William and Mary,[9] but there was no cohesive legal collection at the College during Wythe's law program. Instead, particular treatises were chosen as a basis for classroom study. Apparently Wythe relied heavily on Matthew Bacon's *New Abridgement of the Law*[10] and Sir William Blackstone's *Commentaries on the Laws of England.*[11]

The narrow selection of legal texts seems to downplay the role of a formal law library in the early years of the law program. However, some sort of legal collection must have been envisioned during the

---

[6] Jennings, p. 79.

[7] *Id.* Even still, in 1781 the 3,000 volume library was the second largest academic collection in American, after Harvard (12,000 volumes) and just before Yale (2,700 volumes).

[8] *Id.* at 60–1.

[9] Godson, p. 136. There were at least eight students under Wythe in 1780, "since there were enough to form two moot court teams of four each. One of them was John Marshall, who remained only a few months. In a letter to James Madison . . .Jefferson praised the beginning that Wythe had made, remarking, `Our new institution at the college has had a success which has gained it universal applause'. . . ." *Id.*

[10] W. F. Swindler, "John Marshall's Preparation for the Bar – Some Observations on His Law Notes," *Am. J. Legal Hist.*, vol. 11, p. 207 (1967).

[11] "Although as a professor at William and Mary, Wythe emphasized the study of political economy and public law, his students received a formal grounding in the English common law, with Blackstone's *Commentaries on the Laws of England* being the basic text for his lectures. Students also were encouraged to read much more, to attend other lectures at the college, and to observe proceedings at the capital. Those able to do so received tutorial instruction from Wythe that extended from the classics to contemporary economics and politics; but to study with Wythe in this way, one needed to be a competent reader of Greek, Latin and French." P. D. Carrington, "The Revolutionary Idea of University Legal Education," *Wm. & Mary L. Rev.*, vol. 31, pp. 527, 535 (1990) [hereinafter Carrington].

reorganization of Virginia's legal system. "From the standpoint of education, the most important aspect of an apprenticeship was access to the master's law library and his guidance in reading the law."[12] Jefferson must have contemplated some type of law library that would complement, if not replace, a master's legal collection, for in a 1790 letter to John Garland he stressed the importance of a good library in legal education. "All that is necessary for a student is access to a library and directions in what order the books are to be read."[13]

The infant law curriculum had little time to develop. The College closed its doors on June 1, 1780, as the result of hostilities with the British Forces, and the survival of the law program became in doubt. When, in September 1782, the College's Board of Visitors met to prepare for the reopening of the College, an eminent member expressed his concern about the closing of the law school. "Should the law-school be overturned, the college will be reduced to a desart [sic]."[14] The law school survived, however, despite the later resignation of Wythe in 1789. Jefferson, who referred to Wythe as "the pride of the institution" and "one of the greatest men of the age," commented on the resignation, saying "it is all over with the College."[15]

The school found a worthy replacement for Wythe in St. George Tucker, who began teaching in September 1790.[16] As deserving as this appointment was, the modest Tucker asked that others not compare him to his predecessor, George Wythe, in part because he (Tucker) "had a defective library for a teacher of law. . . ."[17] Tucker altered the requirements for William and Mary's law degree, which may have had an additional effect on the texts used by the law program. The compilation of the College statutes of 1792 provided: "For the degree of Bachelor of Law, the Student must have the requisites for Bachelor of

[12] Bryson, p. 5.

[13] *Id.*, p. 25.

[14] Godson, p. 169.

[15] "In 1788 the courts of Virginia were reorganized, and Chancellor Wythe was required to move his residence to Richmond. This forced his resignation in 1789 of the professorship in Williamsburg after a decade of lecturing." Bryson, p. 24. Another account has Wythe resigning "in anger at the college." Carrington, p. 537.

[16] Tucker was the college rector at the time he succeeded Wythe. "Tucker, learned in the law and closely associated with the college, was the logical choice to replace Wythe. His recognition as a legal scholar was widespread and his connection with the college strong." C. T. Cullen, *St. George Tucker and Law in Virginia, 1772–1804*, p. 118 (1987) [hereinafter Cullen]. "Tucker was arguably the most important American legal scholar of the first half of the nineteenth century." Carrington, p. 540.

[17] Cullen, p. 119.

Arts; he must moreover be well acquainted with Civil History, both Ancient and Modern, and particularly with municipal law and police."[18]

At his introductory lecture, Tucker told his students that he had little to add beyond what his students could get by reading the works of Blackstone, Sir Francis Bacon, Sir Henry Finch, and Sir Matthew Hale. Although Blackstone's *Commentaries* formed the foundation of Tucker's course, his students would read John Locke's *Essay on Civil Government*, Sir Edward Coke's *Institutes*, William Sheppard's *Touchstone*, Bacon's *Abridgment*, James Burgh's *Political Disquisitions*, and Jean Louis de Lolme's *Constitution d'Angleterre*, titles one might expect to find in an early nineteenth century lawyer's library. A challenging instructor, Tucker gave his students a list of sixty-two titles he thought every law student should read (this number included twenty-five reports of English court cases), plus the laws of the young Virginia commonwealth.[19]

Although Tucker lamented publicly the size of his personal library, he often provided the additional materials through his private collection.[20] He was a successful lecturer,[21] and it was during Tucker's tenure that the first earned law degree was granted in America when, in 1793, the College conferred a bachelor of law degree on William H. Cabell.[22]

In the first thirty years of the new century, all parts of William and Mary seriously declined, including the law department.[23] Tucker resigned his professorship in 1803 after a disagreement with the Board

---

[18] R. M. Hughes, "William and Mary, the First American Law School," *Wm. & Mary Qtly.*, 2d ser., vol. 2, p. 42 (1922).

[19] Cullen, pp. 119–27.

[20] "Tucker gave his lectures in his home rather than at the college because he felt he needed to have his books readily available while he lectured. He found it helpful to hold his classes in his own house where he could turn to his library and quickly pull a book off the shelf to illustrate a point. Because there was some criticism of his teaching at home . . . Tucker tried taking a chairbox full of books to class at the college every day, but he complained that he frequently needed a book he had left in his library." *Id.*, pp. 120–21.

[21] "As many as seventeen attended his lectures at one time, and over one four-year period he claimed to have had a total of about fifty students." *Id.*, p. 126.

[22] S. L. Trask, "In Celebration of the Bicentennial of America's First Bachelor of Law Degree Recipient, William Cabell, William & Mary LB 1793," *Wm. & Mary Lawyer*, pp. 6–10 (1992).

[23] Bryson, p. 25. "Despite continuing stress between law professors and the administration of the college, the program at William and Mary survived for several decades in much the form in which Jefferson and Wythe had created it." Carrington, p. 540.

of Visitors over the administration of the College. The law collection, which was segregated from the general library collection, felt the effects of this decline and numbered only 300 volumes in 1829.[24] By the time Nathaniel Beverley Tucker, St. George Tucker's son, assumed the directorship of the law program in 1833 (a position he would hold until 1850), the "discipline had become a thing of the distant past."[25] Additional problems soon befell the College and the law program. "[T]he War Between the States and the College fires of 1859 and 1862 crippled the school, draining it of students and destroying the law library. (From the bits of remaining evidence, it is believed that the library collection was substantial.)"[26]

III. *Era of Decline: 1862–1920*

The College of William and Mary closed in 1862 at the beginning of the Civil War's Peninsula Campaign and did not reopen until 1888. The law program, however, remained closed for more than a generation longer; it would not reappear until 1920. Between the Civil War and 1920, although some occasional courses in law were offered and three law degrees were conferred, there was no real law program.[27]

IV. *Revival: 1920–1980*

A. *1920–1950*

In 1920, William and Mary's newly elected president Julian A. C. Chandler began a campaign to revive the College's law program. The first law courses were reintroduced to the College in September 1920. Still, Chandler did not yet consider this a "law school," primarily

---

[24] "Our library too, which for many years, has been in a state of disorder, has recently been reorganized. The books independently of the law library . . .number 3260. The law library collection contains [300] volumes." Report of the Faculty to the Visitors of William and Mary College Papers (July 1829), Mary Goodwin's Notes (Earl Gregg Swem Library Archives, College of William and Mary). "The Law Library, belonging to the College, is kept in the Law lecture room and the student is allowed constant access to it." *Catalogue of William and Mary College*, p. 19 (1855).

[25] Godson, p. 259. "Harvard, Columbia, Yale, the University of Virginia, and the University of Maryland, among others, had law schools, often headed by judges and scholars of great repute. The general trend in such programs was to make the study of law more professional. . . .Tucker was not part of this mainstream." *Id.*

[26] L. Huevel, "The Highest Aim," Marshall-Wythe School of Law [1983 Annual Report], p. 6 (1983).

[27] Godson, p. 571.

because the College offered only two years of law courses. Even after the Board of Visitors agreed upon a third year of law beginning in 1923–24, Chandler reported that his hesitancy was due to the library's limited size.[28] The program was renamed the School of Jurisprudence, and, under the direction of law professor Oscar Lane Shewmake, it became a division of the newly formed Marshall-Wythe School of Government and Citizenship.[29] The law program was not meant to be merely a training ground for prospective lawyers. "The purpose [was] . . .to permit properly trained students to study law in conjunction with other studies."[30] The reality, however, was that the school was a "modest, largely paper organization" that provided a home for the reinstituted law courses "but otherwise the school merely collected under a new title a number of professors and courses taught in other departments."[31] The small library collection associated with the School of Jurisprudence probably developed in relation to the several fields of study being taught in the liberal arts based law program.

The School of Jurisprudence's debut was not impressive. For several decades it suffered with few students, a small number of faculty, and limited facilities.[32] Funding for the struggling program was equally scarce, and the library suffered as a result. In 1927 Earl Gregg Swem, the College Librarian, reported that the law library collection consisted of only 4,450 volumes, which included a collection the library was about to receive. At least 7,500 volumes were needed to meet the minimum standards set by the Association of American Law Schools, which had been accrediting member schools since the turn of the

[28] *Id.* Although a bulletin from August 1920 announced plans for the reestablishment of the law program, a full three year curriculum was not yet in place. At any rate, the College claimed that the formal re-establishment of the law school had occurred on January 14, 1922, with the inauguration of the Marshall-Wythe School of Government and Citizenship.

[29] It seems peculiar, indeed, to have a "School" of Jurisprudence within the Marshall-Wythe "School" of Government and Citizenship. However, that is what the College called the resurrected law program.

[30] *Id.*, p. 571, quoting subsequent Dean Theodore S. Cox.

[31] *Id.*, p. 570.

[32] "After its reestablishment the school awarded its first bachelor of law (B.L.) degree in the summer of 1924. . . . [B]ut by the end of 1939, nearly two decades after the program began, only twenty-eight students had earned law degrees at William and Mary. During this period, enrollments in law classes usually ranged between forty and seventy students each semester, but many were undergraduates who were not preparing for a career in law." *Id.*, p. 572. "From 1924–34 graduates received a B.L. (Bachelor of Laws) degree. From 1935 to 1966 graduates received a B.C.L. (Bachelor of Civil Laws) degree. Law graduates began receiving the J.D. (Doctor of Jurisprudence) degree beginning in 1967." Godson, p. 572, n. 42.

century. To reach this size, Swem estimated that at least $7,500 would have to be spent over the next five years to develop the law collection.[33] Others considered the collection even poorer. In 1928 John Garland Pollard, a distinguished Virginia lawyer who helped Chandler revive the law program, estimated that more than half of the materials in the law library were obsolete and that no less than $10,000 was needed to provide an adequate law collection.[34]

As late as 1931, the law collection consisted of only 6,500 volumes on the third floor of the main library. Despite – or perhaps because of – the feeble state of the law program, in 1932 the College hired the first librarian to supervise the law collection, and presumably, eventually an independent law library. Soon after John Latané Lewis assumed this new position, the law school secured accreditation by the American Bar Association. The law school was accredited by the Association of American Law Schools (AALS) in 1936.

Insufficient funds hindered Lewis's ability to develop the collection, and the library acquired few new materials.[35] Notes from a 1934 faculty meeting reveal how few items Lewis could acquire with his small budget:

> Mr. Lewis reported that $125.57 is available for the purchase of books. Dean Cox stated that he has been authorized to spend an additional $200 in purchases. It was decided to purchase the following: 2 copies of *Burks' Pleading and Practice*, 2 copies of Restatement of *Conflict of Laws*, 2 copies of *Restatement of Torts*, 2 copies of *Restatement of Agency*, 1 1930 *Code of Virginia*, 1 copy of *Webster's New International Dictionary*.[36]

---

[33] *Id.*, p. 572.

[34] *Id.*, pp. 572-73. In a letter to Thomas W. Shelton, Robert M. Hughes (a supporter, along with President Chandler, of the revival of the study of law at William and Mary) cited the need to return William and Mary's law program to good standing. Funding for the acquisition of the AALS required volumes (7,500) was unsuccessfully sought from the newly available Taft memorial. Papers of John Stewart Bryan, President of the College (Earl Gregg Swem Library Archives, College of William and Mary).

[35] By the new year Lewis was purchasing a modest number of materials for the library. "The Law Librarian was authorized by the faculty to purchase for the Law Library the following: *United States Digest, Barton's Chancery Practice, Wigmore on Evidence, Williston on Sales, Thompson on Private Corporations.*" Faculty Minutes, January 11, 1933.

[36] Faculty Minutes, December 11, 1934.

In June of 1936, the president's annual report indicated that the law library held 8,865 volumes, a modest increase from the 6,500 volumes of 1931. Funding for legal materials, which totaled a scant $1,913.90 in 1936, came from the State and also a small private fund set up for the purchase of law books.[37] The few legal donations at this time were directed to the main library, which housed the law collection as one of its many divisions.

But the modest law collection was not the law school's sole concern. The AALS, when it accredited the law school in 1936, included several demands "all of which would cost more money than the state was likely to provide."[38] When the College's Board of Visitors met in early 1938, William and Mary President John Stewart Bryan convinced the Board to downgrade the School of Jurisprudence to the Department of Jurisprudence because "our law school is not a credit to William and Mary and it cannot be made a credit to us without the expenditure of money which we do not have, and which I see no likelihood of getting."[39] At the same time, a special committee composed of Board members was charged to study further the meager law program, which had bestowed only twenty-three degrees since its revival nearly two decades earlier.

In May of 1939 the Board of Visitors, following the special committee's recommendation, announced plans to abolish the law school. A swift outcry from current law students and law alumni, however, forced the Board to reverse its action only a week later. Ironically, the Board announced not only that it would retain the law school, but that it would strengthen it.[40] One must speculate whether President Bryan hoped to see this result when he recommended downgrading the school.

With renewed hope, the new decade gave birth to escalated interest in the law program and an increase in the number of students studying law at William and Mary. In 1941, enrollment in the Department of Jurisprudence jumped from 79 to 140. The law collection, housed in the main library, began to receive regular and sustained use. Approximately sixty people a day visited the law library,

---

[37] Annual Report of the President, June 6, 1936, Supplement by John L. Lewis. The Sherman Fund was restricted to the purchase of law books.

[38] Godson, p. 649.

[39] *Id.*, chap. 6, n. 58; Report to the Board of Visitors (February 8, 1938).

[40] R. W. Arthur, "How a Small Band of Students Saved the Law School," Marshall-Wythe School of Law [1983 Annual Report], pp. 8–9 (1983).

which was then managed by a staff of five. Presumably all worked part time.[41]

Unfortunately, World War II interrupted the progress of the developing law program and led to a series of rapid changes and instability in the library's leadership. Law Librarian Lewis was on leave for the war from April 1943 until September 1946, but he never returned to William and Mary as law librarian. Charles Harper Anderson became law librarian in the fall of 1946 after his graduation from the Department of Jurisprudence. He remained in that position only until 1947, when he joined the law faculty. Anderson was followed by Virginia Blanche Till, the College's first female law librarian, who served until the end of 1949. Chester Stoyle Baker, Jr., took over in 1950 and managed to stabilize the position nearly through the end of the decade.

B. *1950–1960*

The haltering effects of World War II seemed to dissipate by the early 1950s. In 1953, the Department of Jurisprudence split from the School of Government and Citizenship, and, under the leadership of Dean Dudley Warner Woodbridge, became the Marshall-Wythe School of Law.[42] The establishment of an endowed chair in taxation reflected the addition to the curriculum of a Master of Law and Taxation, the first degree of its kind in the nation.[43] In that same year the law library received its first endowment when Jessie Ball duPont gave the College a bond portfolio valued at more than $33,000 to inaugurate the new tax program. A portion of that amount was expended "for the salary of a renowned specialist in law and taxation, and for the acquisition of books related to that program."[44]

Up to this time the College's legal collection was housed both within the law school (in Blair Hall) and in the College library. Faculty minutes from the fall of 1954 indicate an intent to consolidate the law collection in the law school library.

[41] Annual Report of the President, August 20, 1941.

[42] Godson, p. 784.

[43] *Id.*

[44] "Designation of the Jessie Ball duPont Fund to Function as Endowment." William and Mary Board of Visitors Resolution W-9 (February 23–25, 1978). Today the endowment generates about $5,000 in annual income to the law library for the purchase of tax materials.

> [S]ome materials published by the Government which should be in the law library are in the College general library. . . .The College Librarian had requested Mr. Atkeson [a law professor] to make a list of the most recent of these materials, and promised that they would be moved to the law library immediately.[45]
>
> These items, which became available for shipment in November of 1954, raised the number of volumes in the law library to approximately 21,000.[46]

The total library staff remained modest in size. With law librarian Chester Baker, the staff numbered seven, including student assistants. None of the staff, however, including Baker, were full-time.[47] The library attempted to purchase many badly needed items, and Dean Woodbridge asked the faculty for recommendations on materials to acquire for the collection. He promised that funding would be available for both present wants and to pay for continuations.[48] Notwithstanding the dean's pledge of support, the library was still plagued by inadequate funding. At the close of 1955, Baker indicated that he would purchase no new books that year because all funds were needed for continuations.[49]

Limited resources continued to restrict severely the development of the law collection. In the fall of 1956 Dean Woodbridge acknowledged the collection needs of the library, but the purchase of even these essential faculty-recommended materials was inhibited by poor funding.[50] In April 1957, Baker informed President Chandler "that it would be desirable to have a Law Library budget of $7,000 since approximately $5,300 is needed just to keep up the present contin-

[45] Faculty Minutes, October 28, 1954. In addition, there followed a "detailed discussion of rules and regulations concerning the use of books in the law library."

[46] Faculty Minutes, November 24, 1954. "Mr. Atkeson stated that certain government publications which had been housed in the general library were now packaged and ready for movement to the law library. . . . Mr. Baker stated that the law library now has approximately 21,000 volumes."

[47] D. W. Woodbridge, *A Short History of the Marshall-Wythe School of Law*, p. 3 (Earl Gregg Swem Library Archives, College of William and Mary).

[48] Faculty Minutes, October 7, 1954.

[49] Faculty Minutes, November 3, 1955.

[50] Faculty Minutes, October 16, 1956. The list of needed items included various statutes, journals, and indexes.

uations."[51] About $9,000 was spent for legal materials in 1958, although the budget for that year was only $4,000. Chandler made up this difference with one-time special funding, but the College made no commitments to improve the law library budget. Indeed, only $6,000 was budgeted for legal materials the next year.[52] These financial difficulties came at a time when other deficiencies also began to threaten the law library, including an increasingly inadequate facility.[53] The law school's 1957 move to the Bryan dormitory complex and the library's occupancy of the basement of the adjoining Camm Building, unfortunately, did little to alleviate these space problems.[54]

Unknown to many, the law school survived an external threat in the Spring of 1957. One year earlier the Virginia General Assembly created the State Council of Higher Education, in part, to recommend elimination of duplicate programs in the several state colleges and universities. Davis Y. Paschall, who would in 1960 become president of William and Mary, had only days earlier been appointed Superintendent of Public Instruction. At his first State Council meeting, Paschall learned that the Council listed the William and Mary law school as its number one priority slated for elimination. A passage from a biography of Paschall describes candidly the state of the law school at that time.

> As a member of the Board of Visitors of William and Mary, he [Paschall] was keenly aware of the vulnerability of the law school. It was housed in the basement of a men's dormitory; had a total enrollment of 48; six faculty members, including one part-timer; limited library resources, and was regarded more as a department of jurisprudence than a law school. Its

[51] Faculty Minutes, April 25, 1957. Of the $5,300 spent on continuations, over $2,100 was spent on tax materials. The actual budget for 1957 was $4,000.

[52] Faculty Minutes, September 18, 1958.

[53] In the Spring of 1957 President Chandler asked Baker about the most urgent needs of the law library. "Mr. Baker replied that the Law Library needed at least two ranges of shelving placed in the tax room to take care of the new material and to relieve the crowded condition in the main stock area." Faculty Minutes, April 25, 1957. The College Librarian, citing a need to "take the books off the floor, agreed with this recommendation." Mr. Servies (the College Librarian) also hoped to employ a new cataloger in the "very near future" to provide aid to the new law collection. Faculty Minutes, November 21, 1957.

[54] The law school occupied the first floor of Bryan and most of its basement. The library occupied the basement of the Camm Building, which connected with Bryan. Interview with John Donaldson, law professor, in Williamsburg, Va., by James Heller (November 21, 1995).

> faculty members then met and voted with the Faculty of Arts and Sciences.[55]

Paschall was convinced that the General Assembly would approve the Council's recommendation, should it see it. In an emotional speech he told the Council that "[t]o abolish the law school that Jefferson established would be like removing the very heart of a College that is, indeed, a 'Pearl of Great Price' to this Commonwealth." He further cautioned that abolishing the school "would be a gross and callous disregard of the Biblical admonition: 'Remove not the ancient landmark, which thy fathers have set.' (Proverbs 22:28.) It would constitute an unforgivable betrayal of priceless heritage, and its perpetrators would be silhouetted in infamy."[56] The Council agreed to hold in abeyance its recommendation to abolish the law school and did not send it to the General Assembly. The law school had survived yet another threat to its existence.

Toward the end of the decade it became increasingly apparent to the school and College administration that the law library's deficiencies must be addressed, particularly the weak acquisitions budget, as both the ABA and AALS collection requirements were about to increase.[57] Changes in the law library's budget finally occurred,[58] and extra funding was made available to the library. Baker, nearing the end of his tenure as law librarian, apparently was quite conservative in spending the library allocation, for the library budget actually showed a $1,250 surplus in 1959.[59]

With the departure of Baker, the College and the law school initiated steps for greater formal involvement of the law faculty in

[55] W. Kale and H. L. Smith, *Davis Y. Paschall: A Study in Leadership*, p. 130 (1990).

[56] *Id.*, p. 131.

[57] "The minimum number of volumes in the law library, as well as the type of reference materials in the library, will very possibly become much more stringent." Interdepartmental Communication Regarding Report on Observations, etc., at Convention of Association of American Law Schools, Chicago, December 28-30. Faculty Minutes, January 5, 1959.

[58] The budget for the forthcoming academic year was broken into three sections: "Personal Service," "Expense of Operation for Instruction other than Personal Service," and "Research." Faculty Minutes, February 19, 1959.

[59] "Mr. Baker advised the faculty that there was about $1250 in the Law Library appropriations that had not been spent and he would welcome any suggestions for the purchase of books." Faculty Minutes, March 19, 1959. The faculty experienced these budgetary benefits as well. "Mr. Joseph Curtis stated that he wished to go on record that he appreciated the recent purchase by the Law Library of the 1950 Code of Virginia for use in his office." Faculty Minutes, April 16, 1959.

library affairs, particularly with regard to collection development. In the fall of 1959, William and Mary President Alvin D. Chandler requested formation of a faculty Law Library Committee to suggest and prioritize potential acquisitions to the law library and to inform the law school dean of its recommendations.[60]

C. *THE 1960S*

The overhaul of the law library continued with the arrival of Anna Booth Johnson, who replaced Baker in 1960. Like her predecessors, Johnson remained under the joint supervision of the College librarian and the law school dean. Johnson, only the second woman to run the law library, was Marshall-Wythe's first full-time librarian.[61] The law school's 1963 Self-Study praised her as "a qualified librarian who has taken many steps to prepare herself with respect to the special problems connected with a law library."[62] The Self-Study went on to commend the services of the law library, pointing out the excellence of the "small library, well managed by an efficient staff, which finds increasing use by the general College community and lawyers in the area."[63]

At this time, the Law Library Committee was primarily interested in building the collection. In particular, the library sought to acquire the statutes from each state.[64] Although the committee knew that the

---

[60] Faculty Minutes, October 15, 1959. The Law Librarian meets regularly with the Law Library Committee. The College Librarian meets with this committee several times a year with respect to budget, overall policies, handling of purchases which are made through the general library services, personnel for the library, and facilities. 1963 Law School Self-Study. Appendix A (No. 5) to Faculty Minutes, April 18, 1963, p. 1 [hereinafter *1963 Self-Study*].

[61] Interview with Anna Booth Johnson, former law librarian, in Williamsburg, Va., by Scott Boak, James Heller, and Sue Welch (April 3, 1995). Johnson received a B.S. degree from Longwood College in 1956.

[62] *1963 Self-Study*, p. 1.

[63] The *Self-Study* also described and commented on Ms. Johnson's staff. "While one regular assistant has been available on a part-time basis, she should be made a full-time, permanent member of the law library staff and her salary allocated to the law library funds. An adequate number of student assistants is available to keep the library running smoothly." *Id.*, p. 2.

[64] Faculty Minutes, January 21, 1960. The Library Committee was "to consider costs and order of purchase." The collection of complete state statutory codes was completed in 1965. Faculty Minutes, April 22, 1965. Law Professor William F. Swindler, who had also been employed as Director of Development for the College under former President Davis Paschall, was instrumental in helping to secure funding to build the state collection. Interview with John Donaldson, law professor, in Williamsburg, Va., by

treatise collection also needed much strengthening, it was aware of the inability to house many new volumes within the law library. The faculty apparently also were aware of the importance of volume count, for they discussed the:

> desirability of including some ten thousand peripheral volumes in the law library count which are not now actually in the law library for lack of space. This might be done on the theory that they were now accessible and were being stockpiled against the time when we will have available room for them.[65]

The faculty wisely questioned the propriety of this action, however, as the materials were not readily accessible.[66] Steps were taken to provide additional services in the law library. Mr. Servies, still the College Librarian, offered to purchase a copying machine and microfilm reader for the law library.[67] For once, funding for these items was readily forthcoming. The 1963 Self-Study recognized the College's efforts to improve law library funding, including establishing endowments for that purpose.[68]

This unusual, and much welcomed, infusion of funds from the College clearly was designed to impress the ABA inspection team. Private support also was forthcoming. A $5,000 gift by the late Charles Phineas Sherman, Lecturer Emeritus in Roman, Canon, and Civil Law, enabled the library to build a collection of Roman law materials.[69]

James Heller (November 21, 1995); telephone interview with Davis Y. Paschall, former William and Mary President, by James Heller (November 22, 1995).

[65] Special Faculty Meeting Minutes, February 4, 1960.

[66] *Id.* By 1963, the chief need was for "slightly larger appropriations for purchase of current books, more funds for the purchase of a complete set of state annotated cases (although we are well within the standards of the Association of American Law Schools), more funds for back issues of law reviews, more funds to complete the cataloging of treatises under the standard system." *1963 Self-Study*, p. 2.

[67] Faculty Minutes, January 31, 1960. Again, "[t]he problem of where to find room for this equipment was discussed."

[68] "The administration has made special efforts to aid the law library in its development, and plans are under way to secure partial or complete endowment funds for it. . . . Mr. Curtis announced that an additional $3,500 has been allotted by the President for the law library expenditures as another step in readiness for the forthcoming A.B.A. Committee on Legal Education visitation." Faculty Minutes, April 18, 1963.

[69] "Resolution Acknowledging Charles P. Sherman Bequest to Marshall-Wythe School of Law." Board of Visitors Resolution W-12 (September 12, 1964). Today the Sherman Fund generates about $1,700 in annual income.

Another gift that same year, made by Marie Estaire Baumert in the name of her brother Guillermo Butler Sherwell, eventually also would be used for the purchase of law books.[70]

These efforts were, however, temporary solutions; by 1965 the old financial woes had returned. Faculty minutes from the autumn of 1965 noted that the law library:

> is now without funds for the purchase of additional books in the balance of the session. The [Library] Committee urged that this plight be made known to the College Administration with a request for additional funds of $3,700 to meet immediate needs, and that a special allocation of $15,000 be sought for other long standing needs.[71]

The library's funding and space problems coincided with, and in some sense were due to, a period of steady growth at the law school. By September of 1962 law school enrollment had reached 91 full-time law students, the largest enrollment in the history of the school. Enrollment increases continued throughout the 1960s, and by 1969 the size of the school again doubled, to 190 students.[72] In just ten years the school had quadrupled in size.

Larger enrollment created pressure for additional law school space. Throughout the 1960s and through the next decade, the law library was housed in several different buildings. During most of the sixties, the law library's general collection was divided between a portion of the basement of Bryan Hall and the basement of the adjoining Camm Hall, while the tax collection was housed solely in Camm Hall.[73] Library shelves were nearly full, and student seating was inadequate.

The law school was able to address some of its space problems upon completion of Swem Library in 1967. The law school moved into

---

[70] "Resolution: Guillermo Butler Sherwell Lecture Fund." The Endowment Association of the College of William and Mary Resolution VIII (January 24, 1973). The donation was originally used to fund a series of lectures on contemporary developments in the law. In 1973, however, Dean James Whyte recommended that the fund be used to establish the G. B. Sherwell Memorial Law Book Collection, as the income produced was no longer sufficient to pay the fees and expenses of a distinguished lecture. Today the Sherwell fund generates about $1,100 in annual income.

[71] Faculty Minutes, October 21, 1965.

[72] Special Faculty Meeting Minutes, September 12, 1969. The increases were steady over the course of the 1960s. The school had 148 enrolled students in 1965, 163 students in 1966, and 177 students in 1967.

[73] *1963 Self-Study* (No. 7), p. 2. This haphazard library setup, however, would continue to plague the law school until the completion of the present law building in 1980.

the old general library, which became known as the Marshall-Wythe Building.[74] The library occupied most of the first floor of Marshall-Wythe, plus the entire basement. But satisfaction with the new facility was short lived. At the end of 1968 the AALS revised their standards to require that a law library have the capacity to seat at least 60 percent of its student body at any one time, a requirement Dean Joseph Curtis considered the "most hurtful."[75]

Following the move into the Marshall-Wythe Building, the law library sought to have its own budget. A strongly worded faculty resolution was sent to the College President, Davis Paschall, in the spring of 1968 requesting a budget that complied with the accreditation requirements, autonomous administration of the law library, and that the College make special law library funding its major objective during William and Mary's 275th anniversary.[76] The College administration approved the proposed separate law library budget, which it set at $28,000.[77] This budgetary victory, however, was overshadowed by the inadequacy of the funding; the allocation did not provide sufficient funds for existing subscriptions and continuations, nor for necessary new purchases.[78]

The AALS recommendation that law school libraries have a minimum annual budget of $40,000 and a minimum collection of 60,000 volumes put considerable pressure on the law school to find

[74] Interview with Anna Booth Johnson, *supra*. Johnson described the move, which she coordinated, as an ordeal. She had sporadic help from students with the transportation of boxed materials.

[75] Faculty Minutes, January 23, 1969.

[76] Resolution of Faculty of Marshall-Wythe School of Law Concerning Budget for Law Library, March 28, 1968 (with Faculty Minutes, March 28, 1968).

[77] Law Library Status Report, October 21, 1968 (with Faculty Minutes, October 22, 1968). The law library remained under the College Library's supervision, however, in regards to acquisitions.

[78] "Dr. Swindler . . . noted with pleasure that this year the Law Library at last has been given its own budget, but expressed concern that the budget was charged without Law School authorization with items carried over from last year. He recommended the Law Faculty to resolve that (a) the Law Library budget may include charges other than those for the current year only upon the Law Library Director's express authorization, and (b) restitution be made of funds representing non-current items already assessed against the current budget. Dean Curtis responded, saying that 'it is unrealistic to expect further allocation for the Law Library purposes at this time'." Faculty Minutes, October 28, 1968.

additional funding for the library.[79] The law school understood the need to seek private gifts to the library.[80] "[T]he Law Library Committee urged the immediate expansion of both the budget and the collections by about one-third. . . .The Committee recommended that the long-discussed plans to approach private industry for possible supplementary support in the indicated areas be implemented in the near future."[81] Additional private funding was not immediately forthcoming, but presumably the College was able to supplement the law library budget. By June of 1969, faculty member William Swindler, who chaired the Library Committee, reported that "[t]he $44,500 paid out for acquisitions takes us over the $40,000 minimum set up as a guideline for accredited libraries. We will have approximately 60,000 volumes by 1972."[82]

D. *THE 1970S*

The seventies began with an incredible increase in the size of the student body. The entering class more than doubled, from 76 entering students in 1969, to 182 in 1970. During these changes, Anna Booth Johnson stepped down as law librarian in 1971. She continued to work as associate, however, under the new librarian, J. Madison Whitehead. Whitehead, the first law librarian at William and Mary to hold a law degree,[83] is remembered primarily for two major catastrophes during his tenure: the failed attempt to classify the collection under the Ranganathan Colon Classification System and the 1975 ABA accreditation crisis.

At the time of Whitehead's arrival, approximately one-third of the collection had already been cataloged using the Library of Congress system. For some reason, Whitehead abandoned the LC system in 1972

[79] Faculty Minutes, January 23, 1969, and Report of Law Library Committee, January 21, 1969. It was around this time that the library received additional staff support. Berna Heyman was hired as Assistant Librarian for Acquisitions and Cataloging in December 1968 and held this position through August 1969.

[80] "The [Law Library] Committee notes that, because for a number of years there has been no College funds available for the large scale acquisitions needed to keep up the quality of the Law Library Collection, substantial annual gifts of private funds must be sought. . . ." Law Library Status Report, October 21, 1968 (with Faculty Minutes, October 22, 1968).

[81] *Id.*

[82] Faculty Minutes, June 10, 1969.

[83] Whitehead had a B.A. from the University of Chicago, an M.L.S. from Louisiana State University, and a J.D. from Tulane University.

in favor of the Ranganathan Colon system. By 1975, however, the confusing new classification system had been discontinued due to constant complaints from all sectors of the law school community.[84] In the summer of 1976 the library began re-instituting from scratch the discarded Library of Congress system, which by this time included the American Law (KF) tables.

The seventies also saw the last remnants of College control over the law library disappear. The main library (renamed the Earl Gregg Swem Library in 1966 after the librarian-historian who directed it from 1920 to 1944) had retained oversight over law acquisitions, even after the implementation of an autonomous law library budget. Law school Dean James Whyte, noting that the law library now had in its employment an acquisitions supervisor, stated that there was "adequate personnel to staff the Law Library. . .[and that] the proposed separation from College Library Supervision can be made by January 1, 1970."[85] Although it is impossible to determine whether this event happened precisely on that date, it is clear that in 1973 the school reported that the "law school library administration is totally autonomous from the main library on campus in accordance with ABA standards," and that acquisitions were made "directly by the law librarian to law book publishers, and not through the centralized library acquisition department of the parent institution."[86] However, "Law Library funding requests to the Legislature from the College [were] not grouped with requests from the law school, but [were] grouped under a general library request."[87]

Despite its new independence, the law library continued to experience the usual array of problems. Gaining autonomy from the main library did not necessarily mean additional staffing. Most of the incoming unclassified materials were not cataloged; the law library did not employ a professional cataloger until 1976. The law collection, which in 1973 had approximately 73,000 volumes, was considered adequate in primary materials, but weak in periodicals and recently

[84] "Dean James P. Whyte, Jr., abolished the long-controversial colon classification system last Monday, following an extended meeting with law librarian J. Madison Whitehead. The Dean directed Whitehead to end the colon system because of `100 percent dissatisfaction with it, students and faculty alike'." *Amicus Curiae*, vol. 5, p. 1 (March 11, 1975).

[85] Faculty Minutes, October 16, 1969.

[86] Law School 1973 Self-Study (March 1973), p. 31 [hereinafter *1973 Self-Study*]. The Self-Study was prepared in anticipation of a March 18–21, 1973, ABA/AALS inspection visit.

[87] *Id.* That practice continues to this day with no ill effects.

published texts.[88] The 1972–73 budget of $60,000 permitted the funding of continuations, but not the purchase of new materials.[89] Not mincing words, the law school reported in its 1973 Self-Study that "[b]udgetary support for the library is barely sufficient to sustain life," and that "[w]ith such miserly support, it is unlikely that the deficiencies of the library will ever be rectified."[90]

The increasing number of enrolled law students further strained the library's already limited resources. Total enrollment jumped from 190 students in 1969 to 459 in 1973, a 142 percent increase.[91] The library staff, which now consisted of two professionals, Whitehead and Johnson, and five full-time clerical staff, could not address the massive increase in the use of the library and its collection.[92] The facilities were, in a word, dismal. The 1973 Self-Study noted that:

> the Law Library conducts its business in three different buildings: Marshall-Wythe where the main collection and library administrative offices are housed, the basement of the Wren Building where additional seating space and room for duplicate materials is found and the third floor of James Blair Hall where much processing of incoming books takes place.[93]

The 1975 American Bar Association inspection visit served notice that the law school's ABA accreditation was at risk. The ABA visiting committee found the school to be deficient in several areas.[94] James P. White, Consultant on Legal Education to the American Bar Association and head of the visiting committee, reported that "[t]he Law School has possibly the most inadequate physical plant of any ABA approved law

---

[88] 1972–73 Law School Annual Report, p. 19 (June 29, 1973).

[89] *Id.*

[90] *1973 Self-Study*, p. 31.

[91] Special Faculty Meeting Minutes, September 12, 1969, and 1972-73 Law School Annual Report, p. 1 (June 29, 1973).

[92] 1972-73 Law School Annual Report, pp. 19-21.

[93] *1973 Self-Study*, p. 44. Former students recall "the `classic' experience of Tucker Hall, its tomblike library and various satellite classrooms." The Marshall-Wythe Building was renamed the Tucker Building. "Memories of Law School: The Accreditation Crisis of '75," *Amicus Curiae*, vol. 5, p. 9 (January 23, 1995).

[94] Deficiencies indicated by the ABA report include building, library books and personnel, faculty salaries, admissions interference, and rules regarding promotion, tenure, and appointments. Faculty Minutes, September 5, 1975.

school in the country."[95] Although the library collection had reached the 100,000 volume mark, the library was the source of much of White's criticism: "A law library is the heart of the law school. It is my opinion that the current physical setting and support level for the library limits the academic aspirations and goals of the Marshall-Wythe School of Law."[96] White noted that the unfortunate physical arrangement of the law library greatly reduced the effectiveness of the already attenuated staff. Given the "library's bifurcated physical setting and that professional librarians should man both parts of the Library at all times, it seems to me imperative that at least three additional professional librarians are provided in the forthcoming academic year."[97]

White visited Williamsburg in October 1975, to explain the ABA's report. He commented on the law school's strong academic program and reported that the ABA's primary concerns centered around the law building, the law library facilities, and library staffing. William and Mary President Thomas Graves met with White and commented on their conversation, saying that the law school's accreditation was jeopardized due to woefully inadequate facilities, the limited resources for the Law Library in terms of staff, space and acquisition funds and concern over law faculty salaries.[98] The law school student newspaper reported numerous student complaints with the library, including ineffective use of shelf and reading space, the location of the reserve collection, inadequate space to store superseded materials, the library's small audiovisual collection, and the need to utilize the faculty library differently.[99] In the end, the ABA's biting report, which noted "with very grave concern" the law school's problems, provided the necessary impetus for lasting change within the law school, and in particular, the law library.[100]

---

[95] ABA Visiting Report, May 15, 1975, p. 65.

[96] *Id.*, p. 66.

[97] *Id.* "The auxiliary Library, which among other materials, houses the entire tax collection, is operated by only student helpers during the evening and weekend hours." *Id.*

[98] "ABA Consultant Explains Unaccreditation Problems," *Amicus Curiae*, vol. 6, pp. 1, 4 (October 28, 1975).

[99] "Inadequate Law Library Presents Huge Problems," *Amicus Curiae*, vol. 6, p. 4 (October 28, 1975).

[100] Faculty Minutes, September 5, 1975, Acting Dean Emeric Fischer. In response to the report, "Dean Fischer stated that he intends to mobilize our alumni, the Virginia Bar, and Justices Burger, Clark, and Powell in connection with the school's need for a new

The downward spiral of the struggling law school and law library began to change in 1976. William B. Spong, a prominent and politically well-connected Virginian (he had served for ten years as a Virginia State Senator and was a member of the U.S. Senate from 1967–73), was appointed dean of the law school. On the financial side, the Virginia General Assembly allocated an additional $50,000 for law library collection development.[101] More significantly, the General Assembly appropriated funds for site preparation and utilities for a new law school building to be located approximately one-half mile from the main campus. The law school site was adjacent to land where the National Center for State Courts, having decided to relocate from Denver to Williamsburg, planned to build a new headquarters building.

The College immediately addressed the ABA's staffing concerns, but at the expense of the Swem Library. Two Swem librarians were transferred from Swem to the law library. Paul Roy came to the law library in late 1975 to oversee acquisitions functions,[102] and Sue Welch arrived from Swem in February 1976 to serve as Law Cataloging Librarian.[103] One of her first tasks was to reclassify the collection to the Library of Congress classification system.

In May 1976, as an interim measure to address some of the most pressing space problems – particularly the ABA's insistence on more library seating – the law library relinquished what little space it had in the Wren basement and obtained additional space in the Camm building. Between the two buildings the library offered 269 seats, very close to the AALS 60 percent requirement. Both the Marshall-Wythe and Camm facilities were attended by library staff.

Whitehead departed Marshall-Wythe in mid-1976 and was replaced by Caroline Chandler Heriot. Heriot arrived with an impressive résumé. After receiving her M.L.S. she worked at the University of North Carolina law library while earning a law degree at the U.N.C. law school. She served as law librarian at the Supreme Court of New Mexico and later at the Loyola of New Orleans Law School, where she planned and oversaw the construction of a new law school library. This experience made her particularly well qualified to plan the hoped-for new law library at William and Mary.

---

building." Faculty Minutes, September 5, 1975.

[101] March 17, 1976, Memorandum from President Thomas Graves to the Board of Visitors, Board of Trustees, and Board of Directors.

[102] Roy's tenure would not last long. He left William and Mary sometime during the 1976–77 fiscal year.

[103] In 1981, Welch was promoted to Head of Technical Services.

Heriot quickly transformed the library. She expanded the hours the library was open, but at the same time banned smoking, food, and drinks in the library.[104] The law faculty adopted her proposal that new courses could not be approved without a library impact statement. Those proposing courses had to coordinate with the law librarian in advance to assure that the library had materials to support student and faculty coursework.[105] In that same year the library received a gift from Louis Ellenson, a 1950 graduate of the law school, the income of which was restricted to the purchase of books for the law school.[106]

Laura Sale became the library's first professional Serials/ Documents Librarian in 1978, and later that year Edmund P. Edmonds joined the staff as Associate Law Librarian. Edmonds had received his B.A. from Notre Dame, an M.L.S. from Maryland, and a J.D. from Toledo. He earlier had served as the Head of the Circulation Department at Toledo. Edmonds served as William and Mary's first law-trained reference librarian; until his hiring third year law students provided reference support. He soon integrated the library into the academic curriculum when he assumed responsibility for teaching the Legal Research and Writing course. As 1978 drew to a close, the law library became a selective federal depository library.

V. *The Modern Era: 1980–1995*

Necessarily, Heriot spent most of her time planning and overseeing construction of the library portion of the new law school building. The eagerly awaited building opened in the fall of 1980. With 37,270 net square feet on three floors, the new library was nearly triple the size of the 13,994 square feet occupied previously. Heriot estimated that the library would accommodate 250,000 bound volumes; the existing collection occupied less than 40 percent of the library's 49,000 linear feet of shelving. With seating for 458 patrons (130 carrels and 328 other seats), the new facility could seat more than 80 percent of the student body.

The law library also moved into the electronic age later that year. It acquired its first LEXIS terminal, joined SOLINET, and began using the OCLC online cataloging system. Using OCLC not only boosted production, but it also provided elevated service to library patrons.

---

[104] Faculty Minutes, February 3, 1977.

[105] Faculty Minutes, November 18, 1977.

[106] "Establishment of the Louis Ellenson Endowment Fund." Endowment Association of the College of William and Mary, Resolution 4 (September 23, 1977). Today the Ellenson Endowment Fund generates about $2,200 in annual income.

New books, which formerly remained in cataloging for thirty to sixty days, were generally cataloged within one week of receipt.[107] The library soon began a retrospective conversion project that, in two years, would transfer nearly all cataloging records to machine-readable format.

The move into the new building also enabled the library to obtain an accurate collection count for the first time in many years. Not surprisingly, the collection was smaller than had been reported in the ABA annual surveys. At the time of the move into the new facility, the library had approximately 155,000 volumes and volume equivalents, with about 110,000 volumes in hard copy.

An ABA/AALS site evaluation team visited the law school in 1981 for their sabbatical inspection visit. Now in the new facility, the law school had addressed the 1975 team's primary concern. But this team still had several concerns about the law library, including uneven funding, uneven collection development, and an over-dependence upon gift moneys to purchase new materials. The team reported that the professional staff (now four in number) was still too small in size, that the library relied too heavily on student help for basic library duties, and that salaries for professional, classified, and student staff members were inadequate.[108] These problems the law school could, and eventually would, address. The most difficult burden for the library and law school was the illness and, in December 1981, the death of Caroline Heriot.

Associate Law Librarian Ed Edmonds was named Acting Law Librarian and served in this capacity until he was appointed Director in 1983. One of Edmonds's first tasks was to find a new associate director. He hired Martha Rush, who, like Edmonds, had both M.L.S. and J.D. degrees and had been serving as Chief Legislative Librarian with the Kentucky Legislative Research Commission.

The law library surpassed the 200,000 volume mark in 1985, which represented more than a doubling in the size of the collection from ten years earlier. This swift increase in collection size was made possible by significant growth in the collection development budget–with both public and private funds–between 1975 and 1981.

[107] Interview with Sue Welch, Head of Technical Services, in Williamsburg, Va., by David Elliott (March 22, 1995).

[108] ABA/AALS 1980 Site Evaluation Report, pp. 14–31. Laura Sale left the library not long after the ABA/AALS visit, at which time Heriot reorganized the staff. She promoted Sue Welch to head of the new Technical Services Department and eliminated the Serials/Documents Librarian position. Susan Dow was hired as Reference/ Documents librarian in the fall of 1981. Dow departed in mid-1983 and was replaced by Leslie Loar that fall. Theresa Schmidt filled that position when Loar left in 1986.

In 1985 a small computer lab was established within the law library; by 1987, it had expanded to nine stations, but library staff neither ran it nor procured equipment for it. The College Computer Center provided the equipment (mostly older computers that had been surplused from other departments), and a technologically-oriented law professor and a handful of students provided modest staff support.

Meanwhile, the law school community still suffered from the library's small staff size. A student body of 550 and faculty of 25 put increased strain on the staff to provide adequate services. In the fall of 1986 law school Dean Timothy Sullivan hired Richard Danner, Law Library Director at Duke University, as a consultant to study the library's staffing needs and public service programs. Danner visited the law library in October, and the next month reported his findings to Sullivan. Danner noted that the staff included four professional librarians, a library secretary, two circulation assistants, and five technical services staff. He recommended hiring one more reference librarian to enhance services for faculty and students and to provide evening reference coverage, plus additional clerical help in reference and circulation to reduce excess reliance on student assistants. Danner also recommended physical changes that would increase the visibility and accessibility of the reference staff.[109]

Additional staff were not forthcoming, however, although the school acknowledged the need for greater reference support in its 1988 Self-Study prepared in anticipation of the 1988 ABA/AALS sabbatical inspection. The Self-Study reported that faculty frequently could not locate a professional librarian, that they often left requests with student assistants, and that too often such requests were ignored.[110] Echoing Danner's recommendations, the Self-Study reported that the library's highest staffing priority was another professional reference librarian and that the circulation desk should be attended by permanent staff whenever the library was used heavily.[111] The Self-Study also reported that the treatise collection lacked depth and that inadequate funding for collection development could not sustain substantial growth.[112]

---

[109] Richard A. Danner, Report on Staff Needs and Organization: Marshall-Wythe School of Law Library, November 20, 1986. The Director's and Associate Director's offices were on the library's top floor, and the Reference Librarian's office was hidden away in the back of the library. None of these offices were easily visible to library patrons.

[110] Law School 1988 Self-Study, p. 51.

[111] *Id.*, pp. 49–50.

[112] *Id.*, p. 47.

The library was making additional technological advances, however. In anticipation of the site inspection visit, in 1987 the library finally subscribed to Westlaw. (By that date, all but about ten ABA-accredited law schools had acquired Westlaw.) In that same year the library inaugurated its online public access catalog, "LION." Using the campus-wide VTLS integrated library system, the law library closed its card catalog and provided access to it and other William and Mary library collections through the online catalog. In the meantime, the collection had grown to nearly 250,000 volumes and volume equivalents, moving it, in only a dozen years, from near the bottom to well above the median in the number of volumes held by law school libraries in the Southeastern United States. More good news was in store, for in December 1987 Pearl Jones, who for nearly forty years served as private secretary to five College presidents, bequeathed $500,000 to the College in the name of James P. and Grace Virginia Alexander exclusively for the purchase of law library materials.[113]

Edmonds departed William and Mary in the Summer of 1988 to become director of the Loyola University of New Orleans Law Library. He was succeeded that August by James S. Heller, who had spent the preceding five years as law library director at the University of Idaho. Heller had a B.A. from Michigan, a J.D. from San Diego, and an M.L.S. from California, Berkeley. He had served as director of the U.S. Department of Justice Civil Division Library and as Head of Public Services at The George Washington University Law Library.

Heller noticed immediately that the library subscribed to an inordinately high number of serials.[114] Indeed, the library's materials budget had been exhausted more than two months before the end of the prior fiscal year (nearly four months before Heller's arrival) because the library subscribed to many more serial publications than its budget could support. He initiated a massive serial review project, resulting in the cancellation of 700 serial subscriptions over the next three years. The law library also abandoned the PRIME word-processing system and moved to a PC-based environment using WordPerfect and other off-the-shelf software.

---

[113] Establishment of the James P. Alexander and Grace Virginia Alexander Memorial Fund, College of William and Mary Board of Visitors, December 21, 1987.

[114] For 1987-88, the library ranked thirty-second among the 174 ABA-accredited law school libraries in the number of serial subscriptions, but only eighty-seventh in titles added. Two years later the library ranked sixty-sixth in serial subscriptions, and fifty-sixth in the number of titles added. Office of the Consultant on Legal Education to the American Bar Association, *Law Library Comprehensive Statistical Tables from 1987-88 and 1989-90 Annual Questionnaires*.

During his honeymoon period, Heller obtained funds to hire an additional reference librarian, which would bring to five the number of professional staff. By the time candidates were brought to campus in late 1988, Reference Librarian Theresa Schmid had tendered her resignation. The library, therefore, hired two reference librarians; Mary Grace Hune and Rick Buchanan, each of whom had both M.L.S. and J.D. degrees, began their new positions in February 1989.[115]

The next fiscal year began well. The materials budget was increased, and additional funding was made available to hire part-time, permanent staff to perform much of the work done by student workers. Daytime circulation desk assistance and most shelving and filing was turned over to these "hourly" staff. But, as had happened all too often, the library had little time to enjoy its good fortune. The fall of 1989 saw the beginning of a state fiscal crisis that would last for nearly three years. Many departments throughout the College suffered substantial budget cuts; the Swem Library was particularly hard hit. The law library was not impacted nearly as much, and its budget remained fairly constant over the next three years. But the library did suffer a staff reduction in 1990 due to the crisis; a cataloging paraprofessional position was lost when the incumbent resigned her position, reducing the full-time support staff to eight.[116]

Fortunately, the library had secured funding to relocate and renovate all public services work areas and offices that winter. A new circulation/reserve area was constructed, and new reference offices and a reference room with ample shelving and seating space were created on the main floor. The director, associate law librarian, and library secretary moved their offices from the library's top floor to the new administration/reference area,[117] and a 4,200 volume capacity faculty library was built on the top floor adjacent to faculty offices. Also during the 1989–90 academic year, four dual-degree librarians began teaching the legal research component of the law school's innovative Legal Skills program.

---

[115] Hune had extensive experience as a law firm librarian, and for four years had served as Head of Public Services at the Ohio Northern University Law Library. Buchanan had experience as a public librarian and as a practicing attorney. At the same time, responsibility for government documents and microforms control, previously the responsibility of the sole reference librarian, was transferred to the library's technical services department. Responsibility for ordering and control of library supplies, previously under technical services, was transferred to the library secretary.

[116] Salaries throughout the College were cut mid-year in FY 1989–90 and were frozen in 1990–91 and 1991–92.

[117] *Law Library Briefs*, vol. 1, p. 1 (January 1990). Faculty took over the vacated librarian offices.

In the summer of 1990 the entire collection was relocated in an effort to make it more accessible to library patrons and to use existing space more efficiently. That summer the library also assumed responsibility for overseeing the modest and poorly equipped computer lab and for law school audiovisual playback and production services.[118] Reference librarian Mary Grace Hune was assigned responsibility for coordinating computer-related activities, while Rick Buchanan, the other reference librarian, took over audiovisual services. These new responsibilities created additional pressures on the staff. They were in great part responsible for the decision to create a new Audiovisual/ Computer Technician position in 1993; they also influenced the January 1994 restructuring that created a new Computer and Audiovisual Services department.

In 1991 Heller convinced the College's Computer Services department to oversee the lab in the same manner that they ran other computer labs around the campus. The Computer Center doubled the number of PCs from ten to twenty and consolidated the networked PCs in new carrels on the library's top floor adjacent to the new twelve-station LEXIS and Westlaw Temporary Learning Center. The Computer Center also provided funding for students to staff the lab. In the meantime, the library was installing additional LEXIS and Westlaw workstations; within a year thirty-four CALR stations were available throughout the library. That spring Reference Librarian Rick Buchanan departed for private law practice. He was replaced later that year by Susan Trask, a 1991 William and Mary Law School graduate who had earned her library degree several years earlier and had served as Systems/Automation Librarian at Old Dominion University prior to matriculating at Marshall-Wythe.

The statewide recession resulted in the College's cutting the law library's materials budget during fiscal year 1990–91, leaving it slightly lower than the previous year. Better news was in store for the next year, however. The materials budget increased from about $542,000 in 1990–91 to $607,000 in 1991–92, even though the state was still mired in its economic slump. By mid-1992 the recession had eased, and substantial additional funding was made available to the law library, particularly for collection development. In fiscal year 1992–93 the materials budget increased to nearly $700,000.

Having reduced substantially its subscriptions, the library was able to use much of the new funding to enhance its treatise collection. The changed focus on collection development was reflected in the annual ABA survey. For 1992–93 the library ranked thirty-seventh

---

[118] *Law Library Briefs*, vol. 2, p. 1 (August 1990).

among the 176 law school libraries in the number of new titles acquired, an increase of fifty places from 1987–88. Although the library's acquisition of its 300,000th volume in 1993 was an important milestone, more noticeable was the installation of a CD-ROM network in the reference room during the summer of 1993.[119] Also that year for the first time the law school offered an advanced research course, which was team taught by the dual-degree librarians.

The library, meanwhile, had added another professional position. In early 1993 Haibin Hu joined the staff as Reference/Cataloging librarian.[120] Now with six librarians, the library could finally offer professional reference assistance weekday evenings and Sunday afternoons. Since the 1988 Self-Study, the library had added two full-time professional staff and three part-time hourly staff.[121]

Increasing demands for computer and audiovisual support prompted a 1994 staff reorganization that created a new Computer and Audiovisual Services department. In January 1994, Reference Librarian Mary Grace Hune was appointed to head that department. William Cooper joined the library staff in the Summer of 1994 to fill the reference position vacated by Hune.[122] With the hiring of Cooper, who had both law and library degrees and came to William and Mary with extensive law firm and academic experience,[123] the professional staff now numbered seven.

Meanwhile, little had been done to enhance the size of the technical services staff. But for the reference/cataloging librarian, who split his time between public and technical services, the technical

[119] For many years *Legal Trac* had been the library's sole CD-Rom product. Over the next two years the library added numerous CD-Rom products, including *Index to Legal Periodicals, Wilson Business Abstracts, Social Science Index, Michie's Virginia Law on Disk, CIS Masterfile I and II, CCH Standard Federal Tax Reports, CCH Estate and Gift Tax Reporter, Hein's Treaty Index, RIA State and Local Taxes*, and several titles published by Matthew Bender.

[120] Hu had a law degree from Beijing University and M.L.S. and LL. M. degrees from the University of Illinois.

[121] Student assistants now worked forty percent fewer hours than they had only five years earlier. The six permanent, part-time staff members now performed much of the tasks done previously by students.

[122] The library's materials budget increased again, and significantly so, in 1993–94. The new position was funded by transferring funds from the materials budget. Even after that transfer, the library's 1993–94 materials budget totalled nearly $850,000, a 56 percent increase since 1990–91.

[123] Cooper was a research attorney at the Detroit law firm of Dykema Gossett for fourteen years. Early in his career he had served as Reference Librarian at the University of Pennsylvania Biddle Law Library and as Librarian at the law firm of Hogan and Hartson in Washington, D.C.

services department received no new permanent staff even though nearly twice as many books were being ordered, processed, and cataloged than a decade earlier. (Indeed, a cataloging paraprofessional position had been lost in 1990.) Hiring a temporary paraprofessional enabled the library to complete the cataloging of all periodicals and create coded holdings for nearly all the library's periodicals and newsletters. Good fortune came in the fall of 1993 when a trained preservation librarian, Jennifer Hoh, matriculated at the law school. Over the course of two years she would inventory, organize, catalog, and classify the library's rare books and special collection materials. The entire library collection was growing significantly and was more accessible than ever due to various cataloging and classification projects. To protect the collection more adequately, during the summer of 1994 the library installed a library security system.[124]

Interlibrary loan and document delivery activities also grew dramatically. The number of law journals supported by the law school had increased from one in 1988 to five (arguably six) in 1994,[125] resulting in increased demand for materials from other libraries. A larger and more productive faculty was also making increasing requests for materials not held by the law library. And more and more libraries were borrowing books from William and Mary. Interlibrary loan and document delivery transactions more than tripled between 1987 and 1994; servicing these requests was accomplished without any additional staffing.

The law library completed its Strategic Plan in 1994. The Plan involved the entire library staff and took nearly two years to complete. The Strategic Plan, which will be instrumental in charting the library's course for the next several years, identified the library's primary goals, objectives, and strategies,[126] as well as its mission.

---

[124] Security for the collection had historically been a major problem; in the early 1990s the library spent, on average, more than $6,000 annually replacing missing items.

[125] In addition to the *William and Mary Law Review*, the law school now supported the *William and Mary Bill of Rights Journal*, the *William and Mary Environmental and Policy Review*, the *William and Mary Journal of Women and the Law*, and the *Administrative Law Review* (formally an American Bar Association publication). The *Journal of Bankruptcy Law and Practice*, edited by a law faculty member and published by Warren, Gorham & Lamont, was also run out of the law school.

[126] "*Goal 1 (Management)*: To provide effective management and administration to ensure quality library operations and services. *Goal II (Collection)*: To acquire, process, and maintain a collection of information resources to support law school programs, research, the curriculum, and the needs of library users. *Goal III (Access)*: To facilitate access to and delivery of information resources to support law school programs, research, the curriculum, and the needs of library users. *Goal IV (Instruction)*: To instruct and educate library patrons in the use of legal and law-related information

> The mission of the Marshall-Wythe Law Library is to provide access to law and law-related resources and a wide range of services to support the law school curriculum and programs, promote the advancement of legal scholarship, and fulfill the information needs of library users. The law library provides resources and services to its users in the following order of priority: (1) Marshall-Wythe faculty, students, and staff; (2) the College of William and Mary community; (3) Marshall-Wythe alumni; (4) the Virginia bench and bar, and (5) other library patrons.

During 1995 the William and Mary libraries abandoned the VTLS online library system, replacing it with a system designed by the SIRSI Corporation that is based on the UNIX operating system and uses client/server architecture. Migrating from one system to another will require a tremendous amount of staff time but will result in even better access to the collection and will foster closer ties with the Swem Library. As 1995 moved to a close, in order to implement the Strategic Plan more effectively, the library split the Public Services department into two separate departments. Martha Rush would direct the Information Access department and William Cooper would head Research and Instructional Services.

VI. *Conclusion: Towards the Millennium*

It has been a rocky road, indeed, for the William and Mary law school and Marshall-Wythe law library. From its distinguished beginnings as the young nation's first law school, to its closing during the tumultuous Civil War, to its reopening in the 1920s as the country itself began to roar, William and Mary mirrors the development of the Commonwealth of Virginia and the nation. Since the law school's rebirth in 1923, it came close to closing in the bleak days of the 1930's Great Depression, and then had to survive the re-accreditation threat of 1975. The turning point began in 1976 with new law school leadership and a commitment by the Commonwealth to maintain not just a law school, but a great law school, in Williamsburg.

As the history of the law school chronicles the development of America, the evolution of the law library parallels the development of

---

resources. *Goal V (Technology)*: To use technology creatively to support law school curriculum, research, programs, and the needs of library users and staff. *Goal VI (Staff Development)*: To support and encourage opportunities for staff development, education, and full participation in the life of Goal IV (Instruction), the law school, and the College."

the law school. It survived a long history of weak support, meager staffing, and abysmal facilities. Today it has a solid budget, a strong collection, energetic and dedicated staff, and a Strategic Plan that will guide it towards the millennium.

PUBLIC LAW LIBRARIES

Gail Warren and Courtney A. Christensen

IN CONSIDERING public law libraries of Virginia, one must first specify the scope of the word "public." The use of "public" in this essay refers to two categories of law libraries, including both those libraries open to the general public and those libraries which are financed by government funding. Thus, there are actually three types of public law libraries: libraries which are open to the public, but financed through non-government means, libraries which are not open to the general public but exist through government funding,[1] and libraries which are government funded and are open to the public.[2] The majority of public law libraries in Virginia fall into the latter category.

I. *Virginia State Law Library*

The beginning of the Virginia State Law Library was an Act of Assembly passed in 1666 that directed the purchase of the *Statutes at Large*, Michael Dalton, *Justices of the Peace*, Michael Dalton, *Office of Sheriffs*, and Henry Swinburne, *Testaments and Last Wills*, for the use of the General Court of Virginia and the General Assembly.[3] Later, when the seat of government was moved from Jamestown to Williamsburg, this library was moved also. In 1780, the capitol of Virginia was again moved, this time to Richmond, and the General Court and its library were soon housed temporarily in the Henrico County Courthouse.[4] In 1783, when the courts of Virginia were reorganized, fifty volumes, what remained of the General Court library, were transferred to the new Court of Appeals.[5] When the new State Capitol Building was completed, the library was moved in. The Clerk of the Council acted as the librarian, and there were about 1300 volumes, of which 392 were law books, in 1828.[6]

---

[1] See also above, "Academic Law Libraries."

[2] E.g. the Norfolk Law Library; see below, "The Norfolk Law Library."

[3] Hening's Statutes, vol. 2, p. 246.

[4] *Calendar of Va. State Papers*, vol. 3, p. 538.

[5] Va. Supreme Court Order Book, No. 1, p. 10.

[6] W. L. Hall, "The Virginia State Library," *Commonwealth Mag.*, vol. 8, no. 10, pp. 9, 10 (Oct. 1941); "The Virginia State Library," *Tyler's Qtly.*, vol. 1, pp. 18, 20 (1919); see

The General Assembly of Virginia passed an act establishing a new public library, the Virginia State Library, on January 23, 1823.[7] However, it appears that there were some problems in the execution of this Act because in 1826, the General Assembly expressed concern that the public library had not materialized and stipulated specific steps which were to be taken to create the library.[8] In order to fund the library, the General Assembly ordered the executive to appoint an agent to sell copies of Hening's *Statutes* for $10 a set, Gilmer's *Reports* for $1.50, and Randolph's *Reports* for $17. The proceeds of these sales were ordered to be used "for the purchases of a library, to be located at the seat of government, and to consist of such books in law, literature, science, and the arts, as may be useful to the several departments of the government."[9] Later, in 1829, the General Assembly ordered that the Literary Fund lend the Library Fund $6,000 at 6 percent interest in an effort to provide more funding. In the next year, an additional $4,000 loan was ordered and the payment on the loan was suspended by the General Assembly. A librarian was charged with purchasing books for the library; in order to ensure the librarian's faithful performance, a $10,000 bond was ordered. The librarian's salary was set at $300 a year.[10]

It is clear that the legal section of the Virginia State Library was of utmost importance from its establishment. In describing the books which should be bought for the new library, the first category specified by the General Assembly was "law books." In 1832, the Joint Library Committee authorized the transmission of "the statutes at large, the sessions acts since the revisal of eighteen hundred and nineteen, the Virginia reports, and such other law books whereof duplicate copies are now in the library" to the clerk of the Court of Appeals at Lewisburg for the use of the judges when in session in that city.[11] The libraries were also used as resources for the local communities as a matter of grace.

---

generally B. Tarter, "A Rich Storehouse of Knowledge: A History of the Library of Virginia" in S. G. Treadway and E. D. C. Campbell, Jr., eds., *The Common Wealth: Treasures from the Collections of the Library of Virginia* (1997), pp. 3-64.

[7] 1822-23 Va. Acts, ch. 12, p. 15.

[8] 1825-26 Va. Acts, ch. 7, p. 8.

[9] 1825-26 Va. Acts, ch. 7, p. 8.

[10] 1828-29 Va. Acts, ch. 8, p. 9.

[11] 1831-32 Va. Acts, ch. 10, § 3, p. 12. The library established at Lewisburg was closed following the split of Virginia into two states, Virginia and West Virginia. The 1873 Va. Code explains that "the court has no law library at Lewisburg now" in the footnote to title 10, ch. 18, § 18.

The 1849 Code gives us many details about these early state law libraries. It specifies that the law library in Richmond was to be under the charge of the "general librarian," who was also in charge of the Virginia State Library, and that the law library in Lewisburg was to be under the charge of the Clerk of the Court of Appeals. Prior to assuming the role of law librarian, the Clerk of the Court of Appeals had to post a $2,000 bond. The law librarian at Lewisburg was to be paid no more than $50 a year, which was to be paid out of the treasury. There were also provisions regarding the volumes to be contained in each library. Each of the law libraries was to be given a copy of every law book published in the Commonwealth of Virginia, and the library at Lewisburg was to be provided with a copy of every book available at the law library in Richmond. The Court of Appeals was given the power to make and enforce the regulations of the law libraries. However, the General Assembly's joint library committee was careful to specify that granting the power of regulation to the Court of Appeals did not dilute any of the joint committee's power over the law libraries.[12]

In 1847, a new State Office Building was built in the southeast corner of the Capitol Square, and the Court of Appeals and the duplicate copies of the law books from the State Library were moved in; the Court was also authorized to purchase additional law books.[13] Most unfortunately, this building and the books and the archives of colonial Virginia were destroyed in the Evacuation Fire of 1865.

In 1865, the General Assembly made a provision relating to the creation of a new law library, which was to be at a separate location from the general library, and the Supreme Court of Appeals was to appoint one of its officers to act as law librarian.[14] In 1867, it was provided that all of the law books of the Virginia State Library shall be transferred to the law library.[15] The Court and its library moved to the Sycamore Church Building in 1872.[16] Three years later, the General Assembly ordered the establishment of two additional law libraries, at Wytheville and Staunton (the Augusta Law Library), with a court officer at each location serving as librarian.[17] These additional libraries served the needs of the court during its sessions at those cities and

[12] Va. Code, ch. 19, §§ 19-24 (1849).

[13] 1846-47 Va. Acts, ch. 14, p. 15.

[14] 1865-66 Va. Acts, ch. 60, § 7, p. 174.

[15] 1866-67 Va. Acts, ch. 92, p. 551.

[16] Va. Supreme Court Order Book, vol. 22, p. 177.

[17] 1874-75 Va. Acts, ch. 228, p. 272.

were more accessible to the general public, though they were under the same regulations as the main branch in Richmond.[18] In 1895, the headquarters of the Court and, of course, the law library were moved into a new building in Capitol Square just south of the Governor's Mansion (now the State Finance Building).[19]

There were approximately 45,000 volumes in the State Law Library in 1937. It was the largest law library in Virginia at that time.[20]

In 1944, the General Assembly eliminated the sessions of court in Wytheville. Fearing the loss of this valuable legal resource, the local judiciary petitioned the court to allow the library collection to remain in Wytheville. In response, the court transferred the library to the Circuit Court of Wythe County in January of 1946 "for so long a time as such library is held and kept for the use of the bench, bar, and public. . . ." The legislature also approved this measure in March of the same year.[21] Although the court discontinued sessions at the Staunton location in 1971, maintenance of the library collection continued for some years serving the research needs of Justice George M. Cochran, who lived there. Following Justice Cochran's retirement in the spring of 1987, the existing library collection was transferred to the Augusta County, Staunton, Waynesboro Law Library by court order in February of 1988.

The librarian of the Virginia State Law Library is appointed by the Chief Justice of the Supreme Court of Virginia and serves at the Chief Justice's pleasure.[22] The first librarian for the State Law Library was William Wallace Scott, who had been the librarian of the Virginia State Library before the separate position was created. He served from 1902 until his death in 1929. Prior to his appointment as State Law Librarian, Scott served as the reporter of the *Virginia Appeals* series and was the author of *The Capitol of Virginia and the Confederate States*.

His successor was Lloyd M. Richards, originally the custodian of the building. Richards, who eventually became a member of the

---

[18] The librarian at the Augusta County, Staunton, Waynesboro Law Library in Staunton reports that it has always been accessible to the general public.

[19] 1895-96 House Journal, pp. 620-621; these accommodations had become inadequate by 1903: 1904 Senate Journal, pp. 29-30.

[20] H. Clemons, *Survey of Research Materials in Virginia Libraries 1936-37*, pp. 56-57 (1941).

[21] 1946 Va. Acts, ch. 209, p. 366.

[22] 1902-3-4 Va. Acts, ch. 547, p. 875.

Virginia State Bar, served as law librarian from 1929 until his retirement on June 30, 1961. He catalogued the books with the advice and assistance of Frances Farmer, the law librarian at the University of Virginia. In addition to expanding and cataloging the library collection, Richards participated in local politics, marketed a product called "Gay Paree Syrup," and practiced law, all from the librarian's office.

Richards was followed by H. Elmer Kiser, who had served as the assistant law librarian since June of 1960. Kiser was no stranger to the Virginia judicial system having served as the Clerk of Tazewell County for twenty-four years, in addition to serving as President of the Virginia Court Clerk's Association in 1947. Kiser rearranged the library and did much to increase the exchange of law books with other states. He was the State Law Librarian until his death on September 9, 1966, and was succeeded by his assistant, Walter S. Griggs, Jr.

Griggs, a recent law school graduate, served as law librarian until 1968.[23] On January 1, 1968, Griggs's assistant, Marjorie D. Kirtley, became law librarian and served until August 30, 1982. She was succeeded by Gail Warren, an attorney with a law degree from the University of Richmond. Although several of her predecessors were members of the bar, Warren is the first State Law Librarian to hold a graduate degree in library science (M.S.L.S.).

II. *Local Bar Libraries*

In 1852, an act was passed stipulating that if any member or members of the bar contributed a law library worth $100 or more for the use of the local courts and bar, the clerk of the county circuit court was required to take charge of the library and manage the library in accordance with the rules prescribed by the bar and approved by the court.[24] In 1919, the minimum amount of the donation was increased to its current figure of $500.[25] This provision led to the creation of many local bar libraries throughout Virginia. Most of these libraries were for the use of local courts and bar members only, but a few were open to the general public. Private local bar libraries were established in Norfolk in 1880,[26] in Richmond in 1886,[27] and in Roanoke in 1925.

---

[23] Walter S. Griggs, Jr., "State Law Library" (typescript).

[24] 1852-53 Va. Acts, ch. 36, § 1, p. 52.

[25] Va. Code § 373 (1919).

[26] See below, "The Norfolk Law Library."

[27] J. O. Peters, *Tale of the Century: A History of the Bar Association of the City of*

These libraries were a critical development in the history of public law libraries in Virginia because many were later expanded and opened to the general public. The private libraries of lawyers were often donated for public use after they retired or died. Frequently, these private libraries met the minimum value required for the clerks of the court to take charge of them. Once the original library was established, additional donations by bar members served to update and expand the library collection.

In many instances, the secretary to the circuit court judge acted as the part-time librarian and received a small additional salary. The larger public law libraries now have full time librarians. Some of the smaller ones have merged with local public libraries in order to have the benefit of professional librarians to manage them.

The reason for the growing collections and increased public accessibility of bar libraries lies in a Code provision which enabled additional public funding for law libraries. A provision permitting an assessment for the law library as part of the filing fee for civil actions was passed in 1960.[28] This stipulated the fee could be collected upon the filing of a civil case and used for the operating costs of the law library if the library were open to the general public. The assessment was limited to one dollar and the library was required to be open to the public at convenient hours. This provision was enhanced by the 1977 amendment which stipulated that any two or more adjoining counties or cities who assessed filing fees could jointly establish a regional law library. This was the turning point for public law libraries in Virginia. At this time, many bar association libraries were turned over to local governments, who used the filing fees as a way to maintain the libraries, often in conjunction with continuing contributions from the local bar association. Thus, many of the current public law libraries in Virginia began long ago as an individual donation of a lawyer's private collection to the courthouse or bar association, and they were thereafter opened to the public as funding flowed from court civil filing fees, pursuant to statute.

PUBLICLY FUNDED LAW LIBRARIES

The Abingdon Law Library, Court and Main Streets, Abingdon, Virginia 24210.

Richmond, pp. 2, 6, 28 (1985).

[28] Va. Code Ann. § 42.1-70; Va. Code Ann. § 42-19.4; 1960 Va. Acts, ch. 423, p. 664.

The Alexandria Law Library, 520 King Street, Room L-34, Alexandria, Virginia 22314.

> The William Wools Law Library in Alexandria contains 16,000 volumes, with special collections in the areas of energy, security, bankruptcy, and tax law. Although the law librarian is a city employee, the library is governed by a library board of nine, appointed by the city, the circuit court, and the Alexandria bar.

The Arlington Bar Association Law Library, 1425 North Courthouse Road, Room 501, Arlington, Virginia 22201.

> The Arlington law library was first established in the early 1940s as a bar library open for public use. The library grew out of a donation of books to the courthouse by a bar member, Tom Phillips. Much of the library was destroyed by a fire on May 20, 1990. Since February of 1991, the library has been open to the public. It operates as a nonprofit corporation primarily funded through court filing fees, with about twenty percent of its costs provided by the bar association. The Lawyer Referral and bar association offices are located in the library. The collection contains around 12,500 volumes.

The Attorney General's Law Library, 900 East Main Street, Richmond, Virginia 23219.

> This library is located in the Attorney General's Office. It is for the use of the attorneys who work in that office and is not open to the public. It is a division of Attorney General's Office's budget and receives all of its funding through legislative appropriation. There are approximately 10,000 volumes in the library. The library was created after the Attorney General's assistants were pulled together into one office and pooled their various collections around 1980. Before the large increase in the Attorney General's professional staff, the Virginia State Law Library was sufficiently convenient to serve them, the Attorney General's office being located in the same building.

The Augusta County, Staunton, and Waynesboro Law Library, 13 West Beverley Street, Post Office Box 55, Staunton, Virginia 24402.

> This library was established in the 1870s for the Supreme Court of Appeals and operated as a branch of the Virginia State Law Library. In 1987, the library was opened to the public. It was also at this time that bar members began to be assessed for partial funding of the library. This assessment is used in

> conjunction with the civil court filing fees to finance the library. The library contains around 20,000 volumes.

The Bristol Law Library, City Hall, 497 Cumberland Street, Bristol, Virginia 24201.

The Brunswick Bar Association Law Library, Post Office Box 580, Lawrenceville, Virginia 23868.

The Central Rappahannock Regional Law Library, 1201 Caroline Street, Fredericksburg, Virginia 22401.

> This library was originally established as a bar association library at the old courthouse. In the mid 1980s, it became public and moved to its present location in the public library. The library is funded in conjunction with the local library and through filing fees.

The Chesapeake Public Law Library, Civic Center, 300 Cedar Road, Chesapeake, Virginia 23320.

> The law library functions as a branch of the public library system with funding for the collection from civil filing fees.

The Chesterfield County Public Law Library, 9500 Courthouse Road, Chesterfield, Virginia 23832.

> This was established in 1991 and is funded through filing fees. It contains around two hundred and forty titles.

The Cooperative Law Library, Post Office Box 318, Warsaw, Virginia 22572.

> Formerly called the Northern Neck Public Law Library, this library was organized as a bar library. It is now open to the public and located on the Warsaw campus of Rappahannock Community College.

The Danville Law Library, 212 Lynn Street, Danville, Virginia 24541.

> This is managed under the direction of the public library system and the City of Danville. The library houses approximately 14,000 volumes and is funded through a variety of sources, including bar dues and civil filing fees.

The Fairfax Law Library, 4110 Chain Bridge Road, Fairfax, Virginia 22030.

> This was established over twenty-five years ago. In 1981, the Fairfax Bar Association took over its management. The library is funded through filing fees and contains around 35,000 volumes.

The Fauquier County Law Library, 40 Culpeper Street, Warrenton, Virginia 22186.

> This was established in the summer of 1990. It is a limited general practice collection and is funded through civil filing fees. At the time of the library's creation, it was agreed that the local bar association would supervise the general functioning of the library. In addition, the local bar association donated a collection of books to serve as the foundation for the library. The library is open to the public three days a week.

The Halifax Law Library, Halifax Courthouse, Main Street, Halifax, Virginia 24458.

The Harrisonburg Law Library, Laird L. Conrad Memorial Law Library, Carrier Library, James Madison University, Harrisonburg, Virginia 22801.

The Henrico Municipal Reference and Law Library, Post Office Box 27032, Richmond, Virginia 23273.

> This library was established in 1979 as a branch of the public library system, serving county government. It is completely funded by filing fees and contains about 8,000 volumes.

The Hopewell Law Library, Hopewell Circuit Court, 300 Main Street, Post Office Box 354, Hopewell, Virginia 23860.

The Lynchburg Public Law Library, 900 Church Street, Lynchburg, Virginia 24574.

> This library became public when the City of Lynchburg assumed control of the library in 1987. Now operating as a branch of the public library system, the original collection was organized as a local bar association library. It is funded entirely through filing fees and contains around 10,000 volumes.

The National Center for State Courts Library, 300 Newport Street, Williamsburg, Virginia 23185.

> This library has a specialty collection of books on the administration of justice. It serves the needs of this research institution and the legal information requirements of state and federal courts. This library is not open to the general public.

The Newport News Public Law Library, 2600 Washington Avenue, Newport News, Virginia 23607.

> This law book collection is completely funded through filing fees. It is a branch of the public library system and contains around 13,000 volumes.

The Norfolk Law Library, Dominion Tower Building, Suite 1300, 999 Waterside Drive, Norfolk, Virginia 23510.

> This venerable institution was established in 1880 by members of the local bar. This library was not open to the public until 1987. It has approximately 25,000 volumes and is essentially a practitioner's collection. It is now a nonprofit, independent foundation.

The Portsmouth Law Library, 601 Crawford Street, Portsmouth, Virginia 23704.

The Prince William County Law Library, 9311 Lee Avenue, Manassas, Virginia 22110.

> This library is located in Manassas, Virginia, and operates under the direction of the Clerk of the Circuit Court. It was established in 1983 and currently has over 11,000 volumes in its collection.

The Richmond Public Law Library, John Marshall Courts Building, Room 302, 400 North Ninth Street, Richmond, Virginia 23219.

> This law library was originally established in 1886 as the law library of the Bar Association of the City of Richmond. In 1894, the library was given the use of a room in the City Hall, where the Richmond city courts sat, in return for access by the judges; the Bar Association furnished the room. At that time, the library consisted of forty titles, and there was a full time librarian, Sallie Roddy. Later, the room and library were opened for use by any

> member of the Virginia State Bar Association. (J. O. Peters, *Tale of the Century: A History of the Bar Association of the City of Richmond*, p. 28 (1985).) In 1985, this library, which had grown considerably over the years, was donated to the newly established Richmond Public Law Library, which is open to the general public. The current location of this library is on the third floor of the John Marshall Courts Building in Richmond.

The Roanoke County Law Library, Courthouse Building, 305 East Main Street, Salem, Virginia 24153.

The Roanoke Law Library, 315 Church Avenue, S.W., Roanoke, Virginia 24016.

> This library was established in 1925 by the local bar association. It became public in 1977 and has been funded through filing fees since that time. The collection contains around 27,000 volumes.

United States Courts Library, United States Courthouse, Room 319, 600 Granby Street, Norfolk, Virginia 23510.

United States Court of Appeals for the Fourth Circuit Library, Tenth and Main Streets, Richmond, Virginia 23219.

> This law library is open to federal judges and their staffs, lawyers and their assistants, and librarians. It contains around 65,000 volumes. It is funded by the Administrative Office of the United States Courts in Washington, D.C.

The Virginia State Library, 11th Street and Capitol Square, Richmond, Virginia 23219.

> This library, now called The Library of Virginia, was established in 1823, pursuant to a statute, as a general public library. It has a section on federal and Virginia law-related materials. It is open to the general public six days a week.

The Virginia State Law Library, Supreme Court Building, 100 North Ninth Street, Richmond, Virginia 23219.

> This institution is located at the Supreme Court and is open to members of the bar, judges, and other members of the legal community, but not the general public. The library contains around 100,000 volumes and is funded by the budget of the Supreme Court of Virginia.

The Wahab Public Law Library, Judicial Center, Virginia Beach, Virginia 23456.

> The law library in Virginia Beach, became public in 1975. Prior to this time, it was a haphazard collection of donations. It now operates as a branch of the public library system funded through filing fees and contains around 10,000 volumes.

The Winchester-Frederick Law Library, Judicial Center, 5 North Kent Street, Winchester, Virginia 22601.

> This was established in 1984 through the initiative of the local courts and bar associations. The initial collection was purchased from a retiring attorney, relocated to the new courthouse and has been maintained through civil filing fees. It serves the bar, the judiciary, and the public in the City of Winchester and Frederick County.

The York-Poquoson Law Library, Post Office Box 532, Yorktown, Virginia 23690.

BIBLIOGRAPHY

Bar Association of the City of Richmond. 1901. Catalogue of Books. [Richmond: n.p., 1901]. 8 p.

A Catalogue of the Library of the State of Virginia. Richmond: S. Shepherd & Co., 1828; Richmond: S. Shepherd & Co., 1829; Richmond: S. Shepherd & Co., 1831; Richmond: S. Shepherd, 1835; Richmond: Shepherd & Colin, 1839; Richmond: Colin, Baptist and Nowlan, 1849; Richmond: John Nowlan, 1856; Richmond: Geo. W. Gary, 1877.

> The first and largest section of these catalogues lists the law books.

Norfolk and Portsmouth Bar Association's Library Pamphlet and Book List. Norfolk: Burke & Gregory, 1907; 2d ed., n.p., 1936.

A CATALOGUE

OF THE

LIBRARY

OF THE

STATE OF VIRGINIA,

ARRANGED ALPHABETICALLY,

UNDER DIFFERENT HEADS, WITH THE NUMBER AND SIZE OF THE VOLUME OF EACH WORK SPECIFIED.

TO WHICH ARE PREFIXED,

THE RULES AND REGULATIONS

PROVIDED FOR ITS GOVERNMENT.

RICHMOND:

PRINTED BY SAMUEL SHEPHERD & CO.

1831.

THE NORFOLK LAW LIBRARY

John B. Jenkins, Jr., and Francis N. Crenshaw

ON JUNE 4, 1873,[29] the Circuit Court of the City of Norfolk (Judge George Blow presiding), granted a charter[30] to twelve lawyers of this vicinity under the name of "the Norfolk Law Library Association." The name of Tazewell Taylor appears as president of this corporation, J. G. Holladay as vice-president, W. B. Martin (later Judge William Bruce Martin of the Court of Law and Chancery) was secretary, and W. G. Elliott, treasurer. Two of the incorporators, J. G. Holladay and J. F. Crocker, were residents of the City of Portsmouth.

At that time the Bar of Norfolk was composed of twenty-five practitioners. The census of 1870 listed Norfolk as a city with a population of 19,229.

If this corporation ever functioned, its existence shortly ceased and no permanent law library was founded. It is doubtful if any real collection of books was ever started as a result of these efforts.

The only law books available at that time were the private property of the practitioners and were kept in their offices. These books, in the main, consisted of old standard textbooks. The English treatises were as popular as and more important than the American, if there were excluded those intended for use in the Commonwealth of Virginia. The works of Stephen, Chitty, and Tidd on common law pleading and practice, those of Mitford and Daniell on chancery practice, and the older English texts on real estate were in common use. Blackstone at that time had not been entirely forgotten.

In the matter of reported decisions, the English greatly predominated over the Americans. The English common law reprints, chancery reprints, and various exchequer reports and crown cases were found in the best private libraries, which usually contained only reports of the Commonwealth of Virginia and of the United States Supreme Court.

Many American textbooks ranked as high as English texts. In this category were the works of Story, Greenleaf, Sedgwick, and Chancellor Kent. Such textbooks were treatises in fact, as well as in name, and were far removed from the modern loosely written textbooks, which are hardly more than digests. The authorities cited were few in comparison

---

[29] This article was begun by Robert M. Hughes and read before the Norfolk and Portsmouth Bar Association on July 13, 1936; it was revised in 1941 by John B. Jenkins, Jr., and again by Francis N. Crenshaw; it is printed here with the kind permission of the Norfolk and Portsmouth Bar Association.

[30] This charter was recorded in the Clerk's Office of the Corporation Court of the City of Norfolk, in Charter Book 1, at page 89.

to the modern practice and could be relied upon as being in point. The authors gave their own powerfully reasoned opinions freely and independently of the authority of judicial decisions and were often in defiance of such authority and their opinion carried great weight.

Shortly after his arrival in this City in the fall of 1877, Robert M. Hughes in conjunction with W. B. Martin (later judge of the Court of Law and Chancery of the City of Norfolk) inaugurated a movement for a law library. A canvas of the Bar for that purpose was started and an application was made to the General Assembly for a legislative charter, which was granted on February 10, 1880.[31] The title to this Act is "An Act to Incorporate the Norfolk Library Association." It was a joint stock company with shares to be issued of a par value of $100 each, which could be purchased or acquired either for cash or turning into the corporation law books of an agreed valuation.

The records of this corporation were destroyed by fire when the Columbia Building burned on January 30, 1902, destroying the names of the officers and directors and members of this corporation. The selection and purchase of books were left largely to the judgment of Hughes and Martin, who consulted freely with any lawyer who would lend them a willing ear. It was at that time the ambition of the members of this corporation to acquire as rapidly as their means would permit the reported decisions of the other state courts of last resort.

The census of 1880 listed Norfolk's population as 21,966 with the bar still very small, not over 40 in number. With limited personnel and slender financial resources, the acquisition of these state reports was a long and arduous business. In starting the collection of books, the officers of the Association took over at an agreed valuation the few sets of state reports that were then in Norfolk. From Burroughs and Brother (Judge W. H. Burroughs and Captain J. J. Brother) came a part of the New York State Reports. From Starke and Martin (Colonel L. D. Starke, Sr., and Judge William Bruce Martin) came the North Carolina Reports, and from White and Garnett (William H. White and Judge T. S. Garnett) a large portion of the Pennsylvania Reports. Other reports were acquired from secondhand catalogues, inventories, and sales of law books of deceased lawyers in other localities.

After the West Publishing Company started the National Reporter System, this valuable service was subscribed to by the Library Association and subscriptions to the state reports discontinued. The only state reports which were not acquired prior to the advent of the National Reporter System were those from Delaware and New Hampshire. They were both too expensive. The Delaware Reports were of

[31] 1879-80 Va. Acts, ch. 60, p. 43.

only average rank as authority while the New Hampshire Reports were of very high rank as authority, but both were prohibitory as to cost.

For a long time the only collection of Federal general laws which could be afforded was the *Revised Statutes*, published in 1878 and supplemented in 1891. Later the *United States Statutes at Large* were purchased.

As late as 1890, the population of Norfolk was only 34,871. In February, 1894, at a meeting of the bar held to endorse judges for the Corporation Court and the new Court of Law and Chancery, which had just been created, the total vote cast was only 87, and this was at a meeting of the entire bar, and included many who were not members of the Library Association.

In the late nineties, the growth of the city became more rapid and its business and importance increased correspondingly. In 1898 a movement grew in favor of organizing a bar association to take care of other important professional needs than the mere acquisition and maintenance of a law library. A number of lawyers led by Alfred P. Thom convened a preliminary meeting on November 23, 1898. This movement acquired momentum, later a constitution and by-laws were adopted, and the organization of the Norfolk and Portsmouth Bar Association was perfected. Alfred P. Thom was the first president with Legh R. Watts vice president, Henry H. Little secretary, and Lawrence Waring treasurer. At first this Association was not incorporated, but later, on March 5, 1900, the General Assembly granted a charter.[32] Membership in this corporation increased rapidly. It was natural that this larger and more powerful organization should take over and operate the library accumulated up to that time by the old library association.

The first steps towards doing so were taken at a meeting held February 3, 1903. A committee was then appointed consisting of Richard H. Baker, Robert M. Hughes, and John B. Jenkins to open negotiations with the old library association to accomplish the above mentioned purpose. A plan was devised and adopted to accomplish the acquisition. Payment by the new Bar Association was made by the issuance of its certificates of indebtedness, which were in turn delivered to the living members of the old association and to estates of deceased members proportionate to the amounts of money paid in by them to the old association.

[32] 1899-1900 Va. Acts, ch. 646, p. 684.

The first building designed and erected for a commercial and office building in this city was the old Lowenberg Building, which until about ten years ago stood on the north side of Main Street, opposite the Citizens Bank Building, which has now been demolished. Soon after its completion, many offices on the second floor were rented by members of the legal profession. This building offered to its tenants the "last word" in office service. The first room used to house the law library was in the northeast corner, and each member of the association had a key. The rules prescribed that books could not be withdrawn from the room except for use in court.

At first there was no librarian in charge. The first attendant or librarian was Miss Colie Foster who was also a stenographer and an accomplished typist. Miss Foster was given the use of the room for her work in exchange for acting as librarian. In 1899, she was succeeded by J. Cabell Dabney and Minor Bronaugh, young lawyers who were new to the bar and acted as librarians in return for the use of the library rooms as their office.

At the turn of the century, the Federal Building on the corner of Atlantic and Plume Streets was completed and quarters were assigned there to the Federal Court. A large room on the third floor was fitted for library use with built-in book shelves and alcoves. The Bar Association was allowed the use of this space for library purposes on condition that the library should be used without charge by Federal officials. Soon the regulations of the library were relaxed to permit the withdrawal of books by the members to their own offices as well as for use in the courtrooms. Shortly after this, Dabney and Bronaugh acquired other office facilities and another librarian was secured.

In 1906, the United Owners Realty Corporation built an office building later known as the Law Building, now known as the Seaboard Air Line Building, on the northwest corner of Granby and Plume Streets. As an inducement to secure lawyers as tenants for that building the owners offered the Bar Association a lease of about 1,000 square feet of floor space rent free for use as a library for a term of not more than fifteen years, the offer to include heat, light, and janitor service. In addition, the landlord offered to contribute the sum of $500 *per annum* for the purchase of law books. This offer was accepted and in the fall of 1906 the library was moved to these new quarters. It was shortly after moving into these new quarters that the library committee acquired the Florida and Texas Reports, which completed the acquisition of such state reports, other than Virginia, as are now on hand in the library.

Before removing the quarters of the library to the Law Building, the English decisions prior to the year 1865 were acquired and in 1913 a set of English reprints from 1865 to that date were acquired. Robert M. Hughes at that time gave to the Association his English common law reprint and English exchequer reports. In 1907 the Canadian reports and *Mews Digest* of the English reports were acquired. In that same year, the Bar Association published a booklet containing the rules of the Library and a list of its holdings.[33]

Prior to 1920 the library comprised only books of primary authority, but in that year it was decided to acquire *Ruling Case Law*. Since that time many treatises, textbooks, digests and encyclopedias have been acquired. The *United States Code*, together with the codes of neighboring states, are now found on the library shelves.

In the year 1935 the United Owners Realty Corporation, through Goldsborough Serpell, its president, donated to the Bar Association the sum of $1,000, which was to be used in the purchase of textbooks for the Law Library. In addition to that, about $300 was also borrowed and with these funds were purchased a substantial number of the 400 or more excellent textbooks which are now found on our library shelves.

When in the year 1937, the United Owners Realty Corporation, the owner of the old Law Building, leased that structure to the Seaboard Airline Railway Company for a long term of years, the Bar Association was forced to secure new quarters for its law library. As a result of negotiations, new library space was acquired on the third floor of the Bank of Commerce Building. At that time, the National Bank of Commerce gave to this Association the library quarters rent free for a term of five years beginning August 1, 1937, and in addition, $1,000 per year for the same five years, which sums were to be used for the purchase of new books for the library. The terms of this lease at its expiration were extended for another five years without any annual payment of money. This term expired July 31, 1947, and thereafter the Bar Association occupied the library space rent free under an extension of the terms of that renewal of the original lease.

Robert M. Hughes served faithfully as chairman of both the Library Association and of the Library Committee of the Norfolk and Portsmouth Bar Association from their beginnings until the year 1927. Hughes had retired from active law practice about 1920, but continued to serve this Association as chairman of its Library Committee as long as he felt he could do the day's work. His love of books and their use was always great. The Bar Association is his permanent debtor for the intelligence, time, and strength which he gave to it.

[33] *Norfolk and Portsmouth Bar Association's Library Pamphlet and Book List* (1907). A second edition was issued in 1936; there were 8,790 volumes in the library in 1936.

Since the retirement of Hughes, who practically served as the whole Library Committee, James Elliot Heath, Robert M. Hughes, Jr., Lucian B. Cox, John B. Jenkins, Jr., S. Burnell Bragg, William G. Maupin, J. Walter White, Delamater Davis, Robert B. Tunstall, Frederic G. Swink, Edward R. Baird, Joseph L. Kelly, Jr., Tazewell Taylor, Jr., Francis N. Crenshaw, and William P. Oberndorfer have served as members of the Library Committee.

There has never been any organic law of this Association providing for a continuity of the membership of its Library Committee. But the presidents and executive committees, throughout the years, made comparatively few changes in its personnel. The result was a sustained, unchanging plan with reference to the purchase of books and of the management of the Library. The results seem to justify this policy.

When the Library was moved from the old Lowenberg Building to the then new Federal Building (now the old City Hall), George E. Bowden was appointed Clerk of the United States District Court and custodian of the new building. In 1908 a youngster by the name of Joseph S. Hall was employed as a member of the staff of servants in the Federal Building assigned to the Federal Court. In a short time he was employed as a custodian of the library in conjunction with his other duties with the Federal Court. He was also assigned the duty as bailiff of the United States District Court then presided over by the Honorable Edmund Waddill. Later he became a full time librarian and served the members of the Bar Association of the city in that capacity with intelligence, industry, and courtesy. He acquired a knowledge of the workings of the digests, citations, and books giving cross references to cases. Joe Hall continued without interruption until he was retired and later pensioned on October 9, 1947. He died during the first few days of 1950. Margaret Long was engaged as librarian in July 1947, and served until January 1949. Grace Culbreth succeeded Miss Long as librarian during the closing days of the year 1948.

In 1950, there were in the library over 8,000 volumes of reported cases, 400 textbooks, the digest of the National Reporter System, the United States Codes, the *Code of Virginia* and the *Acts of Assembly*, the codes of North Carolina and West Virginia, *Corpus Juris, Corpus Juris Secundum, Ruling Case Law, Shepard's Citations* complete, several sets of law journals and other used and useful books which brought the total book collection to about 12,000 volumes.

At the beginning of 1951 the Norfolk and Portsmouth Bar Association had 211 members. In 18 years the membership substantially doubled as there were 494 members as of December 1, 1968. This swelling membership generated an increased demand upon the library which was met by substantial and varied book acquisition and by a dramatic change in the quarters which housed the library.

As late as 1948, the *Virginia Law Review* was the only such periodical to which the Library subscribed. Since then, the Law Library has subscribed to or has been given the law reviews published by Columbia, Harvard, University of Michigan, University of North Carolina, University of Pennsylvania, Washington and Lee, William and Mary, and Yale.

The total number of volumes in 1970 exceeded 15,300. In addition to the expected volumes of the National Reporter System, the digests, encyclopedia, codes, old state reports, and the Canadian and English reports, the Library Committee had been sensitive to the desires of the members and had purchased many recommended, pragmatic texts or services. There were 754 volumes of general texts, treatises and form books alone.

This growth in content of the library necessitated capital improvements. In 1952 the then chairman of the Library Committee, Joseph Kelly, recommended physical improvements in the form of improved lighting, replacement of chairs and tables, and the provision of additional shelving. This work was authorized by the Executive Committee at an expense of approximately $1,250. In 1956 the Reading Rooms of the Library were air-conditioned and the Association rented an additional room contiguous to the then library spaces, in which the entire *Decennial Digest* and all of the law reviews were placed. This small room was rented from the Commerce Corporation for $50 per month, the highest rent ever paid for space in the history of the Association.

On September 2, 1955, at a meeting of the Association, the then president, William P. Dickson, Jr., announced that the late George A. Carnegie, who had died in 1954, had made a splendid gift of $5,000 to the Law Library. He commented that this was, "the most remarkable thing that every happened to a group of lawyers." Mr. Carnegie had for many years been the owner of Carnegie Office Appliance Company located on West Main Street in Norfolk. He felt that he had profited over the years from the business given to his firm by members of the Association, and he felt a warm personal regard for his many lawyer friends. By his generous gift, he gave abundant thanks for that enduring friendship. The membership of the Association adopted a resolution expressing its appreciation and specifying that a space within the Law Library be named and dedicated in the honor of Mr. Carnegie. The room which then housed the *Decennial Digest* and the law reviews was so designated and a commemorative plaque was struck and placed at its entrance, bearing the inscription: "This room is dedicated to the memory of George A. Carnegie whose generosity has substantially benefitted this library."

During the late fifties, the need for additional space required successive revisions of arrangements within the Library, but through the ingenious use of available space by Mrs. Culbreth, the needs of the many lawyers were satisfactorily served.

The library has been much more than a mere depository of books. During 1955 a custom was developed to post on the bulletin board in the Library the names of available legal secretaries as well as the names of lawyers seeking employment. This service has proved of considerable help to the members.

In addition, to housing the standard texts, digest, and services, with which most lawyers are familiar, the library has become the depository for file cabinets containing archives, memorials, committee reports, and correspondence produced by the various committees of the Association.

Certain acquisitions merit specific reference. The need for a tax service had become established by 1958 and after lengthy consideration, the Library Committee chose the *Prentice Hall Tax Service*. To augment this service, acquisition was also effected of the reports of the United States Board of Tax Appeals and the Tax Court of the United States.

Sophistication in the methods of recording the information unearthed by the membership during its forays into the Library produced by 1960 a growing demand for a photocopy machine. Torn between the desire for a first rate and easily operated machine on the one hand and the necessity of a financially attainable installation on the other hand, the Law Library Committee leased a Docustat machine which reproduced a double page of a book for 25 cents.

Not only is the membership served by the Library. An unparalleled increase in the population of Tidewater has produced a proportionate expansion of the student body and faculty at Old Dominion University. The study of constitutional law, political science, and related subjects has been substantially assisted by students' research in our Library.

During 1954 Mrs. Culbreth completed the first complete card index showing the title, author, edition, and number of volumes of the various texts, treatises, and form books. This index has been revised and up-dated annually. This index permitted the first comprehensive inventory of all the bound volumes in the Library, which inventory is revised every five years.

In April of 1964, it was announced that the Virginia National Bank was to erect an imposing new structure on the south side of Main

Street directly opposite its then headquarters. Negotiations with the Bank ensued, resulting in a proposition forwarded by the Bank to house the Law Library in the new building. The Library Committee studied the proposition and negotiated a lease for space on the 11th floor of the new building for a period of ten years at a rental of one dollar per year. The new space contained 3,990 square feet of usable space, which could include a conference room, a work room for the law librarian, and sufficient space to accommodate approximately ten years' growth of the Law Library. This generous proposal was refined through consultation between the Library Committee and the bank's architect so that new shelving was provided throughout, as well as study carrels, a new desk for the librarian, appropriate furniture for the conference room, and certain other additional tables and desks. The Executive Committee authorized an expenditure of $13,800 to furnish and equip the new library.

The move to new quarters at once raised the very considerable problem of moving the books across Main Street. It was resolved by the timely creation of the Young Lawyers Section of the Association. The endless enthusiasm of the young lawyers was profitably channeled into a most successful operation which accomplished a near miracle in moving all of the volumes into the new building in such a manner as to result in their rearrangement in an orderly sensible manner. By mid-year of 1968 the Law Library was serenely functioning in bright new offices.

In 1987, the Norfolk and Portsmouth Bar Association, the Circuit Court of the City of Norfolk, and the City of Norfolk entered into an agreement as to the library. A non-profit foundation was established to maintain a public law library to serve the needs of the general public, the courts, and the bar. The Bar Association donated their books, and the courts added a library fee onto their filing fees, and the public was guaranteed access to the library as required by Virginia Code § 42.1-70. The new institution was named the Norfolk Law Library. In 1989, the Library was moved to the Dominion Tower in downtown Norfolk. The collection has over 25,000 volumes and much of the new electronic law retrieval technology is also present.

The legislative charter which was granted to the twelve lawyers in February 1880 has disappeared, and the Norfolk Library Association was taken over by the Norfolk and Portsmouth Bar Association. It is now a public library. That Association has increased in membership nearly nine-fold. Meanwhile, the Library has grown to rank with the best private law libraries in the South. It combines a deep sense of tradition, exemplified by the British and Canadian reports, with the pragmatism which urged acquisition of the modern services designed to facilitate the handling of complex specialized problems. The Library has retained its balance during the past years and should continue to flourish in its fine new quarters.

PRIVATE LAW LIBRARIES BEFORE 1776

W. H. Bryson

OF ALL PROFESSIONALS, lawyers are the most dependent upon books. All of their resource material is in written form. To know the level, the quality of the practicing bar, the bench, legal studies, and legal scholarship in general, one must know the books upon which they are founded.[1] Therefore, a census of law books was undertaken in order to know a little better the legal life of colonial Virginia.[2]

Virginia was the largest British colony in North America in the seventeenth and eighteenth centuries. There was not much legal communication with the other colonies before the beginning of the Revolutionary period; British laws assured that commercial and cultural ties were direct with Great Britain. However, Virginians had a disproportionate influence on the United States for the first fifty years of its existence, and this influence was exerted largely by men trained in the law at the end of the colonial period. It is believed that this study will shed some light on the law that shaped the lawyers who shaped the nation.

To say that this essay covers the colonial period calls for a warning. It does include the entire span from 1607 to 1776 as far as the presence of law books could be discovered. However, the records of seventeenth-century Virginia were not as carefully made or preserved as they were in the following century. Therefore almost all of the information comes from the period of about 1676 to 1776. This

---

[1] See generally A. G. Roeber, " 'The Scrutiny of the Ill Natured Ignorant Vulgar': Lawyers and Print Culture in Virginia 1716 to 1774," *Va. Mag. Hist. Biog.*, vol. 91, pp. 387-417 (1983); W. M. Billings, "English Legal Literature as a Source of Law and Legal Practice for Seventeenth-Century Virginia." *Va. Mag. Hist. Biog.*, vol. 87, pp. 403-416 (1979); W. M. Billings, "Justices, Books, Laws, and Courts in Seventeenth-Century Virginia." *Law Libr. Jour.*, vol. 85, pp. 277-296 (1993); B. C. Steiner, "Law Libraries in Colonial Virginia," *Green Bag*, vol. 9, pp. 351-354 (1897). For a good treatment of lawyers, see A. M. Smith, "Virginia Lawyers 1680-1776: The Birth of an American Profession" (Ph. D. diss., Johns Hopkins Univ., 1967); for colonial libraries in general, see the works listed in D. Gillespie and M. H. Harris, "A Bibliography of Virginia Library History," *Journal of Library History*, vol. 6, pp. 72-90 (1971), and J. M. Patterson, "Private Libraries in Virginia in the Eighteenth Century" (M.A. thesis, U. Va., 1936).

[2] An earlier version of this essay was published as the introduction to the author's *Census of Law Books in Colonial Virginia* (1978), and it is reprinted here with the permission of the University Press of Virginia. After that book had been published, further research has been done, primarily in the county court records of wills and inventories of decedents' estates, and the information of the additional law books found has been added into the statistics given below.

statement in turn requires the explanation that Virginia before 1676 was nowhere near so prosperous or so populous as it was later, and therefore fewer books of any kind would have been present in the early years.

The types of libraries that included law books were varied. There were those of the professional lawyers with extensive and comprehensive law collections, e.g., Richard Hickman and John Mercer. The libraries of the great landowners, William Byrd, II, and Robert "King" Carter, who sat in the General Court in Williamsburg, show that they had more than a superficial understanding of the law. The lesser gentry, an extensive class in Virginia, were justices of the peace and composed the county courts, the quarter sessions of colonial Virginia. In addition they usually handled their own legal affairs, and legal manuals and guides appear regularly in their modest libraries. The larger libraries will be mentioned later in more detail.

This study is based on printed sources, some manuscripts that have come to hand, and the inventories of decedent's estates in the county court archives. These printed sources are for the most part transcripts of inventories of decedent's estates, which were filed among the probate records of the county courts. One of the major limitations of this compilation is that not all of the county records have survived the fires, wars, and other vicissitudes of Virginia's history. Of particular distress is the loss of the probate records of Williamsburg, since this was the colonial capital, the seat of the General Court, and the residence of many prominent lawyers, including the attorneys general. There must have been a large number of law books in colonial Williamsburg that are now unknown to us and thus necessarily not included in this study. Moreover, there must have existed many books that perished in the lifetimes of their owners and were thus never inventoried. Fires were frequent in private homes.[3] Some books were lent and never returned; others must have been lost to overuse, dampness, and vermin. Many of the inventories that we do have are incomplete lists.[4] Many others tantalize with vague entries such as "law books" or "old legal books."[5]

---

[3] For example, Thomas Jefferson's library at Shadwell, which was composed mostly of law books, was burned in 1770 (Smith, pp. 249, 250).

[4] Patterson, pp. 3, 4, 9, 48, 56.

[5] For example, "1 law book" (Benjamin Brown, 1762), "15 law books" (Joseph Heenning, 1718), "13 law books" (Robert Tucker, 1723), "20 law books" (John Eustace, 1702), "Books in Colonial Virginia," *Va. Mag. Hist. Biog.*, vol. 10, pp. 389-405 (1903). There were 38 law books in the estate of Dr. Henry Willoughby on March 3, 1686, in (old) Rappahannock County.

On the other hand, it is possible that a single book has been counted more than once. It has not been possible to trace migrations of books to any degree significant to this study. That the titles were listed demonstrates that books were considered of importance and value by the administrator of an estate and that they were not going to be discarded. Nevertheless, I have not been able to discern any pattern in the acquisition or ownership of the various copies of the same title, and therefore I cannot make any conjecture that a certain person got his copy from any other particular individual, though he may have.

Furthermore, it cannot be said that the number of titles is the minimum number present in colonial Virginia because many entries of the inventories are too laconic to be identified. These may, and probably do, duplicate some of the fully identified entries. It is hoped that these errors of omission and commission will cancel each other. It is my opinion that the size of this census is cautious and conservative.

The results of the compilation of this census are a number of interesting statistics and insights. There are 1,571 copies of 482 identified titles; in addition there are 360 copies of 179 unidentified titles. Probably many of these unidentified titles are additional copies of identified books, but many are not. We must keep this caveat in mind when noting that the census gives a total of 1,931 copies and 661 entries.

The number of volumes cannot be determined with any significant degree of accuracy because it is seldom that this information was recorded. Many works were published in different numbers of volumes with the different editions, but the inventories do not identify editions. Furthermore, it is possible and likely that many titles in these lists represent incomplete sets, especially where the volumes were not issued simultaneously but might have had to be ordered from England separately over a period of several years.

Let us first consider the types of law books found in colonial Virginia and then the libraries in which they were found. There are 345 copies of ninety-one identified reports and accounts of trials, six copies of three or four indexes to reports, and twelve copies of six unidentified collections. These reports would have been of little practical value to a layman, and thus the presence of several in one library would suggest that their owner was a practicing lawyer or a person with aspirations in that direction. Of course, a volume of reports could have strayed into a gentleman's library by gift, bequest, or ill-advised purchase. With this in mind, let us examine the list of reports as a clue to the professional and intellectual level of the bar of colonial Virginia.

As one should expect, the most popular of reporters was Sir Edward Coke; there were twenty copies of his reports (including incomplete sets and abridgments). The next in number of copies in Virginia was Croke with fourteen. There were thirteen copies each of Hobart and of Salkeld, and nine copies of Pollexfen and of Ventris. At least one copy of all the then printed reports were present in Virginia before 1776, except Brooke's *New Cases*, which appeared in several editions up to 1628; Bunbury, 1755; Cunningham, 1766 and 1770; Mosely, 1744; Sayer, 1775; F. Vesey, Sr., 1771, 1773; and Wilson, 1770 to 1775. Of the ninety-eight reports then in print, ninety-one are known to have been available to the colonial Virginia bar.

The holders of the largest numbers of copies of reports were:

John Mercer	97
William Byrd, II	33
Robert Carter	26
George Johnston	25
Peyton Randolph	24
Richard Hickman	21
George Douglas	17
Henry Churchill	15
Charles Burges	11
Daniel McCarty	11
Dabney Carr	10

The libraries of these men will be discussed below.

There were forty-three copies of twenty-four titles of collections of state trials and of individual cases, most of which were criminal trials. These works were probably bought for their general interest value rather than for use for legal research.

Most of the English collections of statutes were called *Statutes at Large*; there were at least 104 copies and sets in colonial Virginia. The Virginia statutory collections are represented by sixteen titles and a total of 133 copies. It was easier to identify these titles than the English ones because the possibilities are fewer. The proportion of unidentified books, however, is much higher than that for the reports of cases.

The number of Continental legal works is not great, but it is larger than one might have expected. There were sixty-five copies of thirty-four titles. Of these sixty-five, the library of William Byrd, II, accounted for twenty-eight, and these twenty-eight were the more esoteric. The remainder, standard texts, were scattered thinly and were often English translations. There were in total twenty copies of Pufendorf's two popular treatises, ten copies of Grotius's *De Jure Belli ac Pacis*, six of Justinian's *Institutes* (a textbook of Roman law), and two copies of Domat, *Loix Civiles*. The other titles were represented by single copies each, eighteen of which were owned by Byrd.

The secondary English legal literature constitutes the great bulk of this census. It includes everything from scholarly treatises to form books and manuals for laymen. There were 1,007 copies of 346 identifiable titles and 305 copies of 162 unidentified ones. This is an appropriate place to inquire of this census what were the more popular categories of treatises and handbooks owned in colonial Virginia.

There was a substantial number of English manuals for justices of the peace, sixty-three copies of twenty-one titles. The most popular of these were the works of Dalton (as might have been expected), whose treatise was represented by seventeen copies, of Keble, five copies, and Burn, five copies. Dalton's *Country Justice* was first published in 1618; it superseded in popularity Lambarde's *Eirenarcha*. Dalton's work was enormously popular in England as well as in Virginia and went through many editions before it was, in its turn, superseded by Burn's *Justice*. The presence of only five copies of this last mentioned book is not really surprising. Burn's manual was highly successful in England, but since the first edition was not issued until 1755, there was serious local competition in the field from George Webb.

This brings us to mention three entries which have two things in common; first, they are the only American treatises found in colonial Virginia, and second, they are all three manuals for justices of the peace. There was one copy of the work by Simpson published in Charleston, South Carolina, and six copies of a handbook by Parker, which went through three editions in the middle Atlantic colonies before 1776. The third was George Webb's *Virginia Justice*, which was printed in Williamsburg in 1736; forty-three copies have been found, but there must have been many more in circulation.

In Virginia the justices of the peace presided over the county courts, which had civil as well as criminal jurisdiction; but in England the justices were invested only with criminal jurisdiction and with quasi-criminal administrative duties. Therefore, these manuals for justices dealt only with matters of criminal law. In addition to these, there were other types of books dealing with the criminal law and its administration.

There were three separate guides for sheriffs. There were at least seven copies of the one by Dalton and single copies of Wilkinson's *Treatise* and of the anonymous *Complete Sheriff*. There were two books for constables, those by Meriton and Wingate, and two for clerks of assize. There were also twelve titles dealing with the criminal law in general; they were represented by forty copies. The most popular of these were Coke's *Third Institute* (ten copies), Hale's *Summary of the*

Pleas of the Crown (eight copies), and Hawkins's *Pleas of the Crown* (seven copies).

By far the most commonly owned law books in colonial Virginia were guides, handbooks, and collections of forms for pleading in court and for the conveying of land. One hundred seventeen titles were represented by 359 copies. These books constituted the foundations of the practicing attorney's professional library and were also very popular with the layman who handled his own legal affairs. The most common of these were:

Duncombe, *Trials per Pais* (15 copies)
Fitzherbert, *New Natura Brevium* (13 copies)
Manley, *Clerk's Guide* (11 copies)
West, *Symboleography* (11 copies)
Bohun, *Institutio Legalis* (9 copies)
Brown, *Modus Intrandi Placita Generalia* (9 copies)
Practick Part of the Law (9 copies)
Style, *Registrum Practicale* (9 copies)
Richardson, *Attorney's Practice in the Court of King's Bench* (8 copies)
Attorney's Pocket Companion (7 copies)
Billinghurst, *Arcana Clericalia* (7 copies)
Richardson, *Attorney's Practice in the Court of Common Pleas* (7 copies)
Hutton, *Young Clerk's Guide* (6 copies)
Jacob, *Every Man His Own Lawyer* (6 copies)
Townesend, *Preparative to Pleading* (5 copies)

There were a few books on various branches of the substantive common law, such as contracts, slander, and fraud, and many on the subject of real property. This large preponderance of books on property law indicates that real estate was by far the major form of wealth in England as well as in Virginia and also that this was the most well developed and sophisticated branch of English law. There were twenty-one titles and sixty-eight copies of books on this subject. By far the most important of these was *Coke upon Littleton*, which constituted the first part of Coke's *Institutes*; it was an elaborate and deeply learned commentary on Littleton's *Tenures*. This was the standard law text until the appearance of Blackstone's *Commentaries* in 1765. There were at least twenty-seven copies of *Coke upon Littleton* in colonial Virginia. The second most popular work was that by Perkins, *A Profitable Book*; eight copies of this one were found here.

Equity, the other major branch of English law, was represented by twenty-six copies of thirteen titles on procedure and practice. In addition there were ten copies of six works on the substantive principles.

In addition were the general works: law dictionaries, abridgments, and encyclopedias. Of these there were twenty-eight titles and 132 copies.

Jacob, *Law Dictionary* (23 copies)
Rastell, *Termes de la Ley* (17 copies)
Wood, *Institutes* (14 copies)
Sheppard, *Abridgment* (7 copies)
Bacon, *Elements of the Common Laws of England* (6 copies)
Cowell, *Interpreter* (6 copies)

These figures do not include the following five works whose antiquity and scholarship entitles them to special notice: Glanvill, *Bracton*, *Britton*, Selden's *Ad Fletam Dissertatio*, and Saint Germain's *Doctor and Student*. There were eight copies of this last-mentioned work in colonial Virginia. All five of these works were on the shelves of William Byrd's library at Westover; King Carter owned copies of *Bracton* and *Britton*; and John Mercer had a copy of *Britton*. Indeed it is the presence of these books and others of equal erudition in other fields which justifies the reputations of Byrd and Carter and of their libraries.

The final categories of law books to be considered are those branches of the civil law of the Continent which were grafted onto the trunk of English jurisprudence: ecclesiastical law (including the law of wills) and the law of merchants (including maritime law and the levy of customs duties). The works dealing with the various aspects of church law, tithes, canons, convocations, parishes, etc., are represented by twenty-four copies of twenty titles. The fact that only two titles were present in more than one copy suggests the relative unimportance of this general group of books. On the other hand, the works dealing with wills and executors were very useful and were present in relative profusion. There were seventy-two copies of eleven titles. The most frequently found of these were:

Swinburne, *Treatise of Testaments and Last Wills* (23 copies)
Wentworth, *Office of Executors* (13 copies)
Godolphin, *Orphan's Legacy* (11 copies)
Gilbert, *Law of Devises* (8 copies)

Anyone of any financial substance would have wanted to make a will then, as now, and the absence of banks meant that many persons would have found themselves serving as executors of wills and administrators of decedents' estates.

Almost all colonial Virginians derived their income from farming, and they were dependent upon British merchants and shippers to provide them with manufactured goods and to market their agricultural products. To aid themselves in these mercantile affairs, the Virginia planters used fifty-five copies of twenty titles. The single most popular book by far was Molloy's *De Jure Maritimo* with eighteen copies. There were six copies of Malynes's *Lex Mercatoria* and nine copies of "the book of rates," which were schedules of the statutory customs duties.

These statistics have shown which were the most popular types of law books in pre-revolutionary Virginia. The most popular individual titles were as follows:

Webb, *Virginia Justice* (43 copies)
Mercer, *Abridgment of Acts of Assembly of Virginia* (31 copies)
Coke upon Littleton (27 copies)
Swinburne, *Treatise of Testaments* (23 copies)
Jacob, *Law Dictionary* (23 copies)
Molloy, *De Jure Maritimo* (18 copies)
Dalton, *Country Justice* (17 copies)
Rastell, *Termes de la Ley* (17 copies)
Coke, *Reports* (16 sets)
Duncombe, *Trials per Pais* (15 copies)
Pufendorf, *Law of Nature and Nations* (14 copies)
Wood, *Institutes* (14 copies)
Fitzherbert, *New Natura Brevium* (13 copies)
Wentworth, *Office of Executors* (13 copies)
Croke, *Reports* (12 copies)
Godolphin, *Orphan's Legacy* (11 copies)
Manley, *Clerk's Guide* (11 copies)
West, *Symboleography* (11 copies)
Wingate, *Abridgment of Statutes* (11 copies)

Before going on to the discussion of individual law collections, let us pause to note the presence in this list of the books by Swinburne and Dalton and the absence of Dalton's manual for sheriffs, of which only seven copies have been located in Virginia. In 1666 these three works were given a measure of official approval by the General Assembly by an act which required copies of each to be provided for the use of every court.[6] Thus one should expect to find them in the possession of many private persons as well.

Having considered the books by intellectual categories, it is now appropriate to consider them as they were collected together in the various private libraries of colonial Virginia. The largest collection of law books in the period was owned by John Mercer of Marlborough, Stafford County. His library included 284 titles and twenty-six duplicate copies. Mercer was a planter and a real estate speculator, but primarily he was a practicing attorney and a highly successful one.[7] Furthermore his legal activities extended to sitting as a justice of the county court and to compiling an abridgment of the laws of Virginia.[8]

Mercer's collecting of law books had begun as early as 1725; his account books show that he was adding steadily to his law library in the 1730s and 1740s, and the *Virginia Gazette* daybooks record several purchases in 1751, 1764, and 1765.[9] He died in 1768 after a long and busy career at the bar, and his library was sold several years later.[10] The information for this census is based upon Mercer's own account books, supplemented by the *Virginia Gazette* daybooks and the inventory of his estate made in 1770. Mercer's library included 101 copies of reports and state trials, 191 copies of a wide range of treatises, and eighteen copies of legislative compilations. It is interesting to note that 114 of the titles in this collection are not known to have been present elsewhere in colonial Virginia. This law library was one of breadth and depth; it was the working library of a practicing lawyer who could and did handle any sort of lawsuit.

The second largest law collection and the largest library overall in colonial Virginia belonged to William Byrd, II, of Westover, Charles City County. Byrd was born into the aristocracy and therefore never practiced law. However, he was closely concerned with the law throughout his life. As a young man he studied law in London at the Middle Temple and was called to the bar in 1695. After his return to Virginia, he was elected to the House of Burgesses and was later

[6] Hening's Statutes, vol. 2, p. 246.

[7] C. M. Watkins, *Cultural History of Marlborough, Virginia*, pp. 21, 23-24, 27, 49, 55 (1968).

[8] *Id.*, pp. 24, 50-53.

[9] *Id.*, pp. 17, 191-192, 198-208; *Virginia Gazette* Day Books, 2 vols., University of Virginia Library, Department of Manuscripts.

[10] Watkins, pp. 59, 61-63; see also the inventory made in 1770, a copy of which is among the Brock manuscripts in the Huntington Library.

appointed to the Council, which also sat as the General Court, the highest court in the colony.[11]

Byrd's law library consisted of 189 titles and 19 duplicates.[12] These can be divided as 52 copies of reports, of which 18 were state trials, 141 copies of secondary legal literature, and 25 copies of various legislative works. Seventy-six law titles in Byrd's library were unique copies in Virginia. The usual manuals and handbooks were present, but the collection is particularly noteworthy for its inclusion of many works on constitutional law, international and Continental jurisprudence, and the older English authors, such as Glanvill, *Bracton*, *Britton*, Fortescue, Littleton, and Brooke. This was the working library of a gentleman who was the manager of his own affairs and who was a statesman occupied with the legislative and judicial affairs of the colony.[13]

William Byrd, II, died in 1744, but his library was not dispersed until 1777 following the suicide of his son.[14] William Byrd, III, was not an intellectual person at all and in all probability did not add much to his father's library; he was addicted to gambling, was a poor businessman, and was constantly in debt. Therefore the books at Westover have been assigned to the collection of the scholarly William Byrd, II.

The third largest law library in Virginia was that of Robert Carter of Corotoman, Lancaster County, who was so wealthy and powerful that he is usually referred to as "King" Carter. Carter was a planter, a land speculator, and the land agent for the Fairfax family, who were the proprietors of the Northern Neck. His public duties included the office of speaker of the House of Burgesses and later a place on the Council and a seat in the General Court. He was very conscious of

---

[11] L. B. Wright, *First Gentlemen of Virginia*, pp. 322, 325, 333 (1940); *DAB*.

[12] Since this work was submitted to the press, the following excellent book has been published: Kevin J. Hayes, *The Library of William Byrd of Westover* (1997). At page 82, Hayes puts the number of legal titles in Byrd's library at 298. This figure includes many works which are not strictly legal in my view. However, Hayes has identified numerous pamphlets on state trials that were bound together and listed as a single item in the catalogs that I relied upon for my count. These should be added to my figures, as should the following: M. Garrati, *De Bello* (1629); *The Compleat Clerk* (1655); Vaughan's *Reports*; and A. Vinnius, *Tractatus Quinque* (1664).

[13] Byrd frequently used his law books: K. J. Hayes, *Library of William Byrd*, pp. 83, 175, 180, 182, 200, 216.

[14] E. Wolf, II, "The Dispersal of the Library of William Byrd of Westover," *Proc. Am. Antiq. Soc.*, vol. 68, pp. 19-106 (1958); K. J. Hayes, *Library of William Byrd*, pp. 95-103.

learning and showed great concern for the education of his children; his library included over 260 titles at the time of his death in 1732.[15]

King Carter owned eighty-seven different law books and nine duplicates. Of these, thirty were reports, sixty were guides, treatises, etc., and six were legislative materials. Although he would not have considered himself a lawyer, he did represent himself and the Fairfax interests in court. Certainly the handbooks and form books dealing with conveyancing were of great practical value to him. His general interest in learning and perhaps also his position as a judge of the General Court in Williamsburg led him to the acquisition of the more erudite legal works, such as *Bracton*, *Britton*, Fortescue, Fitzherbert, Brooke, and Selden, in addition to the standard treatises.

Richard Hickman, who was the clerk of the Council in Williamsburg and who died in 1732,[16] also built up a substantial law collection. It consisted of seventy-three titles and eight duplicates. Reports of cases were represented by twenty copies, treatises and manuals by fifty-six, and statutory material by five. The size and character of this library suggests that Hickman was also a practicing attorney.

George Johnston was an eminent attorney from Fairfax and Alexandria. He was born in 1700 and served in the House of Burgesses from 1758 until his death in 1766.[17] His library included sixty-two legal titles, of which twenty-five were reports, two were statutes, and thirty-five secondary works.

Henry Churchill, a Virginian from the northern part of the colony, had been called to the bar of the Middle Temple in 1754 before beginning the practice of law back in his homeland. He died in 1760.[18] His legal library consisted of fifty-four titles and two duplicates, sixteen law reports, three statute books, and thirty-seven handbooks and treatises.

The earliest known law library of any size is that of Arthur Spicer, who died in 1699. Spicer was a lawyer, merchant, member of the General Assembly, justice of the peace, and county court judge of Richmond County.[19] He owned fifty-three different law books and three duplicates; of these forty-six were treatises, six statutes, but only four

[15] Wright, pp. 248-250; *DAB*.

[16] *Wm. and Mary Qtly.*, 1st ser., vol. 3, p. 248 (1895).

[17] *Va. Mag. Hist. Biog.*, vol. 10, p. 12 (1902); *Wm. and Mary Qtly.*, 2d ser., vol. 2, pp. 75-80 (1922).

[18] *Va. Mag. Hist. Biog.*, vol. 36, p. 31 (1928).

[19] *Wm. and Mary Qtly.*, 1st ser., vol. 3, p. 133 (1894); *Tyler's Qtly.*, vol. 10, p. 163 (1929).

reports. The secondary works were the commonly found books on pleading and conveyancing.

Godfrey Pole studied law for five years at Barnard's Inn in London and was an attorney of the Court of Common Pleas for fourteen years before immigrating to Virginia. He was admitted to practice here in 1715. He built up an extensive practice in the General Court in Williamsburg and in the county courts. In addition he was the clerk of the Northampton County Court from 1722 until his death in 1729 or 1730.[20] The list of his books is dated 1716; it is quite possible that his library was much larger by the time of his death. Pole's working law library included fifty-three titles and three duplicates; of these forty-seven were secondary works, four were reports, and five were statutes.

There were fifty titles and a single duplicate in the collection of law books of Daniel McCarty. These figures include thirty-two treatises, thirteen reports, and six copies of statutory material. McCarty was a wealthy man and a member of the House of Burgesses from Westmoreland County. He died in 1724.[21]

John Herbert of Chesterfield County, who died in 1760, had a law collection consisting of forty-two titles. There were thirty-two treatises, six reports, and four collections of statutes.

On the eve of Independence, Philip Fithian made a partial catalogue of the library of Councillor Robert Carter of Nomini Hall, Westmoreland County. Councillor Carter, the grandson of King Carter, had studied law at the Inner Temple and was later a judge of the General Court and of the county court. He was an intellectually inclined gentleman, and by 1774 he had acquired some 1,400 volumes.[22] Carter's legal collection encompassed at least thirty-nine titles and two duplicate copies. There were thirty-five treatises and guides, three reports, and three statute books. Along with the usual practice manuals were found works by Justinian, Grotius, Pufendorf, and three books by Kames. Although he appears to have inherited his grandfather's love of books, a comparison of the two inventories suggests that he did not inherit the books themselves.

The next library to be mentioned is that of Dabney Carr, who died in 1773. Carr, brother-in-law of Thomas Jefferson, was a practicing lawyer and a burgess from Louisa County.[23] His law collection

[20] *Va. Mag. Hist. Biog.*, vol. 17, pp. 147-150 (1909).

[21] L. G. Tyler, *Encyclopedia of Virginia Biography*, vol. 1, p. 288 (1915).

[22] L. Morton, *Robert Carter of Nomini Hall*, pp. 11, 27, 31, 34, 42, 54, 215 (1945); there is a transcript of the inventory in H. D. Farish, ed., *Journal and Letters of Philip Vickers Fithian*, pp. 285-294 (1943).

[23] *Va. Mag. Hist. Biog.*, vol. 2, p. 221 (1894).

consisted of thirty-eight titles and one duplicate; of these, twenty-six were treatises, nine reports, and four statute books.

The last two collections of law books to be considered have several things in common. They both constitute a fairly small proportion of fairly large libraries, twenty-seven books in a collection of about 375 and twenty-six of about 300. Both were owned by wealthy and influential planters. Ralph Wormeley, II, of Rosegill, Middlesex County, who died in 1701, was a judge of the General Court and of the county court; he was also secretary of state, a receiver of duties, and a naval officer.[24] He had twenty-seven law books, twenty-two of which were treatises and handbooks, two were reports, and three were collections of statutes.

The law library of Richard Lee, II, who died in 1714, was very similar. This collection included twenty-five titles and one duplicate, and of these twenty-one were secondary legal works, three were reports of cases, and two were books of statutes. Lee, of Mount Pleasant, Westmoreland County, was a judge in the General Court in Williamsburg and in the local county court; he was also a collector of customs.[25]

John Chapman of Brunswick County had nineteen law books in 1743. Charles Burges of Lancaster County had thirty-five in 1733; John Edmunds of Sussex County had twenty-nine in 1770. George Douglas of Accomack County had fifty-three law books in 1758, and Richard Coke also of Accomack County had thirty-six in 1764. Coke had fifteen titles that Douglas also had; so it may have been that Coke bought them from Douglas's administrator, they both being from the same county. The other holdings of law books in colonial Virginia ranged on down to a single manual, form book, or statute book. The ownership of law books was widespread throughout the colony. It is obvious that Virginians were concerned with their legal rights and that they looked to the English common law for the definition of them.

This study shows that the legal literature available to eighteenth-century Virginians was remarkably extensive in depth and in breadth of scope. Moreover, there were large and small holdings throughout the settled areas of the colony. It is also to be kept in mind that books were freely lent to neighbors and library doors were always open to friends.

As one would expect, the legal manuals and guidebooks for laymen were most frequently found in colonial libraries. People needed to know what their powers and duties were as justices of the peace, collectors

[24] Wright, pp. 187, 189, 195-197.

[25] *Id.*, pp. 212-217.

of customs, sheriffs, constables, vestrymen, administrators of estates, etc. They needed to know how to make wills, how to convey land, and how to draft bills of exchange. In addition to this type of law book, many of the practicing attorneys and General Court judges had copies of the various reports of cases and collections of statutes. The more wealthy and highly educated had these books and also tomes of jurisprudence, legal history, and international law. The most fabulous library of all, that of William Byrd, II, included books of the Roman and canon laws of the Continent.

BIBLIOGRAPHY

I. *Printed Works*

Bassett, John Spencer. *The Writings of "Colonel William Byrd of Westover."* New York: Doubleday, Page, 1901, App. A, pp. 413-443.

Inventory c. 1751-54; William Byrd, II, who created this library, died in 1744; it is unlikely that his son and heir, William Byrd, III, added many books.

"Books in Colonial Virginia." *Va. Mag. Hist. Biog.*, vol. 7, pp. 299-303 (1900).

Robert Massey inventory of 1753.

"Books in Colonial Virginia." *Va. Mag. Hist. Biog.*, vol. 10, pp. 389-405 (1903).

Inventories of Peter Jefferson, 1757; Cornelius Thomas, 1775; Matthew Kemp, 1717; Thomas Thompson, 1715; Hancock Lee, 1710; William Dare, 1721; John Mottrom, 1657; Samuel Fox, 1723; Matthew Hubard, 1670; Francis Epes, 1679; Charles Pasture, 1736; Nathaniel Hill, 1691.

"Books in Williamsburg." *Wm. & Mary Qtly.*, 1st ser., vol. 15, pp. 100-113 (1907).

Sales catalogue of Dixon & Hunter dated 1775.

Bryson, William Hamilton. *Census of Law Books in Colonial Virginia.* Charlottesville: University Press of Va., 1978.

"Catalogue of the Library of Daniel Parke Custis." *Va. Mag. Hist. Biog.*, vol. 17, pp. 404-412 (1909).

Inventory c. 1759.

"Correspondence Relating to Lord Botetourt." *Tyler's Qtly.*, vol. 3, pp. 106-26 (1922).

Inventory of 1771.

Draper, Lyman C. "The Westover Library." *Va. Historical Register*, vol. 4, pp. 87-90 (1851).

Duncan, Marion Moncure, Adrian Cather Miller, Peyton Sagendorf Moncure. *House of Moncure Genealogy, First Supplement.* N.p., 1968.

Inventory of the Rev. John Moncure, J.P., dated 1764.

"Extracts from the Records of Elizabeth City County." *Va. Mag. Hist. Biog.*, vol. 17, p. 322 (1909).

Inventory of John Tabb dated 1762.

Farish, Hunter Dickinson, ed. *Journal and Letters of Philip Vickers Fithian.* Williamsburg: Colonial Williamsburg, 1943, pp. 285-294.

"The Farrar Family." *Va. Mag. Hist. Biog.*, vol. 8, p. 207 (1901).

Inventory of William Farrar dated 1678.

Hayes, Kevin J. *The Library of William Byrd of Westover*, Madison, Wis.: Madison House, 1997.

This book supersedes the works by Bassett and Wolf.

"Historical Notes and Queries." *Wm. & Mary Qtly.*, 1st ser., vol. 8, p. 275 (1900).

Books of William Nimmo who died in 1748.

"History of York County in the Seventeenth Century." *Tyler's Qtly.*, vol. 1, pp. 231 at 259 (1920).

Books belonging in the York County Court in 1692.

Hoppin, C. A. "The House in Which George Washington Was Born." *Tyler's Qtly.*, vol. 8, pp. 73-103 (1926).

Augustine Washington inventory of 1758.

Hoppin, C. A. "Library of Edward Gouldman." *Tyler's Qtly.*, vol. 8, p. 284 (1927).

Inventory dated 1709.

Houlette, William. "The Byrd Library." *Tyler's Qtly.*, vol. 16, pp. 100-109 (1934).

"Isle of Wight County Records." *Wm. & Mary Qtly.*, 1st ser., vol. 7, p. 248 (1899).

Inventory of Joseph Woory dated 1694.

Jennings, John Melville. "Notes on the Original Library of the College of William and Mary in Virginia, 1693-1705." *Papers of the Bibliographical Soc. of Am.*, vol. 41, pp. 239-267 (1947).

Books in the possession of Gov. Francis Nicholson in 1695.

"Miscellaneous Colonial Documents." *Va. Mag. Hist. Biog.*, vol. 17, pp. 147-150 (1909).

Godfrey Pole inventory of 1716.

Newton, B. T. "The Inventory of Goods and Chattels of Col. George Eskridge." *Northern Neck of Va. Hist. Mag.*, vol. 14, pp. 1311-1315 (1964).

Eskridge died in 1735.

"Notes." *Va. Mag. Hist. Biog.*, vol. 8, p. 61 (1901).

Inventory of Sterling Clack dated 1751.

Stanard, W[illiam] G[lover]. Library of Dabney Carr, 1773, with a Notice of the Carr Family." *Va. Mag. Hist. Biog.*, vol. 2, pp. 221-228 (1895).

Stanard, William Glover. "Major Robert Beverley and His Descendants." *Va. Mag. Hist. Biog.*, vol. 3, pp. 388-391 (1896).

Robert Beverley inventory of 1734.

Tyler, Lyon Gardiner. "Libraries in Colonial Virginia." *Wm. & Mary Qtly.*, 1st ser., vol. 2, pp. 169-175, 247-251 (1894); vol. 3, pp. 43-45, 132-134, 180-182, 246-253 (1895); vol. 4, pp. 15-17, 94-95, 156, 269 (1896); vol. 6, pp. 40-41, 158-164 (1897); vol. 8, pp. 18-22, 77-79, 145-150, 230, 237 (1900).

Inventories of Ralph Wormeley, 1701; Matthew Hubard, 1667; Edmund Berkeley, 1719; John Kemp, 1648; Charles Colston, 1724; Samuel Peachy, 1750; Arthur Spicer (lawyer and J.P.), 1699; James Whaley, 1701; Richard Hickman (Clerk of the Council), 1732; Thomas Cocke, 1697; Thomas Walke, 1704; Christopher Cocke, 1716; Daniel McCarty, 1724; John Waller, 1755; John Herbert, 1760; Southey Littleton, 1680.

Watkins, C. Malcolm. *The Cultural History of Marlborough, Virginia.* Smithsonian Bulletin 253 (Washington, D.C., 1968), pp. 198-208.

These pages transcribe the parts of the ledger of John Mercer where he lists the books in his possession from 1746 to 1750.

"William Dunlop's Library." *Wm. and Mary Qtly.*, 1st ser., vol. 15, pp. 275-279 (1907).

Inventory dated 1740.

Williams, J. R. "A Catalogue of Books in the Library of 'Councillor' Robert Carter at Nomini Hall, Westmoreland County, Va." *Wm. and Mary Qtly.*, 1st ser., vol. 10, pp. 232-241 (1902); vol. 11, pp. 21-28 (1902).

Inventory c. 1772.

Wolf, Edwin, II. "The Dispersal of the Library of William Byrd of Westover." *Proc. Am. Antiq. Soc.*, vol. 68, pp. 19-106 (1958).

Wolf, Edwin, II. "More Books from the Library of the Byrds of Westover." *Proc. Am. Antiq. Soc.*, vol. 88, pp. 51-82 (1978).

Wright, Louis Booker. "The `Gentleman's Library' in Early Virginia: The Literary Interests of the First Carters." *Huntington Library Quarterly*, vol. 1, pp. 3-61 (1937).

Robert Carter inventory of 1732.

Wright, Louis Booker. "Richard Lee, II, a Belated Elizabethan in Virginia." *Huntington Library Quarterly*, vol. 2, pp. 1-35 (1938).

Inventory dated 1715.

II. *Manuscript Works*

Inventories of the following decedent's estates among the county court records were shown to me by Gary L. Cardwell, Cynthia Gianakos Oates, Harold B. Gill, Jr., and Jonathan H. Poston:

Robert Andrews, 1750, Accomack County
Francis Ballard, 1720, Elizabeth City County
Patrick Barclay, 1751, Essex County
Thomas Wright Belfield, 1744, Richmond County
John Bell, 1744, Lancaster County
William Black, 1738, Accomack County
Thomas Blair, 1740, Accomack County
John Bonney, 1767, Princess Anne County
Edward Booker, 1767, Halifax County
George Bowman, 1771, Frederick County
Alexander Boyd, 1766, Augusta County
William Brent, 1742, Stafford County
Charles Burges, 1733, Lancaster County
Thomas Carter, 1734, Lancaster County
John Chapman, 1743, Brunswick County
John Chichester, 1728, Lancaster County
Henry Churchill, 1762, Fauquier County
Francis Clarke, 1771, Princess Anne County
Christopher Cocke, 1716, Princess Anne County
Thomas Cocke, 1697, Princess Anne County
Richard Coke, 1764, Accomack County
George Conway, 1758, Lancaster County
Edmund Custis, 1701, Accomack County
Henry Custis, 1733, Accomack County
John Custis, 1733, Accomack County
John Custis, 1747, Northampton County

Rachel Custis, 1720, Accomack County
Thomas Day, 1774, Isle of Wight County
Isaac Dix, 1744, Accomack County
George Douglas, 1758, Accomack County
John Edmonds, 1770, Sussex County
Rev. Arthur Emmerson, Accomack County
Peter Eppes, 1773, Charles City County
Solomon Ewell, 1736, Accomack County
Abram Farrow, 1732, Stafford County
Nicholas Flood, 1776, Richmond County
James Fontaine, 1746, Northumberland County
John Foushee, 1774, Halifax County
Chandler Fowke, 1745, Stafford County
John Gaston, 1697, Princess Anne County
Samuel Godwin, 1735, Westmoreland County
James Gordon, 1772, Lancaster County
William Gordon, 1728, Middlesex County
Robert Green, 1755, Orange County
Leroy Griffin, 1750, Richmond County
Thomas Griffin, 1733, Richmond County
Philip Grymes, 1762, Prince George County
Peter Hack, 1717, Accomack County
John Hart, 1743, Orange County
George Heale, 1737, Lancaster County
John Heale, 1738, Lancaster County
Nathaniel Hill, 1690, Henrico County
John Holt, 1765, Surry County
George Hope, 1724, Accomack County
John Jackson, 1739, Accomack County
Mary Jackson, 1761, Isle of Wight County
Thomas Jackson, 1773, Augusta County
Joseph Jegitts, 1767, Elizabeth City County
George Johnston, 1767, Fairfax County
Ann Jones, 1749, Northumberland County
Ralph Justice, 1760, 1761, Accomack County
John Kendall, 1739, Accomack County
William Carr Lane, 1771, Loudoun County
Armistead Lightfoot, 1772, York County
Edward McDonald, 1761, Augusta County
John McDowell, 1743, Orange County
Kenneth McKenzie, 1755, York County
John Minor, 1755, Spotsylvania County
William Moore, 1767, Sussex County

Willoughby Newton, 1767, Westmoreland County
John Osheal, 1749, Norfolk County
William Parsons, 1760, Elizabeth City County
Simon Pearson, 1733, Stafford County
Henry Person, 1754, Southampton County
John Person, 1767, Southampton County
Sarah Robins, 1743, Accomack County
James Rule, 1765, Accomack County
John Scott, 1772, Amelia County
James Seaton, 1744, Stafford County
John Scarburgh, 1742, Accomack County
John Shepherd, 1740, Accomack County
John Smith, 1746, Accomack County
Joseph Smith, 1728, Essex County
Warrington Staton, 1761, Accomack County
Charles Stockley, 1764, Accomack County
David Stuart, 1749, Stafford County
John Tabb, 1763, Elizabeth City County
John Tarpley, Jr., 1737, Richmond County
Travis Tarpley, 1768, Richmond County
Charles Taylor, 1773, Southampton County
James Taylor, 1768, Halifax County
Littleton Tazewell, 1759, Brunswick County
Thomas Teackle, 1696, Accomack County
Presley Thornton, 1770, Northumberland County
Anthony Tucker, 1759, Elizabeth City County
John Turbervile, 1728, Lancaster County
John Walker, 1747, Accomack County
William Walker, 1763, Stafford County
Townshend Washington, 1744, Stafford County
John Watts, 1736, Accomack County
Charles West, 1758, Accomack County
Lewis Whitehead, 1760, Southampton County
William Wishart, 1765, Accomack County

"The Library of John Mercer of Marlboro." Henry E. Huntington Library, San Marino, California.

> This manuscript inventory, which is dated 1770, is among the Brock manuscripts.

Virginia Gazette Day Books. 2 vols. University of Virginia Library, Manuscripts Department.

These two manuscript volumes cover the years 1750 to 1752 and 1764 to 1766.

PRIVATE LAW LIBRARIES AFTER 1776

E. Lee Shepard and Kenneth D. McArthur, Jr.

EVEN BEFORE the close of the colonial era in Virginia, the legal profession in the Old Dominion had naturally fallen into two distinct categories, the inferior court bar and the superior court bar. The inferior bar, the group of advocates that Thomas Jefferson disdainfully labeled as "insects," practiced in the colony's county courts, local judicial bodies presided over by justices of the peace who were primarily gentry planters "unlettered in the law." The superior bar, consisting of the best qualified and most successful practitioners in the colony, appeared before the Virginia General Court (most frequently in appellate cases) and before the colonial Court of Oyer and Terminer (as advocates in capital criminal cases). Any ambitious young practitioner set his sights on graduating from the country practice to the superior bar, but very few made it.[1]

With the gradual evolution of legal practice in Virginia and the periodic reform and restructuring of the Commonwealth's judicial system in the decades following the Revolutionary War, this dichotomy within the bar persisted only for a time. Gradually, lawyers settled into two unofficial categories, rural attorneys whose practices tended to be quite routine and urban professionals with broader and often more specialized practices who handled most of the appellate business in the Commonwealth. This division of labor in the legal community, reflecting the very different circumstances of law practice in those disparate settings, alone makes any attempt at identifying or describing a "typical private law library" in Virginia impossible.

The failure of Virginians in general to keep good records of the libraries they amassed complicates matters even more. Benjamin Watkins Leigh, Jr., son of a famous nineteenth-century Virginia attorney and a lawyer himself, complained to antiquarian Hugh Blair Grigsby of "the ways of our fellow Virginians as to books" when trying to reconstruct the library of John Randolph of Roanoke in 1848.[2]

---

[1] Some scholars have argued against the presence of a two-tiered legal profession in colonial Virginia, but see Frank L. Dewey's masterful handling of the issue in Appendix B of *Thomas Jefferson, Lawyer*, pp. 122-126 (1986). For the development of the profession in Virginia after the Revolution, see A. G. Roeber, *Faithful Magistrates and Republican Lawyers: Creators of Virginia Legal Culture, 1680-1810* (1981), and E. Lee Shepard, "Lawyers Look at Themselves: Professional Consciousness and the Virginia Bar, 1770-1850," *Am. Journ. Legal Hist.*, vol. 25, pp. 1-23 (1981).

[2] Benjamin Watkins Leigh, Jr., to Grigsby, November 28, 1848, Hugh Blair Grigsby Papers, Virginia Historical Society, Richmond (hereinafter VHS).

Although sufficient evidence is yet to be gathered, the supposition that the book collections compiled and used by country practitioners in the eighteenth and the nineteenth centuries were quite modest in comparison to the libraries of superior court attorneys is not without considerable merit. Historians have yet to scrutinize the membership of the Virginia legal profession closely, but that future study will no doubt include extensive research into the nature and scope of private legal libraries through the examination of estate inventories and other documentary evidence.

In the absence of such raw data, this essay examines Virginia's private law libraries in two ways: surviving information about the libraries of a sampling of judges, law professors, and prominent practitioners to discover titles held in common, as well as rare and unique volumes in those collections, and some anecdotal perspectives on how Virginia lawyers compiled and used their law libraries. The libraries of such leading advocates in the Commonwealth were built upon a strong foundation of practical legal works that would have been essential to any attorney at any level of practice. Beyond that foundation, each individual built up a library based on his areas of specialization and general interests. Where the contents of these various libraries intersect, in other words, in the titles that each held in common, we can best identify the basic volumes most crucial to any advocate's successful practice of his profession.

The popular image of the country practitioner in post-Revolutionary Virginia was that of the lawyer riding circuit from one county courthouse to another with nothing more than Blackstone and the Virginia statutes in his saddlebag. While this picture could very well describe the travel habits of a great number of practitioners who could certainly not carry their libraries on horseback with them, the image also tended to suggest that most lawyers thought they did not ever really need much more than what they could carry in their saddlebags. Thomas Jefferson, never a fan of the conservative English legalist, worried in 1810 that the new generation of Virginia attorneys felt "that everything which is necessary is in [Blackstone], and what is not in him is not necessary." Jefferson's advice to aspiring attorneys sounded a much different theme, one that subtly emphasized the importance of access to a well-stocked library. "Coke's Institutes and Reports are their first," he wrote of his instructions to students, "and Blackstone their last book, after an intermediate course of two or three years."[3]

[3] Jefferson to John Tyler, Sr., May 26, 1810, in Lyon G. Tyler, *Letters and Times of the Tylers*, vol. 1, p. 248 (1884). On Jefferson's well-known attitude, see Julius S. Waterman, "Thomas Jefferson and Blackstone's Commentaries," in David H. Flaherty,

While the rising generation of attorneys may indeed have been more enamored of Blackstone's *Commentaries* than they should have been, in reality most recognized that the broader their access to legal tomes, the more successful they would likely be before both courts and juries. "Read like Jefferson," the eminent William Wirt once admonished an aspiring attorney, "and speak like Henry." In seven words Wirt had summed up what every young practitioner heard at every turn. Law students, whether reading in an attorney's office or studying in one of the law schools that came into being in the post-Revolutionary and antebellum years, recognized that they had to read widely and thoroughly, and they soon learned that such reading did not stop once one had a law license in hand. "If he will make himself a lawyer," the elder Benjamin Watkins Leigh intoned in the 1830s, any attorney "must be a student as long as he lives."[4]

The value of books, however, stretched even beyond the realm of learning principles and searching precedents. It extended to the most routine elements of everyday practice. Thomson Mason, a veteran of many years before the bar of the colonial General Court, refused to draw even the most routine document in 1779 without recourse to his books. A half-century later, Norfolk attorney Henry L. Brooke worried about the need for constant study of the law and confessed that "the simplest question [always] drives me to my books."[5]

So, attorneys in practice in Virginia after 1776 clearly saw themselves tied to print culture. The size and breadth of the holdings they were able to acquire over the years as they followed their profession became factors of availability, practical need, and success (with its concomitant resource of spendable income).

Like their counterparts in the colonial era, lawyers in post-Revolutionary and antebellum Virginia began to build their libraries with a number of standard categories of books. Reports headed the list, and as few Virginia cases were available in print until the third decade of the nineteenth century, many of those reports were

---

ed., *Essays in the History of Early American Law*, pp. 451-488 (1969).

[4] Wirt to Francis Walker Gilmer, July 23, 1815, in John P. Kennedy, *Memoir of the Life of William Wirt*, vol. 1, p. 342 (1851); Benjamin Watkins Leigh to Thomas R. Johnston, March 9, 1836, Private Papers Collection, Archives Division, Library of Virginia, Richmond (hereinafter LVA).

[5] Thomson Mason to John P. Custis, January 26, 1779, Custis family papers, VHS; Brooke to Robert M. T. Hunter, August 31, 1836, Hunter-Garnett papers, Manuscripts Department, University of Virginia Library, Charlottesville. On this point see particularly A. G. Roeber, " 'The Scrutiny of the Ill Natured Ignorant Vulgar': Lawyers and Print Culture in Virginia, 1716-1774," *Va. Mag. Hist. Biog.*, vol. 91, pp. 387-417 (1983).

of English cases or of judgments from jurists in other American states. Charles Lee, an Alexandria attorney and United States attorney general under George Washington, possessed thirty-eight separate reporters' titles (representing sixty-two volumes) when he died in 1815. Most of these books contained British case law. Both John Marshall and George Wythe gathered a substantial number of the same reports in their libraries as well.[6]

Lawyers also wanted volumes of statutes from the jurisdictions in which they practiced. Charles Lee owned several sets of Virginia laws, including one of the colonial codes, as well as sets of the laws of the United States, Massachusetts, and Pennsylvania, and some parliamentary enactments. Lee apparently found abridgments most helpful in his practice, for he held no less than sixteen such volumes, along with six volumes of Comyn's *Digest* and a copy of Tomlin's *Digest*.[7] The rest of Lee's extensive office library of 318 volumes consisted primarily of a diverse mix of legal treatises, including Wright's *Tenures*, Buller's *Nisi Prius*, and of course, *Coke on Littleton* and Blackstone's *Commentaries*.[8]

Attorneys' libraries grew as they advanced in their profession. As indicated below, Virginia's jurists were able to amass some of the largest and most sophisticated book collections in the Commonwealth, but in some other cases, legal scholars and bibliophiles generally contributed to the increased presence of a diverse range of law books in the Old Dominion.

Thomas Jefferson stands out as a prime example of such a collector. Jefferson, too, developed his library on a firm foundation of standard legal works. Unfortunately, the library that he gathered during the period of his legal training and first years of practice burned in a fire at his Albemarle County home, Shadwell, in 1770. He immediately set about rebuilding the collection, and even when he stopped the practice of law four years later and began to turn in other directions as a book collector, legal titles still made up a sizable portion of his library.[9]

---

[6] Inventory and appraisement of the personal estate of Charles Lee, November 2, 1815, Peyton family papers, VHS; James Albert Servies, "[List of] Books in the John Marshall House Library, Spring, 1963," manuscript copy at VHS; Louise Merriam, "Recreated Inventories of the Libraries of Peyton Randolph and George Wythe," manuscript copy at VHS.

[7] Inventory of the estate of Charles Lee, Peyton papers.

[8] *Id.*

[9] E. M. Sowerby, *Catalogue of the Library of Thomas Jefferson* (1952).

Jefferson's library holds importance on a number of counts. Not only was it compiled by a former superior court practitioner, who knew how to assess both the practical and the theoretical value of a legal volume, but it also proved to be an invaluable resource throughout Jefferson's local community. Some of the leading practitioners and jurists of the day consulted Jefferson and borrowed books from him.[10] Loaning books was not an uncommon practice at that time, nor was Jefferson's willingness, as he advised Governor John Tyler in 1810, to "lend my counsel and books to such young students as will fix themselves in the neighborhood."[11] So, although Jefferson continued to collect legal tomes from the perspective of scholarly inquiry and investigation, the contents of his library in some ways influenced the very practice of law in the Old Dominion.

Without question, Jefferson's collection of case reports and statutes rivaled any in the Commonwealth, but it was his compilation of legal treatises from England, Europe, and America that lifted his collection head and shoulders above any other that could be found at the time within the confines of the Old Dominion, if not the United States. In some cases, the only copy of a volume known to have been in early America shows up in the Jefferson library.[12] Certainly, his international travel and reputation aided his collecting, but the drive to acquire imbued the man himself.

In the 1790s Jefferson began to dispose of a small portion of his legal library, in part to raise funds to finance the purchase of other volumes. Thinking first to offer the volumes to the general public, Jefferson instead eventually sold the proffered volumes directly to his friend, Staunton attorney Archibald Stuart, later an appellate judge. Stuart took most of the volumes Jefferson made available, some thirty-nine in number, the bulk of which were English case reports. The group, however, also contained Hargrave's edition of Jefferson's esteemed *Coke on Littleton*, the English yearbooks, and Fitzherbert's *New Natura Brevium*.[13] All of these volumes would bolster Stuart's

[10] George Hay, United States District Attorney in Richmond for many years, regularly borrowed books from Jefferson. See Jefferson to Hay, February 26, 1815, and Hay to Jefferson, March 8, 1815, Thomas Jefferson papers, Library of Congress. See also Jefferson to Archibald Stuart, June 30, 1795, Archibald Stuart papers, VHS.

[11] Jefferson to John Tyler, Sr., May 26, 1810, in Tyler, *Letters and Times of the Tylers*, vol. 1, p. 248.

[12] H. A. Johnson, *Imported Eighteenth-Century Law Treatises in American Libraries, 1700-1799*, pp. xxx, xxxii (1978).

[13] Jefferson to Stuart, April 18, May 23, June 30, 1795, Archibald Stuart papers, VHS. P. L. Ford, ed., *Writings of Thomas Jefferson*, vol. 7, pp. 7-8 (1896) (letter of April 18, 1795).

growing collection and support a burgeoning practice that would eventually propel the Staunton attorney from the state legislature onto the Virginia bench.

If antebellum attorneys did not have the time or money to pursue the niceties of the law from a strictly scholarly vantage point, success at the bar of the Supreme Court of Appeals in Richmond provided them with the incentive and the capital, if not the leisure, to build significant personal law libraries. Gurdon H. Bacchus, one of those leading practitioners (although hardly a household name today) amassed just such a collection of 436 books by the time of his death in 1834.[14]

An orphaned Petersburg native who had spent most of his young life in New England, Bacchus returned to the Commonwealth to enter his profession in 1810. He rose in the legal ranks quickly, a sure sign of distinguished ability, to became one of the leading advocates at a bar that boasted the likes of John Wickham, Benjamin Watkins Leigh, and Chapman Johnson.[15]

The inventory of Bacchus's library taken in 1835 reveals some of the changes that were beginning to take place in the collecting of legal volumes in Virginia. Along with *Coke on Littleton*, Leitch's *Crown Law*, and Peere Williams's *Reports*, we find William Waller Hening's thirteen volumes of the *Virginia Statutes at Large*, William Munford's *Virginia Cases*, St. George Tucker's edition of Blackstone's *Commentaries*, and Hening's own *Virginia Justice* manual, illustrating the discernible growth in legal publishing in and for Virginia occurring at this time. In addition, Bacchus held copies of some titles that would begin to appear commonly both in law libraries and on law students' reading lists, such as *Starkie on Evidence*, Chitty's *Pleadings*, and Noy's *Maxims*.[16]

Bacchus's was the working lawyer's collection, focused on practical need. Case reports made up no less than 53 percent of his collection (230 volumes), but at the same time reliance on a personal compilation of large numbers of statute volumes had given way to an emphasis on works on specialized branches of practice, especially business law (such as *Parke on Insurance*, *Watson on Partnership*, *Ballentine on Limitations*, and *Marshall on Insurance*).[17]

---

[14] Inventory and appraisement of the estate of Gurdon H. Bacchus, February 11, 1835, Henrico County Will Book 9, pp. 134-146 (1834-1836).

[15] E. L. Shepard, "Sketches of the Old Richmond Bar: Gurdon H. Bacchus," *Richmond Quarterly*, vol. 13, pp. 43-48 (1990).

[16] Inventory of the estate of Gurdon H. Bacchus.

[17] *Id.*

In addition to his law volumes, Bacchus also collected dozens of other works, ranging from his thirty-two volumes of the *Edinburgh Review* and the four-volume *Memoirs of Jefferson* to the *Works of Josephus* and *Tristam Shandy*. Not all of these "miscellaneous books" listed in the inventory came into his library for Bacchus's personal reading pleasure. Like any good attorney, Bacchus knew that jurors in particular could sometimes be swayed by more than the dry precedents of the law books. One of his contemporaries, Judge Lucas P. Thompson, advised the students at his private law school in Staunton that a knowledge of human nature and human experience served an attorney well. "A part of your time may be pleasurably and profitably employed in reading history," he observed, "in which there is much it behooves the accomplished lawyer to know – or in metaphysics, or mental philosophy, or in studying those inimitable portraitures of the passions and the affections, the vices and the virtues, and the crimes, delineated by the great master and high priest of nature, the immortal Shakespeare."[18] Richmond attorney Herbert A. Claiborne went even farther to draw very specific practical applications from a familiarity with polite literature. He wished his law student son to be equipped to:

> draw on history or any of the sciences, poetry, romance or sacred writ for happy illustrations or to give force and point to [your] arguments. I can assure you that a well selected quotation from our best poets . . . and especially from holy writ will sometimes carry a jury as it were by storm when the most learned law argument would produce no other effect on them than to induce them in retirement to say "that may be the law but if it is it ought not to be."[19]

A good lawyer's library, then, might consist of a bit more than just the best law books around.

Another of Bacchus's contemporaries, Benjamin Watkins Leigh, probably the leading Virginia advocate of his generation and for a time a United States senator, listed for one of his correspondents in 1836 the volumes in his library that he thought most essential and valuable to the fundamental practice of law in the South. He noted that every lawyer needed a thorough familiarity with Blackstone's *Commentaries*, with Chitty's first volume on *Pleadings*, and with Buller's *Nisi Prius*. He, too, owned *Starkie on Evidence*, Maddock's *Chancery Practice*, and

---

[18] *Introductory Lecture Delivered by Judge Lucas Powell Thompson, Before his Law School in Staunton, December 3, 1839* (1839).

[19] Herbert A. Claiborne to Herbert A. Claiborne, Jr., October 21, 1838, Claiborne family papers, VHS.

Cowper's *Equity Pleadings.* Other recommended volumes included *Roberts on Frauds,* Sugden's *Law of Vendors, Roper on Legacies, Powell on Mortgages,* and *Marshall on Insurance.* Perhaps most interesting, however, was his suggestion that any lawyer should be thoroughly conversant with Justinian's *Institutes,* Brown's *Civil Law,* and Story's *Conflict of Laws.* Clearly, Leigh looked to national, even international, practice, perhaps characteristic of someone who headed the state superior court bar and likewise practiced before the United States Supreme Court.[20]

Lawyers often did more than simply offer advice to aspiring attorneys. Some loaned volumes to students, and they were especially generous if such learners were members of their own family. In fact, before the Civil War, many libraries were passed down from father to son or uncle to nephew, so that they remained unbroken over several generations or more. When no family member exhibited an interest in a deceased person's library, however, or when debts forced a liquidation of property, executors often found a ready market for book sales.

In 1841, following the sudden death of Philip P. Barbour, a United States supreme court justice from Orange County, his son-in-law, Circuit Court Judge Richard H. Field, inquired of a prominent Richmond attorney where he might best dispose of the justice's library. "Judge Barbour," Field explained:

> left a well selected law library consisting of from 600 to 800 books, which have been left in the neatest manner, and many of them not in the least manner defaced. He read a great deal and in many of his books are very valuable notes of reference in his hand writing. As the family has no further use for the library and as many of the books which are now in demand may be rendered of but little value at a future day by the publication of new and improved editions of the same works, we are all of the opinion that it would be best to sell the law books very soon.[21]

Unfortunately, another event had the effect of dispersing, and in some cases destroying, the libraries of some Virginia practitioners, and in some instances several members of a single family suffered the losses together. The coming of Civil War in 1861 took many attorneys out of the courtroom and on to the battlefield. When they returned

[20] Leigh to Thomas R. Johnston, March 9, 1836, W. H. Bryson, *Essays on Legal Education in Nineteenth-Century Virginia,* pp. 113-116 (1998).

[21] Field to Conway Robinson, April 6, 1841, Robinson family papers, VHS.

home, many found ruined plantations and destroyed homes. Others discovered that they had to sell possessions in order to keep their families alive.[22]

In Fauquier County, Robert Eden Scott had been practicing law since 1829, for a time as Commonwealth's Attorney, and for many years he had served in the Virginia General Assembly. When he was killed in 1862 by marauding Union deserters, colleagues at the Fauquier bar compiled an inventory of Scott's law books. Many of the volumes had been handed down in the Scott family for years. They included six volumes of Bacon's *Abridgment* (1740 edition), ninety-two volumes of *English Common Law Reports*, and the *Virginia Reports* through 15 Grattan. A number of works of Virginia authorship appeared, including John Tayloe Lomax's *Digest of the Laws of Real Property*, Conway Robinson's encyclopedic *Practice in the Courts of Law and Equity of Virginia*, and John A. G. Davis's *Treatise on Criminal Law*. Scott's library also contained among its 524 volumes Guy's *Medical Jurisprudence, Sanders on Uses and Trusts*, Chancellor James Kent's *Commentaries*, and loose issues of such national legal periodicals as *Law Library*, the *Jurist*, and the *American Law Register*.[23]

When Scott's two sons, Robert Taylor and John, returned from Confederate service at the end of the war, the trying economic conditions of the time forced them to consider selling off much of what comprised their law libraries, including many books inherited from their late father. Robert, who had joined his father's practice a few years before the war, planned to sacrifice some of the English, American, and Virginia reports, along with the legal periodicals. John, who in the fall of 1865 was preparing to enter the University of Virginia, had received most of his father's collection of legal treatises, along with about an equal share of case reports. John painfully prepared a "Catalogue of Law Books for Sale" in November, which contained nearly all of the volumes he had inherited from his father. His older brother stepped in, however, and when the two men sent off a parcel to booksellers J. W. Randolph and English of Richmond in May 1866, John's contribution had been significantly reduced. Robert noted

[22] On this period generally, see W. H. Bryson and E. L. Shepard, "The Virginia Bar, 1870-1900," in G. W. Gawalt, ed., *The New High Priests: Lawyers in Post-Civil War America*, pp. 171-186 (1984).

[23] Inventory of the Law Library of Robert E. Scott, February 20, 1863, Keith family papers, VHS. On Scott's life and career see H. E. Hayden, *Virginia Genealogies*, pp. 650-653 (1891); "Robert Eden Scott, A Biographical Sketch," *Fauquier Hist. Soc. Bull.*, pp. 78-92 (1921-24).

that "the miscellaneous lot, being in bulk my property" was sent to Richmond "for sale for cash."[24]

Much of what we currently know about private Virginia law libraries after the Civil War has been derived from surviving auction catalogs, published primarily by Richmond booksellers and auction houses in advance of estate sales. Some two dozen of these catalogs list volumes from some of the finest nineteenth-century collections, as well as from several unidentified collections, the latter clearly examples of the average working practitioner's holdings. Just such a collection was compiled by Thomas P. August of Richmond.

August, known affectionately as "Colonel Tom" for his service in the Mexican War and with the Confederate infantry, had been a popular Richmond practitioner before the war. Although his practice extended into the Virginia Supreme Court, August more regularly appeared before the local courts of Richmond and the surrounding counties. Known for the keenness of his mind and the effectiveness of his delivery before bench and jury, August was ever ready with a pithy story or a clever pun. His reading, judging from the list of his library, tended to be broad and inclusive, incorporating history, English literature, and the classics. But when the 368-page catalog of his library was issued in late 1869 following his death, it included only five pages of law books, and those mostly published after 1850.[25]

These law books consisted primarily of works on corporate and commercial law, criminal law, and equity. Along with Virginia and federal case reports, the collection also contained such standards as Kent's *Commentaries*, Henry St. George Tucker's *Commentaries*, and the more recently published multi-volume *Practice in the Courts of Justice of England and the United States* by Conway Robinson. Perhaps emphasizing his concentration on commercial law, August's library also included codes and reports from a number of other American jurisdictions, including Maryland, New York, and Pennsylvania.[26]

Most attorneys practicing in Virginia in the decades following the Civil War, especially in the rural counties, continued to be general practitioners. As John Sergeant Wise perceptively observed, a lawyer

---

[24] "Catalog of Law Books Belonging to Robert Taylor Scott for Sale," and "Catalog of Law Books Belonging to John Scott, Oct. 27th 1865," Keith family papers, VHS.

[25] *Catalogue Sale of the Law and Miscellaneous Library of the Late Colo. Thomas P. August* (1869); E. L. Shepard, "Sketches of the Old Richmond Bar: Thomas P. August," *Richmond Quarterly*, vol. 6, pp. 48-51 (Spring 1984).

[26] *Catalogue Sale of the . . . Library of the Late Colo. Thomas P. August.*

in that day "took whatever grist came to his mill."[27] Debt collection, estate settlements, and actions over land occupied most of his time in court, while drawing wills and deeds and other legal instruments kept him busy in the office. Lawyers were beginning to find that practice was changing, however, and more frequently they began to encounter situations that introduced them to increasingly complex legal realities particularly involving the world outside of their own local communities, and more importantly, outside of Virginia.[28]

One of the most important ways in which a rising practitioner might equip himself to traverse this changing legal landscape was by stocking his library with books appropriate to the evolving nature of practice. When auctioneers advertised the sale of the law library of John C. Tabb in March 1878, they noted that in this sale "Young practitioners will have a rare opportunity of furnishing their libraries at small cost." Tabb's collection contained 154 titles including Virginia reports, a few English reports, a small number of treatises, form books, dictionaries, digests, and practical handbooks, all of relatively recent publication date.[29]

In 1880, death robbed the Virginia bar of a number of eminent practitioners and judges, while simultaneously offering their colleagues a rare glimpse at the libraries they had amassed over many years. Certainly, the best known of these decedents was William Green, originally from Culpeper County but for many years one of the leading advocates in Richmond.

At the head of the Virginia Supreme Court bar of his day, William Green was acknowledged by contemporaries as a preeminent American lawyer-scholar. Before his death in 1880, he assumed the post of first law professor at what would become the University of Richmond. His collection of 1,439 titles, comprising some 10,000 volumes, reflected the depth and breadth of his legal learning, as well as his personal fascination with the intricacies of the law. He was, as Robert A. Brock of the Virginia Historical Society testified, "an insatiate devourer of books, and bibliography was a passion with him." John William Wallace, reporter of the United States Supreme Court, noted that Green "never seemed to care how much he paid for a book; and his library, I know, had volumes in it which I never heard of being in any library, public or private, elsewhere." In accumulating this collection over more than half a century, his contemporary Conway Robinson

[27] J. S. Wise, *The Lion's Skin*, p. 174 (1905).

[28] Bryson and Shepard, "The Virginia Bar, 1870-1900," pp. 171-186.

[29] *Catalogue of a Valuable Collection of Law, Medical, Scientific & Miscellaneous Books Belonging to . . . John C. Tabb, Esq.* (1878).

added, "There has, I suppose, been no citizen of Virginia owning at his death so large and valuable a library."[30]

Beginning with a 1499 English imprint, Green's library spanned almost four hundred years. Most notable among the many works of his collection was a group of laws and reports from twenty-two different states in the Union, along with an "exceptionally large" collection of British case reports. The auction catalog listed alphabetically sixty-one subject categories covered by treatises in the collection, from arbitration to water rights. The overall value of this collection was reputedly enhanced by the extensive critical and explanatory notes and annotations made on blank pages and in margins by Green. "Many of [the books]," added Brock, "are attractive, too, by reason of past associations, containing as they do, the memorials of distinguished ownership, successively, often, by members of the several Law `Courts' and `Inns' of London, and by those whose names are historic in this country – autographs, bookplates, and manuscript notes."[31]

If the libraries of other Virginia legal luminaries who died in 1880 were decidedly more modest than that of William Green, their contents are no less instructive. Auctioneers combined books belonging to the estate of railroad attorney Raleigh Travers Daniel with a few volumes derived from other sources to present a catalog of 249 entries that year, most of which were standard law texts common to the working lawyer's library.[32] Interestingly, the catalog of the library of George P. Scarburgh, a judge from Norfolk, listed only sixty-nine law books (suggesting it may have been raided by legatees before the sale), a large number of which were New York case reports. Virtually all of the works listed had been published in New York, Philadelphia, or Boston.[33] This circumstance may say more about the jurisdiction of Judge Scarburgh, who once sat on the United States Court of Claims, than it does about the Norfolk book trade.

---

[30] R. A. Brock, comp., *Catalogue of the Choice and Extensive Law and Miscellaneous Library of the Late Hon. William Green, LL. D.* (1880); G. E. Butler and W. H. Bryson, "William Green," *Legal Education in Va.*, pp. 265-268 (1982); DAB.

[31] Brock, comp., *Catalogue Sale of the . . . Library of the Late Hon. William Green.*

[32] *Catalogue Sale of the Law Libraries of the Hon. R. T. Daniel and of Hon. Robt. L. Montague, Together with Additions from Other Libraries* (1880).

[33] *Catalogue of Theological Books Belonging to the Estate of Rev. Dr. A. Wade, Dec'd; and the Law Library of the Late Judge Scarburgh of Norfolk, Virginia* (1880); W. H. Bryson, "George Parker Scarburgh," in Bryson, ed., *Legal Education in Va.*, pp. 557-559. For an impressive library of 589 titles of one of the postwar justices of the Virginia Supreme Court, see *Auction Sale of the Valuable Law Library of the late Judge Wm. T. Joynes* (1877). See also, *Catalogue Sale of the Valuable Law Library of Judge J. M. Gregory, of Charles City County, Va.* (1880).

When the library of Richmond attorney James Alfred Jones was offered for sale in 1894, the title of the catalog covering the sale emphasized the collection's overall importance. It included "state, U.S., and English reports, text-books and some very rare and valuable acts and codes." Actually, Jones's collection represented one of the smallest of Virginia's more significant private law libraries. The important feature of this library was that its contents covered the entire range of legal topics. Virginia materials predominated, but the collection also included a substantial number of national and international legal works.[34]

That same year, the libraries of Judge T. H. Bayly Browne of Accomack County, Edward Y. Cannon and W. W. Cosby, Jr., of Richmond, and Judge Richard Parker of Winchester, were sold together at auction. While the sale catalog did not differentiate among the libraries when listing the titles, the bibliography reveals a number of characteristics of Virginia law libraries as the nineteenth century came to a close. First, of the 455 titles listed, many are digests and legal treatises, not a few of which concerned railroad and insurance law. A fair number of issues of American legal periodicals also appear. So do some rare volumes that had once belonged to such notable Virginians as Lord Fairfax and Philip Ludwell Lee.[35]

In some ways, this last characteristic helps to explain the gradual change in private law collections that has taken place in the twentieth century. Where once the volumes owned by legal practitioners had been obtained by succeeding attorneys for their practical (as well as their associational) value, now collecting for the sake of collecting was becoming a more common practice among lawyers. The library of John Thompson Brown, offered for sale in New York in 1913, underscores this point. The auctioneers advertised it as a "valuable collection of old American law books, the property of John Thompson Brown, Esq., of Evington [near Lynchburg], Campbell County." Consisting of 396 titles, the library included not only antique legal treatises from a variety of authors, but also rare congressional journals, acts of the Virginia General Assembly from 1734 to 1867, journals of the Virginia House of Delegates and Senate from 1778 to 1855, and scarce Virginia law reports signed by George Wythe.[36]

---

[34] *Catalogue Sale of the Valuable Law Library Belonging to the Estate of the Late Hon. James Alfred Jones* (1894).

[35] *Catalogue Sale of the Valuable Law Libraries Belonging to the Estates of T. H. Bayly Browne, of Accomac Co. . . .* (1894).

[36] *Catalogue of a Valuable Collection of Old American Law Books, the Property of John Thompson Brown, Esq., of Evington, Campbell County, Virginia* (1913).

Lawyers now began to indulge their bibliographic interests without necessarily considering simultaneously the practical value of any volume they brought into their library. One need not be a scholar to appreciate fine bindings, rare imprints, or an early work on some specialized subject not even a part of one's own practice.

This freedom to acquire came about not only because of the increased availability of personal funds from which to make such acquisitions. It also developed from the circumstance that more and more attorneys were able to separate and maintain private libraries away from their workplaces. Attorneys no longer primarily worked out of an office attached to their home or located on the same plantation. Moreover, the phenomenon of partnerships, something that had begun to emerge by the 1840s and that blossomed after the Civil War, reshaped the focus, as well as changed the location, of many a lawyer's working library. Partners pooled their resources when it came to practical works incident to the needs of their everyday practices, including areas of specialization. Works not found there might be consulted in a public or academic law library. The nature of law practice was changing; so, too, was the character of private law collections throughout the Commonwealth.

BIBLIOGRAPHY OF PRIVATE LAW LIBRARIES

Administrator's Sale Catalogue of the . . . Library of the Late Hon. John B. Clopton. New York: C. C. Shelley, 1861. 162 p.

Auction Sale of the Valuable Law Library of the Late Judge Wm. T. Joynes. Richmond: Whittet & Shepperson, 1877. 8 p.

Brock, R[obert] A[lonzo], comp. *Catalogue of the Choice and Extensive Law and Miscellaneous Library of the Late Hon. William Green, LL. D.* Richmond: Jones, 1880. 210 p.

Catalogue of a Rare and Valuable Collection of Law, Historical and Miscellaneous Books, Being the Private Library of the Late John Wickham of this City, to be Sold at Public Auction on Tuesday, the 2d Day of May, 1854. [Richmond: n.p., 1854]. broadside.

CATALOGUE

OF THE

CHOICE AND EXTENSIVE

LAW AND MISCELLANEOUS LIBRARY

OF THE LATE

Hon. WILLIAM GREEN, LL. D.,

Comprising Nearly 10,000 Volumes in the Several Departments of Literature.

IN LAW, IT IS REMARKABLY FULL AND COMPREHENSIVE, Ranging from an English Imprint of 1499 to the latest publications, and including the various

TEXT-BOOKS AND ENGLISH AND AMERICAN REPORTS,

Many being Curious Specimens of Typography and Binding. Among the Miscellaneous Books are many that are desirable in the Departments of

Americana, History, Travels, Biography, Belle-Lettres, Political Economy, Philosophy, The Classics, Etc., Etc.

The Collection of Works relating to

VIRGINIA

Is more varied and valuable than has probably ever been offered before, and includes

THE SERIALS OF

Law Reports, Collected Statutes, History, Biography and Ephemeral Pamphlets.

The value of the books is largely enhanced by the Critical and Explanatory

MANUSCRIPT NOTES

Of their late eminently learned possessor. Many of them are attractive also by reason of past associations, containing as they do, Memorials of distinguished ownership in England and America,

AUTOGRAPHS, BOOK-PLATES, MANUSCRIPT NOTES, &c.

To be sold by Auction, January 18th, 1881, at RICHMOND, VA.

Copies of the Catalogue will be furnished on application. It was prepared under the supervision of MR. R. A. BROCK, Corresponding Secretary of the Virginia Historical Society, whom those desiring information as to the condition or special features of volumes may address.

Gentlemen who may be unable to attend the sale may have their orders filled by THE AUCTIONEER, or by either of the local Booksellers—J. W. RANDOLPH & ENGLISH, WEST, JOHNSTON & CO., WOODHOUSE & PARHAM, CARLTON McCARTHY.

JOHN E. LAUGHTON, Jr.,

AUCTIONEER OF LITERARY AND PERSONAL PROPERTY, Etc.,

No. 916 Main Street, Richmond, Va.

Catalogue of a Valuable Collection of Law, Medical, Scientific & Miscellaneous Books Belonging to . . . John C. Tabb, Esq. . . . to be Sold at Auction on Friday and Saturday, March 8th and 9th, 1878. Richmond: Henry Schott, 1878. 22 p.

Catalogue of a Valuable Collection of Old American Law Books, the Property of John Thompson Brown, Esq., of Evington, Campbell County, Virginia . . . To Be Sold at Auction . . . Dec. 2nd, 1913. New York, [1913]. 30p.

Catalogue of a Valuable Law and Miscellaneous Library to be Sold at Auction November 16th, 1874. [Richmond, 1874]. 38 p.

Catalogue of a Valuable Law and Miscellaneous Library . . . to be Sold at Auction March 30th, 1876. [Richmond, 1876]. 43 p.

Catalogue of Law, Theological, Medical and Miscellaneous Books, to be Sold at Auction on Monday, May 30th, 1881. Richmond, 1881.11 p.

Catalogue of Theological Books Belonging to the Estate of Rev. Dr. A. Wade, Dec'd; and the Law Library of the Late Judge Scarburgh, of Norfolk, Virginia, to be Sold at Auction Dec. 14, 1880. Richmond, 1880. 5 p.

Catalogue Sale of Law and Miscellaneous Books, Embracing Many Rare and Valuable Volumes on Law and Miscellaneous Subjects, to be Sold at Auction Thursday and Friday, February 23 and 24, 1888. Richmond, 1888. 19 p.

Catalogue Sale of the Law and Miscellaneous Library of the Hon. R. T. Daniel, Deceased, Together with Many Additions of Law Books From Other Parties . . . to be Sold at Auction July 14th. Richmond [1880?] 8 p.

Catalogue Sale of the Law and Miscellaneous Library of the Late Col. Thos. P. August, Attorney at Law. Richmond: Dispatch, 1869. 368 p.

Catalogue Sale of the Law and Miscellaneous Library of the Late Judge R. C. L. Moncure, to be Sold at Auction April 3d, 1883. Richmond, 1883. 17 p.

Catalogue Sale of the Law Libraries of the Hon. R. T. Daniel and of Hon. Robt. L. Montague, Together with Additions from Other Libraries . . . to be Sold at Auction Sept. 30th, 1880. Richmond, 1880. 8 p.

Catalogue Sale of the Library of the Late Rev. W. F. C. Gregory, Comprising Many Valuable Law, Religious, and Miscellaneous Volumes, to be Sold at Auction June 28th, 1887. Richmond, 1887. 15 p.

Catalogue Sale of the Rare, Curious and Valuable Miscellaneous Library, Collected by the Late Hon. James Alfred Jones, of Richmond, Va. Comprising Books . . . of Literature: American Early-Printed Books, Poetry &c; to be Sold at Auction . . . May 25 & 26, 1894. Richmond, 1894. 27 p.

Catalogue Sale of the Valuable Law Libraries Belonging to the Estates of H. R. Wattles, dec'd, of Alexandria, Va., and of Others. To be Sold at Auction May 29, 1891. Richmond, 1891. 16 p.

Catalogue Sale of the Valuable Law Libraries Belonging to the Estates of T. H. Bayly Browne, of Accomac Co.; Edward Y. Cannon and W. W. Cosby, Jr., of Richmond; and Judge Richard Parker, of Winchester . . . Comprising State and U. S. Reports, Text-Books and Some Very Rare and Valuable Acts and Codes; to be Sold at Auction . . . Mar. 5 and 6, 1894. [Richmond, 1894]. 15 p.

Catalogue Sale of the Valuable Law Libraries Belonging to the Estates of the Late John Murray Forbes and of Others, to be Sold at Auction Friday, Nov. 6, 1891. Richmond, 1891. 12 p.

Catalogue Sale of the Valuable Law Library Belonging to the Estate of the Late Hon. James Alfred Jones, Comprising State, U. S. and English Reports, Text-Books and Some Very Rare and Valuable Acts and Codes; to be Sold at Auction . . . May 24, 1894. Richmond, 1894. 12 p.

Catalogue Sale of the Valuable Law Library of Judge J. M. Gregory of Charles City County, Va. . . . To be Sold at Auction April 1st, 1880. Richmond, 1880. 10 p.

Catalogue Sale of the Valuable Law Library of the Late Charles L. Mosby, of Lynchburg, Va., Embracing U.S., English Law and Equity, and Chancery Reports . . . to be Sold at Auction, on Thursday, February 26th, 1880. [Richmond], 1880.

Catalogue Sale of the Valuable Law Library of the Late Judge Asa D. Dickinson and Others, and a Large Assortment of Miscellaneous Books Belonging to the Estate of Alex. McRae, dec'd, and Others. To be Sold at Auction on Tuesday, February 24th, 1885. Richmond, 1885. 10 p.

Catalogue Sale of the Valuable Law Library of the Late Judge E. H. Lane, of Louisa County, Va. . . . to be Sold at Auction on Wednesday, Jan. 14, 1880. [Richmond, 1880]. 8 p.

Catalogue Sale of the Valuable Miscellaneous Libraries Belonging to the Estates of the Late Judge Richard Parker of Winchester, Va. . . . Comprising Many Rare and Valuable Works and Confederate Miscellany, to be Sold at Auction . . . March 7 '94. Richmond, 1894. 12 p.

Catalogue Sale of Valuable Law and Miscellaneous Books Belonging to the Estate of C. C. McRae, Dec'd . . . to be sold at Auction Friday May 24th, 1889. [Richmond, 1889]. 12 p.

Catalogue Sale of Valuable Law and Miscellaneous Books Belonging to the Libraries of the Late Judge Wharton, the Receiver of J. F. T. Anderson and Others to be Sold at Auction April 5, 1898. [Richmond] 1898. 10 p.

Catalogue Sale of Valuable Law and Miscellaneous Books, Comprising the Library of the Late John Washington, Esq. of Caroline County, with Desirable Additions from other Libraries. To be Sold at Auction Tuesday December 20th, 1887. [Richmond] 1887. 15 p.

Catalogue Sale of Valuable Law & Miscellaneous Books, Contributions from Various Libraries, to be Sold at Auction Friday, June 6, 1888. Richmond, 1888. 13 p.

Catalogue Sale of Valuable Law Books, Including the Virginia and other State Reports, English Law and Equity, Chancery and Other Reports, a Large Number of Standard Textbooks and United States Reports, Together with Many Valuable Law Books Not Included in This Catalogue. To be Sold at Auction . . . Nov. 25th, 1881. Richmond, 1881. 8 p.

Coghlan, Jill Moria. "The Library of St. George Tucker." M.A. thesis, Coll. of William and Mary, 1973.

Sowerby, E[mily] Millicent. *Catalogue of the Library of Thomas Jefferson*. Washington, D.C.: Library of Congress, 1952, 5 vols.; rept. Charlottesville: Univ. Press of Virginia, 1983, 5 vols.

Law books: vol. 2, pp. 192-429.

Steiner, Bernard C[hristian]. "Law Libraries in Colonial Virginia." *Green Bag*, vol. 9, pp. 351-354 (1897).

"Subscribers in Virginia to Blackstone's Commentaries on the Laws of England, Philadelphia, 1771-1772." *Wm. & Mary Qtly.*, 2d ser., vol. 1, pp. 183-185 (1921).

LAW PUBLISHERS' CATALOGUES

Randolph's Law Catalogue 1856. Richmond: J. W. Randolph, 1856. 24p.

Catalogue of Law Books for Sale by George M. West, Exchange Bookstore. Richmond: Chas. H. Wynne, 1856. xii p.

Law Catalogue – No. 10 . . . Catalogue of Second-Hand Law Books. Richmond: J. W. Randolph & Co., [c. 1890]. 40 p.

Catalogue No. 14. Receiver's Sale of Law Stock of J. W. Randolph Company, New and Second-Hand. Richmond: n.p., 1897. 40 p.

A. Morris, Law Bookseller and Publisher, Richmond, Virginia, Would Invite the Attention of the Legal Profession . . . to the Following List of . . . Law Books, Published by Him. Richmond, n.d. 15 p.

PUBLIC PRINTERS

Brandon D. Quarles

PRINTING IN VIRGINIA and the office of Public Printer were born at the same moment, when William Parks established his press in Williamsburg in 1730. The Public Printer was a salaried official of the colony, his duties clearly defined. The Public Printer did more than simply disseminate official information. He also served as a liaison between the government and the public, a possible tool for the formation and direction of public opinion. In turn, the printer's position was improved by direct access to information, suitable interesting or important material to fill up his newspaper columns, enhanced prestige, and greatly increased income from government job printing.[1]

One of two official printing positions,[2] the office of Public Printer was open to competition, chosen after 1732 by the House of Burgesses, from among a number of petitioners. The use of the ballot in the appointment of such office was a comparatively late innovation, not appearing until 1766. The post of Public Printer was later filled by appointment of the Governor and Council and approved by legislative sanction. After 1797, the Public Printer was appointed by a joint vote by both houses of the General Assembly.[3] Between 1733 and 1833, never fewer than three and often as many as seven printers competed for the office when it fell vacant. The real openness of the competition is shown by the fact that Virginia had two women as public printers before 1820: Clementina Rind, who was elected and appointed by the House of Burgesses in 1774, and Deborah Pleasants, who was allowed to complete her husband's term of office in 1814.[4]

The duties of the Public Printer were clarified by the Council of State in March 1787, after printers John Dixon and John Hunter Holt suffered reverses while holding the post. The mandate required the printers: To publish the laws of each session of the legislature, without delay, upon the closing of the session, and without compensation other

[1] A. P. Hubbard, Jr., *Notes on the Book Trade in Richmond, Virginia, Together with a Preliminary Checklist of Richmond, Virginia, Imprints: 1780-1860*, fascicle I.

[2] There was also an official printer to the Senate, which office, from 1777 until 1871, was held by a printer other than the Public Printer. Also from 1820 to 1871, the official reporter of the Court of Appeals jobbed out the printing of the Virginia reports.

[3] S. Shepherd, *Statutes at Large of Virginia*, vol. 2, p. 118.

[4] Hubbard, *supra*.

than their annual salary; to publish the journals of the House of Delegates at each session, under the same terms; to publish in their newspaper, or in other newspapers as they might be directed, all notices of particular laws, orders, proclamations and advertisements from the Governor, the Supreme Courts, the Treasurer, Attorney-General, Auditor of Public Accounts, Solicitor, Justices of the Peace, and other public persons and bodies "acting in their public capacities"; to supply the executive branch of government (Governor, Treasurer, Auditor, Solicitor) and various state inspectors (particularly of tobacco) with blank forms.[5]

In return for being prepared to do all of this, the state offered a salary of £300 *per annum*, later raised to £650 ($2,000). This was a princely sum for work, and there were additional advantages and loopholes by which the printer could profit further. For example, the Advice of 1787 while specifying various forms and blanks for the Executive did not include in the list the office of adjutant general or the militia. These were considered "extra printing" and were paid for at the going rate, above the Public Printer's salary. Also, printing done for the executive branch in general, including circular letters, announcements and the like, were also paid for separately, even though the publication of the same notices in the newspapers were covered by the salary. Likewise, any separately printed acts of the legislature for Executive distribution were seen as "extra printing."[6]

Another area for profit lay in overprinting the quantities of *Acts of Assembly* and *Journals* of the House of Delegates demanded by the state. All copies printed above the required number could be sold by the printer. This was a common eighteenth century practice where the printer was usually also a publisher and bookseller.[7]

In 1804, the General Assembly passed an act which slightly altered the position and duties of the Public Printer and also raised the salary of the office. The act specified that the Public Printer was to publish, within forty days after the rising of the General Assembly in each session, 3,200 copies of the laws of such session. As the quantity demanded would greatly affect the cost, the salary of the Public Printer was raised to $2,500 a year. Another change in the act of 1804 was that the printer was to post a bond of $5,000 as a guarantee of the regular discharge of his duty and that all conditions of his work would be carried on in a satisfactory manner until another Public Printer could

[5] *Journal of the Council of State of Virginia*, vol. 4, p. 63 (1786-1788).

[6] Hubbard, *supra*; Va. Code, chap. 20, pp. 114-116 (1849).

[7] See, for example, R. G. Silver, "Government Printing in Massachusetts Bay, 1700-1750," in *Proceedings of the Am. Antiquarian Soc.*, vol. 68, p. 1 (1958).

ACTS

OF THE

GENERAL ASSEMBLY

OF THE

STATE OF VIRGINIA,

PASSED AT CALLED SESSION, 1862,

IN THE

EIGHTY-SEVENTH YEAR OF THE COMMONWEALTH.

RICHMOND:

WILLIAM F. RITCHIE, PUBLIC PRINTER.

1862.

be appointed or elected.[8] In 1814, the General Assembly raised the annual salary to $2,600, where it remained for another twenty years. The Public Printer's salary was $1,000 to be paid in four quarterly installments of $250 each, to cover actual costs; the balance was paid after printing of the acts of each session was completed.[9] The Public Printer's salary climbed all the way to $4,800 by 1852.[10]

The Public Printer's salary was abolished in 1858, and he was to be paid at the following rates:

> Forty-six and a half cents per thousand ems for plain work, forty-six and a half cents per token for press work, and sixty-nine and three fourths cents, being a price and a half, for rule or figure work, and ninety three cents per thousand ems for rule and figure work; and all blanks, circulars, handbills, advertisements, and other kinds of printing, except book and pamphlet work, shall be paid for at the customary rates of printing for private individuals or concerns. All of which prices are not to include paper, but the public printer is to furnish the paper at the expense of the state, charging ten percent above cost for waste and trouble in procuring the same; and for book binding, the Public Printer is to be paid the usual price or rates established among other book binders in the City of Richmond.[11]

The position of Superintendent of Public Printing was created in 1866. This officer was to be elected every two years by the joint vote of the two houses of the General Assembly.[12] He had to reside in the City of Richmond and was charged with contracting and superintending all the printing and binding authorized by law to be done for the state or any of its officers. His annual salary was $1,000, to be paid monthly.[13] He was required to post a bond of $5,000 for the faithful discharge of the duties of his office.[14]

Among the Superintendent of Public Printing's duties were the following: To cause to be printed, in octavo form, two hundred and forty copies of the Journal of the House of Delegates, as it is furnished by the

[8] S. Shepherd, *Statutes at Large of Virginia*, vol. 3, pp. 129-130.

[9] 1813-14 Va. Acts, p. 66; Va. Rev. Code, vol. 2, pp. 226-228 (1819).

[10] 1852 Va. Acts, chap. 23, p. 24.

[11] 1857-58 Va. Acts, chap. 25, p. 38.

[12] 1865-66 Va. Acts, chap. 30, p. 147.

[13] 1865-66 Va. Acts, chap. 30, p. 150.

[14] 1865-66 Va. Acts, chap. 30, p. 147.

clerk; At the end of each session of the assembly, to cause to be printed two hundred and forty copies of the index prepared by the clerk of the House of Delegates to the said Journal and the Documents printed during the session; To cause to be printed, as soon as practicable after the close of each session, one hundred and fifty copies of the general acts and deliver the same to the secretary of the commonwealth; Within forty days after the termination of the session, to cause to be printed and bound four thousand copies of the acts and resolutions passed during such session, with the tables and index, all of which copies shall be delivered to the said secretary; To cause to be printed, in octavo form, on good paper, and have bound in boards, two hundred and forty copies of such reports as the governor may deliver to him to be printed; To cause to be printed two hundred and forty copies of each public document, which may be directed to be printed by the general assembly, or the house of delegates, or the senate, other than bills, and so many copies of any bill which the senate or the house may order to be printed, as it may direct; To have printed without delay all annual reports of companies, boards or institutions as soon as they are received.[15]

The Superintendent of Public Printing was to let or job out to the lowest bidder all the printing and binding required by the state or its officers, by the Senate or House of Delegates, and authorized by law to be done, and he was to supervise the execution of the same. He was permitted to let out the printing and binding to different persons, and at such times and in such lots or portions as he deemed proper. In every case, he had to require the party undertaking to do the work, or any part of it, to enter into a written contract, stating distinctly the terms of the same and embracing the price to be paid for composition, presswork, folding, stitching, binding, and all other items, in detail, and always providing in such contract for printing, that the printing is all to be executed in a close and compact form, without any unnecessary title pages or useless blank pages. The Superintendent of Public Printing also was to take from the person or persons making any such contract a bond with security, to be approved by the Secretary of the Commonwealth, in the penalty of at least double the amount contracted to be paid for the work.[16]

The Superintendent of Public Printing was to "purchase all the paper needed for the printing let out by him and to furnish the same to the printer as it may be needed; the accounts for the purchase of which (certified by him to be correct), was to be presented by him to the

[15] 1865-66 Va. Acts, chap. 30, pp. 147-49.

[16] 1865-66 Va. Acts, chap. 30, p. 148.

governor, who shall certify the same to the auditor of public accounts; and the auditor shall grant a warrant therefor on the treasury." The Superintendent was not to be interested, in any manner, "directly or indirectly, in any contract for the purchase of paper, or for the printing or binding to be let out by him, [or] to participate in the profits arising from the same." If found to be involved in any of these activities, he was deemed to be guilty of a misdemeanor and, if convicted for such offense, "shall be fined not less than five hundred nor more than one thousand dollars, and shall be confined in jail not less than six nor more than twelve months."[17] By forbidding the Superintendent of Public Printing from doing through his own print shop the public printing, the holder of this office was transformed from a printer who was the holder of a very lucrative printing job into a public administrator.[18]

In 1871, the Superintendent of Public Printing was charged with contracting "for the printing and binding of one thousand copies of the reports, by the reporter of the Court of Appeals, of the decisions of that court, in a style not inferior to the reports published" to that date. He was also to "secure the copyright of the said reports for the benefit of the Commonwealth and [to] deliver the volumes, when completed, to the Secretary of the Commonwealth."[19]

The Superintendent of Public Printing's annual salary was raised to $1,500 in 1873. He was also authorized to employ a porter at a salary not exceeding $30 per month. A joint standing committee of the General Assembly was charged with making investigations into the transactions of the Superintendent of Public Printing. This committee was composed of two members appointed by the Senate and three members appointed by the House. The committee had the authority to supervise and give directions in all that related to the public printing and, at their option, could make a report to the General Assembly of any matter deemed pertinent by them.[20]

The Superintendent of Public Printing's term of office was extended to four years in 1903,[21] and his annual salary was increased

---

[17] 1865-66 Va. Acts, chap. 30, pp. 149-50; Va. Code, §§ 270-287 (1887); Va. Code, §§ 379-401 (1919).

[18] Thus, for example, the Superintendent of Public Printing, R. F. Walker, contracted with James E. Goode for the printing of the Virginia Code of 1873 and with the two firms of Randolph & English and of Simons & Keiningham for its binding. See also 1872-73 Va. Acts, chap. 228, p. 205.

[19] 1870-71 Va. Acts, chap. 238, p. 338.

[20] 1872-73 Va. Acts, chap. 95, pp. 71-76.

[21] 1902-1904 Va. Acts, chap. 226, p. 326.

to $2,800 in 1919.[22] The office of Superintendent of Public Printing was abolished in 1928, when a new Division of Purchase and Printing was created. This move was part of the simplification and reform of the state government, which was initiated by Governor Harry F. Byrd.[23] The director of the new division was appointed by the Governor and ratified by the General Assembly.[24]

PUBLIC PRINTERS

William Parks (1730-1750)

William Parks was born in Shropshire, England, in the late seventeenth century. After six years of printing activity in his native Shropshire, he arrived in Annapolis, Maryland, in March 1726. He was commissioned as Public Printer to the province of Maryland in October 1727 and served in that capacity until 1737. He also started the *Maryland Gazette* (the first newspaper south of Pennsylvania) in 1727. He established a printing press in Williamsburg in 1730 and was, by the appointment of the governments of Maryland and Virginia, printer to both colonies. For this work, he received £200 currency, *per annum*, from both colonies. About the year 1733, he left Annapolis and made Williamsburg the place of his permanent abode. His appointment as printer to the government was continued, and his salary enlarged. In 1736, Parks began the *Virginia Gazette*. For many years, his press was the only one in Virginia.[25] Parks decided to go to England on business in the spring of 1750 and came down with a pleurisy that caused his death in the course of his voyage on the ship *Nelson* on April 1 of that year. Before he died, he undertook to print the collected laws of the colony as revised by the Assembly in 1746 and 1748. He provided in his will of March 30 (two days before his death) that his wife Eleanor and his son-in-law John Shelton should "complete printing the Laws of Virginia which I have undertaken." Two years later appeared this revisal of the Virginia laws, printed at Williamsburg and bearing the name of William Hunter, Parks's journeyman and successor as printer. The colony paid the estate £850 for the job, and after completion of the

[22] Code of Va. § 3438 (1919).

[23] V. Dabney, *Virginia: The New Dominion*, p. 482 (1971).

[24] 1927 Va. Acts, chap. 33, § 11, pp. 111-112.

[25] P. A. Carlson, "William Parks, Colonial Printer, to Dr. Charles Carroll." *Va. Mag. Hist. Biog.*, vol. 86, no. 4, pp. 408-12 (1978).

job, Hunter purchased his former master's equipment.[26]

As Public Printer, Parks printed fourteen volumes of the *Acts of Assembly*, ten volumes of the *Journal of the House of Burgesses*, and the Virginia Code of 1733; this was a major part of his printing output. Parks also printed George Webb, *Justice of Peace* (1736) and John Mercer, *Abridgment of the All the Public Acts of Assembly of Virginia* (1737, 1739).[27]

William Hunter (1751-1761)

William Hunter was born at Yorktown, Virginia, and served his apprenticeship with William Parks, whom he succeeded in 1751. He printed for the House of Burgesses and published a newspaper. The *Gazette* had been suspended for a few months after the death of Parks, but Hunter issued his first number on January 3, 1751. On August 15, 1751, Hunter purchased Parks's printing office. He was a great friend of Benjamin Franklin, and in 1753 he was appointed with him deputy postmaster general, which office he held during his life. Like his predecessor, Hunter printed the laws of Virginia and kept a bookstore. He died in August 1761 and left an infant son. Hunter's will was proved at Yorktown on August 17, 1761, and he bequeathed Joseph Royle £1,000 currency, on the condition that he would continue the business for the joint interest of himself and his infant son, whose name was William.[28]

Hunter printed nineteen volumes each of the *Acts of Assembly* and the *Journals of the House of Burgesses*, and he was responsible for the printing of the Code of 1752, a book of 455 pages.[29]

Joseph Royle (1761-1766)

Joseph Royle succeeded Hunter in 1761. He was bred to printing in England, married one of Hunter's sisters, Rosanna, and was for several years a foreman in Hunter's printing house. He printed for the government and continued the *Gazette*, but died in a few years.[30] He

---

[26] L. C. Wroth, *William Parks: Printer and Journalist of England and Colonial America.* (1926).

[27] S. S. Berg, *Eighteenth-Century Williamsburg Imprints*, pp. 3-48 (1986).

[28] "Old Virginia Editors," *Wm. & Mary Qtly.*, 1st ser., vol. 7, p. 12 (1898).

[29] Berg, *supra*, pp. 49-91.

[30] I. Thomas, *The History of Printing in America: With a Biography of Printers and an Account of Newspapers*, p. 555 (1970).

printed eight volumes of the *Acts of Assembly* and the *Journal of the House of Burgesses*.[31]

William Rind (1766-1773)

William Rind was born in Annapolis, Maryland, in 1733, and was raised there as apprentice to the Public Printer, Jonas Green. To protest the Stamp Act the partners suspended publication of the *Maryland Gazette* in October 1765, and shortly thereafter Rind accepted the invitation of a group of Virginia liberals to publish a "free paper" in Williamsburg. The first issue of Rind's *Virginia Gazette* appeared May 16, 1766, under the motto: "Open to all parties, but influenced by none." The press, the paper, and the printer quickly established a good reputation. The fall General Assembly chose Rind as Public Printer, and in spite of rising costs of paper and other supplies, the business prospered. Rind died August 19, 1773, and his paper was carried on for two years by his widow, Clementina Rind.[32]

He printed six volumes of the *Acts of Assembly* and eight volumes of the *Journal of the House of Burgesses*. In addition, he, in partnership with Alexander Purdie and John Dixon, printed the Virginia Code of 1769.[33]

Clementina Rind (1774)

Clementina Rind was born in Maryland around 1740 and was Virginia's first female printer and newspaper editor. As editor of the *Virginia Gazette*, she was careful to preserve the integrity of the motto and in other respects followed the program set up by her husband. Her choice of subject reveals special interest in new developments and experiments in science, plans for improving educational opportunities, and designs for philanthropic programs. Apparently women were valued readers of her paper, for it carried an unusual number of poetic tributes to ladies in acrostic or rebus form, literary conceits, and news reports with a feminine slant. In many issues of her gazette, contributors expressed healthy respect for her standards and literary judgment. Her bid for public favor was so well received that she expanded her printing program and in April 1774, after six months as editor, announced the purchase of "an elegant set of types from

[31] Berg, *supra*, pp. 91-104.

[32] E. T. James, *Notable American Women: 1607-1950: A Biographical Dictionary*, p. 161 (1971).

[33] Berg, *supra*, pp. 105-125.

London." A month later the House of Burgesses appointed her Public Printer in her own right, and they continued to give her press all the public business in spite of competing petitions from Purdie and Dixon, publishers of a rival *Virginia Gazette*. At the end of August she was in ill health and finding it difficult to collect payments due her. She died in Williamsburg on September 25, 1774, and was probably buried beside her husband at Bruton Parish Church.[34] Since her children were minors, John Pinckney, an apprentice or Rind's partner, managed the press for them.[35]

Alexander Purdie (1775-1778)

Alexander Purdie was born in Scotland. He continued the business at Williamsburg after the death of Royle, for the benefit of the widow of Royle, young Hunter, and himself. The widow Royle soon remarried, taking John Dixon as her second husband. Though Dixon was not a printer, Purdie took him into partnership within a year after Royle's death. The firm of Purdie & Dixon continued until 1774, when Purdie withdrew to establish a *Virginia Gazette* of his own, which appeared in February 1775.[36] There were three different Virginia Gazettes printed at Williamsburg in 1775, and Purdie ran one with the motto, "Always for liberty and the public good." This *Gazette* appeared every Friday. He issued the first number on February 7, 1775, and was soon after made Public Printer to the colony.[37] Purdie served as Public Printer to Virginia from 1775 to 1778, working under the most trying of war conditions. He was paid a salary of six hundred pounds yearly in return for printing the laws and legislative journals.[38] Purdie died at Williamsburg in 1779 of dropsy. His *Virginia Gazette* was continued by his nephew, John Clarkson, and by Purdie's journeyman printer, Augustine Davis.[39]

---

[34] James, *supra*, pp. 161-62; L. M. Hudak, *Early American Women Printers and Publishers 1639-1820*, pp. 300-317 (1978); M. D. Barlow, *Notes on Women Printers in Colonial America and the United States 1639-1975*, p. 72 (1976).

[35] John Pinckney published the *Gazette* that was the successor to Rind's publication. He continued the *Gazette* in 1775 and did other printing after the war began. He died shortly thereafter in North Carolina on September 5, 1777. "Old Virginia Editors," *Wm. & Mary Qtly.*, 1st ser., vol. 7, p. 16 (1898).

[36] D. C. McMurtrie, *The First Printing in Virginia*, p. 10 (1935).

[37] "Old Virginia Editors," *Wm. & Mary Qtly.*, 1st ser., vol. 7, p. 15 (1898).

[38] See generally, "Documents Relating to Alexander Purdie, Public Printer," E. G. Swem, *A Bibliography of Virginia*, part 2, pp. 1063-65 (1917).

[39] McMurtrie, *supra*, p. 10.

Purdie printed the last *Journal of the House of Burgesses* in 1775 and the *Journal of the House of Delegates* from 1776 to 1778. He printed the proceedings and ordinances of the Virginia Conventions of 1775 and 1776 and the Virginia Constitution of 1776. He also was the printer for the *Acts of Assembly* of 1776, 1777, and 1778 and the first *Journal of the Senate* in 1776.[40]

John Clarkson and Augustine Davis (1779-1780)

John Clarkson and Augustine Davis also succeeded Purdie as Public Printer to the state, printing the *Journals of the House of Delegates* in the late summer of 1779 and during the winter of 1779-80, after which the seat of government was moved from Williamsburg to Richmond and the public printing was given to John Dixon and Thomas Nicolson, who had succeeded in setting up a press in Richmond before their rivals could do so.[41] Clarkson and Davis had intended to move to Richmond, but the tremendous shortage of housing and suitable buildings in the new capital made it difficult to locate their printing office there. They dallied in Williamsburg, and in May 1780, petitioned the legislature to continue them as Public Printers, with an increase in salary, promising to follow the General Assembly to Richmond as soon as possible.[42]

John Dixon and Thomas Nicolson (1780-1781)

John Dixon and Thomas Nicolson served as Public Printers from 1780 to 1781. Dixon, after Purdie had left the original *Virginia Gazette*, formed a partnership with the younger William Hunter, and the two continued their paper until the end of 1778, when Hunter joined the British forces with whom he later left the country. Dixon then joined forces with Nicolson, reviving the older *Virginia Gazette* in 1779 and removing it in 1780 to Richmond, where they were the first printers. Just a year after setting up their press in the new capital, where they began to print in May 1780, Dixon and Nicolson discontinued their *Virginia Gazette*, having lost the public printing contract. Shortly after Dixon and Nicolson arrived in Richmond, the General Assembly decided their equipment was inadequate for the demands made upon

---

[40] Berg, *supra*, pp. 138-155.

[41] *Id.*

[42] Hubbard, *supra*, fascicle VI; Swem, *supra*, pp. 1069-70.

it by public printing.[43]

Thomas Nicolson, the fourth son of Robert Nicolson, was born around 1758. He was the first printer to establish his press in Richmond, coming to the new state capital from Williamsburg in the spring of 1780. During the first six years of his career, he worked in partnership: from 1779 with John Dixon, Sr., in Williamsburg; then, he worked with William Prentis in Richmond. From the latter half of 1785 until his death late in 1808, he was the sole proprietor of his own printing office, from which he issued a weekly newspaper, did contract and book printing and functioned as a general job printer. Nicolson's press was in continuous operation in Richmond for more than twenty-eight years. From 1783 to 1803 he also acted as printer to the Senate of Virginia.

Nicolson was apprenticed a printer, perhaps in the office of John Dixon, Sr., his father's political associate. In 1779, Nicolson bought into a partnership in the printing office of Dixon, Sr. in Williamsburg. Nicolson moved to Richmond in April 1780 to establish a printing office there, but the firm of Nicolson and Dixon dissolved in December 1781, while Dixon was still in Williamsburg. Dixon came to Richmond with a new partner (John Hunter Holt of Norfolk) in 1783. On January 1, 1782, Nicolson entered into a partnership for printing with William Prentis, and they presented Richmond with a new newspaper, the *Virginia Gazette or Weekly Advertiser*. On January 6, 1785, their office was badly damaged by fire, and the partnership dissolved by May 14 of the same year. Nicolson remained as the sole proprietor of the *Virginia Gazette and Weekly Advertiser*, which he continued to print until April 1797.

Nicolson was an active Freemason and a member of St. John's Church in Richmond, serving as a vestryman from 1789 to 1795. He died November 10, 1808.[44]

John Dunlap and James Hayes (1781-1785)

After the Assembly decided Dixon and Nicolson's equipment was inadequate for public printing, it authorized Thomas Jefferson, the governor, "to engage with and employ, at the public expense, and for the public service, a good and able printer, of firm and known attachment to the independence of the United States, who may be willing to bring a good and well provided press into this commonwealth." John Dunlap and James Hayes, Jr., printers of

[43] McMurtrie, *supra*, pp. 10-11.

[44] Hubbard, *supra*, fascicle II; *Richmond Enquirer*, Nov. 18, 1808.

Philadelphia and Baltimore, accepted Jefferson's invitation, but the equipment was seized by the British on the way from Maryland to Virginia in October 1780. Clarkson and Davis had still made no move to Richmond, and the legislature, desperately needing a press, considered commandeering their printing equipment. It began an inquiry as to whether the printing press at Williamsburg (which had belonged to the Public Printer, Alexander Purdie) was public property; and if so, that the governor direct the removal of it to the Town of Richmond that Dunlap and Hayes may be availed of its use. It became clear that the press in question was private property, however, and so it was saved to Davis, Hayes having to procure another press at state expense. This press was brought by land rather than by sea. Three wagons were hired to bring the press and types to Richmond, a costly method of sending such bulky freight. The Dunlap and Hayes press was not, however, first established at Richmond, as the General Assembly had been forced by the British invasion to leave that city. Rather, it was set up at Charlottesville, in the central part of the state. The location at Charlottesville was only temporary. No newspaper was established there, and only the official documents of the May 1781 session of the General Assembly were printed there. In the fall of 1781, Hayes and Dunlap moved their press to Richmond. Hayes and Dunlap did the public printing at Richmond from 1781 through 1785.[45]

James Hayes was an Englishman who was born around 1759 and who came to this country in early manhood settling in Richmond, soon after the seat of government of the Commonwealth had been transferred to and established in that city. His first appearance in records as in Richmond was in January 1781 when he is referred to as preparing to engage in the work of printing official publications of the Commonwealth of Virginia. He appears to have immediately established himself in the printing business upon settling in Richmond, contracting for public printing and publishing a weekly newspaper (of which he appears to have been the owner), the *Virginia Gazette or American Advertiser*, the first issue of which appeared December 22, 1781. The paper continued under his management until 1786. Hayes died in Richmond on October 6, 1804.[46]

---

[45] D. C. McMurtrie, *The Beginnings of Printing in Virginia*, pp. 29-32 (1935); see generally, "Documents Relating to Hays & Dunlap, Printer," E. G. Swem, *supra*, pp. 1065-67 (1917).

[46] "Genealogy: Hayes Family," *Va. Mag. Hist. Biog.*, vol. 49, pp. 282-84 (1941).

John Dixon and John Holt (1786-1787)

John Hunter Holt published a newspaper in Norfolk, but when his press fell into the hands of the British, he moved to Richmond and founded the Richmond *Virginia Gazette and Independent Chronicle* in partnership with John Dixon. Holt died June 8, 1787.

Augustine Davis and Thomas Nicolson (1787-1788)

For the period 1787 to 1788, Davis and Nicolson were occasionally also associated with John Dixon in the printing of public papers.

John Dixon (1788-1791)

Dixon, after assisting Nicolson in establishing the first press in Richmond and then separating from him in August 1783, founded the Richmond *Virginia Gazette and Independent Chronicle* in partnership with John Hunter Holt. After Holt's death in 1787, Dixon continued the paper alone until his own death around April 27, 1791. This was succeeded by the *Virginia Gazette, and Public Advertiser*, which was published from 1791 to 1793 by John Dixon, Jr.[47]

John Dixon, Jr. (1791)

John Dixon, Jr., acted as the Public Printer from April 27, 1791, to May 14, 1791, the date of the appointment of Augustine Davis. Dixon, Jr., died May 22, 1805.[48]

Augustine Davis (1791-1797)

Davis was born in Yorktown around 1755. He was the first editor of a Richmond newspaper. His first Richmond newspaper began life in late July 1786, with the title *The Virginia Independent Chronicle. The Virginia Gazette, and General Advertiser*, the final name of the paper, continued until December 1809, when Davis sold control to a group of investors.[49] After relinquishing control of the *Gazette*, Davis undertook a second newspaper, called the *Virginia Patriot*, which began pub-

---

[47] D. C. McMurtrie, *The Beginnings of Printing in Virginia*, p. 32 (1935); "Documents Relating to John Dixon, Sr.," Swem, *supra*, pp. 1071-72.

[48] Swem, *supra*, p. 1072; *Richmond Enquirer*, May 24, 1805, p. 3.

[49] C. Brigham, *History and Biography of American Newspapers, 1690-1820*, vol. 2, pp. 1146, 1151-52 (1947).

lication that same month. This was a more ambitious paper than the weekly *Gazette* in that it appeared twice a week until 1816, and daily thereafter. In April 1821, he ceded the *Patriot* to William Ramsay and apparently retired from the printing business.[50]

Politically, Davis was a Federalist, and political patronage was part of his official life. Under governors Henry Lee and Robert Brooke he prospered. In 1791, he was appointed the Public Printer of Virginia. One of his major printing efforts was the long delayed revision of the laws of Virginia, the Virginia Code of 1792. Not only did the revisors take more time than was foreseen, but the General Assembly took a close look at it before passing it.[51] Then the paper that Davis had ordered from England never arrived and he had to look elsewhere for it, and then his workers got sick.[52]

In 1794 he was acting as postmaster of Richmond, a patronage office in which he was confirmed under the administration of John Adams. Davis also took a small but active role in city and state affairs; for example, in 1791 he was one of a group of Richmond merchants petitioning to have a branch of the Bank of the United States established in Richmond. The merchant and political alliances in Richmond in the 1790s was effectively destroyed by the detested Alien and Sedition laws, and in 1798 the Jeffersonians came to power. The state contracts for printing went to men who supported Thomas Jefferson: Meriwether Jones and Samuel Pleasants, Jr.

Augustine Davis died in Richmond, in retirement, at the end of October 1825. He was buried in the cemetery on Shockoe Hill, final resting place of another, greater, Federalist, John Marshall.[53]

Meriwether Jones and John Dixon, Jr. (1798)

Meriwether Jones was born in 1770, probably in Northumberland County, where his father served as County Clerk until 1781. He married Lucy Franklin Read in February 1789. The focus of Jones's life was political activity. At the forefront was his newspaper, the *Examiner*. His press was established in opposition to the Federalists, and to their printers: Augustine Davis, William A. Rind, and Henry Pace. "A friend of Jefferson and an ardent defender of Republicanism,

[50] L. J. Cappon, *Virginia Newspapers, 1820-1835*, p. 178 (1936); *Wm. & Mary Qtly.*, 1st ser., vol. 5, p. 272 (1897); Virginia Historical Society, Mss2B9407a1 (1794).

[51] C. T. Cullen, "Completing the Revisal of the Laws in Post-Revolutionary Virginia," *Va. Mag. Hist. Biog.*, vol. 82, pp. 84-99 (1974).

[52] See "Petitions of Augustine Davis," Swem, *supra*, pp. 1070-71.

[53] Hubbard, *supra*, fascicle VI.

Jones cut a wide swath through Virginia's political consciousness from 1798 until 1803. He was one of the most combustible elements in the incendiary factional politics of the day." Even as the Printer to the Commonwealth, with that office's salary and emoluments, Jones had to face two financial drawbacks. First, his newspaper printing took up most of his time, his printing for the state consumed his working capital, and he did very little outside book and job printing. Sixty of his sixty-four located separate imprints are directly connected to the political climate or public printing. Second, he was not a printer, and he had to rely on associates for the practical work of the press, causing further pressure on his financial capacity. In the end, despite "patronage," he could not make enough money to survive, and he resigned the position of Public Printer in March of 1804.[54]

Jones was elected to the House of Delegates from Hanover County by the Jeffersonians in September 1792. Here he was appointed to three very powerful committees: Propositions and Grievances, Claims, and Courts of Justice. On December 1, 1796, General James Wood was elected governor, and Jones was chosen to fill the vacancy thus created on the Council of State.[55] He served on the Council of State until December 6, 1798, when, upon his election as Printer to the Commonwealth, the state's rigid conflict of interest laws forced him to decide his political future.[56]

In November of 1798, Jones had entered into partnership with a practical printer of Richmond, John Dixon, Jr. Besides extensive book and job printing, Dixon had published several newspapers in Richmond after 1791. The *Virginia Gazette, and Public Advertiser* was succeeded by the *Virginia Gazette & Richmond Chronicle*, published by Dixon from 1793 to 1795. He also published the *Richmond Chronicle* in 1795 and 1796, the Richmond *Observatory* in 1797 and 1798, and the Richmond *Examiner* in 1798 and 1799. The last issue of Dixon's *Observatory* appeared on November 26, 1798. On December 3, it was transformed into the *Examiner*, published by the firm of Jones & Dixon.[57] Three days later, the firm was elected Printers to the Commonwealth, and Jones resigned from the Council of State. The first contract for state printing made it clear that while Jones and Dixon were Printers to the Commonwealth, Meriwether Jones was Public

[54] Hubbard, *supra*, fascicle VII.

[55] *Calendar of Virginia State Papers*, vol. 8, p. 401; see also, *Virginia Gazette, & General Advertiser*, December 7, 1796.

[56] *Calendar of Virginia State Papers*, vol. 8, p. 531.

[57] Brigham, *supra*, vol. 2, p. 1141.

Printer. The partnership between Jones and Dixon was clearly an unsatisfactory one and lasted only six months. The last joint issue of the newspaper was printed in early May 1799, and at the beginning of June the partnership was dissolved by mutual consent.

Meriwether Jones (1799-1804)

Jones continued at the *Examiner* office until November 1799, when he established his press in his home on Shockoe Hill.[58] He found at least three men to oversee his printing office after 1799: John L. Cook, Seaton Grantland, and William L. Worsley.

Jones's last political appointment took him away from printing. In March 1804 he was named Commissioner of Loans for the state of Virginia. Deciding to accept this office, he notified the governor on March 31 that he was resigning the office of Public Printer. Four days later his fellow Jeffersonian printer, Samuel Pleasants, Jr., assumed the office.[59] After April 1, 1804, Meriwether Jones was no longer connected to the printing business in any form. He filled the office of Commissioner of Loans for a little over two years. He died on August 9, 1805, while visiting Warm Springs in Bath County, Virginia.[60] His widow, Lucy, married again in 1808, a lawyer, George William Smith,[61] who became Governor of Virginia in 1811.

Samuel Pleasants, Jr. (1804-1814)

Samuel Pleasants, Jr., was appointed Public Printer on April 3, 1804, and remained in that office until his death on October 4, 1814. Pleasants was probably born in the mid-1760s. An innovative printer and bookseller, he established the first three-press office in Richmond. He was an apprentice and a member of the household of Augustine Davis in the spring of 1787. Thus, Pleasants was trained to the press in Richmond, and his relationship with Davis preceded his own printing office days.[62] Pleasants married Deborah Lowndes on July 18, 1795,[63] and they had seven children.

In 1803 and 1808, Pleasants published updated versions of the

[58] *Examiner*, December 6, 1799, in a note dated November 11, 1799.

[59] *Calendar of Virginia State Papers*, vol. 9, p. 391.

[60] *Richmond Enquirer*, August 22, 1805; *Impartial Observer*, August 23, 1805.

[61] *Virginia Argus*, June 14, 1808.

[62] Hubbard, *supra*, fascicle I.

[63] *Virginia Gazette, and General Advertiser*, July 23, 1795.

Code of Virginia. He was careful to have them both legislatively approved so that they would be official publications. The 1803 Code was officially approved by George William Smith and James Rind.[64] The 1808 Code was officially approved by William W. Hening and William Munford.[65] A supplementary volume was published in 1812.[66]

On April 15, 1793, Pleasants established a semi-weekly newspaper, *The Virginia Gazette and Richmond and Manchester Advertiser* with Augustine Davis. The partnership dissolved October 16, 1794, and Pleasants became the sole publisher.[67] On April 30, 1795, the title of the paper was changed to *The Richmond and Manchester Advertiser*. The title was changed again to the *Virginia Argus* on November 19, 1796. It was usually referred to simply as the *Argus*.[68] When Pleasants died on October 4, 1814, the *Argus* of the next day was printed with black borders to all columns.[69]

Pleasants also played an active role in the development of a national book distribution network. His first "official" printing contract was not with the state but with the federal government. On January 19, 1802, he was appointed "Printer of the Laws of the present Congress within the State of Virginia" by Secretary of State James Madison. He was reappointed by Madison for another two-year term on December 20, 1803.[70] He continued as authorized printer of the laws of the United States for the eastern district of Virginia until his appointment as Public Printer.

In the summer of 1800, Pleasants and Meriwether Jones were members of a committee to get local Jeffersonian candidates elected (George Wythe for Richmond) and to have Jeffersonian electors for the President appointed (again, George Wythe). From 1801 until April 1802, Pleasants was one of the Board of Inspectors of the Penitentiary. In 1803, he was the Senate Printer. He was also one of the first directors of the new Bank of Virginia, elected by the stockholders in May 1804, and served as a director for a decade. Both Pleasants and Meriwether Jones were members of a committee to plan a great gala

---

[64] Swem, *supra*, p. 1072; Shepherd's *Statutes*, vol. 2, p. 323.

[65] Swem, *supra*, pp. 1073-74; Shepherd's *Statutes*, vol. 3, p. 292.

[66] Va. Rev. Code, vol. 2, pp. 328-330 (1819).

[67] Brigham, *supra*, vol. 2, p. 1148.

[68] Brigham, *supra*, vol. 2, p. 1136.

[69] Hubbard, *supra*, fascicle I.

[70] J. R. Lucke, "Letters from John Quincy Adams and Others Dealing with the Printing of the Federal Laws in Virginia, 1802-1821," *Va. Mag. Hist. Biog.*, vol. 59, pp. 34-37 (1951).

festival in Richmond on May 3, 1804, in celebration of the Louisiana Purchase.[71]

Deborah Pleasants (1814-1815)

Deborah Pleasants was Samuel Pleasants' widow. Upon Samuel's death in October 1814, Deborah successfully petitioned the General Assembly to continue in the unexpired portion of her husband's term as Public Printer. Thus, she became Virginia's second female to hold the office of Public Printer.[72] The *Journal of the House of Delegates* from the session which began October 10, 1814, and continued until February 19, 1815, was printed at the *Argus* office.[73]

She was a remarkable woman, actively involved in her husband's business, but she also set up business for herself, at least briefly. In late summer 1806, she set up as a milliner, offering the latest in bonnets and hats. Like her husband, Deborah was also involved in civic affairs. With the assistance of Jean Moncure Wood, wife of Virginia's governor, she was a prime mover and founding member of the local Society for Assisting Poor Widows and Children, chartered by the legislature in 1811 as the Female Humane Association of Richmond.[74]

Thomas Ritchie (1815-1834)

Thomas Ritchie, one of the greatest editors of his day, was born in Tappahannock on November 5, 1778. He was the son of Archibald Ritchie, a Scottish merchant. Ritchie was the founder and long the distinguished editor of the Richmond *Enquirer*, and one of the leaders of the Jeffersonian party in Virginia. His editorials made him a political force of national significance.[75] He married Isabella Harminson Foushee, daughter of Dr. William Foushee, and they had twelve children.

In 1799, at age twenty-one, Ritchie took charge of an academy at Fredericksburg. He regarded the teaching profession as one of the most honorable and respectable professions, and he made an honest plea for greater educational opportunities for women. He also promoted the cause of free public instruction in Virginia. Ill health would not permit

---

[71] Hubbard, *supra*, fascicle I.

[72] Clementina Rind was the first to do so; see above.

[73] Hubbard, *supra*, fascicle I.

[74] R. A. Brock, *Virginia and Virginians*, vol. 1, p. 91 (1888).

[75] *Va. Mag. Hist. Biog.*, vol. 7, p. 240 (1900).

his remaining in the teaching profession, however, and he sought more agreeable employment in Richmond as the owner and proprietor of a small bookstore. Ritchie arrived in Richmond in 1803. Until the spring of 1804, when he began his newspaper at the urging of Thomas Jefferson, he was a bookseller who had no printing experience.[76]

Ritchie had offered his and W. W. Worsley's services to the Executive for the Office of Public Printer on March 31, 1804, the date it was to be vacated by Meriwether Jones. Previously that month, Augustine Davis, Samuel Pleasants, Jr., and John Dixon, Jr., had all sent solicitations to the Governor for the office. Pleasants was the successful candidate.[77] He was, however, the Senate printer from 1804 to 1814. Ritchie was later the Public Printer of Virginia from March 1815 to 1834 and 1836 to 1839.

The *Enquirer* was edited and published by Ritchie from 1804 to 1843 and then by Thomas Ritchie and Sons from 1843 to 1845.

Samuel Shepherd (1835)

Samuel Shepherd was appointed Public Printer in 1835 as a political rebuke to Thomas Ritchie. Ritchie had recently failed in a political assault on Senator Benjamin W. Leigh, and the loss of this lucrative public contract was the result.[78]

Samuel Shepherd printed the *Statutes at Large of Virginia* in three volumes from October session 1792 to December session 1808, inclusive, pursuant to an Act passed by the General Assembly on February 21, 1835.[79] The contract stipulated that it was not to exceed 500 copies and Shepherd would be paid $3.50 per volume. These volumes were a continuation of Hening's *Statutes*. Shepherd also printed the reports of the Virginia Court of Appeals from 1829 to 1848.

Thomas Ritchie (1836-1839)

Thomas Ritchie was again Public Printer from 1836 to 1839. At the urging of his political friends in Washington, he left Richmond to edit a newspaper in the national capitol, and from 1845 until 1851, Ritchie was the editor of the Washington, D.C., *Union*. He died in Washington,

---

[76] C. H. Ambler, *Thomas Ritchie: A Study in Virginia Politics*, p. 12 (1913).

[77] *Calendar of Virginia State Papers*, vol. 9, p. 391; Ambler, *Thomas Ritchie*, p. 32.

[78] Ambler, *Thomas Ritchie*, p. 164.

[79] 1834-35 Va. Acts, chap. 15, pp. 16-17.

D.C., on July 12, 1855, and was buried in Hollywood Cemetery in Richmond.[80]

Samuel Shepherd (1840-1848)

Samuel Shepherd was again Public Printer from 1840 to 1848. Shepherd's last known imprint was published in 1849, and his partner, Colin, was in partnership with others in 1850; this leads to the supposition that Shepherd retired or died in 1849.

William F. Ritchie (1849-1864)

William Foushee Ritchie was the oldest son of Thomas Ritchie, the founder of the Richmond *Enquirer*. He succeeded his father in the editorship of the *Enquirer* and conducted it for some years.

In addition to his official work as Public Printer, Ritchie was also authorized to reprint volumes one through five of Leigh's *Reports*, which had gone out of print and were unavailable.[81]

He was universally known in the political and social circles of Virginia. The State Convention of the Whigs met in Richmond on February 22, 1843, and the Democratic Convention on March 2. Trouble was narrowly averted between the two editors of Richmond's leading newspapers. Ritchie, of the *Enquirer*, challenged John Hampden Pleasants, of the *Whig*, to a duel over a political discussion in the papers. J. W. Pegram and James Lyons acted as peacemakers and brought about an amicable settlement.[82] Ritchie spent his retirement among relatives at Lower Brandon, where he died on the evening of April 24, 1877.[83]

Joseph H. Pendleton (1865-1866)

Joseph H. Pendleton jobbed out the printing of the journals of the House of Delegates in 1865 and 1866 to the Richmond firm of Allegre and Goode.

---

[80] Cappon, *supra*, p. 171; see generally V. Dabney, *Pistols and Pointed Pens*, pp. 1-15 (1987).

[81] 1853-54 Va. Acts, chap. 28, p. 23; 1855-56 Va. Acts, chap. 35, p. 33; 1857-58 Va. Acts, chap. 27, p. 38.

[82] W. A. Christian, *Richmond: Her Past and Present*, p. 146 (1973). However, Ritchie's brother, Thomas Ritchie, Jr., provoked another duel with Pleasants in 1846 and killed him. V. Dabney, *Pistols and Pointed Pens*, pp. 19-37 (1987).

[83] *Richmond Daily Whig*, April 27, 1877, p. 2.

William B. Allegre, born around 1812, was associated with Nathaniel Tyler, O. Jennings Wise, and others in publishing the *Richmond Enquirer* during the 1860s.[84] Allegre died at age 64 and was buried in Shockoe Cemetery in Richmond on February 15, 1877.[85]

James Edwin Goode was born in Richmond on October 1, 1837, and spent his whole life in that city. He was the son of Joseph Goode, an old-time Richmond grocer, and Eleanor Warrock. He learned the printers' trade under the firm of Ritchie and Dunnavant, for whom he worked many years prior to the war. Leaving them, he went into the office of his grandfather, John Warrock, the founder of the renowned *Warrock and Richardson Almanac.* In 1857 when Warrock became paralyzed, Goode took charge of his business. Warrock had been Printer to the Senate from 1818 to 1857, and at his death, while Goode was only nineteen years old, he was appointed to succeed him.[86] He held this office until 1866; he was again the Senate Printer in 1870. After that, he did much of the state printing. Goode was a widely known and prosperous printer in Richmond. He was well known to the political leaders of the state, having been connected with public printing in one capacity or another almost throughout his entire life.[87]

From 1858 until his death, he continued to publish the *Warrock and Richardson Almanac.* He carried on a job printing business in Richmond for a long time, and he organized the J. E. Goode Printing Company shortly before his death. He was elected president of this company.

Goode was quite prominent in Masonry, having been past master of St. John's Lodge, No. 36, of which he was also secretary for many years. He was also a member of the Second Presbyterian Church. Goode died at his home at 815 W. Franklin Street in Richmond on November 30, 1896, after an illness from heart disease of more than six months duration. He was survived by his wife.[88]

Allegre & Goode reprinted the 1865 *Journal of the House of Delegates* in 1866; they also printed the *Journal of the House of Delegates* and the *Acts of Assembly* for the 1865-66 session. Goode alone was the printer for the *Acts of Assembly* for the 1866-67 and

[84] Cappon, *supra*, p. 171, no. 1262.

[85] A. B. Rudd, *Shockoe Hill Cemetery*, vol. 2, p. 119 (1960).

[86] 1857-58 Va. Acts, p. 288.

[87] Goode tried to stir up trouble for the Public Printer in 1889, but it came to nothing. See 1889-90 House Journ., pp. 345-347; 1889-90 Senate Journ., pp. 179, 231, 341, 376-377, 511, Document No. 18.

[88] *Richmond Dispatch*, Dec. 1, 1896, p. 1.

1869-70 sessions.

John J. Palmer (1866-1869)

John J. Palmer was elected Superintendent of Public Printing in 1866,[89] and under the new system of public printing, he jobbed out all of the work. The Enquirer Press printed the 1866-67 *Journal of the House of Delegates*. The State Journal Office printed the 1869 *Journal of the House of Delegates* and the 1869 *Journal of the Senate*. The Richmond firm of Clemmitt & Jones printed the 1869-70 *Journal of the House of Delegates*.

C. A. Schaffter (1870-1872)

Charles Aurelius Schaffter was born at Grandvai, Switzerland, on June 1, 1837. When he was seven, he came with his parents to the United States, and they settled near Bluffton, Indiana. Both of his parents died shortly thereafter, and Judge Upton, a learned jurist, became his guardian. At the age of twelve he was taught the printing trade, and at age twenty-one, in 1858, he settled in Lynchburg to follow the trade of a printer. He married Lucy Hall, and they had a son, Eugene. In May 1861, Schaffter enlisted as a private in the Confederate Army, and when he was paroled in 1865, he held the rank of First Sergeant.[90]

He was active in the Lynchburg printing trade, doing business as Schaffter and Bryant in 1862. From 1864 to 1867, he was a member of the Lynchburg printing firm of Johnson and Schaffter, then he was back with Bryant from 1868 to 1869.[91] He moved to Richmond in 1870 to accept the position of Superintendent of Public Printing to the Commonwealth, which he held from 1870 to 1872.[92] He was also the Senate Printer in 1871, the last person to hold this position. He also printed volumes 19 and 20 of Grattan's *Reports of Cases Decided in the Supreme Court of Appeals . . . of Virginia*, and he reprinted volumes 3 through 6 of Grattan's *Reports*. He was not renominated for the position of Superintendent of Public Printing. During this period of his life, his wife died, and soon after 1872, he moved to Paxton, Illinois,

[89] 1865-66 House Journ., pp. 451-452.

[90] G. S. Morris and S. L. Foutz, *Lynchburg in the Civil War*, p. 87 (2d ed., 1984).

[91] In 1869, Schaffter and Bryant of 62 Market Street, Lynchburg, published John W. Daniel's *The Law and Practice of Attachment under the Code of Virginia*.

[92] 1869-70 House Journ., p. 119; 1869-70 Senate Journ., pp. 93-94. He was elected over A. P. Bennett of Richmond.

and assumed the position of business manager to the local newspaper, the *Paxton Record.* He married Della Dove, and a year later bought a half interest in the *Batavia News.* In the spring of 1882, he moved to Eagle Grove, Iowa, and founded the *Boone Valley Gazette,* of which he and his son were owner and editor until his death. He died on September 18, 1894, at his residence in Eagle Grove, Iowa.[93]

R. F. Walker (1872-1877)

Major Richard Frederick Walker was born on August 15, 1833, in Buckingham County. He was apprenticed at fifteen years of age at the *Lynchburg Virginian* to learn the art of printing. He came to Richmond to set type for the *Enquirer* in 1851. In the next year, he became shop foreman of the *Examiner* and in 1862 business manager. During the war, Walker was in a company of Home Guards, which was composed of bookbinders, typesetters, printers, and editors. They were frequently called into action in 1864 and 1865, and Walker rose to the rank of major. He also served on the Richmond City Council in 1863 and 1864.

At the end of March 1865, John M. Daniel, the owner of the *Examiner* died and bequeathed it to Walker, but within a month, the Evacuation Fire destroyed the entire plant. His attempt to establish a new newspaper, the *Richmond Republic,* failed after publishing for only one month. In 1865, he was engaged in the printing trade in partnership with J. W. Lewellyn. Walker was one of several men to be appointed to a committee to arrange for the reception of the Governor Francis H. Pierpont and his associates after Richmond had been captured on April 3, 1865.[94] Walker was elected Superintendent of Public Printing in 1872 without opposition.[95]

R. E. Frayser (1878-1879)

Captain Richard E. Frayser, the last of a family of ten children, was born in New Kent County in October 1830. He was the son of Richard Frayser, a well-known Methodist preacher. Frayser was a soldier and an editor, and he was long connected with the press. He served in Co. F., 3d Va. Cavalry, and practiced law in his later years. He married Mary A. Williamson, who was formerly of New Kent; they had no children. Frayser died on December 22, 1899, in Richmond at

[93] Obituary, *Boone Valley Gazette,* Sept. 25, 1894.

[94] Christian, *supra,* pp. 270-71; L. H. Manarin, ed., *Richmond at War,* p. 635 (1966).

[95] 1871-72 House Journ., p. 160; 1871-72 Senate Journ., pp. 136-137.

the Retreat for the Sick after a long illness. He was buried on December 23, 1899, at Hollywood Cemetery beside his widow and sister.[96]

R. F. Walker (1880-1883)

Walker was the Superintendent of Public Printing again from 1880 to 1883. He was a close political ally of General William Mahone.[97] In 1883, the Readjuster Party, the creation of Mahone, lost its control over the General Assembly, and Walker lost his place as Superintendent of Public Printing.

In 1889, he was given a patronage job in the Richmond post office but this was lost to him in 1893 upon Cleveland's election as President. He was listed in the Richmond city directories as a proofreader through 1899, when he apparently left the city.[98]

Rush U. Derr (1884-1885)

Rush U. Derr of Roanoke was the Superintendent of Public Printing of Virginia from 1884 to 1885; he defeated R. F. Walker for the position by a vote of 67 to 40.[99] While Superintendent of Public Printing, Derr also published volumes 77, 78, and 79 of the *Virginia Reports*. In 1892, he was practicing law in Roanoke.

A. R. Micou (1886-1887)

Alfred Roy Micou was born in 1839 in Essex County, where he received his primary education at a private school. Subsequently, he continued his studies at the University of Virginia. When the war broke out, he entered the army in 1861 as a private of the Essex Sharpshooters, who were later on transformed into Company F, Fifty-fifth Virginia Infantry. After the seven days' fight around Richmond, he was promoted to second lieutenant. He was wounded in the left hip at the Second Battle of Manassas and was wounded in the groin during the retreat at Gettysburg in a fight with the Kilpatrick Cavalry. He had to go to the hospital for six months and was taken prisoner.

---

[96] *Richmond Dispatch*, Dec. 23, 1899, p. 3.

[97] J. P. Maddex, Jr., *The Virginia Conservatives 1867-1879*, pp. 48, 87, 98, 112, 159, 245, 249 (1970).

[98] Manarin, *supra*, p. 635.

[99] 1883-84 House Journ., pp. 54-55; 1883-84 Senate Journ., p. 51.

In 1866 Micou went to Mississippi, where he was a school teacher until 1869. He served a short time as commissioner in chancery and as a clerk of the Essex County Court. From 1872 until 1885, he published the *Tidewater Index* at Tappahannock but gave up the publication of the paper towards the end of that year, when he was elected by the Legislature Superintendent of Public Printing.[100] He held that position for only two years, being defeated in 1887 by Captain J. H. O'Bannon.

Micou then engaged in business with Everett Waddey, a Richmond publisher and stationer, and remained there until June 1892, when he received a temporary appointment in the office of the Second Auditor, as Clerk during the funding of the state debt. He also was employed by the Richmond publisher B. F. Johnson, for whom Micou prepared manuscripts for school books. At the time of his death, he served as a clerk in the office of the Auditor of Public Accounts. Micou died at his home at 404 W. Main Street in Richmond on September 27, 1897. He was survived by his wife, Mollie McRae Micou, but no children.[101]

J. H. O'Bannon (1888-1905)

Captain James H. O'Bannon was born in Charlestown, Jefferson County, Virginia, on July 25, 1839. He was the son of Bryant O'Bannon and Harriett Moss. His early education was acquired at the schools of Jefferson County. At the time of the John Brown raid, O'Bannon was a guard at Harper's Ferry, and afterwards he was a private in the Confederate army. He rose to the rank of Captain, commanding Company I of the Second Virginia Regiment, known as the "Clarke Rifles," one of the crack companies of General Stonewall Jackson's Brigade. In April 1864 he was captured near Washington and confined under harsh conditions in Fort Delaware, where he remained a prisoner until the end of the war.

In 1870 he came to Richmond and accepted a position with the *Enquirer*. Later he entered the service of the *State* and remained with that newspaper for twelve years, leaving only to accept the position which he held at the time of his death. Politics had always held a strong fascination for him, and he served for some time on the City Democratic Committee and later as chairman of the Democratic Committee of Henrico County. On April 9, 1873, in Sullivan County, Tennessee, O'Bannon married Flora Summerfield Fhangle, the daughter of Joseph F. Fhangle, a native of Prince George County,

[100] 1885-86 House Journ., p. 64. Micou was elected over R. F. Walker.

[101] *Richmond Dispatch*, Sept. 28, 1897, p. 6; P. Micou, "Paul Micou, Huguenot Physician, and His Descendants." *Va. Mag. Hist. Biog.*, vol. 47, pp. 66-67 (1939).

Virginia.

O'Bannon was a candidate for the House of Delegates in 1887 but was defeated by a small vote. This same legislature elected him to the position of Superintendent of Public Printing.[102] After his first appointment, he was reelected without opposition until his death. He was a member of St. John's Lodge, No. 36, Masons, Knights of Honor, and Richmond Typographical Union, No. 60. He was also a member of the Barton Heights Baptist Church.

O'Bannon died on the evening of August 15, 1905, at his home in Barton Heights in north Richmond. He was survived by six children.[103]

Davis Bottom (1905-1928)

Davis Bottom was born in Richmond on May 2, 1867. He had the opportunity of attending school regularly only until he was ten years of age. His real education was acquired in the great university of a printing office. He began his apprenticeship under Daniel Murphy at Richmond, remaining with him three and one-half years. He completed his apprenticeship in the establishment of Everett Waddey, a general book and job printer, continuing in the employment of this firm for a number of years as a journeyman. Bottom was employed at various times in the larger printing offices in the city and for several years held the position of foreman for the J. Hill Printing Company of Richmond. After this service with local printing houses, Bottom went on the road as a traveling representative, selling printers supplies for the H. L. Pelouze branch at Richmond of the American Type Founders Company. Subsequently, he was traveling representative for the B. W. Wilson Paper Company of Richmond, covering the territory of Virginia and North Carolina; he also represented Charles Helmuth, ink manufacturers, of New York.

In September 1905, Governor Andrew J. Montague appointed Bottom Superintendent of Public Printing to fill the vacancy caused by the death of Captain J. H. O'Bannon. In the next session of the General Assembly, that body unanimously elected him to the office,[104] and he was reelected without opposition until 1928, when the position was abolished. In 1928, The Division of Purchase and Printing was created, and Charles A. Osborne of Keysville was appointed its director. However, Bottom was hired as the head of the printing branch of the

[102] 1887-88 House Journ., p. 49; 1887-88 Senate Journ., p. 47. O'Bannon was elected over R. F. Walker.

[103] Richmond *Times-Dispatch*, August 16, 1905, p. 3.

[104] 1906 House Journ., pp. 39, 156.

new department. He retained this position until his death, upon which it was abolished.[105]

He was elected a member of the City Council of Richmond in 1902 but resigned during his second term to take up his public printing duties. He was a devout Baptist who taught the Baraca Class at Northside Baptist Church Sunday School. He was also a member of the following organizations: Magnolia Camp No. 20, Woodmen of the World, Aurora Council No. 28, Junior Order United American Mechanics, Sons and Daughters of Liberty, Richmond Lodge No. 2519, F.A.U., Richmond Typographical Union No. 90, and the Board of Directors of the Funeral Benefit Association of the United States. Bottom gave all the time and rendered every assistance in his power to further the success of local war campaigns, assisting the Richmond Draft Boards. His home was in the Highland Park section of Richmond.[106] Bottom married Ella V. Alley in Richmond on September 20, 1892, and they had nine children. He died in Richmond on October 4, 1935.[107]

[105] Richmond *News Leader*, Jan. 6, 1928, p. 1, Oct. 24, 1935, p. 8.

[106] "Davis Bottom," *History of Virginia*, vol. 4, pp. 136-137 (1924).

[107] Richmond *Times Dispatch*, Sept. 6, 1935, p. 16, Oct. 5, 1935; Richmond *News Leader*, Oct. 5, 1935, Oct. 7, 1935.

J. W. RANDOLPH

Robert F. Strohm

JOSEPH WILLIAMSON RANDOLPH was born at Chester Lodge near the now extinct town of Warwick in Chesterfield County, Virginia, on August 19, 1815. His parents were Henry Randolph (1784-1840), a direct descendant of William Randolph of Turkey Island, and Elizabeth Norment (1785-1825).[1] After his mother died when he was ten, his father remarried and sent him to Richmond to be raised by his grandmother.

In 1829, he commenced work, at age fourteen, for a Richmond bookseller named John W. Nash. Two years later, when Nash's business failed, young Randolph was retained by the Nash trustees to liquidate the remaining stock at retail. At the final sale, he purchased $200 worth of books and stationery on his own account and set himself up in business at 121 Main Street in Richmond. In conjunction with this business, he also operated a circulating library. By 1834 he was able to purchase the entire inventory of a bookseller in Norfolk, where he lived for a short while. He soon returned to Richmond and took his uncle, Josiah B. Abbott, into partnership. Regrettably, the uncle's business acumen was not equal to the nephew's, and when the elder man endorsed the note of a friend who declared bankruptcy, the company fell liable to a $17,000 debt, which took four years to repay. The partnership was dissolved in 1842, and Randolph continued on alone. (Abbott died in 1849.[2])

On November 28, 1842, Randolph married Honoria Mary Tucker. Nora was a second cousin and the sister of John Randolph Tucker (1812-1883), who served actively as an officer successively in the United States Navy, the Confederate Navy, and the Peruvian Navy.[3] Nora was a Roman Catholic, and Joseph joined her in that faith. They had two sons: Joseph Tucker Randolph, who was a captain in the Confederate Army and was killed in the Battle of Cold Harbor, and Norman Vincent Randolph. J. W. Randolph served the Confederacy in the Ambulance Corps.

During the 1850s, J. W. Randolph so prospered that, by the outbreak of hostilities in 1861, he was not only one of the leading bookmen in Virginia, but in the entire South as well. But Richmond

---

[1] G. L. Randolph, *Randolphs of Virginia*, pp. 799-800 (1990).

[2] "Joseph W. Randolph," Richmond *Dispatch*, March 28, 1893, p. 4. See also Joseph Williamson Randolph letters at the Virginia Historical Society.

[3] D. P. Werlich, *Admiral of the Amazon: John Randolph Tucker*, pp. 2, 8, 134 (1990).

burned on April 3, 1865, and with it Randolph's shop and all his resources; this calamity was compounded by his heavy investment in Confederate bonds and other war securities. A lesser man might have despaired. But Randolph borrowed $100 and reestablished himself as J. W. Randolph & Co. on the same site where he had begun in 1832. He was soon joined by Joseph J. English in the firm of J. W. Randolph & English. The business was later moved to 1318 East Main Street in Richmond.

If not the most prominent, certainly Randolph was one of the most active of publishers, booksellers, bookbinders, and stationers in Richmond. (Printing was jobbed out to a number of different printers.) Randolph's first publications appeared in 1845, being *The Virginia Warbler: A New Collection of . . . Songs* and E. Hagerty's *The Farmer's Calendar*. His first legal publications were issued in 1850.

His publishing activities were general, and his law books were a very small proportion of his total output. However, the legal works that he did publish were important. His contribution to Virginia legal scholarship is significant and worthy of notice. Even though he did not create it, he disseminated it and thus encouraged it. Perhaps if he had not, another would have, but what is undeniable is that he did, in fact, do it. Furthermore, even though it was a small proportion of his publishing output, his law publishing was a steady business covering the years 1850 to 1896, the year before the business was ended. In terms of significance to the Virginia bar, Randolph's books were of major importance. Even though he was never the official printer for the Commonwealth and thus never issued lucrative legislative materials, he published the first two law journals in Virginia and the first seven volumes of the third. Furthermore, his authors included the most distinguished legal scholars of the time: James M. Matthews, Alexander H. Sands, B. B. Minor, John B. Minor, Robert T. Barton, and Conway Robinson.

Randolph published numerous catalogs of books for sale, some of them specializing in law,[4] theology, American history, politics, and the Confederacy.[5] Though virtually unlimited in scope, they not only yield illuminating insights into what was being published and read in nineteenth-century Virginia, but they also provide invaluable bibliographic data on arcane and antique volumes. He was well known as a bibliographer and a bibliophile.

His business thrived until his ill health forced him into retirement

[4] E.g. *Randolph's Law Catalogue 1856* (1856), 24 pp.

[5] R. F. Strohm, "J. W. Randolph, Bookman Extraordinaire," *Va. Hist. Soc. Occasional Bull.*, vol. 42, pp. 7-11 (June 1981).

in 1890.[6] Randolph died in Richmond on March 26, 1893, and his funeral was held at St. Peter's Cathedral. The firm passed into receivership a scant four years after his death.[7]

After his death, it was written that "[t]here was little that had been published about Virginia that he had not read, while his familiarity with general literature was considerable. He was of vast help to all literary workers in [Richmond]. . . ."[8] Commenting on Randolph's phenomenal success, John Tebbel wrote "It was said of him that 'when he commenced his business he could have taken his stock in a wheelbarrow and that now [near the end of the century] it would have taken a steamboat to remove it'."[9]

BIBLIOGRAPHY OF LAW BOOKS PUBLISHED BY J. W. RANDOLPH

1850

Matthews, James M[uscoe]. *A Guide to Commissioners in Chancery with Practical Forms for the Discharge of Their Duties, Adapted to the New Code of Virginia.* Printed by Colin, Baptist and Nowlan.

The Virginia Report of 1799-1800, Touching the Alien and Sedition Laws. C. Sherman, Printer.

1852

Wythe, George. *Decisions of Cases in Virginia.* 2d ed. by B. B. Minor. Elliott & Nye, Printers.

1853

Brockenbrough, [William], and [Hugh] Holmes. *A Collection of Cases Decided by the General Court of Virginia.* Volume 1, 2d ed.

---

[6] See *Law Catalogue – No. 10, Clearance Sale to Retire from Business . . . Catalogue of Second-Hand Law Books* (n.d.), 40 pp.

[7] See *Catalogue No. 14. Receiver's Sale of Law Stock of J. W. Randolph Company, New and Second-Hand* (1897), 40 pp.

[8] Richmond *Dispatch*, March 28, 1893, p. 2.

[9] J. W. Tebbel, *History of Book Publishing in the United States*, vol. 1, pp. 475-476 (1972).

DECISIONS OF CASES

IN

VIRGINIA,

BY THE

HIGH COURT OF CHANCERY,

WITH REMARKS UPON DECREES,

BY THE

COURT OF APPEALS,

REVERSING SOME OF THOSE DECISIONS.

BY GEORGE WYTHE,

CHANCELLOR OF SAID COURT.

SECOND AND ONLY COMPLETE EDITION, WITH A MEMOIR OF THE AUTHOR, ANALYSES OF THE CASES, AND AN INDEX,

BY B. B. MINOR, L. B., OF THE RICHMOND BAR.

AND WITH AN APPENDIX, CONTAINING

REFERENCES TO CASES IN PARI MATERIA, AND AN ESSAY ON LAPSE; JOINT TENANTS AND TENANTS IN COMMON, &C.,

BY WILLIAM GREEN, ESQ.

RICHMOND:
J. W. RANDOLPH, 121 MAIN STREET.
1852.

1854

Hening, William W[aller], and William Munford. *Reports of Cases . . . in the Supreme Court of Appeals of Virginia.* 2d ed. by B. B. Minor, 4 vols.

1855

Grigsby, Hugh Blair. *The Virginia Convention of 1776.* W. H. Clemmitt, Printer.

1856

Guigon, A[lexander] B[arclay], ed. *The Quarterly Law Journal.* Volume 1. MacFarlane & Fergusson, printers.

Matthews, James M[uscoe]. *Digest of the Laws of Virginia of a Civil Nature.* Volume 1. Printed by C. H. Wynne.

Randolph's Law Catalogue 1856. Tho's Bailie, book and job printer.

Selections from the Reports of the Revisors of the Statutes of Virginia.

> This work was issued in parts from 1856 to 1859 and was a given a new title page in 1861.

1857

Guigon, A[lexander] B[arclay], ed. *The Quarterly Law Journal.* Volume 2. MacFarlane & Fergusson, printers.

Matthews, James M[uscoe]. *Digest of the Laws of Virginia of a Civil Nature.* Volume 2. Printed by C. H. Wynne.

1858

Guigon, A[lexander] B[arclay], ed. *The Quarterly Law Journal.* Volume 3. MacFarlane & Fergusson, printers.

1859

Guigon, A[lexander] B[arclay]. *A General Index of Grattan's*

Virginia Reports, from First to Eleventh Volume, Inclusive.

> This work was first issued in parts and is sometimes found bound with the *Quarterly Law Journal*, vols. 1-3 (1856-1858).

Guigon, A[lexander] B[arclay], ed. *The Quarterly Law Journal.* Volume 4. MacFarlane & Fergusson, printers.

1860

Sands, Alexander H[amilton], ed. *The Quarterly Law Review.* Volume 1.

1861

Sands, Alexander H[amilton], ed. *The Quarterly Law Review.* Volume 2.

1863

Military Laws of the Confederate States.

1867

Grattan, Peachy R[idgway]. *Reports of Cases Decided in the Supreme Court of Appeals of Virginia.* Volume 16. Enquirer, print[ers].

1871

Matthews, James M[uscoe]. *Digest of the Laws of Virginia of a Criminal Nature.* 2d ed.

Matthews, James M[uscoe]. *A Guide to Commissioners in Chancery with Practical Forms for the Discharge of Their Duties, Adapted to the New Code of Virginia.* 2d ed.

1872

Matthews, W[illiam] B[aynham]. *Guide for Executors and Administrators in Virginia.*

Sands, Alexander H[amilton]. *Practical Forms.* 2d ed.

1873

Matthews, William B[aynham]. *Forms of Pleading in Civil and Criminal Cases and of Deeds, Wills, &c.* Printed by B. W. Gillis.

1874

Robinson, Conway. *The Principles and Practice of Courts of Justice in England and the United States.* Volume 7. Printed by Clemmitt & Jones.

1877

Barton, R[obert] T[homas]. *The Practice in the Courts of Law in Civil Cases, Founded on Conway Robinson's Practice (1832).* Printed by Whittet & Shepperson.

Christian, George L[lewellyn], and Frank W[ood] Christian, edd. *The Virginia Law Journal.* Volume 1.

1878

Christian, George L[lewellyn], and Frank W[ood] Christian, edd. *The Virginia Law Journal.* Volume 2.

Matthews, James M[uscoe]. *Digest of the Laws of Virginia of a Criminal Nature.* Supplement.

Minor, John B[arbee]. *Institutes of Common and Statute Law.* Volume 4, part 1. Printed by Whittet & Shepperson.

1879

Christian, Geo[rge] L[lewellyn], ed. *The Virginia Law Journal.* Volume 3.

Minor, John B[arbee]. *Institutes of Common and Statute Law.* Volume 4, part 2. Printed by Whittet & Shepperson.

1880

Christian, Geo[rge] L[lewellyn], ed. *The Virginia Law Journal.* Volume 4.

1881

Barton, R[obert] T[homas]. *Pleading and Practice in the Courts of Chancery.* Volume 1. Printed by Whittet & Shepperson.

Christian, George L[lewellyn], and Samuel D[avid] Davies, edd. *The Virginia Law Journal.* Volume 5.

In Memoriam. William Green, LL. D.

> This was reprinted from the *Virginia Law Journal* (Jan. 1881).

Martin, William B[ruce]. *An Index to the Virginia Reports.* Printed by the Norfolk Virginian.

1882

Christian, George L[lewellyn], and James M[uscoe] Matthews, edd. *The Virginia Law Journal.* Volume 6.

In the Chancery Court of the City of Richmond. Cabell & McGuire, Trustees vs. Southern Mutual Insurance Co. et als. Amended and Supplemental Bill.

Robinson, Conway. *History of the High Court of Chancery.* Wm. Ellis Jones, Printer.

Sands, Alexander H[amilton]. *History of a Suit in Equity, as Prosecuted and Defended in the Virginia State Courts and in the United States Circuit Courts.* 2d ed. Printed by Wm. Ellis Jones.

1883

Barton, R[obert] T[homas]. *Pleading and Practice in the Courts of Chancery.* Volume 2. Printed by William Ellis Jones.

Lamb, James C[hristian], and Benj[amin] T. Christian, edd. *The Virginia Law Journal.* Volume 7.

Minor, John B[arbee]. *Institutes of Common and Statute Law.* Volume 4, 2d ed. 1 vol. in 2. Printed by Whittet & Shepperson.

1888

Sams, C[onway] Whittle. *A Brief Comparison of the Most Important Statutes of the Codes of Virginia of 1873 and 1887.* Printed by Whittet & Shepperson.

1889

Howard, Overton. *The Life of the Law or Universal Principles of Law.*

Martin, William B[ruce]. *An Index to the Virginia Reports.* 2d ed. Printed by J. W. Fergusson & Son.

1890

Matthews, James M[uscoe]. *Digest of the Laws of Virginia of a Criminal Nature.* 3d ed. Ware, Duke, & Taylor, Printers.

1891

Barton, R[obert] T[homas]. *The Practice in the Courts of Law in Civil Cases.* 2d ed., 2 vols. Printed by William Ellis Jones.

Minor, John B[arbee]. *Institutes of Common and Statute Law.* Volume 1, 4th ed. Printed by Whittet & Shepperson.

1892

Minor, John B[arbee]. *Institutes of Common and Statute Law.* Volume 2, 4th ed. Printed by Whittet & Shepperson.

1893

Minor, John B[arbee]. *Institutes of Common and Statute Law.* Volume 4, 3d ed. 1 vol. in 2. Printed by Whittet & Shepperson.

1895

Eby, Abram C. *Citations to the Code of Virginia.* Printed by Whittet & Shepperson.

1896

Martin, William Bruce. *An Index to the Virginia Reports*. 3d ed. Printed by J. W. Fergusson & Son.

Sams, C[onway] Whittle. *A Treatise on the Law of Attachment and Bail in Virginia and West Virginia.*

[Date Unknown]

Law Catalogue – No. 10, Clearance Sale to Retire from Business . . . Catalogue of Second-Hand Law Books.

THE MICHIE COMPANY

David W. Parrish, Jr.

I. *Introduction*

IN A STUDY of the history of business, one truth is quickly manifested, businesses are started to provide services and products that are perceived to be needed. Businesses fail quickly if there is no need for their services and products.

The need to know the law has always existed and there have always been persons who sought to make it available, e.g. Moses, Hammurabi, and later Thomas Jefferson, who re-codified the laws of Virginia. To the thousands of attorneys and judges who need ready access to the vast field of statutory and case law as well as the expert opinion of authors of legal treatises, it would seem that the businesses that provide this access have always been needed. However, the law publishing industry developed slowly.

Printing businesses are distinguished from law publishing businesses in that printers merely duplicate and replicate the case and statute law presented to them without any intellectual or editorial enhancement.[1] Law publishers, on the other hand, make editorial additions and changes of a non-substantive nature which make the law quicker to find and easier to read and comprehend. They are active participants in the intellectual presentation of the law to the general public and to the legal profession.

The problem with the steady periodic printing of cases and statutes is easily discernible. Without cumulative indexes, without case headnotes, and without the consolidation of statutory amendments, finding a case in point or an applicable updated statute was a nightmare indeed.

Thus editorial enhancements were essential. For many years these were provided in Virginia by the private enterprise of individual lawyers, by individual attorneys on the state payroll, or practicing lawyers on hire as experts. For example, state reporters were appointed to draft headnotes, which in effect digested the court opinions, and to prepare indexes for each volume of printed cases.[2]

---

[1] E.g. J. W. Randolph, a nineteenth century Richmond publisher and bookseller, published numerous Virginia law books, but neither he nor his company participated in the editorial work of the law books that he produced, nor did his company specialize in law publishing. In fact, no one in Virginia before the Michie Company specialized in producing law books, though many produced some. See above, "J. W. Randolph."

[2] See above, "Reports of Cases."

Statutory law needed to be compiled, arranged, and classified into categories of related subject matter and broken down into sections of a reasonable length. At first, attorneys in private practice were engaged to perform this service, and they, perforce, engaged in trial and error training on-the-job.[3]

In a few instances attorneys and printing companies combined to provide case law with headnotes and to compile statutes. Among the earliest of these enterprises which evolved into law publishing companies were the two that were later known as the Banks-Baldwin Company, which was started in Cleveland in the early 1800s, and the Bobbs-Merrill Company, established in Indianapolis in 1855. (Banks-Baldwin is now owned by the West Publishing Company; Bobbs-Merrill was later part of the Michie Company, now Lexis Law Publishing.)

The sheer body of the law, growing larger each year, eventually doomed the efforts of individual attorneys and brought the advent of the law publishing companies. These companies could develop and expand editorial techniques and innovations, concentrate on specific areas of the law, and hire and train a sufficient number of legal editors to perform various functions accurately and expeditiously.

The pioneers in law publishing were individuals who called on family members to assist them, financially or otherwise, resulting in the major companies being family owned. These companies each had a specialty which made their name synonymous with a product, e.g. the West Publishing Company and the National Reporter System.

II. *Founding and Management*

There were numerous printers in eighteenth and nineteenth century Virginia who printed law books along with their other various enterprises. (Before 1730, Virginia law books were printed in London.) However, the first law book publishing company in Virginia was founded by the Michie family in 1897 in Charlottesville. In fact, the Michie Company is the only publisher specializing in law books ever to have existed in Virginia.

After the Civil War, there was hardly a Michie left to start a company; of five brothers, only Henry Bowyer Michie survived.[4] After the War, Henry B. Michie practiced law with his father, Thomas Johnson Michie, in Staunton. Then in 1883, Henry moved to Charlottesville and purchased the *Charlottesville Chronicle*, a weekly newspaper. Printing facilities for the newspaper were primitive even

---

[3] See above, "Codes."

[4] See generally, T. J. Michie, *The Michie Family*, pp. 9-12 (c. 1942).

by turn-of-the-century standards. All type was set by hand and the press was operated by a temperamental steam engine. Nevertheless, these facilities provided an opportunity to enter into law publishing.

Henry Michie fathered three sons: George R. B. Michie, Thomas Johnson Michie,[5] and Armistead Rust Michie. All three sons were to become graduates of the University of Virginia Law School. The oldest, George, managed the business of the *Chronicle* and went into banking; he later became president of the Peoples Bank of Charlottesville, which was subsequently merged into the Virginia National Bank, then the Sovran Bank, and ultimately NationsBank.

The second son, Tom, joined the editorial staff of the Edward Thompson Company in Brooklyn, New York, a law publishing company. Thompson was publishing the *American and English Railroad Cases Annotated* but quite unprofitably. Tom Michie was able to obtain the right to take over the publication of this set of law books and returned to Charlottesville and to the printing facilities of the *Chronicle*.

The two older brothers formed the George R. B. Michie Company in 1897 to publish law books. In 1899, the Michie Company was incorporated with Tom as president and George as treasurer and business manager (after banking hours). Armistead joined the company after graduation from law school in 1901 and subsequently became president and chairman.

The offspring of the brothers affected the future of the company. George had several daughters, one of whom, Virginia Hench, the wife of a University of Virginia English professor, worked part-time preparing advertising copy for the company. Tom had two sons, Thomas and Hewson. Young Tom became a practicing attorney and later a federal judge.[6] He served the Michie Company as an editorial advisor but never as an employee.

Hewson became a company editor and eventually succeeded his uncle Armistead, who had never married, as chief executive officer. Hewson also succeeded his father as the official reporter of the *Virginia Reports*. In 1957, Hewson Michie[7] became chairman and his son-in-law, William O. Lewis,[8] became president and chief executive officer. Lewis

[5] B. Stedman, "Thomas Johnson Michie," *Va. State Bar Ass'n Repts.*, vol. 50, pp. 241-243 (1939).

[6] W. H. Bryson, "Thomas Johnson Michie," *Legal Education in Va.*, pp. 407-409 (1982).

[7] B. P. Chamberlain, "Addinell Hewson Michie," *Va. State Bar Ass'n Repts.*, vol. 69, pp. 191-193 (1958).

[8] D. W. Parrish, Jr., "William Owen Lewis," *Va. State Bar Ass'n Repts.*, vol. 80, pp. 413-414 (1969).

VIRGINIA REPORTS,

JEFFERSON—33 GRATTAN.

1730–1880.

ANNOTATED

UNDER THE SUPERVISION OF

THOMAS JOHNSON MICHIE.

THE MICHIE COMPANY, LAW PUBLISHERS,
CHARLOTTESVILLE, VA.
1900.

served until his death at age 42 in 1969. He was succeeded by the first chief executive officer who was not a member of the family.

The company was purchased by ITT Corporation, then the world's largest conglomerate, in 1971. Bobbs-Merrill became a part of ITT's publishing group in 1976, and its law division was moved from Indianapolis to Charlottesville and merged into the Michie Company. Michie adjusted to the transition from the rather informal management style of a relatively small company to the structured accounting and strict discipline imposed by ITT's presiding genius, Harold Geneen, and continued to flourish.

Following Geneen's retirement, his successors began to consolidate ITT and sell off some of its business units. ITT Publishing was sold to Macmillan Publishing, an old-line trade and text book publisher, in 1985. Michie became part of Macmillan's Information Services Division. While owned by Macmillan, Michie purchased the Allen Smith Company of Indianapolis, a publisher of state codes, and the Kluwer publishing company, a publisher of treatises for the trial bar.

In 1988, after a bitter financial battle, Robert Maxwell, the notorious British publisher, took over Macmillan and in a matter of weeks sold Michie to the Mead Corporation for 226.5 million dollars. Mead's subsidiary, Mead Data Central, originated LEXIS®, the first successful nationwide electronic legal search and retrieval system. In 1995, Mead sold the Michie Company to Reed Elsevier, a British-Dutch publishing conglomerate. One of the numerous other law publishing companies owned by Reed Elsevier was Butterworth Legal Publishers, the English company founded in 1818.[9] The American branch of Butterworths was merged into the Michie Company to form the law publishing firm of Michie Butterworth, which was headquartered in Charlottesville.[10] In 1997, Michie Butterworth was merged into a new corporate entity within Reed Elsevier, Inc., and the Michie imprint was retired in 1998.

III. *Law Books Published*

In the early days of its existence, the Michie Company published whatever seemed expedient and profitable at the time. There were law books written by independent authors; there were books written by in-house authors, who were employees of the company; and there was job

[9] H. K. Jones, *Butterworths: History of a Publishing House* (1980).

[10] The first publication under the Michie Butterworth imprint was volume 34 of *Virginia Circuit Court Opinions*.

printing to keep the presses occupied when they were not otherwise needed.

Many well known Virginia treatises were published by the Michie Company. Burks' *Pleading and Practice* and Barton's *Chancery Practice* were classics. Judge Brockenbrough Lamb's short books, *A Virginia Cause* and *Virginia Probate Practice*, and Professor Arthur Phelps's books on the Virginia Rules of Court were quite well received by practitioners. Charles Friend's several editions of his treatise on Virginia evidence have assumed classic status.

One of the first projects that was wholly the product of the Michie Company editorial staff was the reprinting of the older Virginia law reports. In 1900, the Michie Company received legislative permission to reprint the nominative Virginia reports,[11] and the result was the *Virginia Reports Annotated*, which was published in twenty-six volumes from 1900 to 1904. Another major project of the Michie Company was *The Encyclopedic Digest of Virginia and West Virginia Reports* (1905-1928) in twenty-six volumes. Some "author books" were continued in later editions by the staff editors of the Michie Company; among the more notable are Harrison's *Wills and Administration*, and Vartanian's *The Law of Automobiles in Virginia and West Virginia*.

Examples of job printing for the Virginia law market are Martin P. Burks, *Parol Evidence Rule*; Charles A. Graves, *Questions on Evidence* (1907); William M. Lile, *Notes on Municipal Corporations* (1910); and W. H. Bryson, *Legal Education in Virginia 1779-1979* (1982).

However, it was not until its first state code was published that the Michie Company found its distinct niche in law publishing. Michie developed editorial standards and procedures for the codification of statutes which assured the production of a high quality product in a reasonable time frame. Publication of state codes became a specialty of the company. Michie now publishes 31 codes, more than any other publisher.

The first *Code of Virginia* published by the Michie Company was a private venture that was begun in 1924. Since 1950, the Michie Company has had the contract with the Commonwealth of Virginia to publish the official *Code of Virginia* in cooperation with the Virginia Code Commission.

Michie's Jurisprudence is the largest major publication on Virginia law since its completion in the early 1950s. This multi-volume commentary on the statutory and case law in Virginia and West Virginia was written by Michie's editors over the course of several

---

[11] 1899-1900 Va. Acts, c. 510, p. 545.

years; this encyclopedia was based on an earlier Michie *Digest* of the laws of the Virginias and is updated annually.

The Michie Company has thus served the Virginia legal community in an extraordinarily important way. Many Virginia law books would never have been issued to the public without the local connections of this publishing company.

IV. *Printing Technology*

In the beginning of the company's history, printing was done in the office of the newspaper; all type was set by hand, and the press was operated by a steam engine. However, in 1898, a year after its founding, the Michie Company built its own printing house at 609 Market Street in Charlottesville. This building was substantially expanded in 1937 and again in 1962. A new plant was built at 1317 Carlton Avenue in 1989.

Later on as printing technology was developed, Linotype machines were acquired, and these have now been replaced by computer type setting machines and electric presses. This has made possible books in modified formats.

Pocket parts that can be inserted into slits in the insides of the rear covers of the books has made it possible to keep books up to date without having to reprint the entire volume. This economy of time and paper has reduced considerably the cost of law book production, and this makes it economically feasible to keep law books current. The *Code of Virginia, Michie's Jurisprudence, Virginia Forms, Harrison on Wills and Administration,* and many other Michie books are kept up to date in this manner.

A further refinement on this idea is the looseleaf book. These books are issued unsewn in a looseleaf binding; new pages can then be issued whenever needed and replaced in the looseleaf binding. The Michie Company uses this method of publication for its *Virginia Model Jury Instructions.*

During the Macmillan era, Michie developed a sophisticated computerized, automated editorial system, the end result of which was an integrated electronic master file of each state code. This eased the transition to CD-ROM publishing technology and allowed Michie to become the pioneer publisher of state statutes in this medium. After its association with Mead, Michie had access to the LEXIS® case law database and was able to include cases with statutes so that the entire law of a jurisdiction could be contained in one or two CD-ROM discs with easy search capability.

BIBLIOGRAPHY OF VIRGINIA LAW BOOKS PRINTED BY THE MICHIE COMPANY BEFORE 1950

1899

Lile, W[illiam] M[inor]. *Notes to 1 Minor's Institutes (4th ed.).* 299, x p.

1900

Laws of the University of Virginia, 1900 Together with Ch. LXVIII of the Code of Virginia of 1887, and Subsequent State Legislation in Regard to the University. 98 p.

Virginia Reports . . . Annotated. 3 vols.

Grattan's reports, vols. 28-33.

1901

Lile, William Minor. *Notes to Vol. III, Minor's Institutes: Prepared for the Use of the Students of the Junior Law Class at the University of Virginia.* 67 p.

Virginia Reports . . . Annotated. 5 vols.

Grattan's reports, vols. 16-27.

1902

Michie, Thomas Johnson. *An Index-Digest to Volumes 92-99 Virginia Reports (Both Inclusive) and Volumes 1 and 2 Virginia Decisions.* 500 p.

Virginia Decisions: A Collection of Virginia Cases Not Officially Reported. 2 vols.

Virginia Reports . . . Annotated. 10 vols.

Reports of Grattan, vols. 1-15, Virginia Cases, Call, Leigh, vols. 9-12, Robinson, and Patton & Heath.

1903

Virginia Reports . . . Annotated. 5 vols.

Reports of Washington, Hening & Munford, Munford, vols. 1-3, Gilmer, Leigh, vols. 1-8, Jefferson, and Wythe.

1904

Virginia Reports . . . Annotated. 3 vols.

Reports of Munford, vols. 4-6, and Randolph.

1905

Michie, Thomas Johnson, ed. *The Encyclopedic Digest of Virginia and West Virginia Reports.* Vol. 1.

1906

Burks, Martin P[arks]. *Abstract of Lectures on Conveyancing.* 103 p.

Burks, Martin P[arks]. *Demurrer to Evidence.* 17 p.

Michie, Thomas Johnson, ed. *The Encyclopedic Digest of Virginia and West Virginia Reports.* Vols. 2-6.

Pollard, John Garland, ed. *The Virginia Law Register.* Vol. 11.

1907

Duke, R. T. W., ed. *The Virginia Law Register.* Vol. 12.

Graves, Charles A[lfred]. *Questions on Evidence.* 47 p.

Hank, J[osiah] D[ickenson], Jr. *Annotations to Volumes 75 to 105 Virginia Reports, Both Inclusive.* 1,005 p.

Michie, Thomas Johnson, ed. *The Encyclopedic Digest of Virginia and West Virginia Reports.* Vols. 7-13.

1908

Duke, R. T. W., ed. *The Virginia Law Register.* Vol. 13.

Minor, Raleigh Colston. *The Law of Real Property*. Vol. 2.

Reports of Cases Decided in the Supreme Court of Appeals of Virginia. Vols. 75, 76.

1909

The Code of the City of Charlottesville, Virginia: Containing the Charter as Amended and Re-Enacted as a Whole (Approved March 14, 1908), the Constitutional and Legislative Provisions of the State Relating to Cities, and the General Ordinances of the City Enacted as a Whole August 6th, 1909, in Effect September 1st, 1909. iv, 319 p.

Duke, R. T. W., ed. *The Virginia Law Register*. Vol. 14.

Graves, Charles A[lfred]. *Extrinsic Evidence in Respect to Written Instruments: A Paper Read Before the Virginia State Bar Association, August 2, 1893*. 34 p.

Michie, Thomas Johnson, ed. *The Encyclopedic Digest of Virginia and West Virginia Reports*. Vol. 14 and index vol.

Reports of Cases Decided in the Supreme Court of Appeals of Virginia. Vols. 81, 82.

Staples, Abram Penn. *Notes on Virginia Corporation Law*. 52 p.

1910

Duke, R. T. W., ed. *The Virginia Law Register*. Vol. 15.

Graves, C[harles] A[lfred]. *Notes to Clark on Contracts*. 43 p.

Jas. E. Irvine, Appellant vs. Randolph Lumber Corp., &c, Appellees. From the Circuit Court of Albemarle County. 56 p.

Record No. 1317, 111 Va. 408, 69 S.E. 350 (1910).

Lile, W[illiam] M[inor]. *Notes on Municipal Corporations, Prepared for the Use of the Students in the Law School of the University of Virginia*. 114 p.

Long, Joseph R[agland]. *Notes of Lectures Introductory to the Study of Law*. 45 p.

Long, Joseph R[agland]. *Notes of Lectures on the Law of Wills and Administrations.*

Long, Joseph Ragland. *Outline of the Jurisdiction and Procedure of the Federal Courts Prepared for the Use of Law Students*. v, 88 p.

Lucy Moon, et als., Plaintiff in Error vs. Children's Home Society of Va., Defendant in Error. From the Circuit Court of Albemarle County. 18 p.

Record No. 1321, 112 Va. 737, 72 S.E. 707 (1911).

1911

The Chesapeake and Ohio Railway Co., Plaintiff in Error vs. Andrew Wilson's Admx., Defendant in Error. From the Circuit Court of Albemarle County. 62 p.

Record No. 1336.

Duke, R. T. W., ed. *The Virginia Law Register*. Vol. 16.

1912

Duke, R. T. W., ed. *The Virginia Law Register*. Vol. 17.

Michie, Thomas Johnson, ed. *The Encyclopedic Digest of Virginia and West Virginia Reports*. Vol. 15.

Taxes on Licenses, City of Charlottesville. For the Year Commencing May 1, 1912. 26 p.

1913

Burks, Martin P[arks]. *Pleading and Practice in Actions at Common Law*. lxxvi, 1,168 p.

Duke, R. T. W., ed. *The Virginia Law Register*. Vol. 18.

Lile, William Minor. *Notes on Equity Jurisprudence, to Accompany Merwin's Equity; Prepared for the Use of the Students of the Law School of the University of Virginia.* 190 p.

Perkins, Perkins & Walker. *Brief of Counsel for S. P. Riddle, Trustee. James H. Corbett, Appellant v. S. P. Riddle, Trustee of M. H. Keefe & Son, Bankrupt, Appellee. In the United States Circuit Court of Appeals. Fourth Circuit. No. 1177.* 32 p.

209 F. 811 (4th Cir. 1913).

1914

Duke, R. T. W., ed. *The Virginia Law Register.* Vol. 19.

Graves, Charles A[lfred]. *Questions on Pleading and Practice.* 45 p.

1915

Duke, R. T. W., ed. *The Virginia Law Register.* Vol. 20.

Graves, Charles A[lfred]. *Common Law Pleading.* 101 p.

Lile, William Minor. *Some Practical Hints for the Beginner in the Making of a Brief.* 40 p.

Reports of Cases Decided in the Supreme Court of Appeals of Virginia. Vols. 78, 79.

1916

Duke, R. T. W., ed. *The Virginia Law Register.* New series, Vol. 1.

Graves, Charles A[lfred]. *Questions on Evidence.* 78 p.

Michie, Thomas Johnson, ed. *The Encyclopedic Digest of Virginia and West Virginia Reports.* Vol. 16.

Snavely, Tipton Ray. *The Taxation of Negroes in Virginia.* 97 p.

Publications of the University of Virginia; Phelps-Stokes Fellowship Papers, No. 3.

1917

Duke, R. T. W., ed. *The Virginia Law Register.* New series, Vol. 2.

1918

Duke, R. T. W., ed. *The Virginia Law Register.* New series, Vol. 3.

Lile, William Minor. *Notes on Bigelow's Bills, Notes and Cheques: (2nd ed.) Prepared for the Use of the Students of the Law School of the University of Virginia.* 91 p.

1919

Duke, R. T. W., ed. *The Virginia Law Register.* New series, Vol. 4.

Michie, Thomas Johnson, ed. *The Encyclopedic Digest of Virginia and West Virginia Reports.* Vol. 17.

Minor, James F[ontaine], ed. *The Workmen's Compensation Laws of Virginia and West Virginia, Together with Rules of Procedure and Other Information.* xci, 691 p.

1920

Duke, R. T. W., ed. *The Virginia Law Register.* New series, Vol. 5.

1921

Duke, R. T. W., ed. *The Virginia Law Register.* New series, Vol. 6.

Reports of Cases Decided in the Supreme Court of Appeals of Virginia. Vol. 77.

1922

Duke, R. T. W., ed. *The Virginia Law Register.* New series, Vol. 7.

Michie, Thomas Johnson, ed. *The Encyclopedic Digest of Virginia and West Virginia Reports. Cumulative Supplement.* Vols. 1-3.

1923

Duke, R. T. W., ed. *The Virginia Law Register*. New series, Vol. 8.

Michie, Thomas Johnson, ed. *The Encyclopedic Digest of Virginia and West Virginia Reports. Cumulative Supplement*. Vols. 4-6.

1924

The Code of Virginia as Amended to Adjournment of General Assembly 1924, Together With All Other General Acts in Force July 1st, 1924, With the Declaration of Independence, the Constitution of the United States, the Constitution of Virginia, the Tax Bill, Complete Annotations. cvi, 2,048 p.

Duke, R. T. W., ed. *The Virginia Law Register*. New series, Vol. 9.

Official Building Code and Builders' Directory, Charlottesville, Va., 1924. 96 p.

1925

Duke, R. T. W., ed. *The Virginia Law Register*. New series, Vol. 10.

Graves, Charles A[lfred]. *Extrinsic Evidence in Respect to Written Instruments: A Paper Read Before the Virginia State Bar Association, August 2, 1893*. 32 p.

Gregory, George C[raghead]. *Forms for Virginia and West Virginia Annotated Including Statutory, Common Law and Equity, Commercial, Corporation, and Criminal Forms*. xlvii, 1,390 p.

Michie, Thomas Johnson, ed. *The Encyclopedic Digest of Virginia and West Virginia Reports. 1925 Supplement*. 2 vols.

1926

Barton, R[obert] T[homas]. *Pleading and Practice in the Courts of Chancery*. 2 vols.

Stedman, Beirne, ed. *The Virginia Law Register*. New series, Vol. 11.

1926 Supplement to the Virginia Code of 1924: Containing All the General Laws of 1926 With Full Annotations. xv, 313 p.

1927

The Code of Virginia (Pleading and Practice) An Abridgment of the Virginia Code of 1924 for the Student of Virginia Pleading and Practice. 1 p., l, 1,505-1,824 p.

Harrison, Thomas W[alter]. *Wills and Administration; a Discussion of the Devolution of a Decedent's Estate and the Procedure for the Distribution Thereof for Virginia and West Virginia*. 2 vols.

Michie, Thomas Johnson, ed. *The Encyclopedic Digest of Virginia and West Virginia Reports. 1927 Supplement*. x, 1,252 p.

Stedman, Beirne, ed. *The Virginia Law Register*. New series, Vol. 12.

Tunstall, Robert B[aylor]. *The Proposed Virginia Bar Act: A Reply to Sundry Criticisms*. 15 p.

1928

Michie, Thomas Johnson, ed. *The Encyclopedic Digest of Virginia and West Virginia Reports. 1928 Supplement*. viii, [2], 792 p.

Minor, Raleigh Colston. *The Law of Real Property*. 2 vols.

Stedman, Beirne, ed. *The Virginia Law Register*. New series, Vol. 13.

Vartanian, P[arounak] H[atch]. *The Law of Automobiles in Virginia and West Virginia*. vi, 564. p.

1928 Supplement to the Virginia Code of 1924: Containing All the General Laws of 1927-1928 With Full Annotations and the Revised Constitution. xi, 501 p.

1929

Hulvey, Charles Newton, and William Hamlin Wandel. *Life Insur-*
6 h *ance in Vir* r

Chapter 5: "The Law of Life Insurance in Virginia."

Michie, A[ddinell] Hewson, ed. *Michie's Digest of Virginia and West Virginia Reports.* Vols. 1-3.

Smith, Charles S[amuel], Jr. *Smith's Justices' Guide; a Guide to Justices, Commonwealth's Attorneys, Sheriffs, Sergeants, Constables, and Attorneys Who Practice in Justices' Courts.* viii, 398 p.

Vartanian, P[arounak]. H[atch]. *The Law of Corporations in Virginia.* xv, 719 p.

1930

The Code of Virginia: As Amended to Adjournment of the General Assembly 1930. Together With All Other General Acts in Force July 1st, 1930, with the Declaration of Independence, the Constitution of the Un States, the Constitution of Virginia, the Tax Co
p.

Hawes, Herbert Bouldin. *Prohibition Index-Manual, Virginia and West Virginia.* lxxix, 705 p.

Michie, A[ddinell] Hewson, ed. *Michie's Digest of Virginia and West Virginia Reports.* Vols. 4-7.

1931

Casparian, Harry. *Instructions; the Law and Approved Forms for Virginia and West Virginia.* 2 vols.

Michie, A[ddinell] Hewson, ed. *Michie's Digest of Virginia and West Virginia Reports.* Vols. 8, 9, 11.

1932

The Code of the City of Charlottesville, Virginia: the Charter as Amended and the General Ordinances of the City Enacted as a Whole

June 6th, 1932, in Effect July 15th, 1932. iv, 423 p.

Michie, A[ddinell] Hewson, ed. *Michie's Digest of Virginia and West Virginia Reports.* Vol. 10.

1932 Supplement to the Virginia Code of 1930: Containing All the General Laws of 1932 With Full Annotations. vi, 255 p.

1934

Burks, Martin P[arks]. *Pleading and Practice in Actions at Common Law.* lxxxiv, 1,088 p.

The Code of the Town of Lexington, Virginia. 369 p.

The Insurance Laws of Virginia. 99 p.

Michie, A[ddinell] Hewson, ed. *Michie's Digest of Virginia and West Virginia Reports. 1934 Supplement.* viii, 753 p.

1934 Supplement to the Virginia Code of 1930, Containing All General Laws Enacted at the 1933 Extra Session and the 1934 Regular Session With Full Annotations. vi p., 1 l., 234 p.

1935

Gregory, George C[raghead]. *Forms for Virginia and West Virginia Annotated, Including Statutory, Common Law and Equity, Commercial, Corporation, and Criminal Forms.* 3 vols.

Richey, Homer. *R. J. Reynolds, et als. v. Milk Commission of Virginia (on rehearing). In the Supreme Court of Appeals of Virginia at Richmond (Transferred from Staunton). Brief of Homer Richey.* 20 p.

163 Va. 957, 179 S.E. 507 (1935).

1936

The Insurance Laws of Virginia. 108 p.

Statutes of Virginia Relating to Banks, Trust Companies, Banking, Building and Loan and Kindred Businesses. 104 p.

Statutes of Virginia Relating to Building and Loan Associations. 16 p.

The Virginia Code of 1936, All the General Acts to and Including the Legislative Session of 1936, Complete Annotations. xlviii, 2,082 p.

1937

The Negotiable Instruments Law of Virginia. Complete Annotations. 91 p.

1938

The Fiduciary Laws of Virginia Containing the General Acts to and Including the Legislative Session of 1938. Complete Annotations. 190 p.

The Insurance Laws of Virginia. 112 p.

The Law of Automobiles in Virginia and West Virginia. xi, 742 p.

Michie, A[ddinell] Hewson, ed. *Michie's Digest of Virginia and West Virginia Reports. 1938 Supplement.* viii, 756 p.

Notable Virginia Bar Addresses Delivered Before Annual Meetings of the Virginia State Bar Association. vii, 515 p.

1938 Supplement to the Virginia Code of 1936: Containing All the General Laws Enacted at the 1936-7 Extra Session and the 1938 Regular Session With Full Annotations. vi, 295 p.

1939

Charter of the City of Roanoke, Virginia. 69 p.

The Code of the City of Roanoke, Virginia. The Charter as Amended and the General Ordinances of the City . . . Enacted as a Whole June 26, 1939, Effective August 1, 1939. 455 p.

Cox, Lucian Baum. *A Manual for Title Examiners in Virginia.* 299 p.

Special 1939 Supplement to Michie's Virginia Code of 1936: Completely Annotated with all Decisions Since the Regular 1938 Supplement and Containing Balance of General Laws Enacted at the 1938 Session of the Legislature. 28 p.

Virginia State Bar. *Directory for the Year Ending August 31, 1939; By-laws Adopted by the Council and Approved by the Supreme Court of Appeals.* 13 p.

1940

The Code of the City of Alexandria, Virginia. viii, 352 p.

The Code of the City of Danville, Virginia. The Charter as Amended, and the General Ordinances of the City. Enacted as a Whole July 11, 1940, Effective September 1, 1940. ix, 501 p.

The Code of the City of Newport News, Virginia. The Charter as Amended and the General Ordinances of the City . . . Enacted as a Whole August 26, 1940; Effective October 1, 1940. viii, 589 p.

The Code of the City of Suffolk, Virginia. The Charter as Amended and the General Ordinances of the City (Except as Expressly Excepted in the Adopting Ordinance) Enacted as a Whole March 21, 1940. Effective March 22, 1940. iv, 319 p.

The Insurance Laws of Virginia. 116 p.

Lee, Howard B[urton]. *The Criminal Trial in the Virginias.* 2 vols.

1940 Cumulative Supplement to the Virginia Code of 1936: Containing All the General Laws Enacted at the 1936-7 Extra Session and the 1938 and 1940 Regular Sessions With Full Annotations. 542 p.

1941

The Code of the City of Petersburg, Virginia: the Charter as Amended and the General Ordinances of the City, Except as Expressly Excepted in the Adopting Ordinance, enacted as a Whole, April 15, 1941, Effective May 31, 1941. viii, 600 p.

Michie, A[ddinell] Hewson, ed. *Michie's Digest of Virginia and West Virginia Reports. Permanent Supplement.* Vol. 1.

There were pocket supplements until 1952.

Tax Code of the City of Lynchburg, Virginia. 85 p.

1942

The Insurance Laws of Virginia. 127 p.

Michie, A[ddinell] Hewson, ed. *Michie's Digest of Virginia and West Virginia Reports. Permanent Supplement.* Vols. 2-4.

There were pocket supplements until 1952.

Statutes of Virginia Relating to Banks, Trust Companies, Building and Loan Associations and Kindred Businesses. 109 p.

The Virginia Code of 1942: All the General Acts to and Including the Legislative Session of 1942 Complete Annotation. liv, 3,160 p.

1943

The Code of the City of Lynchburg, Virginia, 1943; the Charter of the City and the General Ordinances of the City (Except as Expressly Excepted in the Adopting Ordinance), Enacted as a Whole January 25, 1943, Effective March 17, 1943. xii, 794 p.

Michie, A[ddinell] Hewson, ed. *Michie's Digest of Virginia and West Virginia Reports. Permanent Supplement.* Vols. 5-6.

There were pocket supplements until 1952.

Zoning Ordinance and Building Code of Lynchburg, Virginia. [317]-335, [440]-730 p.

1944

The Code of the City of Fredericksburg, Virginia. The Charter as Amended and the General Ordinances of the City (Except as Expressly Excepted in the Adopting Ordinance) Enacted as a Whole May 9, 1944, Effective June 1, 1944. Published by Order of the Council. xiii, 283 p.

The Insurance Laws of Virginia. 147 p.

Laws of Virginia Relating to Mental Hygiene and Hospitals. 41 p.

The Public Welfare Laws of Virginia, Annotated. 89 p.

Virginia School Laws. xiv, 182 p.

Virginia State Board of Education, Bulletin, Vol. 27, No. 2 (August, 1944).

1944 Supplement to the Virginia Code of 1942. 289 p.

1945

Charlottesville Building Code and Plumbing and Sewers. 345 p.

The Code of the City of Charlottesville, Virginia, 1945. The Charter of the City and the General Ordinances of the City. Enacted as a Whole April 16, 1945, Effective May 1, 1945. 508 p.

The Code of the City of Norfolk, Virginia, 1944. viii, 691 p.

1945 Supplement to the Virginia Code of 1942. 41 p.

1946

Building Code; Recommended by the National Board of Fire Underwriters, New York. Adopted, as Modified by the City of Newport News, Virginia, March 4, 1946. 395 p.

The Insurance Laws of Virginia. Containing Laws Enacted at the 1945 and the 1946 Sessions for the General Assembly and Supplementing the Reprint of the Virginia Code of 1942 and the 1944 Supplement. 11 p.

Laws of Virginia Relating to Fisheries of Tidal Waters. 64 p.

The Public Welfare Laws of Virginia. Annotated. 14 p.

Statutes of Virginia Relating to Banks, Trust Companies, Building and Loan Associations and Kindred Businesses. 115 p.

Statutes of Virginia Relating to Building and Loan Associations, Industrial Loan Associations, Credit Unions and Small Loan Law. 36 p.

1946 Cumulative Supplement to the Virginia Code of 1942. 501 p.

1947

The Code of the City of South Norfolk, Virginia, 1946. vi, 168 p.

The Code of the City of Winchester, Virginia, 1947. The Charter of the City and the General Ordinances of the City, Enacted as a Whole May 6, 1947, Effective May 6, 1947. vii, 245 p.

The Code of Virginia (Pleading and Practice): an Abridgment of the Virginia Code of 1942 for the Student of Virginia Pleading and Practice.

Cox, Lucian B[aum]. *A Manual for Title Examiners in Virginia.* v, 390 p.

The Law of Automobiles in Virginia and West Virginia. 3 vols.

Report of the Commission on Code Recodification and Proposed Code of Virginia. Prepared by the Commission Under the Authority of Chapter 400 of the Acts of the General Assembly of 1946 and Submitted to the Governor and the General Assembly at the Session of 1948. 2 vols.

1948

The Insurance Laws of Virginia.

Michie's Jurisprudence of Virginia and West Virginia. Vols. 1-2.

1948 Cumulative Supplement to the Virginia Code of 1942. 691 p.

1949

The Charter and the Code of General Ordinances of the Town of Blackstone, Virginia, 1948. Code Enacted as a Whole January 3, 1949; Effective Date January 20, 1949. 297 p.

Code of Virginia, 1950 With Provision for Subsequent Pocket Parts: Annotated. 10 vols.

Cohen, Alfred E[ugene]. *Divorce and Alimony in Virginia and West Virginia; With Forms.* xii, 502 p.

The Insurance Laws of Virginia. 192 p.

The Insurance Laws of Virginia. Index. 28 p.

Labor Laws of Virginia.

Michie's Jurisprudence of Virginia and West Virginia. Vols. 3-8.

Military Laws of Virginia. 71 p.

Motor Vehicle Laws of Virginia. 198 p.

Smith, George P[ayne]. *The Code of Virginia of 1950. An Address . . . Before the Lynchburg Bar Association on June 7, 1949.* [8] p.

Statutes of Virginia Relating to Banks, Trust Companies, Building and Loan Associations and Kindred Businesses. 197 p.

Statutes of Virginia Relating to Industrial Loan Associations and Small Loans. 22 p.

[Date Unknown]

Burks, Martin P[arks]. *Parol Evidence Rule.*

Graves, Charles A[lfred]. *Notes on Torts.* 31 p.

THE EVIDENCE

IN THE CASE

OF

COMMONWEALTH

AGAINST

FRANCIS S. O'REILLY,

FOR STABBING

JAMES MADISON PLEASANTS,

On the 31st October, 1818.

RICHMOND:
From the Franklin Press.
W. W. Gray, Printer.

GENERAL VIRGINIA BIBLIOGRAPHY

Aycock, Margaret, Jacqueline Lichtman, and Judy Stinson. *A Law Librarian's Introduction to Virginia State Publications*. Washington, D.C.: The Association, Government Documents SIS, 1981.

Berg, Susan Stromei. *Eighteenth-Century Williamsburg Imprints*. New York: Clearwater Pub. Co., Inc., 1986.

"Bibliography of Virginia and West Virginia Legal Publications in Library of College of Law, West Virginia University." *West Virginia Law Quarterly*, vol. 26, pp. 43-57 (1919).

Bryson, William Hamilton. *A Bibliography of Virginia Legal History Before 1900*. Charlottesville: University Press of Virginia, 1979; 2d ed., Buffalo, N.Y.: William S. Hein & Co., Inc., 1997.

The appendix lists the Virginia codes, acts of assembly, legislative journals, and the reports of cases before 1900.

Cappon, Lester Jesse. *Bibliography of Virginia History Since 1865*. Charlottesville: University of Va., Institute for Research in the Social Sciences, 1930.

Cappon, Lester J[esse], and Ira Vernon Brown. *New Market, Virginia, Imprints, 1806-1876*. Charlottesville: Alderman Library, 1942.

Chanin, Leah F., Pamela J. Gregory, and Sarah K[irsten] Wiant. *Legal Research in the District of Columbia, Maryland, and Virginia*. Buffalo, N.Y.: W. S. Hein, 1995; 2d ed., Buffalo, N.Y.: W. S. Hein, 2000.

Cornelius, Roberta D[ouglas]. *J. P. Bell's of Lynchburg, Virginia*. Lynchburg: J. P. Bell Co., Inc., 1959.

Dolmetsch, Christopher L. *The German Press of the Shenandoah Valley*. Columbia, S.C.: Camden House, 1984.

Eure, John D. *A Guide to Legal Research in Virginia*. Charlottesville: Committee on Continuing Legal Education, Virginia Law Foundation, 1989; 2d ed., 1994.

Haynes, Donald. *Virginiana in the Printed Book Collections of the Virginia State Library*. Richmond: Virginia State Library, 1975, 2 vols.

Hubbard, A. Paull, Jr. *Notes on the Book Trade in Richmond, Virginia, Together with a Preliminary Checklist of Richmond, Virginia, Imprints: 1780-1860.* Richmond: Richmond Book Shop, Inc., n.d.

> Part I: Argus Office; Samuel Pleasants (1793-1814); John Burke & Associates (1814-1817)
> Part II: Thomas Nicolson (1780-1808)
> Part VI: Augustine Davis (1786-1817)
> Part VII: Meriwether Jones (1798-1804); William A. Rind (1799-1804); Henry Pace (1801-1803)
> Part XI: Seaton Grantland (1805-1809)

Norona, Delf. *West Virginia Imprints, 1790-1863; a Checklist of Books, Newspapers, Periodicals, and Broadsides.* Moundsville, W. Va.: West Virginia Library Ass'n, 1958.

Quenzel, Carrol H[unter]. *Preliminary Checklist for Fredericksburg 1778-1876.* Richmond: Virginia State Library, 1947.

Virginia Imprint Series, No. 4.

Swem, Earl G[regg]. *A Bibliography of the Conventions and Constitutions of Virginia, Including References to Essays, Letters and Speeches in the Virginia Newspapers.* Richmond, 1910. *Bulletin of the Virginia State Library*, Richmond, vol. 3, no. 4 (1910).

Swem, Earl G[regg]. *A Bibliography of Virginia.* Richmond: Davis Bottom, 1916-1955, 5 vols.

> Part 1. Titles of books in the Virginia State Library which relate to Virginia and Virginians, the titles of those books written by Virginians, and of those printed in Virginia, but not including published official documents.
> Part 2. Titles of the printed official documents of the Commonwealth, 1776-1916. This part has extensive appendices relating to the public printers of Virginia.
> Part 3. The acts and the journals of the General Assembly of the Colony, 1619-1776.
> Part 4 (By Wilmer Lee Hall). Three series of sessional documents of the House of Delegates: extra session, January 7-April 4, 1861; called session, September 15-October 6, 1862; and adjourned session, January 7-March 31, 1863.
> Part 5 (By Wilmer Lee Hall). Titles of the printed documents of the Commonwealth, 1916-1925. With part (volume) 5 "the bibliographical account of the printed documents of the

Commonwealth is completed . . . through 1925, at which point the annual *Check-list of Virginia State Publications* begins and continues."

Torrence, William Clayton. *A Trial Bibliography of Colonial Virginia*. Richmond: Davis Bottom, 1908, 1910, 2 vols.

Wroth, Lawrence C[ounselman]. *William Parks: Printer and Journalist of England and Colonial America*. Richmond: William Parks Club, 1926.

Wyatt, Edward A[very], IV. *Preliminary Checklist for Petersburg 1786-1876*. Richmond: Virginia State Library, 1949.

Virginia Imprint Series, No. 9.

Wyllie, John Cook, *Preliminary Checklist for Abingdon 1807-1876*. Richmond: Virginia State Library, 1946.

Virginia Imprint Series, No. 1.

A REVIEW OF THE OPINION

OF

DOCT. WELLFORD,

IN THE CASE OF

GUY RICHARDS, AND OTHERS,

VS.

WILLIAM K. SMITH;

BY COUNSEL FOR THE PLAINTIFFS.

FREDERICKSBURG;
ARENA PRINTING OFFICE.

1836.

INDEX OF AUTHORS AND EDITORS

SUBJECT INDEX

www.ingramcontent.com/pod-product-compliance
Lightning Source LLC
LaVergne TN
LVHW081943200926
848484LV00009B/2500
9780871692399